Y0-DJQ-530

ABNORMAL PSYCHOLOGY IN THE HUMAN CONTEXT

The Dorsey Series in Psychology

Abnormal Psychology in the Human Context

RICHARD H. PRICE
University of Michigan

STEVEN J. LYNN
Ohio University

1981

THE DORSEY PRESS Homewood, Illinois 60430
IRWIN-DORSEY LIMITED Georgetown, Ontario L7G 4B3

Cover photo: Tony Kelly

ISBN 0-256-02301-8
Library of Congress Catalog Card No. 80-70832
Printed in the United States of America

1 2 3 4 5 6 7 8 9 0 H 8 7 6 5 4 3 2 1

To our beloved parents,
Grace and the late Clarence Price,
Barbara and Herman Lynn

Preface

We have written *Abnormal Psychology in the Human Context* as a text for the first course in abnormal psychology. The book was written in the belief that the field of abnormal psychology is one in which the human and scientific concerns of psychology converge. As a consequence, an overarching theme of the book is one in which human problems are alternately viewed from the point of view of the scientist and in terms of the human experience of the individual.

Because we believe that abnormal psychology can emphasize both scientific rigor and appreciation of the psychological experience of the individual, we have provided balanced coverage of both clinical and scientific aspects of abnormal psychology. In a number of places, extensive clinical examples of individual disorders are offered to help the student appreciate abnormal behavior as a living phenomenon. At the same time, at a number of points in the text, we have offered relatively detailed accounts of a particular research program or study because we believe that learning about abnormal psychology involves, in part, telling the story of research as it is conducted by the scientist. Thus, in a sense, we have tried to offer both clinical case histories to provide examples of the phenomenon of abnormal behavior and scientific case histories that help the student to appreciate the process of science.

A number of major theoretical perspectives in the field of abnormal psychology continue to stimulate research on the determinants of abnormal behavior and to provide conceptual frameworks for alternative modes of treatment. The text presents coverage of each of these theoretical perspectives including the learning, illness, dynamic, social, and humanistic points of view. We have introduced these perspectives early in the book and they are discussed again in later chapters concerned with specific disorders. We have been particularly concerned to note the strengths and weaknesses of each perspective and to show how each can illuminate our understanding of various disorders and how they have provided the conceptual rationale for various treatment strategies.

An important development in the field of abnormal psychology has been the new edition of the American Psychiatric Association Diagnostic and Statistical Manual of Mental Disorders (DSM-III). Although this new diagnostic system has not been without its critics, it will certainly be influential in the study and classification of abnormal behavior now and in the near future. We have presented a discussion both of the advantages and the disadvantages of DSM III early in our presentation and, in later chapters where disorders are discussed in detail, they are considered in light of the new DSM III nomenclature.

Psychology as a discipline has contributed much to our understanding of the treatment of abnormal behavior in recent years. We have tried to reflect the extent and detail of this understanding and the real achievements that have been made by providing extensive coverage of the treatment methods. Accordingly we have discussed the insight therapies, behavioral approaches, biological approaches, group, family, and community based treatment in considerable detail.

The text is divided into four parts. Part one, "Approaches to Understanding Abnormal Behavior" offers historical, theoretical, and scientific perspectives on abnormal behavior to the student. Abnormal psychology is seen in light of important historical and cultural changes that have shaped the way we view those suffering from psychological disorders. The chapter on perspectives shows how biological, learning, social, dynamic, and historical perspectives on abnormal behavior shape our thinking and inspire scientific research. The strengths and weaknesses of each perspective are detailed and how they literally shape the way we "see" abnormal behavior is illustrated. Chapters 4 and 5, on research and classification, provide the student with an understanding of how scientists attack the problems of definition, description, how they search for the determinants of abnormal behavior. Chapter 5 is designed to help the student understand the role of classification both in the development of science and in the improvement of diagnostic systems.

Part two, "The Major Disorders," examines the neurotic, affective, psychophysiological disorders, and the major psychoses offering both clinical illustrations and examples of important research now shaping our understanding of the nature of these disorders.

Part three focuses on social deviation, particularly the personality disorders, antisocial personality, sexual dysfunction, and patterns of substance and alcohol abuse. In this section new research on these maladaptive behavior patterns is examined in detail while, at the same time, we examine how social expectations and cultural norms shape our understanding of these disorders.

Finally, in part four, we have sampled a broad spectrum of treatment strategies and the research evaluating their effectiveness. Our survey ranges from biological intervention strategies through insight oriented and behavioral approaches to the more socially oriented group, family, and community based approaches. Major new developments, such as the rise of community based treatment programs and deinstitutionalization are examined both in terms of their current impact and their place in the history of our understanding and treatment of abnormal behavior.

In the writing of this book, the authors have incurred many debts, both intellectual and personal. In addition to the numerous reviewers and consultants, we would like to thank Jonathan Beecher, Allan Harkness, Anne Peterson, Larry Gorkin, Judith Rhue, Jennifer Lynn, Mary Price, and Harriet Field, each of whom contributed special insights. Barbara Toler and Amy Falor typed and retyped numerous drafts combining patience and precision in their efforts. Our deep appreciation goes to Barbara Lynn who contributed most of the material for the chapter on insight therapies. We are also grateful to the staff of the Institute for Sex Research, Indiana University for their assistance in providing material for the chapter on human sexuality. Roger Blashfield made a number of useful contributions to our thinking about classification, and Salvatore Maddi served as a sensitive and thoughtful consulting editor.

R. H. Price
S. Lynn

Contents

PART 1

Approaches to Understanding Abnormal Behavior

Tony Kelly

1

Introduction

• A college senior was finding that it was getting harder and harder to sleep at night. He began to take long walks around campus by himself. While talking to a sympathetic teacher one afternoon, he burst into tears for no apparent reason. He dropped out of college at the end of that term and entered psychological treatment.

• You are standing on a busy city street corner when a man on the corner begins to shout and gesture. You aren't sure what he is talking about. You do notice that, although he continues to shout and even approaches several people, no one looks at him directly and everyone continues on his way.

• A father arrives at the emergency room door of a local hospital with his three-year-old daughter in his arms. X-rays reveal that she has several broken ribs and a skull fracture. There is also evidence of several older fractures that have since healed. Upon careful investigation the authorities find out that this is not the first time the girl and her younger brother have needed emergency medical attention after the father has been asked to care for them.

• Picture an ambitious, successful woman who is a junior executive in a corporation. Her boss questions her judgment in developing a market survey. An hour later she is immobilized by the excruciating pain of a migraine headache.

• Although he was eight, the boy still liked to play "dress up" with his mother's cosmetics and jewelry. When he and his classmates were asked what they wanted to be when they grew up, he answered without hesitation, "I want to be Miss America."

• **Patient:** There are a lot of people in this place that are out to get me.
Therapist: Uh, you feel people have it in for you.
Patient: They are trying to read my mind because they are spies.
Therapist: Would you tell me a little more about that?

• A professor had been invited to give the keynote lecture to his professional society. Preparing the talk had been a source of intense preoccupation and anxiety. When he stepped up to the podium, he found that he had "forgotten" his glasses and could not read his speech.

• A young man who always seemed to get his way impressed new acquaintances with his self-assurance and sincerity. But he had lost nine jobs in the last five years because of periodic drinking bouts that lasted for two to three weeks at a time. If you were to ask him about losing those jobs, he would give you a plausible explanation for each one, but none of the explanations had anything to do with his drinking habits.

In the pages that follow, you will encounter dozens of additional examples of behavior that appear odd, puzzling, or difficult to explain. Some will represent severe forms of abnormal behavior while others may be relatively commonplace. Describing what is known about behaviors like these and their treatment is the purpose of this book.

Abnormal behavior is both a scientific and a human problem. In our discussion, we will examine various forms of abnormal behavior from a scientific perspective. At the same time, we will focus on the experience of the individual as he or she copes with the demands of living in a changing society. Let us first consider some of the scientific issues raised in the study of abnormal behavior.

ABNORMAL BEHAVIOR AS A SCIENTIFIC PROBLEM

The Search for Scientific Definitions

As we shall soon see, scientists from many different disciplines have attempted to understand the causes of abnormal behavior and have searched for effective methods of treatment. Biochemists, anthropologists, psychologists, and many other scientists have conducted scientific research and developed theories to explain various forms of abnormal behavior. Still, no single definition can encompass all the diverse forms of abnormal behavior we will examine. But three major approaches to defining abnormal behavior have been commonly used as a starting point.

One approach emphasizes subjective distress, a second, social disability, and a third, the violation of social norms. Each applies more readily to some forms of psychological disorder than to others. You may find it instructive to reexamine each of the brief examples above and ask yourself whether you think it fits one or more of these three criteria as we describe them below.

Subjective distress refers to the internal psychological state of the person and usually encompasses such emotions as fear, sadness, or feelings of loss of control. The criterion of subjective distress applies especially well to some of the mood-related disorders, such as depression, that we will discuss later in the book. On the other hand, other forms of abnormal behavior seem not to be accompanied by any clear sense of subjective distress.

A second criterion for defining abnormal behavior is that the person appears to be *psychologically or socially disabled*—that is, less able to cope with the demands and stresses of life. Many of the major psychological disorders, such as schizophrenia, can be extremely disabling. Yet, other forms of abnormal behavior may produce almost no social disability and may be tolerated by the person with little or no difficulty.

The third major defining criterion of abnormal behavior is that some forms clearly seem to be in *violation of accepted social rules and norms*. Consequently, the behavior pattern in question may be disturbing to others. But a moment's reflection may suggest to you that whether a certain pattern of behavior is disturbing

Behavior that violates social rules and norms is often seen as "abnormal".

© William S. Nawrocki

Owen Franken/Stock, Boston, Inc.

to others or not depends very much on the situation in which it occurs and the cultural norms and rules of the local setting. Indeed, some social scientists have argued that an adequate definition of abnormal behavior must take into account the culture in which the behavior occurs.

Although the criteria of subjective distress, psychological disability, and the violation of social rules each contribute to the definition of abnormal behavior, we should recognize that none of them are adequate by themselves. There is no clear line between what is considered "normal" and what is considered "abnormal," even though it is possible to find vivid examples of particular patterns of abnormal behavior.

Description, Measurement, and Classification

Even though we have not arrived at a final definition of abnormal behavior, scientists have devised a variety of methods to aid in the measurement and description of abnormal behavior. As we shall see in later chapters, these methods range from the case history, which provides a narrative description of the course of a particular pattern of abnormal behavior, to psychological tests, to sophisticated biochemical and genetic methods. Thus, methods from all of the sciences are being brought to bear on the scientific description of abnormal behavior.

Scientists not only try to describe the phenomenon in which they are interested, they also attempt to find ways to classify it in order to bring order out of diversity. We will study a variety of types of abnormal behavior and consider several ways in which such behavior can be classified. We will take a close but critical look at the latest version of the diagnostic and

THE ROLE OF CULTURE IN UNDERSTANDING ABNORMAL BEHAVIOR

What is the role of culture in understanding the nature of abnormal behavior? Anthropologists use the term *ethnocentrism* to refer to the tendency to view our own culture as somehow automatically better, more "advanced," and "superior" to other cultures both within our own country and elsewhere in the world. This attitude can creep into our thinking without our being aware of it. We might be tempted to regard our own cultural practices as "natural," "good," and "right," while viewing those of other groups as "primitive" and "unnatural." It is important not to confuse that which is different with abnormality.

Another important idea relating the concept of abnormality to the idea of culture is *cultural relativism.* This idea, introduced by anthropologists early in this century, argues that there are no universal standards that can be applied to all cultures and societies. Each culture is unique, and the practices of each must be understood on its own terms. From this viewpoint the idea of "normality" depends greatly on the culture being examined. Some advocates of cultural relativism have gone so far as to argue that there are no universal forms of abnormal behavior that can be found in all cultures. But are there forms of abnormal behavior that are universal, or are they entirely unique to each culture?

Evidence used to support the cultural relativistic view often involves some forms of abnormal behavior that are clearly unique to a particular cultural group. Examples include *susto,* a form of "magic fright" reported to have been observed among Indian tribes in Central and South America and in the highlands of Peru and Bolivia. Susto usually affects young children and adolescents. Victims show a loss of strength, rapid heartbeat, weight loss, intense anxiety, and depression. Usually they are treated by having their bodies rubbed with various plants and animals.

Another unique form of abnormal behavior is *koro,* an anxiety state that is found mainly in Southeast Asia. A man with koro suffers from an intense fear that his penis will withdraw into his stomach, resulting in his death. The fear usually occurs very suddenly and is very intense. It may last for months at a time and the cause is thought to be sexual overindulgence, particularly masturbation. A common cure for it is to have the man hold his penis in a firm grip, thus presumably preventing withdrawal into the stomach.

Still a third example of a culturally unique form of abnormal behavior is *pibloktoq* (Wallace, 1972). It occurs only among polar Eskimos in northern Greenland. It begins with the victim appearing mildly irritable and withdrawn. Suddenly, with little warning, the victim becomes wildly excited, may tear off clothing, shout obscenities, or throw objects. The person may place himself or herself in great danger by climbing on icebergs and leaping into snowdrifts. This period is usually followed by convulsive seizures and deep sleep. After the sleep, the victim seldom has any memory of the experience and behaves normally.

The fact that there are culturally unique forms of abnormal behavior does not suggest that all forms are culture bound. But these examples do help us to appreciate two ways in which culture can affect abnormal behavior.

First, the *style* and *content* of abnormal behavior may be strongly affected by the culture in which it occurs. For example, koro, the fear that the penis will withdraw into the stomach, is related to sexual concerns of the affected cultural group in Southeast Asia. The content of intense beliefs and fears may often be determined by cultural preoccupations.

A second role of culture in abnormal behavior may be seen in *the way a person copes* with the fear or disabling aspects of a disorder. Wallace (1972) points out that in the case of pibloktoq, the Eskimo may try to withdraw from others rather than place them in physical danger. Wallace notes that this way of coping is consistent with the reluctance to endanger or burden others found in Eskimo culture.

Diet is a third source of disorders unique to a culture, but it is often overlooked. Nutritional patterns, eating habits. and ecologically common chemicals or foods may affect the biochemistry of particular groups. Toxic disorders that result in extreme and uncontrolled behavior may occur as a consequence. An excellent example of this is pibloktoq. Wallace notes that there is now much evidence to indicate that this disorder may be produced by a calcium deficiency. The deficiency produces a neuromuscular disorder that is often complicated by emotional and cognitive disorganization. Thus, a *culturally determined dietary and nutritional pattern,* or the *physical ecology* of a particular culture, may play a role in the development of disorders that are culturally unique.

Are there forms of abnormal behavior that are universal? Researchers have studied this question in great detail. Wallace (1972) summarizes the research literature by saying: "*Yes,* different cultures do encourage different styles of mental illness, *but* the major categories of mental illness (the organic psychoses, the functional psychoses, the neuroses, the situational reactions, etc.) seem to be universal human afflictions" (p. 1).

Thus, although culture exerts a variety of powerful influences on the expression of abnormal behavior, it is not the only determining factor. The fact that some common forms of abnormal behavior can be observed in widely different cultures suggests that other biological and psychological causes also play a powerful role.

statistical manual (DSM) of the American Psychiatric Association (1980) which is now being used as one means of classifying abnormal behavior.

The Scientific Search for Causes and Explanations

We have observed that many of the examples of abnormal behavior are puzzling in a variety of ways. We want to ask ourselves what could lead a person to behave in that way? How can we make sense out of the behavior?

Several different theoretical approaches to explaining the nature and causes of abnormal behavior are currently in use (Price, 1978). One is the view that abnormal behavior is a form of illness or disease. Another argues that it is a result of attempts to deal with the inner conflict of motives. Still another view argues that the peculiar or puzzling behavior we observe is actually learned in the social environment. Another viewpoint stresses the importance of the reaction of others to abnormal behavior. Finally, some theories focus on the development of one's sense of self and the psychological experiences of the person as the most critical processes to consider.

Each of these perspectives sheds light on important aspects of the human experience. And ultimately, each will have to be considered in any comprehensive theory of abnormal behavior. Throughout the text we will consider the ways in which each of them helps us to understand a particular form of abnormal behavior.

Scientists not only try to provide a conceptual framework to explain the development of abnormal behavior, they also conduct research to isolate its causes. It is already clear that abnormal behavior is the product of *multiple determinants.* For example, people with severe depression or prolonged feelings of sadness may be responding to causal factors in the larger culture, the economy, their family, their learning history, their own biochemistry, or any combination of these. With such a diverse range of possible causes of abnormal behavior, the scientific challenge is great. In learning about the search for the causes of various forms of abnormal behavior, we will encounter scientific detective stories that can be, in their own way, as exciting as the conventional kind.

ABNORMAL BEHAVIOR AS A HUMAN PROBLEM

We are living in a time of rapid social and economic change. Changes are occurring in social norms and expectations about which behavior is acceptable and which is not. Changes in sex roles, in the structure of the nuclear family, in attitudes toward sexuality, and in our sense of economic security mean that each of us is coping and adapting in the face of uncertainty.

FIGURE 1–1 Distribution of Psychological Impairment Measured in an Urban Population

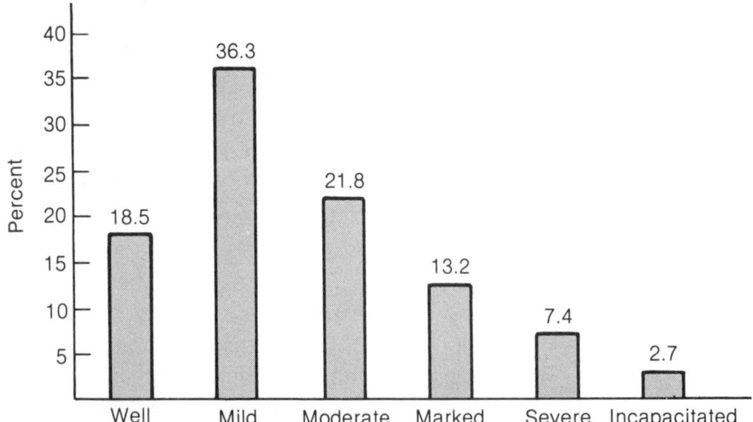

Source: Srole et al., *Mental Health in the Metropolis: The Midtown Manhattan Study* (New York: McGraw-Hill, 1962).

Social and Human Cost

The social and human cost of psychological disturbance is very great. Major studies in both urban and rural areas (Srole et al., 1962; Leighton et al., 1963) have reported relatively high proportions of the population experiencing psychological impairment. These figures will vary greatly depending on the economic status, sex, geographic location, and other characteristics of the people under study; but there is no question that a substantial part of our population will experience relatively severe degrees of psychological distress at some time in their lives.

Because abnormal behavior is a major social and human problem, the development of new methods of treatment and prevention is a critical scientific priority. In the chapters that follow, we will examine a variety of studies focused on the development of more effective treatments. Indeed, the last several chapters of this book are devoted to a description of various biological, behavioral, psychological, and social treatment approaches and the research that has both stimulated them and evaluated their effectiveness.

Abnormal Behavior as a Personal Problem

Many people take a course in abnormal psychology as a way of getting to know themselves better. This can be a helpful experience, but for some it can also provide moments of worry and uncertainty. There may be times, for example, when you are reading a case history or a description in this book and suddenly feel as if you "recognize" something of yourself in it. Then you are likely to wonder, "Is my behavior abnormal?" Or, "Maybe my problems are more serious than I thought."

At times like this, it is useful to know of the pattern medical schools have noticed and call *medical students' syndrome.* As the students begin to become familiar with the symptoms of particular diseases, they may find themselves focusing more on their own bodily processes. Soon it is hard to stop wondering whether a slight twinge in the chest might not be an early warning of

Everyone confronts problems in living from time to time, and this is a normal part of everyone's life.

Monique Manceau/Photo Researchers, Inc.

heart trouble or a headache might not be the first sign of a tumor.

Much the same thing can happen when you are learning about abnormal behavior. It is *natural* to "see yourself" in some patterns of behavior described in this book, partly because our behavior is so complex and multifaceted that everyone will share some of the same impulses and fears from time to time.

It may be that now or at some time in your life you will find yourself with a problem or concern that is disturbing and persistent enough that you will want to talk with someone about it. If so, there are several ways you can find out who to talk with. Your school may have a counseling center or mental health clinic. There also may be a "hot line" or telephone referral service where you can get information about who will be able to discuss your problems with you. Your dormitory counselor may also be able to help. Finally, your instructor is likely to know of appropriate helping services and may be willing to give you some leads. If you are really concerned, don't hesitate to ask.

THE HUMAN CONTEXT

In our discussion of various forms of abnormal behavior, we have tried to keep always in mind that human beings are at the same time biological, psychological, and cultural creatures. Each of these qualities is an equally important facet of the human context in which abnormal behavior must be understood. A rigorous, yet humane, science of abnormal behavior requires no less.

Both the scientific and the human aspects of abnormal behavior and its treatment are mingled in history. How society has understood and dealt with abnormal behavior in the past provides us with an intellectual history of abnormality and is a fitting place for our discussion to begin. It is to this history that we now turn.

2

Historical Views of Abnormal Behavior

INTRODUCTION: THINKING ABOUT HISTORY

To write a history of abnormal behavior that conforms to the "march-of-progress" school of thought is tempting. This version of history sees each age as a step in the progress of human society and humane science. A history written from this point of view tends to focus on scientific breakthroughs in every age and to concentrate its attention on great men and women. This approach is tempting because it prompts us to look only for signs of progress in our thinking about abnormal behavior and our treatment of those who display unusual behavior. Indeed, there are signs of progress and change. But the progress approach to the history of abnormal behavior has some real drawbacks. First, such a history often has a self-justifying, self-congratulating tone. It tends to see the present as the best of all possible worlds, and, if we are not careful, it leads us to use history as a justification for current practices because they are the "latest developments."

Another drawback of the march-of-progress school of thought is that it fails to draw a crucial lesson from history. Not only can history help to tell us how we got where we are, but, more important, it reminds us that the cultural beliefs and the social context of earlier eras shaped the assumptions about what caused abnormal behavior in those times. Likewise, our current social context and culture shape our beliefs about the causes and cures of abnormality. To look at the history of abnormal behavior as a string of chronologically ordered events, then, is to fail to fully understand ourselves today.

We can try, instead, to understand previous events in their social context. With this approach to history, we may begin by looking at the prevailing beliefs about the causes and cures of abnormal behavior. But in order to understand those beliefs, we must ask a number of other questions as well. For example, we might ask about the social institutions of the time. What were people's ideas of the good life? What did people believe about the nature of human beings? What were the economic and political issues of the day? Answers to these questions will help us to make sense of the events of that time. As Reigel (1972) has pointed out, the economic and cultural conditions of society provide a basis for the direction and growth of the science, and that includes the science of abnormal psychology.

History, then, rightly understood, can give us a perspective on ourselves and perhaps make us more humble about our achievements. History abused becomes a justification for our current practices rather than an attempt to deeply and truly understand ourselves.

In this chapter we will examine a brief history of abnormal behavior from ancient times to the present. We will focus on people's explanations of abnormal behavior and their attempts to cope with those displaying the behavior. We will try to keep at least one eye fixed on the context of their beliefs so that when we finish our history, we will be ready to ask ourselves something about our own beliefs and practices today and, perhaps, even to make some guesses about tomorrow.

PREHISTORY: SPIRIT POSSESSION AND EXORCISM

There is very little evidence of how abnormal behavior was thought of in ancient times. Some evidence can be derived from Biblical sources. For example, in the Old Testament, King Saul is described as having killed himself presumably because of a severe depression. Greek myths provide many descriptions of apparently abnormal or irrational behavior. Ajax apparently suffered from the delusion that some sheep were his enemies. He killed them and later killed himself in remorse. The gods themselves could make men mad.

Another sort of evidence is from archeology. Human skulls have been found with holes cut in them, as a result of what we presume was a surgical procedure. This procedure, called *trephining,* is believed to have been used to release evil spirits from the heads of people afflicted with some form of abnormal behavior. A number of people treated in this way apparently survived the operation since there are indications of healing around the skull openings. Selling (1940) believed that while the operation was done to allow evil spirits to escape, brain pressure was relieved in this way, thus confirming for early people the effectiveness of the treatment.

Imagine what the world of primitive people must have been like. They dealt daily with unseen, powerful, and frightening forces in nature. Earthquakes, storms, fires, and illness all occurred without known explanation. And yet to survive, we require an ability to predict and, in some degree, to control our environment. It is not hard to understand how positive, life-sustaining events in the environment would be thought of as possessing good spirits, while unpredictable and dangerous events would be seen as possessing evil spirits.

In this context, the unusual or frightening behavior of a person could easily be explained as possession by evil spirits. The "cure" was *exorcism,* the attempt to drive the evil spirits out of the afflicted person. Exorcism took a variety of forms, including starvation, flogging, or prayers.

These magical and religious beliefs and practices were clearly an attempt to cope with an overwhelming and powerful environment. And exorcism, after all, does provide a sense of mastery over mysterious events. Since it almost surely had an effect in some cases, the idea that abnormal behavior was due to spirit possession was probably strengthened.

Drilling or cutting holes in the skull called trephining, during the stone ages.

Courtesy of the American Museum of Natural History

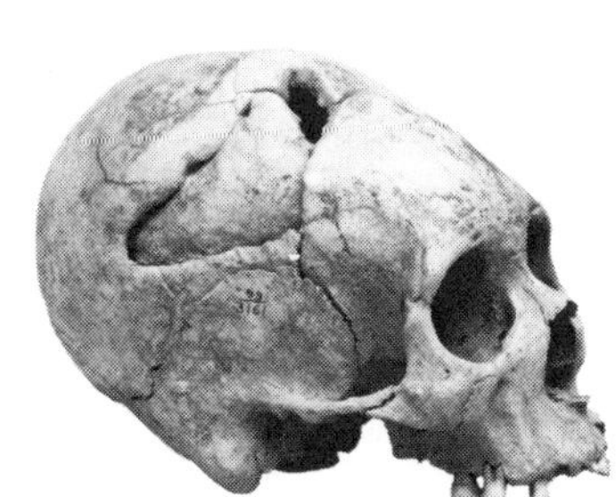

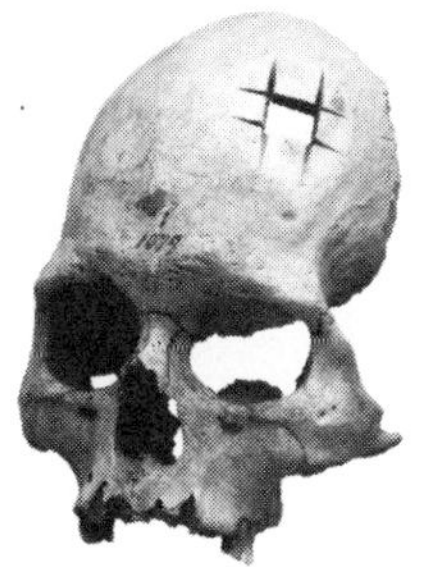

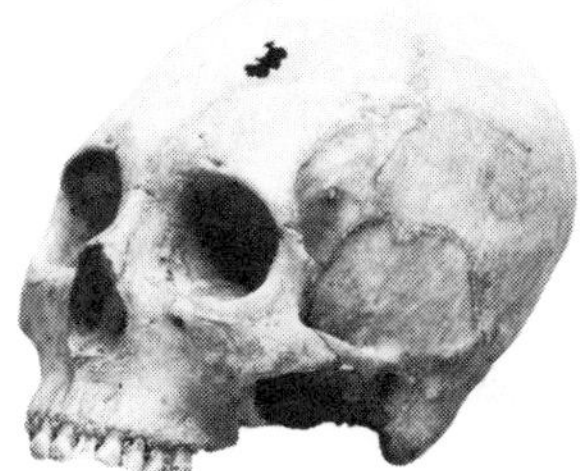

THE CLASSICAL PERIOD: MADNESS AS SACRED AND NATURAL DISEASE

Important early sources of ideas about the nature of abnormal behavior were classical Greece and, later, Rome. During the period of Hellenic enlightenment in Greece, curiosity, observation, and rationality were all highly valued. It was a time of rapid growth in understanding the nature of people and the world in which they lived. There were attempts to understand not only abnormal behavior, but also physiology, architecture, political science, logic, and drama. Zax and Cowen (1972) suggest that the Greeks had the leisure to pursue intellectual problems partly because they were slave owners and therefore had the time and energy to pursue the life of the mind.

Two views of madness prevailed in the classical period. On one hand, irrational behavior was often thought to have supernatural origins, either as a punishment from the gods or as a "sacred disease" indicating special powers as a prophet. On the other hand, Greek medicine rejected supernatural explanations of abnormal behavior and believed it to be a physiological disease of natural origins.

Cleomenes, a Spartan king, illustrates this dual view of irrationality quite well. A vigorous and erratic person, he often struck his subjects in the face with his sceptre for no apparent reason and committed acts of sacrilege. Finally, he was restrained by having his feet placed in stocks. Herodotus, the greatest historian of the time, recorded the explanations offered for the king's erratic behavior. Most informed Greeks saw Cleomenes' behavior as a punishment sent by the gods for various sacrileges. Others, however, were convinced that his behavior was due to heavy drinking and chronic alcoholism. Thus sacred and naturalistic views of abnormal behavior competed for prominence (Rosen, 1968).

Hippocrates (460–377 B.C.), a Greek physician, was a product of this age. He was a keen observer of human behavior and a scientist interested in natural causes. He argued, among other things, that epilepsy was not a "sacred disease" inflicted by the gods but was a result of brain disease. He also believed that madness was due to an excess of bile in the body and that most peculiar or unusual behaviors could be explained by imbalances among the four humors—blood, black bile, yellow bile, and phlegm. For example, a person suffering from too much phlegm in his or her body would appear lazy, sluggish, or phlegmatic. Depression and other mood changes could be traced to other imbalances, it was believed.

Other beliefs about the nature and cause of abnormal behavior by the Greeks had a similar physiological flavor. For example, it was believed that hysteria was a disease that only afflicted women and was caused by the wandering of the uterus throughout the body.

Hippocrates

National Library of Medicine

Roman thought differed in some interesting ways from that of the Greeks. The Romans were practical and political creatures. They were less given to detailed and detached inquiry than the Greeks, and much of their thinking about abnormal behavior was influenced by Greek thought and Greek physicians. Their practical orientation led them to be particularly interested in clinical treatment. Asclepiades (ca. 124 B.C.), a Roman physician, is said to have focused much of his energy on treatment including various physical therapies and baths.

Galen (A.D. 130–200), a physician writing toward the end of the era, summarized a great deal of Roman thought and stated that abnormal behavior was a result of either brain disease or disease of some other bodily organ. In addition, he believed that various environmental events could play a role in the development of abnormal behavior. For example, economic losses, disappointments in love, fear, or shock could be instrumental in producing abnormal behavior.

Although early Greek views of madness invoked supernatural explanations, Greek medicine had a profound influence as well. Perhaps the most important thing to remember about conceptions of abnormal behavior during the classical period is that the Greeks' curiosity about the universe extended to the physiology of the person. Their later thinking about the nature of irrational behavior is best thought of as a natural extension of their interest in physiology and medicine. Thus the classical period marks the beginning of two important themes in the history of abnormal behavior. First, irrational

Exorcism was often attempted in the medieval Church as a cure for deviant behavior.

National Library of Medicine

behavior began to be seen as a natural phenomenon, and second, its causes were located chiefly in the physiology of the person.

THE MIDDLE AGES: WITCHES AND THEIR HUNTERS

To appreciate how abnormal behavior was explained and dealt with in the Middle Ages, we must understand something about the role of the Western church. The church was not just a religious institution but the intellectual establishment. Scholarship resided only within the church, and the church was the final authority on questions of human conduct and faith.

Until around the year 1000, the Western church and the society that it structured and controlled had little reason to doubt themselves. The church continued to grow, and pagans in the north and east were beginning to accept Christianity as a world view and a code of conduct. Like many existing establishments, once the church had gained control, it was reluctant to respond to criticism with internal change. According to historian Norman Cohn, when groups within the church suggested various reforms, they were accused of wishing to destroy the church. These suggested reforms soon became known as heresy, and, by the 13th century, the church developed a new judicial procedure for dealing with alleged heretics. As the church continued to defend its hard-won territory, a Papal Bull was issued in 1231 authorizing a new procedure for dealing with heresy. Anyone accused of heresy could not be found guilty unless he or she confessed, an apparently enlightened procedure. But torture was allowed in order to obtain a confession, and this ruling marked the beginning of the Inquisition.

According to Cohn, witches and warlocks were common in the Middle Ages—part of the neighborhood life of most villages. Few people thought of them as anything more than eccentric people whose danger, if any, was strictly a local affair. But with the coming of the Inquisition, witches came to be thought of as conspirators with the devil, threatening the authority of the church.

By 1484, Pope Innocent VIII issued a Papal Bull that requested all of the clergy in Europe to begin to search out witches and extract confessions. Local witches—those who were in some ways bothersome or different—were promoted from village nuisances to enemies of society.

Two Dominican monks wrote a manual, *Malleus Maleficarum*—"The Witch Hammer"—that described how witches could be recognized—from patches on their skin and other "symptoms"—and how they could be examined to determine whether or not they were truly witches. Janeway (1975) describes the process in the following way:

> Intellectually, the process was convincing. Since what was known about a witch cult was what the Inquisitors racked out of the accused witches, it agreed with itself in a most impressive way. If one witch came up with a new wrinkle, the next was sure to be asked about it, and confirm it for the same reason that she had confessed in the first place. (Increasingly it was a she.) Had she rubbed a stool with black magical ointment and taken off by air to meet with her neighbors to worship a huge toad? Yes. Had she kissed the creature on arrival? Yes. Had she had intercourse with the Devil? Yes, and it was extremely unpleasant since his member was ice cold. Had she murdered children? Yes, indeed, including her own. And so on and so forth (p. 82).

We must remember that the Middle Ages was not only a time in which the church dominated all of society, it was also a time of great tumult and catastrophe. The Black Plague, the Hundred Years' War, peasant uprisings, the kidnapping of a pope, and other events kept medieval society in a turmoil of fear and uncertainty. With the writing of "The Witch Hammer," the witch craze swept across Europe, and people unfortunate enough to behave peculiarly were often described in terms of the dogma on witchcraft.

It is too easy to dismiss the great witch craze as merely the product of a bygone age. The human mind, then as now, sought explanations. It searched for causes. Janeway points out that swarms of demons and evil witches could "explain" the misfortunes of the era. The witch provided a ready target for the fears and uncertainties that threatened social order in the Middle Ages.

Thus the great witch hunts of the Middle Ages can be seen not merely as a curious practice from an earlier time, but as the reaction of the church, the major institution of society, to real and imaginary threats to its existence and authority. Many people were caught up in the net of the Inquisition. Few, if any, were a serious danger to the body politic of the church. Yet, to assert itself, the church required something against which to react, and those who were different became the victims.

Hospital of St. Mary of Bethlehem (Bedlam) in London, shown in this Hogarth engraving, reflects the appalling conditions of the time.

National Library of Medicine

BEGINNINGS OF THE MODERN ERA: THREE STREAMS OF THOUGHT

Early in the 14th century, even as the great European witch craze ended, major changes began to occur in Western civilization. In order to appreciate how the dominant view of abnormal behavior shifted in this period, we must look at the larger historical and social context for a moment.

Perhaps the most basic change in society beginning in the 15th century was the shift in authority from the church to the modern nation state. National armies began to appear late in the 15th century. Hospitals, once exclusively controlled by the church, were taken over by the state. The idea of cure became increasingly associated with secular and medical remedies rather than religious salvation. During the earlier medieval period it was believed that human passions could be controlled only with great spiritual effort. The world was a mysterious and fearsome place in which to live. Now, for the first time in the beginning of the modern era, a new optimism began to emerge; the Italian Renaissance was underway. Copernicus had offered a new theory of astonomy. Shakespeare and Cervantes were writing and Galileo and Kepler were launching a new physics. The world again opened itself to the inquiring mind. A new awareness of the social environment and a humanistic tradition began to emerge.

By the beginning of the 19th century, still other changes showed the shift in intellectual and political climate that had occurred. The early 19th century saw the rise of the factory system in England and the beginning of the Industrial Revolution. The Industrial Revolution did not just represent the coming of factories to our lives but ushered in a new conception of how people ought to be. Alongside the huge growth in technology and science came a change in society's standards of normal behavior. This new morality served the needs of the factory system. The work ethic emerged with a new set of virtues. Diligence and industry, it was thought, spelled success.

Thus the Industrial Revolution represents two changes that ultimately affected our conception of abnormal behavior. The first set of changes were scientific and technological, occurring over the span of time from the end of the Middle Ages to the beginning of the 19th century. These changes laid the groundwork for rapid growth in science and medicine. At the same time, a new morality emerged, with a new set of assumptions about appropriate behavior. Work, diligence, and achievement were considered primary virtues, and this new morality served as a prescription for the emerging working class in Europe and, somewhat later, in America.

Still a third major change in the human and social context began to occur in the later 18th century. At the beginning of the Victorian Age, the virtues of industry and diligence began to be supplemented by still other moral standards. A great tightening of moral norms and a shift in public morality marked the Victorian Age. Shakespeare was published in abridged editions with any suggestive content removed. Victorian women put curtains on the legs of their pianos lest they offend people's moral sensibilities. Legs became "limbs." Great emphasis was placed on suppressing the passionate aspects of people's behavior. The middle class came to dominate society, and its domination changed standards for appropriate and for abnormal behavior.

Against this background we will discuss three streams of thought about the nature of abnormal behavior that emerged in this period and remain with us today. The first of these focuses on the social environment both as the major cause and the source of "cure" of abnormal behavior. This tradition has its roots in the emerging humanism of the Renaissance and the social and political awareness stimulated by the French and American revolutions.

The second major stream of thought is organic and medical. It focuses on physiology as the source of abnormal behavior and sees the solutions to problems of abnormal behavior in medicine. This tradition draws on the steady scientific development beginning in the 15th century and the technological growth associated with the Industrial Revolution.

The third stream of thought to emerge is psychological. Not until the end of the 19th and the beginning of the 20th centuries does a truly psychological approach to human behavior develop. This view, most notably characterized by Freud's psychoanalysis, focused on human sexual and aggressive impulses and was preoccupied with their control, as one might expect of the Victorian Age.

These patterns of thought have alternated, emerged and reoccurred throughout history. In ancient times, magico-religious views predominated, while in classical Greece and Rome, both religious and organic-physiological views were of major importance. During the Middle Ages, the predominant view of abnormal behavior was again religious, and as the authority of the church began to be replaced by that of the state, conceptions of abnormality also changed. The development of nation states can be thought of as a precursor of the environmental view. The Industrial Revolution saw the end of a long development leading to medical organic views, and the Victorians, with their strong emphasis on suppressing the passions, laid the groundwork for the emergence of the psychological view of abnormal behavior.

The First Stream: The Social Environment as Cause and Cure

We said earlier that one of the three streams of thought that emerged in the beginning of the modern era was the idea that the social environment was important in both the causation and the cure of abnormal behavior. This idea took slightly different forms in Europe and in America.

Reform in Europe. For the past two centuries the insane, criminals, and debtors had been housed in large prisons and fortresses. This was a relatively new practice, stemming perhaps from the confining of lepers in leprosariums during the Middle Ages. Although leprosy practically disappeared from Europe at the end of the Middle Ages, as Foucault (1965) points out, the idea of separating the "undesirables" from the rest of society had been established.

The mentally disturbed, criminals, debtors, and other outcasts became the lepers' replacements in fortress-like institutions. By the end of the 18th century, these institutions were appalling in their inhumanity. Inmates lay on straw mattresses on stone floors and were often flooded by sewage when water rose in the spring. Rats and other vermin tormented them. In addition, ships filled with disturbed and disturbing people were sent from port to port in Europe. At dockside the "ship of fools" would be displayed to the public for a fee.

In France, the French Revolution had just ended; it was a time of reform. Phillippe Pinel (1745–1826), a French physician, was placed in charge of a large hospital for the insane in Paris, and he found himself staggered by the conditions he found there.

Philippe Pinel

National Library of Medicine

A humanist and reformer, he believed that disturbed people ought to be treated with kindness and concern rather than be chained in the hospital's dungeon-like atmosphere. As the hospital's superintendent, Pinel unchained the inmates and treated them with kindness. His example was followed by others; soon France had ten new mental hospitals, all practicing benign environmental treatment.

It was not long before the reform movement found its way to England. Among the reformers in England was William Tuke, who established a retreat where patients could live, work, and rest in a benign atmosphere. Of course, we cannot know how many cases of severely disturbed behavior actually were improved by these reforms. But it is clear that many people suffering serious abuses in the asylums of the day were able to lead relatively normal lives once the asylums' oppressive atmosphere was replaced by kindness, concern, and support.

Thus the reform movement in Europe exemplified by the work of Pinel in France and by Tuke in England was stimulated partly by a political and social climate of reform. The target of reform was the oppressive environment of the dungeons that had housed the insane and the afflicted. We will see that this same spirit of reform and focus on the social environment took a different form in America in the Jacksonian Era.

William Tuke

National Library of Medicine

The well-ordered asylum in America. Europe's concern with the role of the environment had not developed alone. In America, too, the role of social and environmental factors began to gain attention and prominence. In colonial times, as David Rothman (1971) notes, it had not occurred to Americans to institutionalize severely disturbed people. They were cared for by the family, relatives, or neighbors, and remained, for the most part, in the community. Suddenly, however, in about 1820, prisons, asylums, alms houses, and retreats for children began to appear and swept across America in a great wave. This was, Rothman suggests, a great revolution in social practice. Before 1810, only a few states in the East had private institutions to care for the mentally ill, and only Virginia had a public asylum. But by 1860, only 50 years later, 28 of the 33 states had public institutions for the insane, and institutionalization of the insane had become standard practice. What caused this revolution in social practice? What were the beliefs in this period about the causes of abnormal behavior, and how did they affect therapeutic practices?

Rothman argues that Americans of the 1820s and 1830s strongly believed that the origins of deviant behavior and insanity lay in the chaotic community organization of the time and the rapid social change present in the Jacksonian Era. In fact, it was not just rapid social change, but other aspects of social life—politics, social mobility, inflation, and even ambition in business—that were seen as the causes of insanity. American physicians of the Jacksonian Era speculated on the causes of abnormal behavior. For example, Edward Jarvis, a prominent physician of the time, explained to a Massachusetts Medical Society meeting,

> In this country . . . the ambition of some leads them to aim at that which they cannot reach, to strive for more than they can grasp. Their mental powers are strained to their utmost tension; they labor in agitation . . . their minds stagger under the disproportionate burden (quoted by Rothman, 1971).

Given these assumptions about the causes of abnormal behavior, it is much easier to understand the rationale underlying the rapid development of the asylum in the United States in the 1820s and 1830s. Rather than try to change American society, medical and scientific men of the time believed that they could create a distinctive environment that would eliminate the tensions and stresses of the social environment. At the same time, they hoped to create a model society that would show the advantages of an orderly, regular, and disciplined routine. It was to be a "demonstration project" to the larger society.

It is important to realize that the asylum of the Jacksonian Era was not a last resort after all other treatment attempts had failed. Rather, the asylum was believed to be the most effective approach to the treatment of abnormal behavior. As Rothman notes, physicians believed that the American environment had become so treacherous that insanity struck American citizens with great regularity. "Create a different kind of environment, which methodically corrected the deficiencies of the community, and a cure for insanity was at hand. This, in essence, was the foundation of the asylum solution, and the program that came to be known as moral treatment" (p. 133).

The heart of moral treatment was disciplined routine. Asylums were placed in the countryside because it was believed that the peace and serenity of the country and removal from the rapid pace of city life were essential to cure. Each patient's day was carefully ordered and each activity had a specified time in the schedule and routine. Even the physical environment was arranged so that it was symmetrical and well ordered. Thus the cure for abnormal behavior, 19th-century Americans believed, was a "well-ordered institution" to provide both a refuge from the chaos of the outside world and a model of what society should be like.

Reformers of the day, such as the famous Dorothea Dix, shared the same general idea. She promoted the mental hospitals in legislatures across the country from 1841 to 1881. She began by condemning the conditions for the insane in jails and poorhouses and then recommended in their place the well-ordered asylum. As Rothman notes, "Her formula was simple as she repeated it everywhere: first assert the curability of insanity, link it directly to proper institutional care, and then quote prevailing medical opinion on rates of recovery" (p. 132).

Claims for recovery during this period of moral treatment were very optimistic. Often 70 percent, 80 percent, and even 90 percent of patients were reported cured. For example, Samuel Woodward, superintendent of the Massachusetts Hospital at Worcester, claimed 82.25

THE RISE AND FALL OF "TENT THERAPY" IN THE 19th CENTURY

The enthusiasm for environmental explanations of the causes and cures of abnormal behavior took a variety of forms in 19th-century America. Ruth Caplan (1969) offers a striking example of this enthusiasm. When the threat of an epidemic of tuberculosis arose, the superintendent of Manhattan State Hospital decided to reduce overcrowding by erecting a tent for some of the patients on the hospital grounds. About 20 patients were moved into the tent. Great enthusiasm and attention to the patients, excellent meals, and extreme sanitary precautions characterized the move. Physicians at the hospital began to note marked improvement in the behavior of a number of these patients. When they were returned to the hospital, many of the patients suffered relapses.

Feeling that a new and effective treatment had been discovered, case histories and articles in learned journals were published attributing the therapeutic success to fresh air, environmental change, and healthy living conditions. Soon the experiment was repeated, and large numbers of patients were moved to tents to profit from the remarkable new treatment. Patients were allowed to participate in

Tent Therapy—This outdoor setting produced a dramatic change in the treatment environment and the change itself may have had beneficial, if temporary, effects.

National Library of Medicine

designing and decorating the tents. Soon "tent therapy" spread to other states, including California, Illinois, and Ohio.

Before long, however, these camps became crowded and the lifestyle became routine and boring. Staff shortages became more apparent, and tent therapy was soon abandoned as ineffective.

Even today, our enthusiasms for new treatments encourage premature adoption of new approaches. An important chance to learn about what were probably the effective ingredients of tent therapy (the participation of patients in their own treatment, enthusiasm, and increased contact with other patients) was lost. Unfortunately, new approaches to treatment are still too often hailed as "scientific breakthroughs" and treated as cure-alls. "Wonder" drugs, new environmental therapies, group techniques, and other approaches to the treatment of abnormal behavior are often overpraised and undertested. Too often the result, like tent therapy, is a cycle of great hope and enthusiasm followed by disillusionment when the promised results diminish and fail to appear.

percent of patients recovered, and a number of other superintendents flatly claimed 100 percent recoveries. Only recently have historians pointed out that sometimes a single patient who had been admitted, discharged, and readmitted several times was listed as having been "cured" each time, thus distorting statistics regarding the effectiveness of moral treatment.

Dorothea Dix

National Library of Medicine

Thus we see one of the main streams of thinking about the causes and cures of abnormal behavior—the social environmental view—beginning in Europe with the reforms of Pinel and extending to its logical extreme in the optimistic, environmentally oriented, moral treatment of the 1800s in America. As we will see in later chapters, strongly held beliefs about the power of the social environment to affect behavior continue to pervade our thinking today.

The Second Stream: Emergence of the Organic and Medical Views

The new age of technology in Europe and England brought about by the Industrial Revolution strengthened the belief that science could solve the problems of

A variety of treatment devices were used even after the Humanitarian Reform movement. Here we see a device for suspending patients to aid in their treatment.

human behavior. Not long before, Darwin had offered his theory of evolution, and Pasteur had shown that disease could be produced by germs. Medical science was looking for new worlds to conquer, and abnormal behavior had, as yet, been largely neglected as a subject of scientific study.

William Griesinger (1817–1868), a German physician, was a product of this belief. Early in his life he published a textbook that flatly asserted that abnormal behavior was due to brain disease. As Zax and Cowen (1972) point out, Griesinger made no distinction between psychiatry and neurology. For Griesinger there was only one form of abnormal behavior. He called it *insanity* and believed that its cause lay in the brain.

To understand Griesinger's assurance and optimism, we must remember that other scientists were making remarkable progress at the same time. Koch, for example, had isolated the bacteria that had caused anthrax in 1876. For the next 25 years, various bacteria and other organisms were found to play important roles in a variety of diseases. There was every reason to believe that microorganisms could explain virtually everything that was wrong with people, even erratic behavior.

In addition, three of the most common diseases of the time, syphilis, tuberculosis, and typhoid, were being better understood. Physicians noted with great interest that these diseases sometimes produced irrational thinking and behavior in those affected. Scientists and physicians reasoned that other forms of peculiar and apparently irrational behavior might also be caused by diseases.

Neurology, too, was becoming an important medical specialty. Areas of the brain were being located that appeared to serve specific functions, such as centers of speech and vision. Earlier, in 1811, Sir Charles Bell had stimulated much of this progress by proposing that sensations were carried along the spinal cord. It is not surprising, then, that a new medical specialty, psychiatry, developed and took as its territory the minds of the insane, who presumably also were suffering from diseases.

The final stamp of the organic and medical view of abnormal behavior was made on psychiatry by Emil Kraepelin (1856–1926). Kraepelin classified irrational behavior in great detail. As we shall see when we discuss schizophrenia, Kraepelin's thinking and influence persist today and provide a major basis for the way we classify schizophrenia. It is important to realize that Kraepelin did more than just classify abnormal behavior. By providing detailed descriptions and classifications, he made the study of abnormal behavior a truly legitimate medical discipline. Irrational behavior could now be described in terms of *disease entities* associated with *symptoms*.

Thus the victory over certain physical diseases which produced abnormal behavior, the rapid progress in medicine—especially neurology, and the scientific and technological optimism of the times all contributed to enthusiasm for the new medical discipline of psychiatry. Irrational behavior, once the domain of witch doctors and then of Inquisitors during the Middle Ages and later the province of social critics and reformers, now came under the influence of medicine. And, like the social-environmental stream of thought we described earlier, the medical organic view of abnormal behavior persists today as an influential approach to understanding abnormal behavior.

The well ordered asylum in America during the early part of the 19th century.

Historical Pictures Service, Inc., Chicago

The Third Stream: The Psychological Viewpoint

Although the psychological view of human behavior did not reach its full influence until the end of the 19th and the beginning of the 20th centuries, it has some roots in the Greek tradition. While Hippocrates was a physician, and because of him much irrational behavior was thought to be a disease, the Greeks also believed that reason could overcome irrational behavior. Later the humanism of Pinel and Tuke also stressed the psychological qualitites of the person.

It was Anton Mesmer (1734–1815), sometimes called the father of hypnotism, who brought the psychological view into focus. Mesmer believed that people had magnetic fluids within them and could be influenced through redistributing these fluids. In 1779 he came to Paris and opened a clinic in which he claimed to be able to cure all sorts of diseases by using "animal magnetism." His treatment involved various forms of suggestion and the use of elaborate rods and mechanical devices thought to affect the magnetic fluids. He was a dramatic figure and often appeared in flowing robes to attend his patients. A variety of complaints were relieved by Mesmer's efforts.

Although Mesmer was attacked as a fraud, the age of animal magnetism in the beginning of the 19th century greatly speeded the development of the psychological approach to human behavior. It helped to establish the ideas of conscious and unconscious thinking; it opened up psychological exploration of mental events; and, most important, it

Historical Pictures Service, Inc., Chicago

revived the idea that one person could help another change his or her irrational behavior.

Psychology was not only the province of physicians and hypnotists. In literature Ibsen, Shaw, and Nietzsche wrote about human behavior in ways that revealed a growing awareness of human motivation and conflict. Dostoevski's descriptions of madness had a richness and complexity that was very different from the classification efforts of the psychiatry of the day. Thus the 19th century was fertile ground for the reemergence of the psychological approach to understanding human behavior.

In psychiatry, changes were also beginning to take place toward the end of the 19th century. Two French physicians—Charcot, a neurologist in Paris, and Bernheim at Nancy—began to explore hypnosis and its relationship to certain

Mesmer in an early setting for hypnosis or "animal magnetism"

Historical Pictures Service, Inc., Chicago

Although Mesmer was often attacked as a fraud, he was also a critic of earlier practices such as exorcism as Hilgard (1977) notes in this fascinating account:

> Hypnosis and exorcism had a confrontation 200 years ago at a time when Father Johann Joseph Gassner (1717–99) was curing many of his parishioners, and others from afar after his fame spread, by using the Church's rituals of exorcism. He had cured himself by getting rid of "the Evil One" while he was a Catholic priest in a small village in Switzerland. There was much opposition to Gassner, because this was the Age of Enlightenment, and many wished to be rid of practices that they considered magical and irrational. The Prince-Elector Max Joseph of Bavaria appointed a commission of inquiry in 1775 and invited Franz Anton Mesmer (1734–1815), then an Austrian physician, to show that the results of exorcism could be obtained as well by his "naturalistic" method of animal magnetism, the precursor of hypnosis. Mesmer was able to produce the same effects that Gassner had produced—causing convulsions to occur and then cursing them. Mesmer won the day, and Gassner was sent off as a priest to a small community. Pope Pius VI ordered his own investigation, from which he concluded that exorcism was to be performed only with discretion" (p. 19).

SOME CONTEMPORARY APPLICATIONS OF HYPNOSIS*

Since the days of Mesmer, some of the world's most eminent scientists such as Benjamin Franklin, Freud, Pavlov, and William James have tried to tease out just what hypnosis can and cannot do. Today hypnosis, as used in treatment, is a private affair between therapist and client; the client is usually given instructions to relax and to focus his or her attention on some aspect of the environment. Those subjects who possess a hypnotic ability will then eventually enter a deeply relaxed state during which suggestions by the therapist are vividly experienced and acted upon as if they were reality (e.g., arm becomes numb, hearing is impaired, client vividly reexperiences past events, client smells odor which is not present).

While psychologists have long since abandoned Mesmer's claims of miraculous healings, hypnosis is still accepted as a treatment technique for a variety of psychological and psychosomatic disorders. Many individuals seek hypnotherapists to gain control of unwanted habits like smoking and overeating, but hypnosis has many other applications.

Enhancement of insight in psychotherapy Some experimental evidence (Nash, Johnson, and Tipton, 1979) suggests that the hypnotic subject has an enhanced ability to vividly reexperience past events and emotions

* Prepared with the assistance of Michael Nash.

associated with events. Some therapists believe that hypnosis enables their clients more easily to recognize and integrate previous repressed feelings or memories which might otherwise remain inaccessible. Hilgard (1977) reports the case of a young man who had not spoken Japanese since the age of about three. He spontaneously conversed in Japanese when, during hypnosis, suggestions were given to him to become three years old. Hypnosis is used by some insight-oriented therapists to help their clients link up past events with current problems.

Enhancement of behavior therapies Hypnosis also has been used as a part of behavior therapies. Behavior therapy relies less on the attainment of insight into problems than on directly changing the problem behavior itself. Systematic desensitization, one such behavior therapy technique, involves helping the client cope with unrealistic fears by vividly imagining the feared object or situation while remaining deeply relaxed. Lazarus (1978), a noted behavior therapist, has suggested the use of hypnosis to help clients more easily relax during desensitization. Hypnosis has also been used to increase the vividness of images in systematic desensitization.

Control of pain One of the most interesting and oldest applications of hypnosis is the control of acute and chronic pain. For acute pain hypnosis has been successfully used as a substitute for drugs in major surgery, childbirth, amputations, and tumor extractions. Complicated operations such as removal of breast tumors, hysterectomies, removal of genital tumors, plastic surgery, and oral surgery have all been carried out painlessly with nondrugged, hypnotized patients (Kroger, 1976). Pain which is more lasting (headaches, cancer-induced pain, arthritic pain) can be minimized and even eliminated by some clients with hypnotic ability who are properly trained in techniques of self-hypnosis and pain control.

Treating physical disorders Dermatitis, warts, rashes, and many other skin disorders may be responsive to hypnotic suggestion. When Sinclair-Giebin and Chambers (1959) suggested to their 14 hypnotized patients that their severe warts would clear from one side of their body, warts on the suggested side did indeed disappear; the warts on the other side did not. But better-controlled studies have not consistently documented skin changes in response to hypnotic suggestions (DePiano and Salzberg, 1979). If hypnosis plays some part in ridding the body of warts, the way in which it works is a mystery (Bowers, 1976). Stress-related disorders such as migraine and tension headaches and asthma have been treated with hypnosis. Of the three disorders, asthma appears to be the most susceptible to treatment by hypnosis (DePiano and Salzberg, 1979).

Treating amnesia and multiple personality Cases of amnesia and multiple personality have been identified and treated by hypnotic procedures. Persons with amnesia cannot recall important personal events in their past. In cases of multiple personality, two or more distinct "personalities" seem to coexist within the same person. Some of the most famous cases of multiple personalities (for example, Sybil and the three faces of Eve) were treated with hypnotherapy. In a classic case study, Prince (1925) used hypnosis to reintegrate the five personalities of Miss Beaucamp. Prince concluded that hypnosis enables the therapist to more easily summon and communicate with any of the personalities.

disorders that seemed to have no organic basis. In particular, the hysterias involving numb parts of the body and paralyses appeared to be curable by hypnotic suggestion. Charcot insisted that these disorders had no organic basis. Pierre Janet, another major French physician in this period, asserted that neurotic behaviors were a result of fixed subconscious ideas. He claimed that these disorders could be treated using "automatic talking" as therapy.

Yet it was a young Viennese physician, Sigmund Freud, who almost single-handedly framed and consolidated a uniquely psychological view of human action and abnormal behavior. Freud studied under Charcot in 1885 and became impressed by the power of hypnosis to affect certain forms of abnormal behavior. He returned to Vienna and worked with another physician, Joseph Breuer, who had developed a treatment called the "cathartic method." This treatment, the talking cure, consisted of hypnotizing the patient and allowing them to discuss their concerns while hypnotized. Often the patients' difficulties began to disappear using the talking cure.

As Freud observed and considered the process by which these cures were achieved, he was struck by the fact that much of the content of the patients' discussions while hypnotized was not

Medical research and treatment were often intertwined, at the turn of the century. Dr. Weir Mitchell (1829–1914) interviewing a patient and taking his pulse.

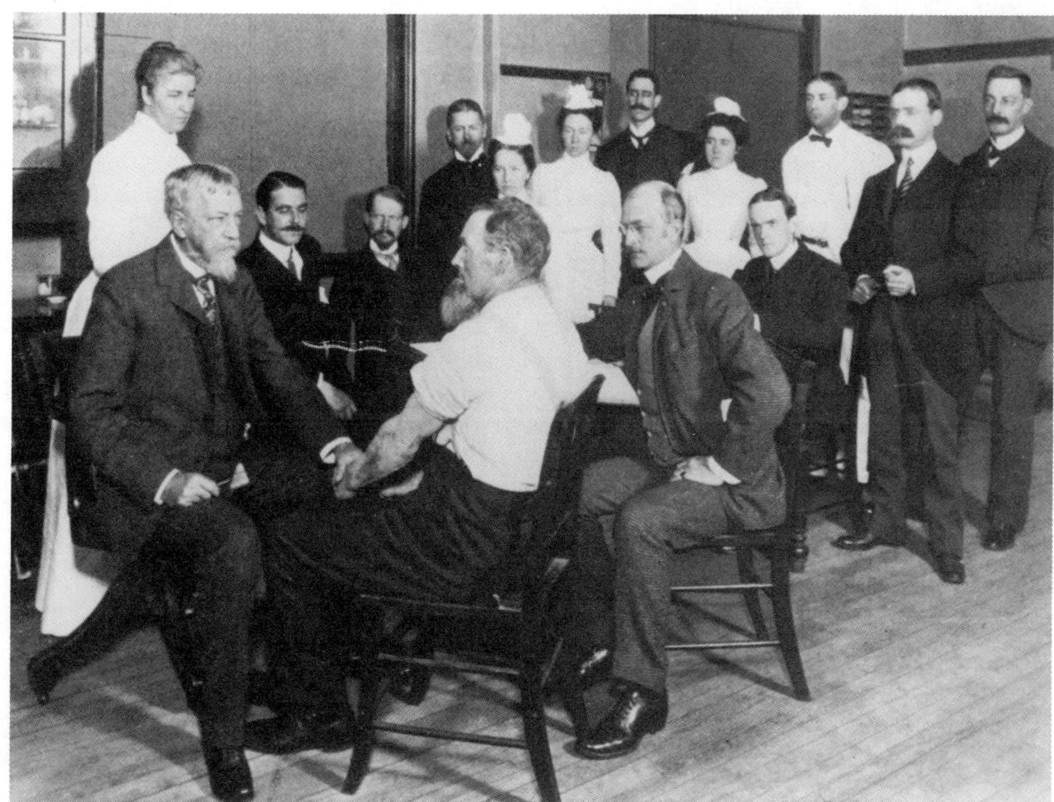

National Library of Medicine

Jean Charcot

National Library of Medicine

accessible when they were awake. These thoughts, said Freud, were "unconscious," and although not available to awareness by usual means, they still seemed to be very important determinants of behavior. Thus hypnosis, the talking cure, and Freud's acute ability to observe human behavior led him to suggest that abnormal behavior could actually be a result of purely psychological processes.

In the next chapter we will discuss Freud's perspective on human behavior, *psychoanalysis,* in more detail. But here it is important to see what became of Freud's thinking in the Victorian Age and late 19th century. Recall that it was an age of new and more restrictive morality. Freud believed that much of irrational or abnormal behavior was really the result of conflicts between sexual or aggressive impulses and the demands of conscience and reality. It is likely that in Vienna, in the late 19th century, moral constraints were so great that much of the content of his patients' discussions did, indeed, reflect conflicts between sexual impulses and strict, prudish social standards. As we shall see later, Freud's view of the role of women and of sexuality both are strongly flavored by 19th-century Victorian thinking.

Thus the psychological stream of thought, culminating in Freud's major contributions, was strongly influenced by the Victorian Age. With its restrictive standards of conduct, Victorian morality

Sigmund Freud

National Library of Medicine

PSYCHOANALYSIS AND THE MEDICAL MODEL

Today many authorities think of Freud's psychoanalysis as yet another version of the medical approach to abnormal behavior or "medical model," despite the fact that its origins were clearly imbedded in the psychological stream of thought. How did psychoanalysis come to be seen as part of the medical model? E. Fuller Torrey (1975), a psychiatrist himself, offers a fascinating analysis of what brought this about.

First, Torrey points out that Freud was a doctor who was strongly influenced by the medical beliefs of his age and by his medical teachers. Furthermore, the 19th century, with its strong belief in scientific knowledge as the solution to the world's problems, led Freud to believe that medical science, with psychoanalysis a part of it, could help to bring order out of chaos. In addition, much of Freud's early thinking involved hysteria, a condition that is similar to neurological conditions. And Freud found the profession of medicine protected him somewhat from the criticism he received for his theories' stress on sexual impulses. Strait-laced Vienna did not welcome theoreticians focusing their theories on sex.

Finally, larger social forces in Freud's time encouraged the idea that psychoanalysis should be part of medicine. A number of medical discoveries had shown a relationship between brain disease and irrational behavior. Psychosomatic medicine, a discipline concerned with showing how emotional reactions can produce physiological changes, was gaining popularity in the early 1920s. The Kraepelinian classification of abnormal behavior had become widely accepted. The mental hygiene movement in America was gaining prominence as it attempted to carry over the principles of public health to the field of psychiatry. Finally, when Dr. Abraham Flexner wrote a report exposing the charlatans who were practicing medicine in 1910, the reaction of psychiatry was to place itself under the protective umbrella of medicine. "Psychotherapy" became a form of "medical treatment."

Thus the psychological approach to abnormal behavior, originating in the animal magnetism of Mesmer and brought to the status of a comprehensive theoretical system by Freud, became another medical specialty.

helped to produce many of the conflicts that would become central to Freud's view of the nature of abnormal behavior.

SUMMARY

Our brief survey of the history of abnormal behavior has carried us from prehistoric times, when trephining was used to release evil spirits from possessed people's heads, to the 20th century, with its psychological, organic, and social environmental approaches to the understanding of abnormal behavior. But a history that does no more than teach us discrete facts is of little enduring value. Let us ask ourselves again a question with which we began this chapter. Are there things that the history of abnormal behavior can tell us about today's views and practices?

Perhaps the most important lesson we can learn from our survey is that the views of abnormal behavior that exist in any given period reflect the major cultural preoccupations of that time. Thus the prevailing ideas about abnormal behavior may tell us something about our own culture, our concerns, our fears, and our hopes for humanity. These ideas about abnormality serve as a kind of mirror. Rather than just accepting them as the "latest" ideas, we can view them as reflections of social and cultural influences to which we are all subject.

Our brief look at the witch hunts of the Middle Ages and the Inquisition should remind us that those who are seen as different, those whose behavior is deviant or peculiar, may at times provide a convenient target for social institutions struggling to maintain authority and control. Although the treatment the unfortunate receive in different ages may vary from persecution or indifference to genuine efforts to help, in each case we learn something about the values and concerns of society in that age.

The history of abnormal behavior in the 19th century provides us with some especially important lessons. The 19th century is recent enough to give us a sense of familiarity, yet distant enough to allow us to look at events with some objectivity. And, the 19th century seems to share some of our current cultural preoccupations—a concern about rapid cultural and social change and an awareness of economic and environmental factors as important in the development of abnormal behavior.

Caplan (1969) suggests several important parallels to current concerns. First, the 19th century was characterized by enthusiastic support of cure-alls for abnormal behavior, followed by disappointment when the treatment was only slightly effective. Second, some treatments were supported with huge investments of public resources before they had been carefully tested. Third, members of the helping professions frequently met public criticism with denial and defensiveness; when further pressed, they withdrew into their professions and institutions.

Finally, Caplan points out, the 19th century was a time in which the social history of abnormal behavior was badly neglected. Instead, the history of psychiatry and abnormal behavior was viewed as a progression of "great scientists" and "scientific breakthroughs." This self-justifying historical view is comforting, but it has little ability to arm us for the challenges of the future. Only a critical understanding of our past and its assumptions about the causes and cures of abnormal behavior can prepare us for those challenges.

3

Perspectives on Abnormal Behavior

Doctor, What's Wrong with Me?

I guess I first started to wonder about myself, seriously, I mean, when I was 13 years old. I was caught stealing some nylon stockings in a department store near where I lived. But the funny thing was, I really couldn't remember even walking into the store. My dad thought I was lying, and he beat me worse than he ever did. In a way I wish I had been lying, at least I could understand that. I was so afraid to tell him about it, because just before the incident he and Mom were fighting and I knew that he had been drinking. That really wasn't all that unusual, you understand; we were all pretty used to his blowing up for no good reason. I wasn't arrested or anything, but, looking back on it, the whole incident made me feel even more worthless, if that's possible. I always felt that I wasn't good enough, smart enough, pretty enough. All the time I was growing up, I felt nervous and awkward. Sometimes I felt that nothing was real, like I was living my life in a dream or a movie. The kids in school stayed away from me. Somehow they sensed that I was "different." You know, I never really had a friend. But I did have my fantasies. One of my favorite ones was being waited on hand and foot by a handsome guy who looked like a prince. But my life sure hasn't turned out that way. Both of my marriages were total disasters. Before Tom took off, he said that he was sick of my "moods" and my constant complaining. During my marriages I did do some pretty strange things. Once I remember walking around the bus station in Cleveland; I had no idea how I got 200 miles from my house or exactly what I was doing there. Since Tom left two years ago, it's been all downhill. I'm afraid to leave the house now. I hate men. I have fantasies of hurting them that I can't seem to get out of my mind. I don't trust myself, and I'm afraid of just about everyone but my mother. She brought me here, you know. When I told my doctor that I was afraid that I was going to "explode" and maybe kill someone, he asked me if I'd come into the hospital. My mother thinks I'm doing the right thing by coming in too. Dad doesn't really care one way or the other. Doctor, what's wrong with me?

Faced with the question, "What is really wrong with this patient?" experts in the field would likely give a wide range of answers. "This person is suffering from an unresolved Oedipal complex." Or, "This person has nothing at all wrong with her, but is merely being labeled 'sick' because of some unusual behavior." Still another might argue, "A functional analysis of this person's living situation suggests that certain behaviors emitted by the patient are consistently receiving reinforcement."

In this chapter we are going to try to understand how those experts, all examining the same patient, could come up with such different explanations of that person's behavior. We are also going to look at some of the conceptions of abnormal behavior currently receiving much attention. We will look, in particular, at the idea of abnormal behavior as *illness,* the *dynamic* point of view, the *learning* approach, the *social* perspective, and the *humanistic* viewpoint.

PERSPECTIVES IN CONFLICT

Disagreements are certainly not unique to the emerging science and study of abnormal behavior. In fact, a look at the evolution of nearly any science will suggest that at some time experts in that field disagreed about fundamental assumptions. Such disagreements mark times of great excitement and controversy in a science.

Thomas Kuhn (1962), an historian of science, has pointed out that most sciences go through periods of what he calls "paradigm clash." At such times several points of view about the nature of a phenomenon under study compete. These are also times when scientists advocating one point of view are unlikely to accept even the most fundamental assumptions of scientists advocating another. But most sciences move through these times of paradigm clash into what Kuhn calls periods of "normal science." During these normal periods, one viewpoint predominates, and important work continues within this dominant framework. Most fields seem to move back and forth between periods of disagreement and periods of normal science, although younger disciplines tend to have more disagreements among fundamental points of view.

The field of abnormal psychology seems to be going through a period of paradigm clash. And so it is important to describe each of these competing views of abnormal behavior and to show what is compelling about each. Let us return to our first question. How can scientists look at the same case and explain it in such radically different ways?

MODELS AND PERSPECTIVES IN SCIENTIFIC THINKING

To answer the question of how scientists can disagree so fundamentally we must look at their thought processes. Price (1978) has suggested that scientists use *analogies* to provide a framework for understanding a puzzling new event. Table 3–1 shows how the process works.

The analogy applies a *concept* that organizes the puzzling event or phenomenon by treating it *as if* it were a more familiar one. The scientist says in effect, "in order to understand the brain I will treat it *as if* it were a computer." Then the scientist can use the computer as a *model* of the brain. This allows the scientist to *select* some events as relevant for study, to *represent* aspects of the puzzling events, and to *make* hypotheses about how the events are organized.

Because adopting a particular model or analogy for representing abnormal behavior exerts such a powerful influence on how we "see" or perceive the events in question, we have chosen the term *perspective* to characterize the approaches we will describe in this chapter.

In fact, we do make sense out of complex events by applying a framework

TABLE 3–1 The Model in Scientific Thinking

Basic Character of Models	*Examples of a Model*	*Functions of Models*
1. *Definition:* A model is any conceptual analogue used to initiate empirical research	Thinks of the brain *"as if"* it were a computer (Familiar set of events or structure) 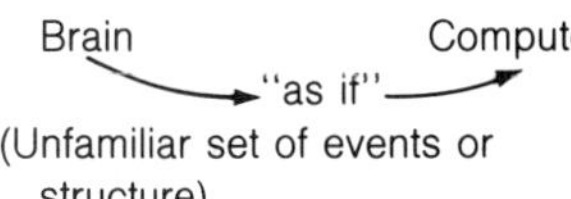 (Unfamiliar set of events or structure)	1. *Aids in selecting events: Stimuli* "as if" input, *cortex* "as if" *storage, behavior* "as if" *output*
2. *Strategy of Models:* Using a set of events or structure to help think about a set of events we do not understand		2. *Provides a mode of representation:* "The cortex is the 'storage component' of the brain"
3. *"As if" quality:* Treats one set of events "as if" it were another set		3. *Aids in organizing events:* "Both behavior and computer output may be corrected via feedback loops"

Source: From *Abnormal Behavior: Perspectives in Conflict,* Second Edition, by Richard H. Price.

that emphasizes some aspects of those events and deemphasizes others. And so we will see that the various views of abnormal behavior emphasize one aspect of a person's behavior rather than another.

For example, the social perspective emphasizes the effect of social forces acting on the person displaying the abnormal behavior. The dynamic view focuses much more on events in the subjective life of the person and how inner needs may conflict. The learning view stresses the role of rewards and punishments on our behavior while the disease perspective focuses on our biological nature. Finally, the humanistic perspective emphasizes the conditions needed for psychological growth. Each view focuses on different aspects of the life of the person and, in doing so, produces a coherent and yet, in some ways, incomplete picture. Let us now examine each perspective.

THE DISEASE PERSPECTIVE

The idea that abnormal behavior is the product of disease has deep historical roots. Psychiatry, a branch of medicine, has long been concerned with the study of abnormal behavior. Important biological advances in the understanding of genetic disorders and infectious diseases have also helped shape our thinking. Furthermore, the idea that abnormal behavior *is* mental illness is not just one promoted by physicians. It is an idea on which public education campaigns have long focused.

The Language of Disease

We are hardly surprised, therefore, to hear the peculiar ways of some people often described as *symptomatic* of an *illness.* Furthermore, we treat such people in mental *hospitals,* giving them *therapy,* and of course, most important, we regard them as *patients.*

These are outward but important signs that the idea of abnormal behavior as illness is commonly accepted. Although the language of the general public reflecting the illness viewpoint may not go farther than such terms as *patient, treatment,* or *symptom,* there are a number of other terms in the illness perspective that we should understand.

Often within this perspective, when we talk about the systematic study of the causes of various disorders, we use the term *etiology*. And when we look at a pattern of symptoms that occur together for a person, we call it a *syndrome*. When a person's behavior is studied in order to decide what sort of disorder he has, that process is called *diagnosis*. We usually expect the diagnosis to tell us something about appropriate *treatments*. We also expect the diagnosis to tell us something about *prognosis*—a statement about the likely course and outcome of the disorder.

Although this language is generally used in the illness perspective, there actually is more than one way to think about diseases. Buss (1966) points out that there are at least three generally accepted kinds of disease in medicine. The first is a *traumatic disease*. This is produced by some external or environmental event or agent. Serious physical damage due to external stress, such as poisoning, or perhaps a skull fracture is an example.

A second major type of disease is the *infectious disease*. Here, some microorganism such as a virus attacks the body through an organ or a system of organs. Probably the most famous such disease in psychiatry is general paresis, a behavior disorder associated with syphilis of the brain.

It is not likely, though, that either of these diseases will provide the best model for understanding abnormal behavior as illness. The third type, the *diathesis-stress* type, probably provides the best and most interesting model. In this type, some organ or organ system breaks down or fails to function properly, mainly because it already has some inherited defect or weakness (diathesis). Thus, the organ or organ system is *predisposed* to break down and may do so if it is subjected to prolonged stress.

The diathesis-stress model is probably the most accepted approach to thinking about abnormal behavior as a disease. Though very simple in its general outline, it takes into account both environmental stresses and the physiology of the person as shaped by heredity. In later chapters we will consider evidence for the diathesis-stress explanation in several disorders.

Meehl's View of Schizophrenia as an Example

Let us consider a clear example of the illness perspective in action. Our example will be drawn from the work of one of the most thoughtful advocates of the disease point of view, Paul Meehl. Meehl has been developing his ideas about one psychological disorder, schizophrenia, for some time. The way Meehl describes his conception of schizophrenia suggests that it is a disease of the diathesis-stress type.

Figure 3–1 shows what Meehl calls a set of causal chains in schizophrenia of minimum complexity. In other words, it gives us a picture of how schizophrenia develops from Meehl's point of view. If you look at the bottom of the figure, you see that it begins with a "dominant schizogene." Meehl is identifying a genetic component in schizophrenia, and he thinks it is important. He believes that the dominant schizogene is the *specific etiology* of the disorder. A specific etiology is any condition that is necessary but not sufficient for the disorder to occur. In other words, Meehl believes that schizophrenia cannot occur unless a person has the

FIGURE 3–1 Causal Chains in Schizophrenia, Minimum Complexity

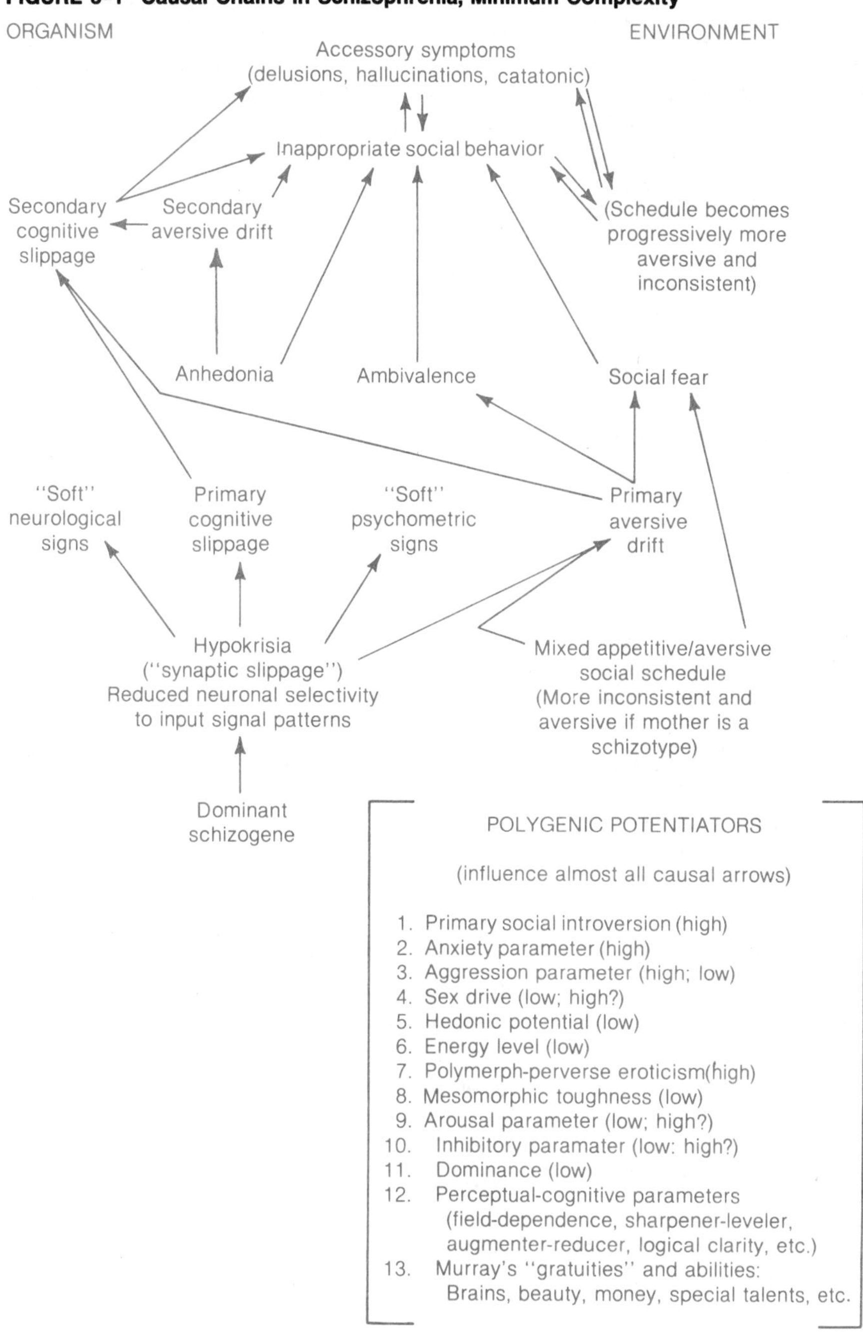

Source: Paul Meehl, "Some Ruminations on the Validation of Clinical Procedures," *Canadian Journal of Psychology,* 1959, Vol. 13, p. 102.

Paul Meehl

"I consider that there are such things as disease entities in functional psychiatry, and I do not think that Kraepelin was as mistaken as some of my psychological contemporaries seem to think. It is my belief, for example, that there is a *disease* schizophrenia, fundamentally of an organic nature, and probably of largely constitutional etiology" (Meehl, 1966, p. 9).

dominant schizogene, but the schizogene cannot, by itself, cause schizophrenia.

Now look again at Figure 3–1. We can see that if people have the dominant schizogene, they will display a number of behavioral traits. These traits, Meehl believes, include "cognitive slippage," that is, loose or odd associations and language, social fear, and others. They are signs that a person could eventually suffer from the disorder. If the person's behavior is seen as inappropriate, he may be exposed to progressively aversive and inconsistent social events. It is at this point that the person will produce the inappropriate social behavior and other symptoms that we have come to know as *schizophrenia*.

Several interesting things should be noted about Meehl's diathesis-stress disease model of schizophrenia. First it suggests that people who develop schizophrenia are genetically predisposed to do so. Furthermore, it suggests that unpleasant environmental circumstances which presumably produce stress are also necessary *but not sufficient* for the disorder to develop. Therefore, other people subjected to the same stress would *not* develop schizophrenia if they were not genetically predisposed to do so.

Finally, notice that, although the environmental events associated with schizophrenia are sketched in, they are only described in the most general way. You will recall that we said perspectives tend to stress certain aspects of the case and minimize others. Here is a clear example of that effect of perspectives on our perception of the problem being studied. Central features of the viewpoint (e.g., schizogenes) are given in detail, and the interpersonal life of the individual is reduced to "aversive and inconsistent events."

Attacks on the Disease Model

As we continue looking at perspectives in this chapter and throughout the book, we will see the disease conception of abnormal behavior has been strongly attacked. One suspects that some of this criticism is justified. The "medical model" of abnormal behavior is often applied on the basis of very little evidence and carries with it much of the institutional authority of medicine and physicians, which in some cases can lead to misjudgments and abuses.

Supporting Evidence

On the other hand, the illness perspective has already scored some important victories. Typically, once the organic etiology or causal basis for a disorder is found, it leaves the domain of psychiatry and abnormal psychology and is treated as just another disease. A classic example of this shift in our view of a disorder is the apparently bizarre behavior that often accompanies pellagra, a nutritional disease. Once vitamin deficiency was discovered to be the disease's main cause and a simple, effective treatment was found, pellagra was reclassified as an organic rather than a functional psychological disorder. Now, although rare

AN ATTACK ON THE CONCEPT OF MENTAL ILLNESS—THOMAS SZASZ

The best-known attack on the notion that abnormal behavior is mental illness has been mounted by Thomas Szasz (1967, 1976). Although Szasz himself is a psychiatrist, he has been one of the most strident critics of the illness perspective on abnormal behavior.

Szasz claims that mental illness is a myth. Instead, the behavior we view as deviant or peculiar in others can be better thought of as simply "problems in living." According to Szasz, the concept of mental illness will not withstand logical analysis. Although *mental illness* is a medical term, it is actually defined by social criteria. And, if a person's problem is actually the result of a neurological defect, it is a disease of the nervous system and should not be called mental illness. Szasz believes that the term *mental illness* really refers to communications that we find peculiar because their content is often unacceptable ("I am Napoleon") and they are often framed in unusual ways; for example, language may be distorted or bizarre.

Szasz argues that the concept of mental illness obscures more than it reveals. He says: "My argument is limited to the proposition that mental illness is a myth, whose function it is to distinguish and thus render more palatable a bitter pill of moral conflict in relations (p. 118).

Thomas Szasz

Courtesy of Thomas Szasz, photo by Jack Orton

in this country, it is not viewed as abnormal behavior even though bizarre behavior can, in some cases, still occur with it.

If, as Meehl argues, certain severe disorders such as schizophrenia are actually diseases, it would follow that some evidence of genetic and biochemical causes would have been found as with other diseases.

As we will see in later chapters, there is indeed evidence suggesting genetic factors in psychological disorders. Rosenthal (1970) has summarized much of this evidence and concluded that for severe disturbances such as schizophrenia, evidence for a genetic factor is relatively strong. Some of the most interesting studies here involve use of the twin method, in which researchers compare the rate of a disorder among pairs of fraternal and identical twins. Since identical twins have essentially the same genetic structures, higher rates of the same disorder among both members of a pair of identical twins suggest that the disorder may have a genetic component. We will examine this evidence in greater detail in later chapters.

Snyder (1975) has reviewed a second line of evidence, the psychological effects of drugs called *phenothiazines.* These drugs appear to have specific effects on the brain chemistry of schizophrenics. This finding, says Snyder, suggests that something in the brain chemistry of schizophrenics is amiss in the first place, and that the phenothiazine drugs have their specific effects because of this biochemical inbalance in the brain chemistry.

In later chapters you will see the amount of biological evidence for various disorders is far from uniform. Some disorders such as schizophrenia and some forms of affective disorder appear to have important biological components. For others, little or no biological evidence as yet has been found. This of course raises the question of the degree to which the disease perspective, or for that matter, any perspective is equally applicable to all forms of abnormal behavior. We will be able to form opinions about that question at several points in later chapters.

We have seen that the disease perspective on abnormal behavior is widely accepted and has its own medical language and concepts. It is likely that the diathesis-stress view is the most plausible account of abnormal behavior now available to us. This view emphasizes the idea that some people may be biologically predisposed to certain diseases such as schizophrenia. We will review evidence for the idea that certain disorders are actually diseases in later chapters. We should note, though, that the disease perspective, like all perspectives, gives an incomplete picture of abnormal behavior. It is a picture that minimizes the importance of social and interpersonal events in the life of the person.

THE DYNAMIC PERSPECTIVE

Sigmund Freud (1856–1939) has probably had the greatest impact of any person on the field of abnormal psychology. During more than 50 years, Freud lectured and wrote scientific papers and books that have profoundly influenced how we think about human behavior. Freud has inspired historians, social critics, and entire schools of literature through his ideas. Even today his influence pervades our thinking and language.

Large segments of the mental health professions are devoted to the psychodynamic point of view originated by

Freud. Psychoanalysis is taught as a primary way of understanding and treating abnormal behavior in a number of medical schools and clinical training programs throughout the country. Even though the dynamic viewpoint has had to compete with other approaches in recent years, it still must be counted as a major source of ideas in the field of abnormal psychology. Actually, a number of dynamic approaches have developed from Freud's original theories both as reactions to some of his propositions and as elaborations of his ideas. In this discussion we will concentrate on Freud's ideas.

Overview of Psychoanalytic Theory

In the following discussion, we will dwell on the *psychological structure of the individual* in understanding the dynamic perspective on the development of abnormal behavior. Nevertheless, as Holzman (1970) has noted, psychoanalysis is not a single perspective; it is a group of perspectives focusing on three general areas. First, Freud wrote on the nature of *thinking and perception.* Second, psychoanalysis formulated a series of propositions and ideas on the *nature and course of human development.* Finally, part of Freudian thinking is devoted to the nature of *abnormal behavior and its treatment.* We will focus on this last aspect of psychoanalytic theory.

Fundamental Assumptions of the Dynamic Perspective

Holzman (1970) has offered an excellent summary of the basic assumptions about human behavior made by the psychoanalytic perspective.

Psychological processes. These may operate outside our conscious awareness. Although Freud did not originate the concept of *unconscious psychological processes,* posthypnotic phenomena and the failure of many of his patients to recall crucial events in their lives convinced him that such processes must be occurring.

Indeed, Freud postulated the existence of unconscious, preconscious, and conscious mental activity. Conscious processes are those which are immediately within awareness at any given time. Preconscious processes are thoughts, ideas, and memories that may be outside of immediate awareness but which are readily available. The ability to recall a telephone number from preconscious processes is an example. Unconscious processes, on the other hand, represent a great reservoir of memories, hopes, fears, and fantasies that cannot easily be brought into awareness. Freud believed there was a "censoring" process that kept these unconscious thoughts from coming into awareness. A summary of this viewpoint process is shown in Figure 3–2.

Freud's theory. Freud also believed that *behavior was purposive,* that is, motivated or caused. Symptoms within the psychoanalytic framework could also serve a purpose.

Developmental determinants of behavior. Psychoanalysts believe that important determinants of behavior are developmental in nature. As Holzman (1970) suggests, for each person the "past persists into the present." According to this view, some motives or behaviors may fixate or "freeze" at infantile levels of development and persist into adult life.

Drives or needs can differ in their intensity. This is often called the "quantitative" assumption in dynamic

FIGURE 3–2 Relationship between the Unconscious, Preconscious, and Conscious Domains of Psychological Life.

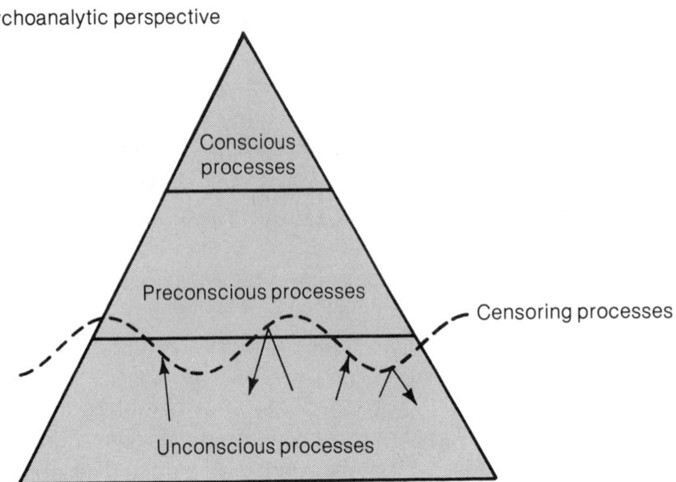

thinking. According to this view, much of what we call abnormal behavior is abnormal in its degree or intensity rather than qualitatively different.

The adaptive nature of behavior. Freud believed that human behavior should be understood as a response to the demands of the physical and social environment. Rapaport and Gill (1967) have called this the "adaptive point of view." It serves to emphasize that the psychoanalytic perspective recognized the impact on people of important interpersonal and social events and saw each person as continuously coping, shaping, and being shaped by the social environment and culture.

Mental Structures, Conflict, and Anxiety

Freud believed there were three major structures in the mental life of each person: the *id,* the *ego,* and the *superego.* Each of these structures operated in dynamic relation to the other two, and the final product of these relationships was the behavior of the person.

The *id* was thought by Freud to represent the primitive biological drives of the person. The id was thought to be in "chaos, a caldron of seething excitement" (Freud, 1933, pp. 103–4). The id's goal was to release this biological energy in aggressive or erotic ways; thus the id was described as operating according to the *pleasure principle.*

Freud called the second major structure in the person's mental life the *ego.* Whereas the id operates by the pleasure principle, the ego operates by the *reality principle.* That is, the ego's function is to assess how realistic it is to engage in sexual or aggressive acts in order to gratify id impulses. One can think of the ego as a kind of executive branch to judge the feasibility, reality, and appropriateness of our actions.

TABLE 3–2 Personal Structure According to the Psychoanalytic Perspective

Structure	*Functioning Principle*	*Mode of Operation*
Id: The instincts; source of psychic energy; biological substratum of personality.	*Pleasure Principle* Seeks to gratify instinctual drives immediately.	*Primary Process* Direct motor discharge of energy or drive, such as dreams, wish fulfillment.
Ego: Developed from the id; reality oriented; judging; executive.	*Reality Principle* "Executive function," that is, moderates demands of instinctual impulses and demands of external reality.	*Secondary Process* Differentiates objective from subjective reality; relies on past experience; judges.
Superego: Developed from the ego; represents introjection of parental moral standards and values.	*Moral Evaluation* Judges right and wrong, "good" and "bad."	*Conscience* Source of moral judgment.
		Ego Ideal Image of person child would like to become.

Source: From *Abnormal Behavior: Perspectives in Conflict,* Second Edition, by Richard H. Price. Copyright © 1978 by Holt, Rinehart and Winston. Copyright © 1972 by Holt, Rinehart and Winston, Inc. Reprinted by permission of Holt, Rinehart and Winston.

Freud described the third major structure in the person's psychological life as the *superego.* As a child is reared, he or she usually learns that certain acts and even certain impulses are "good" and others are "bad." Thus, the superego, as an internal representation of the moral standards of society controls and judges our actions as we plan or fantasize about them, or as we carry them out.

It is the *conflict* between these three structures, Freud believed, that determines much of our behavior. For example, the instinctual demands of the id may conflict with either the reality-oriented concerns of the ego or the moral demands of the superego. When such conflicts occur and are not readily resolved, they are thought to produce tension or anxiety.

Freud thought that people felt different kinds of anxiety depending on which structures among the id, ego, and superego were in conflict. Figure 3–3 shows how conflicts produced various kinds of anxiety. *Reality anxiety* was believed to be produced when the ego perceived some real physical threat in the outside world. *Moral anxiety,* as the name implies, was thought to be a product of conflict between the id and the superego. Finally, *neurotic anxiety* was thought to occur when the id and the ego were in conflict.

In the last two cases, the person undergoes an inner struggle between conflicting impulses. This struggle can be so great, Freud believed, that the person finds the resulting anxiety intolerable.

FIGURE 3–3

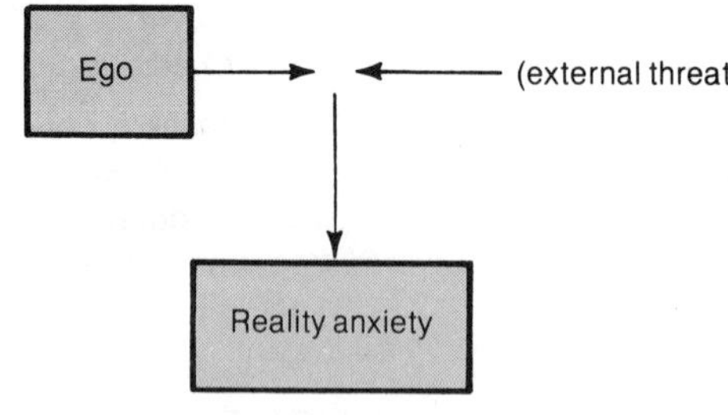

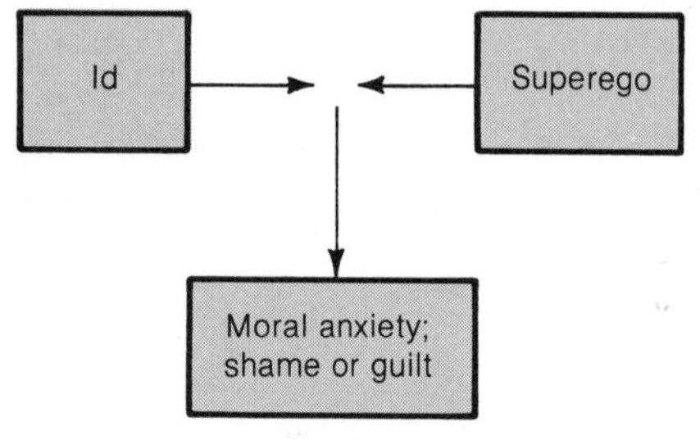

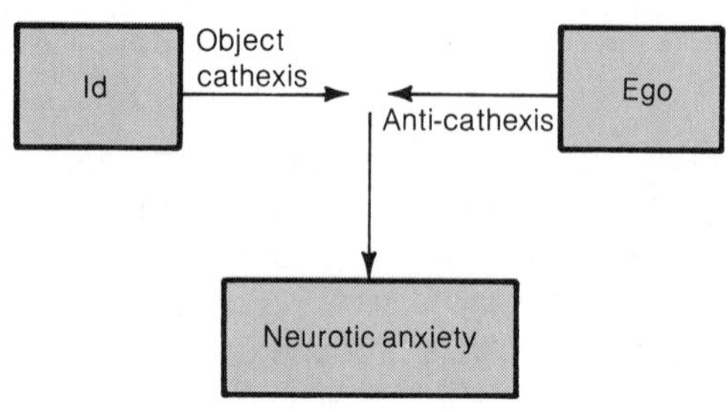

Defense Mechanisms

The ego, in the role of protector, at times had to take irrational measures to shield itself from this conflict-produced anxiety. The means of protection are called *ego defense mechanisms.* They are psychological ways of distorting reality to reduce the anxiety caused by, for example, the id-ego conflict. The most important of them is called *repression.* Here the id impulse, in conflict with the ego or the superego, is totally dismissed from consciousness. That is, repression takes the impulse out of awareness and, by so doing, temporarily relieves us of id-ego conflict and its resultant anxiety.

Another important aspect of defense mechanisms is that they act *without us ever being aware of them.* Therefore, the energy from the original conflict still exists and may manifest itself in anxiety from time to time; but we may not know why we are anxious because the original causes of the conflict are repressed.

Freud thought that much of the behavior that seemed odd, irrational, or abnormal was evidence of defense mechanisms at work shielding the ego. These defenses might at first seem illogical, but actually they have an internal logic of their own. Furthermore, trying to understand a defense mechanism and how it works to protect the person could yield clues about the person's underlying conflict.

Abnormal Behavior Examined from the Dynamic Viewpoint

Recall that we said neurotic anxiety is the product of conflicts between the id and the ego. The id wishes to express some forbidden impulse, but it is blocked by the ego. In Freud's view, the anxiety that we sometimes experience comes to be associated with various objects or situations that almost bring the forbidden impulse into awareness. However, repression forces the impulse back out of awareness. While this struggle is going on, the experience we have is one of intense fear associated with some situation or event. This intense fear is commonly called a *phobia.* But it is a fear for which no rational explanation seems adequate. Phobias are a well known type of behavior

DEFENSE MECHANISMS

Freud was, among other things, a brilliant and perceptive observer of human behavior. When he detected a patient's defensive reality-distorting strategies, he was especially curious and persistent in his inquiries. His years of trying to unravel the complexities of his patients' fantasies, dreams, and apparently irrational behavior patterns yielded the discovery of several distinctive defense mechanisms. Here are some of them.

Repression This is a mechanism for keeping unpleasant thoughts or dangerous impulses entirely out of conscious awareness. Clues that repression might be at work could include unexplainable memory lapses for certain events or "blocking" of names or appointments.

Projection Projection is a mechanism in which an individual attributes his or her own unacceptable impulses to others. For example, a person might accuse others of having "dirty" thoughts and thus "project" his own sexual impulses onto them.

Reaction formation A mechanism in which expressed conscious attitudes are the opposite of an internal wish or impulse is called reaction formation. For example, exaggerated affection may be expressed when internal impulses to injure another are being denied.

Displacement In this case an impulse directed at one person or object is shifted to another more acceptable substitute person or object. When a child strikes a younger brother rather than express anger against a parent, displacement may be at work.

Perhaps now it is easier to see why Freud believed that apparently irrational behavior often had a logic of its own. Defense mechanisms can be thought of as attempts to cope with feelings or desires that are felt to be unacceptable by the ego or superego. Indeed, they are not necessarily abnormal in themselves but are a part of our everyday life. It is only when they begin to interfere with our functioning that they should become a source of concern.

for which the dynamic model can provide an explanation, although we will soon see that other viewpoints can explain them also.

Within the dynamic point of view, the irrationally feared objects or situations are usually thought to symbolize the temptation to the id. So, according to this view, behind each fear there is actually a *wish*—the id's desire—for the object or for something the object represents.

For an example of abnormal behavior as seen from the dynamic perspective, we have taken the famous case of "Little Hans" as described by Cameron (1963). As you read the case, you will see the symbolic nature of the explanation, the conflict between various psychological structures, and the fascinating complexity with which these simple mechanisms and their interrelationship explain an apparently mysterious bit of abnormal behavior.

The most famous case of zoophobia (fear of animals) is also the first one ever to be studied dynamically, the case of little Hans. This boy of five years refused to go out into the street because he was afraid of horses, actually feared being bitten by them. In the course of therapy, it turned out that the horses symbolized the hated and feared aspect of his father. The little patient harbored hostile aggression against his only male rival for his mother's love, but at the same time he also loved his father dearly. Reduced to its simplest terms, the phobic solution was about as follows. The love for his father was retained, while the hatred for him was displaced on the horses. This had the added advantage that the horses could easily be avoided, whereas his father could not. In the usual role reversal of fantasies and dreams, the boy expected primitive retaliation from his father for the primitive hostility he himself felt. This expectation likewise was displaced. It became the regressive oral fear that horses would bite him.

The whole displacement in the case of little Hans was made easy by certain other partial identities: *(a)* the father had often played "horsey" with Hans; *(b)* the horses' bridles reminded Hans fearfully of his father's dark mustache; *(c)* he wished his father might fall and hurt himself, as Hans had seen horses fall, and as his playmate with whom he also played "horsey" had fallen and hurt himself.

As a result of therapy, this patient recovered from his phobia. It is interesting that, years later when Hans chanced upon the account of his illness and its treatment, all memory of the once vivid phobia had been completely repressed. Some of the incidental comments about his parents made him wonder if he could have been this famous little patient and led him to visit Freud, where he found out that he was.

The case history of little Hans is especially instructive for two reasons. First, it shows the role of *conflict* between id and ego or superego in the development of a phobia. The id impulses Hans experienced were, of course, the forbidden possessive sexual love for his mother and his hatred of his male rival, his father. Since these impulses were blocked by the ego or superego, the tension produced was expressed as unbearable anxiety. This anxiety, in turn, was transformed into a more manageable form, the phobic fear of horses, rather than hate and fear of his father.

Also the case shows clearly how crucial the *symbolic* connections in Hans's thinking are to understanding the origins of his phobia. Why should Hans fear horses rather than something else? According to the case history, it is because the hated father is also associated with "playing horsey" and with bridles (father's mustache) and Hans's previous experience with falling horses and hopes that his father might also fall and hurt himself.

The art of the dynamically oriented analyst is also revealed in this brief case history. Notice how Cameron (and Freud before him) managed to understand Hans' apparently "irrational" or "senseless" fear of horses in terms of its symbolic relationship to the father. Like a detective, Freud began to put together the pieces in the puzzle; and surely, once the idea of the symbolic link between horse and father occurred for Freud, it was easy to gather more "evidence" for the validity of his proposition.

The problem of what is *evidence* for the validity of dynamic theories is a difficult one, and it is the basis of most criticisms of the dynamic approach to understanding abnormal behavior. Because the issue of evidence is so crucial both with this approach, and in the scientific understanding of abnormal behavior in general, we will now examine that issue in more detail.

Dynamic Explanations

Freud has been credited with being one of the great original thinkers of this century. Sometimes his contributions are not clearly appreciated. But there is no doubt that his most important one contribution is the idea of *psychological determinism.* This is the idea that purely psychological events, experiences, and mental structures in relationship to one another could be considered fundamental causes of abnormal behavior or symptoms.

In addition to this idea, Freud and his followers developed a treatment technique based on the theory of psychoanalysis. In this treatment individuals and sometimes groups are helped to examine the symbolic meaning of their behavior in order to find the psychological causes of their difficulties or symptoms. The effectiveness of this treatment method is still in dispute; yet it remains one of the most sought-after treatments today.

Some features of Freud's sweeping and complex theories have been much criticized, especially by philosophers of science and empirically oriented scientists. Perhaps the most important of these criticisms is that Freud's concepts often do not meet the criterion of *falsifiability* described by Sidney Hook (1959). What do we mean by falsifiability? Concepts should be constructed so that we can gather evidence that will help us decide whether or not the concept is consistent with the evidence at hand. If we cannot do this,

In psychoanalysis the patient is frequently asked to free associate and to recline to induce a more relaxed state.

Van Bucher/Photo Researchers, Inc.

the concept has little scientific usefulness. This is a slippery but important point. Let us take an example from Hook that illustrates it.

> For example, we hear that someone is "intelligent" or "friendly." Many types of behavior can be cited as evidence for the presence of "intelligence" or "friendliness." *But, unless we are also told what we would have to observe to conclude that an individual is not "intelligent" or "friendly," the terms could be applied to anyone in all situations* (pp. 214–15, italics added).

The important point here is that if a concept does not specify the conditions under which it *is* applicable or is *not* applicable, it is of very little use in science.

Ideas like the Oedipus complex, repression, and defense share this problem of falsifiability. For example, if a person expresses great love for his father, is he expressing genuine affection or is this evidence of a reaction formation? Likewise, if you characterize another person as "hostile," are you reporting an accurate impression or projecting your own hostile feelings, or both? It is problems of evidence and the criteria for application of Freud's concepts like these that have led to criticism of his system. The responsibility of those who follow such a bold explorer is to refine his ideas and to test them against observation and evidence.

THE LEARNING PERSPECTIVE

Perhaps the fastest growing approach to the study and treatment of abnormal behavior is the learning viewpoint. Although American psychologists have long studied the learning process, it is only in the last 30 years or so that they have applied learning principles to the analysis and treatment of abnormal behavior.

Pioneers in this relatively new approach to understanding abnormal behavior were encouraged by the early work of B. F. Skinner. More than 20 years ago, Skinner published a book called *Science and Human Behavior*. The book applied learning principles, in particular those of instrumental conditioning, to a variety of human behaviors ranging from gambling and fishing to learning a language.

Another group of pioneers developing the idea that abnormal behavior could be learned was Jules Masserman and his colleagues. These researchers followed the lead of Ivan Pavlov and began to do laboratory experiments with animals to see if it was possible to create conditions in which abnormal behavior could be learned. They called the behavior they were able to produce *experimental neurosis*. This research led to the optimistic hope that, if we were able to produce abnormal behavior in the laboratory, we would soon understand the naturally occurring circumstances under which abnormal behavior is produced.

A variety of mechanisms have been proposed to explain how abnormal behavior is acquired, how it is maintained, and how it might be eliminated. We will examine (1) classical conditioning, (2) instrumental conditioning, (3) modeling and observational learning, and (4) cognitive processes in the learning perspective.

Classical Conditioning

The first of these processes is called *classical conditioning*. This process was

SKINNER OFFERS A LEARNING INTERPRETATION

Consider a young man whose world has suddenly changed—he has graduated from college and is going to work, let us say, or has been inducted into the armed services. Most of the behavior he has acquired up to this point is useless in his new environment. We can describe the behavior he actually exhibits, and translate the description, as follows: he lacks assurance or feels insecure *(his behavior is weak and inappropriate);* he is discouraged *(he is seldom reinforced, and as a result his behavior undergoes extinction);* he is frustrated *(extinction is accompanied by emotional responses);* he feels anxious *(his behavior frequently has unavoidable aversive consequences that have emotional effects);* there is nothing he wants to do or enjoys doing well—he has no feeling of craftsmanship, no sense of accomplishment *(he is rarely reinforced for doing anything);* he feels guilty or ashamed *(he has previously been punished for idleness or failure, which now evoke emotional responses);* he is disgusted with himself *(he is no longer reinforced by the admiration of others, and the extinction that follows has emotional effects);* he becomes hypochondriacal *(he concludes that he is ill)* or neurotic *(he engages in a variety of ineffective modes of escape);* and he experiences an identity crisis *(he does not recognize the person he once called "I").*

The italicized paraphrases suggest the possibility of an alternative account, which alone suggests effective action. What the young man tells us about his feelings may permit us to make some informed guesses about what is wrong with the contingencies, but we must go directly to the contingencies if we want to be sure, *and it is the contingencies we must change if we are to change his behavior.*

From *Beyond Freedom and Dignity,* by B. F. Skinner.

B. F. Skinner

Courtesy of B. F. Skinner, photo by Christopher S. Johnson

first described by Ivan Pavlov and explains how an event in the environment that originally elicited no reaction can, by being systematically paired with other events, evoke *conditioned responses.* Figure 3–4 shows how this process takes place.

Perhaps the most famous demonstration of how classical conditioning could

Ivan Pavlov

National Library of Medicine

John B. Watson

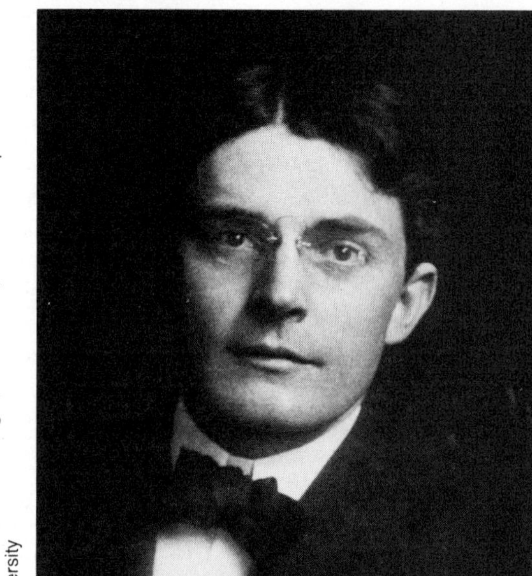

The Ferdinand Hamburger, Jr. Archives, The Johns Hopkins University

produce abnormal behavior was done by Watson and Rayner (1920). They chose as their subject an 11-month-old child named Albert who was very fond of animals. Their goal was to show that through classical conditioning fears that looked irrational and phobic could be learned. In the laboratory, they closely observed Albert's behavior.

FIGURE 3–4 Classical Conditioning Paradigm

Conditioned stimulus (before conditioning) - - - - - - - - - → No response

Conditioned stimulus - - - (learned) - - - → Conditioned response

Unconditioned stimulus - - - (unlearned) - - - → Unconditioned response

Source: Adapted from Introduction to Psychology, Third Edition by Ernest R. Hilgard, copyright © 1962 by Harcourt Brace Jovanovich, Inc. Reprinted by permission of the publisher.

Whenever he reached out for a white rat to which he was attracted (the white rat represents the *conditioned stimulus*), a loud noise was created. Not surprisingly, Albert was startled and began crying. (The boy's reaction is considered the *unconditioned response,* and the loud noise is thought of as the *unconditioned stimulus*). After a number of such pairings of the white rat with the loud noise, Albert was terrified whenever the rat was presented to him. Furthermore, his reaction generalized to other furry objects as well. Watson and Rayner then argued that they had demonstrated that apparently irrational fears (phobias) can be learned through classical conditioning. That is, by pairing a previously neutral stimulus (the rat) with a stimulus that could evoke a strong response (the loud noise) it was possible to obtain a fear reaction to the rat when it was later presented by itself.

Instrumental Conditioning

The second major mechanism used to explain how abnormal behavior is acquired and maintained is called *instrumental conditioning.* With this process, the *consequences* of a particular behavior affect the likelihood that the behavior will occur again. This idea, developed by a number of psychologists including Thorndike and elaborated most by B. F. Skinner, suggests that *contingencies* are extremely important in understanding the development of abnormal behavior. In this approach, events that immediately follow particular behaviors on a systematic basis are called *reinforcements.*

Instrumental conditioning of symptoms. Is it possible to reward a behavior using instrumental conditioning procedures so that, after a while, the very persistence and frequency of the behavior makes it seem strange and abnormal? An example of the development of abnormal behavior using the instrumental conditioning process has been provided by Haughton and Ayllon (1965). They created "abnormal behavior" in a hospitalized 54-year-old woman and then eliminated it using principles of instrumental conditioning. After having deprived the patient of her cigarettes, the researchers proceeded to "shape" the behavior they had selected arbitrarily. They decided to demonstrate that it was possible to have this patient stand upright holding a broom. All that was needed to increase this behavior was to follow it quickly (contingent reinforcement) with a cigarette. A staff member approached the patient whenever she happened to be holding the broom, handed her a cigarette, and left with no explanation. As time went on, the broom-holding symptom became very pronounced and was accompanied by a number of other abnormal behaviors. For example, the patient became quite stereotyped in her broom-holding behavior; she resisted giving up the broom and remained in a circumscribed part of the hospital ward for long periods.

These researchers then took their demonstration a step further: they asked two psychiatrists holding a dynamic perspective to "explain" the behavior of the patient. Of course, they did not reveal how the patient had acquired the broom-holding behavior. The psychiatrists interpreted the behavior as a "magical act" in which the broom might represent either a "phallic symbol" or a "scepter of an omnipotent queen."

Even if it is possible to create artificial situations in which abnormal behavior can be produced, we might well ask, are these same mechanisms responsible for the production of abnormal behavior in natural settings? Certainly, Haughton and Ayllon have shown that instrumental conditioning

FIGURE 3–5

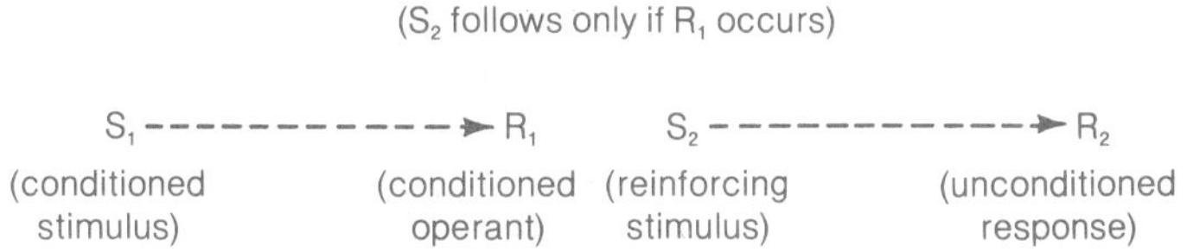

(S_2 follows only if R_1 occurs)

S_1 - - - - - - - - - - - ► R_1 (conditioned stimulus) → (conditioned operant)

S_2 - - - - - - - - - - - ► R_2 (reinforcing stimulus) → (unconditioned response)

Source: Adapted from *Introduction to Psychology,* Third Edition by Ernest R. Hilgard, copyright © 1962 by Harcourt Brace Jovanovich, Inc. Reprinted by permission of the publisher.

LITTLE HANS'S PHOBIA—OEDIPAL COMPLEX OR CLASSICAL CONDITIONING?

Reinterpreting a case history from your own theoretical viewpoint is a favorite tactic in the conflict between perspectives on abnormal behavior. Wolpe and Rachman, (1960) advocates of the learning viewpoint, have reinterpreted little Hans's phobia, first offered as evidence for the dynamic view, in terms of the classical conditioning process much like that described in the case of Albert. These authors argue that little Hans's fear of horses, rather than being a product of an Oedipal complex, is a conditioned response resulting in the pairing of a frightening accident (unconditioned stimulus) with the previously neutral horse and van (conditioned stimuli). So we might diagram Wolpe and Rachman's version of little Hans's phobia like this:

1. Before accident:
conditioned stimulus ------------ no response
(horses, vans)

2. At time of accident:
conditioned stimulus
(horse, van) --- conditioning ---
unconditioned stimulus (accident) unconditioned response (fear)

3. After the accident:
conditioned stimulus ----- conditioned response
(horse, van) (fear of horses and van)

Furthermore, Wolpe and Rachman argue that the way little Hans recovered from his phobia was just what we would expect from a case of classical conditioning. First, events and objects remote from the accident stopped evoking fear; only later did events central to the accident stop being fearful to Hans. This, they argue, is evidence for *stimulus generalization,* a learning process.

As advocates of the learning point of view, Wolpe and Rachman wish to interpret clinical accounts offered by other perspectives within their own framework. This is typical of most of the approaches to abnormal behavior. Advocates of various viewpoints recognize that the more phenomena their perspective explains, the more plausible their interpretation becomes.

mechanisms, can produce behavior that is perceived as abnormal, particularly when the reinforcement contingencies are not known to the observer.

The example of depression: Lewinsohn's model. One recent account of the development and maintainance of depressive behavior offered by Lewinsohn (1974a, 1974b) argues that depression is best thought of as resulting from a low rate of response-contingent to reinforcement. Figure 3–6 shows a schematic view of this theory.

Lewinsohn makes three assumptions in

FIGURE 3–6 Schematic Representation of the Causation and Maintenance of "Depressive" Behavior According to Lewinsohn

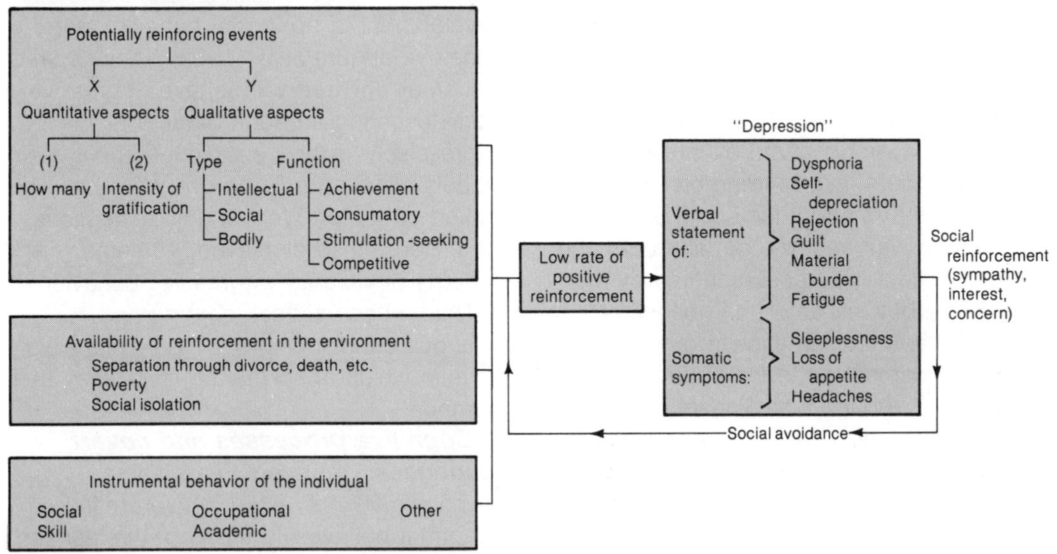

Source: P. M. Lewinsohn, "Clinical and Theoretical Aspects of Depression," in *Innovative Treatment Methods in Psychopathology,* K. S. Calhoun, H. E. Adams, and K. M. Mitchell, eds. (New York: Wiley, 1974).

his reinforcement theory of depression. First, he believes that a low rate of positive reinforcement for behavior makes most people fatigued and unhappy. Second, this low rate of positive contingent reinforcement, Lewinsohn believes, is enough to explain the lack of activity observed among most depressed people. Third, how much positive reinforcement anyone receives depends on (1) the *range* of events that are reinforcing for that person; (2) the environment's ability to supply those events; and (3) the person's ability to actually elicit them from the environment.

When the three sources of reinforcement are relatively low, for whatever reason, a low rate of positive reinforcement exists for the person. This in turn, Lewinsohn argues, produces the clinical syndrome of depression. Expressions of sadness and guilt are in turn rewarded by sympathy, interest, and concern and this actually strengthens the depressed behavior through the mechanism of reinforcement.

Social Learning and Modeling

In addition to the mechanisms of classical and instrumental conditioning, observational learning and modeling represents a'third possible mechanism that may play an important role in the development of abnormal behavior. In general, as Bandura (1966) has suggested, the observation and imitation of others may be an important factor in the development of new maladaptive behavior even when no direct classical or instrumental conditioning of responses has occurred.

Bandura and Rosenthal (1966) have

demonstrated one of the most interesting examples of this process. This was in a study in which they were able to produce "vicarious conditioning" of phobic behavior. In the demonstration, a person who was actually the researchers' accomplice was observed by experimental subjects while attached to an electrical apparatus that made it look as if the accomplice was about to get a shock. The apparent shock was accompanied by the sound of a buzzer. Later the observers showed dramatic increases in emotional response themselves to the sound of the buzzer even though it had never been directly paired with the aversive event as would have been required with classical conditioning.

Albert Bandura

Courtesy of Albert Bandura

Perhaps the most famous illustrations of the power of observational learning in the development of abnormal behavior were done by Bandura et al. (1963). They showed that small children will behave aggressively after observing an adult model behave aggressively. In the classic experiment, adult models attacked a Bobo doll while children looked on. Later, without any instructions, the children also displayed the same patterns of violently aggressive behavior.

Thus, observational learning and vicarious conditioning are highly plausible ways in which abnormal behavior may be learned.

Cognitive processes and covert responses. In recent years some psychologists interested in interpreting abnormal behavior in terms of the learning perspective have shifted their interest from external, directly observable behavior to internal psychological events such as thinking, images, fantasies, and inner speech.

This shift is important primarily because it allows the learning framework to be applied to the rich inner psychological world of the person.

The new stress on cognitive rather than motor events in the learning perspective has taken a variety of forms. Table 3–3 shows the variety of ways in which covert responses such as thoughts and fears have been incorporated into the learning perspective in recent years.

As we see in Table 3–3, researchers have used various "covert responses" in the *treatment* of abnormal behavior. *Covert* responses have been the *target* behaviors to be changed in treatment, used as *consequences* to shape behavior preceding them, and as *antecedents* of behavior that therapists wish to change.

As Price has observed, "it is clear that researchers working within the learning

This series of pictures shows an adult exhibiting aggressive behavior which is then modeled by children who have observed it.

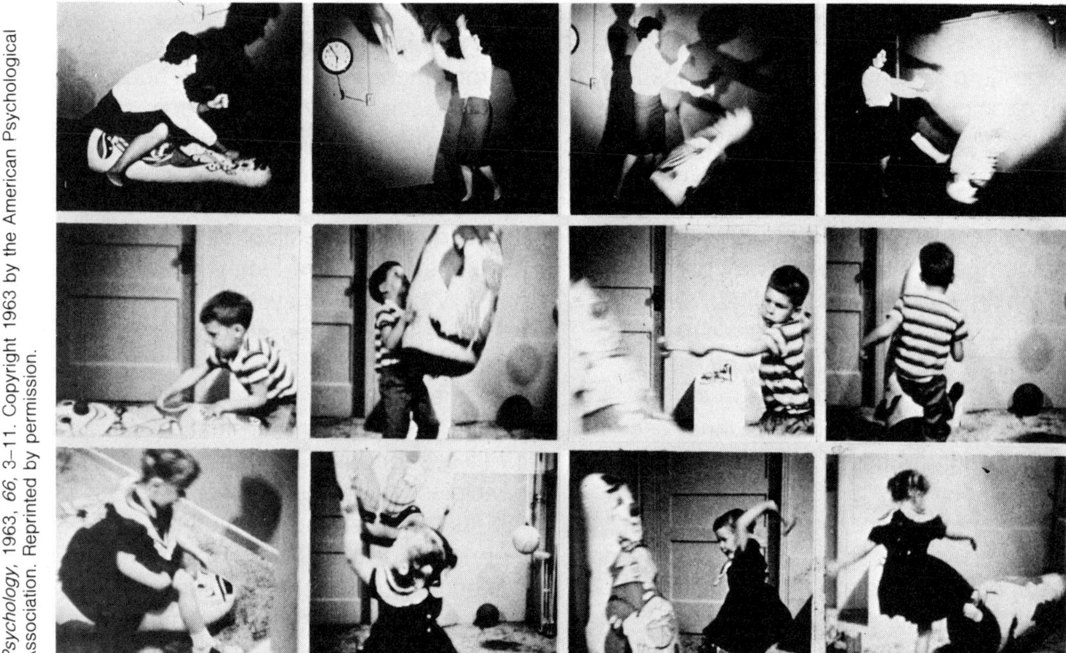

Source: Albert Bandura, Dorothea Ross, and Sheila A. Ross, "Imitation of Film-mediated Aggressive Models." *Journal of Abnormal and Social Psychology,* 1963, *66,* 3–11. Copyright 1963 by the American Psychological Association. Reprinted by permission.

perspective have no lack of imagination in their attempts to include private cognitive events within the realm of behavior" (1978, p. 137).

Overview of the learning perspective. As we said earlier, the learning viewpoint has gained considerable support over the last several decades in American psychology. Yet one of the strongest objections to this view is raised because of the assumptions learning theorists make about human

TABLE 3–3 Use of Covert Responses in Treatment of Undesired Behavior

Covert Responses as Antecedents	*Covert Responses as Target Behaviors*	*Covert Responses as Consequences*
Images of feared situations (Wolpe, 1958): Images of feared social situations, heights, and so forth, used in desensitization	*What clients say to themselves: Self-statements* (Meichenbaum et al., 1974): "Crazy talk," creative ideas, task instructions, fearful self-statements	*Covert sensitization* (Cautela, 1971): Fantasy of aversive event following undesired behavior (e.g., violent nausea following urge to smoke)
"Flooding—implosion": (Stampfl et al., 1967) intense use of feared situations without relief	*Coverants* (operants of the mind) (Homme, 1965)	*Covert responses as positive reinforcement:* Self-reward (Kanfer, 1970)

Source: From *Abnormal Behavior: Perspectives in Conflict,* Second Edition, by Richard H. Price. Copyright © 1978 by Holt, Rinehart and Winston. Copyright © 1972 by Holt, Rinehart and Winston, Inc. Reprinted by permission of Holt, Rinehart and Winston.

nature. Often objections have focused on B. F. Skinner's views, in particular those in his book, *Beyond Freedom and Dignity* (1971). There he argues that our underlying assumptions that humans are autonomous have had a destructive effect on our society. Some of the byproducts of these assumptions are overpopulation, pollution, and war. Traditional views about man's freedom and dignity, Skinner argues, have stood in the way of meaningful change. Instead, we should see humans for what they are—behaving organisms controlled largely by the reinforcement contingencies in the environment. The task, as Skinner sees it, is to design a culture that squarely faces the responsibility to control human behavior for the collective benefit of all.

Skinner's critics argue that the learning perspective offers an overly mechanical view of humans and human behavior—it fails to take account of the individual's inner experience and subjective life. Most likely Skinner does overstate his case, perhaps for polemic reasons. We should recognize, however, that it is not necessary to deny the subjective experience of humans in order to assert that some or even all aspects of abnormal behavior are learned. In the nature of perspectives, however, both advocates and critics tend to take an "all or nothing" approach to understanding abnormal behavior.

The fact that the learning perspective has gained such support recently probably has little to do with the plausibility of the view that abnormal behavior is learned. Instead, strong support for the learning viewpoint comes mostly from the many impressive demonstrations that learning principles can be applied to *treatment* of abnormal behavior. One of the most impressive aspects of the learning viewpoint is that it has closely tied assessment methods and behavior-change strategies.

A variety of techniques based on instrumental conditioning have been used to shape the behavior of children and hospitalized patients. These treatment methods have met with a fair amount of success, and one of the great merits of the learning perspective is that it has developed treatment techniques that can not only be applied systematically, but whose results can be effectively measured.

Some supporters of the learning perspective have argued that, *because* we can treat abnormal behavior using learning principles, the behaviors were learned in the first place. Tempting as this logical leap is, it does not follow from the evidence. Buchwald and Young (1969) make this point using the example of a person who has lost the ability to speak because of a brain injury. A person can sometimes be taught to speak again using learning principles. Yet this does not mean that the loss of speech was "learned" in the first place.

In sum, the learning perspective has in recent years greatly influenced our thinking about the nature and origins of abnormal behavior. The perspective has grown as a result of both creative insights and research on problems like observational learning and cognitive events and because of the development of learning-based treatment methods.

THE SOCIAL PERSPECTIVE

Still another important perspective on abnormal behavior shifts our attention away from the behavior of the individual to that of people around the person and their reactions to his or her behavior. It argues that "mental illness" exists to a great degree in the eyes of those people who come in contact with the "labeled" person. This is a unique departure, one which calls attention to the social environment of the individual. It suggests that other approaches to abnormal behavior mistakenly remove the behavior of the person from the context in which it occurs.

Norms and Roles and the "Career" of a Mental Patient

Not surprisingly, many of the advocates of the social perspective, such as Erving Goffman (1961) and Thomas Scheff (1975), were not trained in medicine or psychology but rather in sociology. Their sensitivity to the social context of the person adds a dimension to our understanding. They stress that people who are called "abnormal" often are viewed as such because they violate certain *norms,* or socially agreed-upon rules of conduct. They also suggest that being a patient in a mental hospital means that one is *cast into the social role of patient.* This role consists of a set of behaviors that are subtly rewarded by those around the patient. Finally, they point out that a great deal of mental patients' behavior can be explained by looking at the social institutions with which patients have to interact, rather than by studying the patients' biochemistry, learning history, or childhood traumas.

How, then, do people become mental patients, according to this view? In general, both Goffman and Scheff agree that when a person behaves in a way that is puzzling or frightening to us, we are likely to seek an explanation. If an obvious one is not forthcoming, we may at last settle on the explanation that the person is "mentally ill" or "sick."

The mental hospital environment can often subtly reward patients in the hospital for engaging in the role of patienthood.

Zalesky/Black Star

Once the person has been labeled, it is quite natural to begin to see different aspects of the person's behavior as consistent with the view that he is crazy or ill. The labeling itself, then, alters the way we behave toward the person. And the labeled person, in turn, seeing our change in attitude, may further change his or her behavior toward us. This cycle of events may continue until eventually the person is led through a series of interactions with social workers, ministers, or others who may recommend that the individual be hospitalized. Thus, the social perspective suggests that the series of interactions that a person has with others may produce a "deviation amplifying system" that finally leads to hospitalization. This is often described as the *"career"* of a person on the path to patienthood.

Being Sane in Insane Places: An Example of the Social Perspective in Action

We have said that the social viewpoint stresses others' reactions to the person who is labeled mentally ill. This view also suggests that the person is cast in the role of mental patient by relatives, friends, and employers, and by medical personnel who accept the view that abnormal behavior is an illness.

One of the most dramatic and fascinating studies offered in support of the social perspective has been done by Rosenhan (1973). Rosenhan asked the question, "Can the sane be distinguished from the insane?" and decided to do a study he thought would help him find out. He began with a group of friends and collaborators. In the group were three psychologists, a psychiatrist, a pediatrician, a painter, and a housewife. These people were asked by Rosenhan to become "pseudo-patients"—that is, they were each to report to a mental hospital and request admission.

The only "symptom" they were allowed to report to the examining physicians during the intake interview was that they heard voices which were unclear but sounded empty, hollow, or made a thumping sound. The pseudo-patients also falsified their names and their work but otherwise presented themselves as they really were. All of them were admitted to the hospital upon reporting their symptom, even though the symptom had never been recorded in the psychiatric literature as an indicator of severe psychiatric disorder. Furthermore, all but one of them were diagnosed as being schizophrenic. All were later discharged, most of them with a diagnosis of "schizophrenia in remission."

Rosenhan believes that the results of his study dramatically demonstrate that it is not possible to tell the "insane" from the "sane" in the psychiatric hospital. Perhaps more important for our purposes is that Rosenhan believes he has demonstrated the power of labels to affect our perceptions and behaviors. Once the person is labeled "schizophrenic," the hospital staff comes to expect that the person will continue to behave like a schizophrenic.

This shows how *patienthood* can be thought of as a social role. Once hospitalized and diagnosed as schizophrenic, these people found themselves cast in the role of patient and treated as if they were mentally ill. It is hard to resist being cast into this role; any protests denying one's status are likely to be seen as evidence that the individual does not yet have "insight" into his own behavior.

Let us look at some examples of how

Rosenhan's pseudo-patients were cast in the role of the mentally ill.

> One tacit characteristic of psychiatric diagnosis is that it locates the sources of aberration within the individual and only rarely within the complex of stimuli that surrounds him. Consequently, behaviors that are stimulated by the environment are commonly misattributed to the patient's disorder. For example, one kindly nurse found a pseudo-patient pacing the hospital corridors. "Nervous, Mr. X?" she asked.
>
> "No, bored," he said (Rosenhan, 1973, pp. 250–58).

Or consider what happened to pseudo-patients when they asked doctors when they would likely be discharged from the hospital:

> The encounter frequently took the bizarre form. (Pseudo-patient) "Pardon me, Doctor X. Could you tell me when you are eligible for grounds privileges?" (Physician) "Good morning, Dave. How are you today?" (moves off without waiting for a response) (Rosenhan, 1973, p. 256).

We should not assume that nursing and psychiatric staff are the only people within the psychiatric setting who help convince the people that they are indeed ill. Consider this example Scheff gives (1966, p. 86).

New patient: I don't belong here. I don't like all these crazy people. When can I talk to the doctor? I've been here four days and I haven't seen the doctor. I'm not crazy.

Another patient: She says she's not crazy [laughter from patients].

Another patient: Honey, what I'd like to know is, if you're not crazy, how did you get your ass in this hospital?

New patient: It's complicated, but I can explain. My husband and I . . .

First patient: That's what they all say [general laughter].

So, we see that the reactions of others, including other mental patients, can help cast a person in the role of someone who is mentally ill. Ultimately, in these circumstances, the person cast in such a role begins to accept the role as appropriate and realistic for him or herself and to question his or her own stability.

We can conclude that the social perspective sees mental illness as a set of expectations, stereotypes, and labels that we apply to people whose behavior or motives are difficult for us to understand. Once applied to a person these labels shape not only how we see that person, but how we interact with that person and how that person sees himself or herself.

Reactions from the Medical Perspective to the Social Viewpoint

Rosenhan's study is certainly not the first in which a social scientist had himself hospitalized in order to find out what it was really like inside a mental hospital. Predictably enough, though, the study has brought intense reaction from the scientific and medical community. Again we see advocates of various perspectives (in this case mainly advocates of the illness perspective) reacting strongly to evidence that they see as threatening the basic assumptions of their viewpoints. Let us look at a sampling of reactions published in letters to the journal, *Science,* where Rosenhan's study was originally published.

> I am deeply concerned about the state and fate of psychiatric care in this country. I am also deeply concerned about the

destructive potential of such pseudo-studies as the one under discussion. Appearing in *Science,* it can only be productive of unwarranted fear and mistrust in those who need psychiatric help and make the work of those who are trying to deliver and teach about quality care that much harder (*Science,* vol. 180, p. 358).

If complaints of isolated auditory hallucinations are believed by the doctor, they can require neurological investigations including lumbar puncture, skilled x-ray series, radio-isotope brainscans. None of these procedures is without risk to the patient, but the risk is less than leaving undiagnosed brain disorders that can give rise to isolated hallucinations. One wonders if the volunteers for this reckless experiment were informed of this risk (*Science,* vol. 180, p. 360).

A much more impressive demonstration of his point could be made by Rosenhan if he were to take obviously insane persons and, by giving them a new name and releasing them to a new community where they were not known, successfully pass them off as sane (*Science,* vol. 180, p. 361).

The attack on psychiatric nomenclature as some kind of pernicious labeling comes very close to a denial that any mental disorders characterized by objectively ascertainable symptoms, behaviors, and tests altogether exist. In the not so distant past, "tuberculosis" and "syphillis" were words shunned by polite society. Fortunately, this did not deter physicians and researchers diagnosing and treating these conditions (*Science,* vol. 180, p. 364).

Contributions of the Social Perspective

Although this view of abnormal behavior has become very popular recently, it has received a great deal of criticism as well. Walter Gove (1975) has done a series of evaluations of studies of hospital admissions and of mental patients returning to the community. The social perspective would predict that hospital admissions would be very perfunctory, would seldom result in patient release, and would presume that ex-mental patients would suffer discrimination because of having been labeled. Gove's evidence, however, fails to support any of these predictions. There is little doubt that stereotypes and erroneous beliefs about the nature of mental illness affect our behavior and even that of mental health professionals and social policy decision makers. It is quite another thing, however, to argue that abnormal behavior is nothing but a labeling process.

Perhaps the greatest strength of the social perspective is its persistent focus on the *social context* of behavior as a crucial element in the development of a more complete understanding of abnormal behavior. Its greatest weakness, on the other hand, probably lies in its lack of attention to the initial causes of the person's abnormal behavior and subsequent "career."

THE HUMANISTIC PERSPECTIVE

Advocates of the humanistic perspective have suggested that, in addition to behaviorism and psychoanalysis, there was a "third force" in American psychology, with a distinctly different orientation and emphasis. Actually, the humanistic movement in psychology reflects a number of different viewpoints including self-theories, existentialism, and a phenomenological view. In recent years,

A SOCIAL AND CULTURAL PERSPECTIVE ON PSYCHOLOGICAL TREATMENT

In his book, *Persuasion and Healing,* Jerome Frank notes that a theory of illness and methods of healing are basic parts of the cultural assumptions of any given culture. He suggests that psychological treatment, like psychiatric diagnosis, cannot be separated from its social and cultural context. In fact, it may be that psychological treatment is unlikely to be successful unless it is consistent with the cultural assumptions of the person being treated. Let us look briefly at two examples of psychological treatment that are not based on assumptions of European and American psychotherapy but instead are based on very different cultural assumptions.

The first of these is *espiritismo,* a Puerto Rican folk healing art. This form of healing is currently practiced in *centros* or centers for treatment in the Puerto Rican community in New York. Although this type of treatment has been viewed with skepticism by Western psychotherapists in the past, it is now of great interest to psychologists and anthropologists interested in effective, culturally based treatment.

A wide variety of problems in living are treated in the centros including nervous disorders, marriage and family crises, and general health problems. Espiritistas, or spiritualists, who treat the people who come to them are careful to distinguish between physical and psychological disorders and often refer their clients to a medical physician as well. The basic assumptions of espiritistas include the idea that there are many different levels of spiritual development. Each person has spirits that reflect his or her particular stage of development. These spirits may be either benevolent or malevolent, and people suffering from psychological disturbance are believed to have been afflicted by malevolent spirits.

Frequently, espiritistas spend a considerable amount of time learning about the background of the person in order to gain a broader understanding of his or her difficulties. The interpretations of the *causas,* or reasons, for the person suffering usually reflect a great deal of insight into the life circumstances of the sufferer. Anthropologists studying this form of healing suggest that espiritistas are at least as effective, and in some cases much more effective, than traditional mental health services in helping members of the Puerto Rican community (Fields, 1976).

A second example of folk healing is the practice of Navajo healers in the Southwest. These healers are highly valued as treatment personnel by the United States and Indian Health Service. As healers they are acutely aware of the cultural traditions underlying their approach to treatment. As Carl Gorman says in *Navajo Philosophy,* "We have to acknowledge to ourselves that our philosophy is different from that of the white man. We do not have to accept the white man's verdict that because it is different, it is wrong. We do not have to abandon that which sustained our people for hundreds and probably thousands of years" (Fields, 1976, p. 12).

To understand the Navajo healer's approach to healing, we must appreciate something about the Navajo philosophy of life. This philosophy emphasizes the unity of all experience. Sickness is thought of as the state of being fragmented. To be healed, one becomes whole again and in harmony with one's friends, with one's family, and with nature.

In the Navajo culture, there is no difference between the church and the hospital. Healing ceremonies conducted by Navajo medicine men are actually both healing and worship. Of Navajo medicine men, Robert Fulton says, "Each man must have a prayer; he must dream of something and believe in something which is more than himself. The Navajo word for prayer is *sodirzin.* It means to grow."

Navajo healing rituals include friends, family, and others and take place in a simple shelter called a *hogan.* The healing ceremonies themselves involve a religious story that describes a problem similar to that of the suffering person along with its resolution. There are a wide variety of different ceremonies; which one is to be used depends on the symptoms or difficulties of the patient.

These ritual ceremonies are often effective at relieving depression, grief, and anxiety in patients. This is not so surprising when one remembers that such ceremonies help to bring a person closer to his family and his society. "The Navajos have been pulled between two cultures . . . often with tragic results. The medicine man, as he offers tales of noble adventures, sparks a renewed pride in Indian tradition. The ceremonies provide a structure to develop, support, and affirm this cultural pride and identity" (Fields, 1976, p. 18).

it has been broadened further, and a new stress on psychological growth has emerged.

In this section we will examine some of the main themes of the humanistic perspective and see how the humanistic view of abnormal behavior is distinctive.

Carl Rogers's View of the Development of Abnormal Behavior

Rogers's viewpoint represents one of the most important intellectual traditions within the humanistic perspective. Deeply concerned about inner psychological experience and strongly focused on questions having to do with the conditions that promote psychological growth, Rogers's approach to the understanding of the development of abnormal behavior is a clear example of the humanistic perspective.

Rogers's viewpoint focuses on the concept of the *self;* it identifies the course of early development as crucial in whether the person develops defensive or disturbed behavior or continues on a path of psychological growth.

Rogers's view of the development of defensive behavior can be seen in Figure 3–7 below.

Rogers argues that unconditional positive regard is a state in which a person (e.g., a parent) values another (e.g., child) for himself, not for what the person wishes him to be. Rogers believes that this is essential for the child's psychological development. When this condition is missing, the child does not regard him or her self positively. Instead the child values himself in terms of certain

FIGURE 3–7 The Development of Defensive Behavior

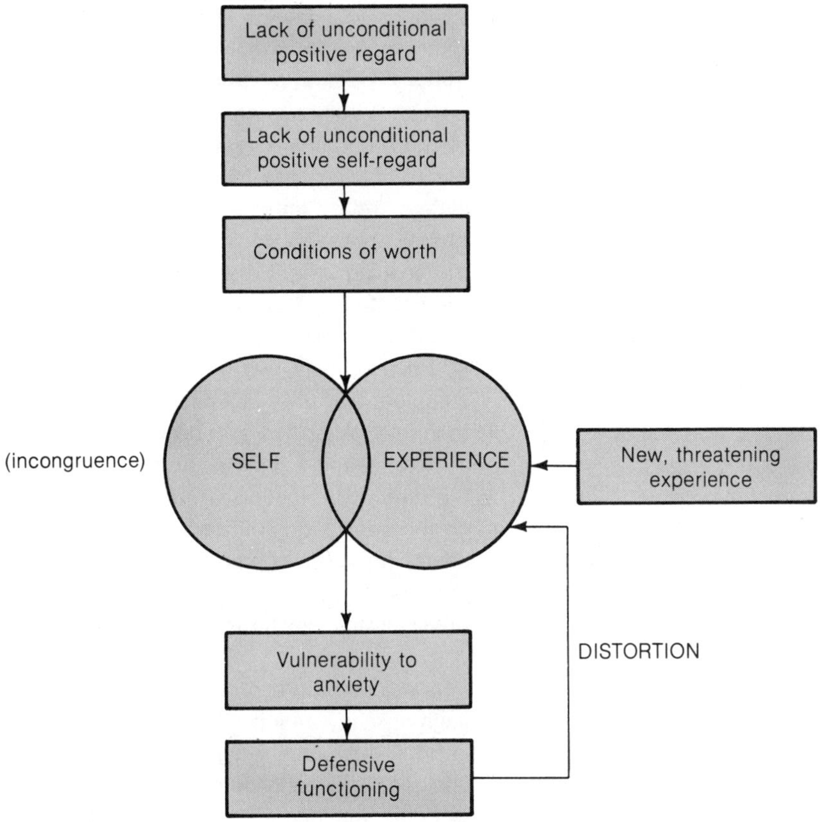

Source: Carl R. Rogers, *On Becoming a Person* (Boston, MA: Houghton Mifflin, 1961). Copyright © 1961 by Houghton Mifflin Company. Reprinted by permission of the publishers.

external standards such as achievement or an attractive appearance. This produces what Rogers calls "conditions of worth" within the self.

When one experiences such conditions of worth, it is inevitable that one's sense of self and one's experience will not be congruent, as shown in Figure 3–7. If one

ROGERS DESCRIBES THE SEARCH FOR THE AUTHENTIC SELF

I have been astonished to find how accurately the Danish philosopher Søren Kierkegaard pictured the dilemma of the individual more than a century ago, with keen psychological insight. He points out that the most common despair is to be in despair at not choosing, or being willing, to be oneself; but that the deepest form of despair is to choose "to be another than" oneself. On the other hand "to will to be that self which one truly is, is indeed the opposite of despair," and this choice is the deepest responsibility of man. As I read some of his writings I almost feel that he must have listened in on the statements made by our clients as they search and explore for the reality of self—often a painful and troubling search.

This exploration becomes even more disturbing when they find themselves involved in removing the false faces which they had not known were false faces. They begin to engage in the frightening task of exploring the turbulent and sometimes violent feelings within themselves. To remove a mask which you had thought was part of your real self can be a deeply disturbing experience, yet when there is freedom to think and feel and be, the individual moves toward such a goal. A few statements from a person who had completed a series of psychotherapeutic interviews will illustrate this. She uses many metaphors as she tells how she struggled to get to the core of herself.

> As I look at it now, I was peeling off layer after layer of defenses. I'd build them up, try them, and then discard them when you [sic] remained the same. I didn't know what was at the bottom and I was very much afraid to find out, but I *had* to keep on trying. At first I felt there was nothing within me—just a great emptiness where I needed and wanted a solid core. Then I began to feel that I was facing a solid brick wall, too high to get over and too thick to go through. One day the wall became translucent, rather than solid. After this, the wall seemed to disappear but beyond it I discovered a dam holding back violent, churning waters. I felt as if I were holding back the force of these waters and if I opened even a tiny hole I and all about me would be destroyed in the ensuing torrent of feelings represented by the water. Finally I could stand the strain no longer and I let go. All I did, actually, was to succumb to complete and utter self-pity, then hate, then love. After this experience, I felt as if I had leaped a brink and was safely on the other side, though still tottering a bit on the edge. I don't know what I was searching for or where I was going, but I felt then as I have always felt whenever I really lived, that I was moving forward.

I believe this represents rather well the feelings of many an individual that if the false front, the wall, the dam, is not maintained, then everything will be swept away in the violence of the feelings that he discovers pent up in his private world. Yet it also illustrates the compelling necessity which the individual feels to search for and become himself. It also begins to indicate the way in which the individual determines the reality in himself—that when he fully experiences the feelings which at an organic level he *is,* as this client experienced her self-pity, hatred, and love, then he feels an assurance that he is being a part of his real self (Rogers, 1961, pp. 110–11).

then encounters a new and threatening experience, the person, already vulnerable to anxiety, will begin to behave in a defensive way in order to protect his already fragile identity. This defensive functioning distorts experience and may lead to chronic interpersonal difficulties and a deep personal sense of inadequacy.

Maslow: Self-actualization and Psychological Help

Another major proponent of the humanistic perspective is Abraham Maslow (1954), who introduced the concept of *self-actualization* as a critical goal for personal development. He saw it as a kind of growth principle and an indication of positive psychological health.

Maslow has argued that what is essential for positive mental health is meeting a variety of basic human needs. These needs have been arranged in a hierarchy: (1) physiological needs, (2) needs for love or belongingness, (3) a need for the esteem of others, and (4) the need for self-actualization. Self-actualizers were people who had a need for spontaneity, to be creative, and to show interest in others.

Maslow and Rogers both see external social events as having the potential to block the satisfaction of needs, or in the case of Rogers, producing conditions of worth. Thus, although the humanistic perspective is primarily concerned with psychological growth and development, it sees social events as playing an important role in enhancing or blocking that growth.

Abraham Maslow

Courtesy of Bertha G. Maslow, photo by Marcia Roltner

R. D. Laing: Psychosis as Growth

One group of humanistic psychologists offers us a strikingly different perspective on the nature of abnormal behavior. Theorists such as R. D. Laing (1959, 1967), Dabrowski (1964), and Perry (1962) have argued that an episode of seemingly abnormal behavior may actually represent an opportunity for personal growth rather than a disintegration or disorganization of behavior. Laing (1967) has argued that "madness" may in fact represent a split between the person's true

R. D. Laing

Peter Southwick/Stock, Boston, Inc.

inner self and a false outer self, which develops over time in response to other peoples' social expectations.

Thus the emergence of psychotic behavior in Laing's view may actually represent a stripping away of the false outer self, revealing the essential truth of one's preoccupations, fears, fantasies, and distortions. For example, Gordon (1971), describes the case of a woman named Mary who led an anxiety-ridden life until she had a dramatic breakdown. She stopped eating, tore off her clothes, could only be fed milk from a bottle, and behaved in a variety of other infantile ways. Slowly, however, she began to recover, using drawing and painting as a medium for self-expression. Gordon believes this episode represented a major stripping away of Mary's outer self and a new reintegration of her creative needs and impulses that only could have been possible after this extreme disturbance in behavior.

Rollo May: The Social Context of Anxiety

We have suggested that in much of the humanistic perspective there lies the notion that society demands a falseness in behavior from each of us that exacts a psychological cost. Humanistic psychologists believe that for some these costs can be very high. Rollo May, a psychiatrist with strong interests in existentialism and a commentator on the contemporary social scene, has suggested that the modern person is faced with a dilemma. Society, May believes, rewards the individual only for being a "team player," and this produces a sense of anxiety and depersonalization in all of us. He notes

> the loss of the experience of one's own significance . . . leads to that kind of anxiety that Paul Tillich called the *anxiety of meaninglessness,* or what Kierkegaard terms anxiety as the fear of nothingness. We used to talk about these things as psychological theory, and a couple of decades ago when I was undergoing my psychoanalytic training, we discussed them as psychological phenomena shown by "neurotic" people. Now such anxiety is endemic throughout our whole society. These are some of the considerations which impel me to suggest that there is "no hiding place" with respect to the psychological dilemmas of our times (p. 37).

We can see that the humanistic perspective, as represented by such

Rollo May

TABLE 3–4 Perspectives on Abnormal Behavior

	Psychoanalytic	*Illness*	*Learning*	*Social*	*Humanistic*
Basic metaphor	Intrapsychic conflict	Disease	Learning	Deviance; norm violation	Actualization; growth
Subordinate concepts	Id, ego, superego, anxiety, defense	Nosology, etiology, symptom, syndrome, prognosis	Stimulus, response, reinforcement, classical and operant conditioning, modeling	Norms, rule-breaking, career, stigma	Experience, self-concept, incongruity, conditions of worth; consciousness expansion
Causal factors	Intrapsychic conflict	Organic, biochemical, genetic	Reinforcement; classical and operant conditioning	Diverse factors: Organic, psychological, social; labeling	Conditions of worth, deficiency needs; social demands
How abnormal behavior is described	Defense and anxiety	Symptoms, syndromes, disorders	Maladaptive behavior; helplessness	Behavior is deviant; audience reaction emphasized	Defensive and disorganized behavior; false outer self
Means of therapeutic intervention	Psychoanalysis	Medical treatment; drugs, shock treatment, surgical procedures	Behavior therapy, desensitization, shaping	Institutional reform; community mental health	Client-centered therapy; sensitivity training; Gestalt therapy; yoga; meditation
Major proponents	Freud	Kraepelin, Meehl, Snyder	Bandura, Eysenck, Krasner, Seligman, Skinner, Ullmann, Wolpe	Becker, Goffman, Sarbin, Scheff	Laing, Maslow, May, Ornstein, Rogers, Tart

Source: R. H. Price, *Abnormal Behavior: Perspectives in Conflict,* 2nd ed. (New York: Holt, Rinehart & Winston, 1978), p. 215.

theorists as Rogers, Maslow, Laing, and May, focuses on those social and personal conditions that provide the opportunity for psychological growth. Humanistic psychologists believe that when this opportunity for personal growth is thwarted, either by external social constraints or by the lack of fulfillment of basic needs, psychological disturbance may result. However, some theorists, such as Laing, believe that, paradoxically, the disturbance may offer the potential for personal growth.

SUMMARY

In this chapter we have surveyed the rich array of perspectives on the nature of abnormal behavior. Each conceptual approach begins with its own basic set of concepts to provide a framework for understanding the nature, causes, mechanisms, and description of abnormal behavior. A summary of those ideas is given in Table 3–4.

We saw that each of these perspectives exerts a powerful influence on how we perceive abnormal behavior, what elements seem most important to understand, and what research questions need to be asked. In later chapters we will meet each of these perspectives again as we consider theory research and treatment approaches for specific disorders!

4

Research Strategies in the Study of Abnormal Behavior

PERSPECTIVES AND CAUSES

In Chapter 3, you will recall, we discussed five different perspectives on abnormal behavior: the disease, dynamic, learning, social, and humanistic perspectives. Each of these perspectives focused on a different aspect of abnormal behavior, and each perspective also thought about the *causes* of abnormal behavior differently. In effect, each viewpoint places different bets about the nature of the cause of abnormal behavior.

The disease viewpoint argues that the causes of abnormal behavior are found in the physiological makeup of the individual. For example, genetic errors may predispose the individual to certain types of mental illness or lead directly to faulty development of structures necessary for normal functioning. Another version of the disease perspective suggests the cause can be found in disease-producing microorganisms or toxic chemicals. In either case, the locus of the cause of abnormal behavior is the physiology of the person.

The dynamic view, on the other hand, locates causes in the psychological dynamics of the person. The major causes of abnormal behavior from the dynamic viewpoint involves intrapsychic conflicts that cannot be resolved. Various defense mechanisms evolve to protect the individual from anxiety generated by the conflicts. The defense mechanisms, in turn, are frequently perceived as abnormal.

The learning perspective suggests that the causes of abnormal behavior are learned and that they may be due either to a failure to learn necessary adaptive behaviors or to the direct learning of maladaptive behaviors. In either case, the abnormal behavior is learned and the causes are presumably located in the stimulus environment of the individual.

The social perspective says little about the origins of abnormal behavior but suggests that abnormal behavior is maintained by social processes. In particular, the reactions of other people to the individual labeled as abnormal are thought to have a powerful influence on subsequent behavior.

Finally, the humanistic perspective sees the origins of abnormal behavior as arising from a world too demanding of facades, and surface qualities that too little appreciate qualities like authenticity and openness.

LSD AND THE SEARCH FOR THE CAUSES OF SCHIZOPHRENIA

Consider the account of an LSD experience by Solomon Snyder (1974). After a moderate dose of LSD, little was experienced for the first 30 minutes, except possibly slight nausea. "Then visual effects began. Objects of all sorts took on a new beauty and richness. Colors and textures and lines, even the pores in one's skin, began to stand out visually." Snyder says that the contours of objects may become distorted. For example, when he stared at his thumb, the thumb began to swell, undulate, and then to move toward him. Time-sense alters dramatically. A minute may seem like an hour or a day. The sense of distance also changes. "Flicking one's finger seems like hurling it across the room, and walking across the room is like traversing the corners of the universe" (p. 43).

Another striking effect of psychedelic drugs is *synesthesia.* During the experience of synesthesia, one may seem to "see" sounds or "hear" colors. Snyder reports that under the influence of LSD someone clapped his hands and he thought that he could see the sound waves undulate before him. Still another commonly reported experience is the loss of self-identity. Many people experience a merging of themselves with their environment or the entire universe. This experience is sometimes reported to be much like experiences of Christian and Hindu mystics. Yet it also strikingly resembles the loss of identity frequently reported by people diagnosed as schizophrenic. These drugs have been described as *hallucinogenic* (capable of producing hallucinations), and as *psychotomimetic* (capable of producing states which mimic psychotic states).

Reports of the LSD experience soon began to capture the imagination of the scientific community. It was not long before scientists began to wonder whether the chemistry and subjective states of the psychedelic experience might not provide some insight into the nature of one of the most puzzling forms of abnormal behavior, schizophrenia. The analogy between the LSD experience and schizophrenia was too compelling to be ignored. Scientists began to speculate on how the experience and biochemistry of LSD might inform their thinking about schizophrenia.

One hypothesis argued that it was possible that the bodies of schizophrenics might be producing some toxic substance resembling LSD. If this were the case, then, one should examine the body chemistry of schizophrenics to discover what was producing a chemical agent that in turn produced the schizophrenic symptoms.

In 1952 two British scientists, Osmond and Smythies, noted a striking chemical similarity between adrenalin and the mescaline molecules. Adrenalin is a chemical secretion of the adrenal gland that prepares the body for emergency action during periods of stress. Osmond and Smythies reasoned that, if the body were able to change adrenalin into some chemical resembling mescaline, this might be the toxin they were seeking that produced schizophrenia.

Soon afterward, Dr. Abram Hoffer reported an apparently exciting breakthrough that seemed to confirm this idea. His research strategy appeared to be deceptively simple. Hoffer had found a derivative of adrenalin called *adrenochrome* in blood and urine samples of schizophrenics but not in nonschizophrenics. Adrenochrome is a pink-colored chemical that results when oxygen combines with adrenalin, as is the case when adrenalin is exposed to air. Thus Hoffer felt he had isolated a chemical substance, adrenochrome, in the blood of schizophrenics that might be related to their illness. To test this possibility, he administered this substance to normal subjects. He reported that they experienced psychedelic effects similar to those of LSD.

A great wave of excitement swept through the scientific community. Scientists all over the world attempted to repeat Hoffer's experiments. These attempts almost universally failed, and careful measurement indicated that adrenochrome did not appear to a greater degree in the blood of either schizophrenics or nonschizophrenics. Apparently Hoffer had allowed the blood samples of schizophrenics to remain in the open air longer than those of nonschizophrenics, thus producing the pink color.

But what about the effects of the schizophrenic blood samples when they were administered to the normal subjects? Possibly Hoffer and his colleagues were so eager to demonstrate their theory that they unwittingly suggested the expected effects to their subjects. Their subjects then displayed the well-known *placebo* effect. That is, even though the chemical was no more potent than tap water, the suggestion that it would make subjects slightly schizophrenic led them to behave in the manner expected of them. Thus, even though there are other lines of evidence that do indeed suggest that biochemistry plays an important role in schizophrenia, these results had a more prosaic explanation.

For every scientific breakthrough there are hundreds of stories like that of the "pink spot" studies. The search for the causes of various forms of abnormal behavior is governed by strict rules of evidence that demand public, repeatable findings and acceptance of findings only when as many alternative explanations as possible have been ruled out. In this chapter we will examine the rules and the research strategies that scientists have used in the study of abnormal behavior.

SCIENTISTS AND DETECTIVES

Both scientists and detectives are basically *determinists.* That is, they are both primarily concerned with the causes of events. For a detective the "causal agent" may be a criminal, and for the scientist it may be a chemical in the blood. But in each case the search is for causes. In addition, both detectives and scientists must reconstruct past events. A detective has only the victim and the scene of the crime. A scientist may have only a pattern of symptoms and a sketchy life history to work with.

Both scientists and detectives rely heavily on *observation* to gather evidence in their search for the truth, and both are concerned about the reliability or dependability of their observations. Detectives take photographs, search for fingerprints, and question witnesses independently. Scientists use standardized interviews and tests. Both gather evidence to increase the reliability of their observations.

Detectives and scientists also have hunches or *hypotheses* about the cause of the events, and during their investigations try to rule out less plausible hypotheses. Each draws on a body of knowledge to form hypotheses and excludes less plausible possibilities. For the detective the body of knowledge may include information about the chemical composition of cigar ashes. For the scientist it may concern a description of the distribution of some disorder across different ages. But in each case, prior knowledge is used to test their hunches.

Finally, both scientists and detectives tend to be extremely cautious about the conclusions they draw, and for similar reasons. Their conclusions must withstand critical scrutiny of a jury of critical peers or a court of law.

The analogy between detectives and scientists should not be carried too far. One important difference is that a scientist is concerned with arriving at general statements that allow grouping apparently dissimilar events under a single rule or *generalization.* Detectives, on the other hand, wish to narrow their search to a single person, and they are much less interested in the generalizations that might be produced from their work.

TYPES OF CAUSES

Although scientists frequently ask questions like, "What is *the* cause of abnormal behavior?" it is unlikely that any major disorder is due to any single cause. Instead, scientists tend to think about *classes* of causes. For example, some causal factors are described as *predisposing causal factors.* That is, events or conditions that occur long before any abnormal behavior is observed may predispose the individual to later difficulties. Predisposing causes can be a consequence of previous events or some genetic condition or both. The important point is that they pave the way for later psychopathology.

A second major type of cause is the *precipitating causal factor,* described as the "trigger" for a disorder. A precipitating life event could be a sudden loss of a loved one, a disaster, a major failure in one's life, or a sudden physiological change. The ingestion of LSD, for example, can sometimes precipitate severe reactions in individuals who are predisposed to react in that manner.

Finally, a third type of cause is the *maintaining causal factor.* These factors reinforce abnormal behavior and thus

The death of a loved one can be a precipitating factor in the development of psychological distress.

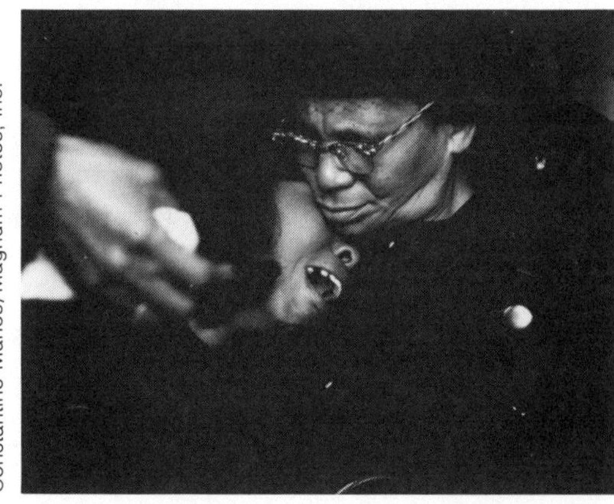

Constantine Manos/Magnum Photos, Inc.

maintain it over time. For example, poor conditions in a mental hospital could maintain a person's withdrawal and depression for a considerable period of time.

Even thinking about classes of causes rather than one cause is somewhat arbitrary: it may be difficult at times to decide whether a particular event or condition served as a predisposing event, a precipitating event, or both. The advantage of classifying causal events in this way is that one can construct a *complex* model of the causal process underlying abnormal behavior that is more likely to capture the complexity of the actual causal process.

RESEARCH METHODS

Even if an investigator has some hunches or hypotheses about the determinants of abnormal behavior, evidence that supports the hypothesis is required. We will consider some of the most commonly used methods to gather evidence below.

Case Histories and Clinical Observation

The life history of a patient can provide a rich source of information about the patient's difficulty. This information may suggest some unique or unusual feature in the patient's background. This striking feature may then be incorporated into a crude hypothesis such as "parental permissiveness leads to delinquent behavior" or "early loss of a loved one leads to later episodes of depression."

In the case history a crude hypothesis can be formed, but very little more can be learned using the case history approach. For example, in the above hypothesis on

UNDERSTANDING CHILDREN'S SEX ROLE DEVELOPMENT: THE USE OF CASE HISTORIES AND OBSERVATIONAL TECHNIQUES

If you were working on Michael Lewis' research team, studying the relationship between mothers and their children (Lewis, 1971; Goldberg & Lewis, 1969) you would probably observe a scene that looks something like this: A mother and her 13-month-old child are seated in a room that has its floor marked off in squares. There are toys on the floor and the mother is seated a few feet from the child. Your research team is particularly interested in *attachment behavior,* both *proximal* behavior, such as touching, holding, rocking, kissing, and caressing, and *distal* attachment behavior, such as looking at, talking to, gesturing at, and other activities that are intended to achieve or maintain contact between the mother and the child. Having observed a series of 13-month-old children interacting with their mothers, you would have noticed the following differences between the behavior of boys and that of girls. Boys venture farther away from their mothers than girls do. They stay away longer. They look at and talk with their mothers less. They play more vigorously with the toys in the observation room. When your research team erected a barrier between the mother and the child, girl infants stood at the barrier, but boy infants made vigorous attempts to get over and around it to reach their mothers. Clearly, even at 13 months, boys and girls are behaving very differently toward their mothers.

The children are displaying distinctive patterns of behavior that, in this culture, we associate with sex role differences. How they acquire these behaviors and how they are maintained is an interesting question in itself, but it also provides us with an excellent example of how biological and environmental events interact during early development. These interactions and how they come about will also provide us with useful lessons later when we attempt to understand how maladaptive or inappropriate behavior develops in children and adults.

Lewis points out that it is extremely difficult to disentangle sex differences that reflect basic biological mechanisms from those that are learned. An interesting illustration of this point is that observations by Lewis and his colleagues indicate that parents tend to talk more to girl infants than they do to boy infants. However, other studies have shown that girl infants tend to respond more to auditory stimuli than do boy infants. Thus it is quite likely that parents, who are highly involved and motivated observers of their own infants, are responding to basic biological differences in responsiveness to auditory stimuli. But, through their attention and reinforcement, they actually magnify the behavioral differences in auditory responsiveness between boys and girls.

This example provides us with several important points to remember. First, sex-linked behavior is *phenotypic.* That is, it is the product of interactions between biological and environmental events. Second, behavioral sex differences tend to become *magnified through social learning* as the child continues to interact with his or her environment. The differences between boys and girls in their responsiveness to auditory stimuli provides an example. Third, it is important for us to remember that the shaping of behavior between caretaker and infant is *reciprocal.* That is, the child is an active shaper of the parents' behavior as well as the reverse. Thus we must remember that socialization is a two-way process involving a reciprocal relationship between child and caretaker in which mutual shaping occurs.

Let us return to our original question. Why do the infant boys in Lewis' study venture farther from their mothers, play more vigorously, and appear generally more adventuresome? Lewis suggests that for both boys and girls, between birth and two years of age, parents engage in a number of *socialization acts* that are intended to involve the child in its environment, to teach the child to separate himself or herself from the parent. Parents engage in a number of different strategies in order to accomplish this socialization task. They frequently point out objects in the environment to the child; they face the child away from them and toward the environment. They suggest that the child play with objects in the environment.

Yet, Lewis suggests, American mothers tend to move their male children through this socialization process more rapidly than they do their female children. This is clearly a cultural difference. Presumably in other cultures differences of this sort may not occur. Thus Lewis suggests that the relationship between caretaker and infant produces a variety of early behavioral influences that differ for boys and girls and help account for important later sex role differences.

"early loss" and "depression," we could look at additional case histories of depression and search for instances of loss. But we could not be sure of how representative the case histories were, and therefore the generality of our hypothesis would remain doubtful.

The case history approach would also leave us in doubt about the definition of the key terms in our hypothesis. Are "depression" and "early loss" defined in comparable ways in other case histories? If not, we could not be sure that we were looking at the same phenomenon in succeeding cases.

The primary value of the case history approach lies in generating hypotheses or hunches that can then be tested by more rigorous means. The case histories can also provide accounts of unusual or rare clinical phenomena or demonstrate new treatment techniques. This approach is best thought of, however, as a method of "hypothesis finding," not hypothesis testing.

Correlational Approaches

If we are on the track of a possible relationship between early life events and depression, we may draw on case history evidence, but, by itself, this evidence would hardly convince skeptical colleagues. Our next step should be an attempt to discover whether a relationship between early loss and depression actually does exist.

In order to establish a relationship, we will first have to provide *operational definitions* for key terms in our hypothesis. That is, we will have to develop standard ways of defining "depression" and "early loss." We may use psychological tests, a checklist of behaviors, or a definition that independent observers can use reliably. Whatever our method, we will have provided *public* and *repeatable* operations that other investigators could duplicate.

Our next step should be to try to discover whether there is a statistical relationship between the variables in question. A common method for doing so involves the application of *correlational techniques.* If our hypothesis is viable, there should be more cases of depression that report early loss than those that do not; or the degree of depression should correlate with the extent of early loss. This outcome would be reflected in a *positive correlation* between the two variables. Figure 4–1 shows three possible outcomes of such an investigation. In the first case it appears that individuals who show more signs of depression also experienced more early loss. In the second there is no relationship, and in the third the opposite of what we expected has occurred and a negative correlation was obtained.

If at this stage of our research we still find positive correlation between early loss and depression, we should find this encouraging but far from conclusive. A number of alternative explanations exist that might "explain away" the relationship and show that it tells us nothing of real importance about the causes of depression. The fact, for example, that early loss and depression seem related to each other may be due to a *third variable* that affects both reports of early loss and depression. A third variable such as socioeconomic status could affect both loss and depression and lead us to believe that loss and depression were related when both were being affected by the experience of poverty. Or perhaps when depressed adults recall events in their childhood they report negative events selectively without being aware of doing so. In this case the direction of the relationship is the opposite of what we suspected.

FIGURE 4–1 Three Possible Correlational Relationships between Previous Life Events Reflecting Loss and Rated Current Severity of Depression

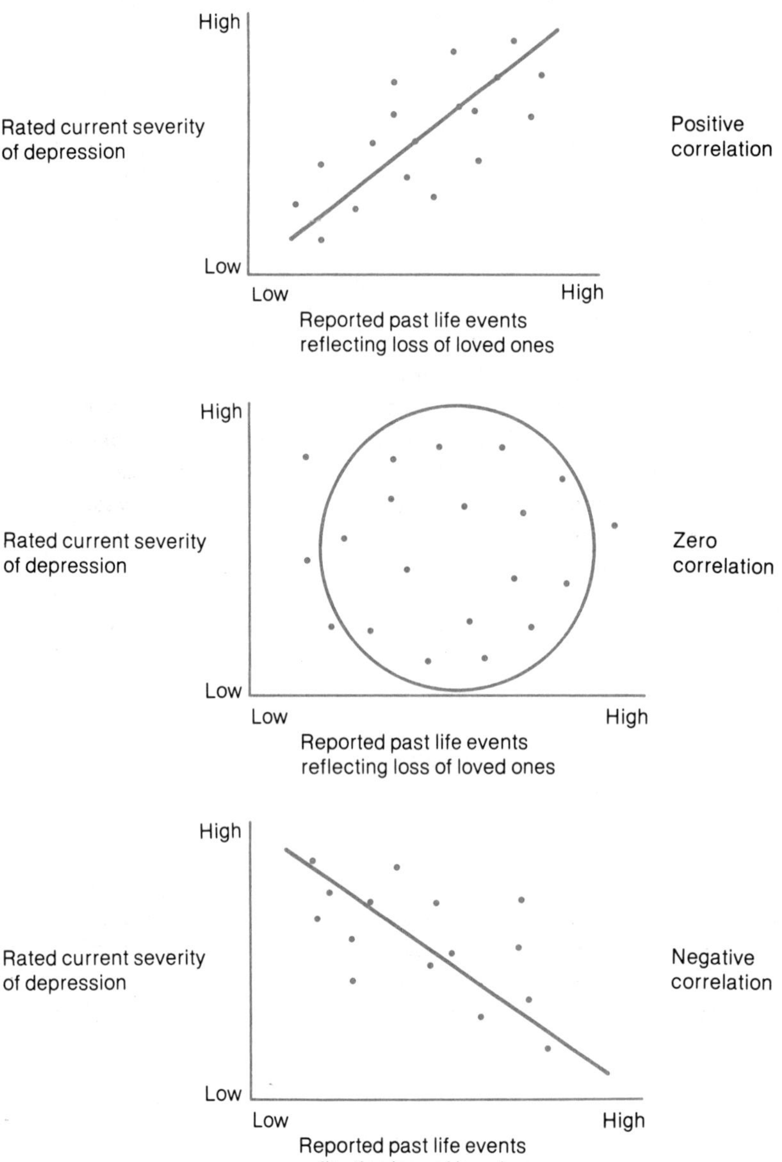

ECONOMIC CHANGE AND PSYCHOLOGICAL DISTURBANCE: AN EXAMPLE OF CORRELATIONAL RESEARCH

Think for a moment about the possible life changes or coping strategies that might be produced by marked economic change. Perhaps you or your family have experienced some of these changes yourself. Individual stress associated with negative economic changes might include job loss, the necessity of moving from one home to another, the necessity of taking part-time jobs, less leisure time, continued concern and worry about bills and outstanding debts, and increased family conflict over financial matters. Not only do individuals experience additional stresses, but entire families may be made more vulnerable to stress.

One study (Pierce, 1967) examined the relationship between economic change and suicide rates in the United States during the period from 1919 to 1940. Common stock prices were used as the economic change indicator and were examined in relation to the suicide rate. Pierce found that suicide rates increased in relation to economic downturns. How does one explain this relationship? Pierce believes that economic changes reduce social cohesion—and the closeness with which people relate to one another. Like Emile Durkheim (1951), Pierce speculates that this reduction in social cohesion leads to the loss of social support in the face of stress and therefore to an increase in the frequency of suicide.

Perhaps the most detailed and well-known recent study on the relationship between economic instability and abnormal behavior has been done by Harvey Brenner (1973). Brenner has compared changes in employment figures with rates of mental hospitalization over a period of approximately 50 years. His most recent studies show that, throughout the United States, as the rate of employment drops, the rate of hospital admissions increases.

An interesting feature of Brenner's findings is that hospitalization rates do not increase immediately after economic downturns, but that they do so in a systematic way approximately one year later. Perhaps this is because the effects of the stress associated with economic change are not immediate. After a year, however, the impact of economic change is felt strongly enough to increase hospitalization rates.

Who is most severely affected by economic downturns? According to Brenner, the most noticeable effects of a falling economy occur for men from 35 to 54 and for women 25 to 44. Certainly these are periods during which men and women bear a particularly heavy burden of responsibility in providing for their families and, therefore, are more likely to experience stress associated with unemployment.

We should be cautious, however, in interpreting first admissions to mental hospitals as a direct indicator of the rate of mental illness in the country at any given time. Consider for a moment some other possible explanations for changes in the rate of mental hospitalization. One explanation might be that hospital admissions policies change systematically over time. Another possible explanation is that the definition of mental illness could have changed, affecting hospitalization rates. Or perhaps in times of economic stringency the community's

Unemployment during the Great Depression produced massive psychological distress and depression.

Historical Pictures Service, Inc., Chicago

tolerance for various forms of abnormal behavior is reduced, thus producing more mental hospitalizations. Although these are all plausible explanations for changes in hospitalization rates, any other explanation must show that it can predict changes in the rates more accurately than economic changes can. So far, no factors have been found that are capable of predicting hospitalization rates as accurately as economic changes.

We should also be clear that it is not correct to suggest that changes in the economy "cause" mental illness in a direct fashion. But certainly any changes in the economy that increase stress for the population are more likely to function as either *predisposing* or *precipitating causes.*

The discovery and exploration of a relationship between psychological distress and economic changes suggest opportunities for planning mental health service to respond to increases in the need for psychological support and treatment. In addition, as Dooley and Catalano (1976) note, the one-year lag between economic change and severe psychological disruption suggests that it might be possible to engage in preventive efforts as well. For example, knowing that economic changes may make working class and poor people even more vulnerable than others suggests that immediately after such economic changes would be an ideal time to provide supportive services. Perhaps preventive efforts are best applied by the federal government itself. Various alternative employment programs, retraining, and income maintenance programs might be developed to buffer the damaging effects of recessions or inflation.

Instead of early loss producing later depression, later depression is eliciting "evidence" of early loss. If the relationship survives any speculation about directionality or the effects of a third variable, then you will want to test it, using other, more rigorous methods.

Experimental Methods

One of the most powerful methods for gathering evidence about the effect of one event or variable on another is the *controlled experiment.* In its most basic form, a controlled experiment involves the manipulation of one variable or event while holding constant or controlling all others. If the expected effects occur under these circumstances, then we can be fairly sure it was the event or variable we manipulated rather than something else that had the observed effect.

The classic experimental design involves manipulating the environment of an *experimental group* in some systematic fashion. The experimental group and a *control group* are both measured in one or more ways that presumably will show the effect of the manipulation on the experimental group as compared to the control group. To be sure that the experimental and control groups are comparable in all ways, the subjects are randomly assigned to one group or the other. By allowing chance to dictate group membership, we can be assured that no selective factor will affect group membership or the later comparison of the two groups.

A moment's reflection will indicate that this method in its pure form is of limited use in understanding the causes of abnormal behavior. No one would seriously consider randomly assigning children to experimental and control groups, producing traumatic life circumstances for the experimental group and later comparing the experimental and control groups for differences in the degree and type of abnormal behavior they display.

Researchers have tried to use the power of the experimental method, however, in other ways. One of the common strategies is the use of *experimental analogues*—recreating a particular phenomenon under laboratory conditions with normal people or animals. For example, laboratory animals could be subjected to different experiences of "loss" and observed for later behavioral indications of "depression." The potential problem with this use of experimental analogues is fairly evident. The analogy between children and rat pups, for example, may be slight. The laboratory operations used to produce "loss" may not provide a good analogy to the emotional loss suffered in childhood, and the laboratory definitions of depression may be only distantly related to the clinical phenomenon in which we are really interested.

In certain circumstances, especially in biochemical research, experimental analogues can provide useful evidence about the determinants of abnormal behavior. Usually, however, the evidence produced might provide only little support for the hypothesis in question, rather than definitive evidence.

Single Subject Experimental Strategies

Just as it is possible to use the principles of experimental design with groups of individuals, it is also possible to apply the same logic to research with a single person. Instead of applying an experimental condition to one group and comparing it with a control group, the single subject strategy applies an

LABORATORY ANALOGS OF ATTACHMENT AND DEPRESSION

Most people tend to be skeptical about the degree to which animal behavior can be generalized to that of humans. The scientific strategy used in making these generalizations is crucial. The strategy adopted by Harlow and his colleagues at the University of Wisconsin has been to search for important patterns of behavior in human interaction and then attempt to produce analogous behavior in lower species.

Harlow and Suomi have been studying rhesus monkeys for several decades and have become particularly interested in the question of human attachment. After having carefully examined research on attachment carried out with humans, Harlow and his colleagues created several very different rearing situations for infant monkeys. They were able to show that the attraction infant monkeys show to their mothers is not merely learned by associating the mother's face with hunger satisfaction, as was previously thought, but had a great deal to do with the sheer pleasure of contact with her body, or "contact comfort."

Currently, Harlow and his colleagues are studying analogs of human depression by isolating infant monkeys in order to produce pathological behavior patterns such as depression. What is especially interesting about their work is that they have taken their analog research approach one step further by placing the monkeys reared in total isolation with three-month-old normal monkeys which they call "therapists." These isolated adult monkeys have no fear of the infant therapists, who then begin to interact with the depressed adults and to rehabilitate them through contact and play.

experimental condition to the individual at one point in time and compares the effect to another time period when no experimental condition has been applied.

Consider the example offered by the research of Allen, Hart, Buell, Harris, and Wolf (1964). Ann, a four-year-old in a preschool setting, was observed by the investigators to have become isolated from other children. The investigators observed her behavior carefully and noticed that she used a variety of strategies for gaining the attention of adults. Since adults did attend to her behavior and since this was incompatible with interacting with her peers, Ann had placed herself in a social situation in which she would become increasingly isolated from her peers.

Allen et al. developed an intervention program in which the reinforcement contingencies were changed so that she received reinforcement in the form of adult attention only as a consequence of playing with other children. Figure 4–2 shows the initial *baseline* period in which an estimate of the proportion of time spent with children and adults was obtained. The second period was one in which interaction with other children was reinforced. In this case, the portion of time Ann spent with children substantially increased.

Then the investigators used one of the classic strategies of single subject experimental designs. They *reversed* the condition, thus returning to the original

An infant monkey receiving "contact comfort" from surrogate mother.

Courtesy Harry Harlow, Wisconsin Primate Laboratory

A previously isolated monkey learning contact and play from younger normal "therapist" monkey.

Courtesy Harry Harlow, Wisconsin Primate Laboratory

situation. Not surprisingly Ann reverted to her original behavior patterns and the proportion of time that she spent with adults again increased. Returning again to the original experimental condition, the investigators again reinforced interaction with other children and the rate of interaction with children again increased.

These results provide impressive evidence for the effect of an experimental condition and are very much favored by behaviorally oriented researchers studying abnormal behavior. We will see still other examples of the use of this research strategy in later chapters.

Longitudinal and High Risk Methods

One of the unique difficulties of doing research on the determinants of abnormal behavior is that clinical groups suffering from a particular disorder are also likely to display other behavior due to associated, but causally unrelated, conditions. Schizophrenic patients, for example, may display behavior patterns resulting from years of hospitalization rather than from the schizophrenia itself. Similarly, family disturbance or the reactions of a family to having a chronically disturbed member of the household could reflect a possible set of causal factors in the schizophrenic. Once the patient has begun to display signs of disturbance, disentangling possible causes from consequences of the disorder is very difficult.

Longitudinal methods of research study the development of behavior over extended periods of time. In principle, longitudinal studies can be very useful in obtaining information about possible determinants of abnormal behavior because the information may be obtained

FIGURE 4–2 Percent of Time Ann Spent in Social Interaction with Adults and with Peers during Approximately Two Hours of Each Morning Session

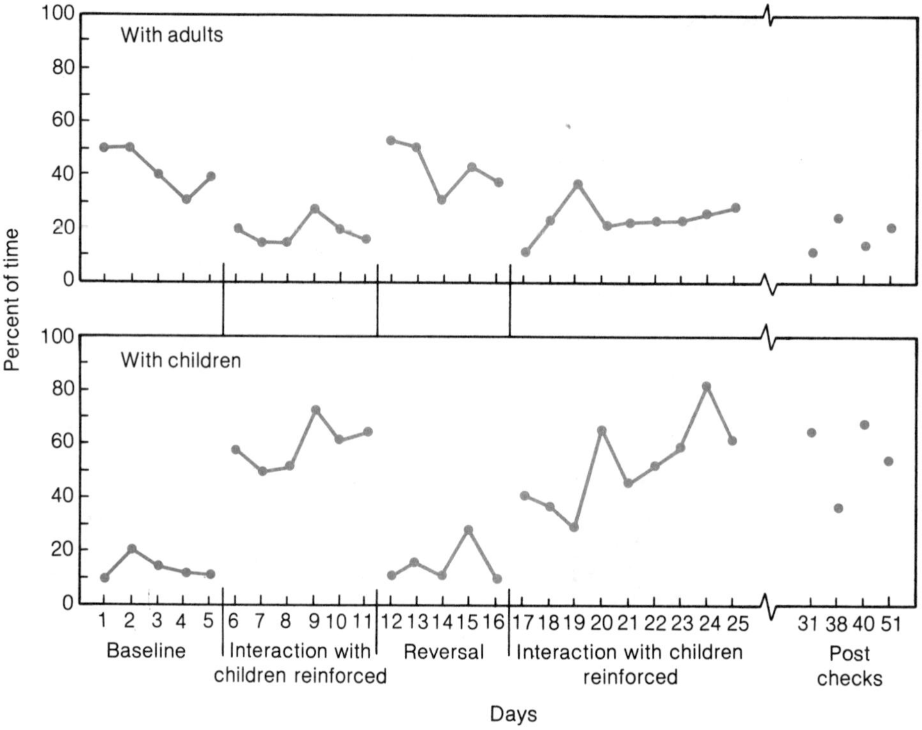

Source: Adapted from Allen, Hart, Buell, Harris & Wolf, "Effects of Social Reinforcement on Isolate Behavior of a Nursery School Child," 1964, *35*, pp. 511–518. © The Society for Research in Child Development, Inc.

before the clinical disturbance becomes evident. So this information is not complicated by associated but causally irrelevant evidence.

One way to obtain longitudinal information on adult disturbance is to study the childhood records of adults who later develop a particular disturbance. If we compare information on this group with that of adults who did not develop the disturbance, we may be able to isolate important childhood determinants of the disorder. Although this method has been used effectively in some cases, difficulties may arise in assuring that the "disturbed" sample and the control adults are representative of the population sampled. Frequently the two groups will also differ markedly in social mobility, making comparison of them with clear inferences difficult.

An important new approach to studying the development of abnormal behavior that takes advantage of the longitudinal approach is the *high risk method* (Mednick, 1966). A general design for a high risk study is shown in Figure 4–3.

You can see that Mednick chose 100 "low-risk" children, who have normal mothers, and 200 "high-risk" children, whose mothers are schizophrenic. The children of schizophrenic mothers are

FIGURE 4–3 Design for a Study Using High Risk Samples of 200 Children with Schizophrenic Mothers and 100 Low Risk Control Subjects

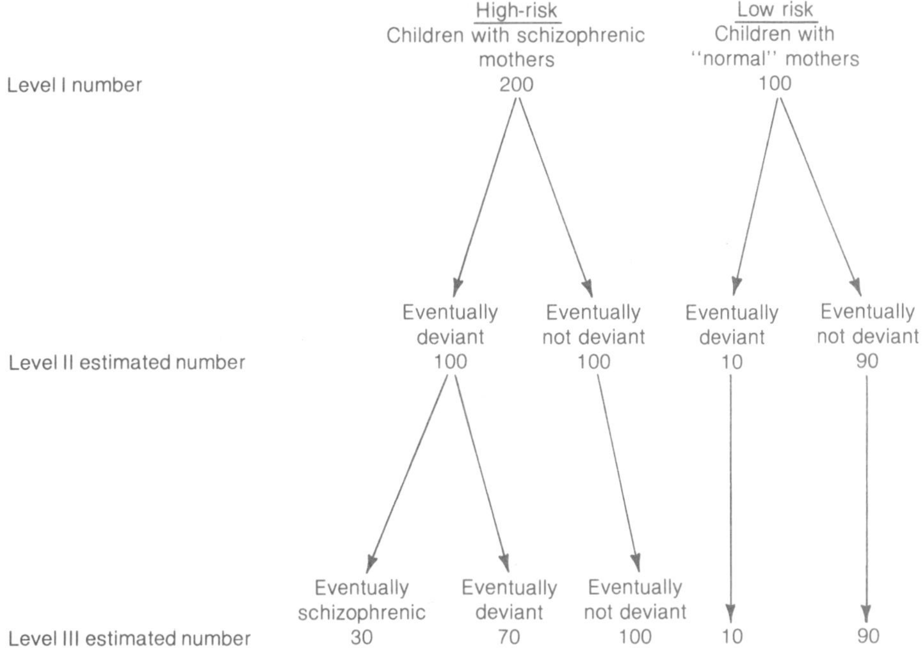

Source: S. A. Mednick and F. Schulsinger. Some premorbid characteristics related to breakdown in children with schizophrenic mothers. In D. Rosenthal & S. S. Kety (Eds.), *The transmission of schizophrenia* (Elmsford, N.Y: Pergamon Press, 1968).

considered to be high risk cases because it is known that 15 percent of such children will eventually become schizophrenic, and another 35 percent will develop some form of deviant behavior. Thus a longitudinal sample of children of sufficient size for careful study is assured.

The investigators measure the high risk and low risk groups of children on a broadly based battery of physiological and psychological tests at the beginning of the study and periodically in subsequent years. Eventually some of the high risk children will develop schizophrenic behavior. It will then be possible to compare the results of earlier tests on these children with results for (1) high risk children who did not develop schizophrenia, and (2) low risk children, to discover differences that are of potential causal significance among the groups.

Despite the great cost and effort involved in conducting longitudinal studies, a number of investigators concerned with the causes of schizophrenia have adopted this strategy recently and we can expect new evidence on the nature of schizophrenia in the near future.

ETHICAL ISSUES IN THE STUDY OF ABNORMAL BEHAVIOR

Imagine, for a moment, that you have carefully developed a procedure for helping people to cope effectively with their anxiety. The only way to know whether your new procedure is more effective than other approaches is to test it with individuals suffering from anxiety, in carefully controlled conditions, comparing your treatment with existing treatments. Proper experimental procedure would require that you randomly assign people with severe anxiety problems to your new treatment and to the other treatment approach. How can you know whether your treatment will be as effective as the current treatment? If it is not, then those people assigned to your new treatment might justifiably argue that they were given inferior care. Yet we can never know whether your treatment procedure is superior unless it is subjected to a rigorous experimental test. Thus a dilemma arises between the need for increased knowledge about a promising treatment that ultimately might help thousands of people and the danger of possibly inferior treatment to several dozen patients.

In searching for chemical causes of schizophrenia, or a new drug to relieve anxiety, or a more effective behavioral treatment for depression, scientists must ultimately work with people suffering abnormal behavior. As Henry Beecher has noted, "Man is the final test site." Inevitably, then, scientists studying abnormal behavior will be confronted by ethical dilemmas and concerns. Bernard Barber, a social scientist who has studied medical researchers' attitudes toward ethical issues in research, suggests that the public has recently become much more aware of these issues.

In understanding the ethical issues in human experimentation, two major issues should be considered. The first has to do with the possibility of exposing people to *undue risk.* The second major issue has to do with assuring that people who agree to participate in scientific experiments are able to give *informed consent.* That is, people should ideally agree to participate only if they have a clear understanding of the risks involved. As a student of abnormal behavior, you may find yourself, someday, in the role of subject in a scientific experiment. Or perhaps some years from now you will find yourself in the role of scientist, actually conducting an experiment. In either case, the complex and difficult issues of risk and informed consent need to be considered in detail.

Consider some examples. In the 1930s a group of black subjects with syphilis were kept under observation in an effort to understand the course of the disease. By 1945 penicillin had become available as an effective cure for syphilis. Despite this, these individuals were not given the cure, and, instead, observation of the course of their disease was continued. This is clearly a case in which people were subjected to undue risk. An example of a flagrant violation of informed consent involves two respected cancer investigators who, in the 1960s, injected live cancer cells into a number of geriatric patients without first obtaining the patients' informed consent.

It is difficult to know how common such flagrant violations of codes of ethics actually are. Barber (1976) has conducted extensive surveys of medical scientists who work with human subjects to discover their attitudes toward undue risk and informed consent. Barber surveyed scientists across the country and asked them to judge experimental proposals that varied in the amount of risk potential for the subjects involved. In addition, Barber and his colleagues examined the way in which scientists reviewed research proposals that held possible risk for human subjects. In general Barber found that the vast majority of scientists were extremely cautious and concerned about ethical issues in working with human subjects. A consistent minority, however, were likely to approve projects with undue risk or without providing for adequate informed consent.

Why does even a consistent minority of scientists fail to be adequately sensitive to these ethical issues? Barber believes that defects in professional training, lax procedures by review committees, the occasional conflict between the desire for knowledge and the need for adequate treatment, and scientific competition all can play a role in the occasional insensitivity to ethical issues in human experimentation. Concern about ethical issues in experimentation may sometimes get lost among other issues. For example, when Barber asked the 350 scientists in his sample what three characteristics they would want to know most about another researcher before entering into a collaborative relationship, 86 percent mentioned scientific ability, 45 percent mentioned motivation to work hard, but only 6 percent listed anything that could be classified "ethical concern for research subjects."

It is important to realize that not all people undergoing psychological or medical treatment are equally vulnerable to careless ethical practices. As Barber points out, his results and those of other scientists suggest that some groups are more vulnerable than others. Poor people who are more likely to be treated in a hospital ward, institutionalized patients, prisoners in correctional facilities, and children are most vulnerable to unethical experimentation. This is because they are living in a context in which there are implied constraints against refusing to participate in experiments, or because they are unable to provide informed consent for participation. These vulnerable groups are also the most likely to suffer at the hands of thoughtless experimenters.

In the arena of research in abnormal psychology, it will frequently be necessary to work with humans. The conflict between the search for new knowledge and the danger of risk to human subjects will always be present. Increased awareness is, in the long run, our best safeguard.

ETHICAL PRINCIPLES OF PSYCHOLOGISTS

As the major national organization of psychologists, the American Psychological

ETHICAL STANDARDS OF PSYCHOLOGISTS IN RESEARCH*

PREAMBLE

Psychologists[1] respect the dignity and worth of the individual and honor the preservation and protection of fundamental human rights. They are committed to increasing knowledge of human behavior and of people's understanding of themselves and others and to the utilization of such knowledge for the promotion of human welfare. While pursuing these endeavors, they make every effort to protect the welfare of those who seek their services or of any human being or animal that may be the object of study. They use their skills only for purposes consistent with

[1] A student of psychology who assumes the role of a psychologist shall be considered a psychologist for the purpose of this code of ethics.

these values and do not knowingly permit their misuse by others. While demanding for themselves freedom of inquiry and communications, psychologists accept the responsibility this freedom requires: competence, objectivity in the application of skills, and concern for the best interests of clients, colleagues, and society in general. In the pursuit of these ideals, psychologists subscribe to principles in the following areas: 1. Responsibility, 2. Competence, 3. Moral and Legal Standards, 4. Public Statements, 5. Confidentiality, 6. Welfare of the Consumer, 7. Professional Relationships, 8. Utilization of Assessment Techniques, and 9. Pursuit of Research Activities.

PRINCIPLE 9. PURSUIT OF RESEARCH ACTIVITIES

The decision to undertake research should rest upon a considered judgment by the individual psychologist about how best to contribute to psychological science and to human welfare. Psychologists carry out their investigations with respect for the people who participate and with concern for their dignity and welfare.

a. In planning a study the investigator has the responsibility to make a careful evaluation of its ethical acceptability, taking into account the following additional principles for research with human beings. To the extent that this appraisal, weighing scientific and humane values, suggests a compromise of any principle, the investigator incurs an increasingly serious obligation to seek ethical advice and to observe stringent safeguards to protect the rights of the human research participants.

b. Responsibility for the establishment and maintenance of acceptable ethical practice in research always remains with the individual investigator. The investigator is also responsible for the ethical treatment of research participants by collaborators, assistants, students, and employees, all of whom, however, incur parallel obligations.

c. Ethical practice requires the investigator to inform the participant of all features of the research that might reasonably be expected to influence willingness to participate, and to explain all other aspects of the research about which the participant inquires. Failure to make full disclosure imposes additional force to the investigator's abiding responsibility to protect the welfare and dignity of the research participant.

d. Openness and honesty are essential characteristics of the relationship between investigator and research participant. When the methodological requirements of a study necessitate concealment or deception, the investigator is required to insure as soon as possible the participant's understanding of the reasons for this action and of a sufficient justification for the procedures employed.

e. Ethical practice requires the investigator to respect the individual's freedom to decline to participate in or withdraw from research. The obligation to protect this freedom requires special vigilance when the investigator is in a position of power over the participant, as, for example, when the participant is a student, client, employee, or otherwise is in a dual relationship with the investigator.

f. Ethically acceptable research begins with the establishment of a clear and fair agreement between the investigator and the research participant that clarifies the responsibilities of each. The investigator has the obligation to honor all promises and commitments included in that agreement.

g. The ethical investigator protects participants from physical and mental discomfort, harm, and danger. If a risk of such consequences exists, the investigator is required to inform the participant of that fact, secure consent before proceeding, and take all possible measures to minimize distress. A research procedure must not be used if it is likely to cause serious or lasting harm to a participant.

h. After the data are collected, the investigator provides the participant with information about the nature of the study and removes any misconceptions that may have arisen. Where scientific or humane values justify delaying or withholding information, the investigator acquires a special responsibility to assure that there are no damaging consequences for the participant.

i. When research procedures may result in undesirable consequences for the individual participant, the investigator has the responsibility to detect and remove or correct these consequences, including, where relevant, long-term after effects.

j. Information obtained about the individual research participants during the course of an investigation is confidential unless otherwise agreed in advance. When the possibility exists that others may obtain access to such information, this possibility, together with the plans for protecting confidentiality, is explained to the participants as part of the procedure for obtaining informed consent.

k. A psychologist using animals in research adheres to the provisions of the Rules Regarding Animals, drawn up by the Committee on Precautions and Standards in Animal Experimentation and adopted by the American Psychological Association.

l. Investigations of human participants using drugs should be conducted only in such settings as clinics, hospitals, or research facilities maintaining appropriate safeguards for the participants.

REFERENCES

Psychologists are responsible for knowing about and acting in accord with the standards and positions of the APA, as represented in such official documents as the following:

American Association of University Professors. Statement of Principles on Academic Freedom and Tenure. *Policy Documents & Report,* 1977, 1–4.

American Psychological Association. *Guidelines for Psychologists for the Use of Drugs in Research.* Washington, D.C.: Author, 1971.

American Psychological Association. *Principles for the Care and Use of Animals.* Washington, D.C.: Author, 1971.

American Psychological Association. Guidelines for conditions of employment of psychologists. *American Psychologist,* 1972, *27,* 331–334.

American Psychological Association. Guidelines for psychologists conducting growth groups. *American Psychologist,* 1973, *28,* 933.

American Psychological Association. *Ethical Principles in the Conduct of Research with Human Participants.* Washington, D.C.: Author, 1973

American Psychological Association. *Standards for Educational and Psychological Tests.* Washington, D.C.: Author, 1974.

American Psychological Association. *Standards for Providers of Psychological Services.* Washington, D.C.: Author, 1977.

Committee on Scientific and Professional Ethics and Conduct. Guidelines for telephone directory listings. *American Psychologist,* 1969, *24,* 70–71.

Association has been concerned with the ethical practice of psychology and psychological research for many years. The organization has developed an important document entitled *Ethical Principles for Psychologists* that describes the obligations of psychologists who are working with human beings in a variety of professional capacities.

In the area of research, the principles have been carefully formulated to deal with questions of confidentiality of records, knowing use of procedures that might harm others, disclosure of results, scrutiny of the procedures of any study in which a person participates, and the requirement that an individual give fully informed voluntary consent when participating in any research study. The portion of *Ethical Principles* regarding the conduct of research is shown above.

SUMMARY

In this chapter, we have examined a variety of research strategies used in the scientific study of abnormal behavior. We noted that each perspective of abnormal behavior suggests its own set of causes, and that scientists favoring a particular perspective are more likely to look for the causes of behavior in areas suggested by that perspective. We also noted that we may think of several different kinds of causes of abnormal behavior including predisposing causal factors, precipitating factors, and maintaining causal factors.

The research methods used to understand abnormal behavior are agreed upon procedures that emphasize repeatable observations that constitute evidence about the nature and the causes of abnormal behavior.

Each research method has its own particular strengths in helping us to understand the nature and causes of abnormal behavior. Case histories and clinical observation may provide a rich background of detail about a particular phenomenon but do not provide the basis for generalizations to other cases or individuals. Correlational approaches are particularly useful for identifying potential relationships between variables but can tell us little or nothing about the causal structure of the phenomenon that we are investigating.

Experimental methods are the most powerful approach for gaining evidence of the potential causes of behavioral phenomena but have had limited use in the study of abnormal behavior. This is because of the ethical and practical constraints associated with subjecting humans to independent variables that we think may be causal factors in the development of abnormal patterns of behavior. Consequently a good deal of experimental research in the area of abnormal behavior has been focused on the use of experimental analogs. The analog may test the effects of a particular independent variable on another species or test the effects of conditions in the laboratory that we think are analogous to those associated with the development of abnormal behavior. In addition, the systematic use of experimental designs with individual subjects has increased substantially, particularly among behaviorally oriented psychologists. We also suggested that longitudinal and high risk methods for studying the development of abnormal behavior promise to uncover important findings about the causes of abnormal behavior.

Finally, we discussed the question of ethical issues in the study of abnormal behavior and noted that the danger of undue risk to experimental subjects and the need to obtain informed consent are two major issues in this field. The *Ethical Principles of Psychologists* provide an example of the way in which scientists regulate their own behavior to safeguard the public welfare while pursuing their scientific objectives.

5

Classification and Assessment of Abnormal Behavior

CLASSIFICATION AND SCIENCE

We are always classifying objects, events, and people in order to make sense of our world. If we have no label for an object or person, we are likely to invent one. As any science evolves, one of its first concerns is classification. Although initial classifications are always tentative, the scientist tries to assign whatever is being studied to groups within a system of categories; and members of these groups are expected to resemble each other in one or more important ways. Classifications are tools and, like other tools, they survive because they are useful. For example, classification can aid the process of discovering previously unseen similarities between events, objects, or people.

Classification systems are always in a state of evolution. For example, the periodic table in chemistry has undergone considerable extension over recent decades, and zoological classifications are continually undergoing change. Classification in the field of abnormal psychology is at a preliminary stage. It is likely that a number of the classifications we now use confidently to describe the characteristics of people will undergo a great deal of change in the near future. Later we will look at some of those changes.

The Uses of Classification

We noted before that one could think of classification as a tool with very specific uses. We are now going to look at those uses in greater detail, following a scheme developed by Blashfield and Draguns (1976).

Classification as a basis for communication. Specialists in nearly every field develop a common language to communicate effectively with one another. Lawyers, plumbers, physicians, used car salesmen, and even confidence men have developed their own specialized language to help them discuss the details of the objects and events of their work. One way to view a classification system in the field of abnormal psychology is as a dictionary of terms that allows us to discuss a person or a disorder as a member of a class. In doing so, we are communicating information about that individual in a kind of shorthand. When a mental health worker says that an individual is a "reactive depressive," or that the person displays "schizophrenic features," he is using abbreviations to imply a much larger spectrum of features.

Classification as a key to scientific literature. The classification of abnormal behavior assumes that the name of a disorder is the key to scientific information describing it. By looking at the literature discussing "obsessive-compulsive neuroses," we ought to be able to find information on its description, what is known about its causes, and, perhaps, how people have tried to treat it.

Critics of current classification schemes have suggested that we abandon current classifications and start again. But throwing out the current system would bring an enormous loss of information, since most of our scientific knowledge about various disorders is catalogued according to this system.

Classification as a means of description. One goal of both clinical practitioners and research scientists is to describe the characteristics of the people whose behavior they study. If a classification system categorizes individuals so that the groupings are fairly homogeneous, then the name of a grouping will provide a fairly accurate summary of the important characteristics of the person, at least insofar as abnormal behavior is concerned. Many of the classes in the current classification system are *not* very homogeneous. Thus our system is seriously limited.

Classification for prediction. A major purpose of classifying disorders in the field of abnormal psychology is to predict certain important characteristics or behaviors of people belonging to each class. Once we have classified a disorder, it should be possible to predict (1) what the causes of the disorder are likely to be, (2) how an individual affected will respond to treatment, and (3) the probable course of the disorder. Indeed, a very large portion of the efforts of scientists in abnormal psychology are devoted to discovering these relationships.

Classification as a building block for scientific theories. There is a final important way that a classification scheme can be useful. A category in the scheme can become a concept in a theory about abnormal behavior. For example, the classification "schizophrenia" has long served as the reference point for a set of ideas about people who are thought to share characteristics that include social withdrawal and severe disorganization of perception, thought, and emotion. Schizophrenia is an *idea* shared by scientists. It is not a theory, but a scientific concept used to summarize a set of characteristics of people's behavior. And, like scientific concepts, its usefulness is subject to scientific verification.

The Diagnostic and Statistical Manual of Mental Disorders: DSM III

Over the years, a number of classification schemes have been developed to distinguish various patterns of abnormal behavior from each other. The single most widely used classification scheme has been the *Diagnostic and Statistical Manual of Mental Disorders* published by the American Psychiatric Association. The earlier version of this manual, published in 1968 (DSM II), was developed so that it conformed closely to the international classification of diseases described by the World Health Organization.

Problems of reliability and validity of DSM II. Although the second edition of the *Diagnostic and Statistical Manual of Mental Disorders* remained in use for over a decade, it received substantial criticism because of a number of shortcomings. Among them was the fact that within the broad diagnostic classes in the classification system, patterns of behavior included were very heterogeneous. Zigler and Phillips (1961), for example, reported a study of the hospital records of nearly 800 patients in which they examined the overlap in symptoms in different diagnostic categories reported for patients. Essentially, the study demonstrated that based on the pattern of symptoms reported it would be difficult to predict the diagnosis a patient should receive.

In addition, the reliability of the DSM II was poor, particularly in the broader categories. As we shall see later in this discussion, the ability of two diagnosticians to agree on the diagnosis to be given to a particular individual is critical in the effective use of the system. To illustrate the problems, consider the following case example:

You are sitting in your office, having just interviewed two people. One was a 36-year-old married woman whose speech patterns were very disorganized and confused. She looked to you as if she was displaying a classic thought disorder. You wonder, is she schizophrenic? The other patient you have just seen was a 30-year-old unemployed, single man. He has a number of beliefs that could be classified as delusional. He also reported hearing and seeing things that sound to you very much like hallucinations. In the last months he has shown marked mood swings, ranging from deep depression to elation. All of these signs of disturbance have only occurred within the last two months.

Both of these people seem severely disturbed to you. Part of your job is to provide a carefully considered diagnosis of each patient that you see. You haul out your copy of the DSM II and again read the definition of schizophrenia.

> Schizophrenia. This large category includes a group of disorders manifested by characteristic disturbances in thinking, mood, and behavior. Disturbances in thinking are marked by alterations of concept formation which may lead to misinterpretations of reality and sometimes to delusions and hallucinations which frequently appear psychologically protective. Corollary mood changes include ambivalent, constricted and inappropriate emotional responsiveness and loss of empathy with others. Behavior may be withdrawn, regressive, and bizarre (American Psychiatric Association, 1968, p. 33).

Should either of the people that you just saw in the interview be classified as schizophrenic? The woman surely showed some evidence of thought disorder. The man provided a number of indications that he is suffering from delusions and hallucinations, but there are 13 distinct signs in that definition of schizophrenia. You ask yourself, how many and which of these signs are necessary for me to make a diagnosis of schizophrenia? But there are no instructions in the DSM II to tell you which signs are more important than others.

Now you can appreciate some problems inherent in the DSM II. How can you expect another clinician to agree with you *(inter-rater reliability)?* How can you expect to use this definition consistently over a period of time *(test-retest reliability)?* There are no rules to tell you which characteristics of the person's behavior are necessary for the diagnosis of schizophrenia, nor how many are necessary.

The value of specific descriptions and decision rules. But a classification system need not be so vague (Blashfield & Draguns, 1976). Let us look at another definition of schizophrenia. This one has been developed by a research team working on new experimental methods for developing diagnostic and classification systems.

For a diagnosis of schizophrenia, (1) through (3) are required.

1. Both of the following are necessary:
   a. A chronic illness with at least six months of symptoms prior to the index evaluation without return to the premorbid level of psychosocial adjustment.
   b. Absence of a period of depressive or manic symptoms sufficient to qualify for affective disorder or probable affective disorder.
2. The patient must have at least one of the following:
   a. Delusions or hallucinations without significant perplexity or disorientation associated with them.
   b. Verbal production that makes communication difficult because of a lack of logical or understandable organization.
3. At least three of the following manifestations must be present for a diagnosis of "definite" schizophrenia and two for a diagnosis of "probable" schizophrenia:
   a. Single.
   b. Poor premorbid social adjustment or work history.
   c. Family history of schizophrenia.
   d. Absence of alcoholism or drug abuse within one year of onset of psychosis.
   e. Onset of illness prior to age 40.

Using this last definition, would either of the two people that we described earlier be classified as schizophrenic? The answer is that neither one of them would qualify.

If the diagnostic system at your disposal were as specific as the one we have just looked at, you should have no trouble agreeing with other clinicians on whether certain behaviors are signs of schizophrenia or not. It is carefully spelled out in the system. Systems of this kind have now been tested and the initial findings suggest that experienced clinicians can agree very well about the diagnosis of individuals (Zubin et al., 1975). This represents an important advance in the development of classification systems. Research aimed at developing highly specific systems for classification will probably do a great deal to influence the way we classify abnormal behavior in the future. Indeed, the newest version of the diagnostic manual, to which we now turn, attempts to improve the specificity of diagnostic criteria and therefore improve upon the reliability of DSM II.

DSM III. The most recent edition of the *Diagnostic and Statistical Manual of Mental Disorders* (DSM III) was published in 1980. It represents a radical departure from DSM II and is a clear effort to meet the criticisms leveled at that version. DSM III notes that clear descriptions of diagnostic categories and the provision of diagnostic criteria to produce greater agreement among diagnosticians was the major purpose of the revision.

It is also important to note that DSM III does not attempt to account for how various psychological disturbances come about, and acknowledges a wide variety of theories to account for the development of various disorders. Instead its primary purpose is an accurate description.

The framers of DSM III have attempted to be inclusive rather than exclusive in categorizing various patterns of abnormal behavior. A major criterion for deciding to include a disorder was whether clinicians would be likely to encounter the condition in their clinical work. (DSM III, 1980). Thus a variety of relatively mild disorders or problems that may not be in the strictest sense "abnormal" are included in this comprehensive classification system (see Table 5–1). In fact, every disorder receives some sort of classification under this system since one of the categories is "conditions not attributable to a mental disorder."

The removal of the term *neurosis* from the DSM III represents still another change. The term *neurosis* has been replaced by new concepts, such as somatoform, dissociative, and personality disorders, which we will discuss in later chapters.

Multiaxial classification. DSM III classifies disorders not along one dimension, but five. This has produced a substantial increase in the amount of information that a classification will communicate about a disorder. The five axes of the current system are shown in Table 5–2 below. The first axis provides for the classification of a person on the basis of a major pattern of symptoms. The second axis classifies personality disorders. Medical disorders are included on Axis III. The severity of stressors that may have served as precipitating events is rated on Axis IV. Finally, Axis V is for an estimate of the current level of functioning of the person. An example of the way in which a particular patient might be classified is also shown in Table 5–2.

The multiaxial classification system is, in effect, five classifications applied simultaneously to a particular individual.

TABLE 5–1 Major Diagnostic Headings in DSM III (1980, pp. 15–19)

DISORDERS USUALLY FIRST EVIDENT IN INFANCY, CHILDHOOD OR ADOLESCENCE
- Mental retardation
- Attention deficit disorder
- Conduct disorder
- Anxiety disorders of childhood or adolescence
- Other disorders of infancy, childhood or adolescence
- Eating disorders
- Stereotyped movement disorders
- Other disorders with physical manifestations
- Pervasive developmental disorders

ORGANIC MENTAL DISORDERS
- Senile and presenile dementias
- Substance-induced dementias

SUBSTANCE USE DISORDERS

SCHIZOPHRENIC DISORDERS

PARANOID DISORDERS

PSYCHOTIC DISORDERS NOT ELSEWHERE CLASSIFIED

AFFECTIVE DISORDERS

ANXIETY DISORDERS

SOMATOFORM DISORDERS

DISSOCIATIVE DISORDERS (OR HYSTERICAL NEUROSES, DISSOCIATIVE TYPE)

PSYCHOSEXUAL DISORDERS
- Gender identity disorders
- Paraphilias
- Psychosexual dysfunctions

FACITIOUS DISORDERS

DISORDERS OF IMPULSE CONTROL NOT ELSEWHERE CLASSIFIED

ADJUSTMENT DISORDERS

PSYCHOLOGICAL FACTORS AFFECTING PHYSICAL CONDITION

CONDITIONS NOT ATTRIBUTABLE TO A MENTAL DISORDER THAT ARE A FOCUS OF ATTENTION OR TREATMENT

TABLE 5–2 Multiaxial Classification System of DSM III

Axes of DSM III		Example
Axis I	Formal psychiatric syndrome	296.80 Atypical depressive disorder
Axis II	Personality disorders (adults) and specific developmental disorders (children)	301.81 Narcissistic personality disorder
Axis III	Nonmental medical disorders	Diabetes, hypertension
Axis IV	Severity of psychosocial stressors one year preceding disorder (range: 1–7)	Psychosocial stressors: 5, severe (business failure)
Axis V	Highest level of adaptive behavior one year preceding disorder (range: 1–7)	Highest adaptive behavior past year: 3, good

Source: Adapted from T. Schacht and P. E. Nathan, "But Is It Good for Psychologists? Approval and Status of DSM III," *American Psychologist*, December 1977, p. 1017.

Each major classification, or category, has diagnostic criteria associated with it in DSM III. The importance of these criteria is that they are an attempt to improve the reliability of the DSM III over that of DSM II by providing a checklist of patterns of behavior that are required in order to make the diagnosis. We will discuss many of these criteria when we consider specific patterns of behavior disorders in later chapters.

The structure of DSM III allows the diagnostician to systematically make decisions about the disorder exhibited by an individual. This is accomplished by providing diagnosticians with a "decision tree" that allows them to begin with the most general pattern of behavior and to rule out alternatives until a final decision is reached. An example of a decision tree for the differential diagnosis of psychotic features is shown in Figure 5–1.

Criticisms of DSM III. Despite the radical departure of DSM III from the previous version, some observers have already offered criticisms of it. Schacht and Nathan (1977) express considerable concern for the lack of evidence of the reliability of the judgments required within the five axes of the diagnostic system. They suggest, for example, that the rating scales used in Axes IV and V are not carefully designed for reliable and culture-fair assessment. In the case of Axis V (level of adaptive behavior), Schacht and Nathan suggest "the authors of DSM III have failed to consider [culture-fair assessment] since variables like socioeconomic status, ethnicity, cultural milieu are clearly germane to considerations of level of adaptive functioning" (p. 1019).

Schacht and Nathan also suggest that, although the operational criteria for defining each diagnostic category are desirable, they do not measure up to the careful research criteria that originally inspired the classification system.

Despite these criticisms, it is unquestionably the case that the DSM III will be a dramatic improvement over the DSM II and will provide substantial information for future research as well as an organizing set of principles for describing and classifying abnormal behavior. Throughout this text, we will frequently refer to DSM III in our discussions of various types of disorders.

FIGURE 5–1 A Decision Tree Based on DSM III Differential Diagnosis of "Psychotic" Features

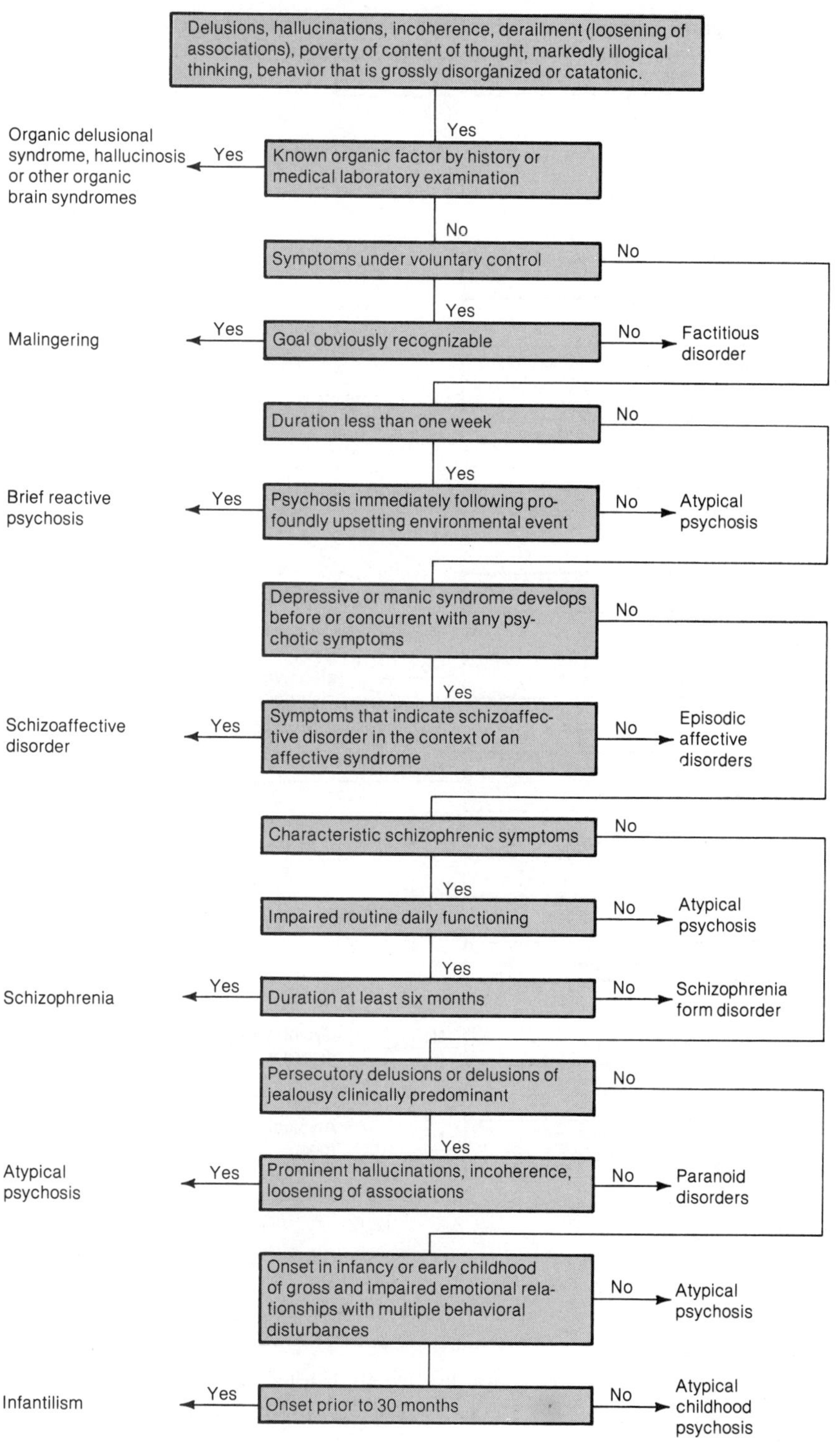

FIGURE 5–1 ***(continued)*** **Differential Diagnosis of Mood Disturbance**

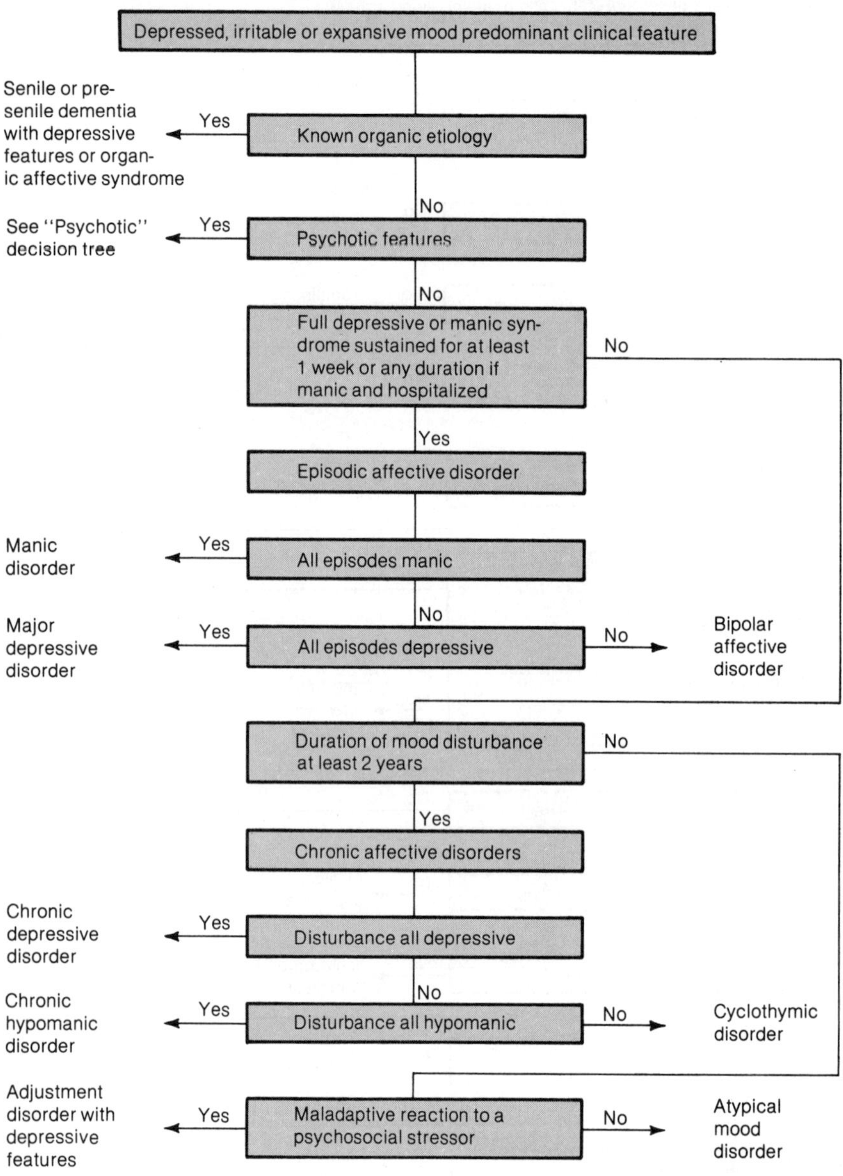

A BEHAVIORAL APPROACH TO CLASSIFICATION

Although the DSM is the most popular system currently in use, a number of other classification systems have been developed and suggested for general use. We are going to look at a behavioral system, both to examine its virtues and to compare it with the DSM.

Psychologists have been particularly interested in developing classification systems that focus on people's behavior. Salzinger (1975) suggests that behavioral classification systems have several distinctive features in common. First, behavioral systems focus on those aspects of the person and the environment that can be directly used in therapeutic efforts. Second, behavioral analysis approaches are more concerned with those environmental conditions that produce a particular behavior than they are with detailed descriptions of the behavior itself. Third, the primary focus in behavioral systems is on classifying the behavior of people, rather than the people themselves. Finally, behavioral systems are concerned, for the most part, with describing the conditions that *maintain* a problematic behavior, and they tend to be much less concerned with the underlying causes of the problem.

Let us look at an example of a behavioral classification system developed by Bandura and shown here in Table 5–3. Notice that the categories listed in this classification use a different language from the *Diagnostic and Statistical Manual.* The language reflects different assumptions; it implies different mechanisms and would lead us to look for very different events both in the person's behavior and environment.

An important thing to notice about this

TABLE 5–3 A Behavioral Classification System Developed by Bandura (1968) and Elaborated by Goldfried and Sprafkin (1974)

Behavioral Class	*Example*
I. Difficulties in Stimulus Control of Behavior	
A. Defective stimulus control: Individual is unable to respond to discriminative stimuli that dictate appropriate response.	Situationally inappropriate behavior, for example, laugh at a funeral.
B. Inappropriate stimulus control: Intense and maladaptive emotional responses that are elicited by previously neutral cues.	Fear of furry objects. Fear of flying
II. Aversive Self-Reinforcing Systems Self-generated feelings of misery associated with unfavorable ratios of self-reinforcement to work. Adequate behavioral repertoires and stimulus control exists, however.	Unrealistically high standards for own performance. Self-blame, self-doubt. Unfavorable self-comparison.

TABLE 5–3 (continued)

Behavioral Class	Example
III. Deviant Behavioral Repertoires Absence of behavioral skills needed to cope due to failures in early learning or absence of prior experience	Socially inept behavior. Lack of social or other behavioral skills.
IV. Aversive Behavioral Repertoires Responses to life situations in ways that alienate others	Overly aggressive or antisocial behavior.
V. Difficulties with Incentive (Reinforcing) Systems	
A. Defective incentive systems in individuals: When social stimuli that for most people are effective at controlling behavior are not effective for an individual	Autistic child. Antisocial people for whom reinforcement has little effect.
B. Inappropriate incentive system in individuals: Existing reinforcers are physically harmful, culturally disapproved of, or both	Drug addiction. Alcoholism. Deviant sexual behavior.
C. Absence of incentives in environment: Problem is function of person's environment. The environment has few incentives available.	Shifts in status. Loss of loved one. Many result in depression.

Source: Based on M. R. Goldfried and J. N. Sprafkin, *Behavioral Personality Assessment.* © 1974 General Learning Corporation. Adapted by permission of Silver Burdett Company.

system is that every classification also contains suggestions for a particular form of treatment or behavioral intervention. Furthermore, in every case, the treatment involves rearranging the stimuli or life events of the individual in order to rearrange the rewards and punishments associated with a particular behavior.

SCIENTIFIC AND PRACTICAL CRITERIA FOR EVALUATING A DIAGNOSTIC CLASSIFICATION SYSTEM

We have just finished looking at some of the uses of classification in the study of abnormal behavior and at some examples of classification systems. But is one system better than another? If so, how will we know which system is better? What makes a ''good'' classification system? The answers to these questions depend on what purpose you want the classification system to serve. Remember, we said there were five different purposes that classification systems could serve, and these included description, prediction, communication, scientific theory building, and the organization of scientific literature. The two most basic of these purposes are description and prediction. If the classification system can serve the purpose of accurate description of behaviors and events and can predict how people will behave in the future, then probably it will also be able to serve the other purposes.

Now we can begin to figure out what characteristics to look for in a good classification system (Blashfield & Draguns, 1976). We know that the features of a classification system that allow accurate descriptions and valid prediction of future behavior are the features we should look for. As we consider the characteristics listed in Table 5–4, we must keep in mind the goals of accurate descriptions of behavior and accurate predictions of future behavior. If we keep these goals in mind, then the characteristics of a good classification system will make a good deal of sense.

TABLE 5–4 Criteria for Evaluating a Classification System

Inter-rater Reliability

Can two judges independently agree on the classification a person should receive?

Test-retest Reliability

Can a judge give the same classification to a person on different occasions?

Descriptive Validity

Is the classification homogeneous? Does knowing that a person is a member of the class tell us what we should expect to see when we observe the person?

Predictive Validity

Can we predict which treatments will be effective based on the classification? Can we predict the outcome of the disorder?

Coverage

Does the classification actually apply to all individuals for whom it was intended? Is it excessively narrow or unreasonably broad?

The first thing a good classification system should do is to allow two observers of the same set of events and behaviors to come up with the same classification. The technical term for this requirement of agreement among observers is called *inter-rater reliability.* A little reflection shows the importance of this requirement. If two observers cannot look at the same person over the same period of time, using the same system, and come up with the same classification on a regular basis, accurate description and prediction will not be possible.

A good classification system should also fulfill the requirement of stability over time. That is, an observer should be able to look at the same person showing essentially the same pattern of behavior on two occasions and arrive at the same classification both times. The technical term for this characteristic of stability is *test-retest reliability.* If a classification system is affected by factors that change over time, it loses its ability to describe and predict accurately.

In a classification system, just knowing that a person is a member of a particular class should tell us about other characteristics of the person that we cannot expect to observe. That is, classification has to be homogeneous. For example, if we look at the classification of metals, we find that simply knowing a piece of metal is made of gold tells us a great deal more about that metal. It tells us about its weight, its hardness, and even its melting point. The technical term for this characteristic is *descriptive validity.* You can imagine that a class containing all sorts of different objects is not very useful in telling us about the characteristics of any particular object in that class. So for a classification system to do a good job of description, the classes within it must be homogeneous.

What about the practical payoff of a classification system? Does the classification system relate to important future events that we would want to be able to predict? It is possible to have a homogeneous classification system for behavior that allows raters to agree with each other without having any practical payoff at all. For example, it would be possible to classify people reliably on the basis of their eye color or their foot size and to produce very homogeneous classes of people. But does knowing that a person falls in one of these classes allow us to predict future events that we care about? When we are studying abnormal behavior we want to be able to predict the causes of the behavior. Is the behavior we are observing caused by a vitamin deficiency or a complex set of events in the life of the individual? Perhaps we want to predict whether the person will recover from his or her difficulties, and if so, how rapidly? Another important payoff for any classification system, of course, would be whether it tells us which treatment will be more effective for which class of people. The technical term for this characteristic of a classification system is *predictive validity.* Developing a classification system with good predictive validity, for practical and scientific purposes, is the main reason to have a system to begin with.

There is one last characteristic that classification systems should have that is frequently overlooked. A classification system should apply to all of the people we wish it to apply to, and not arbitrarily leave out some people. This characteristic is called *coverage.* For example, if we want a classification system to apply to both adults and children, we should be careful to design it to include both groups. Frequently classification systems are developed that are very good in most respects but refer to such a narrow group of people that their practical usefulness is very limited.

PSYCHOLOGICAL ASSESSMENT

When we began our discussion of classification we noted its value in helping us to predict behavior. Psychological assessment serves a similar important function. The assessment of individual characteristics and abilities can provide us with important information to help an individual cope with future life challenges.

Sundberg, Snowden, and Reynolds (1978) define psychological assessment as "discerning individual characteristics important for decisions in person-society relationships." An analysis of this definition suggests a psychological assessment involves several elements.

First there must be a strategy or method for *discerning individual characteristics.* Over the years psychologists have developed a variety of tools to discern individual characteristics and we will discuss a number of them in this section.

A second element in this definition concerns *decisions.* Decisions may involve a recommendation for one treatment plan rather than another or even a legal decision regarding the competence of a person to care for himself. This emphasis on social decisions clearly indicates that assessment is no idle exercise. Psychological assessment may have substantial impact on the life of a person.

The final element in the definition involves *person-society relationships.* The underlying notion here is that decisions made about an individual based on psychological assessment may alter in important ways the manner in which that individual interacts with his or her society in the future. A decision to recommend family psychotherapy will unquestionably alter the relationship of the family members, not only to the community of psychological professionals but also to one another and perhaps even to their outside social world. Similarly, psychological assessment may provide information for legal decisions regarding whether or not a particular defendant is competent to stand trial. Thus, psychological assessment can play a pivotal role in a variety of social decision making situations.

All techniques of psychological assessment attempt to obtain a *sample of behavior* that is assumed to be representative of the behavior patterns displayed by a type of individual in a particular range of situations. Psychological assessment assumes that these samples of behavior allow us to predict other important outcomes in the individual's life. Let us now turn to an examination of some of the major approaches to psychological assessment.

Tools of Assessment

Three of the most commonly used tools of psychological assessment are *behavioral observation, interviews,* and *psychological tests.* Each tool makes a unique contribution to the assessment process. We will examine each of these approaches.

Behavioral observation. Perhaps the most basic way to gather information about a person is to observe him or her in a natural setting. Gerald Patterson and his co-workers at the University of Oregon have developed a system for observing the behavior of young boys in their family context.

Table 5–5 illustrates Patterson's observation system. On the left, a list of some of the behaviors that an observer will look for in observing the home setting is shown. The second column shows how 30 seconds are interpreted using Patterson's behavioral coding system.

If you look closely at this example, you can learn several important things from it. First, Patterson's system, like many behavioral observation systems, is very carefully defined and detailed. It takes the "booming, buzzing confusion" of family life and turns it into a series of coded behaviors that describe the way people are behaving toward each other. It was Patterson's goal to be able to use this information not only to understand the usual patterns of behavior in the home but also to measure progress in treatment. Another thing that you can see from this example is that Patterson's system achieves great accuracy at the expense of being very narrow. This system would not work very well in settings other than the home, nor was it designed to do so.

Patterson and his co-workers designed this system so they could discover the *contingencies* that exist in family interactions. Once behavior is coded in six-second segments, systematic relationships between parent and child behavior patterns can be discovered. This information then provides specific ideas for future behavioral intervention in the family interaction to help deal with problematic behavior patterns.

Interview strategies. The interview is one of the most widely used strategies for obtaining psychological information. A

TABLE 5–5 Illustration of the Use of Patterson's (1969) System of Behavioral Observation: Thirty Seconds in the Life of a Boy Named Kevin

Some Typical Behavior Classes in the Behavior Coding System	*Thirty Seconds in Kevin's Life as a Rater Using the BCS Might See It*	*Narrative Description of Thirty Seconds in the Life of Kevin*
TA (TALK): This code is used if none of the other verbal codes are applicable *AT (ATTENTION):* When one person listens to or looks at another person, and the categories AP or DI are not appropriate	0–6 seconds Kevin engages in "normative" behavior (i.e., appropriate behavior not falling under any specific category) and father shows positive physical contact INO 2PP	Kevin goes up to father's chair and stands alongside it. Father puts his arms around Kevin's shoulders.
NO (NORMATIVE): A person is behaving in an appropriate fashion and no other code is applicable	7–12 seconds Kevin talks and his mother ignores him ITA 3IG	Kevin says to mother as Frieda looks at Kevin, "Can I go out and play after supper?" Mother does not reply.
NR (NO RESPONSE): When a person does not respond to another person. Applicable when a behavior does not require a response, or when behavior is directed at another person, but the person to whom the behavior is directed fails to perceive the behavior	13–18 seconds Kevin yells and both mother and father show their disapproval IYE 2/3DI	Kevin raises his voice and repeats the question. Mother says, "you don't have to yell; I can hear you." Father says, "How many times have I told you not to yell at your mother?"
DI (DISAPPROVAL): The person gives verbal or gestural disapproval of another person's behavior or characteristics	19–24 seconds Kevin is involved in self-stimulation, and Frieda engages in other activities and shows no response ISS 4NR	Kevin scratches a bruise on his arm while mother tells Frieda to get started on the dishes, which Frieda does.
SS (SELF-STIMULATION): Repetitive behaviors which the individual does to himself and cannot be coded by any other codes *CM (COMMAND):* This category is used when an immediate and clearly stated request or command is made to another person	25–30 seconds Kevin engages in self-stimulation while mother and Frieda are involved in other activities and show no response 10S 3/4NR [For purposes of scores, Kevin is considered 1; 2 signifies the father; 3 the mother; and 4 the sister.]	Kevin continues to rub and scratch his arm while mother and daughter are working at the kitchen sink.

Source: Based on G. R. Patterson, R. S. Ray, D. A. Shaw, & J. Cobb, "Manual for Coding of Family Interactions, 1969 ASIS/NAPS c/o Microfische Publications 305 46 St New York NY 10017 Document #01234 skillful interviewer may seem to be carrying on a casual conversation with the person being interviewed, but usually such interviewers collect valuable information for the assessment of individual behavior.

The most commonly used interview in assessing abnormal behavior is called the *mental status interview.* Table 5–6 shows the general areas of behavior covered in the mental status interview and also provides an example of a report that might be based on such an interview. The major limitation of the mental status interview is that the interview itself is quite unstructured. Consequently two different interviewers could obtain quite different results using it.

One solution to this problem is to structure the interview so that the same type of information is obtained in every case. An example of such a structured interview is the Psychiatric Evaluation Form developed by Spitzer and Endicott.

The psychological interview is a valuable source of information for assessment and treatment planning.

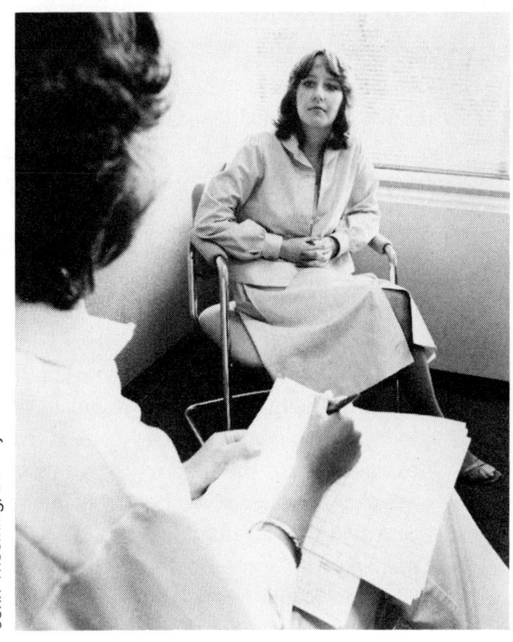

John Thoeming/Dorsey Press

TABLE 5–6 Excerpts from a Mental Status Interview of a 29-Year-Old Male

Category	*Example of Report*
General appearance, attitude, and behavior	He is friendly and cooperative. Has made no complaints about ward restrictions. He smiles in a somewhat exaggerated and grotesque manner.
Discourse	He answers in a deep, loud voice, speaking in a slow, precise, and somewhat condescending manner. His responses are relevant but vague.
Mood and affective fluctuations	His facial expressions, although not totally inappropriate, are poorly correlated with subject of discourse or events in his environment.
Sensorium and intellect	The patient's orientation for place, person, and time is normal. His remote and recent memory also are normal. Two brief intelligence measures indicate about average intelligence.
Mental content and specific occupations	He readily discusses what he calls his "nervous trouble." He complains of "bad thoughts" and a "conspiracy." He reports hearing voices saying "Hello, Bill, you're a dirty dog."
Insight	The patient readily accepts the idea that he should be in the hospital. He feels that hospitalization will help him get rid of these "bad" thoughts. He is not in the least defensive about admitting to auditory and visual hallucinations or to the idea that everyone on earth is his enemy.

Source: Reproduced with permission from B. Kleinmuntz, *Personality Measurement: An Introduction* (Homewood, Ill.: Dorsey, 1967), p. 159.

AN INITIAL CLINICAL INTERVIEW

The following description provides an example of an initial clinical interview and illustrates how it can both elicit background information and initiate the helping process.

Ms. Stewart, an attractive 24-year-old woman, was referred to me for counseling by an emergency ward following a suicide attempt. When Ms. Stewart entered the office, I asked her to have a seat. I said that we would talk today mainly about her background. I explained that I needed to know this in order to help her solve her problems. She said that she had just had a meeting with some doctors and nurses who had asked her a lot of ridiculous questions. I asked her what some of the questions were. She listed them off as "How did I feel when I took the pills?" "Why was I depressed?" "Had I felt that way before?" She did not know how to answer the questions. She did not remember how she had felt when she took the pills. I realized that Ms. Stewart was trying to tell me she wasn't ready to talk about her suicide attempt.

So I changed the subject and asked her to tell me a little about herself, where she was raised, where she went to school, etc. She related that she was born and raised in Connecticut. She has a younger sister who is 21 years old and married. Without further discussion of her family, she said she had been an excellent student in high school and had gone on to become a laboratory technician. I asked her if her parents approved. She said it didn't matter much to them but she supposed that they were glad she had a career. I asked her what she had done after she graduated from school. She had worked at a local hospital and then moved to California, where she easily got a job in another hospital.

We discussed her experience as a laboratory technician at some length. I asked her why she went to California in the first place. She said that she wanted to see the country. She had never been outside of Connecticut and thought that this would be a good way to do it. I asked her if she liked it in California. She said no, not really, as it was not what she had hoped for. I asked her why. She described the jobs she was given as being below her ability. She didn't like taking orders from her supervisor, nor did she like to give orders to the aides. I said I didn't understand and asked if she could tell me more. She related that instead of working directly with the patients she had to do a lot of administrative paper pushing. This was too much responsibility and she couldn't handle it.

I asked if she had any good experiences at her work. No, she couldn't think of any. She said that, fortunately, the social life in California was pretty good. I asked her to tell me more about it. She said it was great. There were lots of parties and other social activities. She dated mainly other hospital workers. Her boyfriend, to whom she had almost been engaged, worked as a hospital administrator.

I then asked her about her social life in high school. She said that she had dated some but did not have a steady boyfriend. I asked her if she would describe her childhood. She related that she was a very friendly child until about age 8, when all of a sudden she became shy. I asked what she meant, and she explained that she stayed home after school and watched TV and ate until she got fat and ugly. I asked her how she felt about that. She said that people made fun of her and she retreated even more. Her family also joked about her and called her names. I asked how she felt about her family calling her names. She said that she did not become bothered by it at first but after a while she felt hurt.

Finally when she was around 13 she decided to lose weight. I asked why she decided to lose weight then. She was in junior high school and had begun to take an interest in boys and wanted to be more attractive to them. When asked if she dated much, she said no but she did date a little but no one serious. I asked if she had many friends. She said not many. She did have one special guy that she dated in high school but he wasn't a steady boyfriend. Recently she heard that he was killed in an automobile accident. I asked if that upset her. She said it did, especially since she had known him so well. I asked her to tell me more about her high school years—what activities she was involved in. She liked sports because she liked to win and worked very hard to do so. I asked what happened when she lost. She explained that she became quiet and usually walked away. I asked if she became hostile toward the winner. She said she didn't, she just got depressed. In fact, she's been depressed for a few years now, and that's why she took the pills.

We then switched to her current situation, and I asked her to tell me more about her taking the pills. She explained that the whole thing started when her boyfriend broke up with her and married someone else. This really upset her. However, she didn't express it by crying. Ms. Stewart said she realizes now that her problem is that she keeps things inside and lets them boil. I asked her what happened then. She decided to leave California and come to Boston where she easily obtained work at a hospital. She started dating, but after each date she'd return to her apartment and feel depressed. I asked about what. She said she pretended to have fun on dates but she really didn't care about any of the guys. I asked if she ever talked to her friends or family about her depression, and she said no, she just kept it all inside.

I asked her when she took the pills for the first time. She explained that 4 months ago she took a handful of phenobarbital pills after the man she had been dating told her he didn't want to see her anymore. Her roommate found her and took her to the emergency ward. Things went OK for a while after that until two weeks ago when she again took an overdose of sleeping pills.

Her most recent suicide attempt was explained in some detail. She had been asked to leave her job when a friend with whom she worked falsely accused her of stealing. In dismissing her, her supervisor implied that because she had had previous psychological problems it would be better if she left work. Again I asked Ms. Stewart if she had talked to anyone about this, and again she said no, she just kept it all inside. She returned to her apartment and again resorted to pills. Ms. Stewart said she knows there is something wrong with her. She didn't really want to die and realizes that she needs help in getting out of her depression. I asked how often she got depressed. She said quite often. She's been depressed since her boyfriend broke up with her. She puts everything into a relationship, and when things go wrong, she takes it as a personal rejection. After a silence, I told Ms. Stewart that she and I would be meeting on a regular basis to discuss her problems. I asked her what day she preferred to come in. She said she wasn't sure which day she'd be able to get a ride to the clinic. I told her I would call her in a few days to discuss an appointment time. She agreed, and we said goodbye (Edinberg, Zinberg, and Kelson, 1975, pp. 102–4).

In Table 5–7 you can see an example of the type of questions asked by the interviewer using the Psychiatric Evaluation Form. An advantage of this method is that the interview results can be translated into ratings that are useful in making decisions about treatment diagnosis and the likely course of the individual's difficulties.

Psychological tests. Perhaps one of the most important contributions of psychology has been its development of tests to measure and predict behavior. Tests provide a distinct advantage over interviews and observations since, usually, they are easier to quantify, and therefore it is easier to compare scores among respondents. Psychological tests are designed to sample, in a standardized way, some important aspect of behavior.

Literally thousands of tests have been developed to measure various aspects of personality and individual abilities. We will consider two examples of psychological tests that have been widely used in assessing abnormal behavior.

The Minnesota Multiphasic Personality Inventory (MMPI) (Hathaway and McKinley, 1943) is a self-report inventory consisting of 550 statements to which one can respond "true," "false," or "cannot say." Each statement is included in one or more scales on the MMPI. The overall result of the test for a person can be portrayed as a profile of the kind shown in Figure 5–2. Profiles of this sort can be used in a number of different ways. Some clinicians use them to make "configural" interpretations. By looking at the overall pattern of scores on different scales, clinicians are able to develop a personality description of the individual. It is possible for the clinician to use either his or her own experience with these scales or standard personality descriptions to describe particular MMPI profiles.

Another major form of psychological testing involves the use of *projective tests.* They are called *projective* because it is assumed that, seeing a relatively ambiguous picture or situation, the person will project his or her own needs, concerns, or values into an interpretation of the picture. The most famous of all projective tests is the Rorschach Test developed by the Swiss psychiatrist Hermann Rorschach in 1921.

The story of the development of the Rorschach Test is an interesting footnote in the history of psychology. Hermann Rorschach was known to many of his high school friends as "Kleck," a word which means inkblot or painter. This nickname reflected Rorschach's early interest in art and his fascination with creating fanciful

TABLE 5–7 Psychiatric Evaluation Form—Diagnostic Version

Interview Guide

ORIGINAL COMPLAINT

If a psychiatric patient: Now I would like to hear about your problems or difficulties and how they led to your coming to the (hospital, clinic).

GENERAL CONDITION

Tell me how you have been feeling recently. (Anything else been bothering you?)

PHYSICAL HEALTH

How is your physical condition?
Does any part of your body give you trouble?
Do you worry much about your health?

If necessary, inquire for doctor's opinion about symptoms or illnesses.

When you are upset do you react physically . . . like [stomach trouble, diarrhea, headaches, sick feelings, dizziness]?

APPETITE-SLEEP-FATIGUE

Disturbances in these areas are often associated with depression, anxiety, or somatic concerns.

What about your appetite for food?
Do you have any trouble sleeping or getting to sleep? (Why is that?)
How easily do you get tired?

MOOD

This section covers several moods. The interviewer must determine to what extent the symptoms are associated with either one or the other or several of the dimensions.

What kinds of moods have you been in recently?

What kinds of things do you worry about?
(How much do you worry?)

What kinds of fears do you have? (Any situation . . . activities . . . things?)

How often do you feel anxious or tense?
(When you are this way, do you react physically . . . like sweating, dizziness, cramps?)

Scales

The time period for this section is the past month.

PHYSICAL HEALTH

214 **SOMATIC CONCERNS**
Excessive concern with bodily functions; preoccupation with one or more real or imagined physical complaints or disabilities; bizarre or unrealistic feelings or beliefs about his body or parts of body.
Do not include mere dissatisfaction with appearance.
? 1 2 3 4 5 6

215 **CONVERSION REACTION**
Has a motor or sensory dysfunction which conforms to the lay notion of neurological illness, for which his doctors can find no organic basis (e.g., paralysis or anesthesia)
? 1 2 3 4 5 6

216 **PSYCHOPHYSIOLOGICAL REACTIONS**
Is bothered by one or more psychophysiological reactions to stress. Examples: backache, headaches, hypertension, dizziness, asthma, spastic bowel. **Note: the reaction may or may not involve structural change.**
? 1 2 3 4 5 6

MOOD

217 **ELATED MOOD**
Exhibits or speaks of an elevated mood, exaggerated sense of well being or optimism, of feelings of elation. Examples: Says "everything is great," jokes, witticisms, silly remarks, singing, laughing, or trying to get others to laugh or smile.
? 1 2 3 4 5 6

218 **ANXIETY**
Remarks indicate feelings of apprehension, worry, anxiety, nervousness, tension, fearfulness, or panic. When clearly associated with any of these feelings, consider insomnia, restlessness, physical symptoms (e.g., palpitations, sweating, dizziness, cramps), or difficulty concentrating, etc.
? 1 2 3 4 5 6

Source: R. L. Spitzer, J. Endicott, A. M. Mesnikoff, and G. M. Cohen, *Psychiatric Evolution Form,* Biometrics Research, New York State Department of Mental Hygiene, Department of Psychiatry, Columbia University, January 1968.

FIGURE 5–2

ROCHE PSYCHIATRIC SERVICE INSTITUTE ROCHE

CASE NO: 718365 MMPI PROFILE RPSI NO: 10000
AGE 39 MALE JULY 29, 1980

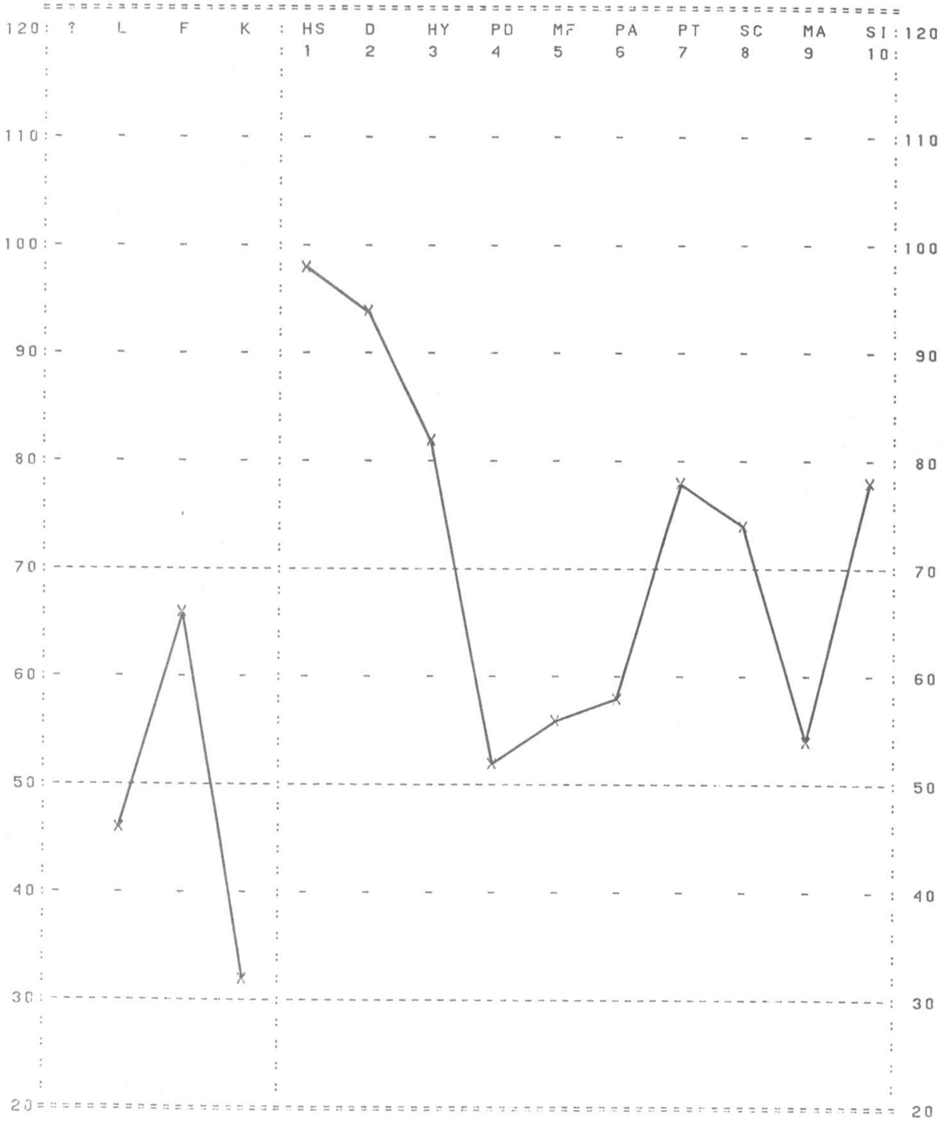
? L F K HS 1 D 2 HY 3 PD 4 MF 5 PA 6 PT 7 SC 8 MA 9 SI 10
120
110
100
90
80
70
60
50
40
30
20

	?	L	F	K	HS	D	HY	PD	MF	PA	PT	SC	MA	SI
R	7	3	10	3	28	35	34	19	24	11	34	32	18	52
K	7	3	10	3	30	35	34	20	24	11	37	35	19	52
T	OK	45	66	33	98	94	82	53	57	59	79	74	55	79

inkblots, a pursuit then known as klecksography. But long before Rorschach's first dabblings with inkblots, artists and poets had used relatively formless stimuli to enhance their creative imaginings. In the 15th century, Leonardo da Vinci was intrigued by the possibility of achieving artistic inspiration by perceiving the forms created by throwing a piece of sponge blotched with colors of paint against a wall. To stimulate the creative process, Kerner, a 19th-century poet, produced inkblots by folding paper over drops of ink. Some of the poems which Kerner wrote and the inkblots which inspired them have been published (Zubin, Eron, & Schumer, 1965). So, before Rorschach developed his now-famous inkblot test, there was ample precedent for their use to spark the creative imagination.

Rorschach, however, suggested the use of inkblots to probe the unconscious. After medical training with the eminent psychiatrist Eugen Bleuler, one of Freud's colleagues, Rorschach became a firm believer in the reality of the unconscious. And Rorschach came to believe that a person's personality dynamics could be discerned by examining his or her responses to inkblots. He also believed that associations to such vaguely defined forms were stimulated by unconscious processes characteristic of the individual's personality makeup.

Rorschach conducted experiments with inkblots during his medical school years; and after he received his M.D. in 1912, his research with inkblots continued. Nine years later, Rorschach published his famous monograph, *Psychodiagnostik,* which described his methods of using inkblots to study personality. In order to get his book published, Rorschach had to agree to omit five of the fifteen blots used in his research studies. The ten blots which were finally included were reduced in size and altered in color from the original ones that he used. Even the shading of the cards was changed by the printing process used to produce the book. Thus, the ultimate product was somewhat different from what Rorschach actually intended. And it is this product that is today known as the Rorschach Test (Aronow & Renzikoff, 1976).

The Rorschach is administered and interpreted by an examiner well trained in its use. The examiner shows the subject the cards one at a time and records verbatim the subject's responses and his or her social behavior during the testing.

Beck (1961) recommended giving the following instructions to the subject: "You will be given a series of ten cards, one by one. The cards have on them designs made up of inkblots. Look at each card and tell the examiner what you see on each card, or anything that might be represented there. Look at each card as long as you like; only be sure to tell the examiner everything that you see on the card as you look at it. When you have finished with a card, give it to the examiner as a sign that you are through with it" (p. 2).

After the subject responds to all ten cards, the examiner shows each of the cards to the subject a second time. After determining which aspects of the blot prompted the response (color, shading, form, movement, and so forth), and learning which parts of the blot the subject responded to, the examiner is ready to interpret the results.

Clinicians rarely analyze responses in isolation; instead, they are more likely to consider patterns of responses to the inkblots. Many scoring systems and scales have been devised to measure such personality characteristics as anxiety, hostility, impairment of brain function, and so on. Clinicians who use the Rorschach

WHAT'S IN AN INKBLOT?

Look at this inkblot. What does it suggest to you? No doubt you will have several impressions. Write them down in the order in which they occur to you. When new concepts no longer emerge read the list to yourself.

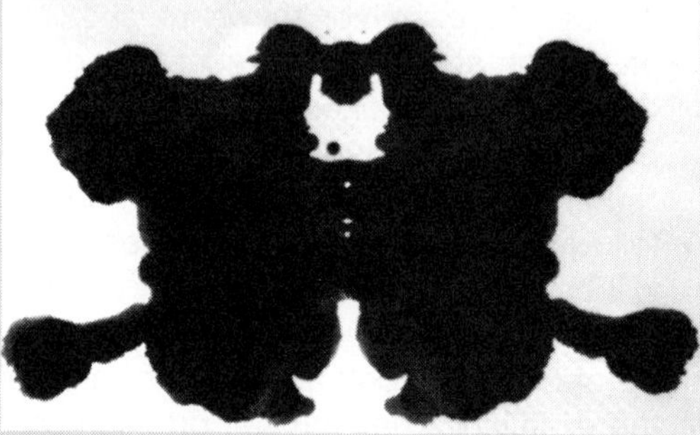

Now compare your impressions with the responses to the same inkblot given by some individual in the course of a diagnostic evaluation:

The center white area near the top reminds me of the heads of two women who are talking.

Near the bottom, the parts sticking out remind me of ice cream cones. They're chocolate, because they're dark. I think I said that because I'm hungry. I have this terrible sweet tooth, you know.

Holding the card upside down, I can see two funny shaped Idaho potatoes.

The lower white area reminds me of the head of a wolf or a coyote.

The whole thing makes me think of a kind of odd butterfly.

The left side of the blot makes me think of a man with a party hat with one of those New Year's favors in his mouth, the kind that shoots out when you blow into them.

Were your responses to this inkblot similar? Were they very different? Even a randomly created inkblot reveals the fact that no two people perceive what we call reality in exactly the same way. The fact that we project our own personality upon our view of the world makes the projective tests a useful assessment tool.

believe it can provide valuable information regarding the client's capacity for original thinking, empathy, impulsivity and emotional reactivity, and contact with reality.

While experts in the use of projective tests have sometimes achieved impressive results in personality description or the prediction of future behavior, the research indicates that even trained assessors' interpretations of responses to the Rorschach can vary a great deal. Thus, the reliability of this technique is frequently quite low. Defenders of the Rorschach claim that when experienced clinicians well trained in the use of the same scoring system evaluate the subject's responses, reliability increases (Rickers-Ovsiankina, 1961).

For a number of years projective techniques have been severely criticized for their lack of reliability and validity. We will discuss this issue in much more detail when we consider the concept of "illusory correlation" later in the chapter. Perhaps the most appropriate question to ask about the Rorschach test, as with any other assessment tool, is: "What is the instrument valid for?" It is impossible for any one test or evaluation instrument to answer every question that we might wish to pose about a person. Indeed, the Rorschach surely cannot live up to some early claims that it can provide a "mental X-ray" of the personality. Sundberg et al. (1978) suggest that perhaps the most valid approach to the Rorschach system may be to regard individual responses as a sample of an individual's thinking processes. It is important to conduct additional research to specify the range of personality characteristics that the Rorschach and other personality tests can validly measure.

Since many clinicians do not have complete faith in any one instrument's ability to provide all of the information to fully evaluate a client, a *battery* of carefully selected assessment devices often is administered. In order to arrive at a diagnosis of a client, the assessor might interview the person and administer an MMPI, a Rorschach, or any number or combination of other assessment devices. The choice of methods used with a particular individual will probably depend on a number of factors, such as the nature and purpose of the evaluation (is the client a danger to others, suicidal, or schizophrenic, and what decisions need to be made about the client, i.e., hospitalization, medication, treatment), the examiner's training and biases, and his or her confidence in a particular test.

THE COMPUTER AS CLINICIAN

In our survey of assessment methods we have looked briefly at observation, interview, and psychological tests as clinical assessment tools. Within the last 20 years computers have become part of the psychological assessment process as well.

What can a computer do better than a clinician can? Computers have the advantages of speed, flexibility, and objectivity, and this greatly aids the computer in performing the sensitive and difficult task of psychological assessment. For example, a computer has a "perfect memory." While a clinician may interpret the same psychological test information differently at two different times, the computer's program will always produce the same interpretation of the same test information. The computer is reliable in its responses. In addition, the computer can have a much larger bank of "clinical experience" than can any clinician. It is possible to program a computer with rules for classifying individuals that have been developed on the basis of testing hundreds of thousands of individuals. Furthermore, it is possible to program the computer so that it can efficiently store new information to alter its own "memory." Finally, the rules used by a computer to assess an individual's psychological test data and to make predictions about that person are public and explicit. They are part of the computer program itself. The clinician also uses rules to assess psychological test data, but they may be private and intuitive and difficult for the clinician to articulate. With such abilities the computer appears

This psychological interpretation of a Minnesota Multiphasic Personality Inventory was composed by computer. The statements consist of the most probable description of a person with the MMPI profile shown in Figure 5–2.

ROCHE PSYCHIATRIC SERVICE INSTITUTE

MMPI REPORT

CASE NO: 718365 RPSI. NO: 10000
AGE 39 MALE JULY 29, 1980

THE PATIENT'S RESPONSES TO THE TEST SUGGEST THAT HE UNDERSTOOD ITEMS AND FOLLOWED THE INSTRUCTIONS ADEQUATELY. IT APPEARS HOWEVER, THAT HE MAY HAVE BEEN OVERLY SELF-CRITICAL. THE VALIDITY OF THE TEST MAY HAVE BEEN AFFECTED BY HIS TENDANCY TO ADMIT TO SYMPTOMS EVEN WHEN THEY ARE MINIMAL. THIS MAY REPRESENT AN EFFORT TO CALL ATTENTION TO HIS DIFFICULTIES TO ASSURE OBTAINING HELP. IT FURTHER SUGGESTS THAT HE CURRENTLY FEELS VULNERABLE AND DEFENSELESS, WHICH MAY REFLECT A READINESS TO ACCEPT PROFESSIONAL ASSISTANCE.

THIS PATIENT MAY EXHIBIT CONCERN OVER PHYSICAL SYMPTOMS WHICH, ON EXAMINATION, REVEAL NO ORGANIC PATHOLOGY. HE MAY BE IRRITABLE, DEPRESSED, SHY AND SECLUSIVE, WITH A RIGIDITY OF OUTLOOK AND AN INABILITY TO FEEL COMFORTABLE WITH PEOPLE. HE SHOWS LITTLE INSIGHT INTO HIS PERSONAL ADJUSTMENT. PSYCHIATRIC PATIENTS WITH THIS PATTERN ARE LIKELY TO BE DIAGNOSED NEUROTIC, CHIEFLY WITH SOMATIC FEATURES. MEDICAL PATIENTS WITH THIS PATTERN ARE DIFFICULT TO TREAT BECAUSE THEY APPEAR TO HAVE LEARNED TO LIVE WITH AND TO USE THEIR COMPLAINTS. ALTHOUGH THE PATIENT MAY SHOW A GOOD RESPONSE TO SHORT-TERM TREATMENT, THE SYMPTOMS ARE LIKELY TO RETURN.

IN TIMES OF PROLONGED EMOTIONAL STRESS HE MAY DEVELOP PSYCHOPHYSIOLOGICAL SYMPTOMS SUCH AS HEADACHES AND GASTROINTESTINAL DISORDERS. HE APPEARS TO BE A PERSON WHO REPRESSES AND DENIES EMOTIONAL DISTRESS. WHILE HE MAY RESPOND READILY TO ADVICE AND REASSURANCE, HE MAY BE UNWILLING TO ACCEPT A PSYCHOLOGICAL INTERPRETATION OF HIS DIFFICULTIES.

THERE ARE SOME UNUSUAL QUALITIES IN THIS PATIENT'S THINKING WHICH MAY REPRESENT AN ORIGINAL OR INVENTIVE ORIENTATION OR PERHAPS SOME SCHIZOID TENDENCIES. FURTHER INFORMATION WOULD BE REQUIRED TO MAKE THIS DETERMINATION.

THIS PERSON MAY BE HESITANT TO BECOME INVOLVED IN SOCIAL RELATIONSHIPS. HE IS SENSITIVE, RESERVED AND SOMEWHAT UNCOMFORTABLE, ESPECIALLY IN NEW AND UNFAMILIAR SITUATIONS.

THIS PERSON IS LIKELY TO BE AN INDECISIVE INDIVIDUAL WHO LACKS SELF-CONFIDENCE AND POISE AND IS LIKELY TO BE INHIBITED AND SLOW IN RESPONSE. HE HAS DIFFICULTY CONCENTRATING, AND MAY BECOME DISORGANIZED UNDER STRESS. ALTHOUGH SUPERFICIALLY CONFORMING AND COMPLIANT, HE MAY EXHIBIT CONSIDERABLE PASSIVE RESISTANCE.

THIS PATIENT HAS A TEST PATTERN WHICH SUGGESTS THE POSSIBILITY OF SEVERE EMOTIONAL PROBLEMS. PROFESSIONAL CARE IS INDICATED

THIS PATIENT'S CONDITION APPEARS TO FALL WITHIN THE NEUROTIC RANGE. HE IS USING NEUROTIC DEFENSES IN AN EFFORT TO CONTROL HIS ANXIETY.

qualified at least to be a partner with the clinician in the task of psychological assessment.

Computers have been used as an aid in psychological assessment in a variety of ways. For example, Spitzer and Endicott (1968) have developed a computer program that is similar to the game of "20 questions." In this system the computer program examines psychological test data for an individual and asks a question of the information that can be answered "true" or "false." Depending on the answer to the question, the computer then rules out one or more possible diagnoses and decides which question to ask next. Just as in 20 questions, the possibilities are finally narrowed down to one or two that are most likely.

How does this system compare to the performance of an expert clinician? When expert clinicians were given the same test data as that presented to the computer, both experts and computer did well. The clear advantage of the computer is that it can do the same job much more rapidly and much more cheaply than the clinician can.

Until now the use of computers in assessment and diagnosis has relied on those characteristics of the computer that make them superior to the clinician—its speed and its large and perfect memory. But will the computer ever replace the clinician? It is doubtful that many of the subtleties observed by a clinician in an interview situation can be detected by a computer program, but researchers have not exhausted their ingenuity in developing ways that computers can use information to help the clinician in the task of diagnosis and prediction. It is likely that we will see computers working in still other roles with the clinician in the future.

ASSESSMENT IN THE HUMAN CONTEXT

Psychological tests and other assessment instruments have been developed with the aim of providing good descriptions of the characteristics of individuals and good predictions about their future behavior. Yet various sources of bias in the use of tests remain that are part of psychological assessment in the human context.

Test Results and Illusory Correlation

In interpreting the results of projective tests such as the Rorschach, the clinician must interpret the response given to each inkblot. That interpretation provides the clinician the opportunity to use creative insight, but it also leaves him or her open to making an incorrect interpretation.

Two psychologists at the University of Wisconsin, Loren and Jean Chapman, have done a series of studies to help us understand how clinicians interpret projective tests and make inferences. They have been very interested in a projective test called the Draw-a-Person Test (DAP). In using the Draw-a-Person Test, the clinician gives an individual a pencil and a blank sheet of paper and requests that a person be drawn on the paper. By examining the way a person is drawn, clinicians believe that they can infer something about the patient's internal conflicts, motivations, and personality. For example, the Chapmans surveyed large numbers of experienced clinicians and asked them about certain characteristics of drawings of people and how they might be related to individual concerns and conflicts. The results they found seem to make "psychological sense." Eighty percent of the clinicians agreed that drawing broad shoulders and a muscular body reflected worries about manliness. Ninety percent of the clinicians agreed that atypical eyes in the drawing indicated suspiciousness of others, and 82 percent of the clinicians agreed that a large or an emphasized head in the drawing indicated that the person worried about intelligence.

These interpretations seem to make good sense, but, as the Chapmans have pointed out, careful research has shown that *none* of these characteristics in drawings predict the symptoms or concerns of the patient as the clinician believed. Chapman and Chapman note that clinicians respond to this finding by saying, "I'll trust my own sense before I'll trust a journal article," and one psychologist said, "I know that paranoids don't seem to draw big eyes in the research labs, but they sure do in my office."

The Chapmans have conducted a series of studies to show that this strong belief in an association between certain aspects of the drawing and certain psychological characteristics are a result of *illusory correlation.* They define illusory correlation as the tendency to see two things as occurring together more often than they actually do. Most of the illusory correlations seen by both experienced clinicians and the undergraduate students they later studied were a result of associations between the test indicator and the interpretation. That is, we tend to associate large eyes and suspiciousness with each other and therefore assume that suspicious clients will draw faces with large eyes. The association makes the test interpreter feel as if the two things "go together," even when they don't actually go together in the real world.

The Chapmans point out that projective tests such as the Rorschach do indeed produce some valid signs that allow clinicians to predict the behavior of the person taking the test. However, the valid signs are seldom intuitively obvious. For example, homosexuality is frequently indicated in people seeing snarling beast or human-animal crossbreeds in inkblots, but these are not intuitively obvious signs of homosexual behavior. The intuitive signs are almost always a result of illusory correlation.

Is it possible that the theoretical grounding of a clinician's training causes him or her to see certain kinds of behavior patterns as abnormal? Langer and Abelson (1974) assembled two groups of therapists with very different training backgrounds to find out. One group was drawn from a university department that had a very strong learning theory and behavioral bias. The other group was drawn from a training program that had a strong psychodynamic training emphasis. Each of these groups was shown a videotaped interview of a man, but half of the subjects in each group were told that the person was being interviewed as a job applicant. The other half were told that he was a psychiatric patient.

Langer and Abelson found that when the person was described as a job applicant, both the dynamically oriented clinicians and the behavioral clinicians saw the person as fairly well adjusted, but, when the interviewee was described as a psychiatric patient, the dynamically trained clinicians saw him as much less well adjusted than did the behaviorally oriented clinicians.

It seems, then, as if prior training can strongly shape the clinician's perceptions when seeing a patient. The study by Langer and Abelson tells us very little about why the behaviorally trained clinicians were relatively immune to the biasing effects of labeling. Perhaps their training led them to respond to the actual behavior of the patient to a greater degree than did that of the dynamically trained clinicians.

Sex Role and Race in Psychological Assessment

If you were doing a psychological assessment of an individual, you would not be confronted with an abstract list of symptoms or behaviors but with a living, breathing person. This person would come from a particular ethnic and cultural background and would be the product of a lifetime of socialization in different roles.

PERSONALITY DESCRIPTION AND THE "BARNUM EFFECT"

Does this personality description fit you? You tend to be critical of yourself and have a strong need to have other people like you. Although you tend to be pretty well controlled on the outside, inside you frequently feel insecure. At times your sexual adjustment has been a problem for you. You like a certain amount of change in your life and become unhappy when you are hemmed in by restrictions and limitations. Sometimes you feel sociable and extroverted, but, at other times, you feel very reserved and introverted. Overall, you have some personality weaknesses, but you are generally able to compensate for them.

If you felt that that personality description fit you pretty well and described some of your unique individual qualities, you are not alone. You have just experienced what Paul Meehl has called "personality description after the manner of P. T. Barnum." Barnum, the great showman, believed that to succeed you had to have a little something for everybody, and, like Barnum, the personality description that you just read had a little something for everyone—it was composed of *statements that are true about almost everyone.*

Astrologers, handwriting analysts, and fortune tellers have long known that people who hear very general statements about themselves are likely to feel these statements are accurate descriptions, if they have been told that the description has been prepared especially for them. What is important about this phenomenon from the point of view of psychological assessment is that some test interpretations may contain a great many "Barnum" statements and therefore appear much more valid than they actually are. Test results that are true of everyone obviously do not allow us to discover the distinguishing characteristics of people. And "Barnum" statements do not allow psychological assessment to make accurate differential predictions or clinical decisions. Thus it is well to remember that a psychological test instrument that only generates statements that are true of everyone may appear "accurate" but is of no value in the psychological assessment of abnormal behavior.

Furthermore, this person's political attitudes might be very different from your own. It is possible that some of these differences might seem quite strange or alien to you. But could your reactions affect your professional judgments about the psychological state of the person you are interviewing? We will consider several different kinds of evidence for this possibility in the following section and we will also discuss the implications of the evidence that we review.

Sex role stereotypes and judgments of maladjustment. If a person were described to you as independent, objective, active, logical, worldly, direct, adventurous, and self-confident, what sort of judgment would you make about his or her adjustment? If, on the other hand, the person were described as having his or her feelings easily hurt, being more emotional, disliking math and science, and being easily influenced, what would you say about his or her adjustment? These two sets of descriptions conform to conventional sex role stereotypes that are widely held in our society. Inge Broverman and her colleagues wanted to know whether there was a relationship between sex role stereotypes and the clinical judgments made by professionals about mental health.

In order to discover whether there was such a relationship, they asked 79 clinically trained mental health workers to respond to a questionnaire that contained a large number of bipolar adjectives like

Sex role stereotypes can affect clinical judgment.

John Thoeming/Dorsey Press

"strong—weak." In each case, the mental health professional was asked to choose the adjective description that best characterized a "male," a "female," and a "mature, healthy adult."

Broverman and her colleagues found that there existed a great deal of agreement among mental health professionals about the attributes characterizing healthy adult men, healthy women, and healthy adults whose sex was unspecified. This is not so surprising. Most of us can call up images of each of these general stereotypes. What was particularly interesting about these investigators' findings was that clinicians have different concepts of mental health for men and for women, and that these concepts seem to parallel the sex role stereotypes prevalent in our society. That is, men who are perceived as conforming more closely to the male sex role stereotype are also judged to be healthier than men who do not. Similarly, women who conform to the female sex role stereotype are also judged to be healthier than women who do not. This seemingly obvious finding, the authors note, conceals a powerful negative assessment of women. Clinicians are likely to suggest that healthy women are more submissive, more dependent, less adventurous, more easily influenced, and less objective. They note that this constellation of characteristics seems to be an unusual way to describe a mature, healthy individual.

Broverman and her co-workers also found that the male stereotype more resembled the mental health professional's conception of an "adult, healthy individual" than did the female sex role stereotype. Thus, mental health professionals' concepts of mental health appear to be biased in a male-oriented direction. Furthermore, this was true regardless of whether the mental health professional was a male or a female.

Broverman and her colleagues point out that we should not be so surprised to discover that mental health professionals display this bias. It reflects, they feel, the general acceptance by mental health professionals of an "adjustment" notion of health—the assumption that individuals who conform to sex roles in which they were socialized are healthier than individuals who do not. We should remember, however, that mental health professionals are frequently assumed to have special knowledge about the nature of psychological adjustment. Consequently, when they accept sex role stereotypes in their judgments of mental health, they may at least implicitly be helping to perpetuate those stereotypes.

Race differences. We have seen that differences in sex role can produce biases in judgments about abnormality. So far our examples of biasing effects have been due to the "norms" of the clinician, that is, the mental health professional's lack of experience or his or her ingrained beliefs about a particular group of people. But biases can also exist in the norms of a test used as a tool for assessment. For example, if people from a particular ethnic or cultural group are given a psychological test that was originally developed for another group, the test results may erroneously indicate a higher proportion of those people as maladjusted. And, if that test is used for job screening or decisions about treatment, systematic biases in the test norms can result in serious discriminatory practices.

Gynther (1972) has reviewed the evidence for test bias in the MMPI when it is given to blacks. After reviewing a number of studies, Gynther has concluded that there are differences in the MMPI

Interpreting minority group test performance in terms of white normative information can produce misleading interpretations.

John Thoeming/Dorsey Press

profiles of black and white individuals and that these differences appear to be due to differences in cultural background. Gynther has examined those items on the MMPI that are answered differently by black and white populations. A common theme which runs through Gynther's results is the marked distrust of society exhibited by blacks and reflected in their test performance. A major finding that emerged from his analysis was that blacks answered many more items reflecting "social cynicism" than did whites. Gynther notes that the dimension of social cynicism is an important and realistic value in black culture.

However, Davis (1975) found no differences in MMPI profiles between races when education and degree of disturbance were held constant. Thus the question of the degree to which the MMPI is appropriate for use with nonwhite populations remains in dispute.

THE ASSESSMENT OF COMPETENCE

One of the consequences of the recent criticism of psychological tests and psychological testing has been a broadening interest in what can and should be measured by psychological tests. At the beginning of this section, we defined assessment as the process of discerning individual characteristics that were important for decision making about people in their relationship to their society. The shift in interest to assessing social competence reflects concern that pathologically oriented definitions of individual differences will miss many of the traits important for the assessment of individuals.

In their recent and important review, Sundberg, Snowden, and Reynolds (1978) defined competence as "personal characteristics (knowledge, skill, and attitudes) which lead to achievements having adaptive payoffs in significant environments" (p. 196). They go on to point out that the idea of adaptation points to the need to assess not just the individual motives of a person, but also the ways in which the person's social environment provides resources as well as demands on him or her.

As Sundberg and his colleagues point out, "consideration of competence raises such questions as: 'In which situations can a person best function?' 'What things can a person do in various environments?' It moves from the 'how much' question of traditional trait psychology to 'where' and 'which' questions concerning the surroundings people encounter and their coping resources and their active interests" (p. 196).

This new orientation to competence has

had an influence on a wide variety of strategies for assessing behavior. For example, McClelland (1973) has recently argued in favor of replacing the concept of intelligence with the concept of competence and would assess aptitudes used in real life rather than hypothetical concepts such as I.Q. A similar development is exemplified in the work of Mercer and Lewis (1977). These investigators have developed a "system of multi-cultural assessment" which provides a battery of measures that has been standardized on Anglo, Hispanic, and black children. The system uses a structured interview with the child's parent and guardian as well as standardized assessments of the child. It is Mercer and Lewis' goal to provide a measure of learning potential that is sensitive to different cultural backgrounds of children. As Sundberg et al. (1978) note, "potential is permitted expression which sociocultural differences ordinarily might camouflage" (p. 199). It should be clear, however, that this system of multicultural assessment is still in its early stages of development and will require continued careful research.

Another strategy for assessing competence is reflected in the work of Spivack and Shure (1974). These investigators have hypothesized that interpersonal problem solving skills are crucial aspects of one's social adjustment and have developed strategies for measuring these skills. One such measure, the Preschool Interpersonal Problem Solving Test, is designed to measure the degree to which a child is able to solve social problems. Such measures, if carefully validated, open new avenues for studying individual differences in adaptive ability.

Although this relatively new orientation to assessment is in its earliest stages, there is little question that it will continue to be influential in the assessment of abnormal behavior. Rather than narrowly focusing on indications of pathology, we are likely to see a shift in the direction of assessing an individual's ability to cope and adapt in his or her social environment as it is encountered in everyday life.

SUMMARY

In this chapter we have seen that classification and assessment are basic strategies for the scientific understanding and practical application of knowledge about abnormal behavior. Classification serves a variety of important functions for the scientist, including communication, key to the scientific literature, description, and prediction; and it can serve as a building block for the development of scientific theories.

The latest version of the *Diagnostic and Statistical Manual of Mental Disorders* (DSM III) provides several new approaches to the description of abnormal behavior. DSM III is intended to improve the reliability of diagnosis by specifying more exactly the criteria for membership in a particular diagnostic category. Unlike previous classification systems, DSM III classifies each person not only in terms of the predominant pattern of abnormal behavior but also on the basis of existing personality disorders, medical disorders, the severity of psychosocial stressors, and level of adaptive functioning. Although DSM III is far from proven at this point, it represents a substantial change in the direction of both increased specificity and comprehensiveness. Diagnostic systems must meet rigorous scientific criteria including reliability, validity, and coverage of a broad range of disorders in order to be useful.

Psychological assessment is the process of discerning individual characteristics that may be important for decisions about treatment or referral. Psychological assessment attempts to obtain a sample of behavior from the individual that will allow us to predict other important outcomes in the person's future. Behavioral observations, interviews, and objective, as well as projective, psychological tests can be used for the purpose of psychological assessment.

A variety of sources of bias may exist in the assessment process. Illusory correlations and inadequate normative data regarding racial and sex role differences can affect the results of psychological assessment unless careful precautions are taken.

Finally, we noted that a relatively new emphasis on the assessment of competence has recently emerged in the field of psychosocial assessment. The competence orientation focuses on positive personal characteristics of individuals and has implications for the social adaptation of people in their social context. It is likely that we will continue to see a shift in the direction of assessing competence as well as pathology in the field of psychological assessment.

PART 2

The Major Disorders

6

Neurotic Disorders: Anxiety, Somatoform, and Dissociative Disorders

INTRODUCTION

Neurotic is a term familiar to most people whether they have had formal training in the study of abnormal behavior or not. In general, people assume that it refers to a variety of anxiety ridden, peculiar, self-defeating, but not necessarily bizarre, behavior patterns.

Until recently, neurosis was part of the official nomenclature of the *Diagnostic and Statistical Manual of Mental Disorders,* but in DSM III the term was deleted. The behavior patterns previously included under the term *neurosis* are listed separately and emphasize the observed pattern of maladaptive behavior rather than underlying anxiety, as did DSM II.

Over the centuries, our ideas about the meaning of neurosis have changed several times. In Chapter 2 we noted that the 19th century was heavily influenced by an *organic orientation* to abnormal behavior. At that time it was believed that neurotic disorders were due to weak or damaged nerves and that the fatigue and anxiety experienced by neurotic people was a consequence of neurological impairment.

The turn of the century and the emergence of psychoanalysis offered another interpretation of the meaning of neurosis. Rather than focusing on organic causes, Freud and his followers believed that neurotic symptoms, particularly *anxiety* and the *defense mechanisms,* were an expression of underlying id-ego conflicts. In Chapter 3, we discussed the *psychoanalytic perspective* on abnormal behavior in some detail.

Today the controversy about the meaning of neurosis continues. Some researchers are still convinced that there is an *organic,* or genetic, basis for many neurotic disorders. These researchers continue to do research to identify genetic causes. Other researchers and clinicians believe, as did Freud, that neurosis is best understood in dynamic terms. Still another group of scientists argue that neurotic symptoms are *learned* either through classic or instrumental conditioning. Early pioneers in the field of learning, such as Pavlov and Watson, conducted studies that they believed demonstrated that neurotic symptoms were the product of learning mechanisms. Today, this controversy remains unresolved, and the organic, dynamic, and learning explanations each have strong advocates.

Perhaps the most important recent turn in the controversy is reflected in the elimination of the term altogether in DSM III. This decision almost surely reflects a shift in the direction of a more empirical orientation to classifying abnormal behavior and a less inferential approach.

In the present chapter, we will follow the DSM III format and discuss three of the most distinctive of the disorders previously classified as neurotic: *anxiety disorders, somatoform disorders,* and *dissociative disorders.*

ANXIETY DISORDERS

Each of us has specific fears and even moments of panic. But imagine fear as a way of life. What must it be like to have an unexplainable fear well up inside of you, sometimes with no warning at all? How do you live your life when so many things seem terrifying, and when those around you can't possibly imagine what it is like to experience constant, pervasive fear. That girl on the Vermont hillside, described in the example "A Life Ruled by Panic," is not as unusual as you might guess. She is suffering from an *anxiety disorder.*

We know that large numbers of people experiencing severe anxiety turn to their family doctor. Redlich and Freedman (1966) estimate that between 10 and 75 percent of the cases seen by general medical practitioners involve anxiety problems. As the girl experiencing a panic attack, many of these people use such minor tranquilizers as Valium or Miltown to control their anxiety.

In the case of the young woman, M., we have just described, her panic attack was one of a series of such experiences that made the world around her an

A LIFE RULED BY PANIC

"Agoraphobia? Fifteen years ago the word meant nothing to most people. Certainly, it meant nothing to the college girl about to sled down the hill in Vermont. As a cold wind hit the hill, she stood holding her chin, looking back at the house in the distance. Her friends heard her mutter something—that she had snow in her boot, or needed the bathroom—some such lie. Then she began to run looking down at the snow. She couldn't look at the house, it seemed too far away. She started to sweat and her legs went soft. She could not feel her feet, but they were running. Her heart was pounding, her face flushed. She began to panic. She felt as though she were coming apart, as if she had been running forever through the syrupy snow of a nightmare. Six Miltowns rattled against four Valiums in her pocket. The sweat on her body tripped triggers in her brain. The adrenalin signaled the nerves to further panic, 'What if I die?,' she thought. 'Oh my God, I'm going crazy.' Then she was at the house, the 'safe' place, but she had added more fears to an already long list. She was afraid of snow. She was afraid of hills. And above all, she was afraid of ever again feeling the way she did running from that snowy hill in Vermont" (Baumgold, 1977).

increasingly fearful place in which to live. She began to anticipate and avoid situations that might start still another panic attack. To avoid attacks, she shrank her world to situations that seemed "safe." She developed a terror of crowds; as she would drive into a tunnel, she would become terrified that it would not be possible to find an opening at the other end; entering an elevator became impossible. She could only go outside in the company of a friend who would reassure her and stay by her through what most of us think of as routine errands. She found she could not go above the first floor in a department store and often, unaccountably, bolted from games, dentist chairs, and restaurants. It became necessary to make excuses and to even lie to her friends when she missed appointments. Because of her crippling fear, her marriage relationship deteriorated and ultimately ended in divorce.

In DSM III, phobias and obsessive-compulsive disorders are two of the most distinctive of the anxiety disorders. It is to these two patterns of behavior that we will now turn.

Acrophobia—fear of heights is obviously not this man's problem.

Robert Houser/Photo Researchers, Inc.

Phobias

A phobia is a continuing intense fear of some specific object or situation that presents no actual danger to the individual. Typically, people suffering from phobias react to the object or situation with a degree of intensity that is out of proportion to its actual threat. Irrational phobic fears may develop in response to a variety of objects and situations, including animals, fire, disease, crowds, darkness, blood, storms, and closed, open, or high places.

It is important for us to distinguish between *anxiety* that appears to be attached to no specific object and *phobic fear* that always is associated with some particular object or situation. Anxiety may be diffuse, but a phobic fear is highly focused and can seldom be explained or reasoned away. Furthermore, the fear is largely beyond voluntary control and typically leads the phobic person to avoid the feared situation.

In the Box opposite, there are some examples of phobic reactions. Clearly, although the fears may seem unreasonable to you, they are very intense and real to the people suffering from them and may be endured only at great personal cost.

In fact, one of the distinctive features of phobias is that the avoidance of the feared object may lead to a severe *constriction or narrowing in life activities.* In the case of agoraphobia, the number of feared objects may increase so rapidly that there are soon few places where the sufferer feels safe. Originally agoraphobia meant "fear of the marketplace." Now, as Baumgold (1977) notes, it has come to mean fear of the marketplace of life. In the case of the young woman we described at the beginning of the chapter, her fears multiplied to such a degree that few normal life activities were available to her.

> M. soon realized there was no safety; she could get an attack halfway through a movie or at a wedding where she was a bridesmaid. . . . Once she was walking home from school, the streets were very quiet and empty and suddenly M. shot into a total panic. . . . One day on the way to the beach for a picnic, she and her boyfriend stopped at a cliff. The moment M. saw the path they would have to take to get to the beach below, she knew she couldn't make it. . . . Later, on a flight to Germany, she called the steward and urgently asked to talk with the pilot. She told him she had to get off the plane. Only when the pilot brought her into the cockpit as if she were a child and showed her the bodies of land they would pass over on their course was she able to relax. After her marriage, she could not drive to the army base or go into stores without her husband. She would visit a neighbor every day, running through the streets to get there even though she knew she was not wanted by the neighbor (adapted from Baumgold, 1977, p. 46–48).

Incidence and developmental course. How common are phobias? Although only a few systematic studies are available, Agras et al. (1969) report finding 77 phobias per 1,000 population in a New England study. But of these, only 2.2 per 1,000 were severely disabled. Thus, although nearly 8 percent of the population reported a phobic fear, many did not suffer from the severe life constriction we found in the case of M. Instead, their phobia were focused on a single situation or object and, through careful maneuvering, they were able to avoid the situation or conceal their fears so that they were hardly noticed.

It is useful to examine developmental research on fears in children, since they may give us some important hints about the characteristics and possible determinants of phobic neuroses. Marks (1969) reports that the common fears of children change as they grow older. In children two to four years old, fear of animals tends to predominate, but from the age of four to six these fears are replaced by fears of the dark and of imaginary creatures. After six, few children develop new animal phobias, and by the time children are nine or ten years of age, they exhibit few fears of animals, although many children exhibit specific fears of thunder and lightening, cars, strong winds, and trains.

Frequently, fears in children disappear

VARIETIES OF PHOBIC REACTIONS

Acrophobia: Fear of High Places such as Cliffs, Roofs, High Windows, Ladders, or Stairwells

Case example "Agnes W., an unmarried woman of 30, had been unable to go higher than the second or third floor of any building for a year. Whenever she tried to overcome her fear of height, she only succeeded in provoking intolerable anxiety. She remembered when it all began. One evening she was working alone at the office when she was suddenly seized with a terror lest she jump or fall out of the open eight story window. So frightened was Agnes by her impulse that she crouched behind a steel file for some time before she could trust herself to gather up her things and make for the street. She reached the ground level acutely anxious, perspiring freely, her heart pounding, and breathing rapid" (Cameron, 1963, p. 282).

Claustrophobia: Fear of Enclosed Places, such as Small Rooms, Closets, Elevators, Alleys and Subways

Case example "Bert C. entered therapy in part because of his fear of elevators. He walked the four flights to his office whenever possible. If he rode in the elevator, he was terrified over the possibility of being trapped and of being mutilated or killed in trying to escape. He often pictured these possibilities to himself" (Cameron, 1963, p. 287).

Agoraphobia: Fear of Wide Open Places such as Halls, Wide Streets, Fields, Parks, and Beaches

Case example "Ethel H., a married woman of 26, had suffered her first acute anxiety attack two years before she began therapy. She was arriving alone by plane from England after visiting her parents there. As she entered the high-ceilinged terminal where no one met her, she suddenly felt terrified at the huge, empty spaciousness. She began "shaking like a leaf"; she could not get her bags through customs without constant help, she had the impulse to tell everyone around who she was in case she went mad. A porter, sensing her anxiety, expressed his concern over her openly, and this comforted her. She managed the rest of the trip by train without mishap, but reached home exhausted and unnerved, certain that something awful was happening to her." (Cameron, 1963, p. 291).

Zoophobia: Fear of Animals such as Dogs, Cats, Snakes, Frogs, Bats, Horses, Tigers, and Lions

Case example Little Hans, a boy of five years old, refused to go into the street because he was afraid of horses. Actually he feared being bitten by them and no amount of rational persuasion could rid him of his fear.

Ocholophobia: Fear of Crowds and Public Gatherings

Case example "M's first phobic attack occured when she was returning home by airplane. It was night and the place was crowded. The people pressed in around her, and M was seized by an overwhelming feeling of panic that seemed to come 'out of the blue.' Her stomach turned, she couldn't breath, she was shaking and sweating and frightened by the very thought of the people pressing around her" (Baumgold, 1977).

FIGURE 6–1 Relative Frequency of Various Fear Responses.

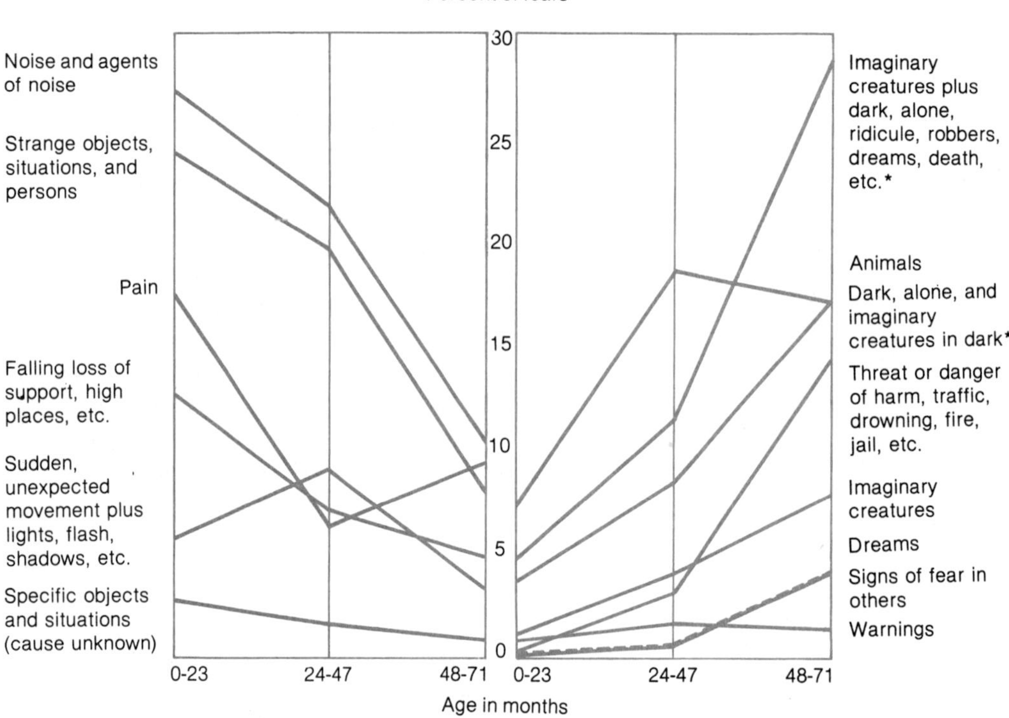

Source: Reprinted by permission of the publisher from Arthur T. Jersild and Frances G. Holmes, *Children's Fears* (New York: Teachers College Press, © 1935).

over time, whereas specific fears in adults are much more stable. Figure 6–2 show the results of a five-year longitudinal study of people with untreated phobias. You can see that children under 20 years of age showed a rapid decline in their specific fears, while in adults the phobias remained relatively unchanged. As Marks (1977) notes: "Fears and rituals appear in children for little or no apparent reason and disappear just as mysteriously" (p. 180). Perhaps this suggests that we should not be overly concerned with the initial appearance of a specific fear in young children since the chances are very great that it will disappear in the normal course of development.

Phobias in childhood: school phobia. The term *school phobia* is generally used to describe a child's refusal to attend school and implies that the child is irrationally frightened by something in the school environment. However, initially, we should make a distinction between children who are truant and those who are genuinely frightened of the school environment. Hersov (1960) did find striking differences from truants and school phobic children. School phobic children were characterized by parental overprotection, expressions of abdominal pain and nausea, numerous sleeping problems, and other indications of pervasive anxiety.

The incidence of school phobias is difficult to estimate, but figures reported in treatment settings and children's clinics vary from 1 percent to 2 percent with

FIGURE 6–2 Untreated Phobias Tend to Persist over Five-year Follow-up in Adults, but Improve without Treatment in Younger Subjects

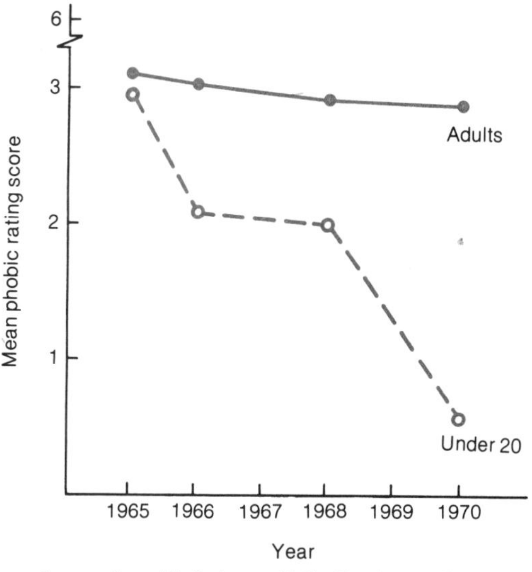

Source: From W. S. Agras, H. N. Chapin, and D. Oliveau, "The Natural History of Phobias: Course and Prognosis," *Archives of General Psychiatry,* 1972, *26,* 315–17. Copyright 1972, American Medical Association.

The transition from home to school produces separation anxiety in many children. A certain amount of distress during this period is normal.

United Press International Photo

estimates in the general population being even higher and estimated to be approximately 5 percent (Kahn and Narstein, 1962).

One of the best known hypothesis regarding the determinants of school phobia has to do with the idea of *separation anxiety* (Eisenberg, 1958). The underlying assumption is that it is not school itself that is feared, but fear of being separated from the mother that produces school phobia. Yates (1970) has suggested that a combination of factors, including the child's fear of separation from the mother, the mother's or other caretaker's expressions of concern and reaction to the child's fears, and the child's ability to obtain social rewards in school from academic achievement and friendships independent from the mother all may be important in the development of school phobia.

Kennedy (1965) has developed a rapid procedure for returning children to school that begins with a differentiation between what he believes to be two types of school phobia. These types are shown in Table 6–1. Type I, Kennedy argues, is a "true" phobia and begins with an acute onset and is much more treatable than Type II "phobias," which Kennedy describes as "a way of life."

Kennedy's method for treating Type I school phobias includes (1) establishing an effective relationship with school personnel, (2) avoiding an emphasis on the somatic complaints reported by the child, (3) extremely strong encouragement to attend school from the parents, (4) a training interview with the parents designed to give them the confidence to execute the program of encouraging the child to attend school, (5) a brief interview with the child after school expressing the advantages of facing the fear directly, and

TABLE 6–1 Differential Patterns of School Phobia Symptoms

Type I	*Type II*
1. The present episode is the first.	1. Second, third, or fourth episode.
2. Monday onset following an illness the previous Thursday or Friday.	2. Monday onset following minor illness not a prevalent antecedent.
3. An acute onset.	3. Incipient onset.
4. Lower grades most prevalent.	4. Upper grades most prevalent.
5. Expressed concern about death.	5. Death theme not present.
6. Mother's physical health in question: actually ill or child thinks so.	6. Mother's health not an issue.
7. Good communication between parents.	7. Poor communication between parents.
8. Parents well adjusted in most areas.	8. Mother shows a neurotic behavior; father, a character disorder.
9. Father competitive with mother in household management.	9. Father shows little interest in household or children.
10. Parents achieve understanding of dynamics easily.	10. Parents very difficult to work with.

Source: Reprinted from Wallace A. Kennedy, "School Phobia; Rapid Treatment of Fifty Cases," *Journal of Abnormal Psychology,* 70, 286. Copyright 1965 by the American Psychological Association. Reprinted by permission.

(6) a follow-up interview with the parents to assure academic progress and to check on other fears and issues in the case.

The essence of the treatment program is carried out by the parents themselves. They are told not to discuss the issue of school attendance but simply on Monday morning to take the child to school and matter-of-factly leave him or her and return home. Any attendance at school in the first few days is to be praised, but otherwise there should be no discussion of school. Each day the child is taken to school in a similar manner and praised for attendance. Kennedy reports substantial success with this particular treatment method, especially with Type I school phobics.

Origins of Phobic Behavior

Where do phobias come from? Are they merely the accidental result of some previous traumatic event? Do they serve some purpose in balancing the psychological drives and needs of the individual? Or is there, perhaps, a genetic predisposition to become phobic?

Three major points of view have developed to account for the pattern of specific, irrational fear and avoidance that we see in phobic reactions. They are the dynamic explanation, the learning explanation, and the idea of biological preparedness.

The dynamic view. Freud was intrigued by phobias and one of his most famous case histories, that of Little Hans, is an attempt to use psychoanalytic theory to explain the development of phobias. One of the clearest modern expositions of this view is offered by Cameron (1963).

Cameron argues that the dynamic organization of all phobias involves four basic steps. First, a threatening impulse, usually of an aggressive or sexual nature, is experienced by the person. In the case of Little Hans, published by Freud in 1909, Freud theorized that Little Hans had an unacceptable sexual desire for his mother and hate for his father. The second step in the development of a phobia is that the person is not capable of preventing these impulses from becoming conscious. Presumably in the case of Little Hans, conflict with his father and sexual desire for his mother, although forbidden, continued to intrude into his awareness. Third, these intrusions became crystalized in the form of fearful fantasies. In the case of Little Hans, he feared being harmed by his father. In the fourth stage these fantasies are attached to an external object which then symbolizes the internal danger. In the case of Little Hans, an accident involving a horse drawn carriage in which he and his mother were riding led him to be terrified of being bitten by horses. This *displaces* the fear from the actual object and gives the person something tangible that he or she can avoid. So we see that, according to the psychoanalytic view, forbidden impulses and the fear associated with them become transformed and externalized. The result is an irrational fear of an external object or situation.

Cameron also notes that there is frequently a *symbolic relationship* between the feared object and the actual fear. Thus, the fear of heights may actually symbolize the fear of falling in the esteem of other people. Claustrophobia, or the fear of closed places, actually symbolizes the fear of being left alone with ones own dangerous impulses and fantasies. And the fear of open places, agoraphobia, is, according to Cameron, actually the fear of helpless exposure and abandonment. So we can see that the dynamic view suggests that phobias speak in a symbolic language about underlying fears and impulses.

The learning viewpoint. Although these dynamic speculations are intriguing, advocates of the learning perspective have severely criticized them and argued that *classical conditioning mechanisms* can more simply account for the development of phobic behavior. As Wolpe and Rachman (1960) argue,

> In brief, phobias are regarded as conditioned anxiety (fear) reactions. Any neutral stimulus, simple or complex, that happens to make an impact on an individual at about the time that a fear reaction is evoked acquires the ability to evoke fear subsequently. . . . It is our contention that the incident to which Freud refers as merely the exciting cause of Hans' phobia was, in fact, the cause of the entire disorder. The evidence obtained in studies on experimental neurosis in animals and on phobias in children indicate that it is quite possible for one experience to induce a phobia (Wolpe and Rachman, 1960, p. 143–44).

Earlier, in Chapter 3, we discussed the famous case of Little Albert reported by Watson and Raynor (1920). In this case, Albert, who was 11 months old at the time, was shown a white rat. Initially, he showed no fear of the animal, but as he reached for the rat, the experimentor struck a steel bar behind his head (the unconditioned stimulus) creating a loud noise and eliciting an unconditioned response of fear. After five such experiences, Albert had acquired a conditioned response of fear to the white rat, so that whenever he was presented with it, he exhibited great fear and anxiety.

This experiment is often used to argue that phobias can be developed by traumatic classical conditioning in which some previously neutral object becomes associated with an intense fear reaction. The previously neutral object, then, acquires the ability to illicit fear in the person by itself.

There are, however, two major

problems with this explanation, as plausible as it may seem. The first, as Marks (1977) notes, is that clearly traumatic events (a definable, unconditioned stimulus) can rarely be pinpointed at the beginning of human phobias. Second, Marks argues that it is unnecessary to make the untestable assumption that phobias are conditioned responses. Instead, we should simply identify *evoking stimuli* (ES) that trigger the phobia and label the phobia itself the *evoked response* (ER). The advantage from the point of view of treatment, argues Marks, is that the therapist's task simply becomes one of identifying all those events that evoke a phobic response. Then the patient may be exposed to these evoking stimuli until the evoked response or phobia no longer occurs, presumably by a process of *extinction.*

Biological preparedness. Why are phobias involving heights, snakes, or spiders relatively common while phobias involving plastic or filing cabinets almost nonexistent? Phobias do not develop in a random fashion. There is, according to Marks (1977), a very limited range of objects to which phobias typically occur. Fearing snakes, spiders, dogs, and cats makes evolutionary sense. They are fears that, although exaggerated in some people, have clear survival value.

But this does not rule out a learning explanation for the development of phobias. Instead, the idea of biological preparedness suggests that certain objects may, for biological reasons, be *prepotent targets* for phobias. As Marks (1977) puts it, "Preparedness is the lightening rod that conducts associations selectively along certain nervous pathways rather than others" (p. 192). Thus, for phobias at least, the laws of learning may make evolutionary sense. Preparedness to make particular associations goes hand-in-hand with the evolutionary history and survival tactics of the organism. If it is true that some objects are prepotent targets for phobic responses, then it should be easier to condition a fear response to some objects rather than others. This is precisely what English observed in 1929.

In an attempt to put the Watson and Rayner study in perspective, English sat a 14-month-old girl in a high chair and presented her with a wooden toy duck. As the child grasped it, he struck a large metal bar behind her, producing a resounding noise. The duck was repeatedly presented, reached for, and withdrawn. But even after fifty trials, no conditioned fear response was established. As English noted, "The writer must confess his surprise and admiration at the child's iron nerves. In a later trial when the duck was grasped, the metal bar was struck such a tremendous blow with a two pound hammer, that professors in remote parts of the building, students, and children able to make a verbal report spoke of the distasteful and alarming nature of the sound." Yet a month later, the child showed no fear of the duck but of new patent leather boots she had never seen before. When English used the same unconditioned stimulus on another child, the child readily developed a conditioned fear of a stuffed black cat. Findings like these led Valentine (1930) to suggest that fears might be much more easily conditioned to furry or leathery objects than to objects such as opera glasses.

Similar results to those of Valentine have been reported in a recent study by Ohman et al. (1974). They found that skin conductance measures of anxiety in response to pictures of snakes and spiders took longer to extinguish than did responses to neutral pictures such as houses.

Marks also offers clinical examples to illustrate the prepotency of certain stimuli. "A four-year-old girl was playing in the park. Thinking she saw a snake, she ran into her parents car and jumped inside, slamming the door behind her. The girl's hand was caught by the closing door resulting in severe pain and several visits to the doctor. Before this, she may have been afraid of snakes but was not phobic. After this experience, a phobia developed, *not of cars or car doors, but of snakes.* The snake phobia persisted into adulthood. . . .

A similar case was reported by Larson (1965). An 18-year-old woman was a passenger in a car that was involved in an accident. At the moment of the accident, the woman happened to be looking at a photograph of a snake. The sudden fear and noise became associated only with the snake and not with the car or photographs in general. Why did these people who have justifiable reasons for fearing cars develop phobias for snakes?" (Marks, 1977, p. 192 italics added.)

These results, if they can be repeated, suggest that both learning mechanisms and biological predispositions may interact in the development of phobias.

Obsessive-Compulsive Disorders

The song that seems to repeat itself again and again in the back of your mind, the frightening thought that recurs even as you try to shut it out, the little superstition that you half believe. . . . If you have experienced any of these thoughts or feelings, even for a moment, you understand something about the experience of obsessive-compulsive disorders.

Clinical description. The hallmark of obsessive-compulsive disorders is the experience of persistent thoughts, impulses, or actions. Often they are accompanied by a compulsion to actually engage in the behavior and a conflicting desire to resist it (Carr, 1974). These impulses or thoughts are usually frightening and seem irrational or senseless. At times they may involve recurrent impulses to harm someone or they may involve sexual fantasies. In some cases, they may involve exaggerated concerns with neatness or cleanliness. Consider the following examples:

- "A clergyman was obsessed with the idea of singing 'Dim dam, dimity damity' to the tune of a church hymn" (Bucklew, 1960, p. 75).
- "A middle-aged woman occasionally had so strong an impulse to choke her husband while he slept that she would have to get up and leave the bedroom" (Cameron, p. 374).
- "A housewife came for consultation because of sudden impulses to destroy objects which did not measure up to her perfectionistic standards. She tore up wallets and clothing which suddenly seemed to displease her because of some imperfection. If she did not give into her impulses, she became nervous and jittery. It took her many hours to clean the three rooms of her apartment. Everything had to be in exactly the right place, and often she went to the extreme of measuring the distance between objects on the top of her dressing bureau to see that they were systematically arranged. Often, she had an impulse to soil objects after having

cleaned them; for example, after having spent a great deal of time cleaning and polishing the surface of a mirror, she would feel compelled to spit on it and then clean it all over again" (Bucklew, 1960, p. 82).

- "A man suffered from irresistible impulses to utter blasphemies. He actually taped his mouth shut at times, both to control and punish himself" (Cameron, p. 374).

A moments reflection will suggest that these people may be severely incapacitated by their obsessive-compulsive behavior. In particular, it is easy to understand how two features of neurotic disorders, a constriction of life activities and interpersonal difficulties, could result from obsessions and compulsions.

Distinguishing features of obsessive-compulsive disorders. There are several other clinical phenomena that are easily confused with obsessive-compulsive disorders and so some distinctions are in order.

First, we should make a distinction between the repetitive acts found in obsessive-compulsive disorders and the stereotyped, repeated activities that are often associated with severe brain pathology. In the case of organic diseases

CASE EXAMPLE: OBSESSIONAL SLOWNESS

"The disorder called primary obsessional slowness insidiously invades all aspects of the victim's life. The middle-aged accountant is a clear example of the obsessional life style of someone affected by this brand of the disorder. As his need to engage in increasingly prolonged and meticulous self-care activities increased, he was obliged to rise earlier and earlier in order to get to work on time. He would start his preparations at 3 or 4 o'clock in the morning and, with a great deal of effort and concentration, be ready to leave for work by about 10 o'clock in the morning. Even when he began his preparations at such an ungodly early hour, he was unable to arrive at work on time and as a result was discharged from successive jobs. When he came to the hospital for his initial assessment, it was taking him up to ten hours to wash, shave, and dress himself. This meant that he awoke at 6 in the morning and finally was able to leave his apartment by 4 o'clock in the afternoon. As the preparation of a meal was such an arduous business, he left his apartment each day in midafternoon in order to eat at a restaurant. Upon completion of his meal, he would either return home or pay a short visit to his parents before going home. His preparations for retiring took approximately three hours, and he would start the process by about 9 o'clock in the evening. In an unsuccessful attempt to come to his assessment appointment at the hospital, scheduled for 2 P.M., he spent the entire night preparing himself. He spent virtually all of his waking time planning and carrying out his self-care rituals. Most of his life was devoted to the execution of these rituals, and as is true of most of the patients who sink into an obsessional life style, it was impossible for anyone to live with him. Most of these patients live in isolation" (Rachman & Hodgson, 1980, p. 60).

of the central nervous system, the repeated behaviors that are observed have no accompanying subjective experience of any kind. That is, repetitive motor acts occur outside of the awareness of the person engaging in them. In the case of obsessions and compulsions, on the other hand, there is an urge to engage in the behavior and a strong desire to resist it. The person appears to be in an inner struggle to both suppress and act out the behavior.

Second, as Carr (1974) notes, there appears to be a sharp difference between the so-called compulsive personality, who is characterized by traits of thoroughness, consistency, punctuality, and neatness, and the sufferer of obsessive-compulsive disorders. Sandler and Hazari (1960) have conducted a factor analytic study that suggests that there is a cluster of personality traits involving punctuality, thoroughness, and consistency. But these traits are not necessarily related to the occurence of obsessive-compulsive symptoms. Thus, it appears that orderly, punctual behavior is not necessarily a mild form of obsessive-compulsive disorder.

Finally, the dual term *obsessive-compulsive* may be somewhat misleading. Carr (1974) notes that the term obsessive-compulsive has been traditionally used to identify cases in which *both* recurrent thoughts and repeated actions occur. But, Carr argues that in all cases the person is disturbed by *a feeling of loss of control* over his or her own behavior. He also argues that there is no reason to suspect that there are different determinants of obsessions and compulsions and that the separate terms are therefore misleading. He suggests instead use of the single generic term *compulsion* and specifying whether the compulsion is primarily cognitive, as in a recurrent thought, or motor, as in repetitive acts.

Let us now turn to some current views about the origins of compulsive disorders.

Origins of Obsessive-Compulsive Disorders

A dynamic view. The dynamic interpretation of obsessive-compulsive disorders suggests that the symptomatic behavior is acutally an attempt to control dangerous or unwanted impulses. You may recall in Chapter 3 that the psychoanalytic viewpoint sees symptoms as attempts to reduce anxiety associated with id-ego conflicts. In the following case, we see both id impulses and forces opposing them called *countermeasures* in open conflict with one another.

> Frances T. was an unmarried typist, aged 24. She was trying to control erotic fantasies which she could not repress. Her countermeasures put into practice, in a compulsive way, the advice often given to adolescents who are struggling with sex problems, "Think of something else!" Walking to work was an activity that permitted erotic fantasies to emerge easily. So each time Frances stepped on or off the curb at a corner, she made herself think of a different person. This kept her mind busy preparing for the next intersection. If she ran out of persons,' she allowed herself to change streets and start the list over again.
>
> This obsessive countermeasure cost Frances time and effort. As it became entrenched, it made her shun company to avoid having to explain her preoccupations and her zig-zag course as she changed streets. She needed to concentrate upon the task of having names ready in time for the next block. The device failed, however, to eliminate all her erotic fantasies, it tended to

> sustain rather than reduce her anxiety, and it kept her from the benefits and pleasures of sharing in the company of others.
>
> In time the countermeasure generalized to other activities. As Frances dressed and undressed, she found that she had to think of a different person with each article of clothing she put on or took off. Later this became necessary for each mouthful of food, and for each act in washing dishes, doing laundry, and other housework. It began creeping into her office work, as she opened or sealed envelopes, filed away or got out letters, inserted paper and carbon in her typewriter, etc. Ultimately, the countermeasure had to be applied to the details of typing—a different person at first for each new page, then for each new paragraph and line, and finally for each word. The girl had to give up her job (Cameron, 1963, p. 383).

This case provides an excellent illustration of psychodynamic thinking about obsessive-compulsive disorders. Clearly, we can see the sexual fantasies as representations of id impulses in conflict with ego restrictions against acting out the impulses. Thus, from the dynamic viewpoint, Frances' symptoms—thinking of a new person in order to block out her sexual fantasies—are attempts to reduce anxiety. The anxiety, in turn, has been generated by the conflict between id and ego forces at war within her.

The case is notable in other ways as well. Frances seems to feel the characteristic loss of control we regard as one of the distinguishing features of compulsive disorders. Further, as the compulsive thoughts become more widespread, the disorder appears to have an increasingly constricting effect on her life. And, of course, ultimately it even meant that she could not retain her job. Clearly, compulsive disorders in their severe form can have a crippling effect on one's life.

Learning theory explanations. One of the earliest accounts of compulsive behavior framed in a learning theory context was offered by Dollard and Miller (1950). They regarded compulsive behavior as behavior reinforced by anxiety reduction. That is, any behavior that has reduced anxiety in the past is reinforced by the anxiety reduction and is therefore more likely to occur again.

Dollard and Miller suggested that the actual *content* of compulsive acts, such as handwashing, checking switches, or turning gas caps, tend to be exaggerations of previously employed anxiety reducing behavior. For example, handwashing in childhood is frequently associated with escape from parental criticism. Therefore, it is the basis upon which an adult handwashing compulsion might develop.

Compulsive handwashing can be a distressing affliction for those who suffer from it.

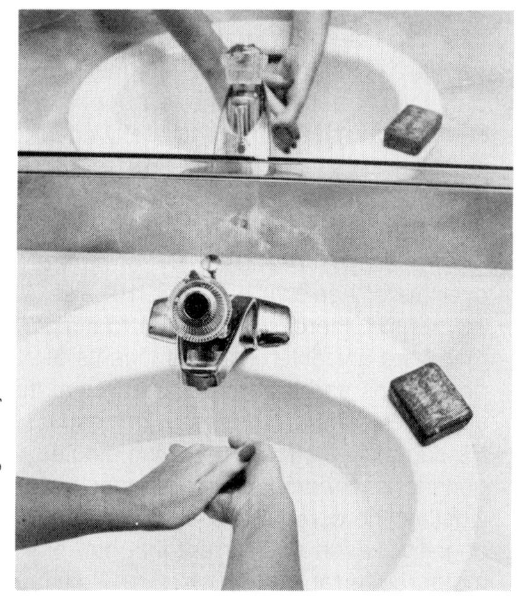

John Thoeming/Dorsey Press

But, can obsessive or compulsive behavior develop on the basis of a single traumatic learning experience? It seems unlikely. Research by Pollitt (1957) and Grimshaw (1964) suggests that there is little firm data to implicate traumatic learning as an important aspect of the etiology of compulsive disorders. The classic example of Lady MacBeth, who developed her compulsive handwashing behavior in order to reduce her guilt for her role in a murder, may be dramatically convincing but scientifically inaccurate.

In attempting to understand how learning theorists might account for the development of compulsive behavior, a famous experiment by Skinner (1948) is of interest. Skinner placed hungry pigeons in an experimental cage in which food was automatically presented at regular five-second intervals. He observed the birds' behavior closely and discovered that in six out of eight cases the birds developed clearly defined "ritualistic" or "superstitious" behavior.

One bird, Skinner reported, began to turn counterclockwise in the cage, making two or three turns before receiving the food reinforcement. Another repeatedly thrust its head in one of the upper corners of the cage. These ritualistic responses seemed to develop because the bird happened to be executing a particular response as the food reward appeared. The response tended to be repeated and subsequently to be reinforced again. As Skinner notes, "A few accidental connections between a ritual and a favorable consequence sufficed to set up and maintain the behavior, in spite of many unreinforced instances."

We should note that in Skinner's procedure the compulsive behavior was not reinforced by anxiety reduction but instead by the administration of positive reinforcements. Thus, Skinner's explanation differs from that of Dollard and Miller (1950), although both explanations invoke the idea of reinforcement.

Social origins of obsessive-compulsive behavior. It is possible to argue, as Cameron (1963) has, that obsessive-compulsive symptoms are merely exaggerations of normal human behavior. Superstition, magic, and ritual enter into our everyday life in a great many ways. He says, "Unless we recognize that the relationships between normal and abnormal in this area are more than superficial resemblances, that both go deep into human nature, we cannot begin to understand obsessive-compulsive behavior. We will not recognize neurotic devotion to exact repetition, rigid uniformity, strict taboo, and severe self-punishment, as pathological variants of universal human trends" (p. 374).

To convince us of the continuity between daily rituals and more severe obsessive-compulsive behaviors, Cameron reminds us that children's games illustrate the need for order, repetition, and ritual. If you watch a group of children playing hopscotch in the street, you will discover that they insist on inflexible rules and exact repetition down to the finest detail.

Furthermore, our social and legal institutions also show what Cameron calls a "passionate insistence upon maintaining inflexible, arbitrary rules" (p. 375). If the law requires three witnesses for a signature to be valid, supplying only two may invalidate the document even though the true intent is clear. And supposedly rational people may design a hotel without a thirteenth floor or value a rabbit's foot for its lucky qualities.

Are obsessive-compulsive behaviors merely exaggerations of behavior we usually regard as acceptable or only slightly eccentric? At the least, Cameron has suggested some important parallels. Perhaps it is most accurate to say that the *goals* of compulsive behavior and superstitious behavior are quite similar. Both of them represent attempts to increase control over the events in our lives. Private rituals and self-imposed penalties become ways of anticipating danger and warding it off when you live in an uncertain, and sometimes frightening world.

SOMATOFORM DISORDERS

As we noted earlier, in the third edition of the *Diagnostic and Statistical Manual,* the neurotic disorders have been reclassified. One major group is called the *somatoform disorders.* The essential feature of somatoform disorders are *physical symptoms for which there are no demonstrable organic findings* but where there is some reason to suspect psychological conflicts or problems. An important feature of somatoform disorders is that the *symptoms are not under voluntary control.*

The point to remember about somatoform disorders is that, despite continual complaints or actual loss of physiological function, upon medical examination there is no evidence of actual or chronic damage, while there is some reason to believe that anxiety or conflict is associated with the disorder.

Let us now turn to the first of the somatoform disorders we will discuss—somatization disorders.

Somatization Disorder

The essential features of this disorder are "recurrent and multiple somatic complaints for which medical attention is sought but that are not apparently due to any physical disorder, beginning before early adulthood (prior to age 25), and having a chronic but fluctuating course" (DSM III 1980, p. 241).

This disorder, once called *hypochondriasis,* has as its most striking clinical feature the fact that the person is continuously preoccupied with fears and that he or she is suffering from some physical disease. They are occupied with their own bodily health and are constantly observing their own bodily functioning with the expectation that a symptom will appear.

It is not uncommon with people suffering from a somatization disorder to go from physician to physician with the conviction that they are suffering from a physical disorder. While most of us would be relieved to hear from a physician that our concerns about the possibility of a physical disease are unfounded, the person with a somatization disorder remains unconvinced and will continue to "shop around" for a physician to confirm his/her suspicion or fear.

The person may fear that they are suffering from cancer, liver disease, diabetes, heart disease, or a variety of other physical disorders. Every heart palpitation or ache or pain is seen as an indication that they are suffering from some disease. Typical complaints include headaches, fatigue, palpitations, fainting, nausea, vomiting, abdominal pains, bowel troubles, allergies, and menstrual or sexual difficulties.

It is important to distinguish between somatization disorders and the more bizarre physical complaints sometimes seen in psychotic disorders. Often, the person with a somatization disorder will know a fair amount about the physical symptomatology of a particular disease and may even feel

AN EXAMPLE OF SOMATIZATION DISORDER

John M. was admitted to a psychiatric hospital following a history of job failure and an unstable family background. He made numerous complaints about his physical health. His concerns began when he experienced a swelling of his glands, which led him to seek help from numerous doctors, all of whom gave him treatments, but no treatment yielded relief. Ultimately, his physical complaints became so severe that he was unable to work.

He is a friendly, pleasant, docile person expressing deep concern about his physical health. He reports that he believes his sex glands are infected, that he has a hernia, suffers from constipation, and has continuous feelings of tightness and pain in his abdomen. While discussing his physical health, he shows deep preoccupation; but later, on another topic, seems relatively indifferent and even cheerful (adapted from Kisker, 1964).

that they know more about their disorder than the examining physician.

The life pattern of the person displaying a somatization disorder may reflect not only a continuous preoccupation with physical symptoms, but also a continuing pattern of failure in school or work partly attributed to the alleged disease. Kisker (1964) noted that Elizabeth Barrett Browning fell from a horse at the age of 15 and remained an invalid for the next 20 years, receiving extra care and attention in her own room, and, by so doing, she escaped competition with her brothers and sisters. Interestingly, Kisker notes that when she was forty she met Robert Browning and, after their marriage, her symptoms promptly disappeared.

This leads us to some hypotheses about some of the gains associated with adopting the "sick role," as in the case in somatization disorders. In many cases a continued preoccupation with bodily disorders may serve a variety of purposes. It may provide sympathetic attention and an opportunity to avoid life's challenges and to rationalize feelings of inadequacy or failure. Many of us have experienced the temptation to rationalize a loss in an athletic contest on the basis of a pain in one's leg or some other physical complaint. In the case of somatization disorders, this motivation is presumably much more pronounced.

Thus, in its milder forms, this disorder may affect all of us as a part of the "psychopathology of everyday life." It is a form of adaptation to the uncertainties, anxieties, and threats we encounter every day. Our cultural norms excuse people suffering from physical illness from many of the obligations of everyday life. Thus, for some people, a somatization disorder may serve an important adaptive function.

We should be clear, however, that this disorder is *not* the same thing as malingering, which is a deliberate attempt to escape some obligation by claiming sickness. Instead, the person suffering from somatization disorders is convinced that they are suffering from a physical disorder. They retain an unshakable belief that they are actually suffering from or are about to contract some serious disease.

Conversion Disorders

A second major type of somatoform disorder is the conversion disorder. You will recall that the primary focus of somatization disorders is the preoccupation with physical symptoms of disease where no real disability can be found. Conversion disorders, on the other hand, actually involve some form of physical impairment but with no known organic basis. The clinical picture of the client is very different from that of somatization disorders. There will be an actual observed physical disorder such as paralysis, blindness, or deafness, but the person may appear relatively indifferent to it.

In earlier diagnostic classifications, conversion disorders were thought to be one form of hysteria. The Greeks believed that hysteria was a disorder suffered by women as their uterus wandered about the body causing various physical disorders. Today, we believe that hysterical conversions, or conversion disorders as they are now called, are actually an expression of some internal psychological

Sudden psychological stress such as that occuring in combat can sometimes precipitate conversion symptoms such as paralysis or, hysterical blindness.

Martin Gershen/Photo Researchers, Inc.

conflict. The function of the conversion disorder is both to excuse the individual from various responsibilities in his or her life, and to block out the individual's awareness of whatever internal conflict motivated the physical disorder.

Woolsey (1976) has suggested that persons suffering from hysterical disorders tend to show four major psychological characteristics. First, they tend to be extremely *suggestable.* In many cases, hysterical symptoms can be made to disappear if the person treating the sufferer is able to provide a convincing treatment. This *placebo effect* may be accomplished by religious faith healing, hypnosis, or administration of inactive sugar pills.

Second, and perhaps most important, the conversion symptoms, whether they involve paralysis, visual impairment, or loss of feeling in some limb, do not correspond to the pattern of loss one would expect if there were actual organic damage. This is perhaps the single most important distinguishing feature of hysterical disorders.

Third, Woolsey notes that often people suffering from the disorder display what Charcot first termed *La belle indifference.* That is, they seem totally unworried and indifferent to their physical symptom. This sometimes occurs in people suffering chronic severe disease, however, and is not always a reliable indicator of conversion disorders.

Finally, many people suffering from conversion disorders appear to be obtaining *secondary gains* in the form of sympathy or attention from their symptoms. This characteristic is not unique to hysterical disorders but can often be found in cases of somatization disorder.

We should also note that conversion symptoms often appear soon after a sudden, extreme psychosocial stress, such as warfare or the death of a loved one. There will often be a *temporal relationship* between some psychologically meaningful environmental event and the development or worsening of the symptom.

Typically, conversion disorders are expressed either through the sensory system or the motor system. Let us examine some of the typical conversion disorders that occur in each of these systems.

Sensory symptoms. The three typical forms of sensory conversion disorders are complete loss or partial loss of vision, hearing, or sensation in the skin. It is much less common to observe sensory symptoms involving smell or taste.

In the case of the loss of skin sensation (anesthesia), the person no longer feels pain or perhaps any sensation in the affected part of the body. Often this lack of sensation will be restricted to one part of the body, and these types of anesthesia are typically called *glove anesthesias,* or *stocking anesthesias* because they occur in parts of the body that *make psychological sense rather than physiological sense.* The patient's idea of nerve supply is what seems to produce the area of insensitivity rather than the actual area of the skin affected by sensory nerves (see Figure 6–3). This clearly shows that the anesthesia is psychological rather than physiological in nature.

In addition to anesthesia, sometimes people suffering from conversion disorders may experience an increased sensitivity of the skin and report tingling, pins and needles, or crawling sensations.

Visual conversion symptoms are also sometimes reported. The person will appear to be unable to see certain objects, particularly those of psychological

FIGURE 6–3 Example of Glove Anesthesia (a Conversion Disorder) and Pattern of Anesthesia that Would Occur if Actual Neurological Damage Were Involved.

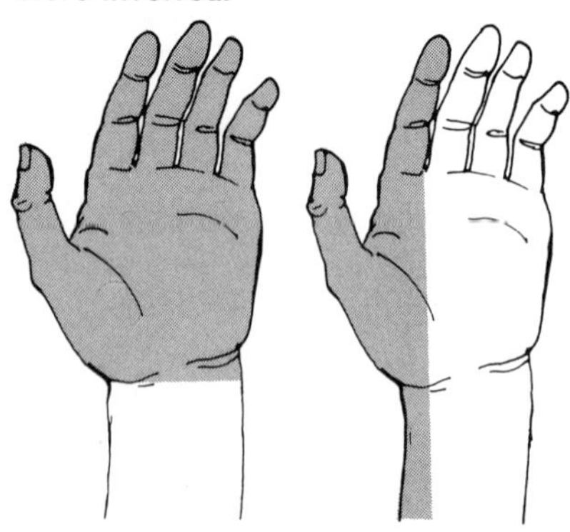

significance. Sometimes only a portion of the visual field will be affected, but again, in ways that do not correspond with the neurological structure of the visual system. In wartime, following the extreme stress of combat, a person may suffer from conversion blindness as a way of expressing his refusal to continue to watch the terrifying features of combat.

Hearing may also be affected by conversion symptoms. People appear to listen selectively, in any case. Many conversion reactions appear to be exaggerations of this tendency. As Kisker (1964) notes "in conversion reactions, the patient may become deaf so he does not hear the unpleasant things the world has to say" (p. 282).

Motor symptoms. The motor system can also be affected in several ways in conversion disorders. Perhaps least serious is a tic. A *tic* is an involuntary twitching or movement of the muscles in some part of the extremities or face or head. A twitching of the corner of the mouth or the winking of an eyelid are fairly common forms of a tic. These movements are automatic and usually occur without the individual being aware of them.

Perhaps the most dramatic form of motor conversion disorder is that of *paralysis.* The onset of conversion paralysis can be sudden and dramatic. The person seems literally to be paralyzed which, in many cases prevents them from engaging in some frightening or unpleasant task. A form of this disorder is "writer's cramp." In order to avoid confronting the psychological risks associated with writing, some people develop a conversion symptom—a cramp of the hand which makes it impossible to write, thus escaping the threatening task of committing oneself to paper (and perhaps experiencing rejection from an editor).

More severe forms of conversion paralysis may involve the paralysis of both legs or other limbs. The function of hysterical paralysis would appear to be to disengage the person from unpleasant tasks or experiences that they otherwise would have to confront.

Although we have pointed out that conversion disorders in both the motor and sensory system do not involve actual organic impairment, there is always the possibility that actual organic damage exists in cases which are misdiagnosed as conversion disorders. Slater and Glithero (1965) followed up a number of patients who had been earlier diagnosed as suffering from conversion reactions. Sixty percent of these patients later developed symptoms of physical disease or had died, and a large proportion of these diseases were in the central nervous system. Similarly, Stefansson et al. (1976) found that, after evaluating the records of several hundreds of people suffering from conversion disorders, most had real physical disorders along with their conversion symptoms. He speculated that

DIAGNOSING A CONVERSION DISORDER

Kate Fox, an adolescent of 13 years of age, was admitted to a hospital complaining of extreme nervousness, a partial paralysis of the left leg, and marked loss of appetite. She had an excellent record of health prior to a time approximately nine months before her admission. At that time, her left leg suddenly became paralyzed in school and she felt as if needles were pricking it. She was put to bed, and after a week in a local hospital, showed a partial recovery, although she continued to use crutches and lose weight.

Careful clinical examination showed that Kate displayed muscle twitches around her throat and chest but was able to use her left leg when lying down; therefore, organic disease was ruled out as a possible cause of her problem.

When given a psychological interview, Kate described the paralysis, lack of appetite, and other facts of her illness with intelligence and sensitivity, but she was unable to give any explanation for her problem. After considerable probing, she told a story of family conflict in which her mother fell in love with a roomer in the home, eloped, and numerous parental conflicts ensued. It was a terrifying experience for Kate. She was particularly terrified by the idea of strife and bitterness in her once happy home.

School was a welcome relief from this strain of her home life, but soon she became fearful in social situations. Her paralysis occurred one day right before recess. Apparently, the threat of social interaction and the potential conflict that might ensue led her to develop a paralysis that would allow her to remain in school but avoid the frightening possibility of social interaction.

After long discussions of the meaning of her symptoms, Kate showed a slow, but steady recovery from her paralysis and is now functioning normally in her home and school setting (Adapted from Pronko, 1963, pp. 169–71).

DSM III lists a number of criteria for distinguishing a conversion disorder from other disorders. Several are listed below. Examine them and decide whether you think Kate Fox was suffering from a conversion disorder or not.

- A loss or alteration of physical functioning suggesting a physical disorder.
- Psychological factors are judged to be etiologically involved in the symptom; that is, either temporal relationship between psychologically meaningful event and initiation of the symptom or symptom allows individual to avoid a noxious activity or symptom allows the individual to get support from the environment that otherwise would not be available.
- Symptom is *not* under voluntary control.
- Failure to explain symptom by a known physical disorder after investigation.

real organic disorders can, in some cases, help to trigger or suggest additional psychological complaints or pains. Thus, we must be careful to distinguish between psychologically induced conversion disorders and organic disorders that appear psychological in nature. It may be that many people who actually have organic or physical problems may have been diagnosed as conversion disorders and therefore did not receive proper treatment.

DISSOCIATIVE DISORDERS

Among the most fascinating and puzzling of neurotic conditions are the dissociative disorders. Consider the following four cases.

- Joseph L. woke up one morning in what appeared to be a strange place. He had no memory of who he was or who was lying in the bed next to him. He appeared bewildered and confused. He was suffering from a dissociative disorder, *amnesia.*
- Jackie, age nine, was found wandering in her nightgown down the sidewalk in front of her house by a policeman at 3:00 in the morning. The policeman approached her cautiously and woke her from what appeared to be a sound sleep. Her parents were unaware of her having left the house and were surprised to discover she had been sleep walking. She was suffering from a dissociative reaction called *somnambulism.*
- Steve L. had just taken on a challenging new job in a law firm. It had not been going well. One day, he disappeared from his apartment and did not report to work. Two weeks later, his parents, having hired a private detective agency, located him working as a dishwasher in a restaurant in a nearby city. He had no recollection of his previous identity and had been drifting from job to job. Steve L. was suffering from a dissociative disorder known as *fugue.*
- "Christine is a loving three year old who likes to draw pictures of flowers and butterflies. David is a withdrawn little boy who bangs his head against the wall when upset. Adelena is a young lesbian. These distinct personalities, along with at least seven others, presented a bizarre puzzle in a Columbus, Ohio courtroom: they all exist within the same individual—William Milligan, 23, who was accused of rape. Last week after a brief trial, the ten faces of Billy were found not guilty by reason of insanity" (Newsweek, December 18, 1978, p. 106). William Milligan is an apparent sufferer of a dissociative disorder known as *multiple personality.*

Each of these forms of dissociative disorder appear to involve a *splitting off or dissociation of one part of a person's experience from another.* Let us consider each of them in more detail.

Amnesia

A loss of memory with no organic involvement is one of the most common forms of dissociative disorders. Typically the person is unable to recall events or people which are associated with his or her own personal identity. Episodes of amnesia may last a few hours or days or in some cases weeks or months. When stopped by the police or interviewed by a mental health professional, the person may also appear to be dazed and mildly confused.

Victims of dissociative reactions

involving amnesia usually are experiencing intense emotional conflict or stress in their social, sexual, or economic life. They literally appear to be escaping from their distressing and conflict-ridden experience by forgetting who they are.

Fugue

In the case of fugue, which may be thought of as a special form of amnesia, victims not only forget their own identity and other significant events in their lives but actually flee their life circumstances. In many cases the person may move to another city some distance from home, and in some cases a secondary personality appears that has little or nothing to do with the person's previous life. The person may change his or her name and carry on an entirely new life-style for some period of time.

In one recorded case (Kisker, 1964), a 22-year-old man disappeared from his fishing boat in Florida and was assumed dead by his family. Six years later, he telephoned his brother to say that he had been working in a convalescent home in New Orleans as an orderly and suddenly remembered his name. He had no memory of what had transpired during the six years since he had left his home in Florida.

Somnambulism

In the DSM III, this disorder is considered a sleep disorder. However, it may also qualify as an example of the dissociative disorders. Typically, in the case of somnambulism, a person will get out of bed and perform some complex act while apparently asleep. The episode may only last a few minutes, and in most cases, at the end of the episode, if uninterrupted, the sleep walker will return to bed. Upon wakening, typically, a somnambulist has no recollection of the episode.

In children, somnambulism is not considered an indication of any serious psychological disturbance, whereas, in adults it may indicate a more serious disorder. Typically, somnambulists can be awakened without any danger but will normally be confused when they are awakened.

Multiple Personality

Perhaps the best-known form of dissociative disorder is that of multiple personality. We should note that in popular literature, this disorder is often confused with schizophrenia, but it is a very different disorder. Whereas multiple personality typically involves an alternation between two or more relatively well-defined personalities, schizophrenia refers to a much more severe psychotic disorder in which thought disorder, blunted affect, and severe reality distortion predominate.

The most famous case of multiple personality was documented in Thigpen and Cleckley's book *The Three Faces of Eve* (1954). In this case, Thigpen and Cleckley reported different personalities associated with "Eve White," the original personality, "Eve Black," who typically was flamboyant and uninhibited, and Eve White, a much more quiet, inhibited, and serious person who appeared very different from the other two personalities.

Eve White began to suspect that something was going on when Eve Black would engage in carefree spending, promiscuity, and drinking that later Eve White would have to account for. During her treatment, a third personality called

Though extremely rare, cases of multiple personality have been documented in recent years.

Jean-Claude Lejeune

"Jane" emerged who was aware of the activities and personality of both Eve White and Eve Black. Finally, a fourth personality developed which seemed more stable than either of the three earlier versions.

More recently, Jeans (1976) has documented a case of multiple personality in very great detail. Jeans, who had treated this person in therapy for some time, was able to document the strikingly different personalities that emerged as "Gena," "Mary," and "Evelyn." Subsequent to Jeans's discovery and documentation of this case, Osgood, Luria, and Smith (1976) attempted to do a blind analysis and interpretation of the strikingly different personalities displayed by Gena, through data collected using the semantic differential.

When Osgood, Luria, and Smith (1976) attempted to do a careful analysis and interpretation of these semantic differential reports collected by Jeans, they found surprising concurrence between Jeans' clinical reports and their own interpretations.

What are the possible determinants of multiple personality? In almost all documented cases, there has been severe conflict and unhappiness in the life of the person suffering from the disorder. The emergence of the different ego states seems to be an attempt to cope and adapt to conflicting impulses and life circumstances and stands in marked contrast to the subtle and complex adaptations most of us make to changing circumstances and needs. The multiple personality seems to be an "all or nothing" shift in an attempt to accommodate to new demands, impulses, and needs that the person experiences.

A NEO-DISSOCIATION THEORY OF DISSOCIATIVE AND CONVERSION REACTIONS

Are there psychological threads that hold the dissociative reactions and conversion reactions together? New research and theory by Ernest Hilgard, reported in his book *Divided Consciousness: Multiple Control in Human Thought and Action,* give us some clues to the possible underlying dimensions of these apparently puzzling forms of psychological disorder. In fact, Hilgard goes much farther and suggests an interpretation of psychological functioning that ties together such disparate phenomena as possession states, fugues, multiple personality, hypnosis, amnesia, automatic writing, conversion reactions, and others.

He begins his argument by reminding us that the study of normal personality has been kept apart from that of the study of the abnormal for reasons which have to do with the social history of science rather than scientific logic. Abnormal psychology, Hilgard reminds us, remains largely a human psychology, and that the principles of learning and cognition discovered in the laboratory should be equally applicable to the phenomena of abnormal behavior.

Hilgard also reminds us that the "unity of consciousness is illusory. Man does more than one thing at a time—all the time—and the conscious representation of these actions is never complete. His awareness can shift from one aspect of whatever is currently happening inside his body or impinging on him from without, or events that are remembered or imagined. Furthermore, as an active agent, he is always making decisions and formulating or implementing plans, and he likes to believe that he exerts control over what he is doing; often however, he may be deceived about the causes of his behavior" (p. 1).

Drawing on his extensive experimental work in the area of hypnosis, Hilgard suggests that even when the hypnotic subject is apparently unaware of what is going on around him because of hypnotic suggestion, there is a part of consciousness, which Hilgard calls the "hidden observer," that continues to monitor external circumstances and later can report on what was going on. The metaphor of the "hidden observer" is Hilgard's way of describing what experimental psychologists have called *parallel processing* in which conscious cognitive events tend to be divided into executive functions (where decisions are made) and monitoring functions (where we continue to observe events even when we are not overtly aware of doing so).

Thus attention is divided all the time in our everyday functioning, argues Hilgard. It may be that many of the apparently puzzling events of conversion reactions and dissociations represent extreme forms of divided attention. The value of Hilgard's explanation is that it ties many of the clinical phenomena of conversion disorders and dissociative reactions to the phenomena of mainstream experimental psychology.

SOME NEW EVIDENCE FOR THE ORIGINS OF NEUROTIC DISORDERS

Recently Silverman (1976) has reviewed a series of laboratory studies pointing to evidence for the relationship between neurotic symptoms and unconscious wishes that suggests that psychoanalytic theory may have explanatory power to help us understand the origins of a variety of anxiety, somatoform, and dissociative disorders.

You will recall from our discussion in Chapter 3 that, according to the dynamic perspective, abnormal behavior develops as a reaction to the conflict between forbidden id impulses and ego-oriented operations to ward off these wishes and impulses using a variety of defense mechanisms. When these defensive operations are successful, few maladaptive consequences occur. But when they are unsuccessful, anxiety and other pathological phenomena, including phobias, conversion reactions, and obsessions, are assumed to emerge.

Silverman (1976) notes that conducting laboratory experiments to confirm these hypotheses is particularly difficult since, "one must attempt to manipulate an unconscious wish and observe the consequences of the manipulations on psychopathology" (p. 624). One strategy for dealing with this problem is to induce conflictual impulses hypnotically. This strategy has been used by Reyher and his associates (Reyher, 1967).

The method is essentially as follows. Relatively normal college students without any clear psychological disturbance are hypnotized and provided with a false memory of a made-up story. The false memory is designed to activate certain unacceptable impulses, such as Oepidal sexual desires. After this, a posthypnotic suggestion is given so that when the subject awakens certain words associated with the memory will lead the subject to have the impulses to express the forbidden feelings.

After the hypnotic trance and posthypnotic suggestion have been given, the person is awakened and presented with a series of words, some of which have been carefully associated with the hypnotic experience. After the words are presented, the subject is simply asked "how are you doing?" and their reactions are recorded and scored to test for the appearance of neurotic symptoms. The following hypnotically induced memory and posthypnotic suggestion provide an example of the procedure.

> One evening while you were out for a leisurely walk, your attention was drawn to an attractive, older woman who seemed quite upset. She had lost her purse and did not have money for her bus fare. Wishing to help the woman, you took out your wallet, but discovered that you only had a $10 bill. Still wanting to help, you offered to accompany her to the bus stop and pay her fare. She, however, insisted that you accompany her to her apartment in order that she might repay you. You agreed, although somewhat reluctantly. Once within her apartment, she suggested that you might find some money. There were pieces of brass, gold, lead, steel, tin, platinum, bronze, iron, copper, silver, chromium, and other kinds of metal. If you saw all of these as I mentioned them, raise your right hand. You also remember seeing some coins. There was a penny, a dollar, a nickel, a peso, a pound, one cent, a mill, a quarter, a dime, a shilling, a farthing, a franc, assorted coins, cash, and other kinds of money. If you saw all of these as I mentioned them,

raise your right hand. When she returned, she seemed very friendly and was reluctant to have you leave. After talking about the collection, she offered you a drink and snack. She then turned on the record player and invited you to dance. Gradually you became aware of some stimulating, but disquieting, thoughts and feelings. She was very good looking, and it seemed like such a pity to have all her beautiful softness and curves go to waste. She seemed to be silently inviting you by her physical closeness, glances, and words. Her heavy breathing indicated that she was becoming extremely aroused sexually. You were just starting to make love to her when it occurred to you that she was older, respectable, perhaps married, and undoubtedly, very experienced. You wondered if you would be able to satisfy her, and thought of how traumatic it would be if she laughed at your advances. In spite of these thoughts, you found yourself becoming increasingly excited and aroused. You wanted to make love to her right there, but the telephone rang. While you waited, you became so aroused and excited that you could hardly speak. You made a hurried excuse for leaving, promised to call her back and left the apartment. Later you learned that the only way you could attain peace of mind was to completely push the whole experience into the back of your mind.

The posthypnotic suggestion was the following:

Now listen carefully. The woman I have told you about actually works in this laboratory. In fact, you will meet her briefly later on. [That did not actually happen.] After you are awakened, you will not be able to remember anything about this session. However, sexual feelings will well up inside of you, whenever words associated with money or metal are mentioned. You will realize that the sexual feelings are directed toward the woman you will see shortly and you will want to tell me how you would like to express these feelings toward her" (From Silverman, 1976, p. 631).

A number of studies have been carried out by Reyher and his associates using this general experimental method. As Silverman (1976) observes, "In each of these investigations, a large number of symptoms were reported by the great majority of hypnotized subjects (75 percent or more) in whom the paramesia (hypnotic memory) was implanted. These symptoms have included disturbances of the autonomic nervous system (feelings of nausea, headaches, tachycardia, sweating, etc.); disturbances of the somatic and muscular nervous systems (stiffness, pains, tremors, etc.); disturbances of affect (lack of feeling, feelings of guilt, shame, disgust, etc.); states of confusion and disorientations; and dissociative reactions (limbs feeling detached, compulsive urges, etc.)" (p. 631). These subjects have been followed carefully and debriefed so that symptoms evoked do not continue beyond the laboratory session. Silverman argues that these studies "support the view that the activation of aggressive and libidinal mental contents can stimulate pathology" (p. 632).

We noted in Chapter 2 and Chapter 3 that the dynamic view of abnormal behavior, developed by Freud and his colleagues, first focused on the symptoms of neurotic disorders and suggested that their origins lay in unconscious conflicts. This research suggests that relatively recent efforts to bring these phenomena into the laboratory provides provocative support for the dynamic view of the development of neurotic symptoms. However, we should note that the "symptoms" produced in this study resemble only superficially the ingrained, disabling behavior patterns of neurotic disorders.

TREATMENT STRATEGIES

The treatment of anxiety, somatoform, and dissociative disorders has been undertaken using a wide variety of methods, including individual and group psychotherapy (Chapters 16 and 19), the prescription of tranquilizing drugs (Chapter 18), and behavioral techniques (Chapter 17).

In our current discussion we will focus narrowly on several methods of treating specific anxiety related complaints, including phobias, obsessions, and compulsions.

Marks has described a dual process framework for the behavioral treatment of neurotic disorders which is shown in Figure 6–4).

According to this framework, the client first must be motivated to seek and complete treatment. The variables affecting this process of seeking and completing treatment include the clients' commitment of change, social pressure, suggestion, therapists credibility, and other factors. The second process involves therapeutic actions executed by the patient that lead to his or her improvement. This may involve a few hours of exposure to a phobic stimulus, or even a complex interaction with others in a social training program. The important point is that the person must, according to Marks' framework, actually *execute* these actions in order for therapeutic influences to be maximized.

The Principle of Exposure

You will recall from our discussion of phobias earlier in the chapter that Marks described what he called the *evoking*

FIGURE 6–4 Therapeutic Influences: An Operational Framework

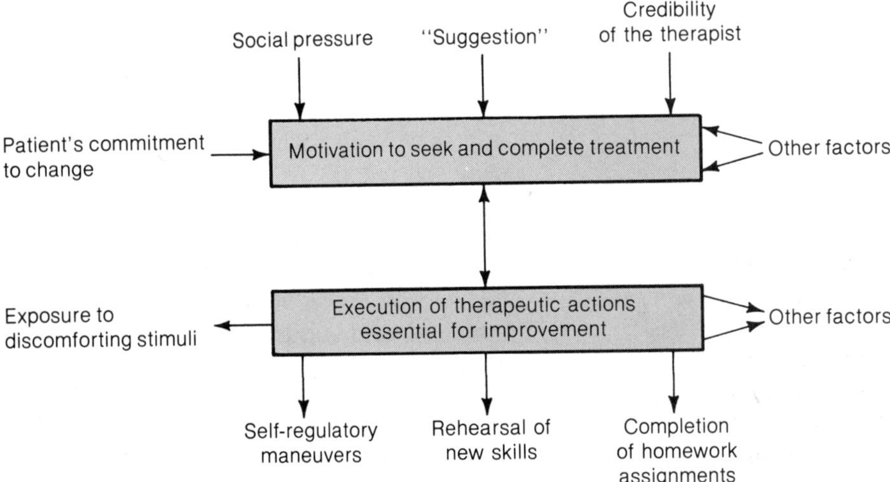

Source: I. Marks, "Behavioral Psychotherapy of Adult Neurosis." In S. L. Garfield and A. E. Bergin (eds.), *Handbook of Psychotherapy and Behavior Change: An Empirical Analysis*, 2d ed. (New York: Wiley, 1978), p. 497.

stimlulus as the critical factor in identifying the development of phobias. In essence, the principle of exposure in treatment argues that relief from phobias and compulsions occurs when the person suffering from them maintains continued contact with those situations that evoke discomfort until the discomfort subsides (Marks, 1977).

Marks goes on to argue that most behavioral approaches to the treatment of anxiety syndromes employ the principle of exposure in one form or another regardless of the specific technique. Of course, the exposure principle does not explain why improvement occurs but only indicates the strategy which the therapist must follow.

> "*Clinicians need to search for the E.S.—those cues that trigger phobias and rituals—and to persuade the patient to come into contact with these cues until he or she is comfortable in their presence.* The noxious stimulus may be a troublesome fantasy, a feeling of insecurity, a shopping expedition, or sexual contact.
>
> Once situations repeatedly produce discomfort, as in phobias and obsessions, then sufferers usually lose this discomfort by agreeing to remain exposed to those situations until they feel better about them" (Marks, 1978, p. 499 authors italics).

Marks offers us results of several studies that seem to support his claim that the principle of exposure is the most important in the reduction of a variety of different types of anxiety-related complaints. For example, Figure 6–5 shows the effects of psychotherapy (P), pseudotherapy (RP), the exposure of clients to a hierarchy of anxiety-provoking events (H), and systematic desensitization (SD). It can be seen that the exposure to the anxiety-provoking elements appears to be the major factor in effective treatment, and that whether or not relaxation accompanies treatment is irrelevant.

Similarly, the results shown in Figure 6–6 compare two methods of exposing clients to frightening events in fantasy and a control condition. The study produced marked effects in both of the exposure conditions when compared with the control condition. As Marks notes, "It is thus clear that phobias and obsessions improve with exposure treatment, but it is not crucial whether patients are relaxed, neutral or anxious during such exposure."

CONSUMER CHOICE IN TREATMENT

Marks (1978) has argued that the evidence is now strong for the value of certain behavioral methods in treating some narrowly defined neurotic behavior patterns such as chronic, phobic, or obsessive-compulsive disorders. Furthermore, he suggests one could actually question the ethics of giving other approaches of dubious effectiveness to clients for these particular problems. "Eyebrows might be similarly raised by the withholding of antidepressant drugs . . . for severe depression or phenothiazines for florid schizophrenia" (p. 538).

If the client defines the goal of treatment as the reduction of phobias or obsessive-compulsive rituals, than inert or expensive procedures might be considered unethical.

If, on the other hand, the client is told that the aim of long-term treatment is the development of increased self-awareness, but that the specific problems are not likely to be improved as a result, then the offer of long-term therapy for certain clearly defined neurotic disorders would not be unethical.

As Marks observes,

> The time has come where our knowledge of treatment effects is sufficiently sound to be able to offer certain patients an informed choice. As an example, a compulsive ritualizer might be told that with up to 20 sessions of behavioral exposure, in vivo, he or she has a good chance of losing most of the compulsive rituals, though wider aspects of his or her personality function will not be touched; alternatively, the patient could have intensive psychotherapy aimed at heightening self-awareness, but in all likelihood, leaving him or her with the same rituals as before. It is then up to the patient, the consumer, to decide according to what he or she wants out of treatment (p. 539).

Obviously, Marks is an advocate for the behavioral approach to treatment and others might argue about whether the evidence is yet as strong as he suggests for the differential effects of certain approaches to treatment. Whether he is correct or not, the general question remains: should the psychotherapist be in a position to tell his or her client what methods are most likely to be effective for a particular problem? Does the therapist have an obligation to tell the client beforehand what to expect from treatment and how long it will take?

FIGURE 6–5 Treatment Results in Patients with Phobias.

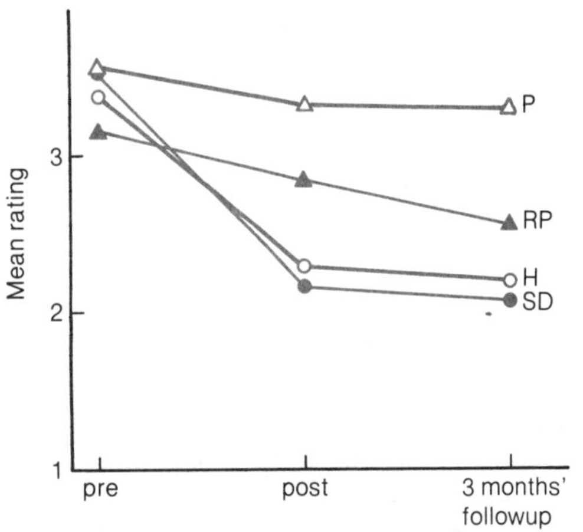

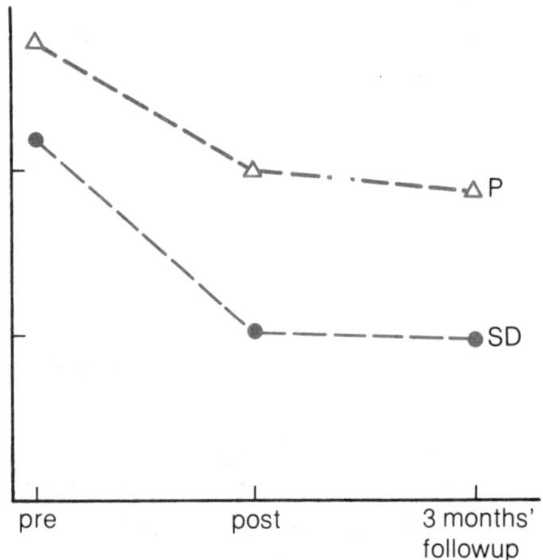

P = Psychotherapy
RP = Pseudotherapy
H = Hierarchies (i.e. SD without relaxation)
SD = Systematic Desensitisation in fantasy

Source: I. Marks, "Behavioral Psychotherapy of Adult Neurosis." In S. L. Garfield and A. E. Bergin (eds.), Handbook of Psychotherapy and Behavior Change: An Empirical Analysis, 2d ed. (New York: Wiley, 1978), p. 501.

FIGURE 6–6

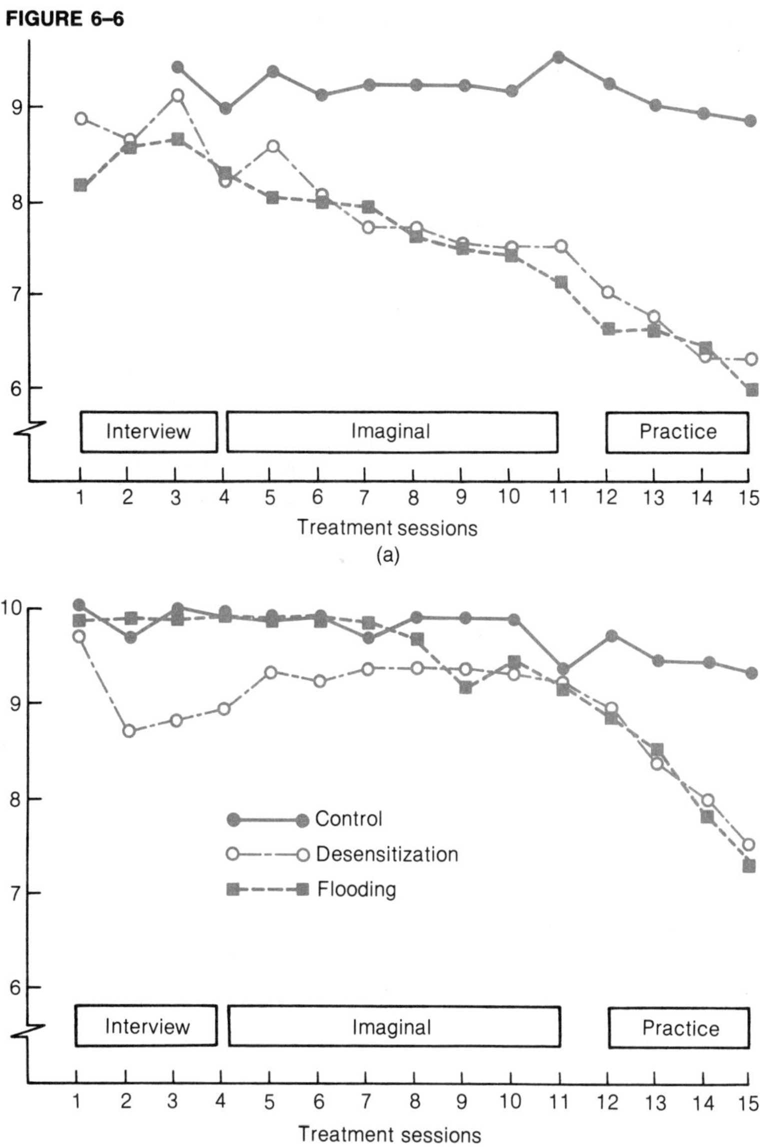

(a) Mean scores for anxiety "when thinking about" phobic situations for each treatment group.

(b) Mean scores of anxiety estimated for phobic situations 'in real life' for each treatment group.

Source: I. Marks, "Behavioral Psychotherapy of Adult Neurosis." In S. L. Garfield and A. E. Bergin (eds.), Handbook of Psychotherapy and Behavior Change: An Empirical Analysis, 2d ed. (New York: Wiley, 1978), p. 503.

Let us return to Marks' overall framework for the treatment of neurotic or anxiety-related disorders. Essentially these results suggest that if it is possible to motivate a client to be committed to change then this is a necessary but not sufficient condition for behavior change itself. The second crucial component is that the person actually carries out activities that allow him to be exposed to the evoking stimulus until tolerance develops. Marks notes that exposure itself might be acting by encouraging clients to develop their own particular self-management or coping strategies in the face of discomfort, although this particular hypothesis is difficult to test rigorously.

Treatment of Obsessional Slowness

In their program of research on obsessions and compulsions, Rachman and Hodgson (1980) had occasion to treat a number of patients experiencing various obsessive and compulsive difficulties. In working with people displaying obsessional slowness, they developed a technique which they called "prompting, shaping, and pacing." Essentially a

FIGURE 6–7 Treatment Progress with One Aspect of S. N.'s Obsessional Slowness, Cleaning His Teeth. Large Early Improvements Were Followed by Slower and Smaller Changes, Interspersed with Plateaus.

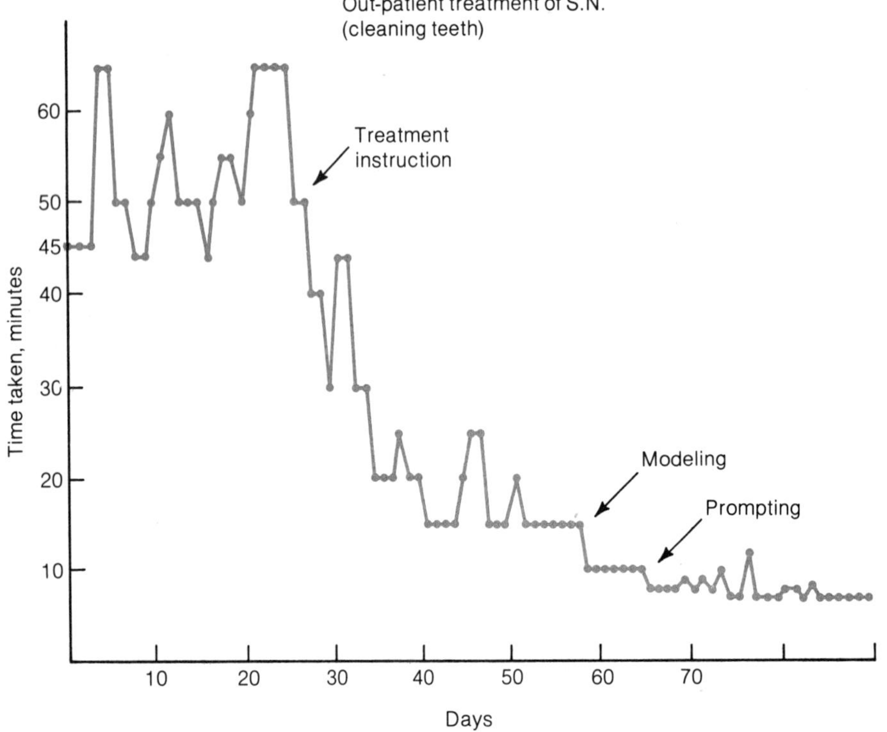

Source: S. J. Rachman and R. J. Hodgson, *Obsessions and Compulsions* (Englewood Cliffs, N. J.: Prentice-Hall), © 1980, p. 229. Reprinted by permission of Prentice-Hall, Inc.

behavioral approach to treatment, the method consisted of providing instructions and modeling for appropriate behavior, shaping instructions to encourage improvement and to discourage errors, and some form of external pacing of behavior.

An example of this treatment technique is shown in Figure 6–7. The patient, S. N., was a 38-year-old man suffering from severe obsessional slowness. He had been admitted to psychiatric hospitals in the past and was hoping to attain greater control over his daily tasks. At the beginning of treatment, the patient was taking approximately three hours each morning to prepare himself for work. The results of treatment instruction for one aspect of S. N.'s problem, cleaning his teeth is shown in Figure 6–7.

A second patient had experienced repeated admissions to the hospital for a 20-year-period and had been taking up to eight hours to prepare himself for work. The authors report that each aspect of his obsessional slowness needed to be treated separately, using essentially the same prompting, shaping, and pacing

FIGURE 6–8 The Effects of Treatment on T. N., a Chronic and Severely Incapacitated Obsessional Patient.

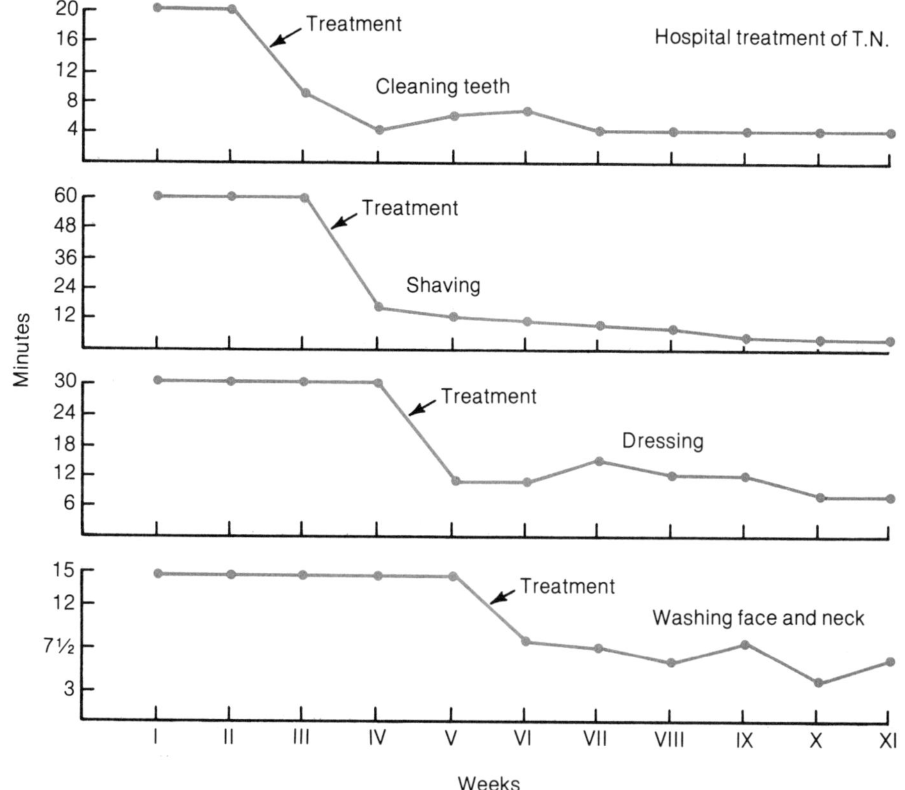

Source: S. J. Rachman and R. J. Hodgson, *Obsessions and Compulsions* (Englewood Cliffs, N.J.: Prentice-Hall), © 1980, p. 230. Reprinted by permission of Prentice-Hall, Inc.

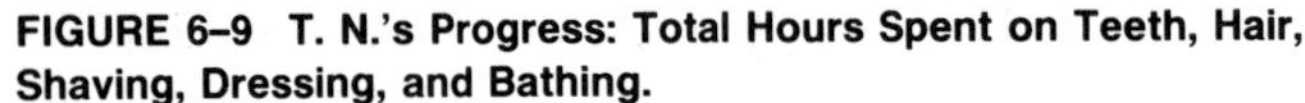

FIGURE 6–9 T. N.'s Progress: Total Hours Spent on Teeth, Hair, Shaving, Dressing, and Bathing.

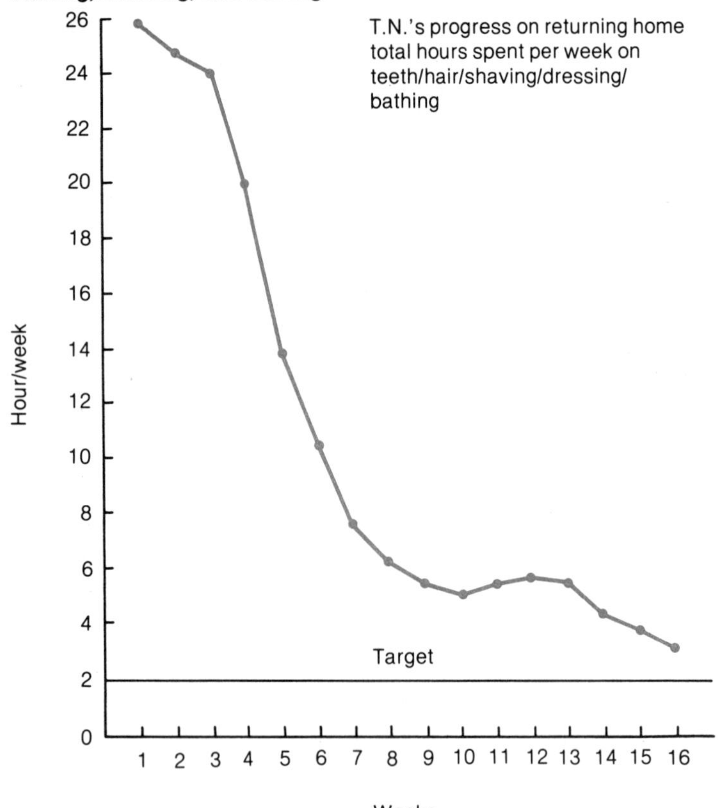

Source: S. J. Rachman and R. J. Hodgson, *Obessions and Compulsions* (Englewood Cliffs, N.J.: Prentice-Hall), © 1980, p. 231. Reprinted by permission of Prentice-Hall, Inc.

method. Results of that treatment are shown in Figures 6–8 and 6–9. This patient ultimately returned home and to full employment although he required several "booster" treatments during a four-year follow-up period.

These examples show that obsessional slowness can be a socially crippling disorder, but that with proper treatment it can be controlled, returning the person to a productive personal and occupational life.

SUMMARY

In this chapter we have taken a broad ranging look at psychological disorders characterized by anxiety, specific physical complaints, and disassociated psychological states.

According to DSM III, phobias and obsessive-compulsive reactions are the two major types of anxiety disorders. Phobias are characterized by intense fears of specific objects or situations. Obsessions involve persistent repeated thoughts that the individual is unable to avoid while compulsions, which often occur with obsessions, consist of fixed stereotyped patterns of behavior that are repeated again and again in an attempt to reduce anxiety about a particular fear or concern. We have noted that both of these types of anxiety disorders appear to be effectively treated by behavioral methods, particularly those methods that adhere to the principle of stimulus exposure.

Our discussion of somatoform disorders led us to note that these types of disorders can take two distinctively different forms. On the one hand, continuous preoccupation about physical health can be socially crippling, whereas conversion disorders involve some form of physical impairment such as paralysis or anesthesia but with no known organic basis. The symptoms prominent in conversion disorders may either be sensory, involving a loss of vision or hearing, or motor, involving a loss of movement or the development of paralysis.

Finally, we discussed several forms of dissociative disorders in which there appears to be a splitting off or dissociation of one part of the person's experience from another. These disorders include amnesia, involving a loss of memory with no organic involvement; fugue, in which the person actually flees life circumstances as well as forgets his or her identity; and some somnambulism or sleepwalking. Finally, multiple personalities in which several distinctive personality patterns appear to emerge and alternate with one another in a single individual.

In examining the determinants of neurotic symptoms, we reviewed biological, social learning, and dynamic points of view. In particular, we noted that recent evidence for the biological preparedness of phobic behaviors is gaining increasing acceptance. At the same time, new evidence from the laboratory supporting the possible dynamic origins of neurotic symptoms suggests that the dynamic perspective is mounting a new challenge to learning theories of the development of neurotic disorders. Thus we see evidence from a number of different points in the human context suggesting a broad range of biological, psychological, and social origins of neurotic disorders.

Although these disorders were all once grouped together as *neuroses,* the increasing acceptance of new diagnostic schemes, such as DSM III, and the specific nature of each of these patterns of behavior suggest that in the future they will probably be studied separately.

7

Affective Disorders and Suicide: Description and Classification

INTRODUCTION

Imagine, for a moment, that you are a clinical psychologist interviewing someone who has just come to you for help. The young man sitting across from you finds it hard to talk about what is bothering him. At first his conversation was animated, but now as he continues to talk his voice flattens into a monotone. His face loses its expression and becomes mask-like, suggesting the despair below the surface.

As the hour goes on, you begin to get a picture of his life. He maintains a pleasant, active facade only at great personal cost. Even the simplest activities, like dressing or driving to work, have become enormous acts of will. He reports difficulty sleeping, and, unaccountably, he wakes before dawn each day. Frequently at night this man withdraws into his apartment, refusing to answer the telephone. He lies listlessly for hours in front of the television set. Lately, he reports, he has begun to think about suicide.

As you listen to him you are struck by several things. His mood is obviously downcast and occasionally tears well up in his eyes. His thinking seems pessimistic and he frequently talks about himself in a disparaging way. The stains on his suit and his rumpled appearance suggest that he no longer cares as much as he once did about his appearance. The bagginess of his suit also suggests that he has lost a fair amount of weight recently. His world is gray and bleak, not very promising.

As you sit there, listening, you begin to notice your own reactions to his man. First you notice your own mood. The world seems less exciting to you, too, now, and you feel somewhat depressed. As time goes on you begin to feel some mild irritation with this person. His apparent inability to "shake off" his feeling of sadness and his lack of response to your encouragements are frustrating and vaguely annoying.

You have just interviewed a person suffering from the typical symptoms of a moderately severe depression. Depression has been called the "common cold" of psychological disorders, and over a quarter of a million Americans are hospitalized for the disorder each year. The chances are about one in five that each of us will suffer at least one severe depression during our lifetime. Students, musicians, laborers, physicists, clerks, psychiatrists, and housewives all are subject to depression. Lincoln and Hemingway, F. Scott Fitzgerald and Sylvia Plath all suffered from severe depression.

Return to your clinician's chair again and consider another man. You are jolted by the fact that the person now in your office seems filled with almost boundless energy. He cannot stay in his chair and paces up and down. He is gesturing as he talks about his plans for the future. His speech is rapid and filled with puns and jokes. He winks at you occasionally. This man seems to have no problems at all. On the contrary, he is filled with optimistic plans for the future. As you listen you discover that he is a salesman at a local automobile dealership and has decided to open his own agency. He has simultaneously borrowed money from at least four different banks, has rented a large warehouse, and hired a number of salesmen for his agency. As you listen, you are astonished to hear that even though this agency is not yet open for business, he is now planning to develop a statewide network of automobile dealerships.

At several points you try to interrupt his seemingly endless flow of speech to ask some questions. But he brushes the questions aside and becomes mildly annoyed when you ask him why he is consulting you. Finally, you discover that his wife, who is very distressed at his current behavior, has convinced him to see a clinician because he has plunged his family deeply into debt. Slowly, as the interview proceeds, you notice that his rapid speech reveals sudden changes in the content of his thoughts. This flight of ideas makes it hard to follow his line of thought, but clearly he sees himself as a perceptive, powerful, and engaging person. His energy seems endless and at the end of fifty minutes you are at a loss as to how to terminate the interview.

Reflecting on your own feelings and reactions to this man, you begin to feel sympathy for his family, who must struggle not to be swept up in his barrage of projects, ideas, schemes, and sudden shifts of interest. You sympathize, too, with his wife's concerns about his apparently thoughtless squandering of their financial resources. His wife reports that he has slept only an hour or two a night for the last ten days and yet he seems as full of energy as ever.

This person is displaying what is known as a *manic episode.* As we shall see, the extremely intense level of motor activity, sleeplessness, boundless energy, and grandiose ideas that characterize a manic episode are a second important form of affective disorder. The two cases seem in some ways to be polar opposites. And yet, as we shall see in this and the next chapter, there may be common threads that bind these two apparently different disorders together. In both instances we will be trying to make sense of behavior that involves the *affect* or emotional tone of the individual.

In this chapter we will consider several approaches to the description and classification of *affective disorders.* In addition, we will examine the act of suicide* which is sometimes, but not invariably, associated with affective disturbance.

CLASSIFICATION OF AFFECTIVE DISORDERS: DSM III

According to the DSM III, the essential feature of affective disorders is *a primary disturbance in mood* accompanied by a variety of related symptoms. Mood refers

* The authors wish to thank Howard Beazel for providing some of the background research material for the section on suicide.

to a prolonged emotion that colors the entire psychological life of the individual and, in the case of the affective disorders, generally involves either elation or depression.

DSM III divides the affective disorders into three general groups: (1) the episodic affective disorders, which involve a sustained disturbance that we can clearly distinguish from a previous level of functioning, (2) the chronic affective disorders that are long standing and have no clear onset and, finally (3) the atypical affective disorders, which involve some mood disturbance but are not easily classified elsewhere. In our discussion we will focus on the episodic affective disorders. These are clear-cut changes in functioning that can be most easily distinguished from personality disorders.

The episodic affective disorders are further subclassified into three major groups. There are (1) *manic episodes,* involving a distinct period when the person's mood is elevated, (2) *major depressive episodes* in which the predominant mood is depression, and (3) *bipolar episodes* in which elation and depressions alternate or exist simultaneously. Let us now examine each of these major subtypes of affective disorders in more detail.

Manic Episodes

Clinical picture. As we suggested earlier, the essential feature of a manic episode is a distinct period in the person's life when their mood becomes elevated and expansive. Frequently a person suffering from a manic episode will appear hyperactive and excessively involved in activities with no apparent concern for the consequences to others. The person will feel euphoric and appear excessively cheerful. This quality can alternate with periods of irritability, particularly when the person's goals are frustrated. Frequently the person will be involved in extensive and sometimes grandiose planning of occupational, sexual, religious, or political activities.

Such persons are often quite sociable and extroverted in their appearance. DSM III suggests, "Almost invariably there is increased sociability such as renewing old acquaintances or calling friends at all hours of the night. The intrusive, domineering, and demanding nature of these interactions is not recognized by the individual. Frequently expansiveness, grandiosity, lack of judgment regarding possible consequences lead to such activities as buying sprees, reckless·driving, foolish business investments, and sexual behavior unusual for the individual. Often the activities have a disorganized, flamboyant or bizarre quality, for example, dressing up in strange, colorful garments, wearing excessive or poorly applied makeup and distributing bread, candy, money, and advice to passing strangers." (DSM III, 1980, p. 206).

These behavior patterns are often accompanied by speech that is loud, rapid, and sometimes difficult to interpret. People experiencing manic episodes frequently appear very witty and are fond of puns, jokes, and plays on words. In addition, the manic individual may be easily distracted by irrelevant events in his or her environment. The person will also often display an uncritical self-confidence. Ambitious projects will be taken on and a person experiencing a manic episode will feel no reluctance to offer advice to anyone who will listen. Sleep disturbances is also a characteristic of manic episodes and during the episode the individual may go for several days without sleep or wake well before his usual time, full of energy.

Manic episodes may begin before the age of 30 and typically begin with a rapid increase in symptoms over the period of a few days. Some people appear to have episodes separated by many years and then have a cluster or series of episodes, one following rapidly after the other.

A manic episode can produce several problems in social and occupational functioning and substance abuse may accompany a manic episode. Because the individual's judgment is impaired, he may also incur financial losses or run into trouble with the law. The actual proportion of the

MANIC EPISODE

Fieve (1976), in a recent book on affective disorders, quotes one of his patients, a 45-year-old housewife, who describes her manic depressive moodswing.

> When I start going into a high, I no longer feel like an ordinary housewife. Instead I feel organized and accomplished and I begin to feel I am my most creative self. I can write poetry easily. I can compose melodies without effort. I can paint. My mind feels facile and absorbs everything. I have countless ideas about improving the conditions of mentally retarded children, of how a hospital for these children should be run, what they should have around them to keep them happy and calm and unafraid. I see myself as being able to accomplish a great deal for the good of people. I have countless ideas about how the environment problem could inspire a crusade for the health and betterment of everyone. I feel able to accomplish a great deal for the good of my family and others. I feel pleasure, a sense of euphoria or elation. I want it to last forever. I don't seem to need much sleep. I've lost weight and feel healthy and I like myself. I've just bought six new dresses, in fact, and they look quite good on me. I feel sexy and men stare at me. Maybe I'll have an affair, or perhaps several. I feel capable of speaking and doing good in politics. I would like to help people with problems similar to mine so they won't feel hopeless.
>
> It's wonderful when you feel like this. . . . The feeling of exhilaration—the high mood—makes me feel light and full of the joy of living. However, when I go beyond this stage, I become manic, and the creativeness becomes so magnified I begin to see things in my mind that aren't real. For instance, one night I created an entire movie, complete with cast, that I still think would be terrific. I saw the people as clearly as if watching them in real life. I also experienced complete terror, as if it were actually happening, when I knew that an assassination scene was about to take place. I cowered under the covers and became a complete shaking wreck. As you know, I went into a manic psychosis at that point. My screams awakened my husband, who tried to reassure me that we were in our bedroom and everything was the same. There was nothing to be afraid of. Nevertheless, I was admitted to the hospital the next day (Fieve, 1976, pp. 17–18).

population experiencing manic disorders is not known. It is a relatively rare phenomenon when occurring without a depressive mood swing following it.

A person experiencing a manic episode may not really be said to be suffering since the experience is one of elation. Box 7–1 offers a first-person account of what it feels like to experience a manic episode.

Diagnostic criteria. Table 7–1 shows the current DSM III diagnostic criteria for a manic episode. The DSM III not only describes the episode and its characteristics, as in Table 7–1, but also attempts to rule out schizophrenic-like symptoms and organic disorders.

Manic episodes are also rated according to their severity in DSM III from "moderate" through "marked" severity involving social impairment, to "severe" levels of the disorders in which meaningful conversation is not possible, through "psychotic" levels of severity when the person is also experiencing delusions or hallucinations.

TABLE 7–1 DSM III Diagnostic Criteria for a Manic Episode

A. One or more distinct periods in which the person's mood is elevated, either expansive or irritable
B. At least four of the following symptoms must also be present:
   1. More active than usual, socially, physically or occupationally
   2. More talkative than usual or experiencing a pressure to continue talking
   3. A subjective experience that one's thoughts are racing or "flight of ideas"
   4. Inflated self-esteem
   5. Decreased need for sleep
   6. Distractability
   7. High involvement in activities without recognizing their potential negative consequences including buying sprees, sexual indiscretions, foolish business investment, or reckless driving.

Major Depressive Episodes

Clinical picture. The essential feature of depressive episodes is a depressed mood or a generalized feeling of a loss of interest or pleasure in the world. In addition, the person may experience a sleep disturbance, feel unable to eat, lose weight, have feeling of decreased energy and a subjective sense of worthlessness or guilt. At times some depressed people have thoughts of death or suicide.

Often, a person experiencing a depressive episode will begin to withdraw from family and friends and may appear agitated. The person may ceaselessly pace, wring his or her hands, and pull at the skin or hair or clothing.

The depressed person often reports feeling unable to concentrate, that his or her thinking is slowed and that he (she) are unable to act decisively. At times even the smallest task may seem difficult or impossible. In severe cases the person will burst into tears without warning, become extremely preoccupied with

Depression can be particularly incapacitating for older people.

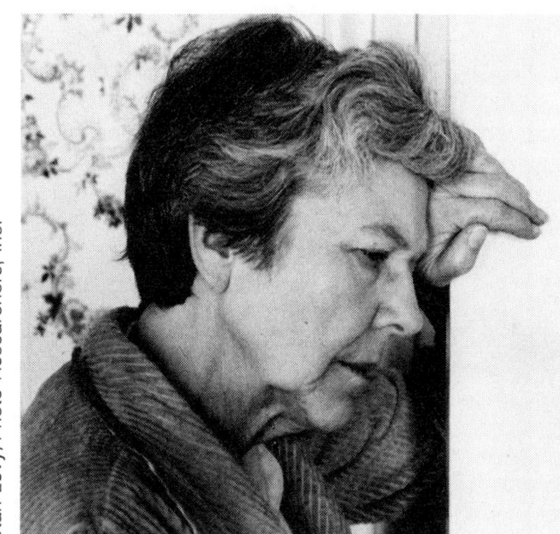

Stan Levy/Photo Researchers, Inc.

physical health or his or her financial status.

Diagnostic criteria. The DSM III diagnostic criteria for a depressed episode are shown in Table 7–2.

As is the case for manic episodes, the DSM III criteria require that at least one week from the time of the first noticeable change in the person's usual condition occurs before one can diagnose a depressive episode. And, as with the manic episode, the critiera require that schizophrenic or organic disorders be ruled out.

Unlike the manic disorders, however, depressive disorders can begin at any age, including childhood. The symptoms may develop gradually over days or weeks or be relatively sudden in onset.

TABLE 7–2 DSM III Symptom Criteria for a Depressive Episode

A. Loss of interest or pleasure in nearly all activities or past times. Dysphoric mood that is characterized as depressed, sad, blue, hopeless, etc.
   Does not include rapid mood shifts and must be prominent in the behavior pattern
B. At least four of the following symptoms are required for the diagnosis of a depressive symptom:
   1. Poor appetite or weight loss, or increased appetite or weight gain
   2. Sleeping too much or too little
   3. Feelings of fatigue, tiredness, and loss of energy
   4. Agitation or actual physical slowing down of behavior
   5. Loss of interest or pleasure in usual activity or decrease in sexual motivation
   6. Feelings of inappropriate guilt or self-blame
   7. Complaint of a decreased ability to think or concentrate or other indications of indecisiveness
   8. Recurring thoughts of suicide or death, or any suicidal behavior including the wish to be dead.

The degree to which a depressive episode can impair the functioning of the person can be quite variable, but some interference almost always is noted. In the most extreme cases, a person may be unable to feed or cloth himself or herself, function socially, or even take care of personal health needs. As we will see, the most serious complication of depressive episodes is suicide, and the likelihood of serious suicidal attempts increases with age.

Epidemiological studies indicate that18 to 23 percent of the females in western countries will experience a depressive episode at some time in their life, whereas approximately 8 to 11 percent of the males will experience such an episode (DSM III, p. 217).

Unitary versus typological approaches to the description of depression. For some years scientists conducting research on depressive affective disorders have been divided on whether there is only one type of depression that varies in severity, or two types of depression that are distinctively different from one another. Advocates of the latter view have offered distinctions such as *neurotic* versus *psychotic* depression and *endogenous* versus *exogenous* depression. As we have seen, the DSM III does not distinguish two types of depression, but rates each case in terms of its severity. However, not all researchers agree with this single-depression approach.

The importance of the controversy involves more than a desire for neat classification systems. If there really are two depressions rather than just one, it may mean that these two distinctly different types of disorder have different sets of causes and require different treatments. On the other hand, if depression is a unitary phenomenon

Young adults and children may suffer from depression which goes unrecognized.

Jean-Claude Lejeune

varying only in severity, the most reasonable assumption is that there is a single set of causes and that a single treatment is more appropriate. Thus, both our strategies for attempting to discover the causes of depression and our treatment strategy could be strongly affected by whether or not one or two depressions exist.

Recently a number of researchers have attempted to resolve the controversy. Their approach has been largely statistical. They begin by obtaining clinical descriptions of depression using a standard assessment instrument. Then they subject large numbers of these descriptions of patients to statistical analyses designed to isolate distinctive groupings of patients and symptoms. According to this strategy, if depression is a single unitary disorder, the results of the analysis should show a single underlying factor. On the other hand, if the two-depression description is more accurate, two distinct factors should emerge from the analysis.

This way of solving the controversy seems, on the surface, to be a reasonable one. But Kendall (1969) has cleverly pointed out the problems inherent in using this strategy as a way of solving the dilemma. He has shown that the clinician's theoretical biases about whether depression is actually unipolar or bipolar strongly affect the study results.

Kendall illustrates this point by showing distributions of symptoms on two very similar samples of patients examined using the same assessment instrument but examined by two different groups of clinicians. One group of clinicians strongly believes in the unitary view of depression. The other group believes that depression is bipolar. Figure 7–1 shows the distribution of symptoms of patients as rated by the two groups.

Each group has generated results that are congruent with its own theoretical bias. In the top distribution, symptoms are normally distributed, and presumably patients in this distribution vary from severely depressed to mildly depressed. On the other hand, the bottom distribution shows data from clinicians who believe that there are two kinds of depression. This distribution is clearly bimodal, with raters grouping patients in two distinct groups—one mildly depressed, the other severely depressed.

FIGURE 7–1 Distributions of Depression Scores Obtained by Psychiatrists with Unitarian Views (A) and Those with Binary Views (B)

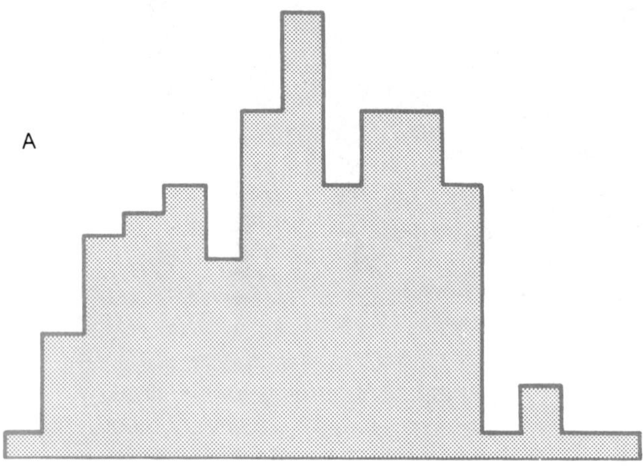

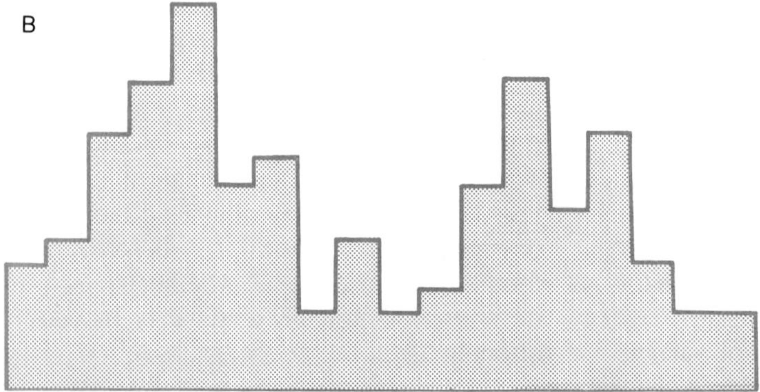

Source: Reprinted from R. E. Kendell, "The Classification of Depressive Illness: Uses and Limitations of Multivariate Analysis," *Psychiatrica, Neurologia, and Neurochirurgia,* 1969.

The lesson seems clear. Statistical analysis can only summarize the data submitted to it. By itself, it is not a way of obtaining objectivity or truth. If the scores of patients are affected by theoretical biases, the biases will emerge as *findings* once the analysis is completed.

One further possibility is frequently overlooked. *How depressed patients respond to treatment* can be used as a basis for classifying cases after the treatment. After all, as we noted, one of the primary purposes for engaging in classification is to make a decision about appropriate treatment.

Having decided about treatment, we can then work backwards. If the two-depression distinction is valid, then different depressions should respond differently to different treatments. It is widely believed that only endogenous depression responds well to electroconvulsive therapy (Levitt & Lubin, 1975). Reactive depressions have been thought to respond poorly to this form of treatment. Indeed, research results indicate that a larger percent of patients classified as endogenous have positive responses to ECT than do patients classified as reactive. However, almost all of the studies are complicated by selection biases, the simultaneous application of other treatments, such as drugs, and unreliable diagnosis.

So the question of whether there are one or two types of depression is not yet answered. It remains, however, an important question both for treatment and for scientific understanding.

Bipolar Episodes

As we indicated above, bipolar disorders involve either an alternation between manic and depressive mood states at different times or the simultaneous occurrence of both symptom patterns in an intermixed fashion.

Like manic disorders, bipolar disorders tend to begin before the age of 30. Typically, in the course of a bipolar affective episode, the first episode is usually manic and both the manic and depressive episodes tend to be more frequent and shorter than those of either the manic or depressive disorders alone. At times, there is a normal period in between the two mood swings. In other cases, there is no normal period but a rapid cycling from one mood to another.

In general, between 0.5 percent and 1.2 percent of the adult population is estimated to have experienced bipolar episodes, and bipolar episodes appear to be equally common in men and women.

Joseph Mendels (1970) notes that bipolar cases of affective disorders have been recorded in which the individual alternated between manic and depressive episodes every 24 hours for months on end. This suggests the intriguing possibility that bipolar affective disorders may involve biological rhythms of the individual in ways that are as yet unclear to us. Although persons suffering from bipolar disorders may report that some environmental stress triggered their episode, frequently episodes may occur with no obvious precipitating environmental event.

It is tempting to think of mania and depression as merely opposites of one another. Psychoanalytic formulations of depression reinforce this idea by suggesting that mania is best thought of as a "defense against depression." The idea is that depression is such a painful experience that people deny these painful feelings and escape into a manic state.

A very different way of thinking about the relationship between mania and depression is suggested by Mendels (1970). He notes that frequently both manic and depressed symptoms can occur virtually simultaneously in the same patient. Thus, a patient in the middle of a manic episode may actually burst into tears. Furthermore, Mendels notes that evidence is emerging to show that the changes in physiological functioning found among manics and depressives may be very similar. If this is so, then it is clearly an oversimplification to think of mania and depression as opposites of one another.

The advantage of this way of thinking about affective disorders is that it allows us to include mixed symptom pictures among disorders as well as to include the usual classifications of mania, depression, and bipolar reactions. In this scheme, the severity of the disorder is not correlated with one of the polar opposites of mania and depression, thus allowing a more complex and yet more inclusive picture of manic-depressive disorders.

In our examination of the affective disorders, we have noted that DSM III distinguishes between *manic* episodes characterized by elevated mood and activity, *depressive* episodes characterized by unhappy mood and lowered activity level, and *bipolar* affective episodes in which mood extremes alternate or occur almost simultaneously. In Chapter 9 we will examine a number of hypotheses and research studies that provide clues to the possible causes of affective disorders.

In describing depressive affective disorders, we noted that suicide was a potential outcome of severe depression in some cases. It is to this problem that we now turn.

Suicide continues to be one of the ten leading causes of death in the United States. We have chosen to discuss the phenomenon of suicide here not because it is only associated with affective disorders, since it is clearly not, but because both attempts or successful suicides are more frequently associated with depressive affective disorders than with other patterns of abnormal behavior.

Although the act of suicide is not a homogeneous clinical entity, nevertheless, its social importance has led researchers to attempt to understand the phenomenon, its distribution in the population, and its psychological components.

In this section we will examine factors associated with the risk of suicide to provide us with a broad understanding of the phenomenon. We will then turn to the question of the prediction of suicide. As we shall see, the challenge of assessing individuals for suicide risk is especially difficult but must be pursued because of its obvious social importance. Finally, we will consider recent research on the cognitive characteristics of people who have attempted suicide. New research in this area suggests that people who attempt suicide may have certain cognitive patterns in common.

Factors Associated with Suicide Risk

Research over the last 30 years has uncovered a substantial amount of information about how suicide is distributed in the population and other characteristics of the individual who attempts or completes a suicide attempt.

Psychological disturbance. Depression is by far the most likely pattern of abnormal behavior to be associated with suicide. On the other hand, less than half of all suicides are believed to have suffered from depressive symptoms. According to Choron (1972), only 5 to 15 percent of severely depressed individuals will eventually commit suicide. Schizophrenia and personality disorders

A concerned policeman begins to help his fellow officer who is restraining an elderly woman who is contemplating suicide.

United Press International Photo

SUICIDE

Carol was referred to a crisis center for help by a physician in the emergency room of a nearby small suburban hospital. The night before, she had attemped suicide by severely slashing her left wrist repeatedly with a large kitchen knife, and she had severed a tendon as a result.

When she was first seen by the therapist at the center, her left wrist and arm were heavily bandaged. She appeared tense, disheveled, very pale, and tremulous. She described her symptoms as insomnia, poor appetite, recent inability to concentrate, and overwhelming feelings of hopelessness and helplessness.

Carol was a 30-year-old woman, single, who lived alone. She had come to a large midwestern city about four years ago, immediately after graduating with a Master's degree in business administration from an eastern university. Within a few weeks she had obtained a management trainee position with a large manufacturing distributor company. In the next three years she had been advanced rapidly to her current position as manager of the main branch office. She stated that she was considered by her co-workers to be highly qualified for the position. She denied any on-the-job problems other than "the usual things that anyone in my position has to expect to deal with on a day-to-day basis." As a result of her rapid rise in the company, however, she had not allowed herself much leisure time to develop any close social relationships with either sex.

About one year ago Carol met John, a 40-year-old widower who had a position similar to hers with another company. His office was on the same floor as hers. Within a few weeks they were spending almost all of their leisure time together, though still maintaining separate apartments.

Carol's symptoms began about two weeks ago when John was offered a promotion to a new job in his company, which he accepted without mentioning it to her first. It meant that he would be transferred to another office about 30 miles away in the suburbs. She stated that she did feel upset "for just a few minutes" after he told her of his decision; "I guess that was just because he hadn't even mentioned anything about it to me first."

They went out that evening for dinner and dancing to celebrate the occasion. Before dinner was even over John had to bring her home because she "suddenly became dizzy, nauseated, and chilled" with what she described as "all of the worst symptoms of stomach flu."

Carol remained at home in bed for the next three days, not allowing John to visit her because she felt she was contagious. After she returned to work she continued to feel very lethargic, had difficulty concentrating, could not regain her appetite, "and felt quite depressed and tearful for no reason at all."

Convincing herself that she had not yet fully recovered from the "flu," she cancelled several dates with John so that she could get more rest. She described him as being very understanding about this, even encouraging her to try to get some time off from work to take a short trip by herself and really rest and relax.

During this same time, John had begun to spend increasing amounts of time at his new office. Their coffee-break meetings became very infrequent. Within the next week he expected to be moved completely.

The night before Carol came to the crisis

center she had come home from work expecting to meet John there for dinner; instead she found a note under her door written by her neighbor. It said that John had telephoned him earlier in the day and left word for her that he had "suddenly been called out of town . . . wasn't sure when he would be back . . . but would get in touch with her later."

She told the therapist, "Suddenly I felt empty . . . that everything was over between us. It was just too much for me to handle. He was never going to see me again and was too damned chicken to tell me so to my face! I went numb all over . . . I just wanted to die." She paused a few minutes, head down and sobbing, then took a deep breath and went on, "I really don't remember doing it, but the next thing I was aware of was the telephone ringing. When I reached out to answer it, I suddenly realized I had a butcher knife in my right hand and my left wrist was cut and bleeding terribly! I dropped the knife on the floor and grabbed the phone. It was John called me from the airport to tell me why he had to go out of town so suddenly—his father was critically ill."

Through sobs she told him what she had just done to herself. He told her to take a kitchen towel and wrap it tightly around her wrist. After she had done that he told her to unlock the front door and wait there, that he would get help to her.

He immediately called her neighbors, who went to her apartment and found her with blood-soaked towels around her wrist and sitting on the floor beside the door. They took her to the hospital, and John continued on his trip. After being treated in the emergency room, Carol went home to spend the night with her neighbors. They drove her to the crisis center the next morning.

During her initial session Carol told the therapist that she had no close relatives. Her father and mother had died within a few months of each other during her last year in college. Soon after, she had fallen in love with another graduate student, and at his suggestion they had moved into an apartment together. She had believed that they would marry as soon as they had both graduated and had jobs.

Just before graduation, however, her boyfriend had come home and informed her that he had accepted a postdoctoral fellowship in France and would be leaving within the month. They went out for dinner "to celebrate" that night because, she said, "I couldn't help but be happy for him . . . it was quite an honor . . . I just couldn't tell him how hurt I felt.

The next morning after he had left for classes she stated that she "suddenly realized I would never see him again after graduation . . . that he had never intended to marry me . . . and I was helpless to do anything about it." She took some masking tape and sealed the kitchen window shut, closed the door and put towels along the bottom, and turned on all of the stove gas jets.

About an hour later a neighbor smelled the gas fumes and called the fire department. The firemen broke into the apartment, found her lying unconscious on the floor, and rushed her to the hospital. She was in a coma for 2 days and remained in the hospital for a week. Her boyfriend came only once to see her. When she returned to the apartment she found that he had moved out, leaving her a note saying that he had gone home to see his family before taking off for France. He never contacted her again. A month later Carol moved to the Midwest.

For the first few months after meeting John, Carol was very ambivalent about her feelings toward him. She frequently felt very anxious and fearful that she was "setting myself up for another rejection." Even when John proposed marriage, she found herself unable to consider it seriously and told him that they should wait a while longer "to be sure that they both wanted it." Continuing, she stated, "Until about 2 days ago I had never felt so secure in my life . . . I'd even begun to seriously consider proposing to him! Then, suddenly the bottom began to fall out of everything."

When John accepted the new job without telling her first, Carol saw this as the beginning of another rejection by someone highly significant in her life. As her anxiety increased, she withdrew from communication with John "because of her flu." John's well-intentioned agreement to cancel several dates so that she could get more rest further cut off her opportunities to communicate her feelings to him. His suggestion that she take a trip alone compounded her already strong fear of imminent rejection by him.

Finding the neighbor's note under the door was, for her, "the last straw," final proof that he was leaving her, "just like my boyfriend did in college."

Unable to cope with overwhelming feelings of loss and anger toward herself for "letting it happen to me again," she impulsively attempted to commit suicide (Agvilera and Messick, 1978, p. 117–19).

also are associated with suicide attempts, as is alcoholism. Approximately 25 percent of successful suicides suffer from chronic alcoholism.

Previous suicide attempts. A persistent myth exists suggesting that if a person has unsuccessfully attempted suicide, they are not serious and therefore the likelihood of a subsequent successful suicide attempt is low. This is simply untrue. Studies have consistently shown that in surveys of completed suicides, the presence of a previous attempt is a primary factor in predicting the risk of a successful subsequent attempt (Choron, 1972). In addition, the method of the previous attempt is an important predictor of suicide. Previous attempts with highly lethal methods such as guns are much more predictive of later successful suicide than public gestures such as swallowing pills.

Suicide in the elderly and in children. Shneidman and Farberow (1970) indicate that the older the individual, the more likely that a suicide will occur. And indeed, the majority of people who kill themselves are elderly. The peak age for successful suicide is between 55 and 65 years of age. But suicide attempts are much more likely in the 24 to 44 age range.

As we have seen, the greatest risk for suicide is in older age groups. On the other hand, suicide among children and adolescents has attracted considerable attention in recent years, primarily because suicide is the second leading cause of death of people under the age of 20.

It is difficult to determine the reliability of the reported rate of suicide among children. Children are unlikely to leave suicide notes or other evidence of suicide. In addition, many people are likely to assume that the child met with an accident because the idea of childhood suicide is unthinkable to most of us. Children may not view death as irreversable or suicide

"Hotlines" and other telephone crisis intervention services can be a valuable community resource.

John Thoeming/Dorsey Press

as taboo. They may make suicide attempts because of a fear of an impending punishment, a desire to punish others, or in an attempt to join a loved one who has died.

Adolescent suicide ranks as a leading cause of death among the 15–19 age group. More than 10 percent of all suicides are made by teenagers. Among young people two particular subgroups are apparently a higher risk for suicide; black males in urban settings constitute one such group. The second group, college students, are twice as likely to commit suicide as their same-age counterparts.

In recent years, many colleges and universities have developed hot lines and telephone crisis services to provide a sympathetic listener to students who feel distressed and hopeless. It is very likely that such a service exists in your own college or university.

Marital status and social support. In general, divorced persons are a higher risk for suicide than either single, widowed, or married individuals, and the lowest suicide rate is found among married people. It is quite likely that the social support associated with the marital relationship is a critical element in preventing suicide.

Sex differences. In general, approximately, four times as many men as women actually commit suicide, but women are nearly three times as likely to attempt suicide (Shneidman et al., 1970). Beck (1975) has found that disruption in personal relationships is more likely to precipitate suicides in women than in men. On the other hand, men tend more often to use highly lethal methods of attempting suicides, such as firearms. This may account for the substantial difference in successful suicides among the two groups.

The Prediction of Suicide

The social importance of predicting a possible suicide attempt is obvious on the face of it. As Shneidman et al. (1970) have indicated, most people are acutely suicidal for only a short period of time. Thus intervention during that critical time could be decisive. In light of this fact, the importance of accurately predicting a suicide attempt becomes even more compelling.

Despite its importance, the prediction of suicide presents extremely difficult methodological problems. First of all, suicide is an extremely heterogeneous phenomenon and therefore adequate classification is necessary for accurate prediction (Neuringer, 1974). On the other hand, several critical issues confront the researcher hoping to design an effective prediction method or the clinician hoping to screen clients for the likelihood of suicide.

In order to validate the predictive power of an instrument, the typical procedure is to conduct a *prospective* study. That is, a large number of people are given a test or are screened on variables that are assumed to predict the outcome of the phenomenon under study. In the typical prospective study, events are allowed to run their course and then those factors in the test or a measurement instrument associated with the outcome can be isolated using correlational techniques. However, the ethical constraints against actually letting someone suspected of attempting suicide complete the act make it obvious that a prospective study would not be ethically feasible.

Another problem confronting the researcher is that the psychological state associated with the likelihood of a suicide attempt may be very brief. Consequently reliable observations of the state may be difficult to obtain. Furthermore, to be useful, a prediction of suicide must specify the period within which the act may occur, since otherwise the prediction will be of little practical use for the purposes of preventive intervention.

Perhaps the greatest difficulty associated with the prediction of suicide is the relative infrequency (low *base rate*) of the event. Most estimates suggest that approximately 11 out of 100,000 people in the general population successfully complete a suicide attempt. As Goldfried, Stricker, and Weiner (1971) have pointed out, when the occurrence of an event substantially departs from 50 percent in the population, the problems in predicting its occurrence increase. In the case of suicide, it is reasonable to assume that in the general population, only one-tenth of 1 percent of the population will actually complete a suicide. Thus, on the basis of the probability alone, you will be correct 99.9 percent of the time if you predict that *no one* will commit suicide. No psychological test administered to the general population can be as accurate. Obviously, whatever satisfaction one might obtain from being correct this often, the social cost of failing to predict a suicide is so great that attempts to devise methods to accurately predict the occurrence of a suicide attempt continue.

Most researchers now try to overcome the base rate problem by identifying population characteristics that substantially increase the likelihood of suicide *in that population.* Then instruments can be developed which can predict within this population having a higher base rate. Let us now turn to a line of research that may improve our ability to predict the occurrence of suicide attempts.

Suicidal Intention and Ideation

Recently, Beck and his colleagues (Beck, Kovacs, & Weissman, 1979) began developing measurement instruments to study suicidal ideation. Suicidal ideation or thought patterns, they believe, may be an important psychological indication of the intent to commit suicide. However, as they point out, intention is only one component of suicide risk. They note:

> Whereas suicidal intent may be regarded as a psychological phenomenon subject to exploration and measurement, suicidal risk is a predictive statement of the probability of a fatal suicide attempt and can be conceived in terms of a complex (although not fully formulated) equation. *Suicidal intention* would represent an important variable in this formula. Other essential components of the suicidal risk formula are factors such as the *lethality* of the method contemplated by the suicidal individual: his or her knowledge of lethal dosages of drugs or skill and familiarity with other forms of self-destruction, and his or her *access to the contemplated lethal method* (such as an adequate number of sleeping pills or firearms or ammunition). Another variable to be factored into the equation is the presence of *environmental resources that would facilitate the detection of suicidal intent* and intervention by another individual who would provide assistance in obtaining immediate and adequate *medical help* following a suicide attempt. Of course, the presence of a viable *social support system* that may diffuse the intensity of the suicidal wish is also an important and tangible factor (p. 345, italics added).

Thus Beck and his colleagues are suggesting that a variety of factors must be taken into account in the prediction of suicide, but that suicidal ideation, if it can be adequately measured, may be a useful predictor.

In this regard, Beck and his colleagues have developed a scale called the Scale for Suicidal Ideation designed to measure the intensity of an individual's conscious suicide intent. This scale is completed by a clinician based on the individual responses to a structured interview. Examples of some of the items from the SSI are shown in Table 7–3 below.

TABLE 7–3 Internal Consistency of the Scale for Suicide Ideation

Item and Rating	*Item-total Score Correlation*
1. Wish to live	.51**
0. Moderate to strong	
1. Weak	
2. None	
2. Wish to die	.61**
0. None	
1. Weak	
2. Moderate to strong	
3. Reasons for living/dying	.59**
0. For living outweigh for dying	
1. About equal	
2. For dying outweigh for living	

TABLE 7–3 *(continued)*

Item and Rating	*Item-total Score Correlation*
4. Desire to make active suicide attempt	.72**
0. None	
1. Weak	
2. Moderate to strong	
5. Passive suicidal desire	.63**
0. Would take precautions to save life	
1. Would leave life/death to chance	
2. Would avoid steps necessary to save or maintain life	
6. Time dimension: Duration of suicide ideation/wish	.58**
0. Brief, fleeting periods	
1. Longer periods	
2. Continuous (chronic) or almost continuous	
7. Time dimension: Frequency of suicide ideation	.63**
0. Rare, occasional	
1. Intermittent	
2. Persistent or continuous	
8. Attitude toward ideation/ wish	.67**
0. Rejecting	
1. Ambivalent; indifferent	
2. Accepting	
9. Control over suicidal action/ acting-out wish	.49**
0. Has sense of control	
1. Unsure of control	
2. Has no sense of control	
10. Deterrents to active attempt (e.g., family, religion, irreversibility)	.66**
0. Would not attempt because of a deterrent	
1. Some concern about deterrents	
2. Minimal or no concern about deterrents	
11. Reason for contemplated attempt	.50**
0. To manipulate the environment; get attention, revenge	
1. Combination of 0 and 2	
2. Escape, surcease, solve problems	
12. Method: Specificity/planning of contemplated attempt	.47**
0. Not considered	
1. Considered, but details not worked out	
2. Details worked out/well formulated	
13. Method: Availability/ opportunity for contemplated attempt	.22*
0. Method not available; no opportunity	
1. Method would take time/effort; opportunity not readily available	
2a. Method and opportunity available	
2b. Future opportunity or availability of method anticipated	
14. Sense of "capability" to carry out attempt	.39**
0. No courage, too weak, afraid, incompetent	
1. Unsure of courage, competence	
2. Sure of competence, courage	
15. Expectancy/anticipation of actual attempt	.56**
0. No	
1. Uncertain, not sure	
2. Yes	
16. Actual preparation for contemplated attempt	.46**
0. None	
1. Partial (e.g., starting to collect pills)	
2. Complete (e.g., had pills, loaded gun)	
17. Suicide note	†
0. None	
1. Started but not completed; only thought about	
2. Completed	
18. Final acts in anticipation of death (e.g., insurance, will)	.15

TABLE 7–3 *(continued)*

Item and Rating	*Item-total Score Correlation*
0. None	
1. Thought about or made some arrangements	
2. Made definite plans or completed arrangements	
19. Deception/concealment of contemplated suicide	.04
0. Revealed ideas openly	
1. Held back on revealing	
2. Attempted to deceive, conceal, lie	

Note. N=90.

† Item-total correlation could not be computed, since all subjects had a 0 coding.

* $p < .05$.

** $p < .02$.

Source: A. T. Beck, M. Kovack, and A. Weissman, "Assessment of Suicidal Ideation," *Journal of Consulting and Clinical Psychology,* 47 (1979), pp. 346–47. Copyright 1979 by the American Psychological Association. Reprinted by permission.

A factor analysis of the items in this scale suggests that there are three major components in suicidal thinking: (1) active suicidal desire, (2) preparation and (3) passive suicidal desire. Future studies will allow further refinement of the scale and examine its usefulness in longitudinal studies.

Another study by Patsiokas, Clum, and Luscomb (1979) attempted to isolate cognitive characteristics that might be important precursors of suicidal acts, using a group of suicide attempters and a group of nonsuicidal controls. They found that suicide attempters tended to be more cognitively rigid. These researchers interpret this rigidity as a low ability to cope with stressful events. However, suicide attempters were found to be no more impulsive or dependent on their

TABLE 7–4 Varimax Rotated Principal-Components-Analysis of the Scale for Suicide Ideation

	Component			
Item	*Factor I*	*Factor II*	*Factor III*	*Communality* (h^2)
Wish to live	*.77*	.09	−.19	.64
Wish to die	*.69*	.10	.13	.50
Reasons for living/dying	*.75*	.23	−.06	.62
Desire to make active suicide attempt	*.79*	−.04	.20	.67
Passive suicidal desire	.48	−.09	*.71*	.74
Time dimension: Duration	*.71*	.08	−.13	.53
Time dimension: Frequency	*.82*	.12	−.10	.70
Attitude toward ideation/wish	*.83*	.15	.03	.70
Control over suicidal action	.42	.38	−.04	.33
Deterrents to active attempt	*.51*	.48	.04	.49
Reason for contemplated attempt	*.64*	−.06	.32	.51
Method: Specificity/planning	.19	*.83*	−.12	.73
Method: Availability/opportunity	−.06	*.52*	.25	.34
Sense of "capability" to carry out attempt	.07	.19	*.73*	.57
Expectancy/anticipation of actual attempt	*.68*	.42	.08	.65
Actual preparation	.06	*.75*	.05	.56
Final acts	.36	.04	−.28	.21
Deception/concealment of contemplated attempt	−.22	.04	*.73*	.59
% of variance	35.3	10.9	9.8	

Note. N=90. Factor I = active suicidal desire; Factor II = preparation; Factor III = passive suicidal desire. Numbers in italics identify the meaning of each factor.

Source: A. T. Beck, M. Kovack, and A. Weissman, "Assessment of Suicidal Ideation," *Journal of Consulting and Clinical Psychology,* 47 (1979), p. 350. Copyright 1979 by the American Psychological Association. Reprinted by permission.

external environment than control subjects. Thus, we see that a psychological rigidity and inability to see alternative solutions to problems may also be a cognitive component of the disposition to attempt suicide.

SUMMARY

In this chapter we have examined the clinical characteristics of affective disorders. In particular, episodes involving elevated moods, depressive episodes involving sad or depressed mood, and bipolar affective disorders involving mood swings were examined. We noted that there is still some dispute in the research literature about the question of whether the depressive affective disorders represent one or two distinctively different patterns of behavior. An answer to that question could be important for decisions about the treatment of affective disorders as well as predictions of prognosis.

We also examined the phenomenon of suicide and considered a number of factors associated with increased suicide risk. As important as it is for clinical and humanitarian reasons, the prediction of suicide is difficult because it is a statistically infrequent event in the general population and the period of highest risk may be relatively brief. However, recent research on suicidal patterns of cognition may prove helpful in identifying psychological factors that increase suicidal risk.

You may recall the three criteria of our initial scientific definition of abnormal behavior: subjective distress, social disability, and the violation of commonly accepted social rules and norms. The affective disorders and suicide clearly reflect all three of these criteria. There is little question that severe alterations of mood both produce psychological stress and are socially disabling to the individual experiencing them. And, in our culture, suicide continues to be a phenomenon that evokes profound social concern. In the following chapter we will examine theory and research that searches for the causes of affective disorders.

8

Affective Disorders: Theory, Research, and Treatment

INTRODUCTION

In Chapter 7 we examined several approaches to the description of affective disorders. In this chapter we will examine a variety of different theories and research approaches to understanding the causal factors and treatment of affective disorders. We shall see that our understanding of the role of the social environment and of biological determinants of affective disorders has greatly expanded in recent years.

PRECIPITATING AND PREDISPOSING FACTORS IN DEPRESSION

Perhaps you recall feeling depressed after a major stress or problem in your own life. Can we reasonably say that stressful events *cause* depression? What is the role of events like the death of a relative, the loss of a job, serious illness in the family, or divorce in the development of depression?

Life Events as Precipators of Depression

These events seem so serious that our first reaction is to assume that they are obviously involved in the development of depression. But, as Hudgens (1974) points out, most people who experience these kinds of life events do not become seriously disturbed at all. Those who do become psychologically disabled appear to regain their equilibrium in a relatively short period of time. Thus, only a few people who experience catastrophic life events show any serious psychological impairment as a result. This fact is important for us to keep in mind, because it is tempting to assume that all serious life events produce psychological disturbance in those who undergo them.

How stressful life events are related to depression is complicated in other ways as well. Look at Figure 8–1 in order to gain an appreciation of some of the ways in which life events could be associated with depression.

As you can see in the first case, it may

FIGURE 8–1 Possible Relationships between Precipitating Stress and Depression

Role of stress	Event sequence
Stress as a major cause of depression	Stressful event (e.g., loss of valued person) → Depressive episode
Stress as a consequence of depression	Depressive episode → Stressful consequence (e.g., job loss)
Stress in temporal coincidence with depression	Stress → Other cause of depression → Depressive episode
Stress interacting with a preexisting predisposition	Stress (e.g., job loss) and predisposition (e.g., genetic makeup or early social learning) → Depressive episode

be that a precipitating stress could act as the *major cause* of depression. For example, if a person suddenly lost his entire family in an auto accident such a catastrophic stress could act as a major cause of depression. But stress can be related to depression in other ways as well.

In the second part of Figure 8–1, stress is a *consequence* rather than a causal factor in the development of depression. Someone suffering from depression could lose efficiency and motivation in his or her work. As a result he or she might be discharged. But clearly here we have a case in which a stressor follows the depression rather than precedes it.

In studies that examine people's past life events in order to discover whether the events are operating as possible causal factors, this particular problem is especially serious. Frequently, when a person tries to recall past events in his or her own life, the exact starting point of a depressive episode may be hard to pinpoint. Stresses that were actually consequences of the depression may easily be mistaken as possible causes.

A third way in which stress and depression might be related is through *temporal coincidence.* That is, it is possible, as in Figure 8–1, to experience a stressful event that is in no way casually associated with a depressive episode, even though it precedes the depression.

Finally *stress can interact with some already existing predisposition* or vulnerability in the individual and produce a depressive episode. Thus, for example, a person predisposed by reason of genetics, constitution, or past experience may react even to a moderate stressful life event with an episode of depression. It is likely that most depressions are of this last kind. In most cases some form of predisposition is probably necessary for stress to have its "triggering" effect. Let us now turn to the question of how a person might be predisposed to depression. We will find, as we did when thinking about precipitating causes, that several possibilities present themselves.

Predisposing Factors in Depression

When we talk about predisposing factors in the development of abnormal behavior, we generally mean some underlying condition that increases the likelihood that the person may develop the disorder. Scientists have long suspected that there were predisposing factors associated with most severe forms of abnormal behavior. But frequently they have disagreed on the *nature* of the predisposition. Some scientists, beginning with Kraepelin, have argued strongly for *organic* predispositions. Both Freud and advocates of the learning perspective have argued vigorously that *prior experiences* are important predisposing factors.

What sorts of previous life experiences or biological characteristics might make a person vulnerable to depression?

ENTRANCE AND EXIT LIFE EVENTS AS TRIGGERS OF DEPRESSION

Some careful research on the relationship between various life events and depression has been done by Paykel and his colleagues (1973). He compared depressed patients with control patients from the general population and asked both groups about previous events in their lives. Events associated with *employment,* such as demotion, promotion, and retirement, *health-related events,* such as personal illness or pregnancy, and *marital events,* such as separation and divorce, tended to be most reliably associated with depression.

Furthermore, undesirable events such as divorce or unemployment tended to occur in the lives of depressed patients much more frequently than in control patients' lives. Desirable events, on the other hand, tended to occur equally often in depressed and control patients.

One of the most interesting ideas that Paykel tested had to do with the life events that involve some sort of *entrance* into the social field, such as engagement, marriage, or birth, and events that involve an *exit* such as death or departure of a family member and divorce. Paykel found that depressed patients tended to have more exit life events in their lives than control groups but did not differ from controls in the number of entrance life events. This is an intriguing finding and suggests that the life events most likely to precipitate depression are those that involve some rupture or break in the person's social relationships. We might speculate that a useful strategy for preventing depression could involve emotional preparation for predictable exit events in our lives.

Evidence on this question is not extensive, but some research is yielding promising results. We will look briefly at three types of predisposing factors here and consider this issue in more detail later, in the context of various theories of depression.

Genetic Predisposing Factors

One major source of hypotheses is *genetic factors.* Winokur (1969) has done a series of studies examining the frequency of affective disorders in the

MOOD AND MONEY

Although at some time almost everyone has felt depressed, until recently little has been known about the characteristics of the average person who feels depressed. As we have seen, most research has been done with people who seek treatment.

In order to provide balance, Levitt and Lubin (1975) conducted a carefully designed national survey of individuals using the Depression Adjective Checklist as a basic measure. This checklist allows people to check a number of mood adjectives associated with depression. Higher scores on the checklist indicate more severe expressed moods of depression. The researchers then proceeded to examine the social and demographic charateristics of their sample in relation to the severity of feelings of depression. A number of interesting findings emerged.

Feelings of depression are related to annual income, but in a *curvilinear* fashion. That is, those people whose income was *below* $6,000 or *above* $25,000 a year tended to have the highest depression scores. People whose financial status had recently improved had low depression scores, and people whose financial status had recently deteriorated tended to have higher scores.

Although there was an expected

It is often the poor and disadvantaged who are most vulnerable to depression.

Charles Gatewood/Magnum Photos, Inc.

relationship between depression and social class, with people in lower socioeconomic strata being more depressed, the most important aspect of this relationship had to do with education. More highly educated people tended to be less depressed.

Levitt and Lubin concluded that people who are most likely to become severely depressed tended in their sample to have poor educational backgrounds, lower annual incomes, and an apparent inability to improve their financial status.

In a striking conclusion the authors suggest, "In the ultimate analysis, a therapy for some forms of depression may be money" (p. 139).

families of manic depressive patients. He found that, when these patients were compared with people in a control group, more of them had parents who also had a history of affective disorder. We have already considered the evidence for genetic factors in manic-depressive disorders, where it appears to be compelling. For unipolar depressions the evidence is mixed, but twin studies by Slater (1953) and Da Fonseca (1959) suggest that at least some forms of severe depression do involve a genetic predisposing factor.

A second way of thinking about predisposing factors involves the idea of a *depressed personality.* This sort of personality marks someone who is overly conscientious, subdued, vulnerable to rejection or disappointment, and who denies feelings of anger and hostility. Laughlin (1965) believes such a person would be vulnerable to depression if they experienced a severe life stress. The idea of a depressed personality seems to be a useful one at first; but left unclear is whether such a personality type qualifies as a predisposing factor or is simply a clinical description of an already existing mild depression. Yet some social roles may predispose people to depression more than others. Bernard (1976) has suggested that several aspects of women's roles may predispose them to depression.

Still a third kind of predisposition may involve *losses or stresses during childhood* that occur at special periods of development. Such losses or stresses could sensitize the person to depression in later life. This might be especially true if a similar event later in life reactivated the feelings of depression and anxiety that had occurred at the time of the original stress. Thus, for example, a child who had lost a parent at a very young age might find feelings of despair and loss reactivated when a close friend or relative dies later in his or her life. The relationship between early separation of infants from love objects and its effects on later behavior has been studied both in clinical populations and in the laboratory context. Let us now turn to that evidence.

Separation and Depression

Akiskal and McKinney (1975) note, "there is abundant evidence that the disruption of a significant attachment bond may well represent the most traumatic kind of withdrawal of reinforcement in primate

WOMEN'S ROLES AND DEPRESSION

Careful studies of the incidence of depression suggest that women are more prone to depression than men. Let us consider some possible reasons for this finding. One possibility is that women are simply more willing to admit to the experience of depression than men. This would suggest that the difference observed in previous studies have only to do with one's willingness to engage in self-disclosure. Involutional melancholia, a depressive disorder that commonly affects women at the age of menopause and is presumed to be, in part, a metabolic disorder, could account for some of the differences, although psychological and physiological changes also occur at the time of the male menopause, or climacteric.

But recently social scientists have begun to advance a very different kind of explanation for the higher incidence of depression among women. This explanation is based on the *social role* into which women have traditionally been cast and the role's effects on one's sense of optimism or hopelessness. Jessie Bernard (1976) has suggested that several aspects of the female sex role can lead to depression. Traditionally, the woman's subserviant role in marriage, lower socioeconomic status, and sense of vulnerability all can predispose her to depression.

Furthermore, in much of our culture, the expectations and perceptions of women's roles are changing. New standards for achievement and independence can clash strikingly with the actual situation in which women, and mothers in particular, may find themselves. This change in social expectations can often intensify women's sense of helplessness.

Possibly this way of thinking about the relationship between sex roles and depression implies possible prevention strategies for depression in women. As socialization practices regarding sex roles change, the incidence of depression among women may be reduced.

One of the most interesting lines of research evidence to support these ideas comes from a careful study of depressed women conducted by Weissman and Paykel (1974). They found that among women who were clinically depressed, those who worked outside the home were often able to continue in their jobs and showed less impairment than women whose activities were confined to the home. Weissman and Paykel suggest that outside occupation may have a protective effect on people vulnerable to depression. After all, having a job outside the home provides a separate arena in which women can find rewards and cope with their world. If this is true, the "protective effect" of an outside job may also be a contributing factor to the lower incidence of men who seek treatment for depression.

Increasingly women are engaging in more active work roles.

Ray Ellis/Photo Researchers, Inc.

species, including man. Therefore it is not surprising that theorists of depression have paid great attention to the possible depressionogenic effects of separation events that disrupt the interpersonal attachment bonds" (p. 293).

Separation can be thought of in two interrelated ways. First, separation could serve as a precipitating stress or "trigger" for depression. Second, loss of a love object during childhood could predispose the person to later adult depression.

If we look at the evidence for separation as a precipitating stress, several generalizations emerge. Studies of groups of people who have just suffered an important loss provide one source of evidence. A study of recent widows during their mourning indicated that 35 percent of the widows developed symptoms of primary depression (Clayton, et al., 1972). These depressions appeared self-limiting and disappeared after a few months, particularly if the individual had other close family ties and friends to provide a substitute interpersonal bond. Other studies suggest that, although separation is capable of triggering depression, it is also capable of precipitating other forms of abnormal behavior and other medical symptoms.

Thus, separation appears capable of starting depression but also other forms of disorder. Yet many individuals who have suffered separation do not develop depressive symptoms and therefore separation is not a sufficient cause of depression. Furthermore, a number of individuals displaying depressed behavior have not suffered separation of any kind. Therefore separation is not a necessary antecedent of depression. Although separation may play a critical precipitating role in some forms of depression, we do not yet fully understand its role as a precipitant.

Depression in Children: Attachment and Loss

Remember we said that separation in childhood could also serve as a predisposing event for later adult depression. Much clinical research on attachment and loss (Bowlby, 1973) has focused on the question of attachment early in life and its implications for later behavior. Perhaps some of the most famous work on early emotional deprivation has been done by Renée Spitz (1945). Spitz reported the reactions of infants separated from their mothers in the second half of their first year of life. The behavior these children displayed has been called *anaclitic depression.* Typically these children displayed continued crying, apprehension, withdrawal, stupor, inability to sleep, loss of weight, and retardation in their growth and development. Similar reactions to separations of children from their mothers have been observed by other investigators.

Perhaps the most famous research on separation was done, not with human beings, but with primates. The work of the Harlows (1969) on the relationship between mother monkeys and their infants has shed considerable light on the importance of attachment and the effects of separation.

The Harlows and others have shown that separating infant rhesus monkeys from their mothers can profoundly affect the infants' behavior. Research with rhesus monkeys on separation has the advantage of allowing the investigators to control carefully extraneous variables so that they could observe the effect of separation itself. Separation can now be studied as an independent variable; the length, type, and age of separation can be controlled to observe the effects of each.

This infant monkey raised in social isolation shows an exaggerated fear of strangers, apathy, and immobility.

Harry F. Harlow, University of Wisconsin Primate Laboratory

Harlow and his colleagues have shown that separating primate infants from their mothers, once the mother-infant bond has been developed, had clinical effects on the baby very similar to those reported by researchers observing the behavior of human infants following separation. Furthermore, separation from peers (monkeys of the same age) once a bond has been established also produces reactions that look very much like despair and depression.

Recent research by the Harlow group suggests that separation can indeed play an important role in predisposing rhesus monkeys to later psychopathology. When peers are separated from one another at three to four years of age they show more abnormal behavior if they have a history of traumatic separation during infancy than if they do not have such a history. Thus experimental research with primates also suggests that separation can play an important role both as a precipitating and as a predisposing event in depression.

THEORIES OF DEPRESSION

In trying to untangle the puzzle of depression, researchers have placed their bets in different places and have pursued their hunches using very different research tactics. In the theory and research that we will examine now, you will see some researchers placing their bets heavily on the importance of cognitive events in depression. Others will place their bets on prior learning experiences, while still others believe that it is the biochemistry of depression to which we must attend.

Each of these investigators uses a different strategy to collect evidence. Some draw on their own clinical experience with depressed patients. Others attempt to construct laboratory analogues of the phenomena that they believe are crucial in the development of depression. Still other researchers focus their attention on the metabolism and brain of depressed individuals. And finally, some researchers find it most meaningful to focus on the social field of the depressed person. Their attention is on the social interaction of the person suffering from depression.

Psychoanalytic Theory

Of the several well-known theoretical accounts of the development of depression, the psychoanalytic view is unquestionably the most widely quoted. Indeed, some of the earliest thinking in the field of psychoanalysis was devoted to understanding the nature and development of depression. Sigmund Freud wrote his famous paper, "Mourning and Melancholia," in 1917. As we will see, the psychoanalytic approach has been modified in recent years in several important ways. Nevertheless, Freud's early theories of the nature of depression continue to have substantial influence.

Depression as hostility turned inward. Freud viewed depression as the inward turning of aggressive instincts. When we discussed the psychoanalytic perspective in Chapter 3, we noted that the id was described as the source of both sexual and aggressive impulses. Freud believed that the child's early attachment to a loved object, such as a mother, involved both feelings of love and hate. When the child lost the love object or was frustrated in his or her dependency needs, feelings of loss were mingled with feelings of anger. The child could not openly accept feelings of anger toward the love object, however, and therefore, turned the hostility inward. The clinical result, Freud argued, was depression. This concept of depression as hostility turned inward suggests that aggression has been *dammed up* and is only capable of being expressed in the form of depression.

A useful question is whether there is any evidence to support this idea. Akiskal and McKinney (1975) indicate that even though the psychoanalytic idea of aggression turned inward is the most widely quoted psychological theory of depression, little systematic evidence substantiates it.

Some research has been reported that tests the idea that if depression represents anger turned inward then people who are depressed should express considerably less outward anger than would normal nondepressed people. Yet a number of studies conducted by Paykel et al. (1970, 1973) suggest that it is possible to find substantial numbers of depressed individuals who also express a considerable amount of anger outwardly toward others in the environment.

Depression as a reaction to object loss. Since the early psychoanalytic formulations of depression as hostility turned inward, a second, more important, aspect of the psychodynamics of depression has been emphasized. This second formulation focuses on the idea of *object loss,* the loss of some loved object or individual in the person's life.

The basic idea behind this formulation is that early ungratified dependency needs lead to fixation. Cameron (1963) describes the idea this way:

> The adult who develops a neurotic depression when he regresses is one whose major points of fixation belong to a phase of development when dependency needs were more powerful than needs for self-assertion. We assume that, as a child, such an adult had unusual difficulties in separating himself emotionally from the protective custody of his mother. His need to be taken care of as a baby was either left ungratified or else it was gratified in such a way that only feeble impulses toward mature independence could emerge. What we see in the symptomatology of neurotic depressive adults are derivatives of an early dependent infantile fixation (p. 427).

This idea argues that hostility turned either inward or outward is not an important cause of depression. It is only a secondary reaction to the fact of the loss of a loved object.

The psychoanalytic perspective on depression focuses on early childhood events and their impact on later behavior. Basically this view argues that if a child's dependency needs were not fully met early in its development concerns about dependency and loss of love are *fixated* at that time. Later, as an adult, the loss of loved objects or even the threat of the loss of love triggers this feeling of vulnerability. The clinical result is depression.

In evaluating the psychoanalytic view of depression it is safe to say that early formulations of anger turned inward were incomplete and have not been substantiated by recent evidence. The emphasis on loss of valued relationships in the more recent dynamic formulations touches on a critical issue. We have already seen that among the precipitating events in depression are negative social and vocational life events, such as divorce, death of someone important to the person, job loss, and other such object losses. In addition, the research on separation as a predisposing factor in some forms of depression seems compelling. Thus, the current formulations focus on what appear to be important environmental events in the development of depression.

Beck's Cognitive Theory

The primary emphasis of most theories of depression is upon the emotions and mood of the person. This emphasis is not surprising since a depressed mood is the outstanding clinical feature of the disorder. Recently, however, a new emphasis is being placed on *cognitive* events in the psychological life of the depressed person.

For example, Beck (1967) believes that the most striking aspect of the depressive's behavior involves the negative expectations and thoughts that are a continuous part of the depressed person's experience. Beck focuses on what he calls the *cognitive triad,* three aspects of negative thinking that characterize depression. The first aspect is *negative conceptions on the self,* the second, *negative interpretations of one's experiences,* and the third, *a negative view of the future.* Note that these are features of the thought patterns of the depressive, rather than qualities of emotional experience. They are essentially "logical errors" to which depressed people tend to be more prone. Depressed people are more likely to accept the blame for negative events in their lives or to interpret negative events as being their responsibility when there is no logical reason for doing so.

Beck believes that a habitual characteristic of depressive thinking involves the use of *schemas* that shape the depressed person's experience. These schemas are habitual ways of thinking that actually reinforce the negative experiences the depressive typically reports. Box 8–4 below summarizes some of the logical errors Beck describes.

We have seen that Beck's formulation argues that the most important aspect of depression is the way the individual perceives and interprets his or her world. The implication is that the cognitive schema of the person shapes his or her emotional tone rather than the reverse. As interesting as this speculation is, no evidence is offered to support it. Although even casual clinical observation suggests that some depressed individuals do indeed display the cognitive distortions Beck describes, whether they are the cause or consequence of depressed affect is unclear. Nevertheless, the emphasis on cognitive events provides a useful balance to other theoretical approaches to depression.

Beyond merely describing the state of depression, Beck has proposed a treatment strategy based on his formulation. Basically it involves helping the depressed person to recognize the fallacies in his or her own thinking and the negative expectations that characterize his or her style of thought. Once having recognized these negative interpretations, or logical errors, Beck argues, one can slowly modify them so that the depressed

EXAMPLES OF DEPRESSED COGNITIONS

Overgeneralization When a person draws an extremely broad conclusion based on some specific fact or minor event they are engaging in overgeneralization. To conclude that one is worthless and that life is hopeless from having just received a parking ticket would be an example of overgeneralization. Another example Beck offers involved a man who, when he observed that his children were slow in getting dressed, concluded "I am a poor father because the children are not better disciplined."

Magnification and minimization Extreme overemphasis of negative factors (magnification) and extreme underemphasis of positive events (minimization) are also examples of logical errors. For example, a person who has just won a lottery, might express guilt because someone more worthy had not won.

Selective abstraction If a person draws a conclusion based only on a selected aspect of a situation and then engages in self-blame on the basis of this selected event, the person is engaging in what Beck calls selective abstraction. A person who consistently singles out his or her role in a softball game and accepts the blame for the loss is engaging in selective abstraction.

Arbitrary inference Drawing a conclusion without any evidence to back it up is an arbitrary inference. Feelings of worthlessness based on the fact that something outside of one's control such as a drought has occurred is an example of arbitrary inference.

Inexact labeling Labeling an event in an exaggerated fashion (bouncing a check becomes "our bankruptcy") and then subsequently referring to the label ("bankruptcy") with extreme negative emotions while omitting the original, relatively minor event from consideration (Beck, 1967) is an instance of inexact labeling.

person then perceives the world in a more positive fashion.

Learned Helplessness and Depression

About 20 years ago a psychologist drowned two rats in the interest of science. He dropped the first rat into a tank of warm water. It swam for about 60 hours before it finally drowned. The second rat was treated differently. Before being put in the water, the psychologist held the rat in his hand until it stopped struggling. When the rat was finally dropped in the water it swam around for only a few minutes and then sank to the bottom. The psychologist, Curt Richter (1957, 1958), believes that the second rat had given up hope of escape even before it entered the water and drowned much sooner because of a sense of helplessness.

Since that first bit of research more than 20 years ago, psychologists have been actively investigating the question of how prior experiences can affect our willingness and ability to cope with loss, change, and stress. In the last few years, the idea that a learned sense of helplessness might be an important component of the phenomenon of depression has gained increasing attention from scientists.

Actually, the idea of *learned helplessness* is only one of a number of behavioral formulations of depression (Eastman, 1976). Behavioral formulations are based on a learning theory approach to understanding human behavior. Their basic assumption is that depression results from certain reinforcement contingencies in the individual's environment. Specifically, learning formulations view the depressed person as someone experiencing *extinction,* that is, someone who is not receiving reinforcement for his or her behavior. In addition, evidence that a person is depressed, from the learning point of view, has to do with how frequently that person engages in particular behaviors (Ferster, 1973). Affective and cognitive aspects of depression typically do not enter directly into learning formulations. So the essence of all learning formulations of depression is the view of depression as a state in which the person is not receiving reinforcement for his or her behaviors. Consequently the person emits very few behaviors. For the learning theorist this *low rate of response* is the most crucial aspect of depression.

The learned helplessness formulation offered by Seligman (1975) was first introduced as an animal *analogue* of reactive depression. In the original experiments Seligman and his colleagues subjected dogs to a series of inescapable shocks and then placed them in a shuttle box where a warning signal came on before shock occurred. The animals' task was to learn to leap over a hurdle in order to avoid the shock. Animals that had been previously exposed to inescapable shock did not learn to escape when placed in the shuttle box. Presumably they had learned earlier that nothing they could do would help them to escape shock. On the other hand, animals that had not been previously exposed to inescapable shock easily learned the task. Seligman and his colleagues concluded that the inability of the animals that had been exposed to inescapable shock to learn simple escape behavior was an example of learned helplessness.

Furthermore Seligman and his colleagues showed that the same dogs could be "immunized" against learned helplessness by exposing them to escapable electric shocks and allowing them to develop effective escape behavior. Learning effective escape behavior had the immunizing effect. When these same dogs were later exposed to inescapable shock and then placed in an escape situation, they learned to escape quickly. They were no longer helpless.

But what, you may ask, does an experiment on dogs using electric shock in a laboratory have to do with clinical depression? The answer is that Seligman believes there is an important *analogy between learned helplessness and depression.* Recall in Chapter 4 we noted that *experimental analogues* offer a strategy for conducting research on the problems of abnormal behavior. Experimental analogues allow much more experimental control over the problem of interest and create a set of circumstances that the scientists believe are analogous to those that occur naturally in the social environment.

But, for an experimental analogue to be convincing, it is not enough to show a few interesting similarities between the

THE VALUE OF EXPERIMENTAL ANALOGUES

Seligman (1975) believes that there are some necessary ground rules for testing whether laboratory phenomena can be used as natural models of psychopathology in human beings. For him four kinds of evidence are necessary for asserting that the laboratory phenomenon and the naturally occurring phenomenon are similar: (1) one must show that behavioral and physiological symptoms are similar, (2) the causal factors are similar, (3) cure or change can be affected in analogous ways, and (4) prevention of the behavior can be produced in similar ways.

We must take this issue seriously for a moment, since virtually all of the research on learned helplessness uses some form of argument by analogy. For example, if it can be shown that the behavioral symptoms of learned helplessness and depression are similar and it can be shown that the same sorts of causal factors can be discovered in both learned helplessness and depression and that both learned helplessness and depression can be cured using similar approaches, then the model of learned helplessness is strengthened. But if such similarities are not discovered the model is weakened.

There are some other interesting aspects of the analogue strategy. Seligman notes that a useful behavioral model has the advantge of sharpening the definition of the phenomenon in question. As we have seen, the clinical characteristics of depression are numerous, and no single behavior is by itself the defining characteristic of depression. As Seligman puts it, a laboratory model "clips the clinical concept off at the edges" by imposing some specific features on the concept. Critics of the experimental analogue strategy have always argued that this is one of its greatest weaknesses. That is, much of the richness of the phenomenon and its complexity is lost when we use a simple analogue, particularly one involving the learning processes of lower animals. However, it also can be argued that this is a useful feature of the model. For example, it may be that the learned helplessness model will clarify our understanding of only some types of depression. Others may be excluded or the entire concept of depression may be redefined as a consequence of rigorously applying the analogue.

laboratory situation and the clinical phenomenon. It is necessary to spell out the parallels in as much detail as possible. In the next section we will examine the similarities between the phenomenon of learned helplessness as it is produced in the laboratory and the clinical phenomenon of depression.

Parallels between learned helplessness and depression. One of Seligman's most important contributions has been to examine the clinical literature on depression in the light of his own research on helplessness. He has then carefully drawn out the parallels between the two sets of phenomena. These parallels are summarized in Table 8–1. Notice that Seligman has looked for similarities between learned helplessness and depression in *symptoms, causes,*

TABLE 8–1 Parallels between Learned Helplessness and Depression

	Learned Helplessness	*Depression*
Symptoms	Passivity	Passivity
	Difficulty learning that responses produce relief	Negative cognitive set
	Dissipates in time	Time course
	Lack of aggression	Introjected hostility
	Weight loss, appetite loss, social and sexual deficits	Weight loss, appetite loss, social and sexual deficits
	Norepinephrine depletion and cholinergic activity	Norepinephrine depletion and cholinergic activity
	Ulcers and stress	Ulcers (?) and stress
		Feelings of helplessness
Cause	Learning that responding and reinforcement are independent	Belief that responding is useless
Cure	Directive therapy: forced exposure to responses that produce reinforcement	Recovery of belief that responding produces reinforcement
	Electroconvulsive shock	Electroconvulsive shock
	Time	Time
	Anticholinergics; norepinephrine stimulants (?)	Norepinephrine stimulants; anticholinergics (?)
Prevention	Immunization by mastery over reinforcement	(?)

Source: From M. E. P. Seligman, *Helplessness: On Depression, Development and Death* (San Francisco: Freeman) 1975, p. 106.

cures, and *prevention.* Let us now survey the evidence for convincing parallels between learned helplessness and depression in each of these areas.

Seligman's strategy has been to examine the symptoms of learned helplessness and ask whether parallels to these symptoms can be found in depression. We should notice that he has chosen to move from the carefully defined laboratory findings in learned helplessness to the amorphous field of clinical depression. Searching for parallels in the opposite direction would clearly have been much more difficult. There are six kinds of symptoms that one typically finds in learned helplessness that Seligman believes have parallels in depression.

• *Lowered initiation of voluntary responses.* One characteristic of learned helplessness is that animals subjected to inescapable punishment are much less likely to initiate new behavior. Seligman finds this similar to the reduced activity of depressed patients and the "paralysis of the will" that Beck (1967) believes is the hallmark of depression. This lowered level of voluntary response presumably produces the passivity, retardation in physical behavior, intellectual slowness, and the social unresponsiveness that we see in clinical cases of depression.

- *Negative cognitive set.* Depressed patients believe themselves to be ineffective in their behavior. In fact, even the smallest barrier to carrying out a simple task often seems insurmountable. In a series of studies, Seligman (1975) has shown that when depressed people are tested in tasks requiring skill or where only chance determines the outcome, they appear to believe that their own efforts are equally important in skill and chance tasks. Nondepressed people have a much stronger belief in the effect of their own behavior in skilled tasks.
- *Learned helplessness and depression both dissipate over time.* With the passage of time, reactive depression and learned helplessness will dissipate. Similarity in the time course for both laboratory produced learned helplessness and reactive depression are compelling points of analogy for Seligman.
- *Lack of aggression.* There is a similar lack of aggression both in animals that have been subjected to the laboratory experience of inescapable shock and in clinically depressed patients. Seligman notes that aggression is still another response that can be undermined by a belief in one's own helplessness.
- *Loss of sexual energy.* There is also a loss of sexual interest and motivation as well as a loss of appetite in both learned helplessness and in clinical cases of depression.
- *Norepinephrine depletion.* There is evidence to suggest that, both in learned helplessness and in clinical depression, important chemical changes may occur in the brain. These changes have to do with the depletion of neurotransmitters, chemicals that aid in the transmission of chemical impulses. We will consider this parallel in more detail later.

This is a fairly impressive list of similarities, but Seligman wishes to go further. He argues that the analogy goes beyond behavioral similarities. He believes that the causes of laboratory produced learned helplessness are known. Furthermore he believes that these causes provide us with some important clues about possible causes of depression itself. In Seligman's own words, *"I believe that what links these experiences and lies at the heart of depression is unitary: the depressed patient believes or has learned that he cannot control those elements of his life that relieve suffering, bring gratification, or provide nurture—in short, he believes that he is helpless"* (p. 93).

The kinds of events that precipitate reactive depression are just those sorts of events that undermine one's sense of control over one's life. For example, failures at work and at school, the death of a relative or close friend, the loss of friendships, being faced with insoluble problems, physical disease, or financial difficulty are all important triggers in the development of reactive depression.

When one examines the attempts to treat depression, Seligman sees still other parallels. For example, Beck's (1970–1971) cognitive therapy, which is designed to help change the depressed patient's negative expectations and cognitions to more optimistic ones, can be thought of as an attempt to overcome helplessness. Assertiveness training and the use of graded tasks that slowly reinforce active behavior in depressed patients are both focused on moving the patient toward a belief that *doing* something will make a difference in his life. Seligman notes that electroconvulsive shock and other drugs may have antidepressant effects. These treatments have also been shown to be at least moderately effective in changing the learned helplessness of laboratory animals.

Seligman believes that people who are particularly resistent to depression are those whose childhood and later experiences have allowed them to effectively control sources of reinforcement in their own lives. These people see the future positively and believe that they control their own fate. They also have the skills associated with extracting reinforcement from their environment. Therefore they are, presumably, more able to cope with a world that inevitably contains reversals, losses, and failures.

How, then, are we to evaluate Seligman's argument? Seligman has been careful to draw out all the possible parallels between the laboratory phenomenon on learned helplessness and the clinical phenomenon of depression itself. There may be other aspects of depression that have been omitted or deemphasized in the attempt to draw clear parallels. Nevertheless, the list of similarities is impressive.

Second, it is probably true that the learned helplessness model of depression best fits reactive rather than endogenous depression. That is, the parallels are more striking and believable in cases where people fall into a depression following some reversal or life change. The endogenous depressions that seldom, if ever, have clear precipitating events associated with them show fewer parallels.

Third, as Eastman (1976) has noted, it is important to add the qualification that the perceived loss of control probably does not produce helplessness unless the loss of control is absolute. Frequently some alternative or compensating behaviors are available.

Furthermore, a number of researchers (eg. Miller & Norman, 1979) have pointed out that learned helplessness in humans depends on the the factors to which failure experiences are attributed. Thus, the cognitive complexity of humans who search for causes of events in the environment may require a more complex framework than that offered by Seligman. A weakness of the learned helplessness model is that it does not capture the complexity and flexibility with which people cope in real life. If one way of regaining control over our life seems out of reach, frequently others are available. Nevertheless, the learned helplessness model is impressive both in its simplicity and in the range of its application.

A Biochemical Theory: The Catecholamine Hypothesis

Think back for a moment to the learned helplessness experiment conducted by Martin Seligman and his colleagues. Seligman first exposed dogs to conditions in which they were unable to escape being shocked. After being exposed to inescapable shock, they were placed in a box where they had to jump over a hurdle to avoid being shocked. Dogs that had previously been exposed to inescapable shock could not learn the simple task of escaping over the hurdle. They moved around the box and finally became immobilized. Seligman explained the behavior of these dogs by saying that they had learned to be helpless. That is, they had learned that nothing they could do would help them to escape shock.

From these basic experiments Seligman went on to show compelling parallels between clinical depression and learned helplessness in humans. Many researchers feel he has made a persuasive case that learned helplessness is a likely explanation for at least some forms of depression. Scientists exposed to learning theory as a way of explaining behavior find themselves particularly persuaded by Seligman's work. The passivity, low levels of activity, and other indicators of depression appear to have been learned in an environment with the message that nothing will make any difference in whether they are punished or not.

But how would a researcher whose primary interest was in the biochemistry of the brain interpret Seligman's results? In our discussion of perspectives in Chapter 3 we noted that perspectives help us to notice certain aspects of a phenomenon and to pay less attention to others. Jay Weiss and his colleagues (Weiss, Stone, & Harrell, 1970; Weiss, Glazer, & Pohorecky, 1976) are concerned with the biochemical aspects of depression. These researchers have examined Seligman's results and have come up with a very different interpretation. They noticed that dogs tested 24 hours after inescapable shock displayed the usual signs of learned helplessness, but dogs tested 48 hours later displayed no difficulties. From a biochemical point of view this is a crucial observation. Weiss believes that this remarkable recovery is just what we would expect to find if we were observing a *temporary physiological problem* rather than learned helplessness. In fact, Weiss believes that it is the loss of a chemical called *norepinephrine* in the brain that produces the behavior Seligman calls learned helplessness.

Here we have a classic confrontation of perspectives: two apparently different explanations have been offered for the same finding. As we have seen, learned helplessness is one of the most well-known behavioral explanations for depression. Our examination of alternative ways of explaining learned helplessness is likely to clarify and broaden our understanding of the nature of depression.

Neurotransmitters. Before we look at Jay Weiss' research, we need a brief lesson on neurotransmitters. In our brain, the thousands of neurons needed to move a muscle or to perceive an object are not connected directly to one another. Instead neurons send impulses from one to another by means of chemical substances. These chemical substances are called *neurotransmitters.* Scientists are discovering more and more about neurotransmitters and how they interact with each other in the brain, but it is already known that these chemicals play a vital role in brain functioning. One of these groups of neurotransmitters is called *catecholamines.* There is a whole family of catecholamines, including epinephrine (sometimes called adrenalin), norepinephrine, and dopamine.

For some time scientists have suspected that catecholamines, and norepinephrine in particular, play an important role in depression. Most of the evidence for the role of norepinephrine has been indirect. Schildkraut and Ketty (1967) have suggested that when norepinephrine is depleted in the brain, something resembling depression results. What is the evidence?

One line of evidence has to do with the effects of drugs that are currently used to treat depression. These drugs, called *monoamine oxidase inhibitors* (MAO inhibitors), have the ability to keep up the level of norepineprhine available in the brain. Thus, scientists reason, it may be the *lack* or norepineprhine in the brain that is associated with depression. Another line of evidence indicates that drugs that increase the level of norepinephrine in the brain tend to produce overactivity and alertness in laboratory animals. Still other evidence suggests that drugs capable of

FIGURE 8–2 Catecholamine Activity in Neurotransmission

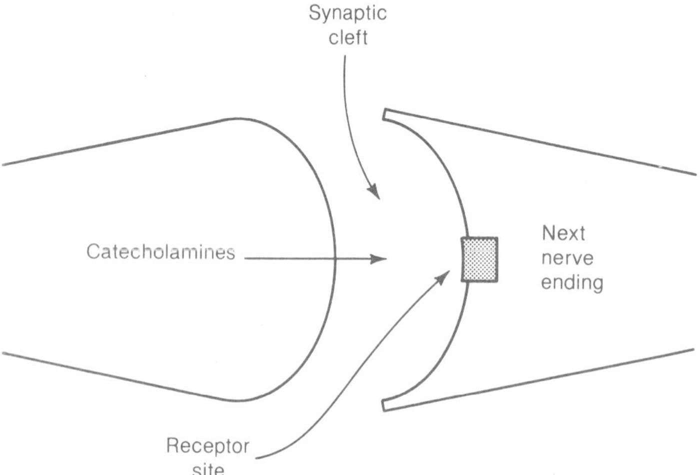

chemically reducing the amount of norepinephrine in the brain tend to produce behavior that looks very much like depression in laboratory animals.

All of this evidence is, of course, indirect. But it is intriguing to say the least. Weiss and his colleagues believe that this evidence for the catecholamine hypothesis is too important to be ignored and that perhaps learned helplessness is not learned after all.

The case for catecholamines. As we discussed the results that appear to support the learned helplessness hypothesis, we noted that most of the evidence was indirect. That is, no direct causal links have been found to show that learned helplessness and depression were the same thing. But it did appear that the parallels between the two were striking and could not be ignored. Similarly, as we examine the series of experiments conducted by Jay Weiss and his colleagues, we will see that none of the evidence is direct. The research involves experiments with laboratory animals rather than humans. But several things are worth noting. First, Weiss and his colleagues have shown remarkable resourcefulness in drawing not one but several lines of evidence that converge on the same general idea. That idea is that at least some aspects of learned helplessness can be explained by the depletion of norepinephrine in the brain of an animal exposed to stressful conditions. Thus, Weiss argues, biochemical events play an important role in the behavior that Seligman has described as learned helplessness.

Weiss is like a prosecutor carefully preparing his case. Each line of evidence by itself is not decisive, but the cumulative effect is impressive. Let us examine the research, both to learn more about depression and to learn how the dialogue between scientists with differing hypotheses proceeds.

1. *The depletion of norepinephrine produces behavior that looks like learned helplessness.* Weiss and his colleagues required laboratory rats to swim for 3.5 minutes in cold water.

This experience has been shown to result in decreased norepinephrine in the brain. When these rats were then later placed in a situation similar to that of Seligman's dogs, they behaved in very similar ways. They were unable to cross the hurdle to avoid shock. In most cases they showed behavior that otherwise resembled learned helplessness.

Thus, a condition that depleted norepinephrine in the brain was capable of producing a behavior that resembled learned helplessness. But, is it possible that the swimming experience itself rather than the cold water somehow produced a learned experience of helplessness? To test this Weiss and his colleagues exposed a control group to a 3.5 minute swim in warm water. These rats avoided shock in the shuttle apparatus in the normal fashion. Thus this evidence suggests that norepinephrine depletion is what produces the helpless behavior.

2. *Norepinephrine is essential for vigorous motor activity.* Weiss and his colleagues believe that is was not learning but the depletion of norepinephrine that produced a lack of vigorous motor activity in the avoidance behavior in Seligman's dogs. The trick for Weiss, then, was to devise an experiment that would allow animals to avoid shock if they were capable of doing so, but that would not require that they engage in vigorous motor activity. If animals could show that they were not "helpless" by engaging in an avoidance task that did not require vigorous motor activity, then Weiss would have shown that it was *motor activity* that was inhibited rather than learning. In order to do this, the invesitgators devised an experiment whereby animals could avoid shock by using a small movement rather than by having to climb over a hurdle in a shuttle box. When animals were exposed to inescapable shock and then later given the opportunity to avoid a shock using a small movement, they were able to do so. They were not *helpless* when the motor activity required to escape was small. Therefore, it appears that it is motor activity that is inhibited by norepinephrine depletion that explains the phenomenon.

3. *Recovery from helplessness by adaptation.* Neurochemical systems of the brain adapt to repeated experiences. If it were the neurochemical system involving norepinephrine that brought on the helpless behavior rather than a learning mechanism, repeated experiences with inescapable shock should produce norepinephrine depletion only at first. Later, as the brain adapted to the experience, depletion would not be great and the helpless behavior should no longer occur. This is precisely what the investigators found. Animals exposed to inescapable shock for only one session showed the expected helpless behavior. But animals exposed over a period of weeks to the same inescapable shock did *not* show helpless behavior when later exposed to the hurdle.

Thus, repeated exposure to the stressful condition did not produce the expected helpless behavior. If learning were the reason for the helpless behavior, we would expect that repeated trials would *strengthen* the helplessness rather than weaken it.

Thus, this test appears to produce particularly strong evidence in favor of a neurochemical adaptation rather than a learning explanation.

4. *Direct measures of norepinephrine depletion also show adaptation.* Weiss then obtained direct measures of the brain level of norepinephrine in laboratory animals. One group of animals had been exposed to one session of inescapable shock, another group was exposed to repeated sessions, and a third group was not exposed to inescapable shock at all. One session produced norepinephrine depletion but repeated sessions and no sessions of inescapable shock showed similarly high levels. Thus, adaptation does seem to be occurring in brain chemistry as well as behavior.
5. *Pharmacological experiments show consistent results.* Other experiments that involved the injecting of drugs with the effect of depleting norepinephrine were also found to produce helpless behavior. If this is true, then the injection of drugs that *maintain* the levels of norepinephrine in the brain should *protect* the animal from the experience of stress. This was precisely what was found. Drug-induced norepinephrine depletion produced helpless behavior. Meanwhile, protecting the animals from the stress of inescapable shock with antidepressive drugs also reduced markedly the amount of helpless behavior observed.

We described these experiments in detail because they provide a fairly strong case for a catecholamine explanation of learned helplessness. This research also illustrates nicely how a scientist can use his or her creativity in the laboratory. This series of experiments draws threads of evidence from very different sources and weaves them together into a fabric of results that all point in a similar direction. The sum of the results strongly suggests that the behavior Seligman has obtained in laboratory animals and called learned helplessness is at least as well explained by a physiological approach that emphasizes the effects of temporary stress and the depletion of norepinephrine, a neurotransmitter in the brain.

What are we to conclude from this? May we reasonably conclude that the learned helplessness hypothesis is incorrect? Is the credibility of biological models of abnormal behavior thus greatly enhanced? May we reasonably decide that learning is not involved in the development of clinical symptoms of depression?

As compelling as this biochemical line of evidence seems, we must be careful not to interpret it too broadly. First, and perhaps most important, it is safe to say that these results help us to sketch a more complete picture of the nature of depression without necessarily ruling out the role of learning. It is clear that stressful experiences like inescapable shock have extremely powerful effects on the adaptation of the organism. Some of these effects are presumably learned, but others, as Weiss' data clearly shows, are neurochemical and involve effects on neurotransmission in the brain.

Second, a relationship is now evident between chemical events in the brain and observable behavior. Thus, a link has been forged in the causal chain between stressful environmental events and their behavioral consequences. These findings do not rule out the important role of learning or the power of the enviornment to affect behavior. But the results help clarify what mechanisms

GENETIC DETERMINANTS OF AFFECTIVE DISORDERS

A number of studies have suggested that there is an important genetic component among the determinants of bipolar affective disorders. Rosenthal (1970, p. 209) has summarized the studies comparing concordance rates for monozygotic and dizygotic twin pairs. His summary is shown in the following table:

Concordance Rates for Bipolar and Affective Psychosis in MZ and DZ Twins

	MZ Twins			*DZ Twins*		
Study	*Total Pairs*	*Concordant Pairs*	*Concordance Rate*	*Total Pairs*	*Concordant Pairs*	*Concordance Rate*
Luxenburger, 1930*b*	4	3	75.0	13	0	0.0
Rosanoff et al., 1934	23	16	69.6	67	11	16.4
Kallmann, 1952*c*	27	25	92.6 100.0*	55	13	23.6
Slater, 1953:						
Only manic-depressive psychosis	7	4	57.1 80.0*	17	4	23.5
Other affective disorders	1	0	0.0	13	3	18.8
Da Fonseca, 1959: affective disorders	21	15	71.4	39	15	38.5
Harvald and Hauge, 1965†	10	5	50.0	39	1	2.6

* Corrected concordance rate.
† According to Zerbin-Rudin, 1967.
Source: Rosenthal, 1970.

You can see that the concordance rates are much higher for monozygotic than for dizygotic pairs, indicating a genetic component in the disorder.

Does this mean that all affective disorders necessarily have a strong genetic determinant? Not necessarily, according to Winokur and Clayton (1967) who examined the family histories of a sample of persons having affective disorders. These researchers were able to distinguish two groups of individuals. The first group they described as "family history positive" (FH+) cases. These people had a clear history of affective disorder for two generations and were clinically depressed and sometimes manic. The second group, "family history negative (FH−), had no evidence at all of family histories of affective disturbance and did not display mania, but only depression. This finding suggests that there may be some forms of mood disorders with strong genetic components and others with largely environmental determinants.

may be involved in linking the environment, the brain, and behavior in the development of depression.

A Social Perspective: Depression as an Interpersonal System

Until now, our focus has been largely on the depressed person rather than on the social field that surrounds the person. For example, the cognitive view of depression offered by Beck leaves us with the idea that the depressed person suffers from persistent negative thoughts, but this view says little about where these ideas originated. The learned helplessness view focuses on the depressed person's passivity and hopelessness. It appears to assume that if only the depressed person would respond, then the environment would react in turn with rewarding outcomes. Of course, the biochemical view of depression sees the passivity and depressed mood of the person suffering from depression primarily as a product of biochemical events.

But what goes on between the depressed person and others in his or her world? Until now, the interpersonal phenomena associated with depression have not been well understood, but clearly they deserve careful exploration. In order to avoid *tunnel vision* about the nature of depression, we need to ask some additional questions. For example, how do other people react to the behavior displayed by a depressed person? Is there something unique about the way others react to the depressive? Is it possible that something about the nature of this interactional system affects the persistence of depressive symptoms?

As Coyne (1976) notes, the depressed person's repeated complaints and self-accusations have distracted researchers from focusing on the social environment and the role it may play in maintaining depressed behavior. Perhaps it is fruitful for us to think about depression as something that goes on *between* people rather than only within individuals.

An interpersonal account of depression does not deny the importance of biochemical or genetic factors in the causation of depression. As Price (1974) has argued, even in disorders where the importance of these internal factors has already been established, there are a large number of links in the causal chain between a specific causal factor and the symptoms ultimately displayed by the person. In order to understand the interpersonal view of depression, we need only assume that the individual has begun to display the depressive behavior. The chain of events between the depressed person and others in his social environment follows in a straightforward way from this initial display of symptoms.

Theory. Recently, Coyne (1976a, b) has offered a theoretical description of the nature of transactions between the depressed person and people in the social environment. His description is summarized in Figure 8–3.

Coyne views depression as a response to the disruption of a person's social space from which they usually obtain support and validation of their own experience and identity. This disruption, as we have seen, can take the form of loss of significant relationships, or life changes such as promotion or retirements, or any of a number of other changes in the person's social structure. The symptoms of depression are seen as a set of messages demanding reassurance of the person's place in their interactional world. Thus, the depressed person's communications of helplessness and hopelessness, their

FIGURE 8–3 Interactional View of Depression

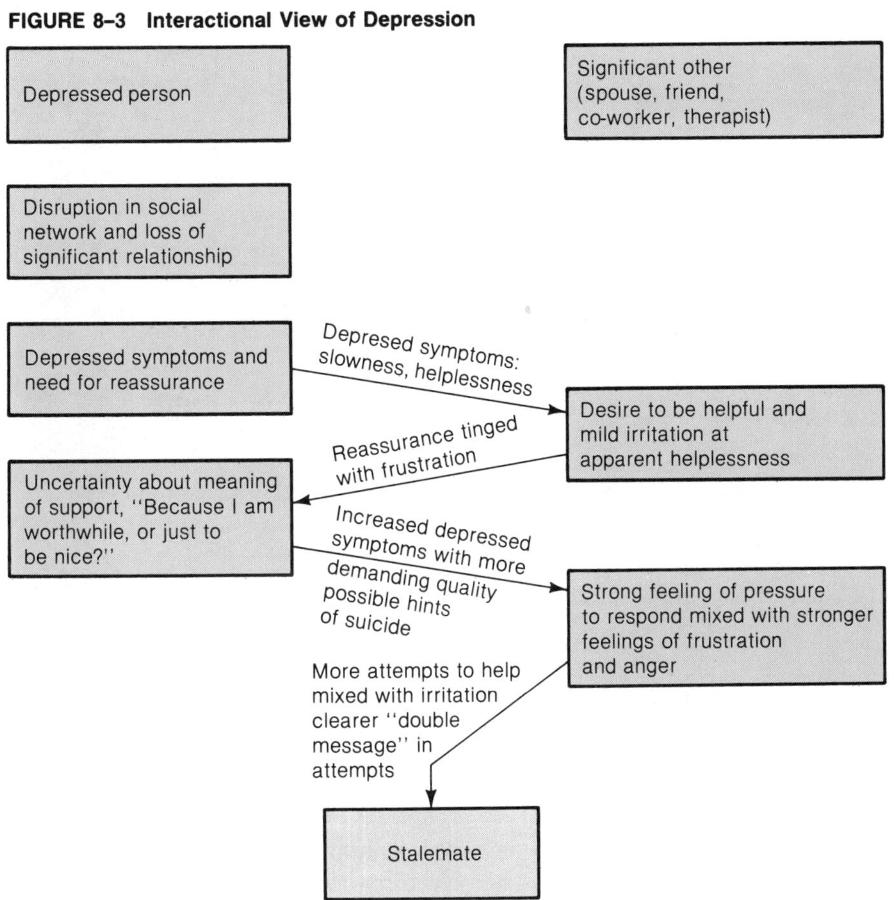

slowing and irritability, make others feel obliged to answer the depressed person's request for support and reassurance.

But direct responses and attempts to support and reassure the depressed person often have other messages associated with them as well. Frequently support and reassurance will be given, but the response will be colored by irritation and frustration. Thus, the message the depressed person receives in response to a request for reassurance is far from unambiguous support. On the one hand, the depressed person desperately needs support and reassurance that what remains of his or her social network is intact. But, on the other hand, the messages of support may frequently have a double meaning because the helper both wishes to reassure and feels frustrated with the lack of effect their efforts have.

In addition, by seeking reassurance in this way depressed people have placed themselves in a dilemma from which they cannot easily escape. The dilemma is this: Are other people assuring them that they are worthwhile and acceptable because those people really feel that way or only because they have attempted to obtain these responses from them?

The social support of even one close friend can be extremely important in coping with depression.

Look at Figure 8–3 again. You can see that this interpersonal process will repeat itself, and even subsequent attempts to seek feedback testing the nature of his acceptance by others cannot reduce the uncertainty. Meanwhile, these requests for repeated assurance become increasingly aversive to others in the person's social environment. As Coyne points out, the depressive has reached the first in a number of possible interactive stalemates in which a pattern of mutual manipulation has been established. There is a paradoxical character to this stalemate. Requesting information about how people *really* view the depressed person becomes indistinguishable from the depressive's symptoms. Continued requests to ask others how they really feel about him will probably only produce denial or an angry defensive response on the part of others.

Anyone who has spent a period of time trying to support, reassure, and be otherwise helpful to a severely depressed person may intuitively agree that they felt compelled to reach out to help and at the same time felt frustrated and perhaps even annoyed when their efforts seemed to have no real effect.

Research. But is there any research that supports this formulation? Coyne (1976a) has conducted an intriguing experiment that has yielded evidence bearing directly on this point. He notes that the behavioral approach to depression formulated by Ferster (1973) and further developed by Lewinsohn suggests that depressed people receive a low rate of positive reinforcement that is contingent on their own behavior. The behavioral view argues that it is the depressed person's lack of social skill that produces this state of affairs. On the other hand, Coyne notes, one could argue that the unwillingness of other people to interact with depressives could explain these findings equally well. More specifically, Coyne argues, the way in which depressed people interact with others may actually induce depression and hostility in those others, and this hostility may in turn lead to social rejection.

In order to test this idea, Coyne selected three groups of *target individuals.* One group consisted of depressed women from a mental health center population, a second comparison group consisted of nondepressed women from the same population, and a third comparison group consisted of normal women drawn from supermarket employees, customers, hospital auxiliary personnel, and neighbors. Coyne then recruited female undergraduates (subjects) to interact with these three groups of target individuals. Each subject was randomly assigned to one target individual and talked with her on the telephone for 20 minutes. Subjects were not aware of which group they were to talk with. Both people involved in the conversation were told that they were engaged in a study of the acquaintance process and that the conversations were taped. In addition, everyone was asked to fill out a questionnaire after the conversation recording their reactions to the other person.

If Coyne's hypothesis is correct, the subjects interacting with the depressed people ought to react very differently from the subjects interacting either with nondepressed patients or with normal individuals. Indeed, that is precisely what Coyne found. Subjects who interacted with depressed individuals became more depressed, anxious, and hostile *themselves* following the interactions than did those subjects who interacted with nondepressed patients or with normal controls. Furthermore, subjects were more rejecting of depressed patients and expressed much less willingness to interact with the depressed group again on another occasion. Analyses of the verbal content of the conversations themselves, however, did not turn up the behavior that led to these strikingly different perceptions.

Thus, the depressed patients in this study did produce negative feelings in other people. They were accepted less even though their activity level and rate of positive responses was no lower than that of other people. Coyne argues that the lower activity level of depressed persons is due to the fact that few people are willing to interact with them rather than because, as learning theorists have argued, their own rate of behavior is initially lower than that of nondepressed people.

Although this study only begins to develop an interpersonal account of depression, it provides promising results. This view of depression, which relies heavily on the social perspective, broadens the arena of inquiry about the nature of depression. Indeed, it suggests that depression is a social phenomenon. It is not only something that occurs within a person, but also something that occurs between people.

TREATMENT OF AFFECTIVE DISORDERS

In the past, severe episodes of depression frequently led to hospitalization. A major reason for the decision to hospitalize a depressed individual often had to do with the danger of suicide attempts. Another major reason for the hospitalization of depressed individuals had to do with the dramatic effect that hospitalization often produced. Clinicians have commonly noted that the simple act of hospitalization without any other active treatment often brought dramatic changes in the individual's depressed mood and behavior. Frequently, of course, these changes were due to the fact that the person was removed from stressful family or work circumstances that maintained the depressed behavior.

Currently, however, clinicians are much less likely to hospitalize severely depressed patients. There are at least two reasons for this. First, in the last few years there has been an increase in the use of various biological treatments for depression. Both pharmacological and convulsive therapies have yielded some measure of success in reducing depressed behavior. Second, psychological treatments for depression have now gone well beyond the traditional talking cures, and behavioral approaches in particular have been shown to be effective in many cases.

Most often biological and psychological approaches to treatment are used in combination rather than singly. Given our imperfect understanding of the mechanisms involved in depression, it is understandable that the treatment-oriented clinician would wish to use a combination of strategies in the hope that the combination would be more effective than any single approach.

But we should still remain skeptical of the effectiveness of various treatments. There are at least two reasons for this. First, as we noted, many depressed people react strongly to suggestion. Substantial research already exists (Mendels, 1970) to show that a person's expectations about treatment can produce a reduction in depressed behavior. Second, we should recall that depression is frequently a self-limiting disorder. That is, with or without treatment, many depressions will dissipate in six months to a year. With these cautions in mind, let us turn to a brief examination of biological and psychological approaches to the treatment of depression.

Antidepressant Drugs

When we discussed the biochemical hypothesis of depression, we noted evidence suggesting that a lowered level of neurotransmitters called catecholamines may be involved in some depressions. This evidence came in part from the research of pharmacologists who were interested in discovering an effective drug treatment for depression. The research was based on what biochemical researchers call the *precursor loading technique.*

The idea behind this technique is to selectively administer certain amino acids that are precursors of a biogenic amine. By administering these chemicals, the researcher is able to manipulate the biochemistry of depression. If a particular amino acid is effective in changing the clinical picture of depression for a particular patient, the researcher may have obtained a double bonus. First, he or she may have discovered an effective biochemical treatment for depression, and, second, a link in the biochemical chain of events in depression may have been uncovered. Some amino acids of this sort are already being marketed in England as antidepressant drugs (Akiskal & McKinney, 1975).

One set of compounds commonly used in the treatment of depression are called *tricyclic drugs,* such as imipramine. These compounds have been shown to have a therapeutic impact in treating psychotic depressions. A second major class of drugs used in the past to treat depression are called the *monoamine oxidase inhibitors* (MAO inhibitors). The evidence for the effectiveness of these drugs is less clear. Since they often produce complicating effects such as severe changes in blood pressure, they have been used much less than the tricyclics in the treatment of depression.

Our knowledge of the action of these drugs is still far from complete, and each of them appears to operate in different metabolic pathways of the brain. Thus, the choice of drugs for treatment has been made primarily on the grounds of clinical effectiveness and lack of serious side effects. The practical effect of the use of

ALCOHOLISM AND DRUG ABUSE AS SELF-MEDICATION FOR DEPRESSION

Of course, many individuals who suffer from depression never seek professional help for their difficulties. In fact, one of the most common patterns of behavior for individuals suffering from anxiety and depression is the use of alcohol or other drugs, such as sedatives, to temporarily relieve the insomnia and feelings of depression and helplessness that they experience. Since the use of sedatives or alcohol can have the temporary effect of reducing feelings of depression and insomnia, they tend to be used increasingly as the symptoms return. Soon a person who was originally experiencing a mild depression may also begin to experience the complications associated with alcoholism or chronic habitual drug abuse. Further, the disorders may be misdiagnosed as alcoholism when, in fact, the original problem may have been depression.

The use of Alcohol frequently occurs as a kind of "self medication" for depression.

Charles Harbutt/Magnum Photos, Inc.

these drugs has been that many depressed individuals have been significantly aided in their recovery and are able to continue functioning in their daily lives without recourse to hospitalization.

Lithium Therapy for Affective Disorders

An important form of pharmacological treatment, described by some writers (Fieve, 1976) as "the third revolution in psychiatry," is the use of *lithium carbonate,* particularly for bipolar affective disorders. Early prescriptions by Greek and Roman physicians of mineral water for affective disorders was probably due to the fact that these waters contained high quantities of lithium. Lithium is not a compound but an element, and one of the lightest of the alkaline metals in the periodic table.

Fieve describes the use of lithium for patients with affective disorders of the "metabolic ward" of the New York State Psychiatric Institute. Patients suffering from mood disorders are brought onto the ward and administered lithium while their behavior and metabolism are monitored using the mood scale shown in Figure 8–4.

Body chemistry and mood are monitored until the individual's mood stabilizes, at which point they are moved to an outpatient treatment status.

Fieve reports that psychotherapy is of little benefit for these patients and that, instead, an outpatient clinic designed to monitor the mood and lithium dosage of patients is both more effective and considerably less expensive than conventional care.

Electroconvulsive Therapy

In the 1930s it was often observed that a few patients suffering from schizophrenia were also epileptic. Physicians hypothesized that the abnormal electrical activity in the brain of epileptics prevented schizophrenic episodes. As implausible as this hypothesis now seems, physicians developed electroconvulsive therapy (ECT) as a treatment for schizophrenia. The treatment consisted of passing a current of electricity through the brain of the patient until a convulsion occurred.

The results of this treatment for schizophrenic patients was almost uniformly disappointing, but ECT had come into widespread use and soon was being used for treatment of depression. Interestingly, some severely depressed patients responded extremely well to the administration of electroconvulsive therapy, and it soon became a standard treatment for depression.

Most people find the idea of electroconvulsive therapy frightening and offensive. The idea of placing a patient on a treatment table and passing 70 to 130 volts through the frontal lobes of the brain, even for a half second, is a terrifying idea. Typically, today most patients are given an anesthetic and an intravenous injection of a muscle relaxant to prevent injury when the convulsions resulting from the ECT occur.

A typical course of treatment for ECT is six to eight treatments given at the rate of three a week. Mendels (1970) notes that more frequent treatment than this is not required since most patients who do not respond to ECT do so after six or eight treatments.

No one knows why electroconvulsive therapy has its therapeutic effects. The

FIGURE 8–4 Mood Scale Used to Monitor Treatment Progress

MOOD SCALE

(To be filled out in Metabolic Unit twice daily, before breakfast and before retiring, by both nurses (0-100) and patients (20-80). Also adaptable to lithium clinic outpatients.)

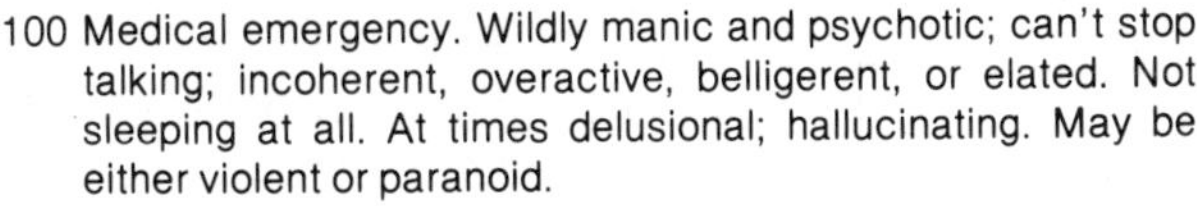

Nurses' and psychiatrists' rating scale (0–100)

Patient's self-rating scale (20–80)

Inpatient (100–90)

100 Medical emergency. Wildly manic and psychotic; can't stop talking; incoherent, overactive, belligerent, or elated. Not sleeping at all. At times delusional; hallucinating. May be either violent or paranoid.

90 Extreme elation so that patient can't rate self; in need of more medication and control. Completely uncooperative.

80 Severe elation. Should be admitted, or if in hospital usually wants to sign out of ward. Sleeping very little; hostile when crossed, loss of control. Needs medication.

70 Moderate elation. Overactivity and talkativeness; irritable and annoyed. Needs only four to six hours' sleep. Socially inappropriate; wants to control. Outpatient treatment has been advised by doctors.

Outpatient treatment

60 Mildly elevated mood and many ideas for new projects; occasionally mildly obtrusive. If creative, the energy is highly useful. Hyperperceptive. Feels wonderful, on top of the world. Increased sexual drive, wants to spend money and travel. Treatment may be contraindicated or not needed.

50 Mood is within normal range (45-55).

40 Mildly depressed mood, but noticable lack of energy; chronic lack of optimism and pleasure. Feels slowed down. Treatment may not be desired, although it may be indicated. Decreased interest in sex. Decreased motivation.

30 Moderate depression. Loss of energy; disinterested in others; early weight, sleep, and appetite disturbance; able to function with effort but wants to stay in bed during day; doesn't want to go to work; feels life is not worthwhile. Little sexual interest. Outpatient treatment advised by doctors.

20 Severe depresion. Takes care of daily routine but needs prodding and reminding; loss or gain of weight; sleep disorder is serious. Volunteers suicidal feelings; very withdrawn, may be paranoid.

Inpatient (10–0)

10 Extreme depression. Actively suicidal, totally withdrawn or extremely agitated. Difficulty rating self on mood scale.

0 Medical emergency. Unable to eat or take medication; can't follow ward routine; delusional, suicidal. Stuporous. Stares into space; very little response on questioning. May require tube feeding.

Source: R. R. Fieve, *Moodswing* (New York: Bantom 1976), p. 187

theories offered to explain its effectiveness range from the idea that depressed patients welcome it as an absolution for their guilt feelings to the suggestion that ECT produces biochemical changes in the brain which in turn alter the depressed person's mood (Mendels, 1970). One problem with the administration of ECT is that little is known about which patients are benefited by the treatment and which are not. However, some evidence does exist to suggest that endogenous depressions are relatively more benefited by ECT treatments.

A major side effect of electroconvulsive treatment is memory loss. In some individuals the loss can be severe, but for most it is temporary. The memory loss can have a negative effect on the recovery rate of a patient since the loss of memory even for the name of a close friend or relative can produce serious interpersonal complications.

With the advent of pharmacological and behavioral treatments for depression, electroconvulsive therapy is used much less than in the past. However, research is still needed to identify those patients who may benefit from the treatment.

Psychotherapy

For many years psychotherapy was a standard treatment for depression and the therapy was of the traditional talking cure type. Normally treatment of this sort was only supportive in nature and its therapeutic benefit seldom was well documented.

Beck's cognitive theory of depression (1970) has led him to develop a treatment technique that attempts to help depressed individuals to recognize and change cognitive habits or schemas that are typical of depression. Individuals are guided to attempt to change their cognitive habits of arbitrary inference or overgeneralization and therefore alter their depressive schemas.

Therapists who treat depressed individuals tend to tailor their therapeutic strategy to the unique psychological characteristics of depressed individuals. Among their strategies are the following:

1. Be sensitive to the fact that the depressive anticipates rejection. The therapist must communicate a careful acceptance of the patient in spite of the patient's own belief in his or her unworthiness.
2. The therapist should avoid encouraging too rapid a release of the suppressed feelings of anger and aggression that the patient may harbor.
3. The therapist must be careful to deal effectively with feelings of frustration and helplessness that the patient frequently induces in the therapist, and carefully control his or her own feelings of aggression.
4. A therapist should communicate an expectation that the depressed episode is self-limiting and that the condition will probably abate even though the patient currently feels desperate with his or her circumstances (Mendels, 1970).

Behavioral Approaches

Recently a number of psychologists have begun to develop behavioral approaches to the treatment of depression that in some ways parallel the learned helplessness formulation of depression we described earlier. Research by Lewinsohn

(1974b), for example, assumes that depression involves a *low rate of response contingent positive reinforcement* and that this low rate is a sufficient condition for explaining depression by itself. According to this view, treatment can involve a number of different strategies. One strategy is to increase the individual's activity level, using a graded task assignment procedure that requires the person to gradually increase the number or complexity of tasks that he successfully completes. Another behavioral strategy recommended by Lewinsohn involves social skill training that presumably improves the individual's ability to elicit positive reinforcement from the environment. Relaxation training, which promotes relaxation in the face of anxiety-provoking events, is also recommended. Lewinsohn further suggests the use of (1) a three-month time limit for treatment, (2) the use of home observations to examine the social environment of the patient and to gauge progress, and (3) the use of daily mood rating and monitors of the patient's activity level.

A unique concept in the treatment of depression suggested by Lewinsohn (1974) is the use of the *Premack principle.* The Premack principle states that the occurrence of a high frequency behavior can be used to reinforce a low frequency behavior. Once the individual emits the low frequency behavior, the high frequency behavior is allowed to occur. Thus the high frequency behavior can be used as a reinforcer to increase the frequency of the low frequency behavior. As we have noted, depressives display certain behaviors that occur with very high frequency. Expressed feelings of unhappiness, guilt, self-deprecation, and rejection are examples. Other behaviors that are desirable occur only infrequently, such as self-assertiveness and realistic judgments. Lewinsohn illustrates the use of the Premack principle in the following case.

Mrs. W, who was suffering from depression, displayed an extremely low activity level (low frequency behavior). In addition, she had many concerns and anxieties and spent a great deal of time telling the therapist about these concerns (high frequency behavior). The therapist then requested that Mrs. W increase the proportion of activity she was engaged in if she wished to talk about her complaints. She could talk about her complaints, the therapist explained, when a certain light in the therapy room was turned on. Mrs. W's initial reaction to this suggestion was angry indignation. When her verbalization rate for planned activities went up during the subsequent therapy hour, the light was turned on as a signal that she could, if she wished, discuss her complaints and concerns. Lewinsohn reported that her verbalizations in the therapy hour changed dramatically and her activity level subsequently changed as well.

Another illustration of the use of behavioral principles in the treatment of depression is offered by Liberman and Raskin (1971). The patient, a 37-year-old housewife, was severely depressed and had been since the death of her mother. She complained about somatic symptoms, paced, withdrew, and frequently cried. Members of her family responded to these depressed behaviors with helpfulness, sympathy and concern.

The therapist began rating two classes of behavior for the patient, *coping behavior,* such as cooking, cleaning the house, and tending to her children's needs, and *depressive behavior,* which included crying and complaining. The therapist then joined the patient's entire family and instructed the husband and children to pay instant and frequent attention to her coping behavior and to ignore her depressed behavior. The therapist taught family members to acknowledge her positive actions with approval, interest, and encouragement and to shift their attention from the "sick woman" to the housewife and mother.

Figure 8–5 shows the effect of the treatment. The first seven days of treatment were used to obtain pretreatment baselines for both depressive and coping behavior. You can see that the daily rates of coping behavior in the first week are very low and the rates of depressive behavior are very high. At the end of the first week the family was instructed to change their response to the mother's behavior. Dramatic decreases in depressed behavior accompanied by marked increases in coping behavior occurred for the next week.

Recall for a moment that we have said that depressed episodes are frequently self-limiting. How then are we to know whether the change in the behavior of the family is producing the behavior change in the mother or not? The answer is that these researchers then conducted a *clinical experiment* to demonstrate the causal link between her behavior and the responses generated in her family. On the

FIGURE 8–5 Modification of Depressive Behavior Using Reinforcement and Extinction Techniques Taught to Family Members

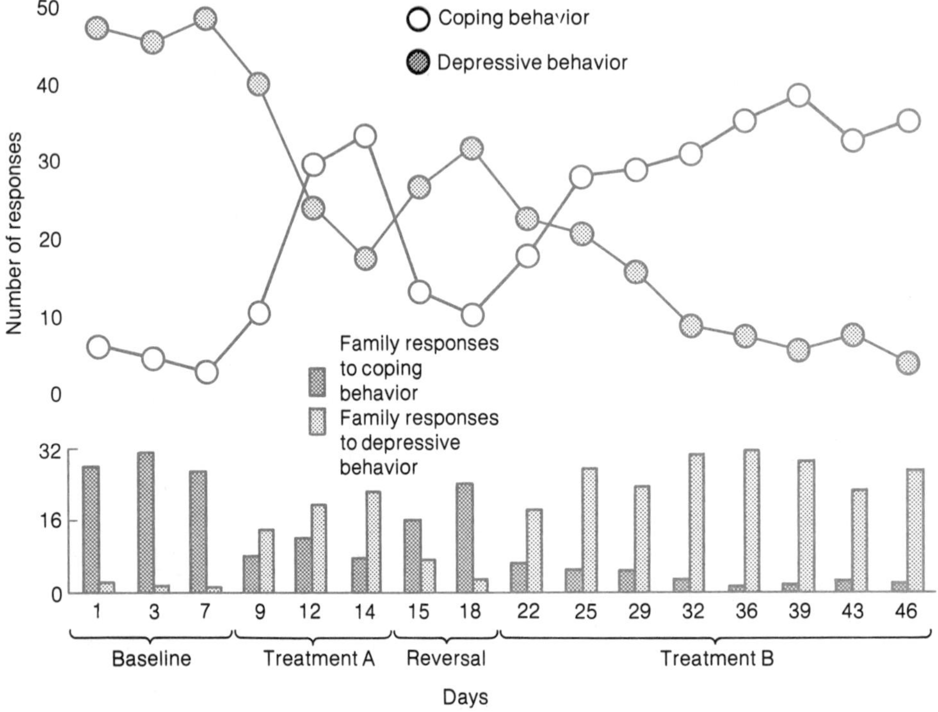

Source: R. P. Liberman and D. E. Raskin, "Depression: A Behavioral Formulation," *Archives of General Psychiatry* 24 (1971), pp. 515–23. Copyright 1971, American Medical Association.

14th day the therapist instructed the family to return to their previous behavior. That is they were again to provide attention and concern for her complaints. Within three days, the investigators note, she was once again showing high levels of depression. The effect can be seen in the "reversal days" of Figure 8–5. After the 18th day the treatment was reinstituted and dramatic improvement again occurred in the behavior of the patient.

This clinical experiment demonstrates the powerful impact the social environment can have on depressed behavior. From our point of view, treatment approaches such as these hold great promise in the clinical management of depression.

SUMMARY

In this chapter we have ranged widely in our survey of research and theory on the possible determinants and the treatment of affective disorders. In surveying predisposing and precipitating factors in the affective disorders, we noted that life events and changes may serve as triggers of affective disorders and that a variety of social and biological phenomena may predispose the individual to depression or manic episodes.

As we examined the various theories of depression, we observed that most of the major perspectives on abnormal behavior are represented. Psychoanalytic views of depression focus on the redirection of hostility or object loss as explanatory factors. Cognitive theories emphasize cognitive styles and distortions in the thought processes of the person suffering from affective disorders. In addition, three major new approaches to depression have become prominent in recent years. Learned helplessness argues that depression tends to be associated with a loss of contingency relationships between behavior and its outcomes. Biochemical theory and, in particular, the catecholamine hypothesis offers a direct challenge to learned helplessness as an explanation of affective disorders. Finally, we reviewed research derived from the social perspective that focuses on interpersonal behavior and its role in the development of affective disorders. Thus, we see that scientific inquiry into the causes of affective disorders is presenting theoretical challenges to previously established points of view from both biological and social perspectives.

Just as various theories of affective disorders emphasize different potential causal factors, the treatment of affective disorders also reflects a diversity of perspectives. Biological treatments including antidepressant drugs and lithium treatment as well as electroconvulsive therapy, all have shown at least modest success in the treatment of affective disorders while psychotherapy and behavioral approaches in particular have developed rapidly and offer new promise for the alleviation of suffering.

9

Psychophysiological Disorders

INTRODUCTION: WILLIAM L.'s ULCER

William L. has just taken a job as city editor in a large metropolitan newspaper. To take advantage of this opportunity for advancement in his profession, he has left a comfortable and satisfying editorial job on a small town newspaper where he worked for over ten years. His wife and two children were reluctant to make the move from their pleasant life in the country but finally agreed to the change.

Anxious to be a success in his new job, Mr. L. has been working long and irregular hours meeting deadlines for the newspaper. Still he finds himself losing sleep worrying about whether the tasks he has delegated to his staff are being completed properly. William L.'s eating habits have become irregular, and he finds himself drinking large amounts of coffee each day. Occasionally he experiences a burning feeling in the pit of his stomach. But he has ignored it since his digestion has always been rather delicate.

Lately Mr. L. has felt nauseated from time to time and has experienced sharp pains shortly after eating a meal. Still he continues working 16 hour days. Indeed, his efforts are beginning to pay off. He is finding himself more and more effective on the job. At the same time, however, the nausea has gotten worse and once when he actually got sick to his stomach, he noticed blood in his vomit.

Thoroughly frightened, Mr. L. decided to consult a physician. He was told that he had a severe duodenal ulcer and was promptly put on a special diet, given some medication, and told in an offhanded way to "take it easy"—something Mr. L. has never been able to do.

You may say, it is not so surprising that someone like William L. would develop an ulcer. He willingly placed himself under a great deal of stress. But how unusual are the stress-related psychophysiological disorders? Pelletier (1977) notes:

> Most standard medical textbooks attribute anywhere from 50 to 80 percent of all disease to . . . stress-related origins. Even the most conservative sources classify the following illnesses as psychophysiological: peptic ulcer, mucous colitis, ulcerative colitis, bronchial asthma, atopic dermatitis, urticaria and angioneurotic edema, hay fever, arthritis, Raynaud's disease, hypertension, hyperthyroidism, amenorrhea, enuresis, paroxysmal tachycardia, migraine headache, impotence, general sexual dysfunctions, sleep-onset insomnia, alcoholism. . . . An awesome statistic is that 30 million Americans

suffer from sleep-onset insomnia. These are the known insomniacs, and practitioners can only estimate how many others there must be who have not sought treatment. Among your friends, how many can you count who have suffered or are suffering from migraine, hypertension, asthma, hay fever, arthritis, peptic ulcer, nervous tension, or alcoholism? If you can answer "None," you have a rare group of friends indeed (p. 7).

Definition

Conventionally, the psychophysiological disorders are defined according to several criteria: (1) they are characterized by physical symptoms; (2) they are caused by emotional factors, (3) they involve a single organ system which is usually under autonomic nervous system innervation; (4) the physiological changes are the same as those associated with normally occurring emotional states, but in the psychophysiological disorders the changes are more intense and last for longer periods of time; and (5) the person may not be aware of his or her emotional state.

If you look back over the brief case history, you will see that Mr. L.'s ulcer bears the earmarks of a classic psychophysiological disorder. His ulcer involves a single organ system, the gastrointestinal system, and the emotional factors associated with the physical symptoms are self-evident. If Mr. L. had experienced intense emotional stress over a few days or even a few weeks rather than months, he would probably have experienced only heartburn associated with hyperacidity. But, the intense stress of his work continued over months at a time.

High stress jobs can lead to a variety of stress related psychophysiological disorders.

John Thoeming/Dorsey Press

He was in a continuous state of high autonomic nervous system activity and ultimately an organ system began to break down.

If you think about this case for a minute, a number of questions may occur to you. First, why did Mr. L. develop an ulcer rather than a heart attack or migraine headaches, or perhaps asthma? For that matter, why do many other city editors operating under the same deadlines and intense stress seem to avoid ulcers or any other psychosomatic disorder? It is these questions and others like them that researchers try to answer as they study psychophysiological disorders.

Range of Psychophysiological Disorders

When we offered a definition of the psychosomatic disorders, we said that they typically involved a single organ system, usually under autonomic nervous system control. In fact, psychophysiological disorders are likely to occur in association with at least six different organ systems. They are: (1) the gastrointestinal system, involving digestion, (2) the cardiovascular system, involving the distribution and flow of blood throughout the body, (3) the genitourinary system, associated with elimination and sexual functioning, (4) the respiratory system, associated with breathing, (5) the musculoskeletal system, associated with the control of muscles, and (6) the skin, which is an organ system in itself.

Distinguishing Features

As you begin to learn more about the psychophysiological disorders, a number of questions are likely to come to mind. What is it that makes these disorders distinctive? How are they different from a number of other disorders which seem to involve physical complaints? In discussing the somatoform disorders, we described hysterical conversion reactions and hypochondriasis, both of which superficially appear to involve physical complaints. How are psychophysiological disorders different from these patterns of abnormal behavior? On the other hand, you may wonder how psychophysiological disorders differ from other forms of organic disease, since both involve some form of actual tissue damage.

These are important questions. Some key distinguishing features of psychophysiological disorders are shown in Table 9–1. The table shows that the two neurotic disorders, conversion reaction and hypochondriasis, do not result in tissue damage to the affected organ and that physical treatment has little effect. Psychophysiological disorders and organic disorders, on the other hand, have a great deal in common. Both may result in tissue damage and both may respond positively to physical treatment, such as the administration of drugs or surgery.

Psychophysiological disorders are most sharply distinguished from other organic disorders by the degree to which they are likely to involve a psychological component or are stress-related. In addition, disorders such as ulcers, migraine headaches, or asthma often involve complete organ systems such as the gastrointestinal system, the cardiovascular system, or the respiratory system.

In fact, it is likely that all diseases or organic disorders may have some psychological roots. Most of us have recognized the experience of being more

TABLE 9–1 Comparison of Organic and Psychophysiological Disorders with Conversion Reactions and Hypochondriasis

	Organic Disease	*Psychophysiological Disorders*	*Conversion Reaction*	*Hypochondriasis*
General definition	Tissue damage resulting from microorganism or physical trauma	Stress-related disorder sometimes resulting in tissue damage	Form of neurosis in which the person suffers a loss of organ function with no organic basis	Irrational or neurotic fear that one is afflicted with a physical disorder
Examples	Appendicitis Common cold Bone fracture Syphilis	Ulcers Migraine headaches Hives Asthma	Hysterical blindness Glove anesthesia Hysterical paralysis Hysterical deafness	Unwarranted belief that one is suffering from cancer unrealistic fear of germs and infection
Tissue damage	Yes	Often	No	No
Structure involved	Any part of organism	Often involves organ systems stimulated by the autonomic nervous system	Sensory or motor systems	None, but preoccupation with all
Effect of physical treatment	Often positive	Often positive	Usually none	Usually none
Effect of suggestion	Usually none	Usually none	Modifies symptoms	May modify symptoms
Patient attitude toward disorder	Concern	Concern	Indifference	Extreme concern

susceptible to a cold after a period of prolonged stress has ended. Our resistance to infectious diseases, then, can be substantially affected by stressful psychological experiences.

At this point in our discussion, we should note that DSM III no longer retains a separate category for psychophysiological disorders. This change from previous classification systems reflects current thinking about physical disorders as having greater or lesser proportions of emotional factors involved in their development. Asthma has been called a psychophysiological illness because it is relatively more affected by emotional states as compared to diseases and disorders in general. However, the specific extent of the emotional involvement depends on the type of asthma *and* the individual. For example, many people who suffer asthmatic attacks are allergic to specific chemical substances in the air. Other asthma sufferers, as we will see, seem to experience symptoms that are clearly associated with emotional factors or stress. In still other cases, psychological and physiological factors may interact to jointly produce an asthmatic attack. In DSM III, the diagnostician can indicate whether a physical disease is present, and also specify the degree to which stress seems to be involved in the symptom picture. So, the boundary line between psychophysiologic disorders and other forms of disease is in some ways unclear.

We are reminded of the artificiality of any distinction between mind and body, or psychological and physical components of disorders. Our bodies are, after all, highly complex, finely tuned, adaptive physical mechanisms. Much of what we call a *psychological response* to events in our world manifests itself in the form of physiological reactions that mobilize our bodies to cope with the situations.

In the remainder of this chapter, we will examine three major psychophysiological disorders: headache, asthma, and ulcers. We consider the physiology of each of these disorders and examine research that attempts to isolate the determinants of the disorder. We will also examine several different theories that try to answer the two major questions we raised earlier: Why do some people develop psychophysiological disorders while others do not? And why do those who do develop psychophysiological disorders develop one form rather than another? We will also examine various treatments. Medical treatment either using drugs or surgery has long been a standard treatment for psychophysiological disorders. But we will discover that there is a range of psychological treatments that can also be highly effective. Finally, we will examine a new body of research on biofeedback as a treatment for psychophysiological disorders and examine some of its limitations as well as its potential benefits.

THE MIND/BODY PROBLEM

Western philosophy and science has made an arbitrary distinction between mind and body at least since the time of Descartes. This *dualism* is so ingrained in our thinking that we commonly refer to the mind and the body as if they were separate entities. Nowhere does this confusion become more acute than in attempting to discuss psychophysiological disorders. Even the term *psycho/somatic* underlines the arbitrary distinction between the psyche (mind) and soma (body). The distinction of course is extremely misleading.

Philosophers and scientists still debate the question of the relationship of our experience to physical matter. For a lively attack on the dualist tradition in philosophy and science, we suggest Gilbert Ryles's book, *The Mind-Body Problem.*

Later in our discussion, when we begin to consider the effects of stress on physiological systems, we will introduce the idea that the human body is continually involved in self-regulation of its own organ systems. Perhaps then, we will see more clearly how arbitrary the mind-body distinction is and begin to be wary of the intellectual traps that it lays for us.

HEADACHE

Nearly everyone has suffered a severe headache some time in their lives. In fact, approximately 20 percent of the population suffers from some form of recurrent chronic headache, and millions of dollars are spent each year for drugs to relieve headache symptoms.

In a general way the psychophysiology of a variety of different kinds of headaches is quite similar. All headaches involve a disturbance of blood flow within and around the brain. Since the brain itself has no nerve endings, the experience of headache is actually the result of blood vessels within the brain expanding or shrinking. These changes stimulate highly sensitive nerve endings within the blood vessels themselves. Thus, a headache is the result of the stimulation of highly sensitive nerve nets within the cranial arteries and veins as they expand or shrink.

A variety of different nonpsychological factors can change the shape of blood vessels in the head and produce a headache. For example, the common hangover is a consequence of chemicals produced as the alcohol is digested, which, in turn, affects the dilation of cranial blood vessels. Similarly, some foods contain chemicals that may stretch blood vessels, such as the common seasoning monosodium glutamate. Our primary interest, however, is not in headaches that are caused by direct changes in chemical composition, but in headaches that are produced, at least in part, as a response to stress.

Tension Headaches

Nearly half of all headaches are a consequence of muscle tension. Feelings of frustration, anger, or anxiety are often accompanied by increases in muscle tension. Similarly, a hard-driving, ambitious person who always seems ready for competition and mobilized for action will often experience chronic muscle tension.

But how does muscle tension lead to headache? When certain groups of muscles, especially those in the face, forehead, or neck, are extremely tense, the demand for oxygen in these muscles increases. And when the blood flow cannot keep up with the oxygen demand, the blood vessels in the head expand. It is this expansion of the blood vessels that produces the pain associated with a tension headache.

Migraine Headaches

Migraines are another form of chronic headache that is usually much more painful than tension headaches. It is estimated that approximately half of all of those people who suffer from chronic headaches are victims of migraines. In addition to the generalized pain associated with most headaches, migraine headaches frequently involve nausea, blurred vision, extreme sensitivity to light and sound, and visual images of light flashes or "scintillating scotoma."

There are essentially two phases of a migraine attack. In the first phase the flow of blood to parts of the head and brain is sharply reduced. This produces a reduction of oxygen available to the brain itself, and as a consequence, certain areas of the brain fail to function effectively. A migraine sufferer may, in this first phase, see various images if the visual area of the brain is affected or slur his or her words if speech areas of the brain are affected. During this first phase, the sufferer experiences no pain but can anticipate it because of these initial signs.

The second phase of the migraine headache occurs when a rush of blood to those areas of the brain deprived in the first phase produces a rapid expansion of arteries in the scalp. This expansion, with its associated stimulation of nerve endings, produces extreme pain which may last from several hours to a day or two.

What do we know about the determinants of tension and migraine headaches? Bakal (1975) concludes from a review of the literature on headache that nonspecific psychological stress is a major triggering event for headaches. He notes that the stress associated with a variety of life changes, including vacations, examinations, increased responsibilities, criticism, and fear of failure, have all been associated with the onset of headache. Furthermore, people suffering from migraine headache tend to attribute the cause to feelings of anger, frustration, anxiety, and other such problem situations in their lives.

There is a fair amount of evidence that migraine headaches have a genetic component. Twin studies have reported very high concordance rates for identical compared to fraternal twins. However, Waters (1971) has conducted a careful study that suggests that the hereditary basis of migraines may be somewhat overemphasized. In any case, it is fairly clear that both environmental stresses and constitutional disposition play a role in the etiology of headache.

Overview of Treatment

The treatment of headache has been approached in three major ways. First, various drugs have been used to treat both tension and migraine headaches. Second, psychotherapy can relieve both kinds of headaches to some extent. Finally, biofeedback methods have become a major approach to the treatment of headache.

Nearly everyone has used aspirin or some aspirin substitute to reduce the pain associated with a tension headache at one time or another. Frequently the simple nonprescription use of aspirin or the use of tranquilizers to reduce the tension associated with tension headaches can be effective in treating this sort of head pain. For migraine headaches a drug called *ergotamine* is frequently prescribed. This drug, which mimicks the effects of serotonin and shrinks the large blood vessels in the brain while expanding small ones, counteracts the usual sequence of events in the course of migraine headaches.

The second approach to the treatment of headaches associated with stress is psychotherapy. If the psychotherapy leads the person to change his or her life situation and to either cope more effectively with stressful situations or to avoid them, it is likely that headaches associated with stress will be substantially reduced. For example, a business executive who decides to change jobs to avoid chronic stress may leave his or her headaches with the old job.

Biofeedback is now being used to treat headache as well as a number of other psychophysiological disorders. Its application provides a new approach to treatment that does not require the administration of drugs. Although we will discuss biofeedback in more detail later, let us examine one example of its use in treating headache.

Biofeedback is the term used to describe any system that allows a person to monitor physiological changes in his or

Person receiving biofeedback of the cranial pulse. When the pulse falls below a given rate a light is illuminated, giving feedback to the subject.

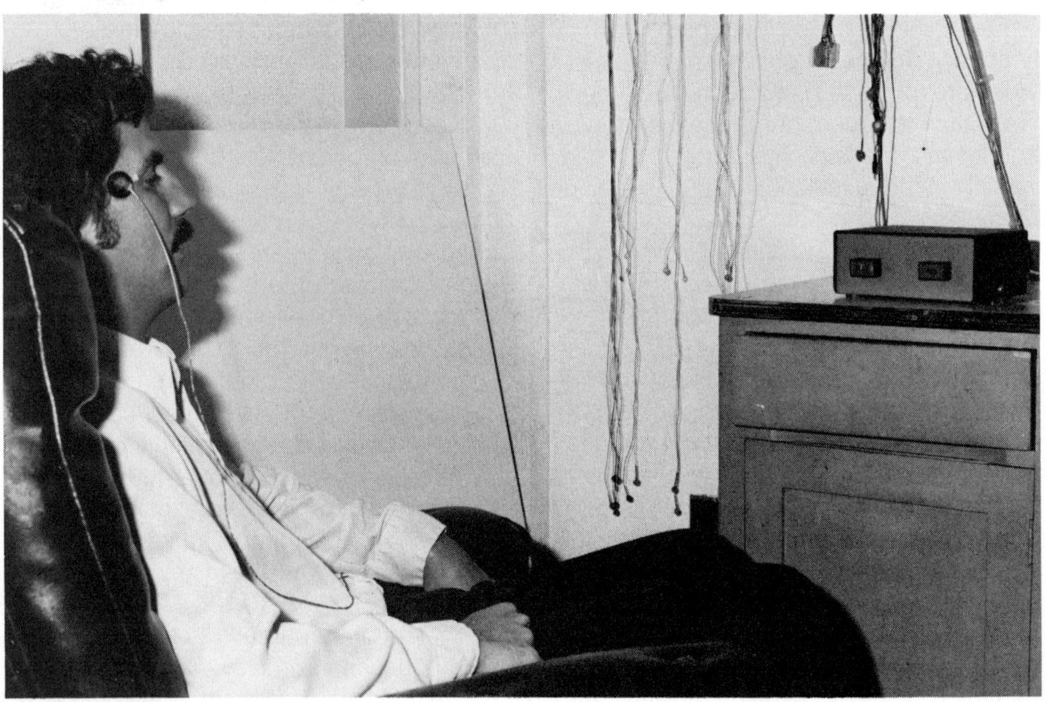

Courtesy of Ronald Fudge, Ph.D., Lafayette Clinic, Detroit

her body and to learn through trial and error to alter those physiological responses. It is possible, for example, to monitor muscle tension, blood pressure, sweating, and a variety of other physiological responses through biofeedback processes.

A recent controlled study examining the effects of biofeedback in treating migraine headaches has been conducted by Friar and Beatty (1976). These investigators taught patients to control the pulse size in their foreheads in order to control blood flow to their heads for the purposes of relieving migraine headaches. To control for the effects of suggestion, they gave half of the volunteers biofeedback of pulse measured from their index fingers and told both groups that biofeedback training would help stop their migraine. Since control of the pulse in the index finger will have no effect on migraine headaches, it was expected that any feedback effect for forehead pulse size group on migraine occurrence would be an actual result of the treatment itself rather than suggestion.

Both groups were asked to report the number and intensity of their headaches during and after biofeedback training. All subjects were told to attempt to lower their pulse size as they had learned during biofeedback training when they felt a migraine headache coming on. The results were impressive. Biofeedback training in the experimental group resulted in a reduction in the number of migraines and a reduction in the use of drugs as well.

Thus, we can see the possibility of biofeedback being used as a tool to help people bring a physiological response under voluntary control and perhaps to prevent the symptoms of headache.

Asthma

Bronchial asthma is a disorder involving the respiratory system. Asthma is characterized by a narrowing of the airways leading to the lungs and leaves the sufferer wheezing and struggling for breath. There are two major types of bronchial asthma. One is called the *extrinsic* type and is a response to some substance to which the person is allergic. The substance may be dust, the chemical composition of some foods, or some other external allergens. The other type, called *intrinsic,* is typically associated with some respiratory infection, such as bronchitis. However, still a third type of asthma appears to be associated with emotional factors or stress and may properly be termed *psychophysiologic* asthma.

Asthma frequently affects children, and it is estimated that more than half of all asthmatics are 17 years of age or younger. Boys are about twice as frequent sufferers as girls, and many asthmatic patients experience relief from the disorder as they grow older.

Family Determinants of Asthma in Children

As we have noted, there are a variety of determinants of asthma attacks, and allergens and intrinsic factors are the major cause. However, according to Rees (1964), 7 percent of cases are precipitated by emotional reactions or emotionally arousing experiences. Indeed, it appears that the home environment can play an important role in precipitating and maintaining asthmatic attacks in some children.

This finding is illustrated by the fascinating study conducted by Purcell, et al. (1969). Purcell selected two groups of families. In one group, a prior study had suggested that emotional factors were important in trigerring asthmatic attacks in the children. In the other group, emotional factors did not seem important. Then Purcell and his colleagues instituted a dramatic experimental intervention. After selection and careful preparation, the children were removed from their homes and a substitute mother lived with the child for a period of two weeks.

During the two week period, a number of measures of asthmatic symptoms were taken, including the frequency and intensity of attacks. For the group of children in which emotional factors were thought to be important, there was a dramatic decrease in the frequency of asthmatic attacks during separation, but in the group where emotional factors were not thought to be important, very little change occurred. When the families of the experimental group rejoined their children at home, the asthmatic attacks increased again.

Thus, Purcell and his colleagues demonstrated that for a proportion of children, emotional factors in the family environment can play an important role in triggering asthmatic attacks. We should remember, however, that these findings are not true of all children experiencing asthmatic attacks, and that infection and allergy also may be frequent causes of asthmatic attacks.

Overview of Treatment

Typically, the medical treatment for asthmatic attacks includes the administration of *epinephrine,* a stimulant that expands the air passages and restores breathing. For persons suffering from allergic asthma, preventive measures to avoid contact with the allergens appear to be the most appropriate strategy. However, it is also possible to use psychological interventions to aid in the reduction of asthmatic attacks.

An example of a behavioral approach to the treatment of asthma has been offered by Neisworth and Moore (1972). These investigators treated a seven-year-old boy who had been suffering from severe asthmatic attacks since the age of two. Although this child had received a variety of medications and had been placed on special diets, none of these measures had substantially reduced the frequency of his asthma attacks. The investigators believed that this child was living in a family environment in which behavior of the parents, particularly the mother, was triggering and possibly maintaining asthma attacks in the child. Consequently, Neisworth and Moore developed a treatment procedure in which the parents were asked to avoid giving attention and medicine to the child during asthmatic attacks which typically occurred at bedtime. In addition, an analysis of what would constitute a positive reinforcer for the child was conducted. Upon discovering that receiving lunch money to buy his own lunch at school rather than carrying a lunch constituted a powerful reinforcer, the child was given lunch money on those mornings that followed a substantial reduction in the asthma attack occurring at bedtime.

After an initial baseline period to measure the level of asthma attacks, the treatment procedure was instituted. It was followed by a reduction in the length of the asthmatic attacks at bedtime from over 60 minutes to less than 5 minutes. When the treatment was suspended briefly to test its effectiveness, the frequency and intensity of asthmatic attacks again increased until the behavioral treatment was reinstated. On a follow-up observation several months later, the child had shown a striking decrease in the length of asthmatic attacks to an average duration of only two minutes.

Thus we see psychological interventions in the family context can be used as a basis for treatment of asthmatic attacks and in some cases, where the emotional climate of the family plays a significant role, such interventions can be highly effective.

ULCERS

A peptic ulcer is a lesion or inflamed focal area that may occur in the stomach lining or the duodenum. These lesions may produce internal bleeding and in some cases the bleeding may be so severe that it is life threatening to the individual.

In normal people, stomach acid secretion occurs when food enters, or is about to enter, the stomach and secretion stops when digestion of the food is completed. However, in people suffering from ulcers, acid secretion may occur when no food is in the stomach. As a result, the stomach acid attacks the tissue of the stomach itself, producing inflammation and the injury that we call an ulcer. People suffering from ulcers tend to produce between 4 and 20 times more stomach acid when the stomach is comparatively empty than do normal individuals (Maher, 1966).

The normal sequence of events associated with acid secretion in the stomach can be described as occurring in two phases. The first phase is called the *cephalic phase* and begins when food is chewed. The action of chewing sets up a series of chemical events so that acid secretion actually begins before food has reached the stomach. During this phase, approximately 20 percent of all the acid secretion occurs and is a result of the activation of vagus nerve. The second phase, called the *gastric phase,* occurs when food actually enters the stomach. Contact of food with the mucus membrane of the stomach produces a substance called *gastrin* which, in turn, activates the secretion of acid in the stomach.

In broad outline, the physiology of ulcers is fairly well understood. It is the secretion of stomach acid attacking the stomach lining itself that produces the ulcer. But what factors, either psychological or physiological, lead people suffering from ulcers to secrete more stomach acid, particularly when no food is in the stomach?

An early set of studies by Brady (1958) suggested that an important psychological factor in the production of ulcers had to do with the ability of the person to control the stressors in his or her life. Brady conducted a now famous series of studies with monkeys that have come to be known as the "executive monkey" studies that illustrate this point. The basic experimental arrangement used by Brady is shown below.

In this study a pair of monkeys was placed in an apparatus in which they would receive a strong unsignaled shock. One monkey, called the "executive," was able to press a lever that would postpone the shock for 20 seconds and if it continued pressing within a 20-second period it could postpone the shock indefinitely. The other monkey received shocks at the same time as did the executive monkey but had no control over whether or not the shock would occur. Brady reported that the executive monkeys in this experiment tended to develop duodenal ulcers while the paired monkey, who did not have to cope with postponing the shock, did not develop ulcers.

As you might imagine, these experiments produced enormous excitement in the scientific community. Here seemed to be an experimental analogue of many of the life stresses experienced by people coping with stress. Unfortunately, attempts by other scientists to repeat the experiment met with mixed

A human stomach (opened) in which there is an ulcer. The esophagus enters at the top center and is seen within the circle of dotted white lines. The point of esophageal entry is surrounded by cells similar to those in the rumen of the rat; the extent of this small region is demarcated by the same dotted circle. Between the two dotted lines, a and b, toward the bottom of the stomach lies the pylorus, and below the lowest dotted line lies the top of the duodenum. The ulcer can be seen at the border of the pylorus and the duodenum.

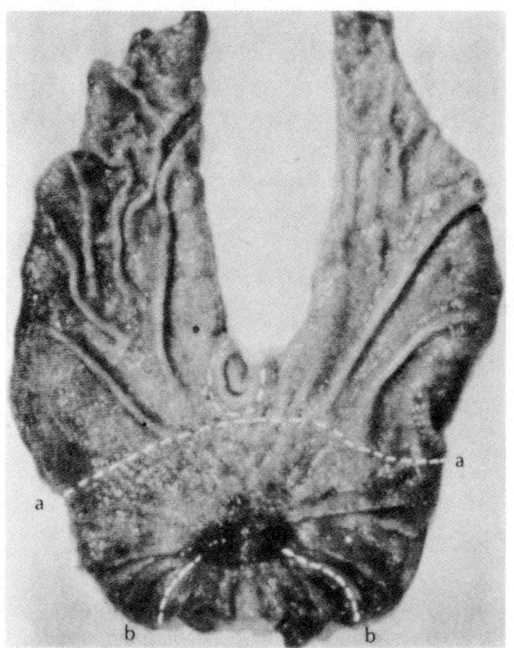

Photo courtesy of Williams & Wilkins Company

Source: Reprinted by permission of the publisher from M. Oi, K. Oshida, and A. Sugimura, "The Location of Gastric Ulcer," *Gastroenterology,* 1959, *36,* pp. 45–56. Copyright 1959 by Elsevier North Holland, Inc.

An "executive" or avoidance-escape monkey (left) and a yoked monkey (right) in primate chairs during the avoidance procedure.

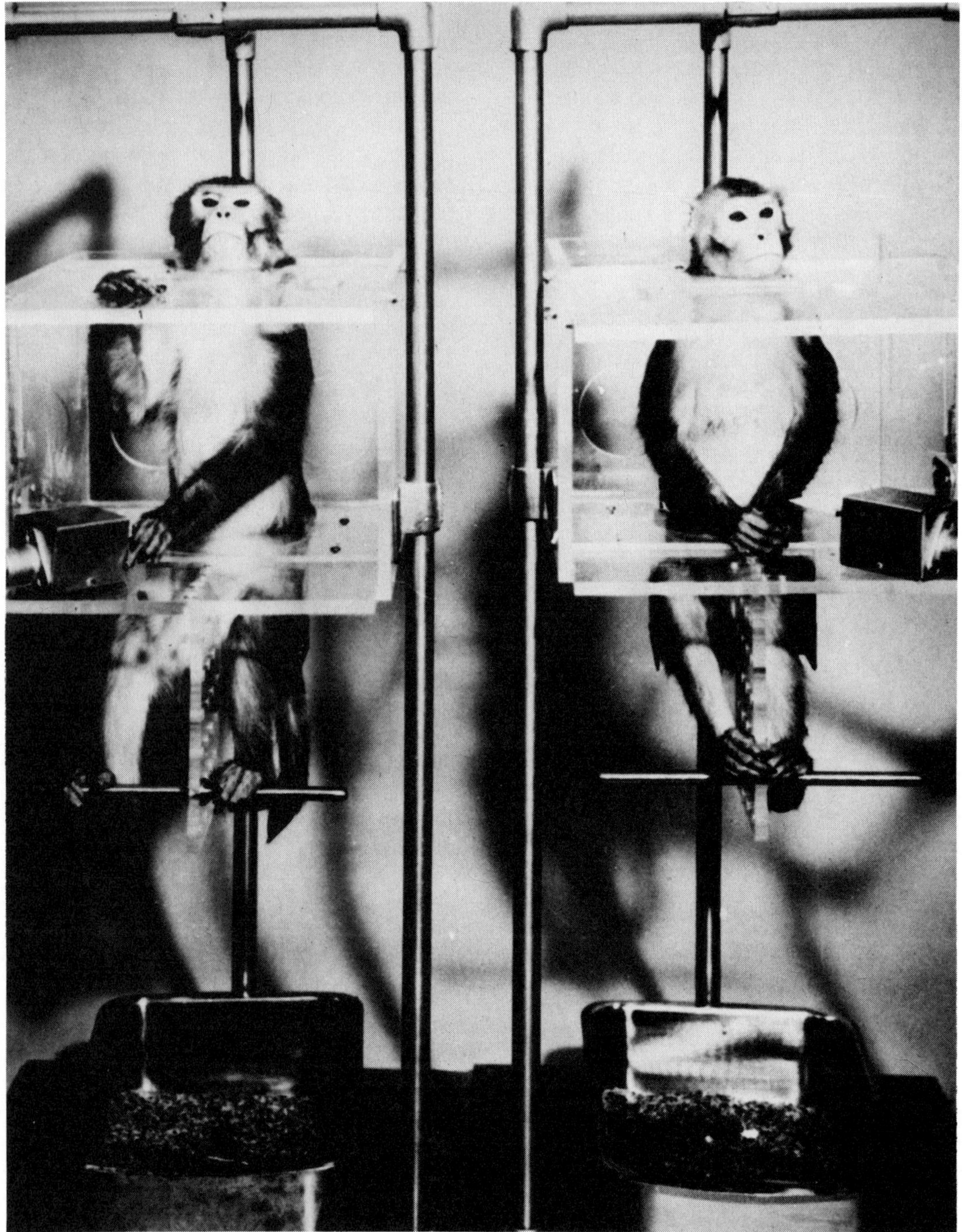

Source: J. V. Brady, Ulcers in executive monkeys *Scientific American,* October 1958, 95–100.

results. For example, Foltz and Millett (1964) reported that they were unable to reproduce the original result. However, additional research using more carefully controlled methods (Weiss, 1971) did show that there was a relationship between the number of attempts to cope with stress and the production of ulcers.

Weiss found that when animals received positive feedback about the correctness of their attempts to avoid stressful shock, they developed fewer ulcers than those animals who did not receive appropriate feedback. Weiss speculated that the high rate of responding to cope with stress and a low amount of feedback were the two critical factors in the development of ulcer lesions. Thus it appears that psychological factors are of great importance in the development of ulcers, but that the picture is much more complex than Brady had originally suspected.

Other factors seemed also to be important in the development of ulcers. How do we explain the fact that even under optimal environmental conditions for ulcer development some people develop ulcers while others do not? It appears that there may be some factor that makes some people more vulnerable to ulcer development than others. A field study conducted by Weiner, et al. (1957) provides an intriguing lead. His work suggests that there is a relationship between ulcer formation and the amount of *pepsinogen* in the digestive system of the individual. Pepsinogen is an enzyme that stimulates gastric activity.

Weiner measured the blood level of pepsinogen in over 2,000 draftees before they underwent the stress of basic training in the army. He found that those trainees who showed high levels of blood serum pepsinogen developed many more ulcers than those with low levels when exposed to the stress of basic training. Furthermore, he found that among those people who developed ulcers, a particular personality pattern emerged. The group who developed ulcers appeared to be more passive and dependent than did those who did not.

Thus we see a complex picture emerging from this study. The results suggest that three factors seem important in the development of ulcers: the presence of stress, a predisposing biological factor, and a pattern of personality characteristics. How these factors combine to produce ulcers and whether all three are equally important is still largely unknown. But, as is the case with other forms of psychophysiological disorders, biological predisposition, environmental stress, and the person's style in coping with that stress all appear to be critical factors in unlocking the puzzle.

THEORIES OF PSYCHOPHYSIOLOGICAL DISORDERS

Thus far we have examined some of the defining characteristics of psychophysiological disorders and discussed headache, asthma, and ulcers as typical examples. But a number of puzzling questions remain unanswered. Why do some people develop psychophysiological disorders while others seem invulnerable? What is it that triggers the psychophysiological response? Can we identify particular psychological events or genetic predispositions that help answer these questions?

Scientists have sought answers to these questions largely in the context of their own favorite theoretical perspective. Let us consider some hypotheses regarding the origins of psychophysiological disorders formulated from the psychoanalytic, learning, illness, and social perspectives.

Psychoanalytic Perspective: The Specific Emotion Hypothesis

A number of psychoanalists, most notably Franz Alexander (1950), argue that *psychophysiological disorders occur when conflicts that have been developed during infancy are repressed but then are stimulated again in adulthood* by some environmental circumstance. Alexander believes that the individual then regresses to this earlier mode of functioning and that the regression is accompanied by some physiological response which becomes the psychophysiologic symptom.

For example, Alexander attempts to explain the occurrence of stomach ulcers by arguing that infantile cravings to be fed are symbolically equated in childhood with a wish to be loved and feelings of dependency. But as the child grows older, these needs for love and dependency come into conflict with adult standards for independence and self-assertion. When these conflicts are reawakened in adulthood, they activate the gastrointestinal system, which has been previously associated with feeding. The result, according to Alexander, is a peptic ulcer.

DO PSYCHOPHYSIOLOGICAL SYMPTOMS HAVE SYMBOLIC MEANING?

Dynamic theorists suggest that many psychophysiological disorders reflect symbolic expressions of interpersonal or internal conflict. They argue that once the individual gains insight into the nature of these conflicts, the conflict will be lessened and along with it the psychophysiological symptom.

An example of this hypothesis is offered by Pelletier (1977). Pelletier reports working with a client whose psychophysiological symptom clearly indicated that the condition was symbolic of an underlying psychological problem. Pelletier reports the case of a nurse who came to him for treatment of *wry neck,* a condition in which the head is turned to face over the patient's right shoulder. The nurse had suffered from this condition for more than five years. In the course of her treatment with Pelletier, she expressed her shame about a long-concealed affair with a younger married man. She noted at one point in her treatment, "if my neighbors ever found out, I couldn't look them in the face." Pelletier suggested that her symptom was a symbolic means of preventing her neighbors from looking her straight in the face even if they found out about the affair. He notes that when she began to have insight into the connection between her psychophysiological disorder and her internal psychological conflict about her affair, her condition steadily improved.

Do you think this is convincing evidence for the symbolic meaning of psychophysiological disorders? Can you offer alternative explanations for Pelletier's report?

This hypothesis, sometimes called Alexander's (1950) *specific emotion hypothesis,* has little controlled experimental evidence to support it. Psychophysiological disorders are often explained *after the fact,* using some version of the specific emotion hypothesis. However, we should remember that it is all too easy to draw selectively on evidence from retrospective clinical reports that is consistent with a psychoanalytic hypothesis while ignoring contrary evidence.

Also, as Maher (1966) notes, it may not be the specific symbolic *content* of the conflict that produces the disorder, but simply the fact that it is a stressor. If this is the case, then focusing on the content of the stressor may lead us to overemphasize its importance while ignoring the more general but important fact that stress may play a role in the development of the disorder.

Learning Perspective: Autonomic Learning and the Vicious Circle

As we might expect, learning theorists have also attempted to offer explanations for the development of psychophysiological disorders. One of the major proponents of this view is Lachman (1972). He argues that most psychophysiological disorders are *learned physiological reactions to stress.* He believes that particular autonomic responses can be learned on the basis of differential reinforcement and that when psychophysiological disorders are rewarded, perhaps by removing the individual from the stressful situation, they are likely to occur again in similar stimulus situations.

> *Autonomic response learning* is another fundamental concept. Not only are autonomic responses learned on the basis of their being conditioned to new stimuli, but also particular autonomic responses are selectively learned on the basis of differential reward or reinforcement. A specific rewarded autonomic response tends to be differentiated out of the emotional response constellation and to be selectively strengthened. Thus, the individual who is rewarded for his expression of gastrointestinal pain by being permitted to stay home from school or from work and who is given special attention, consideration, and love under those circumstances is likely to have strengthened gastrointestinal reactions that led to the gastrointestinal pain, that is, increased gastric acid secretion. This is a statement of the idea that *rewarded autonomic responses may be selectively learned.*
>
> The concept of *vicious-circle effects* is also necessary to understand certain psychosomatic phenomena. Once initiated, a psychosomatic event may produce stimuli that lead to implicit reactions, which

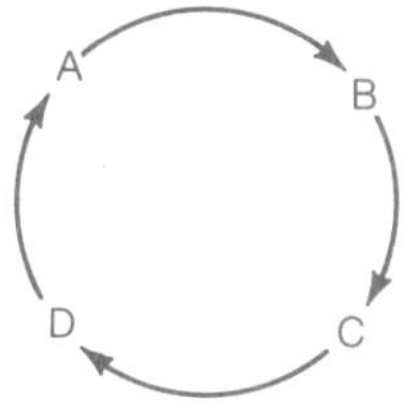

Vicious circle for ulcer development.
A = Noxious stimulation from area of ulcer;
B = Perceptual effect of noxious stimulation;
C = Emotional reaction including gastric gland secretion; and
D = Further inflammation of ulcer.

> rearouse or intensify the psychosomatic event, and so on. For example, the noxious stimulation from a gastric ulcer may elicit implicit reactions including facilitated stomach-acid secretion, which intensifies that ulcerous condition, which leads to further emotional reaction and further irritation of the ulcer. Theoretically, and perhaps in fact, an individual may worry himself to death in such a vicious circle (Lachman, 1972, p. 67–68).

This is an intriguing hypothesis and highly plausible. Certainly it is possible to demonstrate operant learning of specific autonomic responses in the laboratory. For certain disorders, such as asthma, the response of the family to an asthmatic attack in the child may actually reinforce subsequent asthmatic attacks, thus increasing their likelihood.

Furthermore, Lachman's idea that a vicious circle can both maintain and intensify the severity of a psychophysiological disorder is a fruitful one. Thus, a person who suffers from cardiac arrhythmia may worry constantly about the possibility of suffering a heart attack. The worry may intensify the psychophysiological reaction and result in even more instances of arrhythmia.

Illness Perspective: The General Adaptation Syndrome and the Somatic Weakness Hypothesis

Perhaps the single most famous account of stress is that offered by Hans Selye in his famous book, *The Stress of Life* (1956). In that book, he argues that psychophysiological disorders are really *diseases of adaptation.* All individuals are, he argues, equipped with a physiology that responds to stressful circumstances by activating the organism. This general pattern of response to stress he calls the *general adaptation syndrome.*

Hans Selye

Courtesy of Hans Selye, photo © Laszlo

According to Selye, all stressors of life when prolonged, regardless of whether they are due to conflict or frustration, lead the individual through three stages in the general adaptation syndrome. The first stage, called the *alarm reaction,* activates the organism and involves excitation to the autonomic nervous system, the discharge of adrenalin, increased heart rate, and gastrointestinal acid secretion. If the organism remains under prolonged stress, it moves to a second stage of *resistance.* In this stage the organism remains activated but begins to adapt to these physiological changes. However, in the third stage, which Selye calls *exhaustion,* resistance ultimately breaks down and the organism can no longer sustain high levels of activation. The result is tissue damage in one organ system or another.

This account traces the likely developmental course of psychophysiological disorders but tells us little about which organ system is likely to be affected. However, another hypothesis derived from the illness perspective does suggest a possible answer. Often called the *somatic weakness hypothesis,* it argues that there are large inherited individual differences in physiological reactivity in different organ systems. These inherited differences become particularly important when an individual is subjected to stress. Thus, presumably, some organ systems possess an inherited somatic weakness and, with sufficient stress, it is that organ system that breaks down, resulting in a psychophysiological disorder.

We have already noted that a number of disorders, such as asthma and hypertension, tend to run in families. Twin studies, when they have been conducted offer at least modest evidence that there is a genetic component in some psychophysiological disorders. In addition, we noted earlier that large individual differences in pepsinogen, an eynzme involved in digestion, exist among ulcer prone individuals, thus suggesting a possible genetic mechanism.

Certainly, the idea of the general adaptation syndrome and the somatic weakness hypothesis are useful parts of the psychophysiological puzzle and help to account for some of the observed characteristics of these disorders. But, what is the nature of the stressor that Selye talks about? Part of the answer is to be found in the ideas of researchers who work in the tradition of the social perspective.

Social Perspective: Stressful Life Events and Cultural Differences

For the most part, we have been referring to stressors in a very general way. But what are these stressors? Can we identify the most common of them? Holmes and his colleagues have conducted numerous studies directed at identifying life events which appear particularly stressful to individuals.

One product of their research is an instrument they call the Social Readjustment Rating Scale that lists a large number of potentially stressful life events. Table 9–2 provides us with a list of such stressors. It may be instructive for you to examine this list to see how many of these life events you have recently experienced.

A careful look at this list suggests that not all life events that are stressful are necessarily negative in their connotation. Events such as job promotions, outstanding personal achievements, and marriage all may be stressful and are capable of predicting the development of subsequent illness. It appears, then, that life events requiring major adaptations all have the potential to elicit stress reactions and may place the person at risk for the development of psychophysiological disorders.

Holmes and his coworkers have also conducted cross-cultural research on life events. Their findings suggest that the reactions to life events among cultures differ. For example, when they compared Americans and Japanese, they discovered some interesting cultural differences in the importance of different life events.

TABLE 9–2 Social-Readjustment Rating Scale

Rank	*Life-Event*	*Mean Value*
1	Death of spouse	100
2	Divorce	73
3	Marital separation	65
4	Jail term	63
5	Death of close family member	63
6	Personal injury or illness	53
7	Marriage	50
8	Fired at work	47
9	Marital reconciliation	45
10	Retirement	45
11	Change in health of family member	44
12	Pregnancy	40
13	Sex difficulties	39
14	Gain of new family member	39
15	Business readjustment	39
16	Change in financial state	38
17	Death of close friend	37
18	Change to different line of work	36
19	Change in number of arguments with spouse	35
20	Mortgage over $10,000	31
21	Foreclosure of mortgage or loan	30
22	Change in responsibilities at work	29
23	Son or daughter leaving home	29
24	Trouble with in-laws	29
25	Outstanding personal achievement	28
26	Wife begins or stops work	26
27	Begin or end school	26
28	Change in living conditions	25
29	Revision of personal habits	24
30	Trouble with boss	23
31	Change in work hours or conditions	20
32	Change in residence	20
33	Change in schools	20
34	Change in recreation	19
35	Change in church activities	19
36	Change in social activities	18
37	Mortgage or loan less than $10,000	17
38	Change in sleeping habits	16
39	Change in number of family get-togethers	15
40	Change in eating habits	15
41	Vacation	13
42	Christmas	12
43	Minor violations of the law	11

Source: Reprinted from Thomas Holmes and Minoru Masuda, "Psychosomatic Syndromes," *Psychology Today Magazine*. Copyright @ 1972, Ziff-Davis Publishing Company.

A variety of life changes, some of them positive, can also require coping and adaptation from those experiencing them.

Courtesy of Angelo and Gail Lococo

Holmes and Masuda (1972) reported that Japanese and Americans agree that the death of a spouse is extremely stressful. But the Japanese, who use the opinions of others as primary guides to behavior, place detention in jail much higher in their list than Americans did. Family structure differences between the two cultures also seem important. American families that tend to be isolated groupings, with one or two parents and a child, are quite different from Japanese families that involve a much larger group. The addition of a new family member ranked quite high in the American's list of stressful life events, while Japanese respondents ranked it much lower. Thus, we see that cultural differences may be of considerable importance in identifying which events are stressful and may serve as possible triggers of psychophysiological reactions.

Other cultural factors may also play an important role in the development of psychophysiological disorders. For example, Kaplan (1974) has reported hypertension is much higher among black people in the United States than it is among whites. These differences may have to do with the increased stress associated with membership in a minority group. Or, they may also have to do with dietary differences in salt intake among people within the black culture. In either case, they suggest that cultural differences may play an important role in the development of psychophysiological disorders.

We have now surveyed a number of the best known theories that attempt to account for the development of psychophysiological disorders. It should be clear at this point that none of them provides a comprehensive account of the phenomenon. It is almost surely the case that stress is an important precipitant of these disorders. And, it is likely that there are large individual differences in the degree to which particular organ systems are susceptible to stress as a consequence either of innate genetic dispositions or autonomic learning. It is even possible that there are symbolic relationships between the type of psychophysiological disorders developed and current or past conflicts in the individual's life, although evidence for these relationships is much less clear.

What is needed, certainly, is a more comprehensive account of the development of psychophysiological disorders. We need an account that synthesizes the most important contributions of each of these perspectives. At the same time, it should have its own set of organizing principles. Let us now turn to one such promising account.

DISREGULATION THEORY

A moment's reflection will suggest to you that each of the theories of psychophysiological disorders that we have just examined is only a partial explanation. Although it is almost certainly the case that genetic factors, learning, stress, and personality all play a role in the development of psychophysiological disorders, none of these approaches attempts to tell the whole story. Instead, each theory highlights an important set of factors in the chain of events that leads to a psychophysiological symptom. However, Schwartz (1977) does offer a framework for understanding these disorders that may allow us to take all of the factors into account and to weave them into a single explanation.

The brain as master organ of regulation. Schwartz believes that the brain is the master organ of regulation, and it is the brain that directly participates in the development of all psychophysiological disorders. As he notes, . . . the brain constantly regulates itself and thereby controls its multiple output devices, including skeletal muscles, smooth muscles, and glands . . . if this regulation goes astray, causing specific output devices to be either over or under activated, the output devices can develop structural anomalies or injuries diagnosed as disease and require medical intervention (Schwartz, 1977, p. 272).

Despite its key role in regulation, we are seldom aware of the brain's active role in this process.

Feedback. Thus far we have noted that the brain plays a major role in regulating bodily processes even though we are not aware of it. But how does this process work? How do messages get carried to the brain so that it can react to them and carry out its regulatory task? Two systems particpate in the process. The first is called the *exteroceptor system.* Exteroceptors send messages from the external environment to the brain through the senses such as vision, hearing, taste, touch, and smell. It is easy enough to understand how exteroceptors work. When one reaches for an object, for example, visual inputs to the brain allow the brain to adjust behavior in order to carry out the action.

Much more important for our understanding of psychophysiological disorders is the *interoceptor system.* Interoceptors are located inside the body and send messages to the brain regarding chemical and neurological changes in the body. While we are often aware or can make ourselves aware of the operation of exteroceptors, interoceptors tend to operate outside of our conscious awareness. Take, for example, the experience of voluntarily holding your breath. Carbon dioxide builds up in the blood stream which stimulates chemical receptors that feed into respiratory regulation centers in the lower brain. These brain stem mechanisms then activate the respiratory system causing you to take another breath. Even though a complex system of messages is being sent, you only experience the need to take another breath. Thus, Schwartz argues, the brain participates in all of these regulatory processes whether involving interoceptors or exteroceptors. The brain, then, may rightly be called the master organ of regulation.

Gary E. Schwartz

Courtesy of Gary E. Schwartz

But what is the mechanism by which the brain engages in this regulatory process? The answer according to Schwartz is through the use of *feedback.* Feedback refers to the processes whereby information is returned to a regulating system for the purpose of influencing the stability of that system.

The importance of the concept of feedback for our discussion is that it is closely related to a physiological process called *homeostasis.* This process has been described by Claude Bernard and later by Walter Cannon in his famous book, *The Wisdom of the Body* (1939). Homeostasis refers to the biological feedback process whereby physiological variables are kept within certain limits for the purposes of survival. Thus, the brain and other bodily systems participate in a feedback system that allows the body to adapt to demands put on it. Feedback from exteroceptors or interoceptors is sent to the brain, which sends information back to bodily systems to increase or decrease their activity to bring about adaptation.

One final point is important for us to understand. Schwartz argues that the brain participates in *all* psychophysiological disorders, regardless of whether they occur in the gastrointestinal system, the cardiovascular system, or whatever. Thus, each of these systems should be considered a complete functional system with the brain playing a major role.

Psychophysiological disorders as disregulation. With these basic concepts in hand, we are ready to examine Schwartz's conception of how psychophysiological disorders develop. He argues that psychophysiological disorders result from a state of disregulation, regardless of whether the disorder is hypertension, hives, ulcers, asthma, or migraine headaches. Disregulation is most easily illustrated in conditions where the over or under activity of neural control systems are involved. In Figure 9–1, four stages in the physiological feedback process can be identified. A critical aspect of this model is that it suggests that the *determinants of a psychophysiological disorder can occur at any one of these stages or all of them in combination.* Thus, even this simple feedback model begins to capture the complexity of the etiology of psychophysiological disorders.

In stage 1, stimuli from the external environment may be so demanding that the brain ignores negative feedback from some organ system. For example, a person placed in unavoidable stress may experience stomach pain associated with hyperacidity but be unable to leave the stressful situation. Thus, the negative feedback telling the person to change his behavior or situation may be ignored. This class of determinants is similar to our

FIGURE 9–1

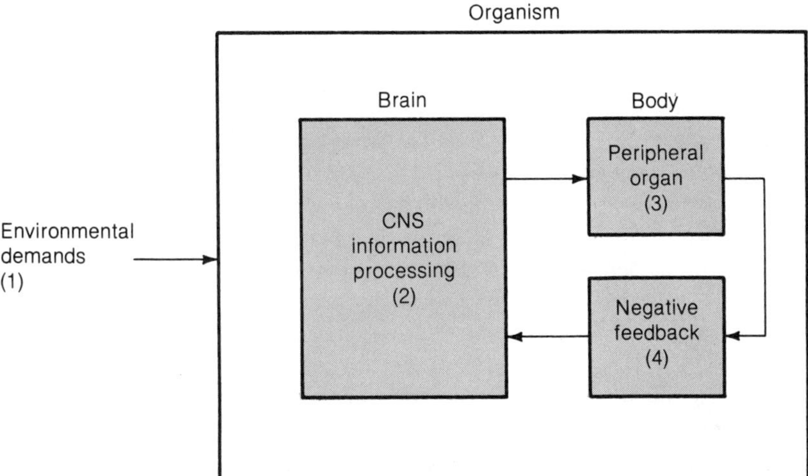

Note: Block diagram depicting (1) environmental demands influencing (2) the brain's regulation of its (3) peripheral organs, and (4) negative feedback from the peripheral organ back to the brain. Disregulation can be initiated at each of these stages.

Source: From G. E. Schwartz, in *Psychopathology: Experimental Models,* ed. J. D. Maser and M. E. P. Seligman (San Francisco: W. H. Freeman and Co., 1977), p. 281. Copyright © 1977.

earlier description of life changes such as divorce or a job change as possible determinants of psychophysiological disorders.

In stage 2, the information processing capability of the central nervous system itself may be faulty. The brain may respond inappropriately to stimuli in the external environment because of faulty programming due to either genetic or experiential causes. At stage 2, then, the brain may act in ways which lead it to ignore the corrective negative feedback it obtains or to use that feedback in ways that place unreasonable demands on a peripheral organ. Interestingly, disregulation originating at this stage could be the result of prior experience, which is consistent with both the learning and the psychoanalytic hypothesis, or could be a result of genetic factors, a view consistent with the illness perspective.

In stage 3, a peripheral organ, for example the stomach, may be under- or overreactive to stimulation coming from the brain. This corresponds closely to the somatic weakness hypothesis we discussed earlier. If the organ is over- or underreactive, the brain may not be able to regulate the behavior of the affected organ.

In stage 4, it is possible that the feedback coming from the peripheral organ itself may be inappropriate. Thus, neuromechanisms sending messages back to the brain may not provide adequate information for control of the peripheral organ.

This model represents an advance in psychophysiological thinking for two reasons. First, it focuses on the feedback system involved in physiological regulation

STRESS AND COPING IN PSYCHOPHYSIOLOGICAL ILLNESS

Throughout our discussion, we have associated stress with the development of psychophysiological disorders. Holroyd (1979) has suggested that confusion surrounds the concept of stress because it has been formulated in several distinct ways. In his analysis of three main formulations of stress, Holroyd provides us with a closer look at the ways in which the person's ability to cope with stress may be related to illness.

According to Holroyd, stress most commonly refers to an environmental event or crisis that requires some adaptive response from the individual. Earlier in our discussion, we noted that life events that require major adaptations may play some role in the development of psychophysiological disorders. Life events, however, are not especially good predictors of the probability of future illness (Rabkin & Streuning, 1976). Our ability to predict the impact of life events on the individual can be improved by knowing something about the resources available to the person for coping with environmental change. This point is nicely illustrated by a study of pregnancy and birth complications conducted by Nuckolls, Cassel, & Kaplan (1972). An interesting relationship between birth complications and coping resources emerged in women with high levels of stressful life events prior to delivery. Women who reported that their personal resources were adequate to cope with the pregnancy and delivery had far fewer birth complications than women who felt they had less adequate coping resources. Thus, when coping resources and stressful life circumstances are considered jointly, the ability to predict birth complications is increased.

The relationship between the ability to cope with stress and the development of illness also can be seen when stress is conceptualized as a physiological response of the organism. Selye, you recall, has argued that the organism responds to stressful circumstances with the general adaptation syndrome. The activation of this response pattern is presumably associated with tissue damage and, ultimately, illness. Recently Selye (1978) has acknowledged the role of psychological factors in influencing a person's physiological response to stress. Adaptive attitudes, values, and motivations may "short-circuit" the general adaptation syndrome or minimize its effects when it occurs (Holroyd, 1979). It seems, then, that physiological responses as well as reactions to stressful life events—two factors related to psychophysiological illness—may be mediated by a person's coping resources.

The above discussion leads us to a third concept of stress and the point of view adopted by Holroyd. That is, stress can be viewed as a particular type of transaction with the environment. Here, stress is seen as resulting from the individual's transactions with the environment which strains his or her adaptive resources. Such a *transactional approach* suggests that stress is a product of the interaction of three factors: life events which require an adaptive response, the individual's response to these events, and, most importantly, psychological mediating processes. As we have seen, the way in which the individual copes with the demands of life can have an effect on his physiology and, thus, the development of stress-related disorders (Holroyd, 1979).

Holroyd contends that dysfunctional patterns of coping with the demands of the environment might contribute to illness in at least three ways. First, if adequate resources are not available to cope with stressful transactions with the environment, physiological disregulation may result, triggering the harmful consequences described by Schwartz (1979). Second, certain ways of coping with stress, like smoking tobacco and drinking alcohol, might prove hazardous to health. Finally, certain ways of coping with the symptoms of an illness can influence the course of the illness or the medical care that is received. For example, minimizing or ignoring the symptoms of cardiac disease, such as attributing chest pains to heartburn, may have serious health consequences for the individual.

Holroyd's arguments suggest that it is important to better understand the relationships between the individual's ways of coping with stress, changes in physiology, and disease outcome. The transactional approach also has important implications for treatment. Holroyd suggests that if we are to effectively treat stress-related disorders, it is important to "focus not only on specific stress responses but on functionally related cognitive and behavioral activity" (p. 217). Later in our discussion we will see how a stress coping treatment for tension headache sufferers provides a more effective treatment alternative than biofeedback, which focuses only on modifying the physiological response presumably associated with headache activity.

and identifies the brain as the central mechanism involved in all of these functional systems. Second, instead of isolating one particular source of the disorder to the exclusion of others, it provides us with a synthesis of previous theories and shows how learning, genetic factors, and external stress all may be involved in physiological disregulation, which leads to tissue damage in psychophysiological disorders.

TREATMENT OF PSYCHOPHYSIOLOGICAL DISORDERS

Biological Treatments

A variety of biological methods have been used to treat psychophysiological disorders. For example, tranquilizing drugs are often prescribed to reduce the emotional tension experienced by the person suffering from a psychophysiological disorder. In addition, the pain of headaches may be relieved by analgesic compounds, and drug treatment of hypertension or for ulcers is frequently employed. In severe cases, surgery has been used in the treatment of psychophysiological disorders. For example, the severing of the vagus nerve which stimulates gastric activity has been used in the case of ulcers. Finally, dietary regulation may also be employed for disorders such as high blood pressure or ulcers.

Although somatic treatment alone is not sufficient for permanent recovery for many psychophysiological disorders, it can be a critical and even life saving component of treatment in severe disorders such as ulcerative colitis or perforation of a gastrointestinal ulcer (Lachman, 1972). In Table 9–3, typical somatic treatments for a number of psychophysiological disorders are listed.

We should also note that careful deliberation should accompany somatic treatments for psychophysiological disorders. Schwartz (1977) has argued convincingly that somatic intervention can sometimes contribute to the disorder as much as to its relief. See the boxed passage, "Some Dangers of Traditional Medical Treatment" on page 250.

Biofeedback

What is biofeedback? Neal Miller, one of the scientifc pioneers in the psychology of learning and in the study of biofeedback, puts it this way:

> Most people are poor at correctly perceiving their visceral responses, such as blood pressure, and some people with tension or neuromuscular disorders are poor at perceiving feedback from certain skeletal muscles. They are like a blindfolded novice trying to learn to shoot baskets. Modern measuring devices can remove the blindfold by supplying better feedback. Feedback provided by a device that provides prompt measurement of a biological function has been called biofeedback (Miller, 1978, p. 373).

We have now seen at least one example of the effectiveness of biofeedback in treating a psychophysiological disorder. We noted that in the study conducted by Friar and Beatty, it was possible to alleviate the distress of migraine headaches using biofeedback training. In addition, biofeedback has been reported as a treatment for a variety of other stress-related disorders, including cardiac arrhythmia (Engel, 1973), chronic anxiety (Raskin et al.,

TABLE 9–3 Somatic Treatment of Psychophysiological Disorders

Representative Disorder	*Somatic Treatment Procedures*
Gastrointestinal system	
Peptic ulcer	Rest. Typically bland diet involving milk as the basis and several daily feedings of easily digested, palatable, nonirritating foods. Multivitamin capsules. Medication to minimize hyperacidity and intestinal spasm. Blood transfusion for hemorrhage of peptic ulcer. Surgical repair of perforation. Surgical removal of intractable ulcer (gastrectomy). Surgical section of autonomic fibers to gastrointestinal tract (vagotomy).
Ulcerative colitis	Bed rest, liberal fluid intake, nonirritating diet. Intramuscular injections of vitamin B-complex. Antispasmodics to depress activity of bowel. Medication to thicken bowel discharges as necessary. Surgery: ileostomy or colonectomy as indicated for extensive bowel damage.
Cardiovascular system	
Anginal syndrome	Physical rest and avoidance of excitement critical. Limited activity and avoidance of overexertion prescribed. Low-fat diet may be helpful. Smoking is discouraged. Drugs to increase coronary blood flow by dilating coronary arteries may be desirable.
Essential hypertension	Administration of hypotensive agents. If obese weight reduction may be desirable. Short-term periods of rest advised. Multivitamin tablets. Diet with restriction of salt: rice emphasized in a special diet that restricts sodium and protein content. Sympathectomy required only in malignant hypertension when less drastic methods have failed.
Respiratory system	
Bronchial asthma	Several drugs may relieve asthma symptoms—ephedrine, epinephrine, aminophylline, cortisone, hydrocortisone, and corticotrophin. Certain antihistaminic drugs may be effective in mild asthma.
Skin system	
Urticaria	Antihistaminic drugs, emollient baths, antipruritic lotions and powders. Cortisone, hydrocortisone, corticotrophin.
Acne	Keep entire body clean; squeezing, pinching, and picking at lesions must be avoided. Steamed towels, antiseptic agents, antiseborrheic lotions, Greasy cosmetics to be avoided. Deep cysts and abscesses may be opened with thin scalpel. Sometimes multivitamin capsules recommended.
Musculoskeletal system	
Rheumatoid arthritis	Cortisone, hydrocortisone, and corticotrophin treatment. Rest and avoidance of fatigue. Proper posture at rest is stressed. Salicylates. Transfusion to counteract accompanying anemia. Local treatment of joints with heat. Certain gold compounds are helpful.

Source: From S. J. Lachman, *Psychosomatic Disorders* (New York: Wiley, 1972), pp. 173–75.

SOME DANGERS OF TRADITIONAL MEDICAL TREATMENT FOR PSYCHOPHYSIOLOGICAL DISORDERS

We have seen that a major treatment approach for psychophysiological disorders involves chemical or surgical intervention with the affected organ system. For headache drugs may be administered to reduce the pain associated with expanding blood vessels. For ulcers antacid medications and surgery are often the treatment of choice. For asthma and for hypertension drugs are routinely administered. But is it possible that using medical interventions of this sort could actually perpetuate psychophysiological disorders rather than relieve them? Schwartz (1977) thinks that this is the case.

You will recall that Schwartz offers the disregulation theory of psychophysiological disorders. In essence the theory argues that the brain maintains the health of various physiological systems by operating as a regulating device, receiving input from various organ systems and altering the level of their functioning. As Schwartz notes, "because the body, as any complex physical device, can only work effectively within certain tolerances, the brain must continually ascertain that all components are working effectively. If any component begins to break down, the brain must adjust itself to bring the disregulation back into balance" (p. 305).

But, when medical interventions are used to treat an affected organ system, *they also have the effect of modifying the feedback from that organ to the brain.* In this case, the brain cannot operate effectively to regulate the organ system.

Schwartz notes that we are no longer constrained to deal with the problem of physiological disregulation by responding in the natural way. Instead, we would rather change our body chemistry than to change our style of life by avoiding stressful situations or changing our environment; we choose to operate artificially on those negative feedback systems that generate natural signals of discomfort. The danger, of course, is that when these feedback mechanisms are removed or altered artificially, the brain loses its capacity to regulate the organ system effectively.

Schwartz offers the example of a simple stomach ache. Rather than to regulate one's diet or to avoid certain foods, commercials suggest that the appropriate remedy is to dose oneself with antacid drugs. In addition, medicine is developing new and even more complex means of bypassing normal adaptive feedback mechanisms. People can now have a surgical procedure to remove the vagus nerve which provides the neural regulation between the stomach and the brain. Again, Schwartz notes "our culture continually reinforces the idea that if the brain and its body cannot cope with the external environment, they will simply have to undergo medical alteration to adjust" (p. 306–307).

The consequences of this approach to dealing with disregulation are, in Schwartz's view, extremely dangerous. He argues that medical procedures should not be the sole approach to treatment. Rather, a thoughtful combination of behavioral strategies, biofeedback, and medical intervention will provide a more adaptive means of coping with the diseases of disregulation—the psychophysiological disorders.

1973), hypertension (Schwartz, 1977), and some rare gastrointestinal disorders (Miller, 1978). This is an exciting development, but, although early clinical tests are promising, most biofeedback treatments have not yet been systematically compared against alternative forms of treatment.

But how does biofeedback actually work? We can gain some insight into the mechanism of biofeedback if we again refer to the disregulation model described by Schwartz. You will recall that Schwartz argues that when there is a disregulation in input or feedback at any one of the four stages in the regulatory system between the brain and an organ system, the organ may suffer tissue damage. Thus, biofeedback works by providing an additional negative feedback loop which provides information about the state of the organ in question to the brain. The brain may then use this feedback to engage in regulation of the affected organ system. This idea is illustrated in the Figure 9–2. Thus, biofeedback provides the individual with new information about his own organ system and allows the brain to regulate the system appropriately.

In the case of hypertension, it has been shown by numerous experiments that it is possible to teach people to either increase or decrease systolic blood pressure by simply providing them with lights or tones indicating when they have succeeded in generating such a change. Furthermore, Schwartz (1972) has demonstrated that, through biofeedback, subjects can regulate their blood pressure and heart rate independently of each other. This

FIGURE 9–2

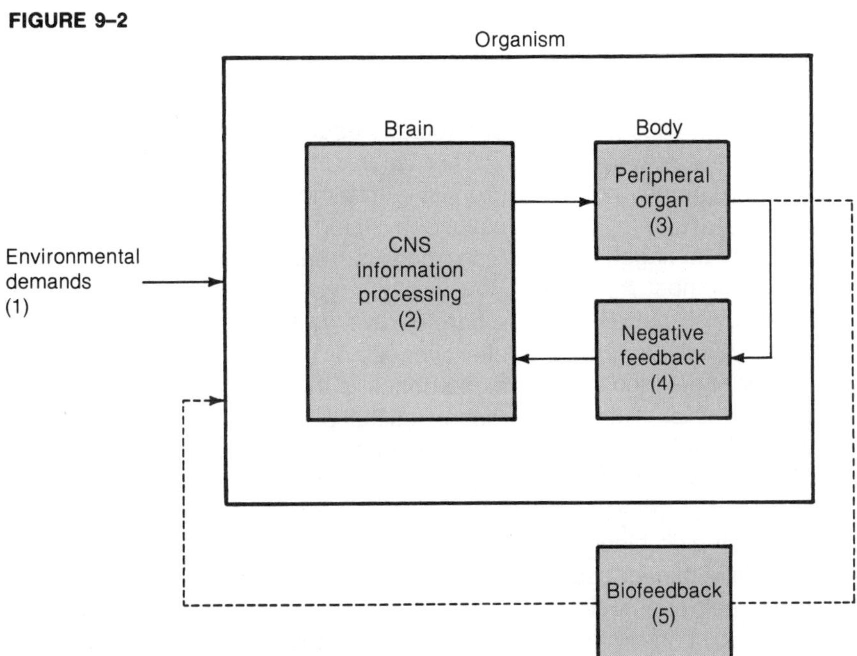

Note: Biofeedback (stage 5) is a parallel feedback loop to stage 4, detecting the activity of the peripheral organ (stage 3), and converting it into environmental stimulation (stage 1) that can be used by the brain (stage 2) to increase self-regulation.

Source: From G. E. Schwartz, in *Psychopathology: Experimental Models,* ed. J. D. Maser and M. E. O. Seligman (San Francisco: W. H. Freeman and Co., 1977), p. 293. Copyright © 1977.

suggests that it is possible to train people with patterned biofeedback, for example, simultaneously lowering their heart rate and blood pressure or lowering one independent of the other. This is an exciting innovation in the treatment of psychophysiological disorders, and it is tempting to assume that all treatment of psychophysiological disorders will ultimately take this form.

However, we should note three serious cautions in examining the effectiveness of biofeedback in treating psychophysiological disorders. First, there are very few studies which have included appropriate control groups to indicate whether biofeedback was the major cause of obtained results. In many cases, merely the patient's adaptation to the laboratory atmosphere or expectations about change can affect biological systems without the benefit of biofeedback. Second, we should clearly recognize that there are real physical limitations on the effectiveness of biofeedback. If the peripheral organ involved is already severely damaged, then it is unlikely that biofeedback will have any effect since the organ may not be responsive to the brain's usual regulatory mechanisms in its damaged condition. Third, and perhaps most important, we should distinguish between the ability to acquire a self-regulation skill, such as the ability to lower one's blood pressure, and the motivation to continue to use that skill for the sake of one's health.

Schwartz (1973) offers an example that nicely illustrates this last point. He notes that in his laboratory patients with high blood pressure were given five daily biofeedback sessions during a typical week and could earn as much as $35 for reducing their blood pressure by a fixed amount. Many patients were very successful at lowering their blood pressure using this system. But Schwartz and his colleagues noted with some puzzlement that when one patient returned on Monday, his blood pressure was again elevated. On questioning him they discovered that after earning his money during the week, the patient would go to the racetrack on the weekend, gamble, and almost always lose. Schwartz remarks that the likelihood of teaching this patient to relax while at the racetrack using biofeedback techniques was slim, and it was clear that effective treatment would require altering other aspects of the patient's behavior that were also related to his high blood pressure.

Recently, Lynn and Freedman (1978) have reviewed a number of possible strategies for transferring what is learned in the laboratory to the everyday stressful situations in which the psychophysiological symptom may actually be triggered. The strategies include overlearning the target response, "booster sessions" in the laboratory, fading the feedback so that subjects learn their own cues for bodily change, and training under stressful circumstances and in real life situations with portable biofeedback units.

Thus, biofeedback represents a promising treatment strategy for psychophysiological disorders, and research is currently very active in this area. However, Lynn and Freedman (1978) offer a careful review of the research of the effectiveness of biofeedback and note that biofeedback is most effective for altering responses that can be easily observed, such as muscle paralysis or stuttering. Results have been much less effective for hypertension. Furthermore they note that if gains that do occur from biofeedback are to be maintained, a variety of behavioral and self-control techniques must be taught to the client. As Lynn and Freedman (1978) note, "the biofeedback patient must be actively engaged in his treatment as opposed to being passively cured by a machine" (p. 479).

This person is wearing an apparatus which allows feedback of skin temperature, at the fingertip, and heard through an earphone. This biofeedback system can be worn by people as they continue through their daily activities.

Courtesy of Robert Freedman, Ph.D., Lafayette Clinic, Detroit

Stress-Coping Training: A Challenge To Biofeedback

As Lynn and Freedman suggest, the initial enthusiasm for biofeedback is being tempered by the results of careful research. Furthermore, other behavioral approaches to managing stress are proving at least as effective. In recent years, behavioral treatment has increasingly drawn upon an understanding of cognitive processes in the appraisal of environmental events. Work by Meichenbaum (1977) suggests that much of psychotherapy is now being conceptualized in information processing and cognitive, rather than in behavioral terms. An example of this cognitive-behavioral approach to the treatment of stress-related disorders is what Meichenbaum calls "stress innoculation training." The goal of this training is to increase the individual's ability to resist the pathological effects of stress.

Essentially, as Holroyd (1979) notes, all treatments of this type have several typical components. First, some explanation for the client's problem is offered that helps the client to attribute his stress response to some specific cognitive or behavioral deficiency. Second, the client is taught to monitor his/her stress response to learn what specific events trigger it, the thoughts that typically accompany the stress, and the typical behavioral responses displayed. Thus, the person learns to identify the pattern of events that precede, accompany, and follow a stressful interaction. Finally, the client is taught to develop alternative ways of coping with the stressful event. Usually instruction, modeling, or some form of practice is used to help develop proficiency with the alternative coping strategy.

A recent study by Holroyd et al. (1977) has offered a direct challenge to biofeedback as the treatment of choice for tension headaches. The effect of the stress coping approach was compared with that of biofeedback. In the stress coping training approach clients were first taught to monitor their own feelings of tension. Specifically, they were asked to identify the cues that would trigger tension and anxiety in them, how they responded when they were anxious, their thoughts before they became anxious, and, then later, the ways these thoughts contributed to their tension and to their headache.

Once clients were taught to monitor their own behavior, they were taught to deliberately *interrupt* the sequence of thoughts that preceded their emotional response. They could either reappraise the threatening situation, focus their attention elsewhere, or use fantasy to divert themselves from the tension producing thoughts.

The stress coping group was compared

with a group of clients requesting treatment for headaches who had been put on a waiting list and with a group receiving biofeedback for tension headaches. You can see the results of the study in Figure 9–3.

It is clear that the stress coping treatment proved to be highly effective in reducing headaches immediately after treatment and was still effective at a 15 week follow-up. The biofeedback group and the wait list control group, however, showed little or no change in the severity or frequency of headaches.

In addition, Holroyd et al. (1977) report that resting levels of muscle tension in the forehead were unrelated to the degree of headache improvement. This suggests that even when clients are receiving biofeedback, the ability to relax these muscles in the laboratory situation is not necessarily helping headache sufferers to use these skills in actual stressful situations (Holroyd, 1979).

As we have seen, researchers have demonstrated that people are able to control their physiological responses to a degree previously thought impossible. Still, as these results suggest, there appear to be real limitations to the therapeutic power of biofeedback, at least currently.

Holroyd (1979) has suggested that in some instances biofeedback training may be effective not because people learn to directly control their physiological responses, but because it sensitizes them to tension producing situations. Once sensitized, they find other ways of coping with those situations. As Holroyd notes, "When biofeedback works in this manner, there may

FIGURE 9–3 Mean Weekly Headache Scores in Two-week Blocks

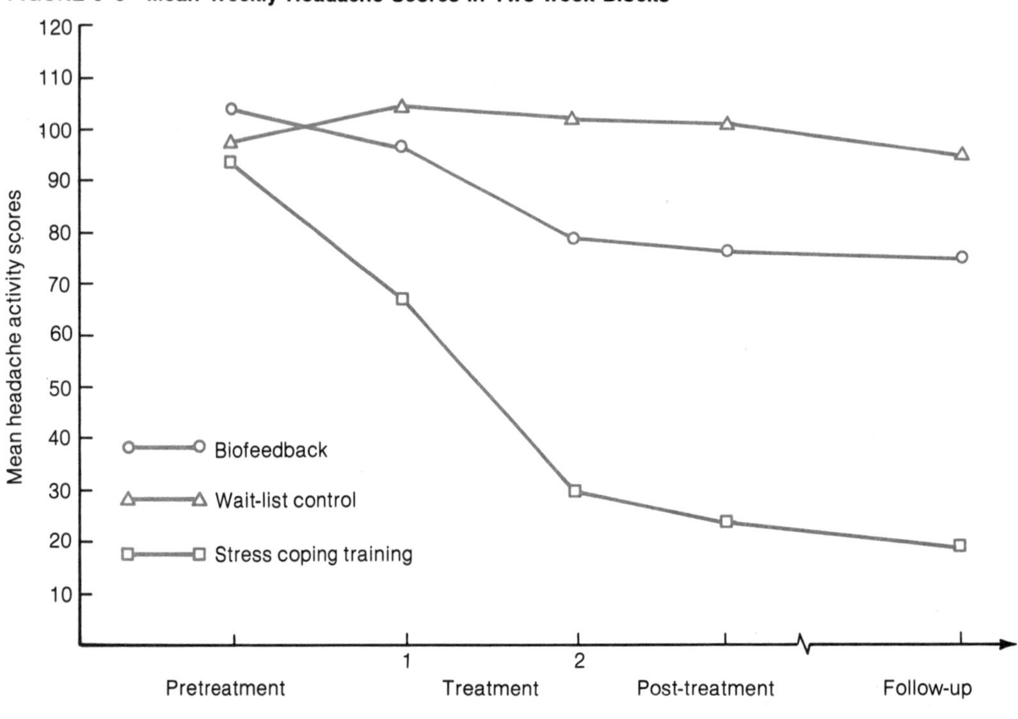

Source: From K. A. Holroyd, in *Behavioral Approaches in Medicine,* ed. J. R. McNamara (New York: Plenum, 1979).

be little relationship between the ability to directly control muscle tension and headache improvement."

A fascinating study with headache victims which demonstrates that this indeed may be the case has been conducted by Andrasik and Holroyd (1978). In this study, the investigators gave feedback for either *increasing or decreasing* frontalis (forehead) muscle activity in separate experimental groups. In another group, the people received feedback from an irrelevant muscle group, in this case the forearm. Furthermore, all clients were led to believe that they were learning to *reduce* muscle tension. When compared to a waiting list control group, all three treatment groups showed a substantial improvement, and subsequent interviews by the investigators suggested that people in all three groups controlled their headaches by changing the way they coped with the headache producing situation to which they were now more sensitive.

SUMMARY

In this chapter, we have examined the stress-related psychophysiological disorders. These disorders are quite common. In contrast with disorders such as conversion reactions and hypochondriasis, psychophysiological disorders involve some form of actual tissue damage. Most diseases have a psychological or emotional component, but considerable variation can be seen in the proportion of psychological factors that contribute to a particular illness. We noted that stress, predisposing biological factors, and personality or family characteristics all may influence the development and course of psychophysiological disorders.

Theories of psychophysiological disorders have attempted to explain their origins from a variety of viewpoints. Psychoanalytic theorists trace the roots of psychophysiological disorders to conflicts developed during infancy which are repressed but then are stimulated again by some environmental circumstance. The learning perspective emphasizes the learned nature of physiological reactions to stress. This viewpoint raises the intriguing possibility that particular autonomic responses related to disease may be rewarded, thereby increasing the likelihood that they will occur again. The illness perspective views these disorders as diseases of adaptation. A pattern of response to stress termed the *general adaptation syndrome* has been related to tissue damage and disease. A particular organ system may be effected because of an inherited somatic weakness, or vulnerability to stress. The social perspective emphasizes stressful life events and cultural factors in the development of illness. Finally we considered Schwartz's disregulation theory, which provides a comprehensive account of the development of psychophysiological disorders. This model focuses on the feedback system involved in physical regulation and shows how learning, genetic factors, and external stress may all contribute to the development of psychophysiological disorders.

In the last section we surveyed a number of treatments of psychophysiological disorders. A variety of biological treatments have been used, including tranquilizer drugs, analgesic compounds, surgery, and dietary regulation. Biofeedback and stress coping treatment, which teaches people to resist the pathological effects of stress, are innovative approaches and merit further attention.

10

Schizophrenia, Childhood Psychosis, and Organic Disorders

INTRODUCTION

Listen as Mark Vonnegut describes (1975) the onset of his first schizophrenic experience:

> Small tasks become incredibly intricate and complex. It started with pruning the fruit trees. One saw cut would take forever. I was completely absorbed in the sawdust floating gently to the ground, the feel of the saw in my hand, the incredible patterns in the bark, the muscles in my arm pulling back and then pushing forward. Everything stretched infinitely in all directions. Suddenly it seemed as if everything was slowing down and I would never finish sawing the limb. Then, by some miracle that branch would be done and I'd have to rest, completely blown out. The same thing kept happening over and over then I found myself being unable to stick with any one tree. I'd take a branch here, a couple there. It seemed I had been working for hours and hours but the sun hadn't moved at all.
>
> I began to wonder if I was hurting the trees and found myself apologizing. Each tree began to take on personality. I began to wonder if any of them liked me . . . (p. 99).
>
> The pages and words [while reading] would twist and blur in the really gruesome spots. I had to stop and catch my breath after every two or three pages. The closer I got to the end the worse it became. I was convinced that I really shouldn't finish the book, that if I did I would die or the world would end or worse.
>
> Since reading was out, I got my old Olivetti and started banging out letters to friends, to Virginia, to various members of the family. I was trying to clue them in about the wonderful things that had been happening to me and all the wonderful new truths I had found. Unfortunately, the typewriter didn't work too well. I had trouble hitting the right letters and even more trouble seeing what was wrong with the wrong letters I hit. One key was as good as the next. While there was a lot of truth to that, I felt it was only fair to the people who weren't quite where I was yet to make an effort to make myself as intelligible as possible. I switched over to longhand. I still had some of the same problems, but to a lesser extent (pp. 100–101).
>
> [Later, talking to his friend, Simon, Mark says,]
>
> "Simon, I keep getting these awful rushes of fear, waves of total terror that leave me shaking and weak. I keep trying to figure out what the hell it is I'm afraid of. Last night I thought my heart was going to stop again. Now I'm keeping you up because I'm afraid to go to bed. It makes no sense" (pp. 105–106).

Mark Vonnegut has described his own experience with a schizophrenic episode.

Courtesy of Peter Vandermark

> Communicating was just about impossible. My tongue and mouth weren't responding very well. It was only with the greatest difficulty that I could tell who was saying what and that I could make any sense out of words. I relied heavily on grunts and gestures (p. 109).

Overview

Although Mark Vonnegut tells his painful story of schizophrenia with insight and good humor, it is not an unusual story. Approximately 1 percent of the American population will be diagnosed as schizophrenic at some point in their lives. But schizophrenia is a worldwide disorder and affects people of all races, religions, levels of intelligence, and wealth. Recent research done under the sponsorship of the World Health Organization (Tsuang, 1976) examined the incidence of schizophrenia in Nigeria, Columbia, Denmark, Russia, India, and the United States. In all of those countries the incidence of the disorder was about 1 percent. The same study suggested that there seems to be universal signs of schizophrenia. These signs include the belief that one is controlling or is controlled by some external agent, a flatness of emotional tone, hearing voices or other sounds, confusion about location or time, and withdrawal from social contact.

Schizophrenics comprise about half of the patients in mental institutions in the United States. Today many more people experiencing schizophrenic disorders continue to live in society but return periodically to hospital settings for treatment. In general, about one third of the people suffering from schizophrenic disorders improve over time, about a third get worse, and about a third stay the same throughout the course of their lives.

You already have a glimpse of the experience of schizophrenia through reading Mark Vonnegut's account. It is a bewildering and terrifying experience. The schizophrenic thought processes are greatly impaired. The person experiencing a schizophrenic episode may have difficulty understanding what is going on or may develop frightening delusions or hear voices. A person experiencing a schizophrenic episode may frequently feel terrified of others and withdraw, avoiding interpersonal contact as much as possible.

Schizophrenia is one of the most important of the *functional psychoses.* Functional psychoses should be distinguished from organic psychoses. Organic psychoses occur as the consequence of known assaults on the brain through, for example, drugs or high fever. Functional psychoses, on the other hand, have no known single cause and remain one of the great puzzles in the study of abnormal psychology.

In fact, learning about schizophrenia is in many ways like a study of abnormal psychology in miniature. Most of the issues and controversies we find across the whole range of abnormal behaviors also occur in the study of schizophrenia. Let us now turn to these issues and controversies. They will serve as our guideposts in this chapter as we learn more about schizophrenic disorders.

Controversies

Despite tens of thousands of scientific studies, schizophrenia remains a puzzle. In fact, we are only now beginning to ask questions that may yield some useful answers. Like much of the study of abnormal behavior, each of these questions has produced controversy. But it is just this controversy that sharpens the issues so that answers can be found. We will focus on three clusters of questions in this and the next chapter.

First, is schizophrenia a single, unitary disorder? Some scientists believe that it is; others argue that it is not a single disorder but a group of similar looking disorders with very different underlying causes. Still others believe that there is no disorder that we could call *schizophrenia* at all. Instead, they argue that schizophrenia is merely a label we use to describe a range of behavior that we do not clearly understand.

Second, how is schizophrenia transmitted? We know that if a child has one parent who is schizophrenic, that child has ten times greater a chance of developing the disorder than someone selected at random from the general population. If that child has two schizophrenic parents, the risk is 40 times greater. Evidence of this kind cannot be ignored, but its interpretation is far from simple. Does the child inherit some disorder through a genetic mechanism? Or is schizophrenia transmitted through social learning in the family context? And what role does society play? We know that the incidence of schizophrenia is much greater among poor people. Does this mean that poverty causes the schizophrenia—or that schizophrenia causes poverty?

While some researchers are attempting to provide us with clearer descriptions of schizophrenia and others are searching for the mechanisms of its transmission, still others are facing the task of offering treatment to people who have already developed the disorder. As we shall see, there have been enormous changes in the treatment of schizophrenia. What treatment lies ahead? Will it be possible for people having experienced schizophrenic episodes to return to fulfilling lives in society? Research continues to evaluate the effectiveness of various drug treatments. Some scientists claim that large doses of vitamins can have dramatic effects. Still others believe that the treatment of schizophrenia is best accomplished by creating a social environment in the community that allows the schizophrenic an opportunity to recover.

In this chapter we will examine the first issue, the scientific description of schizophrenia.

DESCRIPTION

The problem of providing a useful description of the nature of schizophrenia has occupied modern researchers since the 19th century. In Chapter 5 we discussed some of the important purposes of classification. Among them were providing descriptions that would allow decisions about appropriate treatment and provide a common language for behavioral phenomena. The same issues are important to scientists who are trying to provide a description of schizophrenia that has both theoretical and clinical usefulness. Furthermore, in the case of schizophrenia, there is a controversy about whether schizophrenia is a single disorder or a cluster of related disorders with quite different causes. Developing adequate descriptions of the disorder may play a key role in resolving that controversy.

Much of the preoccupation with the description of schizophrenia began in the 19th century. But it is a concern that seems to be reemerging today as our sophistication in developing classification systems and our knowledge about the potential determinants of schizophrenic behavior grow.

Eugen Bleuler

National Library of Medicine

History

You will recall that when we discussed the history of abnormal behavior in Chapter 2, we noted that 19th-century Europe was dominated by a concern with organic disorders and pathology. It is not surprising, then, that the early study of behavioral disorders also was affected by this organic preoccupation. The giant of 19th-century German psychiatry, Emil Kraepelin, was particularly concerned with diagnosis and classification. He chose the *outcome* of a disorder as the basis of classification. Those patients who appeared to deteriorate in their functioning over the course of their lives Kraepelin placed in one category, and those who appeared to recover were placed in another. Kraepelin described the deteriorated group as suffering from *dementia praecox.* Essentially this term means psychological deterioration in youth. Among those individuals who seemed to deteriorate fairly early in their lives, Kraepelin discerned three subtypes: *hebephrenic* patients, who acted in an inappropriate, silly fashion; *catatonic* patients, who either became immobilized or were subject to fits of excitement, and *paranoid* patients, who tended to show delusions or mistaken beliefs about their own persecution or delusions of grandeur.

In the history of schizophrenia, perhaps the most important single figure is Eugen Bleuler. Bleuler was a Swiss psychiatrist who gave us the modern term *schizophrenia.* According to Snyder (1975), one of Bleuler's important

Emil Kraepelin

National Library of Medicine

contributions was that he recognized that there were patients who were suffering from dementia praecox but who never entered a mental hospital at all. They did not deteriorate in the way that Kraepelin might have expected. These people might recover, at least partially, from their symptoms, Bleuler argued, and the clinical picture of schizophrenia, as Bleuler liked to call it, was much more complex than we had imagined.

Perhaps Bleuler's singular genius really lay in his ability to describe the phenomena he observed. He argued that the most important aspect of schizophrenia was not the outcome of the disorder, as Kraepelin has suggested, but that a group of *primary* behaviors could be identified as the central problems of the schizophrenia. The four types of behavior are commonly referred to in descriptive psychopathology as the *four As: autism, associative disturbance, ambivalence,* and *affective disturbance.*

SCHIZOPHRENIA IS NOT "SPLIT PERSONALITY"

One of the most common misunderstandings in the study of abnormal behavior is to confuse the idea of schizophrenia with that of multiple personality. When Bleuler coined the term *schizophrenia,* he was really concerned with emphasizing a *splitting off* of the person's thoughts and emotions from external reality. This is very different from the idea of split, or multiple, personality as in the famous "three faces of Eve" case. In the multiple personality, an individual will behave like one person one moment and another the next. In Chapter 6 you will recall that we discussed multiple personality as a very rare form of neurotic disorder. But multiple personality is very different from the kind of splitting off that Bleuler was talking about.

This confusion persists partly because writers in popular literature continue to mistakenly describe the psychological state in which people are torn between two alternatives or display various forms of inconsistent behavior as a kind of schizophrenia. The use of the term schizophrenia will probably persist, as will the confusion, but, one hopes, not for the reader.

In addition, Bleuler noted symptoms associated with schizophrenia that he called secondary. He described them as secondary because they could be observed in other disorders as well and were not unique to schizophrenia. Included among the secondary symptoms were many of the behaviors we associate with severe psychological disturbance, including hallucinations, delusions, withdrawal, and stupor.

Clinical Descriptions of Schizophrenic Behavior

In saying that the four As were unique to schizophrenic behavior, Bleuler was only partly right. These behaviors are indeed critical aspects of schizophrenic disturbance, but every person who is diagnosed as schizophrenic will not necessarily display all four of them at the same time. Let us look at each of these four types of behavior in more detail.

Perhaps the most important is associative disturbance. Associative disturbance is also sometimes called *loose associations* or *thought disorder.* Consider the following example of schizophrenic thought disorder:

> A man of 39, asked whether he felt that people imitated him, replied: "Yes . . . I don't quite gather. I know one right and one left use both hands, but I can't follow the system that's working. The idea is meant in a kind way, but it's not the way I understand life. It seems to be people taking sides, as I understand it. If certain people agree with me they speak to me, and if not they don't. Everybody seems to be the doctor and Mr. H. [his own name] in turn. The superiors here can't do as they like, they can't come up to speak to you as they like, because they have to take their turn of being superior and insuperior. To say things are all wrong means right in turn, but I don't appreciate it that way. If I go into the stores and say 'Are my cigarettes here?' they say 'No.' But if I say 'My cigarettes haven't come' they give them me" (Mayer-Gross et al., 1969).

You can see that the person's language never seems to be quite on target. It wanders and skips from topic to topic in a vague and disjointed way. Researchers today believe that the peculiar and vague schizophrenic language that one often observes is the result of a fundamental associative disturbance. The usual associations that we make between two words or verbal symbols are considerably weakened or idiosyncratic for the schizophrenic. In mild forms thought disorder of this sort makes speech vague or difficult to follow. In its more severe forms, such speech is almost impossible to understand.

Another form of associative disturbance in schizophrenia is "blocking." An interruption in the flow of thinking and speech occurs in blocking, and the individual seems at a loss to explain where a particular train of thought was going. As we will see later, associative disturbance in schizophrenia has been extensively studied in the laboratory by psychologists. Their hope has been to provide a more precise and detailed description of the nature of schizophrenic thought disorder.

While we are still discussing associative disturbances, think to yourself for a moment of what it would be like to have this sort of difficulty in expressing yourself. The frustration and confusion in communication that would result might drive you to withdraw from others. Thus, it may be that some primary disturbances in schizophrenia may create problems that the person may attempt to cope with using behavior that still further impairs functioning.

The three other core symptoms described by Bleuler were affective disturbance, ambivalence, and autism. By *affective disturbance* Bleuler meant that many of the individuals he observed seemed to have very little emotional response to situations or stimuli that would elicit joy or sadness in most of us. Another aspect of Bleuler's affective disturbance is inappropriate affect. For example, having been told that a relative or friend had just died, the person might burst into laughter.

Schizophrenic behavior is often characterized by inappropriate emotional expression.

Mary Ellen Mark/Magnum Photos, Inc.

Ambivalence is more difficult to describe. In general Bleuler meant to describe the occurrence of opposing emotions or impulses in the person. Frequently schizophrenic individuals report that they simultaneously experience love and hate or depression and excitement in reference to the same person or event.

Finally, Bleuler used the term *autism* to describe the fact that some schizophrenics tend to withdraw from involvement in the external world and become preoccupied by private fantasies. Frequently in these autistic fantasies objective facts become obscured or distorted.

In addition to these core behavior patterns, secondary symptoms of schizophrenia were also described by Bleuler and others. They are thought to be secondary because, although they tend to be very dramatic aspects of schizophrenic disorders, they may be derived as a *response* to the core problems we have just described. And, as we noted, these secondary symptoms are not unique to schizophrenia.

The three most important of these secondary symptoms are delusions, hallucinations, and negativism, or stupor. By *delusions* we mean strongly held beliefs that are not shared by others in our culture. These beliefs are most characteristic of paranoid schizophrenics and occasionally they are highly systematized.

Hallucinations are nicely illustrated in Mark Vonnegut's description of the voices he began to hear during his schizophrenic experience. Hallucinations may be auditory (involving hearing), they may be olfactory

HALLUCINATIONS

"Testing one, two, testing one. Checking out the circuits: What hath God wrought. Yip di mina di zonda za da boom di yaidi yoohoo."

By this time the voices had gotten very clear.

At first I'd had to strain to hear or understand them. They were soft and working with some pretty tricky codes. Snap-crackle-pops, the sound of the wind with blinking lights and horn for punctuation. I broke the code and somehow was able to internalize it to the point where it was just like hearing words. In the beginning it seemed mostly nonsense, but as things went along they made more and more sense. Once you hear the voices, you realize they've always been there. It's just a matter of being tuned in to them.

The voices weren't much fun in the beginning. Part of it was simply my being uncomfortable about hearing voices no matter what they had to say, but the early voices were mostly bearers of bad news. Besides, they didn't seem to like me much and there was no way I could talk back to them. Those were very one-sided conversations.

But later the voices could be very pleasant. They'd often be the voice of someone I loved, and even if they weren't, I could talk too, asking questions about this or that and getting reasonable answers. There were very important messages that had to get through somehow. More orthodox channels like phone and mail had broken down (Vonnegut, 1975, p. 137–38).

(involving smell), or visual. As we noted in Chapter 5, the types of hallucinations experienced by schizophrenics are quite different from those experienced by someone who has just taken a psychedelic drug such as LSD. In the case of schizophrenia, hallucinations are almost always auditory.

Negativism, or *stupor,* refers to behavior displayed by some schizophrenics that tends to make them look paralyzed or immobile. Catatonic schizophrenics in particular tend to display this behavior.

It is important for us to remember that not all people classified as schizophrenic will show all of these behaviors. In fact, very few people suffering from a schizophrenic disturbance would display all of the schizophrenic characteristics, primary and secondary, we have described.

Course over Time

Psychological research and clinical descriptions of schizophrenic behavior help illuminate its possible meaning. But these are only cross-sectional views of the schizophrenia. They give us no idea of the experience and behavior of the schizophrenic over long periods of time. Is it the case that people who display schizophrenic behavior always do so? Or do they have periods of relative normalcy

A person in a catatonic stupor.

Bill Bridges/Globe Photos, Inc.

punctuated by bouts of severe symptomatology?

In Chapter 4 we noted that *longitudinal research* is extremely important for understanding the nature of abnormal behavior. Unfortunately, despite its importance, the expense and time involved in conducting good longitudinal research has discouraged many investigators from doing so. Nevertheless, we do have some information on the life course of schizophrenic disorders.

One of the most important contributors to our knowledge about the course of schizophrenic disorder over time is a Swiss researcher named Manfred Bleuler. He is the son of Eugen Bleuler, the 19th-century theorist, whose ideas have been so influential. His father devoted his career to providing accurate clinical descriptions of the nature of schizophrenic disorders. Manfred Bleuler devoted his energy to following a large number of schizophrenic individuals over the course of their entire lives. This laborious task has yielded important knowledge of the nature of schizophrenic disorders as they develop over time. Figure 10–1 sketches the course of schizophrenic disorders.

About 25 to 35 percent of M. Bleuler's schizophrenic patients had one or two severe episodes and then recovered after these initial episodes. Another 35 to 45 percent also had episodes of severe schizophrenic disturbance, but between these experiences there was some residual impairment. Still others, about 10 to 20 percent, ran a chronic progressive course that got continuously worse and ended in extremely severe continuous psychosis. Less than 5 percent ran a chronic course ending in chronic but mild disorder.

Contrast these outcomes with those of manic depressive disorders and personality disorders in Figure 10–1. You can see that manic depressive disorders tend to be extremely severe, but recovery leaves no residual effect. Personality disorders, on the other hand, develop slowly. There are no marked episodes and no severe deterioration in functioning.

Finally, contrast each of these courses of the disorder with the course of a single person's disorder over time. Although it is difficult to be certain for any single case, it appears that this individual is experiencing an acute onset of schizophrenic disorders with recurrent episodes. These episodes appear in some cases to be triggered by life events and in other cases with no precipitating life events apparent.

Perhaps the most important point to be noted here is that, although schizophrenic behavior at its most severe is extremely dramatic and disabling, it is most often episodic in nature. There are often long periods of time during which the individual

FIGURE 10–1 Course of Schizophrenia over Time

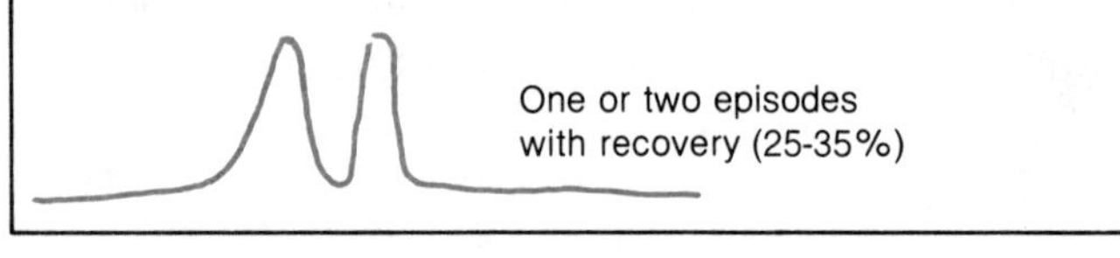

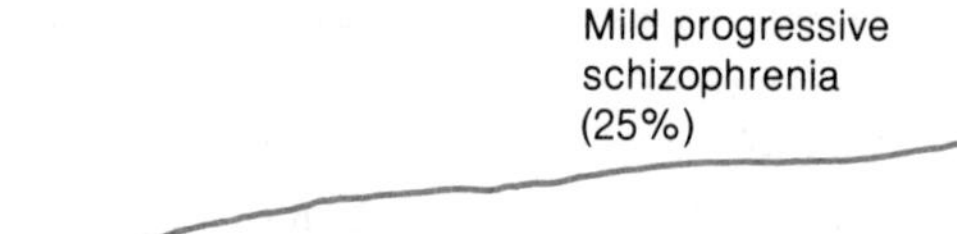

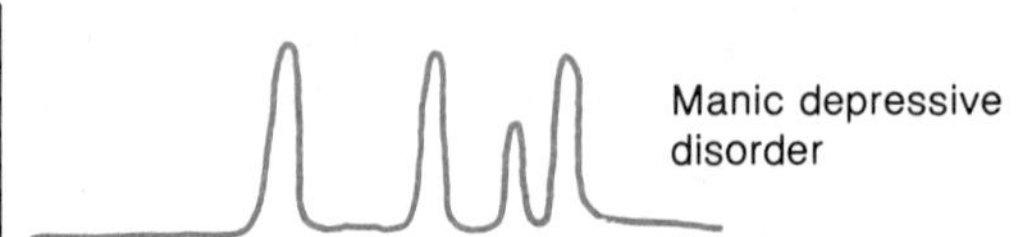

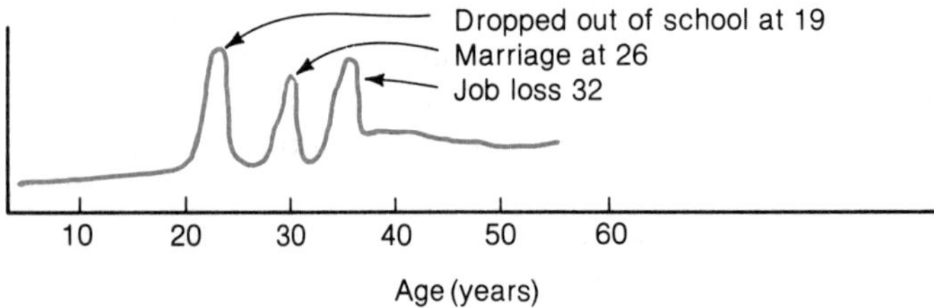

is capable of functioning effectively in his or her social world.

EXPERIMENTAL RESEARCH ON SCHIZOPHRENIC BEHAVIOR

The descriptions and examples that we have drawn from naturalistic and clinical observations lack the precision and explicitness that more carefully controlled studies might provide us. Psychologists have been concerned, in particular, with providing more precise descriptions of the nature of schizophrenic thought disorder. Such descriptions will give us a clearer understanding of the nature of the disorder and provide us with hints about where to search for its determinants. We will now consider examples of psychological research that attempt to describe the nature of schizophrenic thought disorder in more precise scientific terms.

Thought disorder is a good candidate for psychological study because researchers can apply their knowledge about cognitive processes in normal individuals to understand thought disorder as we observe it in the clinical context. Psychologists have been particularly interested in the mechanism of *attention* and the role it may play in schizophrenic thought disorder (Price, 1968). Schizophrenics often report, "I just can't concentrate," or "I'm so distractable I can't keep my mind on anything." This attentional difficulty can even show up in the middle of a sentence as attention wanders from one topic to another.

Wohlberg and Kornetsky (1973) studied unmedicated discharged schizophrenics and compared them with 20 matched controls using a test of attention called the continuous performance test. Patients were rewarded for correct responses and later tested in a session without distracting stimuli. They could fail to respond to critical stimuli (commit errors of omission) or respond incorrectly to noncritical stimuli (errors of commission). Schizophrenics tended to make more errors of omission, especially when they were distracted, than the controls. An important aspect of Wohlberg and Kornetsky's findings is that this basic attentional deficit could even be observed in schizophrenics who were not showing severe symptoms and who were not receiving medication. Much of the previous research on the problem of attention in schizophrenia has been complicated by the inability to rule out these factors as important contributors to the experimental performance of the schizophrenic group. This research suggests that the schizophrenic suffers from some fundamental difficulties in attention. But the delusions and hallucinations sometimes reported by schizophrenics are not accounted for with this research.

However, James Chapman (1966) has argued that delusions may be attempts to make sense out of or cope with the extremely stressful experience of having one's attention and perception so markedly altered. Chapman argues that patients gradually develop less rational and, eventually, bizarre explanations to account for their altered perceptual experiences. Chapman observed people develop delusions of various kinds as an apparent attempt to cope with the altered experience of a schizophrenic episode. Thus, delusions may be attempts to understand what is happening to fragmented and altered experience.

This is also suggested in some research on altered perception in schizophrenia conducted by Price (1966). In this research paranoid schizophrenics, nonparanoid schizophrenics, and normal individuals were compared in their ability to make judgments of the size of standard objects when the distance from the viewer was changed. Normals and paranoid schizophrenics both did fairly well at this difficult task. But paranoid schizophrenics also displayed an intriguing characteristic in their performance. When asked to rate their confidence in their own judgments, paranoid schizophrenics reported that they were "extremely confident" in the accuracy of their reports even when their accuracy was poor. Paranoid patients seemed to be compensating for their uncertainty about their own perceptual world. Thus it may be that some schizophrenics attempt to rigidly restructure the meaning of their world in order to cope with an inability to focus attention.

Schizophrenics Report on Their Own Experience

So far we have examined schizophrenic disorders from the point of view of the clinician who tends to focus on global clinical behaviors such as ambivalence or delusions and from the point of view of the psychological researcher whose goal is to provide carefully controlled analytical descriptions and understand their relationship to psychological processes such as memory or attention. But what about people experiencing schizophrenic disorders? How do they feel about their own schizophrenic experience? Perhaps the reports of people undergoing a schizophrenic experience will give us additional insight into both the experimental research data we have just considered and the clinical behavior of schizophrenics.

As we noted earlier, Chapman (1966) has carefully interviewed schizophrenic patients and asked them to describe the nature of their experience as clearly as they could. Chapman reports that the first signs of an oncoming schizophrenic episode are perceptual. Perceptual distortions can be quite frightening and disorienting. Consider this report: "Last week I was with a girl and she seemed to get bigger and bigger, like a monster coming nearer and nearer. The situations become threatening and I shrink back." Or recall again Mark Vonnegut's experience pruning the fruit trees.

Following these initial perceptual distortions, patients often report that they have extreme difficulty controlling their thoughts. A patient notes, "I can't control my thoughts. I can't keep thoughts out. It comes on automatically. It happens at most peculiar times—not just when I'm talking, but when I'm listening as well. I lose control at conversation then I sweat and shake all over . . . I can hear what they are saying all right, it's remembering what they have said the next second that is difficult. It just goes out of my mind. I'm concentrating so much on little things I have difficulty in finding an answer at the time."

These reports suggest that the person experiencing a schizophrenic episode is having considerable difficulty in focusing attention on external events. Instead, it is almost as if a "filter" that we all use to focus our attention in everyday tasks has temporarily ceased to function.

The idea that fundamental attentional problems in the schizophrenic experiences are important in understanding other schizophrenic behavior has been discussed by a number of researchers. For example, Maher (1968) has suggested that the loss of attentional control and the interference of dominant associations are phenomena that can be combined to help us understand the disordered thought and speech of schizophrenics. As Maher cogently puts it, "uttering a sentence without disruption is an extremely skilled performance, but one that most of us acquire so early in life that we are unaware of this remarkable complexity." He says further, "our successful sentences come from the successful, sequential inhibition of all interfering associations that individual words in the sentence might generate. Just as successful visual attention involves tuning out irrelevant visual material, so successful utterance may involve tuning out irrelevant verbal static" (p. 30).

The "static" Maher refers to is the inappropriate associations that are so characteristic of schizophrenic speech. Thus, it may be that the confused and intriguing patterns of speech are the product of both an inability to focus attention over a sustained period of time on the goal of a particular sentence, and the interference of inappropriate associations that would normally be inhibited. See Figure 10–2 for example. The utterance, "Doctor, I have pains in my chest and wonder if there is something wrong with my heart," can become, when uttered by a schizophrenic, "Doctor, I have pains in my chest and hope and wonder if my box is broken and heart is beaten for my soul and salvation and heaven, Amen." You can see, the sentence has several vunerable points at which irrelevant associations can interfere if one loses focus on the goal of the sentence. Of course, this interpretation of the schizophrenic's speech is only speculative but is consistent with much of the basic psychological research on the nature of schizophrenic thought disorder.

DIAGNOSIS AND CLASSIFICATION

Diagnostic Criteria in DSM III

Thus far we have described schizophrenic behavior as if it were a relatively homogeneous disorder. In fact schizophrenia is a relatively heterogeneous group of disorders. Thus decisions about diagnosis have in the past been notably unreliable. However, in keeping with the goal of increasing agreement among clinicians about the diagnosis of various disorders, the DSM III specifies particular symptoms that must be observed in order to make a diagnosis of

FIGURE 10–2 A Look at a Schizophrenic Utterance

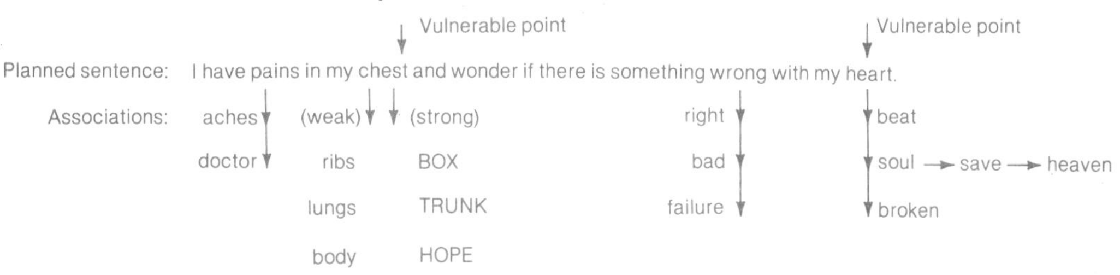

Note: Where a punning word occurs at a vulnerable point, the sequence becomes disrupted and disintegrates into associative chaining until it terminates. The emotional significance of what the schizophrenic plans to say may have little or no bearing on when an intrusion occurs or what it seems to mean.

Source: Reprinted from Brendan Maher, "The Chattered Language of Schizophrenia," *Psychology Today,* 2 (1968), pp. 32–33. Copyright © 1968, Ziff-Davis Publishing Company.

schizophrenia. These symptoms are shown in Table 10–1.

In addition, these symptoms must be associated with the interference of the ability of the individual to function in life situations. DSM III specifies that this diagnosis should be applied only when the person has displayed the characteristic symptoms for at least six months. The system also makes allowance for examining schizophrenic behavior over time and seeks evidence for a disturbance before the actual onset of symptoms, and/or a "residual" phase following the active phase of the disturbance.

Table 10–2 shows the five main subtypes of schizophrenia listed in DSM III. You will note that they resemble the traditional Kraepelinian subtypes with the addition of *undifferentiated* and *residual* types to account for cases that do not fall clearly in one of the other subtypes.

TABLE 10–1 DSM III Criteria for the Diagnosis of Schizophrenia

Characteristic Schizophrenic Symptoms

At least one symptom from any of the following ten symptoms must be present during an active phase of the illness (because a single symptom is given such diagnostic significance, its presence should be clearly established):

Characteristic Delusions

1. Delusions of being controlled: Experiences his thoughts, actions, or feelings as imposed on him by some external force.
2. Thought broadcasting: Experiences his thoughts, as they occur, as being broadcast from his head into the external world so that others can hear them.
3. Thought insertion: Experiences thoughts, which are not his own, being inserted into his mind (other than by God).
4. Thought withdrawal: Believes that thoughts have been removed from his head, resulting in a diminished number of thoughts remaining.
5. Other bizarre delusions (patently absurd, fantastic or implausible).
6. Somatic, grandiose, religious, nihilistic or other delusions without persecutory or jealous content.
7. Delusions of any type if accompanied by hallucinations of any type.

Characteristic Hallucinations

8. Auditory hallucinations in which either a voice keeps up a running commentary on the individual's behaviors or thoughts as they occur, or two or more voices converse with each other.
9. Auditory hallucinations on several occasions with content having no apparent relation to depression or elation, and not limited to one or two words.

Other Characteristic Symptoms

10. Either incoherence, derailment (loosening of associations), marked illogicality, or marked poverty of content of speech—if accompanied by either blunted, flat, or inappropriate affect, delusions or hallucinations, or behavior that is grossly disorganized or catatonic.

Thought Disorder versus Affective Diagnosis

A recent review of the research literature on the diagnosis of schizophrenia and affective disorders by Pope and Lipinski (1978) calls into question whether or not observing any particular cognitive symptoms of schizophrenia can have value in determining diagnosis or predicting the outcome of the disorder and the response to treatment. They argue that in the United States schizophrenic symptoms have been relied upon too heavily in diagnosis, resulting in an overdiagnosis of schizophrenia and an underdiagnosis of affective disorders, particularly mania. Specifically they suggest that affective symptoms do appear to have value in predicting the outcome of psychosis, whereas the

TABLE 10–2 Schizophrenic Subtypes Identified in DSM III

Hebephrenic Type This psychosis is characterized by disorganized thinking, shallow and inappropriate affect, unpredictable giggling, silly and regressive behavior and mannerisms, and frequent hypochondriacal complaints. Delusions and hallucinations, if present, are transient and not well organized. *Catatonic Type (excited and withdrawn)* It is frequently possible and useful to distinguish two subtypes of catatonic schizophrenia. One is marked by excessive and sometimes violent motor activity and excitement and the other by generalized inhibition manifested by stupor, mutism, negativism, or waxy flexibility. In time, some cases deteriorate to a vegetative state.	*Paranoid type* This type of schizophrenia is characterized primarily by the presence of persecutory or grandiose delusions, often associated with hallucinations. Excessive religiosity is sometimes seen. The patient's attitude is frequently hostile and aggressive, and his behavior tends to be consistent with his delusions. In general the disorder does not manifest the gross personality disorganization of the hebephrenic and catatonic types, perhaps because the patient uses the mechanism of projection, which ascribes to others characteristics he cannot accept in himself. Three subtypes of the disorder may sometimes be differentiated, depending on the predominant symptoms: hostile, grandiose, and hallucinatory.
Undifferentiated Type This category is for patients who show mixed schizophrenic symptoms and who present definite schizophrenic thought, affect, and behavior not classifiable under the other types of schizophrenia. It is distinguished from schizoid personality.	*Residual Type* This category is for patients showing signs of schizophrenia but who, following a psychotic schizophrenic episode, are no longer psychotic.

schizophrenic symptoms seem to have little value. Furthermore, they maintain that misdiagnosis of many individuals as schizophrenic rather than as affective disorders may expose large numbers of individuals to social stigma and inferior treatment.

Clearly this research suggests that cognitive disorders may have been overrated in importance compared to affective symptoms in assessing prognosis for schizophrenia. Indeed, recent research by Knight, Roff, Barnett, and Moss (1979) reporting a follow-up study of persons first diagnosed as schizophrenic 22 years earlier, suggests that measure of thought disorders were of little value in predicting the outcome of their disorder. However, measures of affective behavior and interpersonal competence were much more effective in predicting outcome. Thus, there may be a shift in the primary concern of research in diagnosis of psychosis from thought disorder to measures of adjustment such as interpersonal competence and emotional behavior.

Dimensional Approaches

Some researchers have come to believe that there is little value in attempting to classify schizophrenic patients into various types. They feel it is more appropriate to attempt to arrange people suffering from schizophrenia along a dimension that reflects some important clinicial or scientific characteristic.

Perhaps the best known of these dimensional approaches to describing schizophrenia is the *process-reactive dimension.* This dimension was originally designed to help clinicians predict the outcome of schizophrenic disorders. You will remember that Kraepelin was very much interested in classifying patients in terms of the outcome of their disorder, since no organic pathology could be found that would allow an organic classification system. This concern with *prognosis* (outcome of the disorder) is reflected in the process reactive distinction originally developed by Kantor (1953).

Table 10–3 lists the different patterns of behavior thought to exist among process and reactive schizophrenics. One of the most striking differences between the two ends of the process-reactive continuum has to do with the onset of symptoms. In the case of reactive schizophrenics, symptoms almost always occur as a response to some crisis or stressful life event. In process schizophrenia, on the other hand, the onset of schizophrenic behavior is gradual and begins early in the individual's life. Often process schizophrenia is thought to involve some underlying biological cause, while reactive schizophrenia is thought to be triggered primarily by environmental events.

At least three other attempts to distinguish the ends of a continuum of schizophrenia have been suggested in the literature. *Acute* versus *chronic* schizophrenia involves a distinction developed from medical thinking. Acute schizophrenic disorders are characterized by sudden severe symptoms, but the likelihood of recovery is thought to be good. Chronic schizophrenic disorders are usually thought to be irreversible and not necessarily as dramatic in onset. *Premorbid* adjustment has been suggested by Philips (1953) as an important way of delineating a continuum of schizophrenia. Schizophrenics with "good premorbid adjustment" presumably have good social, sexual, and occupational adjustment before the onset of schizophrenia. Patients displaying "poor premorbid adjustment"

TABLE 10–3 Characteristics of Process and Reactive Schizophrenia

	Reactive	*Process*
Premorbid Features	Relatively normal social and intellectual development	Poor early social and sexual adjustment; lower intelligence
Pattern of Onset	Occurs later in life; abrupt acute onset in response to life stress	Occurs earlier in life, in childhood or adolescence; onset is slow and gradual; no apparent environmental stress
Pattern of Presenting Behavior	Depressed or anxious mood; affect preserved disorientation during acute episode	Absence of anxiety or depression; flat affect, bizarre or fragmentary delusions
Course of Disorder	Episodic	Continuous
Prognosis	Good	Poor

Source: Based on R. E. Kantor et al., "Process and Reactive Schizophrenia," *Journal of Consulting and Clinical Psychology* 17 (1953).

tend to have poor social, sexual, and occupational adjustment before the onset of the disorder.

How different these various dimensions are from one another is unclear, and their value in predicting the outcome of disorders is only fair. Nevertheless, the idea of attempting to arrange schizophrenic behavior along the dimension that will predict clinical outcome is a fruitful one.

A Genetic Approach to Diagnosis

Recently, some researchers (Rosenthal, 1970; and Kety, 1967) have proposed the idea of a *schizophrenia spectrum.* This spectrum, shown in Figure 10–3, describes a group of disorders that vary in severity and appear to be genetically related. These researchers argue that "hard spectrum" disorders are those in which a substantial proportion of the relatives of the individual in question also show schizophrenic-like disorders, even when no social relationship exists between the relatives and the patient. "Soft spectrum" disorders, on the other hand, are those where there is substantially less schizophrenic-like behavior among the relatives of the patient.

FIGURE 10–3 Genetic Spectrum Approach to Diagnosis of Schizophrenia

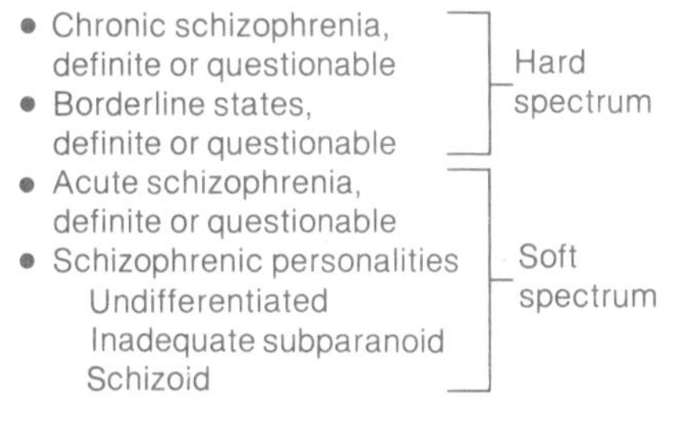

Source: S. J. Keith et al., "Special Report: Schizophrenia, 1976," *Schizophrenia Bulletin* 2 (1976), p. 514.

It is important to recognize that this is a research concept rather than one designed for clinical practice. It is very broad in its application and includes at its extremes a number of types of behavior that are clearly not schizophrenic in the usual sense.

The importance of this approach is that it specifically attempts to develop a classification based on assumptions about the *determinants* (in this case genetic) of schizophrenia. Such a classification system has obvious advantages to researchers like Rosenthal and Kety, who have strong interests in genetic and biochemical determinants of schizophrenia.

INFANTILE AUTISM

Consider the following description of infantile autism as it was first described by the pioneer researcher Leo Kanner in 1942.

> Frederick W. was referred on May 27, 1942, at the age of six years. His mother stated: "The child has always been self-sufficient. I could leave him alone and he'd entertain himself very happily, walking around, singing. I have never known him to cry in demanding attention. He was never interested in hide-and-seek, but he'd roll a ball back and forth, watch his father shave, hold the razor box and put the razor back in, put the lid on the soap box. He doesn't care to play with the ordinary things that other children play with, anything with wheels on. He is afraid of mechanical things; he runs from them. He

used to be afraid of my egg beater, is perfectly petrified of my vacuum cleaner.

Until the last year, he mostly ignored other people. When we had guests he just wouldn't pay any attention. He looked curiously at small children and then would go off all alone. He acted as if people weren't there at all, even with his grandparents. About a year ago, he began showing more interest in observing them, would even go up to them. But usually people are an interference. He'll push people away from him. If people come too close to him, he'll push them away. He doesn't want me to touch him or put my arm around him, but he'll come and touch me.

To a certain extent, he likes to stick to the same thing. On one of the bookshelves we had three pieces in a certain arrangement. Whenever this was changed, he always rearranged it in the old pattern. He won't try new things, apparently. After watching for a long time, he does it all of a sudden. He wants to be sure he does it right.

He had said at least two words before he was two years old. From then on, between 2 and 3 years, he would say words that seemed to come as a surprise to himself. He'd say them once and never repeat them. One of the first words he said was "overalls." At about 2½ years, he began to sing. He sang about 20 or 30 songs, including a little French lullaby. Now he can count up to into the hundreds and can read numbers but he is not interested in numbers as they apply to objects. He has great difficulty in learning the proper use of personal pronouns. When receiving a gift, he would say of himself: "You say Thank You" (Kanner, 1942, p. 217).

Ever since Leo Kanner first described the pattern of behavior captured in the account you have just read and coined the term *infantile autism,* this pattern of behavior has fascinated researchers and clinicians alike. Early in the history of the study of this disorder, it was believed that infantile autism was an early form of schizophrenia. More recently, however, as we shall see, descriptive research has distinguished between infantile autism and childhood schizophrenia, primarily on the basis of the age at which the disorder first appears. It is now fairly clear that infantile autism is a distinct childhood disorder beginning in the first three years of life.

Because of the distinctive pattern of behavior shown by autistic children, researchers have sought to describe the disorder with increasing precision and have searched for the causes of the disorder in the family environment of the child and have also searched for biological determinants. Thus, both social learning perspectives and biological perspectives have stimulated research for the causes of childhood autism. In the discussion that follows, we will consider the clinical picture presented by the autistic child, the course of the disorder over time, and the results of research that has attempted to discover the causes of the disorder. Finally, we will examine recent approaches to the treatment of infantile autism.

Clinical Picture

Stewart and Gath (1978) as well as Rutter and Lockyer (1967) suggest that infantile autism is characterized by three major patterns of behavior. They are (1) lack of social responsiveness, (2) delayed or deviant language development, and (3) resistance to change or stereotyped behaviors. Let us consider each of these major patterns of behavior in turn.

Lack of social responsiveness. The autistic child appears largely uninterested in social interaction with others. While most children will enjoy looking at the face of their parents or other children, the autistic child may avoid eye contact entirely and may withdraw from social interaction. Stewart and Gath (1978) note that some parents first become concerned about their child when they notice that the child is unaware of the mother entering or leaving the room and begin to wonder whether the child may be suffering from a hearing disorder.

Delayed or deviant speech. Wolff and Chess (1965) have described the speech and language of autistic children in considerable detail. Often the speech is automatic sounding, with little change in tone. Autistic children will often imitate or "echo" language that they hear in their environment with no apparent comprehension. Frequently, for example, an autistic child may repeat television commercials, slogans, or highway numbers.

Stereotyped behaviors and resistance to change in the environment. Often autistic children will carry out the same behavior again and again and resist attempting any new activity. These stereotyped behaviors superficially resemble the ritual-like behavior of obsession and compulsive children. At the same time, autistic children often develop attachments to objects or events which are unusually strong and difficult to explain.

> Examples of abnormal attachments are always carrying a mail order catalog or a particular stuffed animal. The range of unusual preoccupations is fascinating. One child recently seen by the authors insisted that his parents stop their car every time they went by a house with a basketball hoop and when they did he would perseveratively question them about the hoop. Resistance to change commonly involves becoming upset when furniture is rearranged in the room, but may extend to pushing a vacationing father out of the house at the time that he usually goes to work (Stewart & Gath, 1978, p. 14).

It is easy to understand the distress of parents who first begin to observe this pattern occurring in their children. Although it may be first dismissed as merely a "phase" through which the child is going, eventually the major difficulties in social development and normal social interaction presented by autistic children lead the parents to seek professional help.

Age of Onset and Distribution in the Population

One of the distinctive features of infantile autism is its early onset. Studies by Rutter and Lockyer (1967) suggest that approximately 75 percent of the children in their sample displayed the distinctive symptoms of infantile autism in the first two years of their life and the remainder by the third year. Only a small proportion of children displaying this behavior pattern display it as late as the fourth or fifth year of life. This is in marked contrast to the development of childhood schizophrenia, which seldom appears before the age of ten.

Although infantile autism has attracted the curiosity of researchers and therapists, it is a relatively unusual disorder of childhood. Studies by Lotter (1966) and by Torrey, Hersh, and McCabe (1975) suggest that autism occurs in between two and five children per 10,000 children in the population. Furthermore, the disorder appears to be about 2.5 times as likely to occur among boys as girls.

Autistic Children in Later Life

What is the fate of these children as they grow older and become adolescents or adults? Since Kanner's original research in 1942, there has been ample opportunity to follow the clinical course of the disorder over time, and several researchers including Eisenberg (1956) and Rutter, et al. (1967) have done so.

Perhaps one of the most carefully conducted follow-up studies was conducted by Rutter and his colleagues (1967). One strength of the study was that they included a comparison group of children who had also been seen in a psychiatric clinic for problems other than infantile autism and matched this comparison group for intelligence, sex, and age.

Although there are a few children showing the pattern of infantile autism who develop into reasonably well-adjusted adults, overall the prognosis is not encouraging, as is shown in Table 10–4. This data, drawn from Rutter, Greenfeld and Lockyer (1967), suggests that nearly half of the children show a very poor social adjustment during adolescence, whereas a quarter of the comparison group shows an equally poor adjustment. Rutter et al. note that for this sample of children a large number of different treatment approaches had been attempted, but they appeared to have little impact on the outcome of the disorder.

Rutter and his colleagues found that when improvement did occur in autistic children, it occurred in a gradual fashion. And children who had relatively higher levels of intelligence, the presence of speech, relatively less severe patterns of disorder, and more time in school were more likely to show relatively satisfactory outcomes later in adolescence.

Research on the Determinants of Autism

Two major schools of thought have predominated in the research directed at discovering the causes of infantile autism. Kanner's early work suggested that there appeared to be something distinctive in the personalities of the parents of autistic children. He described them as unusually reserved and cold and highly intellectual in their behavior. Soon researchers and clinicians began to conclude that it was these qualities in the personality characteristics of parents that influenced the behavior of autistic children.

However, a series of recent studies

TABLE 10–4 Social Adjustment of Autistic Children as Adolescents

Adjustment	*Autistics*			*Controls*		
	Number		*Percent*	*Number*		*Percent*
Normal	1	9	(14)	7	20	(33)
Good	8			13		
Fair		16	(25)		19	(31)
Poor		8	(13)		7	(11)
Very poor		30	(48)		15	(25)
Total		63			61	

Source: Abstracted from Rutter, Greenfeld, and Lockyer (1967). (Reprinted from M. A. Stewart and A. Gath, *Psychological Disorders of Children: A Handbook for Primary Care Physicians* (Baltimore: Williams & Wilkins, 1978), p. 18. © 1978, The Williams and Wilkins Co., Baltimore.

COMPARISONS BETWEEN SCHIZOPHRENIA AND INFANTILE AUTISM

Stewart and Gath (1978) note that schizophrenia in childhood is an extremely unusual phenomenon but can be distinguished from infantile autism, since autism shows an age of onset usually before three and almost never after the age of five. On the other hand, schizophrenia in children is seldom, if ever, seen under the age of ten.

The pattern of behavior in children diagnosed as schizophrenic during childhood or early adolescence resembles that of autism only in the most general fashion. This symptom picture is shown in the table at the right.

When schizophrenia does occur in children, it resembles hebephrenic schizophrenia, as it was described earlier in this chapter. The thought patterns of the child are disorganized and characterized by rapid emotional changes, delusions, and hallucinations.

Symptoms of Schizophrenia in Children and Young Adolescents
Avoids people
Poor relationships with other children
Gives partial answers to questions
Loose or otherwise disordered associations
Thought blocking
Delusions (mostly persecutory or fantastic)
Hallucinations (commonly auditory but also somatic and visual)
Grimacing
Mannerisms
Blunted affect
Perplexity
Incongruous affect

Source: Abstracted from I. Kolvin, C. Ounsted, M. Humphrey, and A. McNay, "The Phenomenology of Childhood Psychoses, *British Journal of Psychiatry* 118 (1971), p. 385. (Reprinted from Stewart & Gath, 1978, p. 25).

comparing the behavior and attitudes of the parents of autistic children with other clinical groups, particularly those of Cox et al. (1975) and Kolvin (1971), have suggested that this is not the case. These comparisons suggest that, if anything, the attitudes and social behavior of the parents of autistic children are more positive, warmer, and more prone to social interaction than those of parents of schizophrenic children or parents of children with speech disorders.

Thus, we see the original clinically derived hypothesis that the "refrigerator parent" is a major force in the development of autistic behavior has not been supported by systematically collected data. This research represents an excellent example of the value of carefully done research to test a clinically derived hypothesis. In some cases it may provide valuable leads and in others may perpetuate conceptions about the nature and causes of a particular pattern of abnormal behavior.

Biological determinants of infantile autism. There is an increasing body of evidence to suggest that there may be significant biological determinants of infantile autism. Folstein and Rutter (1977) conducted a twin study that reported four of eleven monozygotic twin pairs showed concordance for autism while none of ten same sex dizygotic twins did. Although this is a relatively small sample, it does suggest some genetic involvement in the development of infantile autism. Other studies (DeMyer et al., 1972) have reported histories of brain disease or injury in some of their sample and a higher than expected proportion of cases with abnormal patterns of EEGs.

Furthermore, a study by Hauser, DeLong, and Rosman (1975) in which 15 of a sample of 18 autistic children showed an enlargement of one section of the brain, the left lateral ventricle, suggests that atrophy of the temporal lobe may be associated with autism.

Treatment

As we mentioned earlier, early follow-up studies of autistic children suggested that most treatment strategies attempted in the past have had little effect on the outcome of infantile autism. However, recent behavioral approaches, particularly those described by Lovass (1977), suggest that some aspects of the behavior of autistic children can be modified.

Lovass has developed elaborate learning programs to teach normal speech to autistic children. The programs begin with attempts to build verbal responses in autistic children who did not speak at all or whose vocalizations were simply vowels. Once a child has acquired ten recognizable words, he (she) is taught to label events and objects and thus develop a basic vocabulary. Once the child is capable of labeling events, he or she is taught relationships between events, including positions, time, color, and shape.

From this foundation gradually emerges a program of conversation training in which the child is taught to answer questions and comments. This is followed by situations in which the child is placed in a three person interaction and is taught to give and seek information. Further refinements have included attempts to establish grammatical skills, the ability to recall previous events, and attempts to develop spontaneous conversation.

The following example illustrates the training of a child in making discriminations. This particular case is part of a training session for a child in his third month of language training.

E: Ricky, what's your name?

Ricky: Ricky.

E: That's right.

Ricky: How are you feeling?

E: No. Ask me what I asked you. Ricky! Say, what's your name?

Ricky: Ricky.

E: No. Say, what's. . . .

Ricky: What's (pauses). . . .

E: Your. . . .

Ricky: Your (pauses). . . .

E: Say, name.

Ricky: Name.

E: Now, say it all together.

Ricky: What's your name?

E: Joan. Good boy, Ricky. That's good. That's good. Come here, Ricky. Stand up, Ricky. Ricky, how are you feeling?

Ricky: I am feeling fine.

E: That's good. Ricky, come here. Ricky, come here. Now you ask me.

Ricky: How are you feeling?

E: I am feeling fine. That's good. That's good.

Ricky: Lie down, please. Lie down. (Preceding this hour **S** had been taught how to order **E** to stand up, lie down, smile, etc.)

E: Ricky, how old are you?

Ricky: I'm 7 years oid.

E: That's right. Ask me Ricky.

Ricky: Ask me.

E: No. That not what I asked you. Ask me how old I am. Say, how. . . .

Ricky: Are you feeling?

E: No. That's not what I asked you either. I asked you how old you are. Now, you ask me. Say, how. . . .

Ricky: How. . . .

E: Say, old.

Ricky: Old. . . .

E: Say, are you.

Ricky: Are you.

E: That's right. Now say it all together. Say, how old are you?

Ricky: I am 7 years old. How old are you?

E: I'm 21 years old. That's very good. That's good.

(From Lovass, 1977, pp. 74–75.)

ORGANIC BRAIN SYNDROMES: SIMILARITIES AND DIFFERENCES FROM FUNCTIONAL PSYCHOSES

In our discussion of schizophrenia and infantile autism we noted that these were patterns of behavior where no clear cut brain disturbance could be observed. There are, however, several behavior patterns that do resemble psychotic disorders in some ways and yet are associated with brain pathology as it is evidenced by laboratory tests or history of previous injury. These are the *organic brain syndromes.*

It is important to understand how these disorders resemble and differ from the psychotic disorders. We will consider two of the organic brain syndromes—*delirium* and *dementia*—in some detail and briefly describe the other organic brain syndromes.

The DSM III indicates that organic mental disorders have as their essential feature a permanent or temporary dysfunction of the brain that we can attribute to particular organic factors. Furthermore, laboratory evidence, such as brain X-rays, electroencephalograms, or evidence such as a physical examination or a history indicating some organic factor, is necessary before the diagnosis of organic brain syndrome can be made.

If you examine Figure 10–4, you will note that the decision tree for organic brain syndromes in DSM III begins with evidence that the person already has experienced some organic event which is judged to be causing the behavior we observe. These events could be brain injury, infection, a disturbance of the metabolism, the use of an intoxicating substance, brain disease, or even the withdrawal associated with stopping the intake of alcohol or drugs. Thus, we see that the organic brain syndromes may have a variety of different causes, but the causes are clearly psychological and produce either temporary or permanent brain dysfunction.

The patterns of behavior that we will describe below and which are listed in the decision tree in Figure 10–4 reflect differences in the localization of brain injury, the rate of onset of the syndrome, its progression, and the duration of the underlying brain pathology.

Delirium

This organic syndrome is characterized by a very rapid onset and a clinical picture that includes disturbances of attention, memory, and orientation in time and space. Not only is the onset of delirium

FIGURE 10–4 Decision Tree for Organic Brain Syndromes

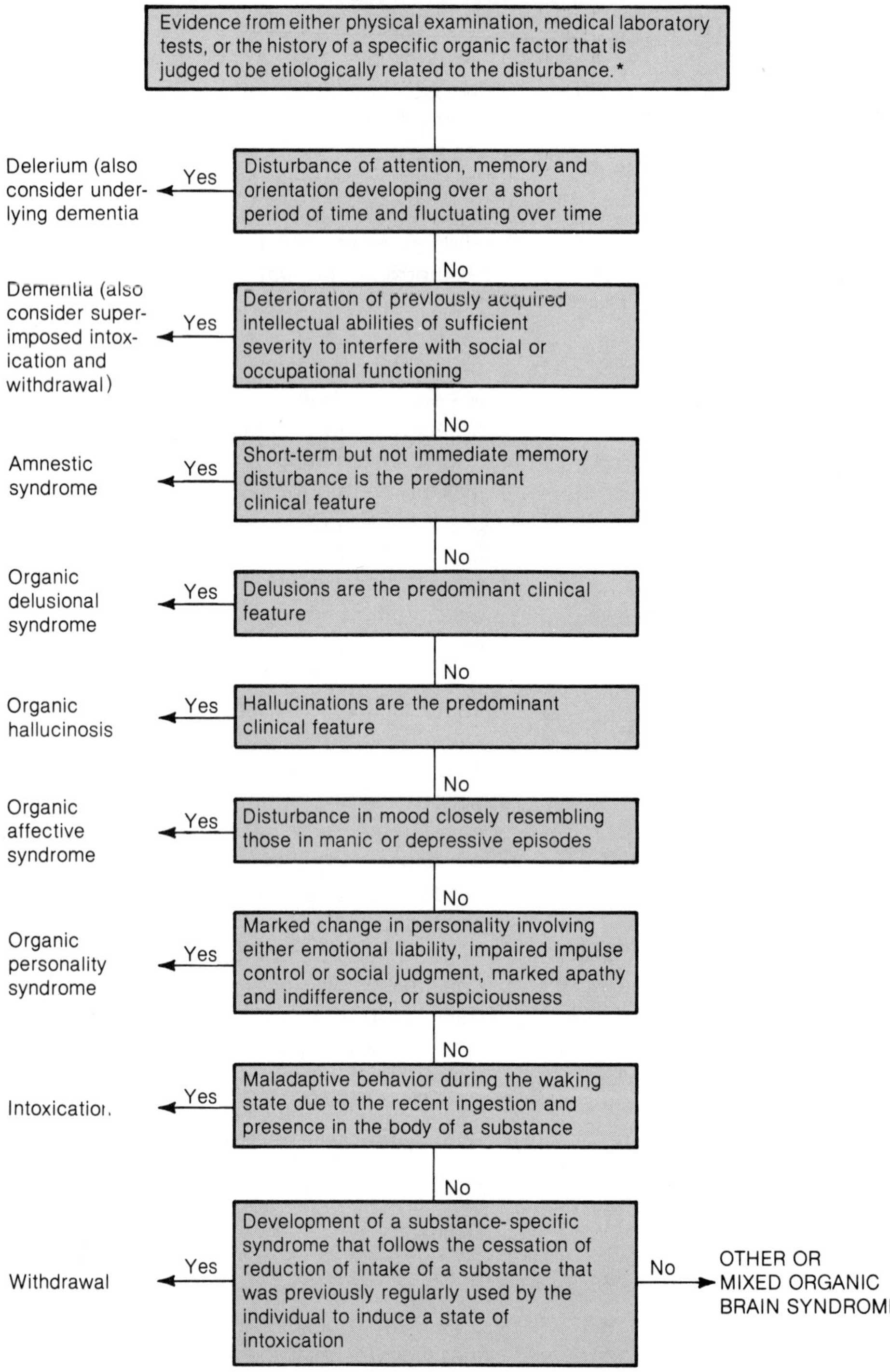

* In the absence of such evidence, an organic factor can be presumed if conditions outside of the Organic Mental Disorders category have been reasonably excluded and if the disturbance meets the symptomatic criteria for Dementia.

Source: American Psychiatric Association *Diagnostic and Statistical Manual of Mental Disorders, (Third Edition) DSM-III.* (Washington, D.C.: American Psychiatric Association 1980), p. 349.

rapid, but frequently its duration is quite brief; as little as a week and seldom more than a month. There may also be a sleep disturbance so that the person suffering from delirium is unable to sleep or sleeps excessively. Frequently, too, the person experiencing an episode of delirium may have perceptual experiences including hallucinations, delusions, and sometimes disturbed speech.

An important difference between delirium and schizophrenia is that in the case of delirium the symptoms rapidly shift and change and are poorly systematized. Thus, the delusions reported by a person suffering from delirium may be only brief and disorganized. Furthermore, dramatic problems of memory and ability to orient oneself are more characteristic of delirium than they are of schizophrenia. This particular pattern has, in the past, been called *toxic psychosis* and *acute brain syndrome.*

The determinants of delirium are often infections, metabolic disturbances, use of alcohol or drugs to excess, or ceasing their use after dependence. Sometimes delirium can occur after a brain injury or after seizures.

TABLE 10–5 Diagnostic Criteria for Delirium

A. Disturbance of attention, as manifested by either:
   1. Impairment in ability to sustain attention to environmental stimuli.
   2. Impairment in ability to sustain goal-directed thinking.
   3. Impairment in ability to sustain goal-directed behavior.

B. Disordered memory and orientation, if testing not interfered with by attention disturbance.

C. At least two of the following:
   1. Reduced wakefulness or insomnia.
   2. Perceptual disturbance: simple misinterpretations, illusions or hallucinations.
   3. Increased or decreased psychomotor activity.

D. Clinical features develop over a short period of time and fluctuate rapidly.

E. There is evidence from either physical examination, medical laboratory tests, or the history, of a specific organic factor that is judged to be etiologically related to the disturbance.

Source: American Psychiatric Association, *DSM III* (1980), p. 107.

Dementia

A second important organic brain syndrome is dementia. As the name implies, the essential features of dementia are a deterioration of previously acquired intellectual ability that may interfere with social functioning or work to produce memory loss and problems in judgment or impulse control.

Unquestionably, the major pattern of behavior that characterizes dementia is memory loss (Table 10–6). A loss of memory for past events as well as the ability to learn new skills are important characteristics. Dementia may begin with a forgetfulness for telephone numbers and directions. A person suffering from dementia may first reflect it by leaving the water running, the iron connected, or perhaps get lost in his or her own neighborhood. Frequently, too, we may observe changes in the person's personality. Changes may either be exaggerations of previous personality characteristics or dramatic changes in personality characteristics.

Although dementia most frequently occurs in older people and is associated with a variety of types of brain disease, it may also occur in children. Dementia may occur because of brain tumors, injuries or neurological diseases, circulatory problems in the brain, intoxication, and infections.

TABLE 10–6 Diagnostic Criteria for Dementia

A. A deterioration of previously acquired intellectual abilities of sufficient severity to interfere with social or occupational functioning.
B. Memory impairment.
C. At least one of the following:
   1. Impairment of abstract thinking as manifested by reduced capacity for generalizing, synthesizing, differentiating, logical reasoning, and concept formation.
   2. Impairment in judgment or impulse control.
   3. Personality change.
D. Does not meet the criteria for Intoxication or delirium, although these may be superimposed.
E. Either (1) or (2):
   1. There is evidence from either physical examination, medical laboratory tests, or the history, of a specific organic factor that is judged to be etiologically related to the disturbance.
   2. In the absence of such evidence, an organic factor necessary for the development of the syndrome can be presumed if conditions outside of the Organic Mental Disorders category have been reasonably excluded and if the behavioral change represents cognitive impairment in a variety of areas.

Source: American Psychiatric Association, *DSM III* (1980), p. 111.

Chronic schizophrenia may also be characterized by some intellectual deterioration and dementia. They key difference is that in the case of dementia there is identifiable brain pathology, whereas in schizophrenia no identifiable brain pathology is present.

Other Organic Brain Syndromes

Let us briefly consider the other organic brain syndromes, described in DSM III and shown in the decision tree for organic disorders.

Amnestic syndrome. This pattern of organic brain disorder involves a memory loss that renders the person unable to remember events that occurred as little as 25 minutes earlier. Such a person may be able to repeat a series of half a dozen digits presented one at a time about one second apart but be unable to recall three objects shown to them 25 minutes earlier. The most common forms of this disorder are associated with chronic alcohol use or vitamin deficiency.

Organic delusional syndrome. In some cases people suffering from some form of brain impairment will develop delusions which may resemble those of schizophrenia. The delusions may be associated with brain tumors on the one hand or brain impairment from drug abuse using amphetamines (see Chapter 14). In differentiating organic delusional syndromes from schizophrenia, the major basis for making distinctions has to do with whether or not there is evidence of the specific organic factor which is necessary for the development of the delusions.

Organic hallucinosis. Another organic brain syndrome may produce recurrent and persistent hallucinations in a person who is fully awake and alert. In some cases, the person may be aware that the hallucinations are not real and in other cases they may be convinced that they are indeed real. The hallucinations may be auditory, but any sensory mode may be involved. Drug use, particularly of the hallucinogens, most frequently produces visual hallucinations, whereas in the case of alcohol intoxication, auditory hallucinations are more likely to occur.

Organic affective syndrome. As the name implies, this syndrome involves major disturbances in mood that look a good deal like manic or depressive episodes. Most commonly this particular pattern of behavior is caused by metabolic factors and certain drugs.

Organic personality syndrome. In some cases a person experiencing a brain dysfunction may display marked changes in personality. They may become very moody and emotional and lose impulse control or social judgment. Temper outbursts are very common, and, at times, the organic personality syndrome will be reflected in a marked apathy and lack of interest. Most commonly tumors or brain injury or stroke are the factors associated with personality change.

Intoxication. As the name implies, this is an organic syndrome involving disturbances of perception, wakefulness, thinking, attention, judgment, and emotional control due to the ingestion of some substance into the central nervous system, most commonly, of course, either alcohol or drugs. DSM III identifies intoxication as being a problem only when it is associated with such maladaptive behavior as fighting and impaired judgment or interference with occupational functioning. Thus, presumably, mild social drinking which does not result in maladaptive behavior would not be defined as intoxication.

Withdrawal. If someone has previously used drugs or alcohol habitually to induce a state of intoxication, stopping the use of that substance or reducing it dramatically may produce the organic brain syndrome described as withdrawal. Most commonly withdrawal is characterized by anxiety, restlessness, irritability, insomnia, and impaired attention. Usually this pattern of behavior is self-limiting and will occur over a few days or several weeks at most.

SUMMARY

In this chapter we have examined the descriptive characteristics of one of the most important of the major psychological disorders, schizophrenia. We have seen that it is both one of the most severe and, from the point of view of social cost, one of the most disabling of the psychological disorders.

Examining the history of attempts to describe schizophrenia, we noted certain key features of the disorder, including autism, associative disturbance, ambivalence, and affective disturbance. We also noted that thought disorder is one of the most salient aspects of schizophrenia, and problems of attention quite probably underlie a variety of the perceptual and language problems displayed by schizophrenics.

The DSM III has identified a number of criteria necessary for the diagnosis of schizophrenia as well as several major subtypes which are in some ways quite similar to the Kraepelinian subtypes we discussed earlier in the chapter. Although the DSM III classification may aid in improving the reliability of diagnosis of the disorder, its usefulness is far from proven. Recent research has suggested that additional emphasis on social competence and affective symptoms may be of more value in predicting the outcome of the disorder.

Finally, we examined approaches to characterizing schizophrenia on the basis of relevant dimensions. Process and reactive dimensions may more directly reflect the course of the disorder over time. Genetic spectrum approaches have also been proposed that reflect the degree to which genetic determinants of the disorder are apparent.

We have seen that among the psychological disorders that affect children, *infantile autism* is one of the most severe and most dramatic in its appearance. Characterized by lack of responsiveness, deviant or delayed speech, and stereotyped behavior patterns, it begins in the first three years of life.

There is growing evidence for biological determinants of autism, but to date the most effective treatments are behavioral. Childhood schizophrenia differs from autism both in having a later age of onset, at age ten or later, and a symptom pattern that resembles hebephrenic schizophrenia in a number of ways.

Though the prognosis for both of these childhood disorders is currently poor, both improved treatment techniques and additional research may make the future more promising for such children.

Our discussion of the organic brain syndrome makes it clear that many of the patterns of behavior associated with actual brain dysfunction do resemble the functional disorders we have described in discussing schizophrenia as well as the affective or neurotic disorders. The distinguishing feature of the organic brain syndromes is, as we have mentioned earlier, the *clear evidence of some underlying brain dysfunction.* But, of course, we should remember that just because a functional disorder such as schizophrenia or the affective disorders do not provide us with clear evidence of a brain dysfunction does not mean that there is none. In the broadest sense, most behavior is mediated in one way or another by brain function. It may be that at least some of the disorders now described as "functional" may one day be identified as organic in their origins.

11

Schizophrenia: Determinants and Treatment

INTRODUCTION

In Chapter 9 we described the schizophrenic disorders. We examined the classical behavior patterns, the course of the disorder over time, and how patients themselves report their schizophrenic experiences. We also considered a variety of research attempts to classify schizophrenic disorders in ways that would allow statements about prognosis or causation.

In this chapter we take up the question of the determinants of schizophrenia more directly and also examine several approaches to treatment. The search for the causes of schizophrenia is one of the most fascinating scientific detective stories in the field of abnormal psychology. The search for causes has ranged broadly; stimulated by a variety of different theoretical perspectives, scientists have examined biochemical, familial, and social phenomena. Perhaps no other major psychological disorder has been examined in such a variety of human contexts. Let us now turn to that search.

DETERMINANTS OF SCHIZOPHRENIA

At the beginning of our discussion of schizophrenia we said that scientists disagree about the underlying causes of schizophrenic behavior. At a general level, most scientists will agree that both biological and experiential factors play some role in the development of schizophrenia. But that is where the agreement ends. Researchers tend to look in different places for the causes of schizophrenic behavior. Some scientists believe that the central mechanisms of schizophrenia are genetic. Quite naturally their search is primarily for genetic factors or for biochemical processes. Others believe that extremely powerful socialization forces in the family play a key role in the development of schizophrenia. They conduct their search within the family itself, attempting to isolate developmental experiences that may play a crucial role in the expression of schizophrenia. Finally, still other scientists are convinced that society, with the inequalities and the stresses it places on the individual, plays a critical role in the development of schizophrenia.

Kessler (1969) notes that, "in general, biologically oriented researchers tend to view schizophrenia as a disease resulting from an unidentified organic or hereditary biochemical or neurophysiological defect, whereas psychologically oriented investigators tend to view schizophrenia as a group of disorders resulting from disturbances in sociocultural, familial, and interpersonal processes. After paying homage to the concept of genotype-environment interaction, most investigators, unwittingly or by choice, slip back into more comfortable modes of thought and place their etiological bets on one or the other side" (p. 1341).

Thus, despite the fact that all scientists recognize that social, familial, and biological factors must *interact* to produce the complex behavior we call schizophrenia, even "objective" scientists have difficulty maintaining the neutral stand that such an interactional view would require. Because of their own training or hunches, scientists usually place their bets (and their biases) on either the experiential or the biological side when searching for the causes of schizophrenia.

But whether a researcher's bias is in the direction of biological or psychological causes, there are certain facts that have to be explained. These are the facts that have to do with the *transmission* of schizophrenia. Remember, we said that a child who has one parent that has been diagnosed as schizophrenic has ten times greater a chance of developing a schizophrenic disorder than someone who does not have a schizophrenic parent. A child with two such parents has 40 times greater a chance. How do you explain that striking finding?

If you are biologically oriented, the first thing that is likely to occur to you (and to scientists) is that this is evidence of genetic transmission. The child must have inherited something physical or biochemical. But a scientist concerned with the family context would argue that these facts can be just as easily explained by recognizing that the child in a family with one parent who is schizophrenic is more likely to learn schizophrenic behavior—perhaps through modeling. It is equally easy for the experientially oriented scientist to explain the increased risk associated with having two schizophrenic parents. Imagine what a child living in such a home must be experiencing. This must be compelling evidence for the power of experience in the causation of schizophrenia.

The important idea to grasp here is that all of these possible causal factors are *correlated* with one another. Each of them looks like a highly likely set of explanations for the development of schizophrenic behavior. Indeed, a look at Figure 11–1 suggests that there are several different "models" of schizophrenic behavior. Now perhaps you can see the puzzle that confronts researchers. Biological, experiential, and social factors all seem to be likely candidates in explaining the causes of schizophrenia. On the surface it seems that each of them by itself could account for the fact of schizophrenic transmission.

In our discussion we will examine the evidence for biological, familial, and social causes in the development of schizophrenia. Having done that, we will examine some of the strategies that scientists are now using to try to untangle the mystery of schizophrenia and we will consider some new views that promise to clear up at least some of the mystery.

FIGURE 11–1 Models of Causation in Schizophrenia

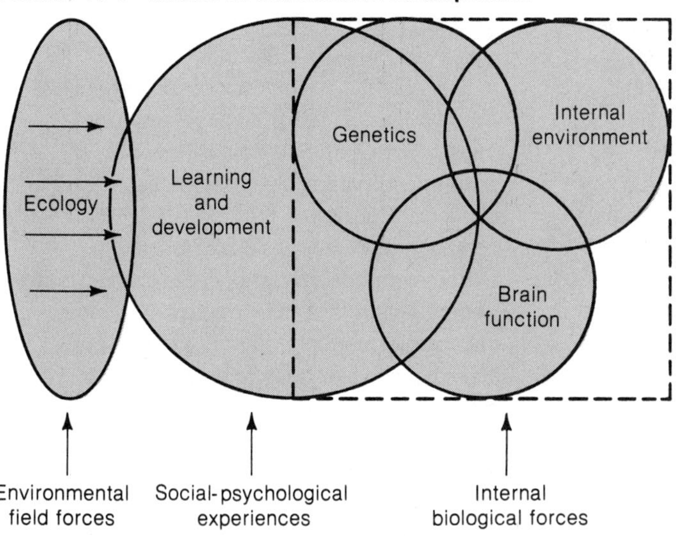

Source: J. Zubin and B. Spring, "Vulnerability: A New View of Schizophrenia," *Journal of Abnormal Psychology* (1977), *86* p. 106. Copyright 1977 by the American Psychological Association. Reprinted by permission.

SCHIZOMIMETIC CONDITIONS AS CLUES TO THE DETERMINANTS OF SCHIZOPHRENIA

A research strategy in searching for the causes of schizophrenia has been to examine conditions that produce behavior resembling schizophrenia. The investigators then ask whether these antecedent conditions might not also be important in the development of schizophrenia itself. This is a version of the *analogue strategy* we described in Chapter 4. An example we discussed earlier is the research on "model psychoses," especially those produced by LSD and other psychedelic drugs.

Chapman (1969) has thoughtfully examined this research strategy and the "schizomimetic" conditions that have been offered as evidence for various theories of schizophrenia. Some of the allegedly schizomimetic conditions are listed below:

Sleep deprivation: The behavior of normal subjects deprived of sleep resembles that of schizophrenics in producing cognitive disorganization, hallucinations, and occasional delusions. Investigators have argued that common biochemical events occur in both schizophrenia and sleep deprivation.

Brain damage: Some behavior of brain-damaged patients resembles that of schizophrenics. Thus it has been hypothesized that brain damage is the real cause of schizophrenia.

Drug-induced psychoses: Certain drugs (for example, LSD) induce behavior that resembles schizophrenia. Therefore it is assumed that altered brain chemistry is a cause of schizophrenia.

Operant conditioning: If normal subjects can be conditioned to behave like schizophrenics, it is assumed that this is evidence for the role of operant conditioning in the development of schizophrenia.

Dreams: Psychoanalysts have inferred that schizophrenic thought reflects the abandonment of the censoring functions of the ego. Thus schizophrenia resembles the "primary process" qualities observed in dreams.

Distraction: Distracting normal subjects in a task may lead them to make errors that resemble those of schizophrenics. Researchers have therefore hypothesized that schizophrenic behavior is a result of "heightened distractibility."

As farfetched as some of these ideas seem, Chapman points out that the schizomimetic strategy is not illogical. If two observed behaviors are indeed indistinguishable, we have to take seriously the hypothesis that they have a similar cause. But Chapman notes that two problems confront us in using this research strategy. The first is that measures of schizophrenic thought disorder are extremely crude. Therefore, concluding that two behaviors are truly identical is almost impossible. Second, current systems of classification are quite imprecise and almost all investigations of schizomimetic conditions avoid specifying what types of schizophrenia are mimicked by the condition being studied. Thus, these schizomimetic strategies may only become useful when more precise measures of schizophrenic behavior and more precise hypotheses can be developed.

THE DISEASE PERSPECTIVE: THE BIOLOGICAL SEARCH FOR CAUSES

Scientists concerned with possible psychological causes of schizophrenia have worked simultaneously on two fronts. First, some scientists have been engaged in an attempt to uncover evidence for underlying genetic factors. Second, other scientists, many of whom are already convinced of the importance of genetic factors, have conducted their search for determinants in the biochemistry of the brain. Their working hypothesis is that something about the biochemistry of the schizophrenic brain is disordered and that finding the nature of this disorder may lead us to understand both the causes of schizophrenic behavior and possibly also lead us to a biological strategy for prevention or treatment.

Genetic Evidence

We have already noted that being the offspring of someone diagnosed as schizophrenic greatly increases one's chances of developing the disorder oneself. This is a major finding in *family studies* of schizophrenia. A typical strategy in genetic research is to ask whether a particular disorder runs in families. If it does, then the scientist considers this a clue to the possible genetic causes of the disorder and looks for evidence that will be more convincing.

Perhaps the best known evidence for a

Comparison of identical twins reared together and apart form an "experiment in nature" which allows assessment of the genetic contribution to a variety of behavior patterns and traits.

Susan Richter/Photo Researchers, Inc.

possible genetic contribution to the cause of schizophrenia comes from *twin studies.* As you may recall, twin studies help rule out the possibility that it is the experience of living in a family with a schizophrenic member that produces schizophrenia in the offspring rather than genetics. Thus, twin studies provide a strategy for obtaining less ambiguous evidence for a genetic component in schizophrenia.

The strategy of twin studies is not hard to understand. We know, of course, that identical twins are *monozygotic;* that is, they develop from the same egg and therefore have identical genetic makeup. Fraternal twins, however, are no more genetically similar than other siblings that have developed from the fertilization of two different eggs. This crucial fact helps us separate the possible effects of environment from those of heredity.

For example, if it is the experience of living in a schizophrenic family that produces schizophrenia, then both members of a pair of identical twins ought to be no more likely to develop schizophrenia than both members of a fraternal twin pair. But now consider the possibility that there is an important hereditary factor in schizophrenia. In this case, if one identical twin is diagnosed as schizophrenic, then the likelihood of the co-twin also being schizophrenic should be greater for identical twins than for fraternal twins.

Table 11–1 illustrates this idea with hypothetical data. In the case illustrating evidence for a possible genetic component, both identical and fraternal twin pairs with one diagnosed schizophrenic member (index case) are compared. In the identical twin group, 90 percent of the co-twins were also diagnosed as schizophrenic, a very high concordance rate. The fraternal co-twins were diagnosed as schizophrenic in only 10 percent of the cases. This would provide strong evidence of a genetic factor. In the other instance no difference in concordance rates are found, suggesting no discernable genetic involvement.

Now look at some actual results of major twin studies summarized by Rosenthal (1970). Table 11–2 shows that, with one or two exceptions, the concordance rate for identical twins is higher than for fraternal twins. Thus, genetic researchers argue we have some evidence that there is a genetic component involved in the development of schizophrenia.

TABLE 11–1 Illustration of Possible Outcomes of Twin Studies Indicating Different Degrees of Genetic Involvement in Schizophrenia (Concordance rate—percent of twin pairs both of whom are diagnosed as schizophrenic)

	Monozygotic Twins (genetically identical)	*Dizygotic Twins (no more genetically similar than siblings)*
Evidence for genetic Component	90%	10%
No evidence for genetic component	15%	15%

The initial twin studies done by Kallman, Slater, and other researchers have been criticized severely even by other genetic researchers. And twin studies by themselves have failed to convince many environmentally oriented critics. These critics point out that even more modern methods of determining zygosity (whether a twin pair is actually identical or fraternal) produce lower concordance rates and make the twin studies by themselves unconvincing. Furthermore, the actual concordance rates for monozygotic twins are highly variable from study to study, probably because of differences in sampling and diagnostic methods.

As a consequence, a number of researchers have begun to use a different strategy for separating possible genetic and environmental factors in the development of schizophrenia. The strategy that they used has been to take advantage of a natural experiment in nature, that of *adoption.* Kety, Rosenthal, and Wender all have made ingenious use of the fact that some schizophrenics' parents have put up their children for adoption early in the child's life.

TABLE 11–2 Concordance Rates in the Major Twin Studies of Schizophrenia

	MZ Twins		*DZ Twins*	
Study	*Number of Pairs*	*% Concordant*	*Number of Pairs*	*% Concordant*
Luxenburger, 1928*a,* 1934	17–27	33–76.5%	48	2.1%
Rosanoff et al., 1934–35	41	61.0	101	10.0
Essen-Möller, 1941	7–11	14–71	24	8.3–17
Kallmann, 1946	174	69–86.2	517	10–14.5
Slater, 1953	37	65–74.7	115	11.3–14.4
Inouye, 1961	55	36–60	17	6–12
Tienari, 1963, 1968	16	0–6	21	4.8
Gottesman and Shields, 1966	24	41.7	33	9.1
Kringlen, 1967	55	25–38	172	8–10
Fischer, 1968	16	19–56	34	6–15
Hoffer et al.	80	15.5	145	4.4

Source: From *Genetic Theory and Abnormal Behavior* by D. Rosenthal. Copyright © 1970 McGraw-Hill. Used with permission of McGraw-Hill Book Company.

Furthermore, some nonschizophrenic parents have adopted children born of schizophrenic parents without knowing the identity or diagnosis of the biological parents. Thus, adoption provides a situation in which entangled effects of heredity and environment can be separated. The trick was to obtain birth records and other information that was detailed enough to allow them to trace adopted children and to discover which of them developed some form of schizophrenic behavior and which did not.

If you think about it for a moment the logic becomes clear. If there is a genetic factor in schizophrenia, then children who were born of a schizophrenic parent but adopted by nonschizophrenic parents will be more likely to develop schizophrenia than will children adopted from nonschizophrenic biological parents and raised by nonschizophrenic adoptive parents.

The early results of a study conducted by Rosenthal et al. (1968) are shown in Table 11–3. Rosenthal and his colleagues took advantage of the fact that some countries, such as Denmark, keep extremely detailed birth records so that it is possible to follow individuals throughout the course of their lives. Consequently it was possible for them to begin with a list of all of the children adopted in Denmark over a 23-year period. The study showed that adopted children with one schizophrenic or manic depressive biological parent are more likely to display schizophrenic spectrum disorders than adopted children whose biological parents had no history of psychological disorder.

A clever study design that makes use of the process of adoption to clarify the roles of genetic and experiential factors of schizophrenia is the *cross-fostering* study by Wender et al. (1973, 1974). Wender compared three groups of children who had been adopted. The first group of children had one biological parent with a schizophrenic spectrum diagnosis but had been raised by parents who had never received a psychiatric diagnosis of any kind. The second group were children who had normal biological parents and normal adoptive parents. The third group of children (cross-fostered) had normal biological parents but were raised by parents of whom one had received a diagnosis in the schizophrenic spectrum. This last group allows us to examine the effects of having been raised in a family

TABLE 11–3 Schizophrenic-spectrum Disorders in Adoptees Who Had a Biological Schizophrenic or Manic-depressive Parent, or Both Biological Parents without Psychiatric History

Diagnosis of Adoptee	*One Parent Schizophrenic or Manic-depressive (n = 39)*	*Parents without Psychiatric History (n = 47)*
Schizophrenia		
Hospitalized	1	0
Never hospitalized	2	0
Borderline schizophrenia	7	1
Near or probable borderline	0	2
Schizoid or paranoid	3	4
Not in schizophrenic spectrum	26	40

Source: From *Genetic Theory and Abnormal Behavior* by D. Rosenthal.

containing a schizophrenic parent while at the same time having a genetically normal endowment.

Wender conducted extensive interviews and tests with each child and then asked trained interviewers to describe each child carefully. These descriptions were then sorted from "least" to "most disturbed" by another group of judges who had no knowledge of the groups from which each description came. The results of Wender's study are shown in Figure 11–2.

There are problems associated with trying to take advantage of "experiments in nature" of the kind we have described here. One clear problem has to do with

THE HIGH RISK STRATEGY IN THE SEARCH FOR CAUSES: PROMISE AND LIMITS

Recently, a number of scientists concerned with the search for causal factors in the development of schizophrenia have been using a research strategy we described in Chapter 4. Commonly called the *high-risk strategy,* it seeks out individuals who are "at risk" for schizophrenia but who have not yet developed the disorder.

The logic, you will recall, is this: once schizophrenic symptoms develop many other complicating factors enter the picture which are *results* rather than *causes* of the disorder, so that no clear inferences about the determinants of schizophrenia can be drawn. Thus, by choosing individuals who have not yet developed any disorder, but who are at high risk, and comparing them over time with individuals who have a low risk, we can discover what events precede the actual schizophrenic episode. Thus we can better be able to distinguish causes from consequences.

We have already mentioned the research conducted by Mednick and his colleagues in which children at risk for schizophrenia have been followed for a number of years. Other high-risk studies have been conducted by Rosenthal and his colleagues. The Wender (1973) cross-fostering study we described earlier in our discussion is another example of a high-risk study of a slightly different sort.

Most of the high risk studies of schizophrenia currently being conducted use genetic background as the criteria for deciding who is at risk. Consequently it has been incorrectly assumed that high-risk studies are designed only to search out genetic or biological causes of schizophrenia. The fact is, any causal factor thought to put a child at risk for schizophrenia could be used in selecting a research sample for a high-risk study.

Even though the high-risk strategy promises to help us answer the questions about the causes and the consequences of schizophrenia, some other cautions must be kept in mind. For example, as Keith Gunderson, Reifman, Buchsbaum, and Mosher (1976) point out, 90 percent of the people diagnosed as schizophrenic do not have a parent or parents who are labeled schizophrenic. Thus, if the current definition of high risk is limited to schizophrenic parenthood, even if it produces important causal evidence, the results will generalize to only approximately 10 percent of the current schizophrenic population.

FIGURE 11–2 Results of Wender et al. (1973, 1974) Cross-fostering Study

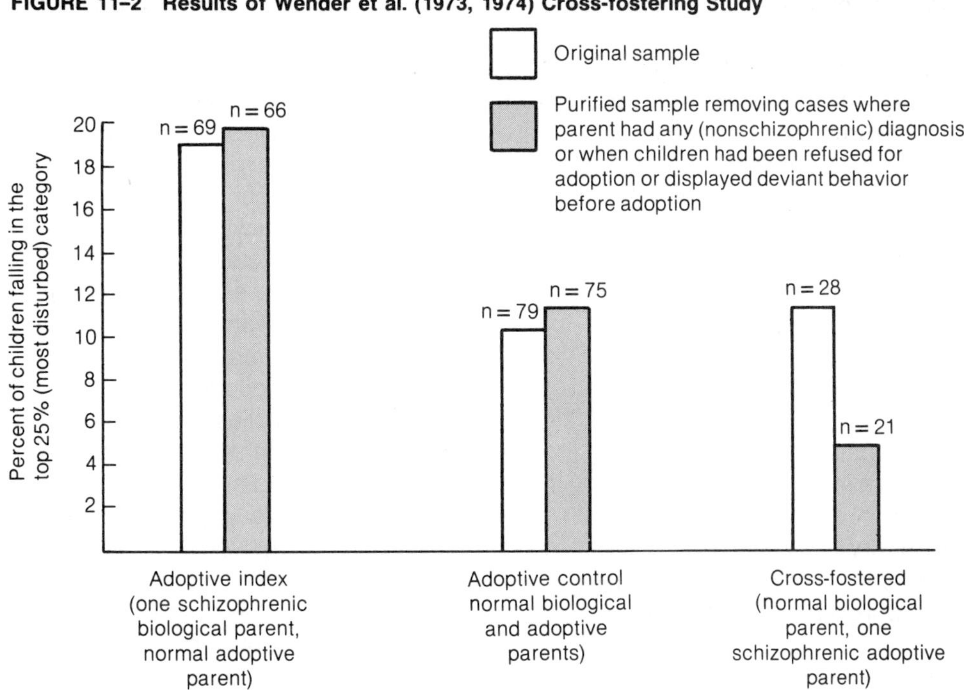

the fact that it is extremely difficult to obtain an adequate sample of cross-fostered children. In any case, this research certainly provides additional evidence for a genetic component in the transmission of schizophrenia.

Genetic Mechanisms

So far we have only established that there may be a genetic mechanism involved in the development of schizophrenia. But what is the mechanism? The question is a critical one since an answer would tell researchers a great deal about the likely nature of the biochemistry of the disorder. Basically, two kinds of theories have been offered to explain the genetic transmission of schizophrenia, a *monogenic theory* and a *polygenic theory.* In fact, the polygenic approach has at least two current versions. Let us consider each of these theories briefly since they will help us to understand the possible modes of genetic transmission of schizophrenic behavior.

Monogenic theories. Monogenic theories are based on the principle that what is transmitted through a *single gene* at one location on a chromosome is all that is necessary to produce schizophrenia. At any given location on the chromosome, a single gene may be *dominant* over another gene. That is, whatever characteristic that particular gene carries will be expressed and that of the recessive gene will not. Thus, at any given locus on a chromosome, a person may have two dominant genes, two recessive genes, or one dominant and one recessive gene. In order to gain a clear understanding of monogenic theories, look at Table 11–4 below.

In this table you can see that the combination of matings of two individuals will produce different combinations of dominant and recessive genes. The actual genetic structure of the individual is listed under the column titled "genotype." Depending on whether the schizophrenic gene is dominant or recessive, the gene combinations will lead to a particular phenotype, or actual expression of the trait. These phenotypes are listed in the last two columns of Table 11–4. You can see that, if the schizophrenic gene is dominant, whenever it occurs the result will be schizophrenia, according to monogenic theory. If, on the other hand, the schizophrenic gene is recessive, the trait of schizophrenia will occur in fewer cases.

This is a relatively simple theoretical model of how schizophrenia is transmitted. And the theory does generate testable predictions. If, for example, the distribution of schizophrenia in families followed a simple monogenic pattern of either dominant or recessive form, this would constitute evidence in support of a simple monogenic theory. As Kidd and Cavalli-Sforza (1973) note, this would allow the resolution of schizophrenia in fairly simple biochemical terms. But, unfortunately, the data describing the distribution of schizophrenia in families does not bear out a monogenic theory. In fact the proportion of cases found among relatives of schizophrenics is always *less* than that which would be predicted either by the dominant or recessive single gene theory.

This poses a peculiar problem for the genetic theorist. If several random factors were involved, the proportion of schizophrenics in families would sometimes be higher than predicted by the monogenic theory and sometimes lower. But, in fact, the results suggest that the proportions are *always lower.* Advocates of a single gene theory of transmission have tried to escape this problem by introducing the concept of penetrance.

Penetrance simply means the percentage of cases that actually manifest the trait in question, given that a particular gene actually exists. The idea of "partial penetrance," then, is advocated by some theorists (e.g., Slater, 1965) as a way of explaining the fact that the actual phenotypes for schizophrenia do not match the proportions predicted by a

TABLE 11–4 Theoretical Outcomes of Monogenic Theory of Schizophrenic Inheritance

*Mating**	*Genotype of Children*	*Phenotype with S Dominant*	*Phenotype with S Recessive*
ss × ss	ss	all normal	all normal
SS × SS	SS	all schizophrenic	all schizophrenic
SS × ss	Ss	all schizophrenic	all normal
Ss × ss	one half Ss one half ss	one half schizophrenic one half schizophrenic	all normal all normal
Ss × Ss	one-fourth SS one-half Ss one-fourth ss	three-fourths schizophrenic one-fourth normal	one-fourth schizophrenic three-fourths normal

* S = "schizophrenic" gene. s = normal gene.

monogenic theory. But other serious students of genetic theories of schizophrenia (Rosenthal, 1973) view the idea of penetrance simply as a way of escaping facts that do not fit the theoretical model of monogenic transmission.

Polygenic theories. Although the monogenic theory is appealing because of its simplicity, it is almost certain that an adequate theory of the genetic transmission of schizophrenia will be more complex. Polygenic theories offer this complexity because they assume that more than one gene at more than one locus of the chromosome is involved.

One version of polygenic theory currently being studied is the *polygene threshold model* described by Gottesman and Shields (1967). Here it is not what is transmitted at a single locus, but the sheer cumulative effect of a number of different "culpable genes" that is thought to produce schizophrenic behavior. A look at Figure 11–3 gives us an idea of how polygenic theories are conceptualized. In this distribution you can see that with increasing numbers of culpable genes the liability or risk of schizophrenia increases. But only when some "threshold" number of genes has been exceeded will schizophrenia actually occur.

Gottesman and Shields (1967) have proposed this polygenic threshold model for schizophrenia partly because diseases such as diabetes seem to fit the model well. In addition, there is good scientific precedent for such a theory since many traits, such as height, weight, and skin color, are believed to be influenced in this way. Thus, in this polygenic theory, schizophrenia is thought to be the result of the cumulative effect of a number of different genes.

Still a third theory, which is neither strictly monogenic nor strictly polygenic, should be considered. The idea of *genetic heterogeneity* (Rosenthal, 1970) is based

FIGURE 11–3 Polygenic Threshold Model of Schizophrenic Causation

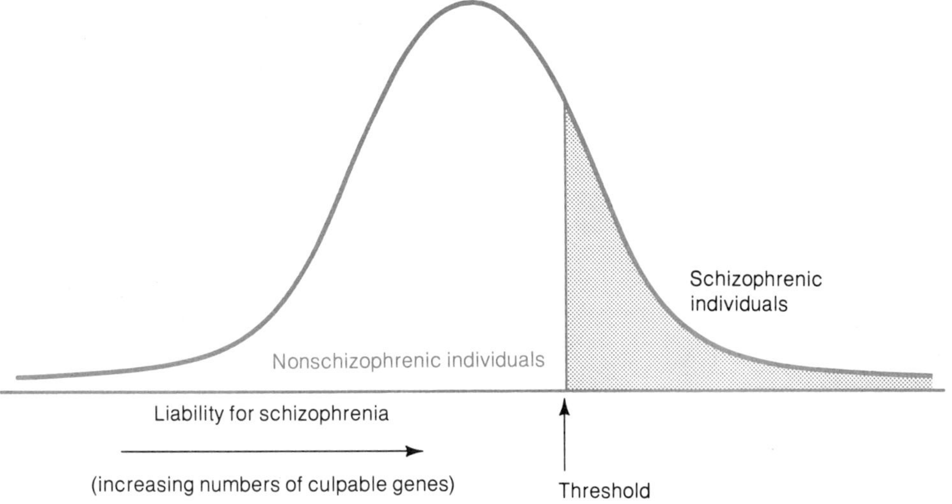

on the idea that more than one gene at more than one locus is required to produce schizophrenia. This is not a simple polygenic theory that argues that a large cumulative number of genes are necessary for schizophrenia. Instead, advocates of genetic heterogeneity argue that very specific genes, when they occur in certain combinations, will produce the schizophrenic phenotype.

The simplest example of a model based on genetic heterogeneity would involve only two genes. In actual practice, of course, many more genes would be involved. Let us look at an example of the two-gene case in Table 11–5 to get an idea of what the consequences might be.

In this two-gene theory, we must assume only that each member of a mating pair carries a dominant or recessive gene for socialization (either S or s) and for coherence of thought (either Z or z). There are, then, nine possible combinations or genotypes that could result. But only four phenotypes result. Further, only one of these would result in schizophrenia (sszz).

This formulation has appealing aspects. For example, you can see that making only a few simple assumptions produces a complex but plausible outcome. Two of the phenotypes (sociable, loose associations and asocial, coherent thinking); although not schizophrenia, resemble "borderline states" and help account for the heterogeneity of behavior actually observed in the clinical context.

The key to choosing between these models is finding some measure, often called a *genetic marker,* that will tell researchers when an individual does indeed show a predisposition for a particular trait. This is the key to unlocking the puzzle for many genetic diseases since it allows the scientist to use the distribution of people who carry a particular genetic marker as a basis for predicting the degree of risk for a

TABLE 11–5 An Example of the Outcome of Genetic Heterogeneity Theory of Schizophrenic Transmission

Resulting Genotypes	*Resulting Phenotypes*	*Frequency*
SSZZ, SSZz SsZZ, SsZz	Sociable, coherent thought	9
SSzz, Sszz	Sociable, loose associations	3
ssZZ, ssZz	Asocial, coherent thinking	3
sszz	Asocial, loose associations ("schizophrenia")	1

Notes: Interest in socialization: S leads to gregariousness (dominant); s leads to social withdrawal (recessive).

Coherence of thought: Z leads to coherent thinking (dominant); z leads to loose associations (recessive).

Source: Drawn from D. Rosenthal, *Genetic Theory and Abnormal Behavior* (New York: McGraw-Hill, 1970).

particular disorder. This prediction can then be compared with actual data on the rates of disorder.

In medicine a classic example with the use of genetic markers is the blood sugar level in diabetes. In the case of schizophrenia it is most likely that such a genetic marker will be biochemical in nature.

It is important to appreciate why researchers build such biological models and pursue data to test them with such vigor. In Chapter 3 we considered the illness perspective with its organic orientation to abnormal behavior. For medical geneticists the idea that schizophrenia is a disease is a highly plausible one. They have successfully pursued other initially puzzling disorders, such as diabetes, to their genetic origins. For them it is no great leap to think about schizophrenia in the same way. In fact, the search for such genetic markers or other unique biochemical characteristics of individuals who are at risk for schizophrenia has a long history. Let us now turn to research on the biochemistry of schizophrenia.

Biochemical Research

Scientists have long suspected that the key to unlocking the mystery of schizophrenia lay in the brain biochemistry or the metabolism of the schizophrenic. If only we could understand how the brain chemistry of schizophrenics was different from that of normal people this would promise both an understanding of the causes of the disorder and the possibility of prevention or cure, perhaps through the regulation of medication.

But the history of the search for the biochemical "X factor" in schizophrenia has been a discouraging one. The fact that psychologists and psychiatrists have placed their bets so heavily on finding some unique biochemical factor in schizophrenia has led to a long series of premature reports of discoveries of the X factor in schizophrenia (Kety, 1967). These reports were withdrawn with much less fanfare when it was belatedly discovered that something in the diet of the experimental group or some other uncontrolled factor actually was producing the biochemical result. (Think back for a moment to our review in Chapter 4 of the research on the "pink spot" conducted by Hoffer.) The exciting possibility that adrenochrome was the X factor in schizophrenia actually turned out to be a result of poorly controlled laboratory procedures. Blind alleys like this have certainly not discouraged researchers who continue to seek an understanding of the biochemistry of schizophrenia.

Another factor scientists have pursued has been research on the "model psychosis." You will recall that in Chapter 4 we described the early interest in the similarity between the behavior and experiences of people who have taken LSD and those who suffer from schizophrenia.

There is, however, an important new set of developments in the biochemistry of schizophrenia that does look promising for the future. This line of research has come to be known as *dopamine hypothesis* (Keith, Gunderson, Reifman, Buchsbaum Mosher, 1976). Snyder (1974) has described the early detective work that led to the implication of dopamine in the biochemistry of schizophrenia. Before we consider that evidence, let us look at Figure 11–4 to understand the role that dopamine plays in normal brain functioning.

FIGURE 11–4 The Dopamine Hypothesis in Schizophrenia.

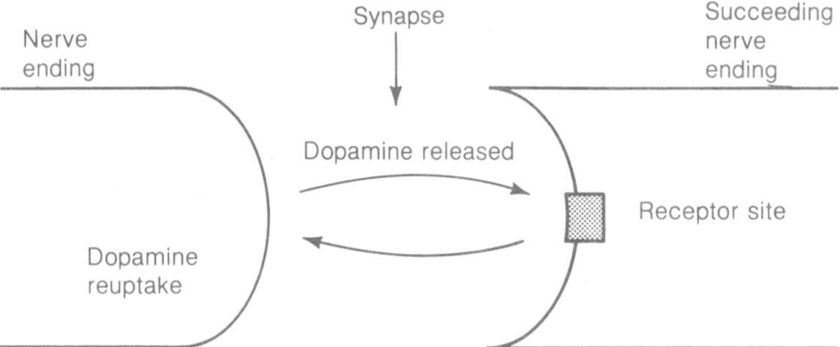

A. Role of dopamine in normal brain functioning

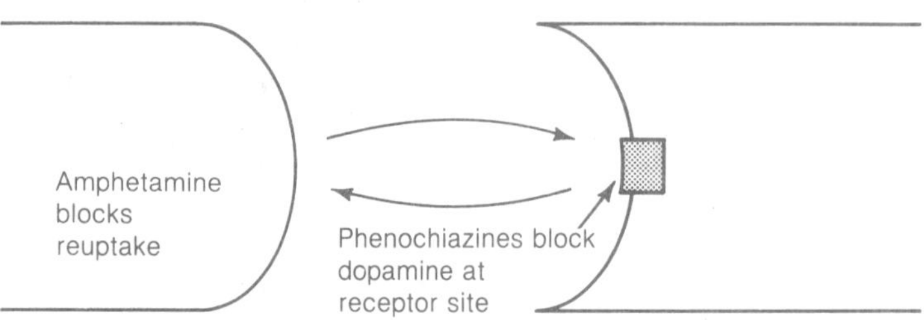

B. Effects of drugs on dopamine transmission in schizophrenia

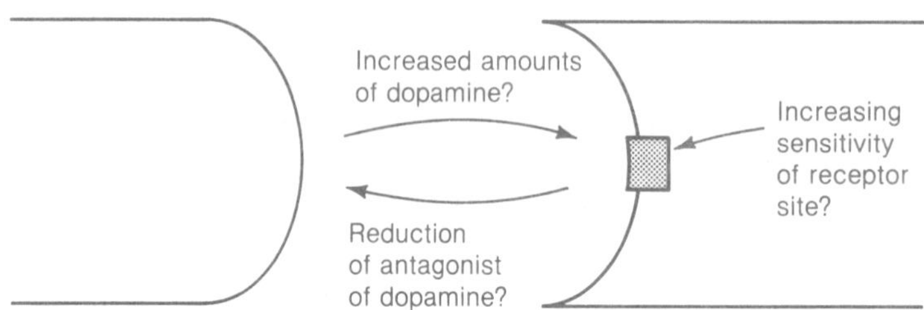

C. Possible dopamine mechanisms in schizophrenia

Dopamine is a *neurotransmitter.* Neurotransmitters are chemicals that transmit electrical signals from one neuron in the brain to the next. They are the message carriers that cross the synapse when an electrical impulse must be transmitted from one neuron to the next. Dopamine is one of a whole family of neurotransmitters that occur in various areas of the brain. In Figure 11–4A you can see that dopamine acts as a chemical messenger by leaving the nerve ending and traveling to a receptor site in the succeeding neuron. Once it has sent its message, it is taken up again *(reuptake)* by the original neuron.

The evidence for the involvement of dopamine in schizophrenia is indirect (Figure 11–4B). First, the effect of antischizophrenic drugs such as the phenothiazines is to block the receptor site for dopamine. Thus, to put it crudely, phenothiazines "slow down" the transmission of nerve impulses by partially blocking the dopamine. Second, amphetamine, a central nervous system stimulant, appears to "soup up" the transmission of nerve impulses by blocking reuptake of dopamine, leaving large amounts of it in the synapse. Amphetamine also makes schizophrenic symptoms much worse (Snyder, 1974).

According to Keith el al. (1976), at least three mechanisms for the increase of dopamine could be operating (Figure 11–4C). Increased amounts of dopamine at the nerve terminals could be producing schizophrenic-like behavior. Second, increased sensitivity of dopamine receptors could be producing the effect. Third, the reduction in some antagonistic chemical which normally reduces the amount of dopamine in the synaptic cleft could also be responsible. Obviously there are many potential mechanisms for the increase in dopamine in the synaptic cleft.

Even if this biochemical process is involved in schizophrenia, as Snyder (1974) and others now suspect, the question of how it produces alterations in behavior still remains. Presumably, the firing of nerve endings and transmission of impulses become increasingly random and rapid and the usual inhibition associated with attentional control becomes difficult for the schizophrenic to achieve.

It is also important for us to note that the search for dopamine imbalances in the brain of schizophrenics is very different from earlier research in the brain chemistry of schizophrenia. Earlier works attempted to find some X factor unique to schizophrenia. Here, instead, we see attempts to understand imbalances in normally occurring brain chemistry processes rather than some biochemical factor unique to schizophrenia. Thus, support for the dopamine hypothesis, particularly if it can be linked to genetic evidence, would be important evidence for for the role of biological factors in the development of schizophrenia.

THE SOCIAL PERSPECTIVE: FAMILY AND SOCIETY AS CONTEXTS FOR SCHIZOPHRENIC DEVELOPMENT

The family is both the genetic and experiential context of human development. Both biological influences and social learning intertwine in the family context. For scientists trying to understand the nature of schizophrenia, the family poses an especially important challenge. It is the family that provides a primary context for the transmission of schizophrenia, whether the actual mechanism is biological, environmental, or some interaction of the two.

For most psychologists, however, the family is seen as a place for learning. Their questions about the relationship between families and schizophrenia are most likely to focus on whether and how symptoms are learned through the process of socialization.

Although it is intuitively obvious to look at the family as an arena for the learning of abnormal behavior, there is actually evidence from genetic studies for environmental determinants of schizophrenia. Think back, for a moment, to our examination of twin studies of schizophrenia. These studies clearly indicated that genetic endowment alone could not fully explain the observed incidence of schizophrenia. Concordance rates among identical twins was far from perfect, whereas an exclusively genetic mechanism for the inheritance of schizophrenia would predict perfect concordance among identical twins.

Thus an environmental search for the determinants of schizophrenia can properly begin with a consideration of the family. But, as we shall see, the larger society may also play a role. We will consider evidence strongly suggesting a role for societal sources of stress and selection in the development of schizophrenia as well. But in the last analysis we will return to the family, for in the family genetics, learning, and society have their most acute impact on the psychological life of the individual.

Family Hypotheses

A common observation of clinicians who treat schizophrenic patients is that much of the content of their preoccupations, fears, delusions, and hallucinations derive from family life. This clinical observation has led a number of different theorists concerned with the causes of schizophrenia to suggest that the family environment operates as an important causal factor in the development of schizophrenia. In fact, their clinical accounts often are very persuasive in suggesting that schizophrenic behavior cannot be understood except in the family context.

But different theorists have different views of *how* the family actually contributes to the development of schizophrenia. Box 11–3 lists a number of different clinically derived hypotheses about the nature of the family of the schizophrenic and its relationship to the development of symptoms.

These hypotheses seem highly plausible

A number of theorists have argued that the pattern of family interaction is an important determinant of abnormal behavior.

Owen Franken/Stock, Boston, Inc.

SIX CLINICALLY DERIVED HYPOTHESES ABOUT THE ROLE OF THE FAMILY IN THE DEVELOPMENT OF SCHIZOPHRENIA

Attachment The difficulties observed in adolescent or adult schizophrenics reflect disruptions in early attachment between the child and caretaker, suggests Otto Will (1970). This disruption in the formation of basic trust results in later fear of loss and separation, withdrawal, panic, odd symbolic communication, and lack of ego development characteristic of schizophrenia.

Schizophrenogenic mother Mothers who are overprotective, smothering, insensitive, rejecting, seductive, and controlling are capable of eliciting schizophrenic behavior in their offspring, according to Arieti (1959).

Marital schism and skew Relationships between spouses may involve a "schism" in which open conflict between them exists and each tries to recruit the child to their side of the conflict. Other relationships may involve "marital skew," in which one parent is dominant and overtly pathological in behavior. Both kinds of relationships may produce schizophrenia in children, suggests Lidz et al. (1965).

Double bind Certain forms of communication between parent and child are productive of schizophrenic behavior according to Bateson, Haley and others (1956). The "binder" communicates to the child in paradoxical fashion, demanding mutually contradictory responses (e.g., "Don't be so obedient"). The dependent child is constrained against pointing out the contradiction and copes in ways that appear schizophrenic, such as withdrawing or searching for hidden meanings in all communications.

Mystification The family of the schizophrenic acts in inconsistent and mystifying ways, suggests Laing and Esterson (1971). The apparently schizophrenic behavior observed in children is really a rational means of coping with a mystifying environment.

Social learning Ullman and Krasner (1975) suggest differential reinforcement is the key factor in learning schizophrenic behavior in the family. Normal behavior is ignored (extinguished) and bizarre behavior is reinforced through attention. The result is a behavioral repertoire that appears schizophrenic.

and are made more so by the rich clinical detail which is often used to support them. But, as important as clinical experience is in *generating* hypotheses, it clearly does not provide an adequate arena for *testing* them.

The reason for this problem is not difficult to grasp. Clinicians are observing families in which a family member has *already developed schizophrenic symptoms*. Thus we are confronted with an unsolvable problem of inference. If we do happen to observe something unique in the patient's family environment, we cannot know whether it played a causal role in the development of those symptoms or whether the unique factor is actually a *response* to the stressful experience of having a severely disturbed person in the family. In short, we cannot know whether the family environment is the *cause* or the *consequence* of schizophrenic behavior.

There is good reason to believe that families who must cope with chronically ill or disabled members show more stress and disturbance than those who do not. Thus, the rival hypothesis that family behavior is a consequence rather than a cause of schizophrenia is quite plausible.

There are still other questions about the role of the family that need answers. For example, if it is true that the families of schizophrenics do show unusual behavior, then we would want to know whether this behavior is *unique* to families that produce schizophrenic offspring or whether it is typical of families with a deviant member.

On the last question we now have some evidence. A recent review conducted by Jacob (1975) was unable to uncover any consistent evidence that conflict or positive and negative emotion were uniquely characteristic of families of schizophrenics as opposed to those of various types of control groups. Jacob did find, however, that there appeared to be *less clear communication* in the families of schizophrenics when they were compared with those of normal controls.

What might this finding suggest? Wynne (1970) has conducted studies of the communication difficulties of the parents of schizophrenic offspring as well as parents of neurotics and normal children. He finds that there is indeed among the parents of schizophrenics communication deviancy that is much greater than that of neurotics and normals.

Wynne emphasizes the importance of the interaction of the family members in interpreting these results. But they are open to still another interpretation. A genetically oriented critic might argue that the communication deviance observed by Wynne might simply be subclinical schizophrenic behavior in the parents and that they, too, are simply "carriers" of schizophrenic genes.

Can family researchers escape from these logical difficulties? One approach is to examine the family over time. *Longitudinal studies* have the potential advantage of examining the family environment *before* the schizophrenic behavior emerges in offspring. The problem here is a practical one. If only 1 or 2 percent of the general population develops schizophrenia, how are we to know which families to observe over time?

In the study of abnormal behavior, one longitudinal strategy is to conduct a *follow-up study.* Follow-up studies examine clinical records of children in various family environments *before* they developed schizophrenic behavior. Later they are examined to determine whether the children themselves developed serious disturbances.

One such follow-up study was conducted by Waring and Ricks (1965). These investigators compared children who had been seen early in their life at a child guidance center, and who later became schizophrenic, with children in a matched control group. Children who had become schizophrenic were divided into groups of those who developed severe, chronic disorders and were hospitalized for long periods of time and those who were released from hospital settings and returned to the community.

Waring and Ricks (1965) studied the clinical records of each child and were able to describe several different kinds of family environments that apparently distinguished children who later became chronic schizophrenics from those who developed schizophrenia but were later able to function in the community.

The severely disturbed chronic schizophrenics were much more likely to come from one of two kinds of family environments. One environment involved "emotional divorce." This describes a family environment in which there is almost no interaction but much hostility and distrust between the parents. The second type of family was characterized as a "symbolic union." This type of family environment usually contains an overcontrolling, dominating spouse and a passive and accepting spouse. A third kind of family environment investigators characterize as "family sacrifice." In these families, the child is openly rejected and frequently forced to leave the home. These children tend to fare relatively well, having the highest proportion of released schizophrenics among them. Although this study cannot tell us that certain family environments are more likely to produce schizophrenia than others, it is important because it suggests that the family may influence the *form* that schizophrenic disorders may take.

Another important controlled study of schizophrenia that throws light on the nature of family interactions in the development of schizophrenic behavior is the *high risk* study conducted by Mednick (1966) that we described in Chapter 4. Mednick and his colleagues carefully examined a group of 207 children who were at risk for schizophrenia because their mothers had been diagnosed as schizophrenic. These children were compared with 104 low risk control subjects. As you may recall, some of these high risk children were expected eventually to develop schizophrenic behavior. Then the data on the schizophrenic children collected *before* they developed schizophrenic symptoms could be compared with the low risk children to discover what if anything was unique to the schizophrenic group. One set of differences reported by Mednick had to do with the degree to which the autonomic nervous system of high risk children was able to recover from stimulation. Now a second major set of evidence appears to be emerging. Daughters, but not sons, appear to be affected by the age at which the mother first became seriously disturbed. In families where the mother was younger when she became disturbed, there is more likely to be a damaging disturbance in the daughter. For boys, separation from their mothers seems to be the key factor. The greater the separation from the mother, the more severe the disturbance among high risk boys who ultimately develop schizophrenic behavior

Thus it appears from these studies that the *form* and *severity* of schizophrenic behavior may well be crucially affected by the family environment. Let us now turn to evidence that suggests that other social and environmental forces are at work as well.

Social Factors

Epidemiology is the study of the distribution of diseases in society. The distribution may be geographical or it may be in terms of income, jobs, or other demographic dimension. In the detective work of searching for the causes of disorders, epidemiologists look for the disproportionate numbers of cases in various geographical, ethnic, income, or occupational groups. When an extremely high incidence of a particular disorder is found, say, in a particular occupational group, it may be a clue to the causes of the disorder. The discovery of the cancer-causing properties of certain industrial chemicals was uncovered in just this way. Workers exposed to the chemicals developed more cases of skin cancer.

In a study of schizophrenia, the problems of the mental health epidemiologist are especially acute. To

SOCIAL AND HUMANISTIC PERSPECTIVES ON SCHIZOPHRENIA

Several theorists have argued that in the case of schizophrenia there is really no mystery to solve. Instead, they argue that the idea of schizophrenia is merely a *myth* that we tend to treat as a reality. Individuals who bear the diagnosis schizophrenia have merely been labeled for their eccentric or socially unaccepted behavior. Thomas Szasz, R. D. Laing, and Theodore Sarbin all have offered slightly different versions of the same argument.

Szasz (1976) in his book, *Schizophrenia: The Sacred Symbol of Psychiatry,* argues that the only thing wrong with the "schizophrenic" individual is that he speaks in metaphors that are unacceptable to his audience. Mental hospitals function to protect society from individuals who are unable to "play the game" of conventional behavior. Psychiatry, argues Szasz, merely uses schizophrenia as a convenient label that allows people who display unconventional behavior to be controlled by the psychiatric profession.

R. D. Laing and Esterson (1971) offer a somewhat different analysis. They argue that people diagnosed as schizophrenic actually are responding rationally to an environment which is "crazier" than they are. Typically the context for this "schizophrenic" behavior is the family, which, for a variety of reasons, tends to use the "schizophrenic" individual as a scapegoat for its own problems and confusion.

Finally, Theodore Sarbin (1972) has argued that schizophrenia is really the result of what he calls the "transformation of social identity." People who behave in an unacceptable way are described by the mental health profession as "schizophrenic." Sooner or later the individual accepts this redefinition of his or her own behavior, thereby transforming his or her personal identity into that of "mental patient" or "schizophrenic."

Recently an anonymous physician who was diagnosed as schizophrenic reported his own experiences in the transformation of social identity. As he described his hospital experience, he reports, "My parents were told by my attending physician, upon my leaving the hospital, that my diagnosis was schizophrenia. Learning of this was very painful for me. I knew then why some staff members had sometimes treated me dispassionately and even cruelly. My label seemed to be the focal point for their debasing behavior. I felt that I had partly lost my right to stand among humanity as a human. . . . For some people I would be forever more something of a subhuman creature."

Name withheld, *Schizophrenia Bulletin,* 3(1977), p.4.

define and diagnose a case of schizophrenia is difficult. Furthermore, schizophrenic disorders are often episodic, making diagnosis even more problematic. Nevertheless, mental health epidemiologists have contributed some important clues to the determinants of schizophrenia.

In 1958, Hollingshead and Redlich published the now classic book, *Social Class and Mental Illness*. They argued that severe mental illness was to be found in disproportionate numbers in the lowest socioeconomic classes of society. Psychotic disorders, and particularly schizophrenia according to their findings, seemed to be much more prevalent in the lower classes while milder psychological disorders, such as the neuroses, were to be found in disproportionately high numbers among middle- and upper-class people. Although other studies (Faris & Dunham, 1939) suggested similar findings previously, Hollingshead and Redlich's book was a kind of watershed, focusing scientists' attention on the stubborn fact and demanding an explanation.

Mental health epidemiologists found this to be an irresistible problem. At least two major hypotheses could be offered to explain the relationship between socioeconomic status and abnormal behavior. The first of these seems more intuitively plausible as we think about the possible effects of poverty. Recall our discussion of the relationship between economics and abnormal behavior in Chapter 4. There we noted that Brenner (1973) had shown that there was a relationship between mental hospitalization rates and economic change. The idea that poverty produces *social stress* which could be a determinant of schizophrenia seems reasonable to most of us.

The second hypothesis, however, is more subtle. The *social drift* hypothesis argues that people developing schizophrenic symptoms will drift into the lower strata of society, primarily because of their reduced ability to cope effectively with the demands inherent in working life.

The social stress hypothesis takes the clear position that the social stress of poverty is responsible for the higher incidence of schizophrenia in the lower classes. But the drift hypothesis takes a more ambiguous stand. It suggests that the incapacity of schizophrenics is what produces downward mobility, but it does not take a clear position on what causes the schizophrenia in the first place.

Actually, the drift hypothesis has been offered in at least two forms. One version of this hypothesis could be called *economic drift*. This version argues that families of schizophrenics tend to drift into the lower classes and are thus found in higher proportions there. The second form, which we could call *geographic drift*, was stimulated by findings of Faris and Dunham (1939). They found that in Chicago the highest rates of hospital admission for schizophrenia tended to be those areas of the city called the zone of transition. The assumption here is that schizophrenics drift into slum areas of the city and are found in higher concentration there. Later studies by Hare (1956) suggested that the geographical concentration of schizophrenics was not associated with poverty but with the number of single-person households and rooming houses in the zone of transition of the city. Was it something about these social conditions that produced schizophrenic behavior or do schizophrenic or preschizophrenic individuals choose to isolate themselves in the central city?

The anomic conditions of some urban settings provide little community support for distressed people.

Ken Firestone

Dunham (1965) repeated the earlier Chicago study, this time in Detroit, and reported an emerging picture of the socially mobile preschizophrenic who leaves his or her family of origin, frequently in rural areas, and migrates to the city where he or she establishes a solitary residence in a rooming house. Several years later, according to Dunham, this person experiences his or her first schizophrenic episode.

The discovery of a relationship between social class and schizophrenia by Hollingshead and Redlich (1958) and Dunham's (1965) description of schizophrenic drift to the center city sets the stage for our discussion. Interestingly we will find that the evidence leads us back to a consideration of the family, but from a new perspective.

Social Class and Schizophrenia

Melvin Kohn (1968, 1969, 1970) has conducted a thorough critical examination of the evidence on the relationship between social class and schizophrenia. Kohn acknowledges the plausibility of the drift hypothesis (schizophrenia leads to lower class status rather than the reverse). The most plausible version of this hypothesis, partly supported by a study conducted by Goldberg and Morrison (1963), would lead to a genetically susceptible concentration of offspring of schizophrenics in the lowest socioeconomic levels. But the drift hypothesis, says Kohn, cannot by itself account for the incidence of schizophrenia in the lower classes.

Instead, Kohn argues it is something about the conditions of life among poor people in the lowest socioeconomic levels that is responsible for the higher incidence of schizophrenia there. Poor housing, illness, criminal victimization, personal degradation, and financial hardship of a life of poverty suggest the most obvious determinant: stress. Furthermore, there is evidence that at all class levels, higher levels of stress are associated with higher likelihoods of psychological disorder.

But stress, by itself, does not account for the differences in incidence either. Kohn (1970) argues that the evidence suggests that when people of lower social class are subjected to equal amounts of stress as people of higher class levels, the lower class persons are more vulnerable to the stress and more likely to develop some form of psychological disorder.

Poor people, because of their life conditions, develop a different world view from that of their more affluent counterparts. The constricting job conditions, limited educational opportunities, and other oppressive conditions experienced in a life of poverty, says Kohn, produce an orientation to the external environment that is more vulnerable to stress and change. It is an orientation of fearfulness, distrust, fatalism, and helplessness.

But how is this world view, born of the oppressive conditions of poverty and social class, transmitted? It is the family, says Kohn, that is the most important mode of transmission.

> The family is important for schizophrenia—not because the family experiences of schizophrenics have differed in some presently undisclosed manner from those of normal people of lower social class background, but precisely because they have been similar. If this be the case, there is no reason to restrict our interest to processes that are unique to the family, such as its particular patterns of role allocation. We should emphasize, instead, processes that the family shares with other institutions—notably those that affect [people's] ability to perceive, to assess, and to deal with complexity and stress. The family's importance comes from its' being the first and earliest institution to shape orientations to self and society (Kohn, 1970, p. 62).

Thus, Kohn argues, the higher incidence of schizophrenia among lower class people may be the result of three sources of vulnerability. Genetically vulnerable people, whether disproportionally represented in the lower classes or not, are subjected to the increased stresses of a life of poverty, and because of the effect of those very conditions on the family, an orientation to the external environment develops that makes coping more difficult and gives stressful events even greater impact. People in the lower classes, then, are in triple jeopardy of schizophrenia, says Kohn.

Schizophrenia and Social Drift

What was it that led the preschizophrenics in Dunham's (1965) study to seek solitude in the roominghouses of the transitional zone of the city? A series of studies carried out at the Institute of Psychiatry in London provide some clues. Interestingly, these studies also center upon the family as the pivotal social environment in the life of a schizophrenic.

Early studies at the British research unit followed schizophrenics after release from the hospital and found that schizophrenics living alone fared much better than those who returned from the hospital to a spouse or parents. Both severity of symptoms and relapse rates were much higher among patients returning to their families.

These researchers reasoned that something about the atmosphere created by those living close to the patient was creating the problem and they set about trying to discover what it was through detailed interviews. The interviews revealed that the *emotional atmosphere* (particularly emotional overinvolvement, hostility, and critical comments) was a crucial variable, and they developed a scale to measure this quality of family life. A subsequent study (Brown, Birley & Wing, 1972) confirmed their hunch. Patients with high emotional expressiveness in their homes relapsed at a rate of 55 percent while only 16 percent of those in the low expressiveness homes relapsed in the nine months following hospitalization.

But was the high emotional intensity in the homes of the relapsed patients just a reaction to the fact that they were initially more disturbed? Or was emotional atmosphere really causing the relapse? When the severity of disturbance was statistically controlled the results remained convincing. Emotional expressiveness was indeed a key factor in relapse.

A subsequent series of studies (Vaughn & Leff, 1976; Leff, 1976) have probed the issue still further. The results of these studies are shown in Figure 11–5. You can see that three factors are critical in relapse rates. First, emotional expressiveness of the family environment has a large overall effect. Furthermore, patients who spend more than 35 hours a week in face-to-face contact with relatives suffer higher relapse rates, but *only* if they live in a highly emotional family environment. Finally, as one might suspect, drug treatment makes an important difference, but, again, the difference occurs in the high emotionality families, not in those with low emotional expressiveness.

We will return to the practical implications of these findings later, but now let us ask what these findings tell us about the nature of social reactivity in schizophrenia. Leff (1976) suggests that reduced social contact has a protective effect in schizophrenia. In fact, patients may monitor their own emotional sensitivity by using social withdrawal to protect themselves against too much emotional stimulation. Leff notes that patients who enter social gatherings and feel tense will withdraw to reduce the feeling of tension.

Mark Vonnegut (1975) describes his own schizophrenic episode similarly.

> The problem is that schizophrenia makes you so . . . fragile . . . my being that fragile and reactive meant I couldn't do many things I wanted to do. I was so distractible that even very simple tasks were impossible to complete, so sensitive that the slightest hint of negativity was crushing, so wired that no one could relax around me (p. 268).

Let us return to the findings on *social drift* reported by Dunham (1965). Perhaps now we have a clue to the reason for the

FIGURE 11–5 Nine-month Relapse Rates of Total Group of 128 Schizophrenic Patients

Nine-month relapse rates of total group of 128 schizophrenic patients[1] after 9 months with their family

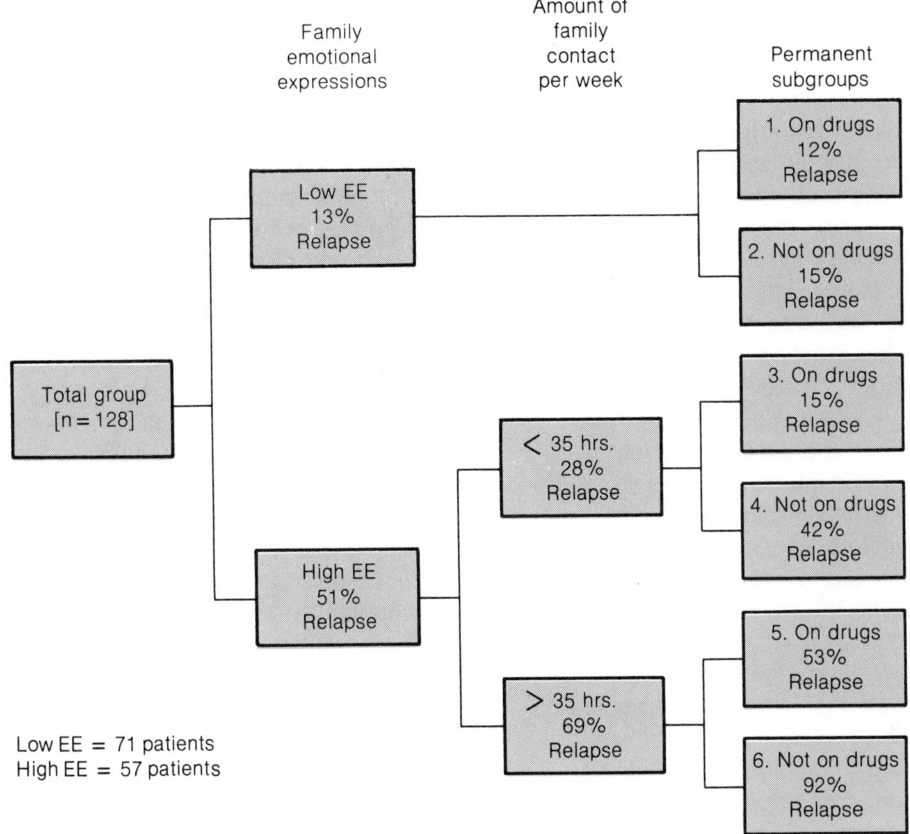

Source: Adapted from C. E. Vaughn and J. P. Leff, "The Influence of Family and Social Factors on the Course of Psychiatric Illness," *British Journal of Psychiatry* 129(1976), p.133.

accumulation of schizophrenics in single person households in the transitional zone of the city. It appears that it is not the conditions of city life by themselves, but the extreme social reactivity of preschizophrenics that led them to withdraw from their emotionally charged homes and seek refuge in the solitude of the city. Again we see the results from the study of both families and social conditions combining to clarify our understanding of the development and course of schizophrenia.

AN INTEGRATION OF PERSPECTIVES: VULNERABILITY

Let us briefly take stock of what we have learned so far about the description and determinants of schizophrenia. It is a heterogeneous disorder or group of disorders. Thought disorder is a primary feature and many sufferers also display hallucinations and delusions. For many it is an episodic disorder, with periods of relatively adequate functioning between episodes.

There is little doubt that the transmission of the disorder is partly genetic. Although almost any single study of genetic similarity and schizophrenia can, by itself, be criticized on methodological grounds, the overall findings are difficult to dispute. No clear answer on the mechanism of transmission is yet available. Whatever is transmitted genetically must have its impact on the biochemistry of the individual. There is promising new evidence that brain chemistry, particularly that involving neurotransmitters like dopamine, may play an important role in the development of schizophrenia. The mechanism is still unclear, although it may be one that involves deviations in some normal regulatory mechanism rather than some biochemical X factor. And even if a neurochemical mechanism is identified, enormous gaps in our knowledge still exist in understanding how the chemical deviation is translated into behavior.

Our survey suggests that family environment and social factors also play a role. The evidence suggests that the social environment has two distinguishably different kinds of impact on the individual. First, it is the source of various learned abilities and skills that may affect the ability to cope with challenge and threats. Second, it is the arena in which stressors or threats are presented. Thus the nature and quantity of stress, and the learned skills available to cope with it, derive from the family and social environment. The evidence also suggests that both the *form* and the *course* of schizophrenia are affected by the social environment.

Now, at least, we have some of the major pieces in the puzzle. Clearly genetics, biochemistry, and familial and social environments are all involved in the development of schizophrenia, but how? It is not simply a matter of choosing one set of determinants rather than another. We recognize that acceptable explanation of the causes and development of schizophrenia must take into account all of the available evidence, not merely that which supports our own favorite hypothesis. Furthermore, as we noted at the outset, problems in genetic background, brain chemistry, family environment, and social class all tend to be correlated with each other. It is likely, for example, that the highest incidence of schizophrenia is in poor, genetically vulnerable families with particularly stressful family environments. Thus the causal factors that we have been discussing as if they were separate are actually intertwined with each other.

There are still numerous gaps in any comprehensive account of schizophrenia. Yet are there models that attempt to incorporate what is already known? One such model has been offered by Zubin and Spring (1977). They call it the *vulnerability model* of schizophrenia.

A basic premise of the model is that each of us is endowed with some degree, however small, of vulnerability, and that under the proper circumstances this vulnerability will express itself in an episode of schizophrenia. They argue further that there are both inborn genetic sources of vulnerability and experiential, acquired sources of vulnerability. This, although very general, is certainly consistent with our review of the evidence.

Thus an individual's vulnerability is determined by some combination of inborn and acquired factors. But vulnerability, Zubin and Spring argue, is not the same thing as the schizophrenic disorder itself. Whether an individual will actually display schizophrenic behavior depends on the impact of challenging life events.

In Figure 11–6 you can see how Zubin and Spring (1977) think of the relation between vulnerability and challenging life events. An interesting aspect of this formulation is that the actual impact of the same challenging event may be very different depending on the person's vulnerability. An event that most of us with relatively low levels of vulnerability would cope with in a routine fashion might exceed the threshold of a more vulnerable person and precipitate a schizophrenic episode.

This brings us to the last important feature of the vulnerability model. The model argues that vulnerability to schizophrenia is an enduring trait that we all possess to a greater or lesser degree. But vulnerability must be distinguished from *episodes* of schizophrenia, which may or may not appear in a particular person. The authors note that this view helps to account for the episodic nature of the disorder which most other formulations have not fully incorporated into their account.

Like all useful formulations, the vulnerability model raises as many questions as it answers. Are there unique challenging events for schizophrenia? How do the inborn and acquired sources of vulnerability interact? Are the inborn sources of vulnerability specific etiological factors (necessary but not sufficient for schizophrenia to occur), as Meehl (1962) has suggested? Does the view have

FIGURE 11–6 Vulnerability Model of Schizophrenia

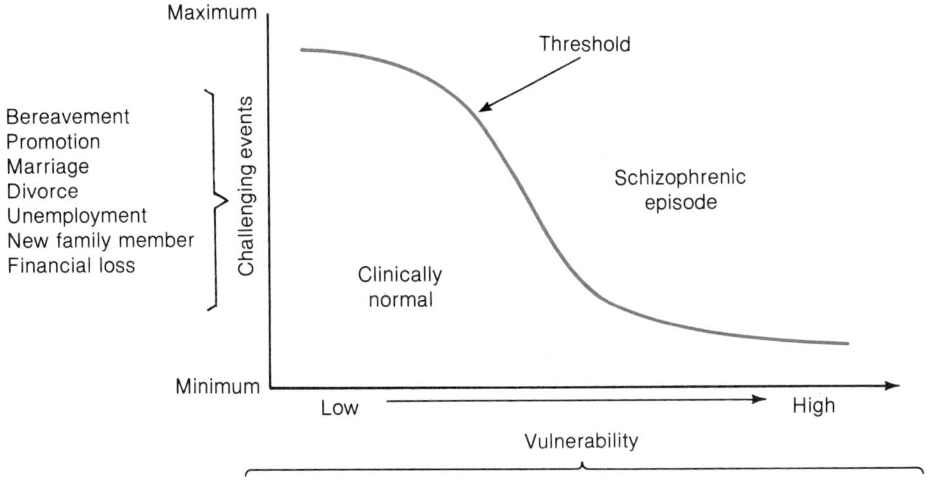

Source: After J. Zubin and B. Spring, "Vulnerability: A New View of Schizophrenia," *Journal of Abnormal Psychology* (1977) *86*, p. 110. Copyright 1977 by the American Psychological Association. Reprinted by permission.

treatment implications that would not have been perceived without it? It is a beginning, at least.

TREATMENT

Early in his account of his schizophrenic experience Mark Vonnegut says, "regular hospitals are places you go to get well. A state mental hospital is where you are put if you don't get well" (p. 21).

Until recently, particularly for schizophrenics, Vonnegut's observation has been correct. A variety of different treatment approaches to schizophrenia have been tried with mixed or only marginal success. And frequently when the treatment failed, Vonnegut's observation held true. More often than not chronic schizophrenics were placed in back wards of state and county mental institutions. There they suffered from the effects of their schizophrenic experience as well as from the effects of an unstimulating, confining life inside the walls of a locked institution.

From Hospital to Community

Today the picture is changing. In order to appreciate how rapidly the treatment of schizophrenia and other severe psychological disorders has changed over the last 20 years or more, let us examine some of the major shifts in treatment as they are described by Keith et al. (1976). There has been a major shift from inpatient hospital care for severe psychological disorders, especially schizophrenia, to outpatient treatment in the community. This major change is shown in Figure 11–7. It shows clearly that the number of episodes of inpatient care has shifted dramatically from 77 percent of all patient care episodes in inpatient settings in 1955 to only 32 percent in 1973. Further, when severely disturbed people are hospitalized, their hospital stay tends to be much shorter.

Keith et al. (1976) claim that there are at least three major reasons for this shift. First, care in state and county mental hospitals has been reduced from nearly half of all episodes in 1955 to only 12 percent in 1973. A second major force for change in treatment patterns has been the development of community mental health centers. These mental health centers treat patients locally and assist in their care in the community. They have played a major role in transforming the treatment of severe psychological disorders from closed institutions to the community. The third major reason for the change in treatment has been the availability of day hospitals which treat severely disturbed patients during the day and allow them to return home in the evening.

Currently more schizophrenic individuals than ever before are living outside the walls of institutions. This is significant change from a number of different points of view, according to Keith et al. (1976). A schizophrenic patient can now, if they wish, retain contact with family friends in his or her own community. This may in turn increase the potential for meaningful employment and the feelings of personal dignity and self-esteem that can accompany work. The families of the schizophrenic patient may be less disrupted as a result of this new pattern of care. Since care is given locally, families are less disrupted when a parent, spouse, or child is away for treatment for only brief periods of time. In addition, the community itself may begin to adapt to more first hand contact with patients experiencing

FIGURE 11-7 Percent Distributions of Inpatient and Outpatient Care Episodes in Mental Health Facilities, by Type of Facility: United States, 1955 and 1973[1]

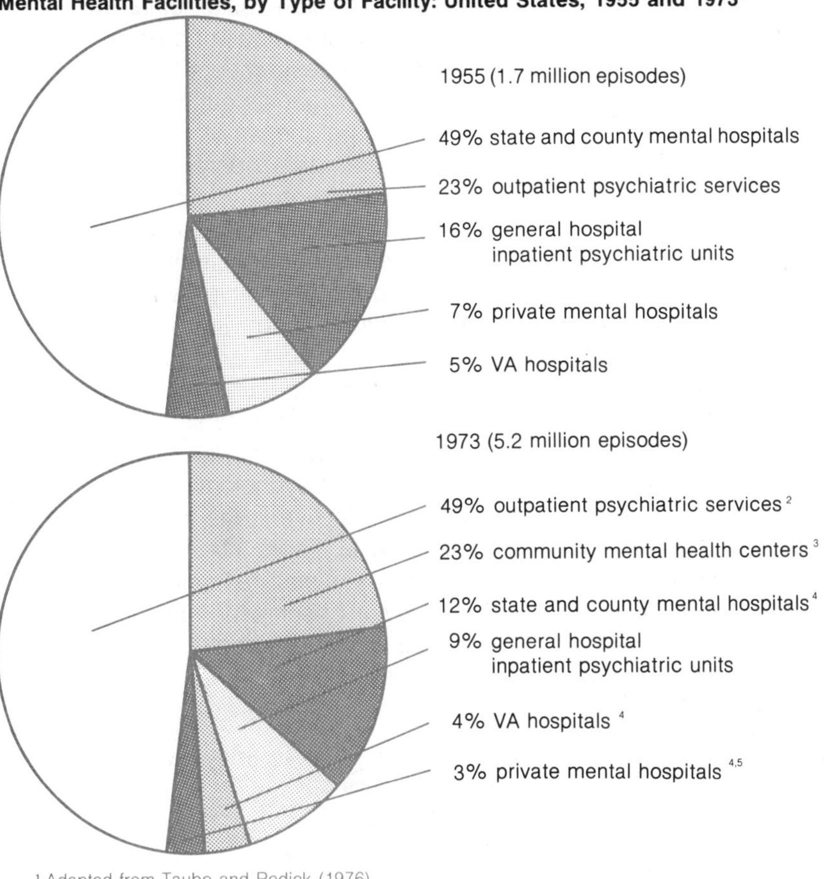

[1] Adapted from Taube and Redick (1976).
[2] Includes free-standing outpatient services as well as those affiliated with psychiatric and general hospitals.
[3] Includes inpatient and outpatient services of federally funded CMHC's.
[4] Inpatient services only.
[5] Includes residential treatment centers for emotionally disturbed children. *Source:* Division of Biometry, National Institute of Mental Health.

schizophrenic episodes. It even may be that some of the problems of stigma (Price & Denner, 1973) associated with being a mental patient may be reduced as a consequence.

Compared with the closed hospitals of the past, Keith et al. (1976) present an optimistic picture. But, think for a moment about our review of the history of treatment in the United States in the 19th century. It may be that this enthusiasm for "community treatment" is no different from the zeal associated with the development of asylums in the Jacksonian era and the enthusiastic reports of "tent therapy" and other innovations of the time. We have little or no reliable information on the quality of life of schizophrenics living in the community. Until data documenting the quality of treatment for released schizophrenics supplements the information we now have on shifting patterns of care, we will have to retain our skepticism. If we do not, we will not have learned the lesson of history.

Drug Treatment

The history of the treatment of schizophrenic disorders has been at times more bizarre than the behavior of the sufferers themselves. As Cole (1970) notes, in the recent past, patients diagnosed as suffering from schizophrenia have been subjected to brain operations, removal of the colon, years of psychoanalytic therapy, playing with mud, psychodrama, token economies, induced comas, huge doses of vitamins, family therapy, artifically induced convulsions, prolonged sleep therapy, seclusion rooms, moral treatment, work treatment, group psychotherapy, summer camping, trips to the French Riviera, cold baths, scotch douches, and a wide variety of different psychoactive drugs.

Out of this strange assortment of treatments, one major approach has emerged that has allowed much of the shift in treatment patterns that we described above to occur. It is the development of *neuroleptic drugs,* especially the phenothiazines, in the treatment of schizophrenia. By 1970 it was very unusual for any patient who had received the diagnosis of schizophrenia not to be treated with one of the major tranquilizers. Today, as Keith et al. (1976) note, many clinicians consider it unethical to fail to use these drugs in the treatment of schizophrenia.

In fact, Synder (1974) has offered evidence to suggest that the drugs usually described as *phenothiazines* have *specific antischizophrenic effects,* rather than merely general tranquilizing properties. Indeed, some researchers have suggested that clinical diagnosis ought to be made on the basis of the way in which patients respond to antischizophrenic drugs because the drugs have been so strikingly effective in treating schizophrenia. The assumption is that people who respond similarly to the phenothiazines may share some common underlying biological characteristic.

Whether this speculation is correct or not, there is evidence to suggest that drug treatment, especially when combined with other forms of psychological treatment, is especially effective in the treatment of schizophrenia. Table 11–6 below, shows how the phenothiazines selectively affect the behavior of schizophrenics as opposed to that of people showing other symptoms.

TABLE 11–6 Analysis of Symptom Sensitivity to Phenothiazines

Bleuler's Classification of Schizophrenic Symptoms	*Response to Treatment*
Fundamental	
Thought disorder	+++
Blunted affect-indifference	++
Withdrawal-retardation	++
Autistic behavior-mannerisms	++
Accessory	
Hallucinations	++
Paranoid ideation	+
Grandiosity	+
Hostility-belligerence	+
Resistiveness-uncooperativeness	+
Nonschizophrenic	
Anxiety-tension-agitation	0
Guilt-depression	0
Disorientation	0
Somatization	0

Source: From *Genetic Theory and Abnormal Behavior* by D. Rosenthal. Copyright © 1970 McGraw-Hill. Used with permission of McGraw-Hill Book Company.

Treatment Combinations

Although the phenothiazines appear to selectively affect schizophrenic symptoms, in practice they are seldom the only form of treatment given to schizophrenic patients. Frequently drug treatment is combined with psychotherapy or some other supportive treatment.

Following suit, researchers have also addressed themselves to more complex questions regarding various treatment combinations for schizophrenia. What is the effect of these drugs when we compare them directly with other forms of treatment? Are some combinations more effective than others?

A classic study conducted by May (1968) compared improvement in schizophrenic patients who received drug treatment, milieu therapy, drugs plus individual psychotherapy, electroconvulsive therapy, and individual therapy. In this study the drug treatment group tended to have shorter hospital stay and showed more rapid change in behavior than other experimental groups. At a three-year follow-up the drug-treated group still maintained some advantage.

Recently, Hogarty et al. (1974a, 1974b) have studied the effects of psychosocial treatment and the phenothiazines in a large sample of schizophrenics recently discharged from hospitals in Maryland. This carefully controlled study compared four groups: (1) drug treatment alone; (2) drugs plus "major role therapy," (3) placebos alone, and (4) placebos plus

In the past chronic schizophrenics have been placed in back wards of public mental institutions.

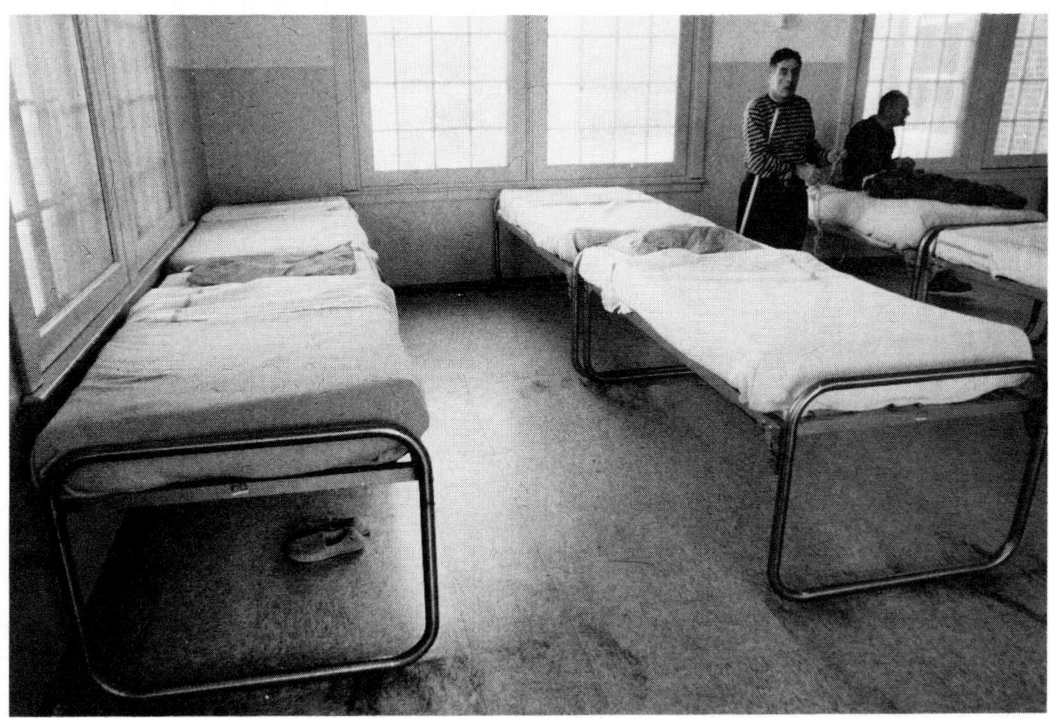

Jeff Albertson/Stock, Boston, Inc.

major role therapy. Hogarty found that 80 percent of the placebo-treated patients had serious relapses by 24 months after discharge, whereas only 48 percent of the drug-treated patients had similar relapses. When he examined the combined effect of major role therapy and drugs, the relapse rate was lowered to 37 percent.

These are impressive results and further demonstrate the effectiveness of the major tranquilizers for schizophrenia. The results also suggest that, even with a disorder as severe as schizophrenia, it may be possible to effectively shift treatment from inpatient settings to the community. Although drugs have had a major impact on the changing patterns of treatment of schizophrenia, other forms of treatment have also emerged as new approaches to the community-based treatment of schizophrenia. It is to these psychological and psychosocial treatment approaches that we now turn.

Social Learning Approaches

Recently, Paul and Lentz (1978) have reported an important research program that promises substantially more effective treatment for chronically institutionalized schizophrenics, both in institutional settings and later in the community. Their goal was to compare two major approaches to rehabilitation of chronic mental patients. First, *milieu treatment* as described by Jones (1975) and others has received considerable attention as a total environmental approach to the treatment of institutionalized individuals, particularly schizophrenics. The second major approach to treatment was the use of a *social learning program* which used learning principles and methods to reduce maladaptive behavior in chronic mental patients. A third control group that received the traditional mental hospital programs was used as a basis for comparing these two types of treatment. Patients in each program were carefully matched on their current level of functioning and various background characteristics to ensure that the groups were comparable at the beginning of the experiment.

The milieu treatment approach was based on explicitly defined principles of milieu treatment. Among the principles employed were the following: (1) the behavior of individuals is controlled by the expectancies of others, (2) group cohesiveness provides a powerful force for the behavior change, and (3) incidents in the treatment program could be dealt with through carefully controlled crisis resolution.

The social learning program, on the other hand, began with a carefully constructed *token economy* in which maladaptive or inappropriate behaviors were ignored and received no reinforcement while adaptive behaviors were consistently rewarded with tokens that could be exchanged for other, more palpable rewards. An important distinguishing feature of the social learning program was that appropriate behaviors had consistently rewarding consequences, whereas inappropriate behaviors did not receive rewards.

Paul and Lentz painstakingly trained the staff to administer each of these programs. Furthermore, the same staff members were used to conduct both the social learning program and the milieu program on rotating shifts. Thus any differences in program results could not be attributed to differences in the staff. Both treatment approaches involved step-by-step programs in which patients were given increased responsibility and increased freedom as their behavior improved. In the case of the social learning program, patients were able to "buy their way out" of the token program by improving their own behavior.

Another way of understanding how the two programs differed is to examine how they each dealt with inappropriate, "crazy behavior." In the case of the social learning program, inappropriate behavior was ignored and some suggestion for positive social behavior was given. In the case of the milieu program, inappropriate or bizarre behavior was never ignored. Instead its psychological significance was interpreted to the patient and the staff communicated alternative expectations to the patient.

It is important to note that the patients in these programs were severely disabled, chronic mental patients. Most of them had experienced at least *17 years* of continuous hospitalization before entering the program. In addition, each of these patients had been previously rejected for extended care in community settings. Thus, they were patients who were so severely disabled that they were unable to benefit from the initial attempts at deinstitutionalization that had occurred in their hospitals.

Despite the extremely severe disturbance of these patients, Paul and Lentz's study has yielded impressive results. Table 11–7 shows the results for the social learning, milieu, and the traditional control programs. Substantially more of the patients in the social learning program ultimately achieved independent functioning in the community. As more and more patients reached the community, Paul and Lentz provided each of them with a carefully designed social learning aftercare program. Of all the patients who received the aftercare program, 97 percent of those released remained out of the hospital at least 18 months and many for as much as four and one half years. Table 11–7 shows the effects of the three treatment programs.

Overall this social learning program was clearly superior in its performance. The social learning program proved superior in changing all classes of measured behavior with the exception of cognitive distortion, where it was equal in impact to the milieu program, although the milieu program produced cognitive improvement more slowly than did the social learning

TABLE 11–7 Effects of Social Learning, Milieu, and Traditional Treatment Programs on Chronic Mental Patients

			Remained Institutionalized		
Type of Program	*Achieved Independent Community Functioning*	*Release with Continuing Community Stay*	*Significant Change*	*No Change*	*Worse*
Social learning program	11%	92.5%	2.5%	2.5%	2.5%
Milieu treatment program	7	71	3.2	9.7	16.1
Traditional treatment control group	0	48.4	12.9	9.7	29

Source: From G. L. Paul and R. J. Lentz, *Psychosocial Treatment of Chronic Mental Patients* (Cambridge, Mass.: Harvard University Press, 1978).

DEINSTITUTIONALIZATION: LIBERATION OR NEGLECT?

It is tempting to assume that a few isolated but impressive programs for community treatment are typical of the community care given to recently released schizophrenic mental patients. Unfortunately, this is not yet the case. It is one thing to close the doors of mental hospitals and quite another to help mental patients make a new life in the community.

The national policy of "deinstitutionalization" that we described earlier has sometimes meant that individuals who have spent 20 years in an institution have abruptly been left to their own devices in the community. The results have often been tragic. Long years of institutionalization cripple an individual's ability to cope with the demands of the external world. These people may have no place to go once they have been turned out of the hospital. As a consequence, they have been neglected, ignored, or far worse, exploited by unscrupulous individuals who have provided substandard housing and care.

As Cohen and Paul (1976) have noted, extended care treatment has been plagued with bureaucratic problems and inadequate funding. And the results of poorly planned attempts at deinstitutionalization frequently have left mental patients as victims rather than beneficiaries of deinstitutionalization.

Single room occupancy hotels in major metropolitan areas have become the only living option available for many newly de-institutionalized patients.

program. The milieu program reduced most maladaptive behaviors, but not as dramatically as did the social learning program, and increased only one of the positive behaviors (self-care) measured by the investigators, while the social learning program increased many positive behaviors.

It should be clear that even those patients who had improved to the point where they could live independently in the community still displayed some residual effects of their psychological disturbance and the prolonged institutionalization that followed it. Paul reports that approximately 30 percent of those patients who had attained independent living status were indistinguishable from other community members, while approximately 70 percent still displayed some marginal behavior.

Nevertheless, the Paul and Lentz study provides striking evidence that carefully designed social learning programs can have substantial impact on rehabilitation, even of severely disturbed chronic schizophrenic patients. Paul* believes that most people currently in extended care facilities in the community could be helped to achieve independent community functioning within approximately two years using the social learning program approach.

Clearly, government policies of deinstitutionalization are not enough. Programs of this sort will be required if effective return to the community is to be a realistic and humane goal.

SUMMARY

In this chapter we have taken up the question of the transmission of schizophrenia. We examined both biological and environmental hypotheses for the transmission of schizophrenia and saw that relatively strong evidence for a genetic role in the transmission of the disorder is available. However, no clear mechanism for genetic transmission has yet emerged.

In the area of neurochemical research, a variety of neurotransmitters, such as dopamine, may be important factors in the development of schizophrenia. Our examination of family and social environmental evidence suggested that both the form and course of schizophrenia may be affected by social and environmental factors and that a vulnerability model of schizophrenia best fits current evidence.

The major advantage of the vulnerability model of schizophrenia is its capacity to incorporate most of the significant observations of other theoretical perspectives in its explanation of the development of schizophrenia. Biological determinants as well as social factors play an important role in the model.

Our survey of treatment approaches to schizophrenia ranged from an examination of the recent movement to deinstitutionalize schizophrenic patients on the one hand, to the use of phenothiazines that appear to have specific antischizophrenic affects on the other.

Social learning approaches have been shown to be effective with chronic schizophrenics in both hospital and community settings, but it is clear that government policies for deinstitutionalization are not yet sufficient to care for chronic schizophrenics. New competencies and coping skills must also be developed if humane treatment is to be available to this population.

* Personal communication, June 1977.

PART 3

Social Deviation

Tony Kelly

12

Personality Disorders and Antisocial Personality

OVERVIEW OF THE PERSONALITY DISORDERS

The DSM III described personality disorders in the following fashion:

> The essential features are deeply ingrained, inflexible, maladaptive patterns of relating to, perceiving, and thinking about the environment and oneself that are of sufficient severity to cause either significant impairment in adaptive functioning or subjective distress. Thus they are pervasive personality traits and are exhibited in a wide range of important social and personality contexts. The manifestations of personality disorders are generally recognizable by the time of adolescence or earlier and continue through most of adult life, although often becoming less obvious in middle or old age (DSM III).

This definition of personality disorders suggests that the traits are pervasive in the life experience of the individual. But these traits are not necessarily associated with ineffective social functioning or the experience of distress. In fact, as we shall see, some of these characteristics are highly adaptive in certain settings. For example, in some cases, suspiciousness may actually allow the person to be vigilant for a real potential threat; while certain compulsive patterns of behavior may actually be very useful in a setting where order and organization is a desirable characteristic.

Another important aspect of our understanding of personality disorders is that they need to be distinguished from episodes of behavioral disruption. The diagnosis of personality disorder should only be made when the characteristics are *typical* of the individual's *long-term* functioning rather than being limited to discrete episodes. Thus, the personality disorders are to be distinguished from acute episodes. They are, instead, long-standing patterns of behavior that may or may not bring the person into conflict with others or produce distress depending upon the demands, expectations, and challenges of the person's social environment.

On the other hand, a person with a personality disorder may express distress or dissatisfaction with his or her life because of the impact that the behavior has on other people in his or her environment. Thus, expressions of anxiety, depression, or moodiness may actually be an indication of the unhappiness the person feels with the social reaction from others to his or her own behavior.

In Table 12–1 below, are listed the major types of personality disorders described in the DSM III. It can be noted that these various disorders have been grouped into three clusters—eccentric, erratic, and fearful—to reflect some general similarities that exist among the disorders. We should note that very little research is available on most of these disorders. In addition, the diagnostic reliability of these particular classifications is not known. In the pages that follow, we will discuss several of these personality disorders in more detail. In particular we will consider the compulsive, the paranoid, and the antisocial personality disorders.

Perhaps more than most patterns of behavior described in this book, whether a person with a personality disorder will be seen as abnormal or not depends heavily on the *situation* or *context* in which the behavior is observed (Price & Bouffard, 1974). Thus, the orderliness of the compulsive personality may be highly valued in an accounting firm, but a handicap in the fluid environment of an

TABLE 12–1 The DSM III Classification of Personality Disorders

Eccentric Cluster

Paranoid personality:
A pervasive and long-standing suspiciousness and mistrust of people in general. Individuals with this disorder are hypersensitive and easily slighted. They continually scan the environment for clues that validate their original prejudicial ideas, attitudes, or biases. Often their emotional experience is restricted.

Introverted personality:
A defect in the capacity to form social relationships; introversion and bland or constricted affect.

Schizotypal personality:
Various oddities of thinking, perception, communication, and behavior. Peculiarities in communication with concepts expressed unclearly or oddly.

Erratic Cluster

Histrionic personality:
Behavior that is overly reactive, intensely expressed, and perceived by others as shallow, superficial, or insincere. Often associated with disturbed interpersonal relationships.

Narcissistic personality:
Grandiose sense of self-importance or uniqueness, preoccupation with fantasies of unlimited success, exhibitionistic needs for constant attention and admiration.

Antisocial personality:
History of continuous and chronic antisocial behavior in which the rights of others are violated. Onset before age 15, failure to sustain good job performance, lying, stealing, fighting, truancy in childhood.

Borderline personality:
Instability in various areas of life including interpersonal relationships, behavior, mood, and self-image. Interpersonal relationships are often tense and unstable with marked shifts of attitude over time.

Fearful Cluster

Avoidant personality:
Hypersensitivity to rejection, unwillingness to enter into relationships unless given an unusually strong guarantee of uncritical acceptance. Social withdrawal, yet a desire for affection and acceptance.

Compulsive personality:
Restricted ability to express warm and tender emotions, preoccupation with matters of rules, order, organization, efficiency, and detail. Excess devotion to work and productivity to the exclusion of pleasure. Compulsive personalíties are often indecisive.

Passive-aggressive personality:
Resistance to demand for adequate activity or performance in both occupational and social areas of functioning. Resistance is not expressed directly. As a consequence, pervasive or long-standing social or occupational ineffectiveness often result.

The traits of the compulsive personality are highly valued in some settings and illustrate that the "fit" between a personality characteristic and the demands of a setting may be critical in understanding human adaptation.

Ellis Herwig/Stock, Boston, Inc.

advertising agency. The suspiciousness about the motives of others of the paranoid personality may be a liability in a cooperative work group, but a useful trait in a homicide detective.

COMPULSIVE PERSONALITY

Each of us has known someone who organized his or her world with such meticulous care that the arrangement seemed almost too perfect. As we shall see, the traits of orderliness and precision can be a real asset but, in extreme cases, can be a liability as well.

Compulsive personalities display stereotyped repetitive patterns of behavior and thought. They are deeply preoccupied with order, organization, structure, and cleanliness and often show some recognition that their patterns of behavior are unusual. Nevertheless, these patterns of behavior show a remarkable persistence over time.

As you can see in the excerpt "The Home Environment of Compulsive Personalities" on page 328, the environment of compulsive personalities often reflects preoccupation with order and organization, but at the same time may show surprising inconsistencies, as in the case of compulsive cleaners who leave one area of their household in disarray. The description offered by Rachman and Hodgson represents extreme examples and illustrates the handicapping effects of some adaptations of this kind.

Origins in Childhood

The determinants of compulsive personality are not yet well understood, but it is believed that family background plays a significant role. Although no evidence for a specific genetic predisposition yet exists, it may be that a general constitutional predisposition or hypersensitivity forms a general vulnerability in the case of compulsive personality. Indeed, Rachman and Hodgson (1980) believe that the compulsive personality is a person who is disposed to develop the disorder because of a constitutional predisposition or vulnerability to criticism. If the person has this sensitivity and if the family environment of the compulsive personality is also pervaded by parental overconcern and overcontrol, two necessary conditions for the development of compulsions exist.

If the child is overprotected, he or she

THE HOME ENVIRONMENT OF COMPULSIVE PERSONALITIES

In their recent research on obsessions and compulsions, Rachman and Hodgson (1980) visited the homes of many people with extremely compulsive patterns of behavior. Their description of how the home environment reflects the life-style of these people is revealing:

> After the first dozen or so visits, our capacity for being surprised was greatly reduced. We learned to expect that the homes of compulsive cleaners would contain a bizarre mixture of excessively clean areas and indescribably dirty parts as well. In the same house, the lavatory might be brightly clean and strongly disinfected while parts of the kitchen were caked with month-old food remains. (Incidentally, this peculiar contrast is often encountered in the patients themselves—a compulsive cleaner who washes her hands 200 times per day may leave her legs and feet unwashed for months and wear the same dirty underwear for weeks on end.) In some cases the accumulation of debris and dirt was directly attributable to the patient's inability to come into contact with dirty or contaminated objects. In other cases the dirt and disarray reflected the patient's inability to cope with the daily requirements of living.
>
> Visiting the home of a patient who engages in compulsive hoarding can also be a memorable experience. Entire rooms are set aside for the collection of old newspapers, used cans, bits of string, nails and screws, and the rest. The inability to start or complete a task, observed in many of these patients, is reflected in the partly completed tasks whose remains are sprinkled throughout the house. One sees cupboards without doors, curtains without seams, rooms that are half-painted, appliances left in their original wrappings, and so on. In one extreme case the patient had been trying to complete the cleaning of the motor of his second automobile for almost three years. He had succeeded in taking out some of the parts and cleaning them, but had gotten no further. This immobilized car was kept in the well-protected garage, while the more valuable vehicle that was in daily use was left unsheltered in the street outside.
>
> Telltale signs of compulsive cleaners are easily spotted. One encounters endless boxes of tissue paper, rolls of paper toweling, bottles of disinfectant, hordes of soap bars, washing powders of all sizes, makes, and varieties, innumerable pairs of rubber gloves, and all the other signs of the dedicated cleaner. Quite commonly the lavatory is the most carefully tended room in the house and is overstocked with extra rolls of toilet tissue.
>
> The homes of compulsive checkers are less obviously different. Here the distinguishing features are excessive tidiness and orderliness. Each piece of furniture has its designated place; the pictures hang straight; and attempts by others to rearrange things quickly produce alarm. Checklists are placed at strategic points, and the common habit of making lists is elevated to a fine art (Rachman and Hodgson, 1980, p. 65).

FIGURE 12–1 A Hypothetical Model of the Relationship between Type of Obsessional Problem and Parental Behavior

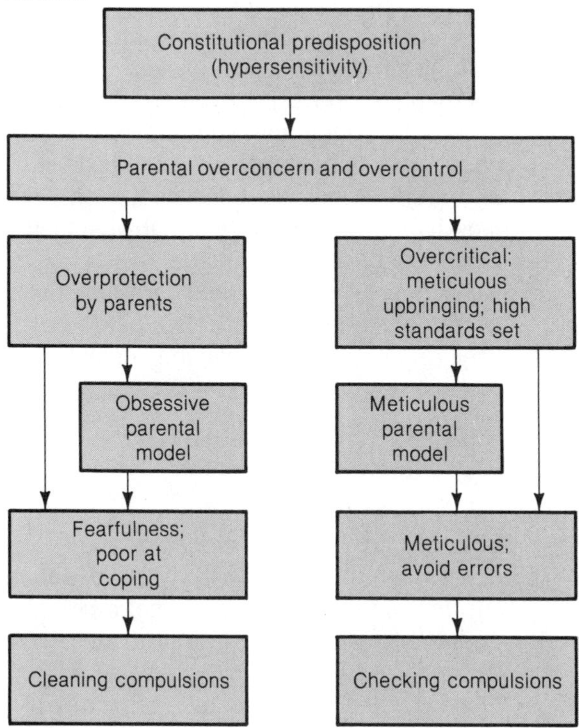

Source: S. J. Rachman and R. J. Hodgson, Obsessions and Compulsions (Englewood Cliffs, N.J.: Prentice-Hall, © 1980), p. 118. Material reprinted by permission.

will develop a fearfulness about the world and be relatively ineffective at coping. Both through modeling from obsessive parents and through a developing sense of fearfulness, cleaning compulsions will develop. On the other hand, if parental hypercriticalness and high standards are the dominant theme of the family background, the child will increasingly be concerned about avoiding errors and become overly meticulous in his or her own behavior. Rachman and Hodgson argue that this results in compulsions to check and recheck the details of one's work or life.

Impact of Task or Setting

We should note that the compulsive personality pattern can be a social asset in some cases or a major handicap or annoyance in others. A great deal depends on the *situation* or *task* confronting the individual. As Rachman and Hodgson (1980) observe:

> When people with creative energy succeed in putting their obsessional personality traits to constructive use, everyone benefits. Orderliness and meticulousness are essential attributes of

> the successful classifier and lexicographer. The best fruits of the combination of creativity and obsessionality can be seen in the works of Samuel Johnson and Charles Darwin.
>
> Among those with less creative talents, controlled orderliness and meticulousness are useful qualities for accountants, information scientists, timetablers, catalogers, and the like. Uncontrolled or controlled obsessionality in bureaucrats can be a source of unending frustration and irritation. When it is combined with gross inefficiency, the results greatly exceed the common, everyday irritations, and quiet desperation sets in (p. 58).

Thus, in some cases, it is not the behavior pattern itself that is maladaptive but the interaction between the behavior and the task or setting in which the person finds himself engaged.

PARANOID PERSONALITY

The paranoid personality is most frequently suspicious, distrustful, and extremely sensitive to criticism. Such people are continually scanning their environment looking for potential threats and for evidence that would confirm their own ideas and their own biases.

An interesting aspect of the paranoid style of thought is that such people may choose to conceal their sense of distrust and suspicion largely because it might "tip their hands" and place them at what they believe to be a disadvantage. Consequently, the paranoid style may not be evident in initial encounters but reveal itself gradually after continued contact.

Paranoid personalities may be cut off from the world by their own suspiciousness and distrust.

Frank Siteman/Stock, Boston, Inc.

Suspiciousness

Shapiro (1965) makes the interesting observation that often when we think about suspiciousness, we refer to what a person thinks rather than their style or mode of thinking. And yet suspiciousness, as Shapiro notes, is, above all else, a way of thinking about the world. Shapiro (1965) describes this cognitive style eloquently: "a suspicious person is a person who has something on his mind. He looks at the world with fixed and occupying expectation and he searches repetitively and only for conformation of it. He will not be persuaded to abandon his suspicion or some plan of action based on it. On the contrary, he will pay no attention to rational arguments except to find in them some aspect or feature that actually confirms his original view. Anyone who tries to influence or persuade a suspicious person will not only fail, but also, unless he is sensible enough to abandon his efforts early, will, himself, become an object of the original suspicious idea" (Shapiro, 1965, p. 56).

Projection

A second major characteristic of the paranoid personality has to do with the use of the psychological mechanism of projection. By projection we mean the attribution to external figures of motivations, drives, or other tensions that are found to be intolerable and are repudiated or rejected in one's self. This is a second major characteristic of the paranoid personality. Impulses or feelings that are unacceptable in oneself are attributed to others as in the following example.

> An actually quite competent and well respected man, who was, however, not convinced of his own competency and was defensive about his professional rank and status in his firm, made a mistake in his work. It was a mistake of no great consequence, easily corrected, and hardly likely to be noticed by anyone else. Nevertheless, for some days afterwards, he was preoccupied with imagining even the most remote possibilities of being discovered and the humiliation that would, according to him, follow from discovery. During this time, when the boss walked by, he "noticed" an irritable glance and imagined the boss to be thinking "this man is the weak link in our organization" (Shapiro, 1965, p. 96).

Interpersonal Impact

The paranoid personality will, almost of necessity, begin to experience a variety of complications in his or her interpersonal relationships as a consequence of the characteristic suspiciousness, distrust, and defensiveness so characteristic of the disorder. The case example given below illustrates this point quite clearly. The young college professor's paranoid orientation to others leads him to see his older colleague as a threat and to overemphasize what were apparently minor slights. Thus, a potentially warm and supportive relationship with a senior colleague soon was turned into a struggle for domination, at least in the view of the young professor.

CASE EXAMPLE OF PARANOID PERSONALITY

A very intelligent 33-year-old college professor, stiff and self-conscious but also quite ambitious and sometimes rather arrogant, had always been sensitive to any rebuff or slight to his dignity, to being "forced" or ordered to do anything arbitrarily, or otherwise treated, as it seemed to him, like a "kid." In this instance, he had recently taken a new job with a different institution and had become interested, although ashamed to admit it, in impressing an important senior professor, obviously with the hope of becoming a protégé of his and probably also with the idea of ultimately outstripping him. At any rate, he was initially quite impressed with this man, and, consequently, he was quite nervous in his presence and concerned with what the older man might think of him. Sometimes, he was concerned that he might be thought "weak" while, at other times, too self-aggrandizing. He watched for signs of both reactions. . . .

However, it soon became clear that this defensive tension and intensified sense of vulnerability was gradually giving rise to an intensification of rigidity and an increasingly antagonistic defensive stiffening. Thus, he not only watched for signs of rebuff or disapproval, but also increasingly anticipated them and, accordingly, braced himself with each hesitant overture. He remembered now that he despised fawning yes-men, and, therefore, he now approached the older man only in a determinedly dignified and equalitarian way.

In the course of some weeks, apparently marked mostly by indifference on the side of the older man, this defensive stiffening progressed further. He watched the older man closely now, no longer with concern, but with suspicion. He angrily seized on some quite ambiguous evidence of disparaging slights and arbitrary, commanding attitudes on the senior man's part. He would not "take it," and he frequently became not merely equalitarian, but defensively arrogant in the relationship. Thus, he refused "menial" department assignments. Once angry and suspicious, he began to watch the colleague, in the way such people do, like a small boy playing cops and robbers around an unconcerned father, only with much more intensity and seriousness, interpreting each movement according to the game—now he is pretending not to notice me, now he is getting ready to shoot, and so on. From this angry, suspicious, and, by now, defensively quite haughty view, he discovered clues that showed him that he had been right; the older man resented his independence, wanted only a mediocre yes-man in the department, and was trying to reduce him to that status. He declared that the situation between them had now come to a "contest of wills" (Shapiro, 1965, p. 90–91).

Similarities between Compulsive and Paranoid Styles

A moment's reflection on the compulsive and paranoid personality disorders may suggest certain similarities between the two types of personality disorders. As Shapiro (1965) notes, both of these personality disorders reflect a kind of tense feeling and a concern about control and autonomy. Both the paranoid and the compulsive personality are strongly purposeful and even willful in their behavior and appear to be experiencing a feeling of external threat. The similarities in cognitive, behavioral, and subjective experience between these two personality disorders is shown in Table 12–2.

This is an intriguing comparison particularly because it emphasizes both the subjectively felt experience associated with each of these personality disorders as well as the observable patterns of behavior.

THE ANTISOCIAL PERSONALITY

Considerable empirical research and theoretical work has been devoted to the understanding of this pattern of behavior. Previously the antisocial personality has

TABLE 12–2 Comparison of the Cognitive, Behavioral, and Subjective Experience of Compulsive and Paranoid Personality Styles

COGNITION

	Mode of Attention	*Object of Attention*	*Response to the Novel or Unexpected*	*Experience of Reality*
Obsessive-compulsive	Acute, intense, and narrowly focused; fixed on what is relevant to its own idea and interest Characterization: rigid	Technical detail	Refuses attention; the unexpected regarded as distraction from own fixed line of thought	World constructed of technical indicators; loss of sense of conviction and sense of substantial truth; extreme manifestation is logical absurdity
Paranoid	Extremely acute, intense, and narrowly focused; fixed on its own idea, searching only confirmation; biased Characterization: suspicious	The clue	Sharply attentive but not to apparent content ("mere appearance"); searches out confirming clue to "real" meaning; the unexpected regarded as threatening	World constructed of clues to hidden meaning; apparent, substantial reality disdained; extreme manifestation is projective-delusion

BEHAVIOR AND SUBJECTIVE EXPERIENCE

	General Behavior Mode	*Response to External Influence*	*Affective Experience*	*Sense of Pressure*
Obsessive-compulsive	Rigid, tense, continuously and intensely directed, purposeful; general aim is accomplishment of work	Imperturbable, determinedly self-willed; obstinate, if pressed	Narrowing of subjective experience in general; narrowing of and estrangement from affective experience particularly (isolation of affect); loss of spontaneity, absence of whim; tense	Lives continuously under pressure of conscience, feeling of "should," experienced as quasi-external but superior to his wants; general reaction is ambivalent submission to authoritative (moral) principle
Paranoid	Continuous, tense, and antagonistic directedness, intentionality, purposefulness; "operating;" general aim is defense against threat	Touchy, guarded, suspicious	General contraction of subjective experience, probably some loss of sensual experience, narrowing of and complete estrangement from much affect (as in projection); loss of capacity for spontaneity and abandonment; extremely tense and usually antagonistic	Lives with awareness of threat of superior force or authority; threat experienced as external; general reaction is defensive

Source: D. Shapiro, *Neurotic Styles* (New York: Basic Books, 1965), pp. 105–6.

been called the "psychopathic personality," the "sociopathic personality," and a variety of other terms as well. In the present discussion, we will use the term "antisocial personality" throughout.

Clinical Picture

According to DSM III, the most marked characteristic of the antisocial personality is a history of continuous and chronic antisocial behavior characterized by the violation of the rights of others, a failure to sustain adequate job performance over several years, commonly lying, stealing, fighting, and truancy in childhood.

This particular personality pattern appears to be much more common in males than females. Most studies indicate that the behavior pattern first emerges distinctly in women about the age of puberty, whereas in men it is observable usually from early childhood. Although estimates of the prevalence of the disorder vary, the typical estimate is 3 percent for American men and approximately 1 percent for women.

Cleckley: The Mask of Sanity. Although early characterizations of the antisocial personality that such people were essentially "moral imbeciles," the most influential modern description has been offered by Cleckley (1968, 1976). In his famous book, *The Mask of Sanity,* Cleckley offered numerous case descriptions of the disorder, and Cleckley attempted to treat many of these individuals in his own clinical practice. The case histories he offers are not merely of criminals or other obviously antisocial individuals, but of prominent businessmen, professionals, and others who also fit the pattern of behavior that Cleckley believes to be essential in diagnosing the antisocial personality.

Hervey M. Cleckley

Courtesy of Hervey M. Cleckley

The essence of Cleckley's ideas of the antisocial personality is the notion that such people are unable to experience shame or anxiety in response to their social transgressions. He offers through case history documentation some evidence that these individuals seem constitutionally unable to experience "normal" guilt in contemplation of their antisocial behavior.

Cleckley's descriptive work on the antisocial personality can be summarized by listing the general characteristics that he believes are critical in identifying this particular form of personality disorder. The behavior patterns consist of the following characteristics:

1. Unreliability.
2. Untruthfulness and insincerity.
3. Lack of remorse or shame.

4. Inadequately motivated antisocial behavior.
5. Poor judgment and failure to learn by experience.
6. Pathological egocentricity and incapacity for love.
7. General poverty in major affective reactions.
8. A specific loss of insight.
9. Unresponsiveness in general interpersonal relations.
10. Fantastic and uninviting behavior with drink and sometimes without.
11. Suicide rarely carried out.
12. Sex life impersonal, trivial, and poorly integrated.
13. Failure to follow any life plan.

It is reasonably clear from Cleckley's descriptive list that a certain amount of moralistic judgment has tinged his clinical description. Nevertheless, the basic concept of the antisocial personality as a remorseless, insincere, manipulative, and aimless individual is clearly portrayed in Cleckley's description. Such people can produce fascinating case histories, and the following case study is no exception.

The case history of Arthur on pages 336–39 illustrates several characteristics of the sociopath that we will encounter later in our discussion. Arthur possesses what Smith (1978) calls "a classic profile of charm and guile" (p. 23). In addition, Arthur appears not at all guilty about his various transgressions. Despite Arthur's antisocial tendencies, his obvious intellectual superiority makes his case history in some ways atypical. Nevertheless, many of the major characteristics of the antisocial individual, as described by theorists in the field, are dramatized in the case of Arthur.

The antisocial personality has fascinated theorists and researchers both in America and in Europe for a number of years. A variety of different theoretical perspectives and research strategies have been employed in the attempt to clarify the nature of the antisocial personality. Attempts to isolate the crucial causal factors in the development of the disorder have been distributed broadly across the theoretical and empirical range of possibilities. Cultural, sociological, behavioral, and biological explanations all have been offered to account for the development of the disorder. Let us now turn to the theory and research.

Charles Manson displayed a number of the characteristics of antisocial and paranoid personalities. These "types" may not always be independent of one another.

United Press International Photo

Theory and Research on the Antisocial Personality

In this section we will consider a variety of theoretical and research approaches to understanding the nature of the antisocial

CASE HISTORY OF ANTISOCIAL PERSONALITY

"I'll Always Remember Arthur"

He was a clever thief, an imaginative liar, and one of the handsomest men I have known, with the innocence of a kitten and the morals of a tomcat. His first name was Arthur; his last name doesn't matter. Arthur's IQ bordered on the genius level. Given just one additional gift—good judgment—he could have left his mark in any field of endeavor; lacking it, he became that rarest of human creatures, a completely happy man doing the one thing on earth for which nature had best prepared him. For Arthur, it was being a full-time problem patient in a large state hospital. I worked as an attendant in that hospital 30 years ago. I was Arthur's attendant for more than a year, and he chose me as a special friend, next only to his psychiatrist, Dr. Kiley, in his affections. With Arthur as your friend you did not, as the Hungarians say, need many enemies.

Nonetheless, when the *Reporter* sent me back to the hospital last summer to write about the changing role of attendants, the one person I most wanted to see was Arthur. I learned that he had left the hospital shortly after I did, and under circumstances that were in complete harmony with his past performances.

Arthur was 34 when I first met him, which was the day I was promoted to charge attendant and put in command of one shift on Crane Cottage. All three shifts of attendants on Crane were new and our supervisor had just transferred from another hospital—a situation that Arthur was quick to note. When I reported for duty, he greeted me with outstretched hand, smiling that engaging smile I came to know so well. "Thank God, they've finally sent us an intelligent young man for this ward," he said. "You are new, but you'll learn. Just come to me if you need help." He hesitated, then added, "Dr. Kiley will be giving me a parole of the grounds when he returns from vacation, but we'll both have to work on him, won't we?"

By 3 o'clock, I was wondering how on earth a man of Arthur's intelligence and poise could possibly be a mental patient on a locked ward. The other attendants felt the same, so when the patient in charge of our clothesroom went home, we agreed that Arthur was the logical man to assume this important job—and it was important because we were responsible for every stitch of clothing owned by our 80 patients.

A few mornings later Arthur met me wearing a well-cut black suit, a white shirt, two-tone shoes, and a bow tie. Before I could comment, he said, "Thought I'd clean up for a change. One of my girl friends from the city may be out today." Watching him strut up the corridor, I could understand why she might.

Reality struck the moment Dr. Kiley returned. "Oh, no!" he cried, "you shouldn't have put Arthur in that job." A careful inspection of his locker and clothes card showed that Arthur now owned 14 suits, 22 shirts, five pairs of shoes, dozens of new ties, not to mention silk bathrobes, much new underwear, slacks, and sweaters. Each article carried a standard tape from the marking room, stamped with Arthur's name, and there was a roll of unused tapes found in his desk, proving that the patient underground system was efficient. It took a stenographer and two clerks from the administration office almost a month to return the clothes to the proper owners. Arthur looked me straight in the eye, and swore that his many girl friends from the city, out of appreciation for his manhood in previous days, had brought the clothes to him.

When I asked Dr. Kiley to tell me a little more about Arthur, he brought me his case history from the record office. Born into a good farm family in the western part of the state, Arthur had graduated from high school and had then gone to work for an elderly German farmer who had married a younger woman—she was 52—as his second wife. When the farmer died suddenly at the age of 70, Arthur, then 23, married the widow, who had inherited widow's rights in the valuable farm. Arthur put in one crop, but after silo-filling in the fall went to bed and did not get up again until early the next spring—and then only to attend his wife's funeral. She had been killed in an auto accident on an icy road while coming from town with Arthur's beer. According to the social worker, the widow had been madly in love with her young husband, humoring his every whim, bringing him magazines and books, cooking his special dishes, milking and doing all the chores while Arthur reclined in bed, taking life easy. Children of the previous marriage offered Arthur $500 for the farm—only a fraction of its value—but he accepted it gratefully. He used his small inheritance to go to the city, where he held numerous jobs, but finally drifted down to Skid Row.

Arthur, who had been classified as a "psychopathic personality" by our medical staff, was completely happy at the hospital and often outlined its many benefits to me. "I never had it so good," he said. "I had $200 worth of free dental care last year, free movies, free dances, a free library with good books, and the food is better than the Salvation Army's soup kitchen." The only blight on Arthur's life occurred with the coming of spring, when he would be struck by an uncontrollable cosmic urge. This was always apparent when his stories turned to his past amours, which he would relate in great detail, eyes sparkling as he remembered. At this point his campaign to get back his parole of the grounds became intense, and Dr. Kiley, a truly gentle and understanding man, was almost as vulnerable as his attendants were to Arthur's appeals.

The year before I came to Crane Cottage, Dr. Kiley had granted Arthur freedom of the grounds and had assigned him to the farm detail to work in the vegetable fields. Directly across from the hospital's farmlands was a fine private farm, with a nice house, several barns and silos. Patients went in from the fields at four, but Arthur, with his parole of the grounds, did not have to report back to his ward until nine. He constructed a collapsible roadside stand directly across from this fine farmhouse, where his sign offered fresh vegetables, "picked today," and home-baked bread, "fresh from the oven." People from town, three miles away, were lining up evenings to purchase these superior products from that "nice farmer" on Town Line Road, paying premium prices. The vegetables were off the state farm, the bread was run in relays, as needed, from the patients' bakery by Arthur's assistants. When he had accumulated enough cash for his fling in the city, he took off, ending up with D.T.'s three weeks later. He was taken to the county hospital, then sent back to us.

Arthur was always delighted to get back "home," and the other patients would hang on his words as he told them in great detail of his conquests in the city, some of them probably true.

As May approached during my year on Crane Cottage, Arthur's cosmic urge became full-blown, and I could see Dr. Kiley weakening. After he finally gave in and assigned Arthur to work in the plumbing shop, giving him a parole of the grounds, he told me, a little sheepishly, that he didn't expect any reformation in Arthur's character. Then added, grinning, "But everyone ought to have the benefit of a second chance."

Five weeks after going on the plumbing gang, Arthur took off for the city. The source of his vacation money became known when the big packing company near the hospital reported that one of our patients had dismantled the copper plumbing of its little soap factory which was used only in the fall when hams were being processed. Unfortunately, Arthur had used a hacksaw rather than a pipe wrench to dismantle the long pipes before hauling them to a junk dealer, who had paid him $107 for his "scrap" metal. It cost the state several thousands of dollars to get it reinstalled in the soap factory. Following this, an edict came down from the superintendent: no more freedom of the grounds for Arthur.

I left the wards to become a staff stenographer. Dr. Kiley retired, and one of the young doctors was given his service. One day this young doctor dictated a progress note to me on Arthur. It read: "This patient is highly intelligent, seems to be totally responsible at present, and has asked for an opportunity to work outside. In view of his past record, I have assigned him to work on a detail at the dairy barn, where he will be under the supervision of an employee at all times." He was a kind, trusting young man, and I did not give him my opinion of his decision about Arthur, but I was smiling inwardly as I went to my desk. June was only a few weeks away.

Late in May, a wave of drunkenness broke out among the working patients. The superintendent had just begun an investigation, suspecting employees of selling whiskey to patients, when the great breakthrough erupted one Friday afternoon. Patients were gathering to sing harmony; fist fights broke out in the laundry, at the powerhouse, in the kitchen. More than 30 patients were picked up intoxicated. Several partially emptied gallon cans of a strange smelling and tasting concoction were found with the patients, and it tested 18 percent alcohol by volume at our lab. Arthur left early that afternoon for the city.

After winning the complete trust of the employee in charge of the dairy barns, Arthur had been given considerable freedom, doing his work well, a veritable model of deportment. However, the many silos connecting to the dairy barns were made of wood. Arthur had tapped the silos like sugar maple trees, filling more than a dozen large milk cans with silage juice, to which he added yeast obtained at the bakery. He stored them in an unused bullshed until their contents were ready for marketing. He sold an estimated 100 gallons of the stuff before leaving on his vacation, from which he returned five weeks later, exhausted but happy to be home.

The rest of Arthur's story I learned last summer from a supervisor who had once worked with me as an attendant on Crane Cottage. He said that a doctor had left a copy of a psychiatric journal on his desk, that Arthur had found it and read with special interest a paper describing a new state hospital on the West Coast where a revolutionary approach to treatment was taking place. No locks were used at this hospital; all patients were free to come and go as they pleased; and they had visiting privileges into town. When they worked, they were paid for their services. Arthur had shown this article to my friend, asking him if he believed it. My friend said that it would not be in that medical journal unless it were true. Arthur left his locked ward through a window a few nights later.

The very last communication contained in Arthur's folder was from a state hospital on the West Coast, asking for "any information you might furnish on Arthur __________, who has just entered this hospital as a voluntary patient, and who has admitted previous treatment in your hospital." Perhaps he is still out there. If so, I am sure his attendants and doctors know him well (W. Van Atta, "I'll Always Remember Arthur," *Psychiatric Reporter, 20,* pp. 8–10).

personality. We will consider role theoretical approaches, social learning accounts, and biological explanations for the disorder.

Social perspective: a role theory explanation. Social theorists have attempted to explain antisocial behavior in interpersonal terms. One well-known account has been offered by Gough (1948). In essence, Gough argues that these individuals are unable to evaluate their own behavior from the point of view of another person which, in turn, produces an inability to empathize with others. The inability to be sensitive in advance to the reaction of other people produces a failure in role taking and role playing skills.

Gough drew heavily on the works of Mead (1934) when developing his role theoretical approach to understanding the antisocial personality. One of the most important concepts in Mead's work is the idea of the *generalized other.* This concept is used to summarize the way each person develops an idea of how other people will react to one's own behavior. People are assumed to refer to this generalized other when judging the appropriateness of a particular behavior or a particular course of action. Thus, the antisocial personality is assumed by Gough to have been unable to develop a consistent generalized other to guide behavior during early social development. In this sense then, Gough suggests that the antisocial personality is undersocialized. Despite an apparent skillfulness at manipulating others, the antisocial personality lacks a common conception of society's expectations and values to guide behavior.

The learning perspective: social learning determinant of antisocial behavior. Learning theorists interested in the possible determinants of antisocial personality have also focused heavily on the socialization process during childhood. One such account offered by Maher (1966) focuses on the pattern of reinforcements that occur when a parent punishes a child for a transgression or some inappropriate behavior. For example, Maher speculates that the child whose parent reduces his or her punishment or who postpones it if the child repents and promises not to repeat the behavior, is actually rewarding repentant behavior, but that no anxiety will be associated with the actual transgression itself. In effect, the behavior being shaped is an elaborate pattern of repentance and excuse making. The result is that the child becomes adept in developing winning ways, offering excuses for his or her transgressions, and, at the same time, fails to develop properly socialized behavior.

Another learning theory account of the development of this pattern of behavior has been offered by Ullmann and Krasner (1969). The essence of their argument is that the antisocial personality is someone who from childhood on has not experienced other people in their personal context as reinforcing. Other people fail to become "acquired reinforcers" to appropriately shape the behavior of the child. In addition, Ullmann and Krasner argue that the antisocial personality may also learn undesirable behaviors from their parents through the mechanisms of modeling and observational learning. Many of the distant or cold behaviors or actions exhibited by parents become acquired by the child in this way. Finally, the social learning account offered by Ullmann and Krasner suggests that the parents of the antisocial personality are often inconsistent in the ways in which they reward behavior. This inconsistency produces a situation in which the child learns to avoid punishment and blame for his or her actions but does not necessarily learn consistent standards for appropriate behavior or consistent concepts of "right" and "wrong."

Antisocial behavior, violence, and intelligence. A critical issue in understanding the antisocial personality has to do with the question of violence. Is it the case that people displaying this personality pattern are more prone to violence than others? Much of the clinical literature would suggest that this is the case, but the findings are far from consistent. Some studies have obtained results suggesting that this group was more violence-prone than others, while other researchers have not (Buck and Graham, 1978).

Recently, Heilbrun (1979) examined the relationship between personality test indicators of antisocial personality, previous records of violent crime, and intelligence. When Heilbrun divided his sample into groups that differed in both the degree of antisocial personality tendencies and intelligence, striking differences in the frequency of violent and nonviolent criminal acts appeared. We can see that among brighter antisocial personalities, the number of violent and nonviolent crimes are nearly evenly distributed. However, among antisocial personalities of lower intelligence, the number of violent crimes is eight times that of nonviolent crimes.

Heilbrun's research suggests that consistent results on the question of whether or not antisocial personality is predictive of violence may have eluded previous investigators primarily because they failed to take the intelligence of the individual into account. As Heilbrun notes, it may be the combination of antisocial traits and lower intelligence that is

TABLE 12–3 Frequencies of Violent and Nonviolent Crime as a Function of Psychopathy and Intelligence

	Level of Intelligence					
	Higher		*Lower*		*Total*	
Level of Psychopathy	*V*	*NV*	*V*	*NV*	*V*	*NV*
Psychopathic	10	9	17	2	27	11
Nonpsychopathic . .	15	7	8	8	23	15
Total	25	16	25	10	50	26

Note: V = violent crime; NV = nonviolent crime.

Source: A. B. Heilbrun, Jr., "Psychopathy and Violent Crime," *Journal of Consulting and Clinical Psychology,* 47 (1979), p. 512.

ANTISOCIAL PERSONALITY AND MACHIAVELLIANISM

Smith (1978) has summarized the recent literature on the personality trait known as Machiavellianism and has drawn some interesting parallels with the antisocial personality configuration.

Christie and Geis (1970) summarized their research in a book entitled *Studies in Machiavellianism*. In that book they describe a general role model for this particular personality pattern which has four characteristics.

1. A relative lack of affect in interpersonal relationships—manipulating should be enhanced by viewing others as objects.
2. A lack of concern with conventional morality regarding lying, cheating, and deceit in general; manipulators should have a utilitarian view of interaction with others.
3. A lack of gross psychopathology—the manipulator is hypothesized to take a rational view of others and is in contact with objective reality.
4. Low ideological commitment—he is more interested in tactics to an end rather than inflexible striving for an idealistic goal (Smith, 1978, p. 87–88).

This general personality configuration is identified by Christie and his colleagues with a personality scale using items such as "True or False: The best way to handle people is to tell them what they want to hear?"

Using this scale, Christie, Geis, and others have conducted a number of studies to illuminate the Machiavellian personality. In one such study, they found that people scoring both high and low in the Machiavellian scale could be led to cheat in an experiment, but what distinguished the two groups was their ability to look their accuser in the eye afterward and to deny cheating.

In other studies involving manipulating people in a group, Christie and Geis created a situation that they called the "ten dollar game." In this situation, three-person groups were formed, each containing a person obtaining a high score on the Machiavellian scale, a second person receiving a middle level score, and a third containing a low score. On the table in front of them lay ten one-dollar bills. The rules of the game indicated that the money would be given to any two subjects who could agree on how to divide the total ten dollars. High scorers on the scale were able to obtain an agreement in each case and earned on the average much more of the ten dollars than did the moderate or low scorers.

Smith (1978) notes the striking similarity between the Machiavellian personality pattern identified by Christie and Geis and the general patterns of behavior reported by clinicians for the antisocial personality. He also observes that there has been little willingness to consider the role of culture in understanding the psychopathic personality. He argues that we should consider "the importance of the broad social climate in which behavior displays occur: the looser the system, the more manipulative practices come into play" (Christie and Geis, 1970, p. 94).

associated with violent and impulsive crime. Heilbrun also suggests that the situational contributions to the prediction of violence would certainly be easier to identify if one knew both the personal qualities of the individual and the level of intelligence rather than just personality characteristics alone. As he observes, a situation involving a barroom argument may represent a very different instigator of violence for the antisocial personality with fewer intellectual resources than for the bright person with antisocial tendencies.

This observation may shed some additional light on our case study of Arthur described earlier. It may be that much of the difference between antisocial personalities of the sort described in this case study and the more aggressive patterns of behavior sometimes observed in antisocial personalities have to do with the social flexibility to cope associated with differences in intellectual ability.

Biological explanations. After reading clinical examples of the behavior of the antisocial personality, several things seem to stand out. First, the person seems remarkably free of anxiety and guilt in instances where most people would react strongly with both emotions. Furthermore, the antisocial personality seems to repeatedly find himself in the same sorts of problematic situations and appears almost constitutionally unable to learn from past experience. It is not surprising that a number of researchers have hypothesized that underlying biological deficiencies are major causal factors for this pattern of behavior. Indeed, researchers have tested a number of interrelated hypotheses about the biological nature of this disorder.

Psychophysiological research. Perhaps the classic study in this field was conducted by Lykken (1957). After noting the striking inability of the antisocial personality to develop feelings of anxiety, Lykken hypothesized that these people were *deficient in their ability to develop a conditioned anxiety response* and undertook to test his hypothesis in the laboratory. Using Cleckley's criteria as a basis for selection, Lykken identified a group of prisoners who fit the criteria well, another group who displayed the behavior pattern but also showed certain neurotic tendencies, and a group of normal students. The three groups were matched for intelligence and then were given a laboratory avoidance learning task in which they were given 20 trials to learn a "mental maze." When they made errors,

David T. Lykken

Courtesy of David T. Lykken

they received a shock of moderate intensity.

Lykken assumed that on those trials where subjects received a shock for performing an error, conditioned anxiety responses would develop. If his hypothesis was correct, then the antisocial personalities who were unable to develop a conditioned anxiety response would show higher error scores on trials where errors produced shocks than would the neurotic or the normal comparison groups. This is exactly what Lykken found. A summary of his findings is shown in Figure 12–2. Furthermore, when Lykken positively reinforced some responses in the task, the groups showed no differences in performance. Thus, the failure of the antisocial personality group to avoid shock was assumed by Lykken to reflect a constitutionally based inability to develop avoidance learning responses and, of course, these are precisely the responses that are assumed to be crucial in effective socialization.

Another well-known study in this area was conducted by Schacter (1971). Schacter also identified prisoners who differed on Cleckley's criteria. An important difference in Schacter's study was that, not only did he submit subjects to Lykken's task including shock, but also administered adrenaline to some students which, he assumed, would arouse the autonomic nervous system of those subjects. Some subjects were actually administered placebos and others received the active drug. Interestingly, those subjects who had been injected with adrenaline showed significantly fewer errors in the antisocial group, but injections with the placebo made no

FIGURE 12–2 Avoidance Ratio (Shocked Errors/Nonshocked Errors) as a Function of Trials. A decrease in the avoidance ratio indicates learning to avoid shocked errors. (After Lykken, 1955)

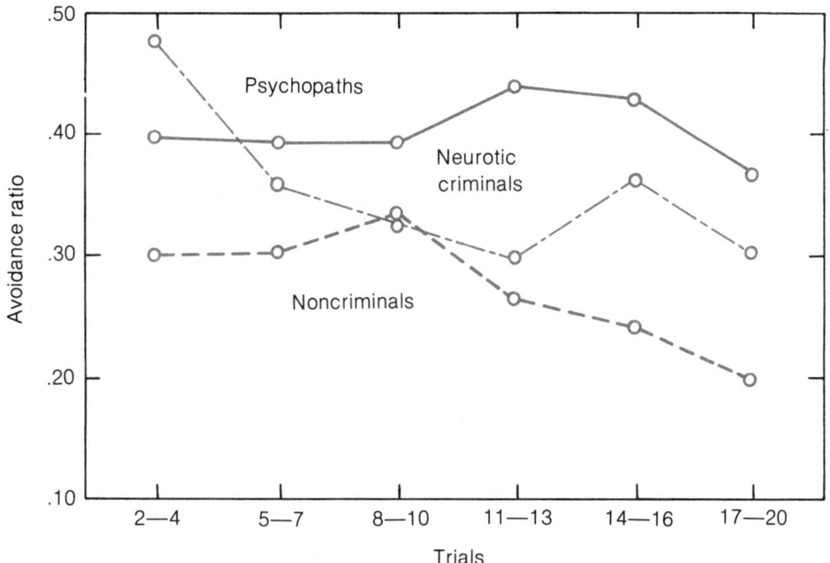

Source: D. T. Lykken, *A Study of Anxiety in the Sociopathic Personality, JASP,* 1957, *55,* pp. 6–10.

difference. Thus, Schacter's study suggests that something about the autonomic nervous system *arousal level* of the subjects is an important factor in the psychopathic personality.

Genetic evidence: adoption studies. One of the most interesting and potentially powerful strategies available to researchers seeking evidence of a genetic mechanism for the transmission of antisocial personality characteristics is the *adoption study.* The basic strategy is simple. Antisocial personality characteristics could be transmitted to offspring either through environmental learning or genetic means. Therefore, family studies that demonstrate a higher proportion of antisocial personality characteristics among the offspring of antisocial parents do not separate genetic and environmental influence from one another. Transmission could be due to either genetic or social learning. On the other hand, if one capitalizes on the "experiment in nature" associated with adoption, it is possible to separate genetic and environmental factors.

The research strategy involves identifying parents with antisocial characteristics who have allowed their offspring to be adopted early in life. These children are then studied some years later in their adoptive home environment and their behavior patterns are compared with children who were also adopted but whose parents did *not* display antisocial characteristics. If the adopted offspring of the antisocial parents display more antisocial characteristics than the control group, we may infer that some genetic transmission is occurring. Of course, it is also necessary to assure that the environment of the adopted children of antisocial parents does not also contain parents with higher than normal rates of antisocial personality, since in that case, environmental and genetic determinants would again be confounded in the control group.

Just such a study was conducted by Cadoret (1978). Cadoret notes that this research strategy allows some estimate of contribution of genetic factors to the disorder and also allows the opportunity to examine the possibility that other similar disorders may also develop even if the antisocial personality pattern does not.

Cadoret found that several factors predicted the number of antisocial characteristics found in the sample. They included (1) antisocial biological background, (2) a background of alcoholism in the biological parents, and (3) psychological problems found in the adoptive family. A moment's reflection will suggest that these factors implicate *both* genetic and environmental causes in the development of antisocial behavior. Indeed, Hutchings and Mednick (1974) conducted a similar adoption study and also found a significant environmental factor in their results. Thus, the adoption strategy appears to yield evidence consistent with both environmental and genetic determinants of antisocial personality.

Childhood anxiety and adult adjustment in antisocial personality. Cass and Thomas (1979) have examined the relationship between the clinical picture of children displaying antisocial behavior early in life and their later adult adjustment. They observe that children who displayed little or no anxiety about their behavior as children are more likely to continue to show the antisocial pattern of behavior in adulthood.

In the first case described below, the person (Larry) did show signs of anxiety and depression in childhood and, later as an adult, appears to be making an adequate adjustment. In contrast, the adjustment of the person in the second case presented below seems not to have improved over time.

LARRY

Larry had been a behavior problem at school for most of the six years prior to his referral to the Clinic at age 12. He was about to be suspended again for disobedience and resistance toward his 7th grade teacher, his cruelty toward other children, and his refusal to do the work assigned. Yet he tested in the superior range intellectually and placed in the 9th grade level on achievement tests. Mother excused Larry's behavior on the basis of his general unhappiness and insecurity. He resented never having had a father in the home; mother, by her own admission, was not strict enough in her discipline. Mother would even excuse the physical abuse she suffered at Larry's hands, seeing it as punishment due her for having given birth to him and his twin sister outside marriage.

Several relatives had helped now and then in the care of the two children but most of the time mother had to struggle with problems of keeping baby sitters while she worked. Larry's anger seemed to be directed especially toward his mother and sister and to have generalized to women teachers. He reached out for a relationship with male father figures, especially one financially successful uncle who was his ideal.

The Clinic recognized the seriousness of Larry's acting out behavior but sensed deep anxiety and depression behind his aggressive bravado. He seemed to be confused and very sad over the loss of the father he had never known. The clinical team thought Larry had the assets to benefit from psychotherapy but recommended that he be placed out of the home in a residential center where the opportunity for male identification and supervision as well as for therapy would be provided. Larry refused absolutely to accept placement. He went to live, for a time, with his aunt and uncle where his school and social adjustment improved temporarily.

During adolescence Larry was arrested for peace disturbance while under the influence of drugs. He dropped out of high school in the 11th grade but later passed the GED tests and enrolled in college courses at night school.

Larry's major improvement in functioning seems to have occurred in the four years before he was seen for follow-up at age 24. It is difficult to pinpoint the bases for the change, but, according to Larry, it was his own realization that he was heading into serious trouble and he had better "shape up." He took on-the-job training as a manufacturer's sales representative and has had several promotions in that occupation. He also gives credit to his wife, whom he met at age 19 and married a year later. She seems to be a very stable person to whom Larry can relate on a collateral level. "We are each other's best friend." They have bought their own home in a very nice suburban area.

Larry seems to be accomplishing many of the goals he had set for himself as a result of his admiration for his uncle. He is still somewhat anxious and his change toward socially acceptable behavior is still largely based on his need to succeed and to avoid punishment. One wonders if he will be able to maintain his new way of life if misfortune should enter in. He feels confident in his ability to do so.

LOUIS

Like Larry, Louis was considered by his family always to have been an "angry child." He simply would not mind. "Father would spank him and put him in a corner, but he would come out and do the same thing again and get spanked again." Both parents were extremely strict. They had come from deprived backgrounds and wanted their children to grow up to be "good citizens" and have a different life than they had had. Mother, who had been beaten by her father many times, felt some obligation to protect Louis when his father lost control in punishing him.

Louis was particularly fatalistic in his attitude toward his problems when he came to the Clinic at age 15. He was aware of his lack of impulse control but had little hope of gaining control through his parents' way of "handling" him. He could envision only further antisocial behavior and eventual destruction of himself. He was unable to identify with a father whom he saw as passive and ineffectual but potentially destructive.

Louis was one of the older subjects seen in the follow-up. At 28, he was an unemployed truck driver. He had been fired for physically attacking his boss, an attack which he felt was justified because the boss was "unfair" to him. He had been discharged from military service a few years earlier as "incapable of adapting to military life."

His relationship to his family was still a hostile, dependent one. He and his father argued constantly. "Sometimes I don't talk to dad or mom at all for weeks at a time." His relationship with peers is equally poor. He described much rowdy, antisocial behavior with a gang of fellows who rode motorcycles in a group. "I used to get so smacked when I was out with them that the guys would put me on my cycle and head me toward my house." He is proud of his marksmanship with a gun. "I keep a pistol and it's loaded. Dad ordered me to get rid of it, but I wouldn't.

Louis' need to prove his masculinity in these symbolic ways is accompanied by an intense hatred of homosexual men. "I can't tolerate bisexual men and if I meet one in a dark alley, I'll smack them up. If they want their teeth, they'd better keep moving." Louis' ambivalence about heterosexuality is clear and his attempts to relate to females have been extremely disappointing. "I just drop girls without even calling them up. I don't trust them. I try to carry on longer with them but I just can't." Louis spends his leisure time with "the boys," at singles dances or at an archery range.

Louis has seen two psychiatrists since he was at the Clinic where he had only the diagnostic. He was referred for psychiatric help after acting out while in the military service and again more recently. He dismissed these therapeutic contacts with the statement: "I was told that I am an angry person and I've decided that I really am."

The consistent, unchanging course of Louis' antisocial behavior seems singularly unrelated to any internal process of learning from experience, let alone to internal anxiety. He does become depressed and pessimistic over his belief that his hostility will lead, eventually to his destruction (Cass and Thomas, 1979, pp. 173, 174, and 175).

Antisocial behavior in childhood appears to remain a fairly stable pattern for some people into adulthood. A major study by Robbins (1966) supports this observation. Robbins selected a sample of 524 children referred to a city child guidance clinic between 1924 and 1929 and then followed them in adulthood to assess their present clinical adjustment. Of her sample of children, the majority (73 percent) were originally referred for antisocial behavior. Robbins was also able to examine a control group of 100 children drawn from the public school records during the same time period, which was matched with the patient group for race, age, sex, intelligence, test scores and socioeconomic status. The control group showed no serious behavioral problems in childhood. When both groups were interviewed 30 years later, 28 percent of those children who had been referred earlier for antisocial behavior still displayed antisocial behavior patterns. The clinic population who had not been referred for antisocial problems displayed a much lower proportion of such cases, only 4 percent.

Thus, it appears that the characteristic pattern of lower anxiety levels noted in research on adult antisocial personalities may also be typical of children displaying this behavior pattern and for some children, at least, may continue into adulthood.

SUMMARY

In this chapter we have examined the personality disorders and have observed that, unlike many forms of abnormal behavior, the personality disorders are not necessarily marked by periods of acute distress. Instead, they reflect *long-standing personality patterns,* which may or may not produce psychological distress in the people displaying them or in others. Whether or not these personality patterns are considered "abnormal" depends heavily on the context in which they occur.

Although DSM III lists no fewer than 11 distinct types of personality disorders, the degree to which they can be reliably distinguished from one another is still unclear and represents an important area of needed research.

We chose to concentrate our attention on three of the most distinctive personality disorders: compulsive personality, paranoid personality, and antisocial personality. In each case we noted the way in which the dominant personality patterns associated with each of these disorders pervaded the home environment, interpersonal relationships, and work lives of the people displaying them.

In the case of the antisocial personality we noted that considerable effort has been devoted to clarifying the nature of the disorder. In particular we reviewed research suggesting that the antisocial personality is less able to develop a conditioned anxiety response and noted that some recent genetic evidence suggests that both biological and socialization factors are important in the development of antisocial personality.

13

Unconventional Sexual Behavior and Psychosexual Dysfunction

OVERVIEW

Consider the following scene: An adult man meets a young boy. They are not related. They go off to a private place, probably the man's house. Then, with mutual consent, they have sexual relations.

Now stop for a moment and consider carefully your feelings about this scene. Do you feel angry? Disgusted? Shocked? You may be surprised to learn that in Siwan, in northern Africa, the above scene is a normal and accepted part of everyday life. In fact, in Siwan, those men who do not engage in such sexual activities are subject to ridicule by their peers.

Now consider a very different scene: A handsome young man and an attractive young woman are walking in Central Park on a clear spring day. They walk hand in hand gazing into each other's eyes. They pause and touch lips and put their arms around each other. Then they walk on, again holding hands.

Now stop reading for a moment and consider your feelings about this scene. You probably feel considerably more positive about what you have just read. Do you feel sympathy, joy, or approval? As unusual as it may seem, when members of the Thonga tribe first saw Europeans kissing, they probably did not react the way you did. The Thonga tribe members first laughed and then one remarked: "Look at them—they eat each other's saliva and dirt" (Ford & Beach, 1954).

The examples of adult and child homosexuality being accepted in Siwan and kissing not being accepted by the Thonga tribe suggest a most crucial point about human sexual behavior: Our ideas concerning the rights or wrongs of sexual behavior are shaped by the norms, values, and standards of the culture we are a part of. The result is the surprising differences in reactions to the sexual practices mentioned in the two scenes we considered.

In addition to the striking differences from culture to culture you would encounter as you travel around the world, there are some surprises to be discovered when you look at the history of sexual behavior within our own Western culture.

We can trace the roots of our current views of sexual behavior to the beliefs of the ancient Israelis and medieval Christians who stressed that the natural aim of sex was procreation. By the 13th century, the Christian theologian Thomas Acquinas summarized the thinking of the day by declaring that intercourse was not only reserved for the purpose of procreation, but that it was also to be restricted to the right person (i.e., the marriage partner) and in the right way (i.e., coitus).

As the church became less powerful, the psychiatrists became the new authorities about sexual matters and translated the old religious doctrine into medical terminology. However, the old doctrines persisted and what once was sin was now considered to be "sexual psychopathology." By the 19th century, a vast array of sexual "deviations," "perversions," and "aberrations" were categorized. People who diverged from the norms of "natural" coitus by choosing the "wrong" sexual object or by choosing the "wrong" sexual activity were believed to suffer from mental disorders (Haberle, 1978). For example, in the sexually repressed Victorian times, people who were known to masturbate were vulnerable to being labeled as having an affliction termed *masturbation insanity.* Frequent intercourse was seen as another cause of mental aberration. Such notions were popularized in the "marriage manuals" which were widely read during the 1830s and gave the stamp of medical authority to prevailing views and taboos. Only when it became clear that nearly everyone engaged in some type of "perverted" behavior did medical authorities begin to acknowledge that many sexual practices considered to be abnormal were in fact exaggerations of normal tendencies. Thus, sexual behaviors which were shared by a wide variety of people which were neither compulsive, destructive, nor personally distressing were no longer regarded as perversions by the medical profession.

Whether you look at the differences in what is acceptable sexual behavior from one culture to another, or whether you look at the differences in what was acceptable in our history compared to today, one thing remains the same. At all times, and in all cultures, no matter what the norms, people who conform to the current societal values are seen as "normal," and those who do not are seen as "abnormal" and deviant.

What is considered normal and what is considered abnormal by the mental health practitioners in our culture? Perhaps the clearest statement of current psychiatric thinking about abnormal sexual behavior are the definitions of the psychosexual disorders presented in the new DSM III classification.

In this chapter we will acquaint you with the major psychosexual disorders listed in DSM III. We will begin our overview of the psychosexual disorders with an examination of the *psychosexual dysfunctions.* These disorders are quite common. They are characterized by a failure to enjoy and/or achieve *accepted* sexual behaviors.

Sexual practices like kissing which are common in our culture are not universally accepted.

Michael Weisbrot and Family

In contrast, persons with *gender identity disorders* and *paraphilias* engage in unconventional sexual activities. More specifically, persons with gender identity disorders manifest their differentness in their feelings of discomfort and inappropriateness about their anatomic sex, and by acting in ways that we generally associate with the "opposite" sex. And, as in previous listings of mental disorders, variations from the norms of conventional choice of sexual objects and choice of sexual activity are considered abnormal. Each of the paraphilias which we will describe involves a variation from socially accepted norms which is distinguished by a diminished capacity of the person to engage in close, affectionate sexual relations with another person. Thus, these disorders can easily be distinguished from widely practiced variations in sexual activity, such as masturbation.

An excellent illustration of how sexual norms are not fixed and may be subject to rapid change is the deletion of homosexuality from the list of mental disorders in the DSM III classification system. This change from previous efforts to classify sexual disorders reflects the growing recognition that homosexual behavior does not necessarily preclude intimate, affectionate, and rewarding relationships. Only when one's homosexuality is unwanted and is personally distressing is it listed as the psychosexual disorder, *ego-dystonic homosexuality*. At the conclusion of our overview, we will devote considerable attention to homosexuality not only because it is the most common unconventional sexual behavior, but also because recent evidence challenges widely held stereotypes about homosexuality.

PSYCHOSEXUAL DYSFUNCTION AND ITS TREATMENT

In about 50 percent of American marriages, some type of sexual dysfunction affects the marital unit (Masters & Johnson, 1970). Indeed, clinical experience suggests that men commonly seek help for premature ejaculation and failure to attain or maintain an erection (impotence). Women may be concerned with a lack of sexual desire or absence of excitement during sexual relations (frigidity and difficulty in reaching orgasm). Pain during intercourse and delay or absence of orgasm in males are less frequently expressed concerns.

The Sexual Response Cycle

Until recently, many misconceptions about sexual functioning created barriers to successful treatment of sexual problems. Little information about how the human body responds to sexual stimulation was available. Consequently therapeutic approaches tended to be largely ineffective. The pioneering research of Masters and Johnson (1966) yielded basic data on normal and dysfunctional sexual responses which proved to be invaluable to clinicians concerned with helping persons with sexual difficulties. In addition, their findings paved the way for their later developing a remarkably successful therapy program for sexual problems.

In 1954 Masters and Johnson launched an innovative research program to study males and females as they were sexually stimulated in the laboratory. At the Reproductive Biology Research Foundation in St. Louis, they collected information on over 10,000 male and female sexual response cycles. Kaplan describes their wide ranging efforts:

> Their observations included a wide spectrum of sexual behaviors under every imaginable condition. They studied coitus in many positions, between strangers, between happily married couples, between couples who had various sexual and interpersonal difficulties. Different techniques of erotic stimulation were explored, as were various types of self-stimulation. The sexual behaviors of men and women of a wide range of ages was studied. Sex was observed during menstruation. The sexual responses of men who are circumcised were compared with those who are not circumcised. The effects of various contraceptive devices on sexual behavior were studied. In addition, sexual responses were investigated in the presence of various pathological conditions, including the artificial vagina, etc. (Kaplan, 1974, pp. 3–4).

At first, Masters and Johnson interviewed male and female prostitutes. While they furnished much valuable information, particularly about sexual techniques, Masters decided not to use them as subjects because they tended to move about the country too much and because the women often suffered from chronic pelvic congestion which affected their sexual response. The volunteers chosen tended to be quite ordinary people. They tended to be patients and students whose participation was motivated largely by curiosity and the desire to contribute to the understanding of sexual functioning.

In order to be accepted into the program, it was essential that the volunteers be able to achieve orgasm in the laboratory. The laboratory was equipped with a bed, monitoring equipment to measure physiological changes, cameras, and a specially constructed transparent penis shaped probe which contained a camera to record changes in the vagina during sexual intercourse. People accommodated to the laboratory with surprising ease; there were remarkably few instances of failure to reach orgasm.

In their first book, *The Human Sexual Response* (1966), Masters and Johnson reported on their findings of the sexual response cycle as males and females attained orgasm. Surprisingly, they found that the basic sexual arousal cycle was the same for both men and women. They defined four phases in this cycle: excitement, plateau, orgasmic, and resolution.

"The excitement phase is initiated by whatever is sexually stimulating for a particular individual. If stimulation is strong enough, excitement builds quickly, but if it is interrupted or if it becomes

The husband and wife research team of William Masters and Virginia Johnson.

United Press International Photo

objectionable, this phase becomes extended or the cycle may be stopped. If effective sexual stimulation is continued, it produces increased levels of sexual tension that lead ultimately to orgasm. This increased tension is called the plateau phase. If the individual's drive for sexual release in this phase is not strong enough, or if stimulation ceases to be effective or is withdrawn, a man or woman will not experience orgasm, but will enter a prolonged period of gradually decreasing sexual tension. The climacteric or orgasmic phase, a totally involuntary response, consists of those few seconds when the body changes resulting from stimulation reach their maximum intensity. During the resolution phase, after orgasm, there is a lessening of sexual tensions as the person returns to the unstimulated state. Women are capable of having another orgasm if there is effective stimulation during this phase. The resolution period in the male includes a time, which varies among individuals, when restimulation is impossible. This is called the refractory period.

In both sexes, the basic responses of the body to sexual stimulation are myotonia (increased muscle tension) and vasocongestion (filling of the blood vessels with fluid) especially in the genital organs, causing swelling. Of course, these basic physiologic sexual responses remain the same regardless of the stimulation—coital, manipulation, or fantasy. However, intensity and duration of responses vary with the method of stimulation used. Masturbation produced the most intense experiences observed in the laboratory, partner manipulation the next, and intercourse the least'' (Belleview & Richter, 1970, 33–34).

DSM III retains much of the basic

FIGURE 13–1 The Human Sexual Response

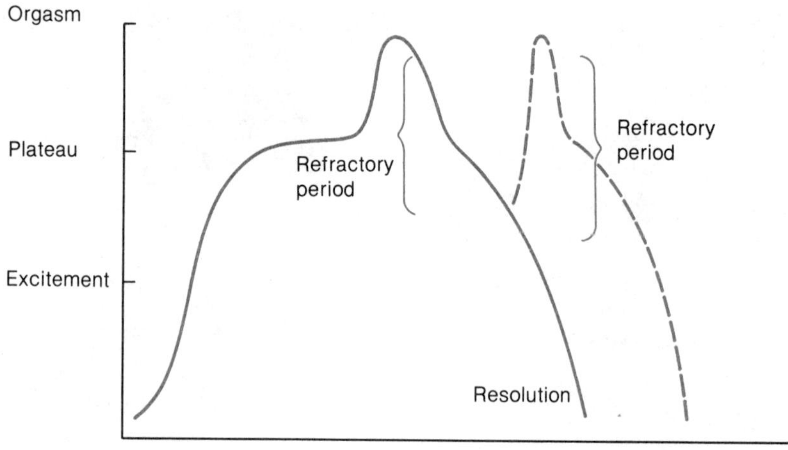

Male sexual response cycle

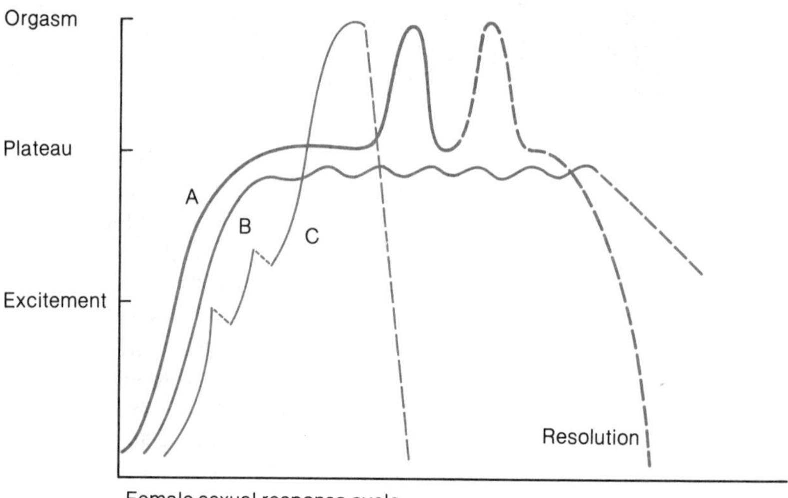

Female sexual response cycle

Source: M. H. Masters and V. E. Johnson, *Human Sexual Response* (Boston: Little, Brown, 1966).

scheme advanced by Masters and Johnson but includes a number of modifications. According to DSM III, the first phase is termed appetitive and consists of the sexual fantasies and interest and desire to engage in sexual activity which initiate the sexual response cycle. The second phase described by the new classification system, excitement, essentially condenses much of what Masters and Johnson term excitement and plateau, into one phase. This simplification is appealing since the plateau phase can be seen as a more advanced state of sexual excitement which occurs just before orgasm (Kaplan, 1974). As in the Masters and Johnson scheme, orgasm and resolution are the final phases of the sexual response cycle.

Explanations and Assessment

Sexual disorders can be associated with each of the three primary components of the sexual response—appetitive or desire, excitement, and orgasm—since each is vulnerable to disruption by emotional responses such as anxiety. Indeed, a diagnosis of psychosexual dysfunction is not made when the difficulty is primarily the result of organic rather than psychological factors.

Kaplan (1977) implicates anxiety as one of the basic causes of sexual dysfunctions. She states, "Sexually disruptive anxiety does not seem to arise from one specific base; rather it appears to originate in a wide spectrum of causes. It ranges from the anxiety produced by ignorance, unrealistic expectations about sexual functioning, and performance anxiety through the more profound fears of rejection and fears of intimacy and commitment to unconscious guilt derived from childhood and the fear of sex with the opposite gender, which originated in childhood pathological family interactions" (p. 8).

Since many diverse etiological factors may have an impact on sexual dysfunctions, it is important to determine their nature and role in any sexual problem. This is often accomplished in the initial evaluation of the dysfunctional sexual behavior. Hogan (1978) describes the following factors which can result in sexual dysfunctions: (1) early environmental problems, for example, problems in the parents' relationship, rape, incest, traumatic experiences with prostitutes, religious orthodoxy, and homosexuality; (2) misconceptions and lack of knowledge about sex; (3) lack of a skilled sexual partner; (4) psychological factors such as anxiety, guilt, fear, depression, and fear of losing control; (5) relationship problems including hostility, marital conflicts, lack of communication, and lack of attraction toward one's partner; (6) other sexual problems; (7) physical and physiological factors such as illness, surgery, irritation from contraceptive materials, and medication.

A complete assessment should also include a determination of the exact nature of the problem, its frequency and severity, its effect on the individuals involved, whether it is generalized or limited to specific situations or partners, and whether it has been present throughout life or developed after a period of relatively normal functioning. Sexual disorders are termed primary when the sexual history suggests that the person never functioned normally. They are termed secondary if the person reports at least one instance of normal sexual functioning with respect to the disorder being evaluated. Secondary sexual dysfunctions tend to have a better therapeutic prognosis than primary dysfunctions.

THE PSYCHOSEXUAL DYSFUNCTIONS

Inhibited Sexual Desire

As we stated previously, sexual dysfunctions are associated with each of the major phases of the sexual response cycle. The disorder associated with the desire, or appetitive phase, is inhibited sexual desire. DSM III suggests that this diagnosis is warranted when there is a "persistent and pervasive inhibition of sexual desire." Since there are no established criteria for "normal" sexual desire, the diagnosis is usually made when lack of desire is problematic either to the individual or to his or her partner.

The independence of the components of the sexual response is reflected in the ability of some people with inhibited desire to experience sexual excitement and even orgasm. Their sexual activity, however, is not motivated by desire, but, perhaps, a wish to please their partner. In other cases, low sexual desire can inhibit other phases of the sexual response.

Inhibited Sexual Excitement

Sexual dysfunctions with inhibited sexual excitement include what have commonly been termed impotence in the male and frigidity in the female. Since both of these terms have negative connotations and have been used to describe a number of different sexual difficulties, it is necessary to clarify their meaning in this context. DSM III considers the male dysfunction with inhibited sexual excitement (impotence) to be reflected in "partial or complete failure to attain or maintain erection until completion of the sexual act." Its counterpart in the woman (frigidity) involves "partial or complete failure to attain or maintain the lubrication-swelling response of sexual excitement until completion of the sexual act" (p. 279). Some women with this disorder consider the sexual experience to be an unpleasant ordeal or endure sexual relations only to preserve their marriage. Others may enjoy touching or physical closeness, yet not experience erotic feelings (Kaplan, 1974).

Occasional failure to achieve or to maintain an erection are not uncommon. Emotional stress, fatigue, and alcohol excess may produce transient episodes of impotence. Since nearly half of all men experience such difficulties at one time or another, a diagnosis of secondary impotence is warranted only when a man fails to achieve an erection in 25 percent of his attempts (Masters & Johnson, 1970).

The incidence of impotence appears to gradually rise with age, particularly after age 45. Before age 35, impotence is relatively rare. By age 70 about 27 percent of males in the Kinsey study reported erectile failure and by 80, 75 percent reported impotence. Many men, however, have no erectile problems well into their eighth and ninth decade of life.

Inhibited Orgasm

Sexual disorders associated with the orgasm component of the sexual response include persistent and repeated delay or absence of orgasm. Failure to reach orgasm can occur in males and females who are responsive to erotic stimuli and experience a normal sexual excitement phase. This disorder is much more common in females than in males. Kinsey, Pomeroy, Martin, and Gebhard (1953) reported that up to 15 percent of women never reached orgasm even after 20 years of marriage. Failure to ejaculate and experience orgasm is rare and probably affects fewer than 1 in 700 men of all ages (Katchadourian & Lunde, 1972).

Premature Ejaculation

Another disorder associated with the orgasm phase is premature ejaculation.

DSM III defines it rather flexibly as ejaculation which "occurs before the individual wishes it, because of recurrent and persistent absence of reasonable voluntary control of ejaculation and orgasm during sexual activity" (p. 280). It is the most common presenting problem of males seeking sex therapy (Kaplan, 1974). Premature orgasm in the female is not considered a sexual dysfunction, since women are responsive to sexual stimulation shortly after orgasm and some regularly attain multiple orgasm.

Functional Dyspareunia and Functional Vaginismus

Vaginismus and dyspareunia can drastically interfere with sexual relations. Dyspareunia refers to painful intercourse not caused exclusively by organic factors. It may be associated with, but is distinct from, vaginismus which is an involuntary spasm of the muscles of the lower third of the vagina. This condition can make intercourse difficult, if not impossible. Dyspareunia can occur in both sexes, but vaginismus is, of course, limited to the female. Vaginismus and dyspareunia are probably the least common of the sexual dysfunctions.

DIRECT THERAPY FOR SEXUAL DYSFUNCTION

Beginning in the late 1950s, Masters and Johnson began to develop a brief, direct treatment program for sexual dysfunctions. The publication of *Human Sexual Inadequacy* (1970) described their research findings and treatment approach and sparked considerable optimism that sexual difficulties could be treated with a high degree of success. Indeed, Masters and Johnson reported an overall success rate of 81 percent for sexual dysfunctions. Their impressive results encouraged others to develop a wide variety of behaviorally oriented programs based on the notion that dysfunctional sexual behavior could be treated directly without emphasizing in-depth personality change. Such approaches have come to be called "direct" sexual therapies. They have proved to be more effective than traditional psychotherapies such as psychoanalysis which stress insight and extensive personality change. As Gagnon (1977)

TABLE 13–1 Overall Results of the Masters and Johnson Treatment Program (1970)

Type of Sexual Problem	*Numbers of Couples Treated*	*Percentage Success at the End of Therapy*	*Percentage Success at Two-Year Follow-up*
Primary impotence	32	59.4	59.4
Secondary impotence	213	73.8	69.1
Premature ejaculation	186	97.8	97.3
Ejaculatory incompetence	17	82.4	82.4
Male totals	448	83.1	80.6
Primary orgasmic dysfunction	193	83.4	82.4
Situational orgasmic dysfunction	149	77.2	75.2
Female totals	342	80.7	79.2
Male and female totals	790	81.1	80.0

Source: G. T. Wilson and D. K. O'Leary, *Principles of Behavior Therapy* (Englewood Cliffs, N.J.: Little, Brown, & Company, 1980), p. 156.

states, "For many people, particularly those with sexual difficulties in their day to day living, talking about the past can be extremely frustrating, since the problems may continue to occur 4 or 5 times a week. . . . After many treatment sessions many patients are still suffering from the presenting problem and have only an apparent understanding of Mom and Dad" (p. 369).

Lo Piccolo (1978) has defined a number of basic principles which are used by Masters and Johnson as well as other clinicians who follow a direct, behavioral treatment approach.

Mutual Responsibility

In direct therapies, sexual dysfunctions are conceptualized as *shared disorders.* Masters and Johnson (1970) emphasize that "there is no such thing as an uninvolved partner in any marriage in which there is some form of sexual inadequacy." Sexual problems are often a source of distress to both partners and can be symptomatic of problems which exist in the relationship. Lo Piccolo (1978) states that "the husband of an inorgasmic woman is partially responsible for creating or maintaining a sexual dysfunction, and he is also a patient in need of help" (p. 3). The couple rather than the individual is the treatment focus, since their attitudes, communication patterns, and sexual interactions are important targets for modification in therapy. In order to minimize one partner's blaming the other for the dysfunctional behavior and to further involvement in the therapeutic enterprise, shared responsibility for the sexual problem is stressed by the therapist. In addition, Masters and Johnson as well as many other direct therapists use a male-female, cotherapy team to provide each person a therapist to identify with.

Information and Education

Since sexual dysfunctions often involve lack of information, and not uncommonly misinformation, providing information and reeducation are major components of direct therapy. Masters and Johnson treat couples in a two-week, intensive program in which educational presentations, therapy sessions, and sexual exercises are individually tailored to meet the unique needs of the dysfunctional couple. When round table discussions reveal an area where additional information is necessary, it is provided to both partners. For example, the notion that sexual intercourse necessarily involves pain can be easily corrected in this context. Discussions, educational reading materials, and educational films have been used to correct misconceptions and instruct couples in effective sexual technique.

Attitude Change

Direct therapy attempts to modify negative attitudes toward sexual behaviors which result in anxiety and, in some cases, disgust in sexual encounters. Some procedures which have been used include providing positive reading materials on sexuality, discussions with sympathetic clergy in the case of religiously based negative attitudes, instructing the husband to express to his wife that he will respect her more, not less, if she becomes more sexual, and encouraging patients to attend workshops and lectures on sexuality and sexual values (Lo Piccolo, 1978).

Eliminating Performance Anxiety

Anxiety and concern about performance interfere with the spontaneous expression of sensuality and inhibit sexual responsiveness. Performance anxiety almost invariably results in the patient assuming the role of "spectator," instead of an involved participant. Performance anxiety can be minimized by reducing the "demands" to perform in sexual situations. Patients are instructed to involve themselves in and enjoy the *process* of lovemaking, instead of "keeping score" and striving for "results." The therapist may give the woman "permission" to enjoy intercourse without striving for orgasm on every occasion. In cases of impotence, the therapist may direct the man to engage in sexual foreplay and to deliberately avoid sexual intercourse, thereby reducing concerns about whether an erection sufficient for orgasm will occur (Lo Piccolo, 1978).

Increasing Communication and Effectiveness of Sexual Technique

Sexual problems often revolve around patterns of negative interactions and expectations. Sensitivity to criticism about sexual performance and pessimistic attitudes about the problem inhibit clear communication and experimentation with new, possibly more satisfying sexual techniques. Direct therapy encourages the sharing of sexual likes and dislikes, sexual experimentation, and furnishing feedback about sexual technique and response. Helping the couple to communicate more effectively during lovemaking may be supplemented with other procedures. These include suggesting that the partners share erotic fantasies, read explicit erotic literature, and see explicit sexual movies to learn new sexual techniques (Lo Piccolo, 1978).

Changing Destructive Life-Styles and Sex Roles

Where patients' life-styles permit little time for relaxed, tension-free interactions, resolving sexual difficulties may be particularly problematic. Sex role separation, where there are no mutual responsibilities for household tasks, diminishes the likelihood that sexual relations will be experienced in a close, sharing manner. Direct therapists assume a very active role in such cases and suggest that the patients arrange "dates" with each other for relaxing times together (Annon, 1974). The therapist may also suggest that the husband assume greater household responsibilities in the evenings so that his wife may enjoy less pressured, shared time to get "in touch with her sex drive and her sexual responsiveness" (Lo Piccolo, 1978).

Prescribing Changes in Behavior

Lo Piccolo (1978) suggests that "if there is any one procedure that is the hallmark of direct treatment of sexually dysfunctions, it is the prescription by the therapist of a series of gradual steps of specific sexual behaviors to be performed by the patients in their own home. These behaviors are often described as 'sensate focus' or 'pleasuring exercises'." (p. 6) Saddock and Saddock (1976) describe this approach:

> Beginning exercises usually focus on heightening sensory awareness to touch,

> sight, sound, and smell. Initially, intercourse is interdicted, and couples learn to give and receive bodily pleasure without the pressure of performance. They are simultaneously learning that sexual foreplay is as important as intercourse and orgasm. Genital stimulation is eventually added to general body stimulation. The couple are instructed sequentially to try various positions for intercourse, without necessarily completing the union, and to use varieties of stimulating techniques before they are instructed to proceed with intercourse (p. 465).

In our discussion of psychosexual dysfunctions we have emphasized the multiplicity of causes of sexual problems, the need for a careful evaluation of a person's sexual difficulties, and the innovative treatment approaches of direct sexual therapies which have proven so remarkably effective in treating psychosexual disorders.

In sharp contrast to the psychosexual dysfunctions which rarely provoke terribly negative reactions from others, the far rarer gender identity disorders and the paraphilias involve activities that are generally not accepted or viewed with tolerance by the majority of people in our society. Indeed, individuals with these psychosexual disorders often encounter reactions of disgust, surprise, and anger when their "different" behavior becomes known to others. Let us now turn our attention to transsexualism, a puzzling, yet intriguing gender identity disorder.

TRANSSEXUALISM: A GENDER IDENTITY DISORDER

Description

The patient appears to be a beautiful woman. None of Martha K.'s friends in the fashion world suspect that "she" is actually a biologically normal male. "She" has worked as a highly successful fashion model for many years, unrecognized by anyone in society as not being a normal woman. But as far back as Martha K.'s memory goes, "she" recalls being feminine and wishing "she" were biologically female. "Her" mother confirms this and says that she never saw masculine behavior in her son. She says they were extremely close and loving but that his father was never present. She never dressed the boy in woman's clothing but was surprised and pleased that her son at age two was already dressing up in girls' clothes and putting on makeup. The patient hates "her" male body, wants it changed to female, but does not deny it is male. "She" does not consider "herself" a homosexual but rather a biologically normal male with completely feminine desires. "She" has never had nor even fantasized sexual relations with a woman, getting no excitement from women's bodies but rather feeling the same casualness in regard to them that a heterosexual woman does. Martha K. is very hopeful that the examining psychologists, psychiatrists, and surgeons will grant her request to undergo a sex change operation (Adapted from Stoller, 1971, p. 233).

It is estimated that about 2,500 persons have undergone sex change operations in order to "make their bodies more like their minds." Benjamin (1966) captures the most characteristic attribute of the male transsexual: "The transsexual feels himself to be a woman trapped in a man's body" (p. 16). This feeling can cause great discomfort and result in severe complications for the transsexual who literally feels like a person of the opposite sex and may attempt to live out that role. As you might imagine, social and occupational problems often result. Severe depression, suicide attempts, and even rare instances of genital mutilation have been reported (DSM III).

Gender Identity Disorder of Childhood: The Development of Atypical Gender Behavior

Martha K.'s experience is typical of transsexuals in that the incongruence between anatomic sex and gender identity (a person's self-concept as a man or woman) begins in early childhood. Richard Green, a researcher whose primary interest is atypical sex role development in children, has attempted to trace the development of atypical sex role behavior.

In order to better understand the acquisition of atypical sex role behavior, Green (1974) has collected detailed information on 50 young boys who show an unusually high degree of feminine behavior but who have normal male anatomy. These children had begun cross-dressing (dressing in clothes typical of the opposite sex) before their sixth birthday and typically have very poor relationships with other boys, but relate to girls. Frequently in their cross-dressing they improvise dresses, jewelry and use nail polish or rouge. They are aware that they are males but wish to be females. They hope eventually to become women rather than men and, when given various projective tests, tend to identify feminine objects and themes. If asked to draw a person, these boys will more often draw girls than boys.

Green has studied the case histories of hundreds of these children, and he argues that no simple explanation of their atypical sex role development is possible. But one can trace a developmental portrait that is typical of these boys.

Usually the mothers of these children believe them to be unusually attractive as infants and devote considerable attention to them. Typically they channel much of their feelings of love and care to the infant. As the child begins to explore his environment he may—as do all children—begin to play with his mother's shoes and cosmetics. Both parents respond positively to the behavior and give him considerable attention for "play acting" of this sort. Often the father perceives the cross-dressing behavior as "cute," but otherwise interacts very little with the child. Later, according to Green, when the father invites the child to play more culturally "masculine" games, the child will display little interest. The father then feels rejected and withdraws still further. By the time the boy starts school, he shows very little assertive behavior, relates poorly to his male schoolmates, and continues to cross-dress at home. The mother continues to regard the behavior as cute, while the father withdraws from the child. By this time, the father frequently feels anxious about the child's atypical behavior and apparently feminine attributes. But still, both father and mother tend to regard the behavior as "only a passing phase." Usually by the time the child is seven, his peers have rejected him and the parents become distressed at the child's unhappiness. They may then consult a mental health professional for an opinion of the child's adjustment.

These young children, according to Green, frequently wish to have sex change operations later in life. They tend to be very unhappy, partly because of the ostracism they feel from their peers and partly because they deeply believe that they are psychologically women, even though anatomically they remain males.

There are many similarities in the backgrounds of male and female

Pictured here in 1960, James Morris was a highly regarded British foreign correspondent and journalist. After fathering five children, he remained convinced that he really should be a woman.

After a sex change operation in 1972, James changed his name to Jan and is now living as a woman. She told the story of her sex change in a moving autobiography entitled *"Conundrum"* (1974).

transsexuals. In the backgrounds of both groups, early parental reinforcement of opposite sex appropriate behavior is common, along with few consistent and effective rewards for sex-role stereotyped behavior (Bentler, 1976). As we have seen in the case of male transsexuals, maternal figures actively encourage opposite sex role behavior, and fathers tend to be nonnurturant, weak, or physically absent from the household. In females, mothers are similarly distant or unavailable and the girl seems to compensate by identifying with her father. Such identification is seen as playing a role in the ultimate adoption of a male gender identity.

The early learning experiences described by Green probably do not account for all transsexual behavior in later life. The life histories of some transsexuals do not seem to fit Green's developmental portrait. Some researchers have wondered whether prenatal exposure of the brain to hormones of the wrong gender may cause transsexualism. However, at present, there is little direct evidence to support this hypothesis.

No one explanation can explain every case of transsexualism. But in both sexes, the complete transsexual pattern usually develops by the middle to late twenties. In adulthood, transsexuals are likely to seek employment in jobs that are consistent with their masculine or feminine identification.

One of the puzzles of transsexualism is why there are so many more male than female transsexuals. The rate of males to females requesting sex change operations varies from 2:1 to 8:1. Green notes that, in our culture, girls who engage in male sex role behavior—"tomboys"—are tolerated and even encouraged. Boys who engage in female sex role behavior, on the contrary, may suffer ridicule and are often rejected by playmates and adults. The greater acceptance of female "cross-gender behavior" may account, in part, for the greater number of male than female transsexuals.

A Typology of Transsexualism

Despite similarities in the backgrounds of transsexuals, groups of transsexuals have been identified which differ from each other in notable respects. Bentler (1976) has developed a typology of transsexualism which acknowledges the heterogeneous nature of this condition and has been adopted by the DSM III classification system. Three major groups of transsexuals are distinguished according to sexual preference. They are termed asexual, homosexual, and heterosexual. Asexual transsexuals deny having ever experienced strong sexual feelings. The homosexual group reports a preference for like-sexed individuals prior to the onset of the full pattern of sexual

SEX CHANGE OPERATION AND THE PSYCHOLOGICAL ADJUSTMENT OF THE TRANSSEXUAL

Since the first sex-change operation was performed more than 30 years ago, hormone therapy and surgical procedures have helped certain transsexuals achieve their goal of "changing their bodies to fit their minds" (Haberle, 1978). The process of "sex change" is gradual and begins with hormone therapy. In males, the hormones stimulate loss of facial hair and growth of breasts; in women, the hormones encourage the development of masculine characteristics. Many clinics and university medical school settings where sexual reassignment surgery is typically performed require that the transsexual successfully live in the role of a member of the opposite sex for six months to one year prior to surgery. To surgically effect a "sex change" in males, the penis and scrotum may be transformed into a vagina, and in women, an artificial phallus may be implanted.

We may think of the desire for a "sex change" operation as unusual or even bizarre, but there is little evidence that the majority of transsexuals who apply for sexual reassignment surgery are psychotic or grossly disturbed. A study by Roback, Strassberg, McKee, & Cunningham (1977) found that 16 of 25 anatomical males seeking sexual reassignment surgery did not show signs of severe psychological disturbance on a self-report personality inventory. In a later study, by the same research group using the same research instrument, considerable variation in self-concept and adjustment were found in a group of 17 female transsexuals applying for sex change operations (Strassberg, Roback, Cunningham, & McKee, 1980). The finding that more than half of the applicants for sex change surgery were not seriously disturbed further suggests that severe disordered thinking or psychosis can not account for transsexual behavior patterns. Both of these studies did, however, find that the transsexuals studied were less well adjusted than the samples of homosexuals and normals with which they were compared.

The assumption that underlies performing sexual reassignment surgery is that the transsexual will be more content and generally better adjusted following the sex change. But this assumption has recently been challenged by a study by Jon Meyer and D. Reter (1979) at Johns Hopkins University Hospital. Prompted by the observation that most transsexuals over the age of 30 tend to adopt alternative life-styles (living in the role of a man or woman) rather than seek sex change operations, Meyer and Reter followed up patients who had undergone sex-change operations and compared their adjustment with transsexuals who did not seek sexual reassignment surgery. Using a number of adjustment indicators, such as psychiatric status, job placement, marital success, and police records, the researchers concluded that the long-term adjustment of transsexuals who underwent sex-change operations was no better than that of transsexuals who lived alternate life-styles and did not undergo surgery.

The findings of Meyer and Reter's study so impressed doctors at Johns Hopkins Hospital that they decided to discontinue the practice of performing sex-change operations on transsexuals. But will the results of Meyer's study signal the demise of sexual reassignment surgery for all transsexuals who seek it? Probably not. Transsexuals, like other individuals with unconventional sexual behavior patterns, differ from each other in many important respects. Some transsexuals may not derive long-term benefits from sexual reassignment surgery, but others may indeed profit from surgical procedures. Meyer and Reter's findings do, however, underscore an important point: A thorough evaluation of the appropriateness of sex-change operations for applicants is crucial, along with carefully weighing the pros and cons of alternatives to surgery before irreversible "corrective" surgery is performed. Additional studies of transsexuals are needed to better predict which individuals are likely to profit from sex-change operations. But until the weight of evidence suggests that all types of transsexuals are likely to benefit from sex-change operations, many transsexuals who desperately seek sex-change operations will continue to find doctors who agree to perform sexual reassignment surgery.

identification. However, they do not view their behavior as homosexual. This stems from their conviction that they are "really" of the other sex. The heterosexual group reports a history of active heterosexual involvement.

UNCONVENTIONAL CHOICE OF SEXUAL OBJECT OR ACTIVITY: THE PARAPHILIAS

Let us now turn our attention to the paraphilias. DSM III defines the essential features of the paraphilias as involving "persistent and repetitive sexually arousing fantasies, frequently of an unusual nature that are associated with either (1) preference for use of a nonhuman object for sexual arousal, (2) repetitive sexual activity with humans involving real or simulated suffering or humiliation, or (3) repetitive sexual activity with nonconsenting partners" (DSM III, p. 266).

It is clear from the above definition that paraphiliac behavior may be harmful to others, may involve nonconsenting partners, or may include other activities that are at variance with community norms for appropriate behavior. When sexual fantasy and behavior is not only compulsive but leads to brutality and violence, it is particularly likely to be regarded as deviant, to be socially condemned, and to be subject to severe legal punishment. Engaging in sexual relations with children (pedophilia), for example, can be punished as a serious violent crime, whereas exposing one's genitals to a stranger (exhibitionism) is generally regarded as a mere nuisance by legal authorities. Thus, the paraphilias are of legal as well as psychological significance. And both social and legal reaction may vary depending upon the nature of the sexual object or the activity involved.

As DSM III points out, many persons with these disorders do not perceive themselves as dangerous or as suffering from a mental disorder. Thus, they may

THE PARAPHILIAS: SOME CAUTIONARY NOTES

When you read about the paraphilias, it is important to keep a number of things in mind. First, there is a tremendous diversity in personal attributes, life experiences, and personality characteristics of individuals with an identical paraphilia. Two individuals with the same diagnosis may differ from each other in very significant ways. Indeed, the only commonality they share may be the behavior pattern that qualifies them for a common diagnosis. This suggests that caution should be exercised with regard to making global judgments about a person based only on a knowledge of his or her sexual behavior.

Using a label such as *exhibitionist* to describe a person, without keeping in mind the true complexity of the individual, may exaggerate the person's differences from others who do not share the label. It is also important for us to keep in mind that the sex life of most persons is rarely limited to one type of behavior or mode of expression but consists of various combinations of activities at various times (Katchadourian & Lunde, 1972).

A final point to remember is that behaviors that might signify a disorder, such as voyeurism, exhibitionism, sadism, or masochism, are common in less extreme or obvious forms in normal heterosexual experience. A theme which recurs through the chapter is that there are many shades and gradations of different types of unconventional sexual behavior. The point at which a particular behavior pattern might be thought of as an "accepted variation" or "normal" sexual behavior and the point at which it might be considered a disorder is somewhat arbitrary and in part dependent upon the values and attitudes of those judging the behavior.

only come to the attention of the medical profession and legal authorities when their behavior has brought them into conflict with society. Since the paraphilias may never come to public attention, reliable estimates of their prevalence are difficult to obtain. But it is likely that persons suffering from one or more paraphilia constitute only a tiny fraction of the general population. As in the case of fetishism, which we will next consider, the paraphilias appear to be far rarer in females than in males.

The mere sight of a shoe may be highly arousing for a shoe fetishist.

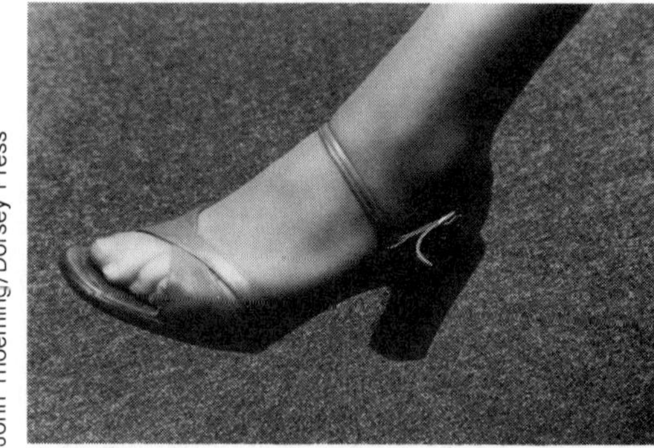

John Thoeming/Dorsey Press

Fetishism

> I can remember an interest in women's shoes as early as my fourth year. . . . When I was 12 years old I was attracted to my sister's shoes. I used to wait for her to sit at the table. I had a strong urge to get under the table. I would pretend to drop something to get under it. I was interested only in her shoes . . . At about age 25, when I would sit opposite of a woman I would concentrate on her shoes and legs. In the earlier stages of this practice I would masturbate through my pocket, concealing this by holding a newspaper over my crossed legs. At a later stage . . . the effect of looking at shoes and legs being enough in itself to produce orgasm . . . I have had only one experience with a girl when the shoe was not needed to make intercourse satisfying. (Adapted from a case study by Grant, 1958, pp. 142–143.)

As can be seen in the case study, fetishism involves the use of an object such as a shoe or an article of clothing to obtain sexual arousal. In partialism, physical attributes or parts of the body assume fetishistic qualities. There are many shades and gradations of fetishistic tendencies. Gebhard (1969) defines a range of fetishistic preferences and behaviors. At one end there exists a mild preference for the fetish. Certain clothes such as high heels, for example, may be especially alluring. A preference for a man with a hairy chest or a woman with large breasts is certainly common and not at all abnormal.

More extreme fetishistic tendencies are evident where Gebhard believes "statistical normalcy ends and fetishism begins." Gebhard illustrates: "This is nicely exemplified by one man who had his first recognition of his own fetishism when he realized he had ignored a beautiful girl to court a plain girl with a particular hair style. The next stage, that of necessity, would be the case of a man who is impotent unless his partner wears a certain type of shoe. The ultimate stage is the man who habitually dispenses with the female and achieves orgasm with only the shoe" (p. 3).

According to DSM III, in true fetishism, the fetish is used as the preferred or exclusive means of obtaining sexual arousal. The object may be incorporated in masturbatory fantasies or activities. A boot, for example, may be touched or fondled. The mere sight of the preferred item may be sufficient to produce an orgasm. Fetishism is much rarer in females than males.

Some commonly chosen items include high-heeled shoes and boots, garter belts, black mesh stocking, and corsets. Gebhard reports that when corset fetishism was common, men paid to look through peepholes at customers trying on corsets at certain shops. Fetishists have been known to steal lingerie items from clotheslines. Collecting fetishistic items can be a favored pastime, even a preoccupation with the fetishist.

For some people with a fetishistic orientation, the material of which the item is made can be a potent source of sexual excitement. For example, the fact that a shoe or glove is made of leather can be even more important than the form of the object. Rubber, plastic, and fur are other common examples.

Little is known about the development of fetishistic tendencies. The onset of fetishism is typically in puberty or adolescence. The preferred object is often associated with a maternal figure or school teacher who provided nurturance and love or was the focus of sexual fantasies during childhood (Caprio, 1973). It has been suggested that the fetish represents, on a symbolic level, a loved or sexually desired person. Unrewarding relationships which are perceived as threatening may also contribute to reliance on objects as a primary source of sexual gratification.

We should note that in DSM III fetishism is distinguished from transvestism, where the fetishistic objects are limited to female clothing used in cross-dressing. Prince (1972) found that only 13 percent of 504 transvestites surveyed reported fetishistic excitement.

Incest and Sexual Exploitation of Children

Sexual exploitation of children has been defined as the involvement of dependent, developmentally immature children and adolescents in sexual activities that they do not fully understand, are unable to give informed consent to, and that violate the social taboos of family roles (Schecter & Roberge, 1976). Sexual activities are not necessarily limited to intercourse. They can include touching the child's genitals or breasts and inducing the child to touch the genitals of the adult. Adults outside the family may sexually exploit children. The term incest, however, is usually taken to mean sexual behavior between members of the same kinship. Let us examine a number of cases of incest and sexual exploitation of children who were seen at a child-serving mental health facility (Slager-Jorné, 1978).

A 13-year-old girl experienced sexual

intercourse at an early age with both her natural father and her stepfather. Presenting problem: evoking seductive responses from strange men.

A 15-year-old girl had sexual relations with her father for several years. The father had sexual relationships with all his sons and daughters. Presenting problem: fainting spells, hysteria.

A four-year-old boy had been sexually abused by his 14-year-old sister. Presenting problem: very aggressive sexually with women and exposing himself.

A 13-year-old girl was raped at age 8 by her minister and later by her brother. Presenting problem: preoccupation with sex and talking constantly about it.

Brief descriptions such as these tend to raise more questions that they answer. One wonders how frequently these kinds of incidents occur. What are the characteristics of individuals who are involved in such activities? What is the nature of the families in which these behaviors occur? What are the consequences of incest and sexual exploitation of children?

Incidence. Unfortunately there are many barriers to obtaining reliable information regarding the problem and estimates of its incidence. Historically the practice of incest has been viewed with disgust, revulsion, and contempt by members of virtually all cultures. Today, violations of the incest taboo, and more generally sexual exploitation of children, continues to be viewed as extremely deviant behavior.

In addition, there are strong religious, moral, and legal sanctions against expressing sexual impulses toward children. Although our legal system is not so harsh as the code of the Ta-ta-thi tribesmen of Australia who punish those who indulge in incest with painful death, legal and social prohibitions make it unlikely that the act will be reported. The child may be fearful of the consequences of reporting, less articulate than the adult, unaware of supportive resources, and may even be unaware that he or she was sexually abused (Swift, 1978).

One source of information comes from studies of the incidence of incest in psychiatric patients. For example, Lukianowicz (1972), working with an unselected population of 650 female psychiatric patients in northern Ireland, found that 4 percent of the females interviewed had been involved in incestuous relationships with their fathers in their childhood. In another group of 700 male and female outpatients, he found an additional 4 percent had experiences with incestuous relationships, excluding paternal incest. Recently, Densen-Gerber and Benward (1976) conducted a detailed study of drug abusing males and females. They found a surprisingly high overall incest rate of 35 percent. Another interesting finding was that the problem did not appear to be limited to any particular race, region of the country, religion, or social class.

Although the actual incidence of incest is not known, it is likely that the true incidence of incest is far greater than many estimates. In addition, instances of sexual exploitation involving strangers are more likely to be reported than those involving family members or friends. The occurrence of some form of child sexual exploitation may be as high as 15 percent of all children (Boekelheide, 1978).

Many cases of child sexual exploitation occur in and around the home. The child has some acquaintance with the offender about 80 percent of the time. In approximately 30 percent of the reported cases, the adult is a member of the child's household; in nearly 25 percent of the cases, the adult is a parent or parent substitute. Slager-Jorné (1978) reports that almost one half of the children are sexually exploited repeatedly over a period of time and 60 percent of the offenders use some form of threat or force. The offender is most likely to be male. In the great majority of cases, the victim is a girl. About ten cases of father-daughter incest are reported for each mother-son case.

Family dynamics. In order to better understand the phenomenon of child sexual exploitation, it is necessary to learn something about the characteristics of the participants involved and the family dynamics in which the problem is enmeshed. Perhaps the most attention has been devoted to studying the fathers in cases of father-daughter incest. Weinberg (1955) has distinguished three groups of incestuous fathers: the first, where incest is part of a pattern of indiscriminate sexuality and the father views his wife and children as objects and is unable to develop warm, tender relationships; the second, where an intense craving for young children may involve seduction of his own daughter and other children; and the third, where the father has an introverted personality and chooses a daughter because of limited contacts outside of the family.

The mother may also play an important role in cases of father-daughter incest (Guthiel & Avery, 1977; Lewis & Sarrel, 1969). Slager-Jorné (1978) describes the mother as depressed, isolated, and withdrawn, with feelings of inadequacy as a mother and wife. The child may become a "replacement" for the mother who may feel overburdened by her sexual and household role. Thus the mother may set the stage for the incestuous alliance. Marital conflict, inadequate supervision of children, financial stress, and a parental history of similar abuse may also be contributing factors.

Psychological consequences. Although the entire family may be implicated in instances of incest, evidence suggests that the consequences of incest and child sexual exploitation are most severe for the victim. Lukianowicz (1972) concluded that only 23 percent of the females involved in incestuous relationships showed no apparent adverse effects. Initially, a child may react with guilt, anxiety, fear, or anger. Guilt may stem from the child enjoying the sexual stimulation, believing that something bad will happen to the seducer, or imagining being responsible for the incident.

The closer the relationship between the child and the adult, and the longer the victimization continues over time, the greater likelihood of psychological problems in later life (Swift, 1978). In many cases, negative aftereffects can be attributed to extreme reactions on the part of adults, who communicate to the child their own belief that irreparable damage has been done.

Pedophilia: a special case. Pedophilia, which means literally, love of children, is characterized by preference for repetitive sexual activity with prepubertal children (DSM III). It is important to distinguish the pedophile from a person who engages in isolated instances of child sexual exploitation as a result of intense loneliness, marital conflict, or the recent loss of a loved one. In pedophilia the person *prefers* to have a sexual relationship with a child rather than an adult.

The common stereotype of the pedophile as a "dirty old man" who molests children who are strangers to him after enticing them with candy, rarely mirrors reality. Actually, in about 85 percent of the cases, the child is known to the adult who lives or works in close proximity to the child. Also, the offender is most likely to be married and in the 20–40 age range.

Some evidence suggests that pedophiles tend to be religious, moralistic, and socially and sexually immature (Walters, 1975). Presumably, they compensate for their feelings of inadequacy by choosing less threatening sexual partners—children. Most often pedophiles look at or touch the genitals of the child; intercourse is rare. The victim is most typically an eight–ten-year old girl.

There are both heterosexual and homosexual pedophiles. However, there appear to be about twice as many heterosexual pedophiles. The average homosexual is no more likely to seduce children than the average heterosexual man. Mohr and Turner (1964) note that the homosexual pedophiliac is a "double deviant." His actions are neither accepted by the heterosexual society in which he lives nor by other homosexuals.

UNCONVENTIONAL CHOICES OF SEXUAL ACTIVITY

Voyeurism

Looking at naked or partially clothed bodies is sexually exciting for many men and women. The commercial success of magazines such as *Playboy* and the recent popularity of magazines catering to women that feature photographs of nude men attests to the widespread appeal of looking at the naked or partially clothed body. These activities, clearly well within the range of normal sexual interest and activity, can be easily distinguished from those of the voyeur described in the following example.

> Beginning at age 16, the patient went into his neighborhood and looked into windows to observe naked women. At age 20, he married but continued to spend at least one hour a night peering into windows on nights when he didn't have intercourse with his wife. He was primarily interested in seeing women's breasts and occasionally enjoyed watching a woman have intercourse. When he observed these forbidden scenes, he usually masturbated, but sometimes would wait to masturbate, fantasizing about what he had seen. He eventually came to enjoy "peeping" more than sexual relations with his wife. The patient was arrested at age 22 and referred for psychological counseling as a condition of his probation.

The voyeur obtains sexual excitement by looking or "peeping" at unsuspecting women who are either naked, in the act of disrobing, or engaging in sexual activity. He is likely to repeatedly seek out situations where it is possible for him to do this. Like exhibitionism, which we will describe below, these actions are not a prelude for further sexual activity and direct sexual contact is not desired. It is not entirely clear why this behavior is sexually exciting for the voyeur. At least part of the excitement may come from the forbidden and dangerous nature of the activity and the knowledge that the person would be embarrassed or humiliated if she were aware she was observed. Support for this idea comes from the observation that the true voyeur is not stimulated by "peeping" at his own wife or sexual partner. As in the case of the person in our example, masturbation while observing or in response to the memory of the stranger is common. In severe cases, the voyeur may prefer peeping to the exclusion of other sexual activities.

The adult voyeur rarely partakes in this activity with another person. He may wait for hours to observe a woman undress and frequently returns to a number of favored places "like an ardent fisherman" (Gebhard, Gagnon, Pomeroy & Christenson, 1965). He is likely to come to the attention of police when neighbors or passersby report his actions. Occasionally, the voyeur may be shot at, mistaken for a burglar, or injure himself falling off a roof or window ledge.

The voyeur is likely to be of normal intelligence, young (average age of first sex offense 22.5), and neither an alcohol or drug abuser, and the person is unlikely to have serious emotional problems. Gebhard et. al's study of peepers (1965) showed that although they are prone to serious antisocial behavior, they are likely to be involved in minor criminality. Only about 20 percent of the offenses involved force, indicating that, as a group, voyeurs are unlikely to be dangerous. Most often, peepers are charged with disorderly conduct. More dangerous voyeurs are likely to enter a building or home in order to observe a woman or draw the attention of the person to the fact that he is watching (Yalom, 1960).

Little of substance is known about the determinants of voyeurism. In psychoanalytic thinking, voyeurism is viewed as related to the primal scene: the child observing the parents having intercourse. Observing individuals making love is interpreted as an attempt to return to the primal scene and gain mastery over it. Unfortunately there is little evidence to support such speculation.

Exhibitionism

The stereotyped view of the exhibitionist is that he is a lecherous, older man who jumps out of bushes and opens his raincoat to expose himself to a terrified woman. Actually exhibitionists tend to be passive and rather young, ranging in age from about 14 to 38. The onset of exhibitionism occurs most frequently in midpuberty and the early twenties. When their sexual behavior is compared with others in terms of frequency of intercourse, number of sexual partners, and age at first intercourse, exhibitionists fall well below the norm (McWhorter, 1978).

Far from being a dangerous criminal, the typical exhibitionist is likely to more closely resemble a respectable average citizen who may even be married and have children. Characteristics attributed to exhibitionists include compulsive tendencies, sensitivity to criticism, low frustration tolerance, and insecurity in social relations. Marital conflict and poor sexual adjustment also have been reported.

The exhibitionist most notably differs from the average man in the way in which sexual excitement is obtained. For the exhibitionist sexual arousal results directly from exposing his genitals to women or children. Almost invariably, the victim is an unconsenting stranger. Physical contact rarely occurs and conversation is initiated only to attract the victim's attention. Most typically exposure takes place in a public place such as a subway, bus, or a park where the exhibitionist may pretend he is urinating.

The compulsive nature of the exhibitionistic act is underscored by the fact that the exhibitionist risks apprehension by exposing himself in highly public places. The act of exposure is not intended as a prelude to further sexual advances. In fact, the exhibitionist is likely to run away if a female observer responds with interest. Sexual excitement can be immediate or it can occur shortly after the incident.

Depression, anxiety, or stress may trigger an exposure in some exhibitionists. Others report a sudden, irresistible urge to expose themselves with no identifiable precipitants. Some exhibitionists report that they were suffering from temporary amnesia and were curiously detached from their actions at the time of exposure. However, such claims may just as easily be seen as denial of responsibility for an act that provokes guilt and shame when the person is identified or apprehended.

One thing is clear, however, the intent of the exhibitionistic act is to evoke a reaction of surprise, embarrassment, or shock from the victim. The victim's strong reaction may bolster the exhibitor's fragile sense of masculinity. This interpretation is supported by clinical observations that threats to masculine self-esteem often precede exposures. The attention displayed by the victim, the reaction of horror, admiration, or awe may strongly reinforce the deviant behavior, increasing the likelihood of future recurrence. For the person lacking in social skills who feels insecure in social relationships, the act of exposure may be a potent, yet inappropriate way of obtaining recognition from others. Even the prospect of apprehension by the police may be exciting and reinforce a sense of power and masculinity for posing such a threat (Mathis, 1969).

A learning theory explanation of the development of exhibitionism and other paraphilias, underscores the importance of sexual fantasies. McGuire, Carlisle, and Young (1965) noted that more than three quarters of a sample of patients with various paraphilias reported the use of a "deviant" fantasy while masturbating. They reasoned that exhibitionistic behavior and other unconventional sexual activities might be reinforced through masturbatory activity. An initial exhibitionistic act may supply the person with a fantasy which may be used during masturbation. Using the fantasy repeatedly during masturbation may reinforce the fantasy *and* the exhibitionistic behavior as a source of sexual arousal. Jackson (1969) successfully treated exhibitionists by having them substitute fantasies of more appropriate content for exhibitionistic fantasies. Maletzky (1974) used a foul smelling substance which was presented to the client as exhibitionistic images were imagined to reduce exhibitionistic behavior. The fact that "deviant" fantasies may be initially tied to unconventional sexual behavior may account, in part, for the success of using such fantasies as the target of behavioral treatments like the one's just described.

Exhibitionism is usually regarded by law enforcement agents as more of a nuisance than a dangerous threat. However, exhibitionism accounts for nearly a third of all arrests for sex related offenses. In addition, nearly 20 percent of exhibitionists are rearrested, the highest rate for sex offenders. Most offenders receive suspended sentences and are placed on probation and urged to seek counseling.

Cases of adolescents who expose themselves on a dare, adults under considerable stress who expose themselves only on a single occasion, and temporal lobe epileptics whose seizure behavior may be mistaken for exhibitionism, should probably be

Societal values differ for male and female bodily exposure.

Jan Lukas/Rapho-Photo Researchers, Inc.

considered separately from the compulsive exhibitionist.

Our society clearly has different values relating to male and female bodily exposure. Women can attract attention and even admiring recognition by wearing revealing clothes. The woman who exposes her body and earns a living by dancing nude on a stage may be considered to be exhibitionistic, but not an exhibitionist. Perhaps there are virtually no reports of compulsive female exhibitionism because society provides women with considerably greater latitude in dress than males.

Our societal attitudes regarding exhibitionistic behavior in men and women are also mirrored in our legal system which clearly favors the woman. Consider the case in which a man observes a woman undressing in front of an open window. The man is the offender (a voyeur), the woman the victim. However, if the roles are reversed and the woman observes the man undressing, she would again be the victim and the male an exhibitionist.

Transvestism

> The patient, in his 30s, is married, the father of three children, and a precision machine operator. His first experience in cross-dressing (dressing in the clothes of the opposite sex) is remembered as a tremendously exciting sexual experience in which, as punishment, an aunt forced him to cross-dress at age 7. While he has no conscious memory of it, however, he has learned that he was first cross-dressed by another aunt at age 4. From puberty on, sexual excitement was invariably and intensely induced by putting on women's shoes, and, as the years passed, this gradually progressed so that with each episode of cross-dressing he now dresses completely as a woman and with proper makeup to hide his beard, passed in society for a few hours at a time. He has never had a homosexual relationship and has no sexual interest in female bodies, but though looking excites him, lying next to a woman is more complicated: he can then only maintain full potency either by putting on women's garments or fantasizing that he has them on (Stoller, 1971, p. 231).

This case provides an excellent illustration of *transvestism.* The transvestite obtains intense sexual arousal by dressing

Two male transvestites in "drag."

Charles Gatewood/Magnum Photos, Inc.

in the clothing of a woman. This pattern of receiving sexual pleasure by cross-dressing may be so habitual and persistent that interference with it can result in intense frustration (DSM II).

As well as representing a source of sexual gratification, cross-dressing may reduce anxiety. Some transvestites tend to cross-dress when they are under stress, and it has been hypothesized that this behavior serves as a comforting retreat from the tensions of everyday life. Curiously, there are almost no reports of transvestism in females. While cross-dressing among women is certainly not unknown, it does not appear to be accompanied by sexual arousal.

Although cross-dressing does suggest that the transvestite has a "feminine side" to his personality, he is generally not effeminate. Transvestites firmly identify themselves as males. Like the patient in our example, most transvestites are family men, who are married with children and work in traditionally male occupations. When not cross-dressed, the transvestite resembles other men in mannerisms and appearance.

Some reports also suggest that transvestites feel inadequate in heterosexual relationships and fear potential rejection. Some may use marriage as a means of bolstering their masculine self-concept. Marriage, however, is often experienced as stressful and is unsuccessful in eliminating compulsive cross-dressing (Bentler, 1976).

It is very important not to confuse transvestites with homosexuals. Confusion can result because a small number of homosexuals do cross-dress on occasion. The homosexual's feminine masquerade is designed to attract another male or to disguise themselves in a theatrical manner as a woman. However, unlike the transvestite, homosexuals do not experience sexual excitement from wearing female clothing. In addition, the overwhelming majority of transvestites have a clear preference for women over males as sexual partners.

Many transvestites are initially sexually excited by one or a few preferred articles of feminine clothing. Lingerie items such as panties and nightgowns are reported to be especially attractive. Some transvestites begin dressing in complete feminine attire and persist with this pattern throughout their lives. Most commonly, more and more articles of clothing are adopted until a complete feminine costume is preferred.

The power of the woman's garment as a sexual stimulus is underscored by the fact that erectile failure may result when clothing is not worn or fantasized during intercourse by transvestites. About one fifth of the wives of transvestites never learn that their husbands cross-dress. Marital complications such as divorce can arise when the wife is aware of and intolerant of her husband's unusual behavior.

The development of transvestism is quite puzzling. The onset is almost invariably in childhood or early adolescence. Observations of transvestites and their families suggest that parents, particularly mothers, may actively encourage and praise the child for dressing in his mother's clothes. Perhaps you noticed that the patient in the case history was forced by his aunt to cross-dress as punishment. Such punishment by a maternal figure is common in the backgrounds of transvestites. Humiliation engendered in this fashion has been cited as a predisposing factor in the development of transvestism. It is not clear, however, exactly how this experience contributes to the later development of cross-dressing.

Sadomasochism

The intermingling of sex and aggression is deeply embedded in our culture. A blend of sex and violence is portrayed in movies and artfully packed in advertisements. Indeed, it is tempting to speculate that the public interest in violence and aggression serves deep-seated sexual needs. Certainly, sexual fantasies that combine sex and aggression are not uncommon. About one in eight females and one in five males studied at the Institute for Sex Research reported being sexually aroused by stories in which the main character either inflicts pain on another or is humiliated and endures personal pain in a sexual context.

Few individuals, however, *prefer* to obtain sexual arousal through giving or receiving physical or psychological pain. The psychosexual patterns in which there is a conjoining of sex, pain, and aggression are termed *sexual sadism* and *sexual masochism.* The consolidated term *sadomasochism* is frequently used since sadism and masochism are often thought of as mirror images of the same phenomenon.

According to the DSM III, the central feature of sexual sadism is physical or psychological suffering inflicted on another person. For the sadist, inflicting suffering is necessary to produce sexual excitement. In contrast the masochist derives sexual pleasure from experiencing suffering. Some masochists find pleasure in being humiliated, bound, beaten, or placed in elaborate restraints. The sadist may enjoy the reverse role: humiliating, degrading, or injuring another as a preferred way of achieving sexual excitement.

Unless they are acted out, sadistic or masochistic fantasies are not sufficient for diagnosing sexual sadism or masochism. In fact, the overwhelming majority of people with sadomasochistic tendencies never act out their fantasies. One important outlet for sadomasochistic impulses is reading "trade magazines" that feature pictures of women dressed in leather and high heeled shoes who dominate, restrain, and torture their "victims" with whips, chains, gags, and ropes.

Sadomasochistic behaviors vary in their degree and intensity. The mildest forms that may accompany intercourse probably should not be regarded as truly sadomasochistic (Levitt, 1971). In fact, in some societies, aggressive behavior and inflicting pain on one's partner are part of normal love play. Women on the island of Truk customarily poke a finger into the man's ear when they are sexually excited. Charotic women spit into their partner's face during intercourse, and the Arpinage woman may bite off her lover's eyebrows and noisily spit them to one side (Ford & Beach, 1954).

Surprisingly few sadomasochists actively seek situations in which extreme pain is involved. The situational context in which the sadomasochistic drama is enacted is perhaps more important than the pain itself. The sadomasochistic session usually follows a "script." The masochist must have transgressed or done something worthy of punishment; threats and suspense precede the punishment. The sadist must be sensitive to the amount of pain that the masochist desires and can tolerate or risk losing a partner. Intermixing love and tenderness with pain and punishment seems to add to the sexual tension and the power of the ritual. The script may be somewhat altered for masochists who prefer bondage. Here, stimulation is derived not from pain but from a sense of helplessness, constraint, and discomfort. Fetishistic paraphenalia such as leather clothing, whips, black stockings, garter belts, and restraining devices may be part of the drama and heighten sexual arousal. Pain, punishment, or bondage may be experienced before, during, or after a sexual act (Gebhard, 1969).

A recent study by Spengler (1976) provides us with a closer look at the characteristics and experiences of the heterosexual and homosexual sadomasochist. Answering contact ads in "trade" magazines and partly with the help of sadomasochistic clubs, Spengler was able to survey 245 German males. Although the sample represented only sadomasochists who were searching for a partner through use of the communications media, the results were of some interest. Spengler found that few men were exclusively sadistic or masochistic. Most sadomasochists enacted both roles in order to accommodate to different partners. Since sadists are far rarer than masochists, role trading is a virtual necessity. When two masochists meet, necessity dictates that they take turns at the sadist role. Spengler also found that nearly half of the men surveyed achieved sexual satisfaction without sadomasochistic experiences. In fact, only about 15 percent experienced sexual excitement exclusively in connection with sadomasochistic activites.

In addition, despite the use of contact ads, about 10 percent of those surveyed were never able to make contact with a similarly inclined partner. The crucial variable determining whether a sadomasochistic relationship would be realized was sexual orientation. There were substantially more available partners in the homosexual group of males. Here, each man could be partner to any other. However, sadistically inclined women are extremely rare and most or all of these women were prostitutes. As one might expect, in the heterosexual group, there was a greater reliance on prostitutes. A larger percentage of men in this group never achieved a sadomasochistic relationship.

A high level of adjustment and self-acceptance was expressed by the majority of the respondents. Only 10 percent of those surveyed required professional help with regard to their sadomasochistic orientation. Very few reported a past suicide attempt. Most of the participants expressed positive attitudes toward their sexual orientation, with only 20 percent preferring to have "no sadomasochistic desires." These results may present an unusually favorable picture of the sadomasochist because the respondents tended to be males who were well educated, held responsible jobs, and enjoyed high social status.

HOMOSEXUALITY

> Homosexuality is assuredly no advantage, but it is nothing to be ashamed of, no vice, no degradation. It cannot be considered an illness; we consider it to be a variation of the sexual functions produced by a certain arrest of sexual development (Freud, 1935).

> I dare to speak out as a mother—as an American—as a Christian, I urgently need you to join with me and my family in a national crusade against this attack on God and His laws. It's really God's battle, not mine (Anita Bryant, speaking about homosexuality, quoted by McNaught, 1977, p. 34).

> Since I've joined the Gay Liberation Movement . . . I've come to an unshakable conclusion: the illness theory of homosexuality is a pack of lies concocted out of the fundamentalist myths of a patriarchial society for the *political* purpose of perpetuating the current societal ethic. Psychiatry, dedicated to making sick people well, is the cornerstone of a system of oppression that makes people sick (Ronald Gold, Chairman, News and Media Committee of the Gay Activities Alliance of New York, in a speech to the American Psychiatric Association, 1973, p. 1).

> The issue has to be decided on the basis of solid clinical and scientific evidence. The overwhelming bulk of data on hand, both clinical and scientific, show that homosexuality is the result of certain pathological patterns. This is not something to decide by popular vote (Dr. Harold Voth, comments after the American Psychiatric Association decision to remove homosexuality from its list of mental disorders, 1974).

Societal Reaction

Homosexuality is a topic that behavioral scientists are struggling to understand. Considerable disagreement persists about its fundamental nature and causes. Sterotypes and misconceptions concerning homosexuality abound both in the general public and in scientific circles. When many people picture a homosexual, they think of a person who is constantly preoccupied with sexual matters, promiscuous, a predator of young children, and unstable and mentally disturbed. It is likely that such thinking accounts for much of the fear, contempt, and distrust of homosexuals.

The findings of recent Gallup polls (1977) reflect pervasive negative feelings and attitudes concerning homosexuals. The results suggest that significant numbers of Americans would deny to the homosexual the right to be an elementary school teacher (65 percent), a member of the clergy (54 percent), a doctor (54 percent), or a member of the armed forces (38 percent). Only 43 percent of those sampled agreed that homosexual relations between consenting adults should be legal. Given such sentiments, it is not surprising that discrimination and withholding of civil rights from homosexuals is common.

At least some of the bias against homosexuality stems from the fact that homosexual life-styles are mysterious and alien to most people. A major new study by researchers at the Kinsey Institute for Sex Research (Bell & Weinberg, 1978) sheds light on the life-styles of a diverse sample of male and female homosexuals. The findings clearly contradict many myths and stereotypes of homosexuality. Coauthors of the study, Alan Bell and Martin Weinberg, contend that their research shows that homosexuals are as different from each other as heterosexuals, that homosexuality is not necessarily pathological, and that some homosexuals are happier, more stable, and better adjusted than heterosexuals as a whole.

The second "Kinsey report" is likely to spark as much controversy as the study reported by pioneer sex research Alfred Kinsey and his colleagues 30 years ago. Before we examine the recent findings reported by Bell and Weinberg, let us consider some of the results and implications of the now famous Kinsey study which preceded it.

The First Kinsey Report

Public furor followed Kinsey's startling revelations that homosexuality was far more widespread than previously believed. Perhaps the most surprising finding was that 37 percent of white American males had at least one homosexual experience leading to orgasm between adolescence and old age. Half of all males reported a homosexual encounter by age 55. Since many of the contacts reported were limited to sporadic experiences in adolescence, a more relevant, yet equally unexpected finding was that 10 percent of the sample was almost exclusively homosexual for at least three years between 16 and 55. In addition, about 4 percent of males reported exclusive homosexuality.

The incidence of homosexuality appeared to be considerably lower in females. Estimates vary, but percentages of males reporting homosexual behavior are consistently twice that of females (Cory & LeRoy, 1961; Kinsey, et al. 1953). Some researchers have suggested, however, that there may be as many female as male homosexuals, but women may be better able to conceal their homosexuality.

After Kinsey's monumental work,

scientists could no longer ignore the fact of homosexuality. Kinsey's efforts were also important because he helped to clarify and sharpen our thinking about homosexuality. Before the first Kinsey report, it was common practice to think of people as either homosexual or heterosexual. Kinsey discovered that people reported widely different amounts of homosexual experience. Some individuals appeared to be exclusively homosexual, while others experienced only a single homosexual contact in early adolescence. Kinsey contended that, "It would encourage clearer thinking on these matters if persons were not categorized as heterosexual or homosexual, but as individuals who have had certain amounts of heterosexual experience and certain amounts of homosexual experience" (quoted by Haberle, 1978, p. 230). Indeed, if we were to categorize as homosexual all persons with one homosexual experience, a sizeable number of males would fall into this category.

Alfred C. Kinsey: The famed and controversial sex researcher who founded the Institute for Sex Research.

Courtesy of the Institute for Sex Research, Inc., photo by Dellenback

In keeping with his view that homosexual and heterosexual behavior ranged along a continuum, Kinsey and his associates (1953) devised a seven-point scale which measured the balance of heterosexual and homosexual psychological reactions and overt experiences. This scale is illustrated in Figure 13–2.

A person's place on this continuum may change as a result of age and life circumstances (Bell, 1973). As Haberle (1978) observes, "There are men and women whose behavior is exclusively heterosexual at one time in their lives and exclusively homosexual at another time. Some engage in both types of behavior but with varying degrees of intensity. Others begin with an equal erotic interest in both sexes and only gradually develop a clear preference for one or the other" (p. 232).

People differ not only in terms of the extensiveness of their homosexual experience, but also in the way they think and feel about their homosexuality. Alan Bell (1973) noted that "it is theoretically possible for a person to be exclusively heterosexual in behavior but exclusively homosexual in feeling. Such a person might be married and sexually engaged only with his wife, all the while fantasizing a male partner" (p. 9).

There may also be a disparity in one's

FIGURE 13–2 Heterosexual-homosexual Rating Scale

Heterosexual and homosexual behavior						
0	1	2	3	4	5	6
Exclusively heterosexual behavior	Incidental homosexual behavior	More than incidental homosexual behavior	Equal amount of heteroxesual and homosexual behavior	More than incidental heterosexual behavior	Incidental heterosexual behavior	Exclusively homosexual behavior
	← Ambisexual behavior →					

Heterosexual-homosexual ratings (ages 20-35)						
0	1	2	3	4	5	6
Single M = 52-78% F = 61-72%						M = 3-16% F = 1-3%
					M = 5-22% F = 2-6%	
Married M = 90-92% F = 89-90%				M = 7-26% F = 3-8%		
			M = 9-32% F = 4-11%			
Previously married F = 75-80%		M = 13-38% F = 6-14%				
	M = 18-42% F = 11-20%					

Note: Scale and figures adapted from Kinsey's data for males (M) and females (F) published in 1953. The ranges of percentages result from different ratios in various subgroups within the seven categories. These categories themselves are somewhat arbitrary, and the whole scale should therefore be read as a continuum.

Source: Adapted from Kinsey et al., "Sexual Behavior in the Human Female," from *The Sex Atlas* by Erwin J. Haberle. Used by permission of The Continuum Publishing Corporation, New York.

behavior rating and ratings of homosexual feelings on the Kinsey scale. Many people who engage in sporadic homosexual activities do not think of themselves as homosexuals. Men with no prior homosexual experience when imprisoned may engage in homosexual activities, yet return to an exclusively heterosexual life-style. Some male prostitutes who cater to a homosexual clientele, consider themselves to be heterosexual. When not earning their living as a prostitute, they are exclusively heterosexual (Reiss, 1961). Humphreys (1970) studied men who occasionally partake in anonymous homosexual activities in public restrooms ("tearooms"). He found that many of the men were heterosexually married and clearly identified themselves as heterosexual.

The San Francisco Study

Now that we have a clearer understanding of the complexities involved in defining and assessing homosexuality, let us turn our attention to the study conducted by Bell and Weinberg.

The way in which the so-called San Francisco study was conducted is perhaps as fascinating as the data itself. Bell (1973) summarizes the mechanics involved:

> We recruited subjects from all kinds of sources: through public advertising of various kinds, in public and private bars and restaurants where approximately 1,000 hours were spent recruiting potential subjects, at small gatherings in private homes or through contacts made on a one-to-one basis in an effort to get at the most covert individuals; we sent information about the study to almost 6,000 individuals, using the mailing lists of various homophile organizations, bars, and bookstores. We recruited in eight different steam baths, at the meetings and social activities of 23 different homophile organizations in the Bay Area, in men's rooms, theater lobbies and balconies, parks and beaches, the streets and public squares. Needless to say, it would have been much easier to rely entirely on the bars or the homophile organizations for our subjects, but we wanted to make sure that we included as many different kinds of homosexuals as possible in our samples. Otherwise, the incredible range of homosexual experience would have been missing (p. 6).

Ultimately, 979 homosexual men and women were interviewed in 1970. In addition 477 heterosexuals drawn from a random sample of San Francisco area residents were questioned. Males, females, blacks, and whites participated in a three-to-four hour face-to-face interview. The study, based as it was in an area well known for its tolerance of gay individuals, may present a somewhat unrealistically favorable picture of homosexual adjustment. However, it represents the first time that a truly diverse sample of homosexuals have been studied, that homosexuals have been compared with one another, and that types of homosexuals have been compared with heterosexuals. Thus while the findings may not be representative of all homosexuals, the results are based on substantial numbers of all types of homosexuals. Previous studies have tended to focus on special groups of homosexuals, such as those undergoing psychotherapy, men in prisons, and members of homophile organizations (Brody, 1978).

A Typology of "Homosexualities"

Based on their data, Bell and Weinberg defined an inclusive typology of homosexuals. This approach is consistent with one of the major aims of their research—to map the great diversity of homosexual life-styles. Homosexuals were categorized into five distinct groups.

1. The *close coupleds* resembled "happily married" heterosexual couples in many ways. They lived in quasimarriages which tended to be long standing. Such relationships were characterized by emotional commitment, fidelity, and a sharing of household responsibilities. Close coupleds expressed few regrets about their life-styles, claimed to have few sexual problems and appeared to be relatively content and self-accepting. In terms of psychological adjustment, they could not be distinguished from the

Alan Bell (left) and Martin Weinberg, co-investigators of the "San-Francisco Study" and authors of the book *Homosexualities: A study of diversity among men and women.*

Courtesy of the Institute for Sex Research, Inc., photo by Dellenback

heterosexuals and actually scored higher on happiness measures. When compared with the other groups of homosexuals, they were the best adjusted. They were more self-accepting, happier, and less lonely and depressed.

2. *Open coupleds* also lived as partners but engaged in substantial sexual activity apart from their primary relationships. This type of independent, nonattached relationship was most common among males. Open coupled women experienced such a relationship as more difficult than men. Males tended to be more self-accepting and less lonely than women in this type of relationship. With respect to psychological adjustment, open coupleds tended to resemble the average homosexual respondent.

3. The *functional* homosexuals were highly active sexually and freewheeling, comparable in behavior to "swinging singles" among heterosexuals. Sexual experiences played an especially important role in their lives. They reported the greatest number of sexual partners, the fewest sexual problems, and expressed the least regret about their homosexuality. Of all groups, they were most involved in the homosexual community. They *cruised* frequently for partners, attended gay bars, and were

most likely to come in contact with the police on account of their homosexuality. Their psychological adjustment was relatively good, but they were more tense, unhappy, and lonely than the close couples.

4. At the less positive end are the *dysfunctional* homosexuals. Bell and Weinberg state, "The dysfunctionals are the group in our sample which most closely accords with the stereotype of the tormented homosexual. They are troubled people whose lives offer them little gratification, and in fact, they seem to have a great deal of difficulty managing their existence. Sexually, socially, and psychologically, whenever they could be distinguished from homosexual respondents as a whole, the dysfunctionals displayed poorer adjustment. If we had numbered only dysfunctionals among our respondents, we very likely would have had to conclude that homosexuals in general are conflict ridden social misfits" (p. 225–226).

As a group, the males were more lonely, worrisome, paranoid, depressed, tense, and unhappy than other

Many homosexuals are not only satisfied with their sexual orientation, but are also psychologically and socially adjusted.

Alex Webb/Magnum Photos, Inc.

homosexual respondents. They reported more job difficulties, robberies, assaults, and extortion on account of their being gay. Furthermore, the dysfunctionals were most likely to have had some contact with the police regardless of the reason. They reported more sexual problems and expressed the most regrets about being homosexual.

5. Finally, Bell and Weinberg identified asexuals who were most secretive and withdrawn, least sexually active and less exclusively homosexual. The asexual lesbians expressed the highest incidence of suicidal thoughts. Together with the dysfunctions, asexuals reported less self-acceptance and more loneliness than other homosexuals and than heterosexuals.

Is Homosexuality a Psychological Disorder?

Whether or not homosexuality should be considered a mental disorder has been the subject of much controversy. In April, 1974, in a history making decision, the American Psychiatric Association supported a motion to remove homosexuality from its list of mental disorders. The decision was accompanied by the creation of a new category in the APA's Diagnostic and Statistical Manual of Mental Diseases (DSM II) termed "Sexual Orientation Disturbance." The term applied only to those who were distressed or in conflict with their sexual orientation. Although it did not go so far as to say homosexuality was "normal," homosexuality by itself would no longer be viewed as a mental illness unless accompanied by internal conflict or social dysfunction.

This classification represents a more tolerant approach than previous attempts to categorize homosexuality. In 1952 the DSM I listed homosexuality as a subcategory of sociopathic personality along with antisocial personality, alcoholism, and drug addiction. In 1968, the revised edition DSM II no longer listed homosexuality as a separate category of sexual deviation. Thus, homosexuality was included among "Sexual Perversions" such as sadism, masochism, fetishism, and voyeurism.

In the most recent revision, DSM III, homosexuality per se is not included. A new category was created, "Ego-dystonic Homosexuality." This is characterized by a desire to acquire or increase heterosexual arousal so that heterosexual relationships can be initiated or maintained. In addition there is a sustained pattern of overt homosexual arousal that the individual explicitly complains is unwanted and is a source of distress. It is obvious that this represents a dramatic change from previous classifications that emphasized the pathological nature of homosexuality.

Bell and Weinberg contend that their data show that homosexuality is not necessarily related to pathology. As we have seen, it is primarily the dysfunctionals and asexuals who are more poorly adjusted. Bell and Weinberg emphasize that similar groups can be found among heterosexuals. In general, homosexual men were found to be quite like heterosexual men in their reports of physical health and happiness. However, homosexual men did indicate that they felt less self-accepting and more lonely, depressed and tense than did the heterosexual men. The homosexual men were also more likely to have considered or attempted suicide and to have sought professional help for an emotional problem. However, homosexual men tended to be more exuberant than the heterosexual respondents.

Few differences in psychological adjustment were found when homosexual and heterosexual women were compared. As a group, however, they reported less self-esteem and more suicidal thoughts than the heterosexual women. Bell and Weinberg concluded that "homosexual adults who have come to terms with their homosexuality, who do not regret their sexual orientation, and who can function effectively sexually and socially are no more disturbed psychologically than are heterosexual men and women" (p. 216).

The San Francisco Study is not, however, likely to dampen the controversy concerning whether homosexuality is a viable alternative life-style. For example, the largest number of male homosexuals stated that they had from 100 to more than 500 different sexual partners. Twenty-eight percent of the white male respondents reported more than 1,000 affairs, the majority described as brief encounters with virtual strangers. Bell argues that the large number of sexual encounters may in part be the result of society affording the homosexual little opportunity to meet on a nonsexual basis. Moreover, long-term, stable relationships were valued by those interviewed and were likely to "involve an emotional exchange and commitment similar to the kinds that heterosexuals experience" (quoted in Brody, 1978).

Certain aspects of the findings may indeed spark further controversy. But the broader point is that "relatively few homosexual men and women conform to the hideous stereotype that most people have of them" (Bell & Weinberg, 1978, p. 230).

Diversity of Experience

At the very least, the San Francisco Study highlights the great diversity of the homosexual experience. With respect to the level of sexual interest and activity reported, little evidence was obtained to support the stereotype that homosexuals are sexually hyperactive or inactive. Thirteen percent of the white male sample asserted that sex was relatively unimportant in their lives. The majority of homosexuals engaged in sexual relations only two or three times a week. Women report they had sexual relations an average of only once a week. Men tended to cruise for sexual partners in gay bars, but 40 percent did so as infrequently as once a month or not at all. Women seldom or never cruised. Furthermore, the majority of men and women had been involved in stable, relatively monogamous relationships lasting one to three years. Most lesbian women had fewer than ten sexual partners. More than three fourths of the women were involved in a stable relationship with another woman. The majority of homosexual men denied they ever had sexual relations with minors or prostitutes. Bell and Weinberg note that heterosexuals are far more likely than homosexuals to seduce minors and make objectionable advances.

Great diversity was also found in the degree of acceptance of one's homosexuality and in the relative overtness of homosexuality. Only one fourth of male homosexuals tended to regret being homosexual, seriously considered stopping their homosexuality, and wished they had been entirely heterosexual from birth. Homosexual women tended to express less difficulty accepting their homosexuality.

Since homosexuals are a distinct minority in the population often the target of prejudice and discrimination, it is not surprising that some go to great lengths to conceal their homosexual life-styles. Only about one fourth of males surveyed indicated their employers and most of their fellow workers knew they were gay. The lesbian women were less likely to report their colleagues or employers were aware of their homosexuality. Some homosexuals whose families knew they were gay were still "in the closet" in their work situation. In the family context, mothers were most likely to know that their sons were homosexual, whereas fathers were reportedly least likely to be aware of their son's homosexuality.

The findings of the Bell and Weinberg study can be seen as congruent with the rationale given by the American Psychiatric Association for excluding homosexuality from the new classification system: "A significant proportion of homosexuals are apparently satisfied with their sexual orientation, show no signs of significant manifest psychopathology (unless homosexuality, by itself, is considered psychopathology), and are able to function quite effectively, with no impairment in the capacity to love or work. These individuals may never come to treatment, or they may be seen by a mental health professional because of external pressure or other problems requiring psychiatric help (e.g., depression DSM III, Draft, 1978, L. 33).

EXPLANATIONS

The Psychoanalytic Perspective

Since for many years homosexuality has been viewed as a pathological condition, it is not surprising that scientists have searched for clues to the etiology of homosexuality. Psychoanalytically oriented etiological explanations emphasize the role of early family relationships in the later development of homosexual behavior. Oedipal conflicts that emerge from the family context and disrupt normal heterosexual development are seen as a prime motivating factor. Freud believed that anxiety resulted from deep-seated incestuous desires for the seductive mother and fear of castration as retaliation by the father. Women come to be feared because the sight of female genitals evokes childhood-based anxiety associated with castration fears. Others have viewed homosexuality as the product of feminine identification stemming from identification with a dominant, attentive mother. Still another view links lack of heterosexual involvement with fears of being psychologically engulfed by women who are equated on an unconscious level with the smothering, overly intimate mother.

Bieber, Dain, Dince, Dielich, Grand, Gondlack, Kremer, Rifkin, Wilbur, and Bieber (1962) discovered a pattern of family relationships consistent with the analytic view that adverse family relationships predispose one to later homosexuality. In a study of 106 male homosexual patients and 100 heterosexual patients, the family constellation most reliably associated with homosexuality was a seductive, overly intimate and protective mother and a detached and/or hostile father. Critics, however, point out that the pattern of intense maternal involvement together with an indifferent or poor relationship with the father is not always evident in the backgrounds of homosexuals. Some homosexuals come from homes with idealized fathers, while others report an intensely ambivalent relationship with an older sibling or an absent mother (Marmor, 1971).

A moment's reflection will reveal that many of the psychoanalytic ideas advanced to explain homosexuality are mutually contradictory. They cannot all be true simultaneously. Marmor states, "The crucial research question is whether any of these patterns exist also in men who are predominantly heterosexual (I believe they do); or conversely, whether none of them exist in some heterosexuals. If so, then none of these patterns can be considered as pathognomic or prerequisite to the development of a homosexual object choice" (p. 55).

The Learning Perspective

Behaviorists, emphasizing explanations based on learning theory, assume that pleasureable and painful experiences shape sexual orientation. Kinsey et al. (1948), for example, contended that early pleasureable homosexual contacts increased the likelihood of ultimately adopting a homosexual orientation. Early pleasant childhood and adolescent sexual and romantic fantasies with homoerotic themes may play a similar role in shaping homosexuality (Saghir & Robbins, 1973). On the other hand, sexual experiences perceived as negative or traumatic may inhibit approaching the opposite sex to obtain sexual and interpersonal reinforcement.

A Biological View

Biological theories represent a departure from both learning theory and family-oriented etiological explanations. Researchers are currently looking for genetic, chromosomal, and hormonal differences between heterosexuals and homosexuals. Kallman (1952) reported an impressive 100 percent concordance rate in overt homosexual behavior in 40 pairs of monozygotic twins. A similar relationship was not found in the degree of concordance for fraternal twins. Such findings are entirely consistent with a genetic explanation. However, other studies have failed to replicate these findings. For example, in one study of seven monozygotic twin pairs only one of the siblings in each pair was homosexual (Kolb, 1963). Nevertheless, researchers encouraged by findings that concordance rates are generally higher in monozygotic than dizygotic twins suggest that evidence for a genetic predisposition toward homosexuality will eventually be forthcoming.

Little evidence has been obtained to suggest that chromosomes are significantly different in homosexual and heterosexual males. Recent studies, however, have found some intriguing hormonal differences between homosexuals and heterosexuals. Several studies suggest that levels of testosterone and its breakdown products are lower in homosexuals than heterosexuals (Loraine, Ismael, Adamopoulous, and Dove, 1970; Margolese, 1973). This finding must be interpreted with caution, however. Other factors such as diet, stress, and general health may account for such results and must be ruled out as causative agents before more firm conclusions can be made. Even if a genetic or constitutional predisposition toward homosexuality were identified, social learning would play an important role in determining whether homosexual behavior and feelings are expressed.

Each of the theories we have considered has emphasized a single set of etiological factors. Bell (1973) cautions against accepting a unitary etiological explanation: "Just as there is such a diversity of adult homosexuality, so there are multiple routes into this orientation, routes which may well account for differences in the way a particular person experiences and expresses his or her homosexuality as well as the nature of his psychological make-up and of his social adjustment. For some, certain kinds of parental relationships and identifications may loom large. For others, negative same-sex peer relationships may be paramount. For still others, early satisfactions associated with homosexual behavior may stand out or negative heterosexual experience during adolescence may be dominant" (p. 16–17).

THE NEW MASTERS AND JOHNSON REPORT

In their new book, *Homosexuality in Perspective,* Masters and Johnson reported the findings of more than 15 years of accumulated research evidence which incisively challenges the myth that there are tremendous differences between homosexuals and heterosexuals in their sexual functioning. Their work also offers new hope that a long-term, reorientation to heterosexuality is possible for many homosexuals who are dissatisfied with their sexual orientation and are highly motivated to change. The new "Masters and Johnson report" centers on a number of research projects which spanned a time period from 1964 to 1977. The first study examined the physiological sexual responses of sexually functional homosexual subjects in a laboratory setting. All of the homosexual volunteers were able to experience sexual arousal and orgasm while engaging in a variety of sexual activities in the laboratory. The research project involved 94 male and 82 female homosexuals who ranged in age from 21 to 54. Their sexual responses and activities were compared with 687 heterosexual male and female volunteers, the majority of whom participated in the study of the sexual response cycle which we described earlier in the chapter. Let us now consider some interesting highlights of the project:

The capacity of heterosexuals and homsexuals to respond to effective sexual stimulation was indistinguishable.

There were no differences between homosexuals and heterosexuals in the physical processes of lubrication, erection, ejaculation, and orgasm.

The rate of failure to achieve orgasm for both homosexuals and heterosexuals was very low—less than 3 percent for both males and females preselected for "sexual efficiency."

Homosexual committed couples (those who have lived together for at least one year) engaged in more foreplay and delayed genital stimulation longer than heterosexual married couples. Homosexuals communicated their feelings about sexual wants and needs more freely than their heterosexual counterparts; they also tended to "take turns" achieving orgasms, allowing them to concentrate more fully on their own pleasure rather than focusing on "distracting" concerns about their partner's pleasure.

Homosexuals occasionally fantasized

about heterosexual loveplay, just as many heterosexuals occasionally have homosexual fantasies.

The results of this project prompted Masters and Johnson to consider treating homosexuals with the same treatment methods that proved so effective in treating sexual dysfunctions in heterosexual patients. Masters and Johnson reasoned that if homosexuals and heterosexuals had identical sexual capacity, they might be treated with equal effectiveness. Thus in their second research program, they treated homosexuals with a variety of sexual dysfunctions using the techniques of direct sexual therapy which they pioneered. Fifty-six male and 25 female couples were treated during a nine year period beginning in 1968. The treatment included a five-year follow-up to evaluate the long-term success of the therapy. The major presenting complaint of males was impotence; the major presenting complaint for females was inhibited orgasm. For all homosexuals during that period, the treatment failure rate was less than 12 percent at the five year follow-up.

In addition to offering hope to those homosexuals with sexual dysfunctions who remain committed to a homosexual life-style, Masters and Johnson's recent work has shown that it is possible to treat certain homosexuals who are dissatisfied with their sexual orientation and desire to change. Using direct sexual therapy procedures, they treated 54 "dissatisfied" homosexual males and 13 lesbian women who first had to prove their motivation to change their sexual orientation. The majority of homosexuals who were treated were married and accompanied by their opposite sexed partners. A sizeable minority of homosexuals came with the heterosexual partners they hoped to marry, the remaining homosexuals came with more casual partners who were committed enough to the patients to engage in the demanding, intensive therapy. The overall failure rate at five-year follow-up, for all 67 homosexuals was 35 percent—an impressive treatment outcome, considering the widely held belief that even highly motivated homosexually oriented clients are difficult to treat.

The finding that the physiological responses of homosexuals and heterosexuals to sexual stimulation do not differ was not surprising to many scientists acquainted with the workings of the human body. But sharp divisions of opinion and criticisms of Masters and Johnson's work have been stimulated by their success with reorienting dissatisfied homosexuals. Questions such as the following ones have been raised: Is the successful application of the therapy limited to only highly motivated homosexuals who enter treatment with partners committed to helping them achieve "reorientation"? Does the therapy simply effect a change in homosexual *behavior* and not a parallel change in feeling and thinking about oneself? Would the therapy be equally effective with individuals with varying degrees of heterosexual/homosexual experience and committment to a gay life-style? Will sexual reorientation therapies be able to effect permanent changes, or will they be relatively short lived? Answers to such questions will surely contribute to our understanding of the limits and potential of treatments designed to "reorient" dissatisfied homosexuals.

SUMMARY

In this chapter we have reviewed the major psychosexual disorders listed in the DSM III classification system. We began our overview with an examination of the psychosexual dysfunctions. These are frequently encountered disorders that are characterized by a failure to enjoy and/or achieve accepted sexual behaviors. We discussed the characteristics of these disorders, their etiology and assessment, and available treatments. We devoted considerable attention to the promising techniques of "direct" sexual therapies based on the pioneering research program of Masters and Johnson. Direct sex therapy programs are aimed at reducing performance anxiety, alleviating shame and guilt through education and attitude change, helping the couple to develop a sense of mutual responsibility for the problem and the treatment outcome, and resolving interpersonal conflict and increasing communication in the context of the sexual relationship.

The psychosexual dysfunctions were contrasted with the gender identity disorders, which are characterized by identification of the self as a member of the opposite sex, and the paraphilias, which involve unconventional sexual behaviors and are characterized by a diminished capacity to engage in close, affectionate sexual relations with another person. We also noted that changes in our thinking about sexual behavior are reflected in the deletion of homosexuality from the list of mental disorders in DSM III. A preference for sexual relations with members of the same sex is now listed as a psychosexual disorder only when it is unwanted and personally distressing (ego-dystonic homosexuality).

We reviewed a number of recent studies which challenge widely held stereotypes of homosexuality. These studies suggest that homosexuality does not preclude intimate, affectionate relationships, that the experience of homosexuals is incredibly diverse, that homosexuals do not differ from heterosexuals in significant ways, that sexual dysfunctions can be treated as effectively with homosexuals as with heterosexuals, and that it is possible to "reorient" certain homosexuals who are dissatisfied with their sexual orientation and desire to change. And finally, we noted that although a number of theories have been advanced to explain the development of homosexuality, at the present time, no one etiological explanation appears to be entirely satisfactory.

14

Substance Use Disorders I: The Illegal and Prescription Drugs

OVERVIEW

Allan H's father is a successful businessman who frequently works overtime to maintain their luxurious suburban home. His wife and 18-year-old Allan scarcely see him. Frequently he feels tired and overwrought, but two Martinis at lunch and another drink when he finally gets home help him to calm his nerves.

Allan's mother feels lonely, bored, and neglected. In attempts to overcome her resentment and depression, she often reaches for a sedative, tranquilizer or barbiturate. Recently she has made increasing demands on Allan to fill the emotional vacuum in her life. Suddenly the H's are communicating. They are both deeply involved with the "Allan problem." It appears that Allan has been missing school, and his grades have markedly dropped. In a recent conference with the school counselor, Allan confided that he has been taking barbiturates from the family medicine cabinet and also buying them from a friend at school. For over one month he has made futile attempts to discontinue this practice. He is deeply unhappy. Allan's mother now recalls that recently he has appeared drowsy and "not himself."

It was an hour before the Alcoholics Anonymous meeting. Richard P. was silently rehearsing the speech he would give when it was his turn to stand up, tell his story, and testify "I am an alcoholic." Since it was his first meeting, he was nervous, but he found that he was repeating to himself, "I have to do this! I have to take the Big Step!" Richard P. made mental notes: "I must not forget to tell the group how I just couldn't quit on my own; how I had to drink more and more just to feel O.K.; I have to confess all the problems and embarrassment I brought to my family; the drinking sprees, the blackouts; I have to tell how I lost the best job I ever had; how I felt on the trip to the hospital emergency room and the horror of the withdrawal symptoms, the D.T.s." "Time to go now." Richard resolutely walked to the meeting.

Ours is a drug-consuming culture and this trend is constantly growing. Allan H. in his first exploration of the family medicine chest probably had a wide choice of drugs. According to the findings of a study by the Standford Research Institute, the average American household had 30 drugs; one out of five was a prescription

TABLE 14–1 Lifetime Prevalence and Recency of Use, by Age, in Percent

	Youth (Age 12 to 17)		*Young Adults (Age 18 to 25)*		*Older Adults (Age 26+)*	
	Ever Used	*Used Past Month*	*Ever Used*	*Used Past Month*	*Ever Used*	*Used Past Month*
Marijuana and/or hashish . . .	28	16	60	28	15	3
Inhalants	9	1	11	(1)	2	(1)
Hallucinogens	5	2	20	2	3	(1)
Cocaine	4	1	19	4	3	(1)
Heroin	1	(1)	4	(1)	1	(1)
Other opiates[2]	6	1	13	1	3	(1)
Stimulants (Rx)[3]	5	1	21	2	5	1
Sedatives (Rx)[3]	3	1	18	3	3	(1)
Tranquilizers (Rx)[3]	4	1	13	2	3	(1)
Any illicit drug "stronger" than marijuana[4]	(9)	NA	(34)	NA	(12)	NA
Alcohol	53	31	84	70	78	55
Cigarettes	47	22	68	47	67	39
Number of persons	1,272	1,272	1,500	1,500	1,822	1,822

[1] Less than 0.5 percent.
[2] Includes methadone.
[3] Nonmedical use. Estimates based on split sample: N = 623,750 and 897, respectively.
[4] "Stronger" drugs defined as: hallucinogens, cocaine, heroin, and other opiates.
NA: Not available.
Source: Originally appeared in H. I. Abelson, P. M. Fishburne, and I. H. Cisin, *National Survey on Drug Abuse, 1977: A Nationwide Study—Youth, Young Adults, and Older Adults* (Princeton, N.J.: Response Analysis Corporation, 1977). This chart appeared in R. Dupont, A. Goldstein, and J. O'Donnell (Ed.), *Handbook on Drug Abuse.* National Institute on Drug Abuse, U.S. Department of Health, Education, and Welfare, Maryland, 1979 pp. 382.

drug and the other four had been bought over-the-counter (Rooney & Nall, 1966).

A recent national survey shows that the use and misuse of drugs is not limited to older individuals, as a glance at Table 14–1 will show.

It may surprise you to learn that among young adults aged 18–25 marijuana use can be considered statistically normal since as many as 25 percent classify themselves as current marijuana users. Furthermore, 20 percent have experimented with hallucinogens or cocaine and approximately 10 percent have used narcotic drugs other than heroin. If all nonmedical drugs more potent than marijuana are combined, it is apparent that about one third of young adults have used one or more of them (Abelson, Fishburne, & Cisin, 1977).

Some Explanations of Drug Use

In view of the prevalence of drug use, you may be wondering what motivates people to use drugs. There are as many answers to this question as there are individuals resorting to drug use. In general drug users are motivated to decrease pain, discomfort, tension, depression, boredom, and other negative feelings. Drug users may also seek to increase pleasurable sensations, find stimulation, and attain feelings of adequacy. Frequently young adults seeking their own identity may find in drug use a source of multiple gratifications of their emerging needs. They may turn to drugs for novel experience, a way of rebelling against parental authority, and a way of gaining approval from peers.

Drug taking is not randomly determined. An individual tends to begin drug use when the drug somehow becomes easily available to him, when it is approved by the particular culture or subculture he lives in, and when, at least initially, he does not expect that there is a possibility of serious consequences of drug use. For example, in the first case we presented, Allan H. found the drug in his own home. The concept of taking a chemical in order to "feel better" was familiar to Allan since his father used alcohol and the probability of becoming dependent on barbiturates seemed remote.

Richard P. had never expected to become an alcoholic. He never even considered alcohol or tobacco, for that matter, as dangerous drugs. In his circle of friends, serving alcohol was an approved method of greeting a guest, and Richard had long ago been conditioned by movies and advertisements to believe that this was an acceptable way to relax, to be sociable, and to "be with it." He kept resisting the growing awareness that as time went on, he had to keep increasing the number of drinks needed to feel "really good." Eventually Richard P. had to confront the fact that a substance that has the potential to give pleasure may also hold the potential for harm.

The effects of drug use vary with the habits of drug usage an individual adopts. When drug usage is limited to occasional experimental use and is motivated by curiosity and the desire to share an experience with friends, the risk of serious, long-term ill effects is relatively low. When drug use becomes more

The ready availability of drugs in our society contributes to problems of abuse.

John Thoeming/Dorsey Press

regular, even though it occurs in a social context, the dangers of serious consequences may increase, particularly with drugs more potent than marijuana. Frequently a narrow line divides recreational use of drugs and what may be considered drug abuse. The new DSM III classification system provides some useful guidelines for clarifying the various dimensions and consequences of drug usage.

Substance Abuse and Dependence

Let us now reconsider the cases of Allan H. and Richard P. and look at them in the light of the DSM III classification system, which clarifies distinction between substance abuse and substance dependence. The DSM III criteria for diagnosing substance abuse disorder are: *duration, social complications, psychological dependence,* and a *pathological pattern of use.*

The case of Allan H. appears to meet the criteria for the classification of substance abuse for the following reasons:

1. He had been taking the drug for a sufficiently long period (more than one month).
2. He suffered social complications: he missed school, his school performance fell off, and his mother noticed that he was "not himself."
3. He manifested psychological dependence: for some time he tried to curtail his drug use but he had been unable to overcome a compelling desire to continue taking barbiturates. One of the factors which may have contributed to his difficulty was that taking barbiturates was pleasant and rewarding. It helped to relieve the tensions engendered by his home situation. Each time he took the drug, his drug-taking behavior was positively reinforced.
4. His pattern of drug usage was pathological: he had used the drug every day for over a month.

The case of Richard P. illustrates all the features mentioned under the substance abuse classification and two additional criteria that define it as a case of the more severe disorder termed *substance dependence.* A number of years ago the term addiction would have been used to describe Richard P's condition. But at the present time the preferred term is drug or substance dependence. In order to apply this diagnosis the user must manifest the criteria of *tolerance* or *withdrawal.*

1. *Tolerance.* As Richard P. continued to drink, he found that he needed increasing amounts of alcohol to obtain the same effect. Thus he exhibited tolerance to the effects of alcohol.
2. *Withdrawal.* Prolonged and excessive consumption of alcohol results in an altered physiological state which demands continued ingestion of alcohol. When Richard P. stopped drinking he no longer satisfied this demand and his body responded to this sudden deprivation with painful and frightening symptoms termed withdrawal. The exact nature of the withdrawal, or abstinence syndrome, will depend upon the drug taken and the duration and intensity of prior drug use.

Richard P., like other users of drugs which lead to physical dependence (presence of tolerance and susceptibility to abstinence syndrome), tended to avoid the withdrawal symptoms by consuming even more of the drug. Thus Richard's alcohol consumption was not only reinforced by the primary pleasurable drinking experience but also by the avoidance of unpleasant withdrawal symptoms.

In this chapter we will consider a number of drugs which have a high potential for dependence and abuse, as defined by DSM III. We will begin our discussion of these drugs with substances which can only be obtained through illegal means. The use of these drugs (heroin, LSD, marijuana, cocaine, PCP) is generally not well accepted or tolerated by society. Following our discussion of the "illegal" drugs, which have been the focal point of much societal concern and anxiety, we will turn our attention to drugs which can be used legally when prescribed by a physician. As we will note, persons who misuse the barbiturates or amphetamines either do not use them as a physician prescribes or obtain them illegally.

In the next chapter we will consider the social drugs: tobacco and alcohol. Even though society sanctions the use of alcohol and tobacco, they exact a tremendous social cost. Although alcohol and tobacco can be purchased legally by adults, they are, nonetheless, the source of significant personal, medical, and social problems. Because their social impact can easily be underestimated, we feel that they deserve separate treatment.

Drugs differ in the way they are perceived by society, the personal and social costs associated with their use, and the legal penalties for their use. Complex social factors can influence each of these aspects of drug use in the human context. A glance at Table 14–2 will inform you of the current federal classifications of drugs of abuse and the legal penalties that can be incurred with their misuse.

Popular attitudes about drugs can change in response to social forces. The prohibited, illegal drug of today, may be the accepted, legal drug of tomorrow. In coming years, marijuana may achieve the status of a social drug, much like alcohol and tobacco. Some would argue that it already has attained that status. As its public acceptance has grown, certain groups have made determined efforts to legalize marijuana. Penalties for its use have decreased or have not been rigorously enforced, as more and more people of different walks of life have tried it. We have decided not to include marijuana as one of the social drugs for two reasons. First, it is an illegal and controlled drug. And second, it is not as widely accepted throughout society as alcohol or tobacco.

We now turn our attention to heroin and the opiate narcotic drugs. Some of the opiate narcotics have legitimate medical uses, but their misuse provokes great alarm in our culture.

THE ILLEGAL DRUGS

The Opiate Narcotics: Heroin

> Heroin is the king of drugs. Heroin is king because it leaves you floating on a calm sea where nothing seems to matter and everything is okay. It is the beatific world of peaceful fantasy where your mind swims in the warm, comfortable, somatic sensation of being held, without pain, and protected from

TABLE 14–2 Summary of Drug Schedules and Penalties for Violation of the Comprehensive Drug Abuse Prevention and Control Act of 1970 (as of January 1, 1978)

					Maximum penalties for illegal	
Schedule	*Potential for abuse*	*Medical use*	*Production controlled*	*Examples*	*Manufacturing distribution*	*Possession*
I	High	None	Yes	Heroin, marijuana, THC (tetrahydrocannabinol), LSD, mescaline; generally, opiates, opium derivatives, and hallucinogenic substances	*Schedules I and II* Narcotics— 1st offense 15 yr/$25,000/3 yr* 2nd and more offenses 30 yr/$50,000/6 yr Nonnarcotics— 1st offense 5 yr/$15,000/2 yr 2nd offense 10 yr/$30,000/4 yr	1st offense 1 yr/$5,000 2nd offense 2 yr/$10,000
II	High	Yes	Yes	Morphine, cocaine, methadone, opium, codeine, secobarbital, amobarbital, pentobarbital, meperidine, methaqualone, all amphetamine-type stimulants		
III	Some, less than drugs in I and II	Yes	No	Nonamphetamine-type stimulants; some barbiturates, some narcotic preparations, paregoric	1st offense 5 yr/$15,000/2 yr 2nd offense 10 yr/$30,000/4 yr	For first offense probation may be given
IV	Low, less than drugs in III	Yes	No	Barbital, chloral hydrate, meprobamate, phenobarbital, propoxyphene, diazepam, chlordiazepoxide, certain nonamphetamine stimulants not listed in previous schedules	1st offense 3 yr/$10,000/1 yr 2nd offense 6 yr/$20,000/2 yr	Penalties for possession are the same for all schedules
V	Low, less than drugs in IV	Yes	No	Compounds, mixtures, and preparations with very low amounts of narcotics; dilute codeine and opium compounds	1st offense 1 yr/$5,000/none 2nd offense 2 yr/$10,000/none	

* Maximum prison sentence/maximum fine/mandatory probation period after release from prison.
Source: O. Ray, *Drugs, Society, and Human Behavior,* 2d ed. (St. Louis: C. V. Mosby Company, 1978), p. 41.

> the concerns and worries that make up your life. Suddenly the emptiness disappears. The great gaping hole that hurts, which you had to hide from everyone, is gone; the terrible growing inadequacy has vanished. And in its place is the power and comfort that's called confidence. No one can get to you when you keep nodding (Rosenberg, pp. 25–26).

Rosenberg's description conveys a sense of the euphoria, anxiety reduction, and dissipation of inferiority feelings which the user of heroin may experience. The pleasureable effects of injecting heroin intravenously may be so powerful and reinforcing, that an overwhelming need to try it again is created. Indeed, a strong psychological dependence can develop as early as the first injection. If a person takes a moderate daily dose of heroin over a two-week period, he becomes physically dependent on the drug (Witters & Witters, 1975).

But there is one fact which every heroin addict knows: the pleasureable effects of heroin are limited to the three or four hours that the usual dose lasts. If another

Intravenous heroin use.

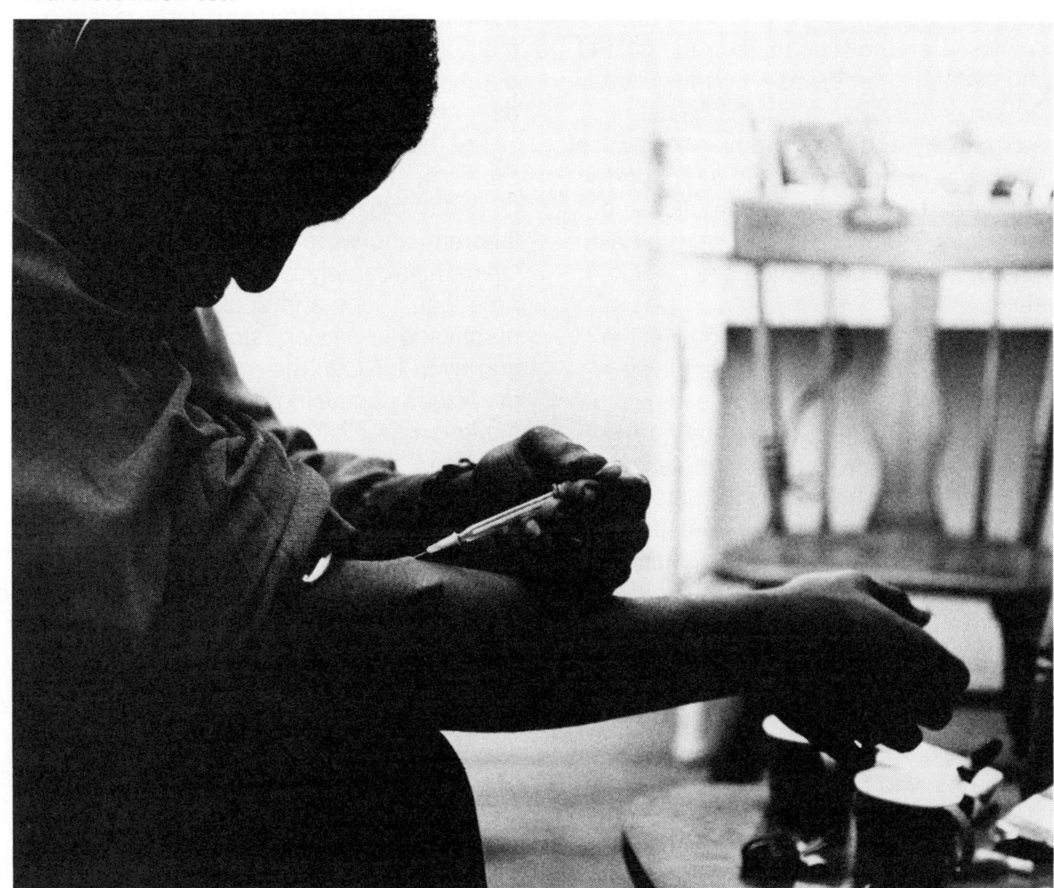

Bob Combs/Rapho-Photo Researchers, Inc.

dose is not taken within four to six hours, abstinence results in the painful symptoms of the heroin withdrawal syndrome: abdominal cramps, vomiting, craving for the drug, running nose, sweating, chills, and yawning. Mild symptoms resemble the discomfort of influenza, but in persons who have developed a high tolerance for the drug, the symptoms can be quite severe.

With continued use of heroin, the euphoric effect of the drug becomes gradually less intense. The addict may feel compelled to continue using heroin as much to avoid withdrawal symptoms as to reexperience the euphoria of the first few injections (Julien, 1978).

Since heroin is illegal and must be purchased on the illicit market, the cost of a heroin habit can be as much as $100–200 a day. Because of the high cost of heroin, many addicts are driven to criminal activities to generate income to support their habit. The Bureau of Narcotics and Dangerous Drugs has estimated the cost of heroin-related crimes to be $3 billion a year.

Heroin addiction is most prominent in large, inner city poverty areas. However, since the 1960s, heroin users can increasingly be found in suburban areas and even small towns. As of April 1977, there were more than 250,000 heroin dependent individuals being treated in government-sponsored programs (Dupont, Goldstein, & O'Donnell, 1979). Ball, Smith, & Graff (1977) have estimated that as of 1975, there were 620,000 persons addicted to opiate drugs in this country.

The opiate drugs include not only heroin but drugs like morphine and codeine derived from the opium poppy, a plant found in abundance in Asia. Morphine is the major ingredient in opium and can be converted into heroin by a simple process: heating morphine in the presence of acetic acid. The action of heroin is virtually identical to that of morphine, but heroin is about three times as potent. Heroin now accounts for 90 percent of opiate abuse.

The opiates are often called narcotics because of their ability to relieve pain and to induce sleep, Medically, they are used to relieve acute and chronic pain, to curb diarrhea, and to depress coughing.

History. The addictive properties of opium were recognized more than 2000 years ago by the Greek physician Erasistratus. But a reference to opium as the "joy plant" on a Sumerian tablet perhaps 6,000 years ago suggests that the euphoria producing aspect of the poppy were discovered long before the dangers of the drug were known.

The history of opium use in the United States begins in the mid-19th century with the influx of large numbers of Chinese laborers who were dependent on opium. Opium use rapidly became part of the American scene and could be legally purchased in grocery stores, pharmacies, and even through the mails. Patent medicines containing opium were marketed as elixirs for "women's troubles," teething syrups for babies, pain killers, cough medicines, and so on. Dependence on opiates was regarded as little more than a vice, on a par with dancing and gambling. But as the population of narcotic dependent persons increased as a result of the widespread use of patent medicines and the large numbers of soldiers addicted to morphine after the Civil War, the medical profession began to exercise increasing restraints in the prescription of opiates.

The Pure Food and Drug Act of 1906

required the labeling of patent medicines that contained opiates and other drugs considered to be dangerous. More restrictive federal legislation was soon forthcoming. The Harrison Act of 1914 declared that addiction was a "willful indulgence meriting punishment rather than medical treatment." It made the sale, purchase, and use of narcotics illegal acts, unless they were prescribed for legitimate medical reasons.

As a consequence of more stringent federal controls, an illegal heroin market developed to cater to the needs of narcotic dependent persons who turned to criminal activity in increasing numbers to pay for the rapidly rising costs of purchasing drugs on the illicit market. By 1924, even physicians could not legally prescribe narcotics to an unhospitalized addict. These legislative actions diverted many heroin dependent persons from the mainstream of medical care and essentially criminalized the unhospitalized narcotics user.

Recent concern with providing adequate treatment for the narcotic addict has been spurred by the belief that treatment would reduce the number of crimes committed by addicts. Expanded treatment and rehabilitation efforts by the federal government were initiated by legislation passed by Congress in 1972 which established the Special Action Office for Drug Abuse Prevention.

Despite extensive legal efforts to control opiate abuse, it is unlikely that addiction will be totally eradicated. As Julien notes, "The use of opiates is deeply entrenched in society, widespread, attractive, difficult to treat, and impossible to stop" (p. 101, 1978).

Explanations of heroin dependence. Why is it so difficult for some individuals to stop using heroin? We have already touched on one explanation for why some individuals continue to use heroin and develop an addiction. As you recall, it stressed the powerfully reinforcing aspects of both heroin induced euphoria and the relief from withdrawal symptoms which heroin provides. Such reinforcement of the drug using behavior may be very strong and insures that such behavior will be difficult to unlearn or extinguish. If an addict continues to live in the style and circumstances in which he or she used heroin, many cues may constantly serve to maintain the addiction.

Nurco (1979) has proposed a number of other explanations, some of which we will discuss here. He is careful to point out that the explanations are not mutually exclusive, and more than one may apply to any given person. One explanation depicts the heroin addict as a person who is unable to delay gratification of needs and wants. The experience of immediate gratification which intravenous injection of heroin provides is especially reinforcing to persons who find waiting intolerable because they experienced significant deprivation as children (Nurco, 1971).

Another explanation views heroin addiction as a means of warding off feelings of boredom. Not only does the drug experience itself counteract feelings of boredom, but the often frantic pursuit of heroin or the money necessary to obtain it alleviates boredom as well. The use of heroin may also help the addict to cope with feelings of frustration and aggression, and thereby to avoid the problems associated with both.

The final explanation is based on the heroin addict's rejection of traditional means for attaining goals which society values, as well as rejection of the goals themselves. The addict's substitution of illegitimate goals for socially sanctioned goals occurs because society does not provide the means for all persons to attain socially valued goals.

Dangers of heroin dependence. Though heroin itself is not a physically dangerous drug, it is important to point out that certain medical complications can arise from using unsterilized and shared needles, contamination of the drug with other substances, and inadequate medical care. The unsterile conditions in which heroin is commonly taken can cause serum hepatitus, pneumonia, skin abscesses, and inflammation of the veins.

In addition, addicts have a considerably higher death rate than nonusers in the general population. A disproportionately high number of addicts die from violent causes such as murder, suicide, and various accidents, as well as from various illnesses and infections (DuPont, 1976). Accidental overdose can be fatal. Most heroin is *cut* or diluted with milk or sugar to give it bulk. Addicts may regularly use heroin that is only 3–5 percent pure. If an addict purchases an unusually potent *bag* of heroin, he or she may die shortly after injecting it. This occurs because of a lack of tolerance to the unusually high dose. Heroin-related deaths may also be caused by the drugs used to dilute it in the street market (Robins, 1979).

Biological and Social Approaches to Treatment

Biological approaches: Methadone and narcotic antagonists. Before the 1960s, heroin addiction was commonly thought to be a chronic disease and the pessimistic veiw prevailed: "Once an addict, always an addict." Treatment programs tended to emphasize a drug-free approach and addicts were often taken off heroin abruptly. The disappointingly high relapse rates reported by such programs only served to reinforce an already existing climate of negative thinking about treatment of addiction.

But in 1964, Vincent Dole, a researcher at Rockefeller University, and Marie Nyswander, a psychiatrist with an interest in treating heroin addiction, made a discovery which had tremendous implications for the rehabilitation of heroin addicts. As part of a metabolic study of addiction, they maintained two addicts on morphine while metabolic tests were conducted. They then transferred the addicts to high doses of methadone—a synthetic opiate—in preparation for detoxification. Detoxification involved administering decreasing amounts of an opiate in order to reduce the severity of withdrawal symptoms.

The administration of methadone had some unanticipated but beneficial effects on their patients. The addicts stabilized physically and emotionally and their social functioning improved. The addicts no longer experienced a narcotics "craving" and methadone prevented the occurrence of withdrawal symptoms. Maintained on daily doses of methadone, the patients were no longer preoccupied with acquiring heroin through illicit sources. After the addicts were stabilized on methadone in the hospital setting, they were released and treated on an outpatient basis. They returned to the hospital for daily doses of methadone and continued to show improvement in their daily functioning (DeLong, 1975).

In an expanded treatment program, Dole and Nyswander were able to demonstrate that methadone could be effective in the long-term treatment and rehabilitation of addicts for another reason: while on maintenance doses of methadone, the addict experiences neither the euphoric effects of heroin nor the lethargy which usually follows the "high." The effects of methadone last considerably longer than heroin (24–36 hours), and it can be conveniently administered in pill form. Unlike heroin which requires an intravenous injection four or five times a day, an addict can be stabilized on a single daily dose of methadone which he receives at the treatment center. Though participants in methadone programs continue to be addicted to an opiate, studies have shown that the criminality of methadone users is substantially reduced (McGlothlin, Witt, Anglin, & Wilson, 1978).

As of 1978, there were approximately 75,000 former addicts receiving methadone in drug rehabilitation programs approved by the federal government. Treatment programs which use methadone may differ from one another in significant ways. Some restrict the use of methadone to treating withdrawal symptoms (detoxification), after which the use of methadone is discontinued. But most programs stabilize users on methadone and place varying degrees of emphasis on therapy and vocational training and counseling. Methadone has become the most widely used mode of treating heroine addiction.

Methadone is far from an ideal treatment for addiction. People are maintained on methadone but rarely become totally independent of synthetic opiates because withdrawal from methadone seems to be about as difficult as withdrawal from heroin (Etzioni, 1973). Methadone is now available on the illicit market, and overdose poses a significant risk of death. Critics of methadone programs legitimately argue that programs

Methadone can be dispensed on an outpatient basis to stabilize narcotic addicts.

Leo Choplin/Black Star

addict the patient to yet another drug and are responsible for leaking methadone to street users. But methadone programs at least offer an alternative to the many addicts who find abstinence from opiates difficult, if not impossible.

Narcotic antagonist programs are the newest entries into the treatment scene. Narcotic antagonists are substances like naltrexone which block the effects of narcotics. Narcotic antagonist programs are usually administered in two phases. The patient is first gradually detoxified, usually with methadone. Then, after the addict is "clean", the narcotic antagonist is administered orally, once a day. Thus, addicts may continue to use heroine, but the drug will no longer have an effect. Research is currently underway to find long-lasting antagonists which can be used in maintenance programs. Researchers hope that it will one day be possible to implant an antagonist under the skin which would release the drug into the body in timed doses over a period of months or longer (National Clearinghouse, 1975).

A social perspective: therapeutic communities. Advocates of therapeutic communities are perhaps the most vocal critics of programs which encourage reliance on drugs as a means of treating addiction. Synanon, the prototypic therapeutic community, was founded in 1958, by Charles (Chuck) Dederich, an ex-alcoholic. Dederich believed that by living in a drug-free community staffed by former addicts, the "junkie" could learn to modify destructive behavior patterns and thereby achieve abstinence from drugs. Addicts who enter the Synanon program are first helped through "cold turkey" or drug-free withdrawal. They are then given a job and encouraged to develop a strong and self-reliant character by participating in small group "games" or encounters known as Synanon. Maslow (1967) comments on the aggressive and direct approach practiced in the group encounters:

> What I have read about Synanon . . . suggests that . . . people are very tough, and not brittle. They can take an awful lot. The best thing to do is get right at them, and not sneak up on them, or be delicate with them, or try to surround them from the rear . . . I've suggested that a name for this might be *no-crap therapy*. It serves to clean out the defenses, the rationalizations, the veils, the evasions and politeness of the world (1967, p. 28).

Synanon's no-holds barred approach to self-understanding has generated much controversey and criticism. Some professionals argue that the group leaders and members may tear down the defenses of some of the ex-addicts and leave them with little foundation on which to build a well-adjusted personality. Indeed, addicts' negative feelings about the "games," may at least partly account for the fact that about half of the addicts leave Synanon before completing the therapy.

Another controversial aspect of Synanon is the belief that an addict can never be cured. According to this line of thought, the addict can never be completely independent of Synanon and successfully reenter the community without remaining affiliated and active in the Synanon program. Many have challenged this belief and some have questioned whether the coercive pressures of the Synanon program are moral or ethical (Ray, 1978). Indeed, over a ten-year period (1958–1968), an average of no more than 20 persons per year have returned to the community drug-free (Murray & Trotter, 1973). Other programs modeled after Synanon, such as Daytop Village and Phoenix House, encourage participants to become involved in activities in the community and to leave the program after a period of time.

The Hallucinogens: LSD

You may recall reading in Chapter 4 a number of personal accounts of the striking effects of ingesting hallucinogenic, or psychedelic, drugs. Indeed, the alterations in perception, in thought, and in mood which you learned about are the trademarks of the hallucinogens. Profound changes in consciousness can result from taking small amounts of hallucinogens such as LSD, mescaline, psilocybin, peyote, and DMT. The amount of LSD contained in pills the equivalent size of two aspirins would provide about 6,500 average doses. When hallucinogens are taken at ordinary doses, they do not cause major changes in the body.

The "psychedelic age" was ushered in by the sensationalistic news coverage of Drs. Timothy Leary and Richard Alpert's experiments with psilocybin with friends and students at Harvard. Their frank advocacy of psychedelics as well as their forced withdrawal from Harvard in 1963 catapulted the hallucinogens into a prominent place among drugs of potential abuse. By the mid to late 1960s, LSD reached its peak in popularity. Psychedelic drugs were commonly portrayed as dangerous and unpredictable drugs in the popular press where stories about fatal plunges, suicides, and psychotic breaks dominated the drug-related news. Though many of these accounts were possibly either inaccurate or exaggerated, they generated sufficient concern among the public and medical profession to lead the federal government to restrict the use and manufacture of hallucinogens in 1965. Since 1968, the use of LSD has declined sharply. Nonetheless, as of 1976, it has been estimated that 17 percent of Americans aged 18–25 have tried some type of hallucinogenic drug (Ray, 1978).

Effects of LSD. One of the most interesting and distinctive characteristics of the hallucinogens is the wide variety of subjective effects they facilitate. Walter Pahnke and his colleagues (Pahnke, Kurland, Unger, Savage, & Grof, 1970) have described five major kinds of psychedelic drug experiences. First is the *psychotic psychedelic experience,* characterized by an intense, negative experience of fear to the point of panic, paranoid delusions of suspicion or grandeur, toxic confusion, depression, isolation, and bodily discomfort; all of which can be experienced very intensely.

Second is the *cognitive psychedelic experience,* characterized by astonishingly lucid thought. Problems can be seen from a novel perspective, and the inner relationships of many levels or dimensions can be seen all at once.

Third is the *aesthetic psychedelic experience,* characterized by a change and intensification of all sensory modalities. Fascinating changes in sensations and perceptions can occur: the appearance of great beauty in ordinary objects; the release of powerful emotions through music, and so on.

Fourth is the *psychodynamic psychedelic experience,* characterized by a dramatic emergence into consciousness of material that has previously been unconscious or preconscious. An actual reliving of events from the past may be subjectively experienced.

The fifth and last type of psychedelic experience has been called by various names: *psychedelic, peak, cosmic, transcendental,* or *mystical.* This type of experience is characterized by a sense of unity or oneness with everything, transcendence of time and space, a deeply felt positive mood, a sense of reverence and wonder, meaningful insights, and a sense of difficulty in communicating the experience by verbal description.

Proponents of hallucinogens like Timothy Leary have emphasized the more positive types of experiences, whereas those who have cautioned about the dangers of hallucinogens have emphasized the psychotic psychedelic experience. In actuality, few psychedelic

Known during the 1960's as the "high priest of LSD," former Harvard psychologist Timothy Leary urges a gathering of "hippies" and spectators in San Francisco in 1967 to "turn on, tune in, and drop out."

Wide World Photos

experiences fit precisely into any one category. Aspects of all five kinds of experience are likely to be evident in any given "trip," although one type of experience may predominate.

Determinants of the LSD experience. What determines the nature of a hallucinogenic drug experience? The subjective effects of any drug are determined by a complex interaction of four factors: the dosage of the drug; the setting or the psychological and social environment; the personality of the user; and the set or the user's expectations of the drug's effects and attitudes about taking the drug (Zetner, 1976).

In the 1960s LSD was used in psychotherapy for the purpose of personal problem solving and self-exploration. Therapists felt that the psychodynamic psychedelic type of experience which we described earlier was easiest to induce at low dosages. It was believed that with higher dosages a more intense and possibly negative experience would be more likely to occur.

But subjects may respond very differently to the same dose of LSD as a result of the influence of set, setting, and personality variables. For example, Blum (1964) found that LSD users who reported the greatest number of religious type experiences were the subjects who indicated that they used the drug with the hope of attaining aesthetic experiences or facilitating personal growth.

Situational factors may also have a great impact on the "tripper." Unger (1963) found that if an experimenter was friendly and relaxed, subjects showed little anxiety; but if the experimenter adopted an impersonal, hostile, or investigative attitude toward the drugged subject, they tended to manifest anxiety, hostility, or paranoid responses.

Barber (1970) notes that whether or not a person becomes suspicious, hostile, and paranoid during an LSD session appears to be functionally related to his predrug personality. Linton and Langs (1964) conducted an experiment in which 30 subjects ingested small doses of LSD after they completed a battery of personality tests. Individuals who were judged as guarded and undefended on the basis of the personality measures showed the greatest number of bodily effects and the greatest degree of anxiety during the LSD session. Paranoid tendencies revealed by the tests were openly expressed by subjects after ingesting LSD.

Tolerance and dependence. The hallucinogens do not produce physical dependence and withdrawal symptoms when their use is discontinued. A tolerance to the effects of most psychedelics develops rapidly, but it is quickly reversed, usually within two days. Users rarely develop a tolerance because the effects of the hallucinogens are so intense that few people take them more than once a week.

Dangers and adverse reactions. During the 1960s much concern was expressed about LSD's effect on the brain and its alleged potential to damage chromosomes. Research suggests that such concerns are, for the most part, unjustified. For example, there is little evidence that LSD damages chromosomes to any greater extent than other drugs and activities like aspirin, coffee, and watching color TV. Also, the use of psychedelic drugs has not been related to a higher incidence of birth defects. However, LSD does cross the placental barrier and it may have yet undetermined effects on the developing fetus. Infrequent and low dosage use of LSD seems to pose little or no threat of damage to the brain. Though there is no firm evidence that long-term use of larger doses of LSD results in detectable brain damage, some subtle form of impaired brain function cannot as yet be ruled out.

Psychotic reactions are occasionally reported to persist long after the end of a psychedelic experience. They appear to occur most often in cases where there is a history of mental problems. But the intensity of negative reactions which a psychedelic experience is capable of eliciting can cause temporary psychosis in seemingly well-integrated individuals.

Flashbacks refer to the reinstatement of a psychedelic experience long after the drug has been ingested and eliminated from the body. Curiously, there is no known pharmacological basis for their occurrence. Flashbacks are apparently rare occurrences. One explanation of flashbacks is that they are triggered by something in the environment or an emotional state that the user associates with a past psychedelic experience.

Marijuana

A recent headline read: "Nation is going to pot, federal survey claims." Nowhere in the text of the Seventh Annual Report on Marijuana and Health does one find the phrase which captures our attention in the headline. But the statistics cited in the report confirm what many of us have suspected: In recent years there has been a sharp increase in the number of Americans who have turned to marijuana as a recreational drug. Marijuana is clearly the frontrunner as the most popular illicit drug in the United States.

Estimates based on a survey conducted in 1977 indicate that 43 million Americans have tried marijuana at least once and

PCP: The "Terror" Drug

PCP, or phencyclidine, is a recent entry into the illicit drug scene. First used as an anesthetic for veterinary purposes, it is still legitimately available from Parke, Davis & Co. under the brand name Sernyl. But in 1967, it made an unheralded appearance in San Francisco under the street name Peace Pill. It was not long, however, before its unpleasant and sometimes debilitating effects on humans received much notoriety.

Indeed, adverse effects of PCP use prompted *Time* magazine to call it the "terror drug" (1977).

As a street drug, PCP may be smoked (sometimes added to low grade marijuana to enhance its effects), injected, taken in liquid form, or ingested in tablets and capsules. The powdered form of PCP is known most commonly as Angel Dust and Hog, but it is also known by a variety of other slang names. Often mixed with other substances or sold in pure forms as LSD, mescaline, THC, or heroin, it may be misrepresented to unsuspecting consumers.

Just how dangerous is PCP? Even at low doses some users may experience numerous negative reactions. These include irritability, depression, paranoia, bodily and perceptual distortions, a feeling of disturbing detachment, and frightening hallucinations. Higher doses produce sedation, catalepsy, general anesthesia, and convulsions. Side effects include abdominal pains, nausea, vomiting, blurred vision, watering of the eyes, and loss of balance. Convulsions and coma can accompany large doses.

Even more unsettling are the reports of deaths by drowning, falls from heights, fire, and auto accidents directly related to PCP use (Burns & Lerner, 1976). Furthermore, PCP has the potential to produce schizophrenic-like symptoms and to exaggerate pathology already present in the individual. Luisada (1977) reports that from 1974 to 1977, one third of the inpatient admissions at a large psychiatric facility in Washington, D.C., were related to PCP poisoning. Luisada delineates three stages in the recovery process from PCP induced psychosis. The initial phase is characterized by a tendency towards violence which makes the person a danger to others and is accompanied by confusion, paranoia, and misperceptions. The second, or mixed phase, usually follows after about five days of treatment. Activity level and hostility decrease, but restlessness may persist. The third stage, recovery, begins after about ten days. Rapid recovery along with some amnesia for the earlier events of the psychosis occurs. Residual problems may be evident in some cases, but recovery is usually complete.

Of course, such marked reactions are not always associated with PCP use. Nonetheless, on the basis of descriptions of the PCP "high" described by chronic users, it is not easy to understand the drug's appeal.

> The common pattern of effects described by users includes an "ozone stage" which occurs 5 to 15 minutes after smoking PCP. In the ozone stage, which usually lasts from two to six hours, a person usually has a difficult time talking and walking, becomes confused, demonstrates repetitive behavior, and has a lack of attention. Things seem to slow down for a person on PCP. As one user described the drug, "It makes me not feel; I can put my mind in a box. It's not like getting high" (Jacob, Marshman, & Carlen, 1976).

The long-term effects of chronic use are in need of further study. Reports of brain damage with repeated use of PCP need to be replicated (Cohen, 1977). The effects of use of PCP along with other drugs such as alcohol also need to be determined before the social costs of PCP use can be accurately assessed. But given what we already know, the costs are likely to be great.

about 16 million had used it within the month before the survey (Abelson et al., 1977). This represents a significant increase since 1976 when corresponding estimates were 36 million and 15 million. In one year's time marijuana use by teenagers increased by about one third. The survey revealed that 62 percent of persons in this age group had tried marijuana. But even among people aged 35 and older who report the least frequent use (about 7 percent), attitudes toward marijuana are becoming increasingly positive. Taken together, these statistics are truly remarkable in light of the fact that little more than a decade ago, marijuana use was largely confined to the inner-city ghetto, to blacks, or to jazz musicians (Jessor, 1979).

Indeed, through much of the 20th century, marijuana was thought to be a dangerous drug that incited violence, led to the use of heroin, contributed to moral degeneration, and was a menace to the public safety. Marijuana's reputation as an "evil" drug dates back to the 1920s when newspapers publicized its use by the "undesirable elements" in society and established a firm connection between marijuana and crime in the public's eye. Before that time, the public was largely unaware of marijuana's use as an intoxicant. Beginning in the 18th century, the marijuana plant, cannabis sativa, was widely grown in Virginia and the colonies and valued for its fiber which was used for rope. However, by 1936, all of the 48 states had enacted laws which regulated the use, sale, and/or possession of marijuana. It was not until the early 1960s that the use of marijuana began to spread to middle- and upper-class youth. Marijuana use increased steadily through the 1960s. But a significant upsurge in the use of marijuana did not occur until the late 1960s, when the use of LSD and other hallucinogens began to decline (Julien, 1978).

As you might imagine, the widespread use of marijuana has stimulated a great deal of interest in better understanding its effects and the social and medical consequences of its use and abuse. Indeed, marijuana has been researched more than any other illicit drug. Recent evidence is transforming our thinking about marijuana and is shedding new light on old stereotypes which have their origin in the days when the drug was seen as an inherently "evil" substance.

What have we learned about marijuana? And equally important, what are some of the gaps in our knowledge about marijuana? Let us first turn our attention to examining the subjective effects of marijuana.

Subjective effects of marijuana. One common belief in vogue in the 1930s was that users who smoked only a portion of a "reefer" (marijuana cigarette or "joint") would become intoxicated. Actually, new users are frequently unable to identify drug related effects and consequently do not experience the marijuana "high" of the more experienced user. Becker (1953) notes that the effects are often subtle, and new users must *learn* to achieve a marijuana high. After marijuana is inhaled and held in the lungs for 20–40 seconds, the user must learn to identify and control the effects. Finally, in order to achieve the high state, the effects must be labeled as pleasant.

The subjective effects of marijuana have been determined, for the most part, by studying more experienced users. The short-term subject effects include a sense of well-being and a tendency to talk and perhaps laugh more than usual. Later the user may become more quiet, introspective, and sleepy. Mood changes are not uncommon. The most prominent physiological changes are an increase in heart rate, reddening of the eyes, and dryness of the mouth.

Other effects have been reported that may be particularly prominent at higher dosages include distortion of the sense of time, spatial and perceptual changes, and an altered sense of self. At very high doses, the effects of marijuana resemble those produced by the hallucinogens—most notably, hallucinations and confusion. There have been rare reports of extreme anxiety and panic at high dosages, which have precipitated a psychotic episode.

The subjective effects of marijuana are caused by the primary ingredient in the plant, THC (tetrahydrocannabinol). Hashish is more potent than marijuana because it contains greater concentrations of THC. The effect of marijuana and hashish are often quite variable and like other drugs, particularly the hallucinogens, depend on the amount taken, the personality of the user, the situation in which the drug is taken, and the user's expectations concerning the drug experience.

Pharmacologically, marijuana is usually classified as a mild hallucinogen, but it also may have sedative or hypnotic qualities. Marijuana does not produce a physical dependence at normal doses, but tolerance to its effects have been verified by research.

Some Consequences of Marijuana Use

Marijuana, criminal activity, and driving. Some definitive conclusions can be drawn with respect to the relationship between marijuana and criminality. Evidence reviewed by the National Commission on Marijuana and Drug Abuse in 1972 suggests that there is no evidence to substantiate the association between marijuana and criminal, violent, aggressive, or delinquent behavior. In fact, marijuana users are less likely to commit violent or nonviolent crimes of a sexual or nonsexual nature than are nonusers.

There is also little question that marijuana, like alcohol, appears to increase the likelihood of an accident when "mixed" with driving. A study of highway accidents in the Boston area found that marijuana smokers were overrepresented in traffic fatalities (Sterlins-Smith, 1976). A relationship between marijuana intoxication and impaired driving performance has been documented in studies of driving related perceptual skills, driver simulation and actual driving performance, and user's own evaluations of their driving skills while high (Peterson, 1977).

The "amotivational syndrome." In 1974, Senator James Eastland cautioned that "If the cannabis epidemic continues . . . we may find ourselves saddled with a large population of semi-zombies—of young people acutely afflicted by the amotivational syndrome" (Ray, 1978). Concerns like those expressed by Senator Eastland are reminiscent of earlier claims that marijuana led to "personality destruction" and degeneration. Indeed, the belief is still prevalent that regular use of marijuana leads to passivity, unproductivity, and a loss of motivation to pursue goals valued by society.

However, a causal link between marijuana use and the so-called amotivational syndrome has yet to be established. Let us examine the findings of a study that is now frequently referred to as the "Jamaican Study." Anthropologists Vera Rubin and Lambros Comitas studied 2,000 working-class Jamaican males, who, like the majority of workers in Jamaica, smoke a potent variety of marijuana called ganga as they are engaged in their everyday labors. The workers smoked an average number of about seven marijuana cigarettes each day, each of which is about 2–20 times as strong as marijuana smoked in the United States.

Over the more than 100-year history of marijuana use in Jamaica, the average user has come to view the consequences of smoking ganga as harmless, if not beneficial. Far from being seen as a substance which dampens motivation, marijuana is most often smoked at work and is even given to school-age children to improve their classroom performance. In the work context, improved concentration and work capacity are attributed to marijuana use.

Rubin and Comitas' analyses of the workers' thoughts before and after smoking ganga were indeed interesting and unexpected. After smoking, workers indicated that they spent more time thinking about their work than they did before taking the drug. Vera Rubin notes that among the Jamaicans, marijuana is "not taken to drop out but to hold on, to eke out a precarious living" (APA Monitor, 1976, p. 5).

Jamaican children smoking ganga.

© Jeffrey Jay Foxx/Woodfin Camp & Associates

A study of chronic heavy marijuana smokers in Costa Rica revealed that the heaviest users were found to have the highest incomes and the most stable job history of those studied. In addition, they reported that their favorite activity while smoking is to work (Coggins, 1976).

These two studies of chronic marijuana use suggest a crucial point: the expectations fostered by a particular culture can play a role in the work-related attitudes and behavior. In everyday conditions, even while consuming high doses of marijuana, the workers reacted in a way consistent with their culture (APA Monitor, 1976).

We must, however, exercise caution about directly translating these results to our more urbanized, industrial American society. The findings may have little relevance to American adolescents at an earlier stage in development and under different social conditions (HEW Report, 1976).

Marijuana and "harder" drugs. Does marijuana serve as a "stepping stone" to more dangerous drugs, as the antimarijuana sensationalism of the 1920s and 1930s would lead us to believe? A recent study by Gould and his colleagues (Gould, Berberian, Kasl, Thompson, & Kleber, 1977) addresses the question of whether college age drug users tend to take drugs in some kind of stepwise, orderly sequence. The study examined the patterns of multiple drug use reported by a random sample of 1,094 high-school students living in Connecticut. They found that respondents who used more than one drug tended to first use alcohol, next marijuana, and then hashish. But the patterns of drug use are not consistent thereafter. Those who progressed beyond hashish were about equally likely to progress next to amphetamines, LSD, barbiturates, or mescaline. Only a small minority of students' drug experience extended beyond these four drugs. For example, over one half of the students had tried marijuana, but only 2 percent of the students had used heroin. Thus, although using marijuana tends to precede the use of heroin, the great majority of users never try heroin. The findings show that the use of marijuana, at least in the population studied, is not causally linked to the use of heroin in a simple, straightforward fashion.

Marijuana and health. Because the adverse effects of cigarette smoking have received so much attention, it is not surprising that considerable concern has been expressed about the hazards posed by smoking marijuana. The available evidence does, indeed, suggest that lung functioning is impaired in chronic marijuana smokers. Long-time heavy users of marijuana sometimes develop a chronic bronchial cough.

Consuming marijuana may be hazardous for persons with cardiac abnormalities. Since marijuana increases heart rate and may also temporarily weaken the muscle contractions of the heart, persons with heart problems who smoke marijuana are exposing themselves to unnecessary risks.

There is considerably less agreement about heavy marijuana use as regards chromosome damage, brain damage, suppression of the body's disease fighting mechanism, and reduced levels of male sex hormones. There are inconsistent and contradictory findings in each of these areas of medical concern. Although the bulk of research studies indicate that physiological changes produced by marijuana tend to remain within normal limits, much more research is needed to rule out possible medical complications of marijuana use.

It seems appropriate to conclude our discussion of marijuana with this quote by Richard Jessor (1978): "It seems safe to predict that marijuana use will continue to increase in prevalence in American society, not only among youth, but in other age groups of the population as well. Its increasingly shared definition as a recreational drug, and the decreasing proportion of the population that disapproves of its use and that perceives any risk associated with its use, signal its likely institutionalization as part of ordinary social life. It is this anticipation that makes it even more important that research on marijuana should be expanded" (p. 349).

Cocaine

Cocaine is the most potent natural stimulant drug. It is obtained from the leaves of a shrub, erythoxylin cocoa, which grows in abundance in the mountainous region of South America. Cocaine has a long and interesting history. About 30 years after cocaine was extracted from cocoa leaves, its anesthetic properties were discovered. And by the late 1800s, cocaine was hailed as a cure-all by doctors who prescribed it for a wide range of maladies. Around the turn of the century, patent medicines, wines, and alcoholic tonics containing cocaine and cocoa extracts were quite popular. Until 1903, cocaine was an ingredient in coca-cola, which was advertised to "cure your headache and relieve fatigue for only 5 cents." Even Freud advocated the use of cocaine to treat morphine addiction and used cocaine himself to improve his mood. But dependence problems began to appear shortly after the drug became popular and Freud reversed his position on cocaine and came out strongly against its use. In 1906 cocaine came under strict control and it is today legally classified as a narcotic drug.

Today, there is a resurgence in the popularity of cocaine. Indeed, it has become a fashionable drug, perhaps *the* status drug because of its very high price and the exotic properties attributed to it (Peterson, 1977). Trends indicate increasing use of cocaine by all age groups over the past decade. The abuse potential of cocaine is probably limited by its high price and somewhat limited availability. Nonetheless, the director of NIDA estimated that over 8 million Americans had experimented with cocaine as a recreational drug (Ray, 1978).

Cocaine can be injected intravenously, but, more commonly, it is inhaled, or "snorted," through the nose where it is absorbed through the nasal mucous membranes. Cocaine is pharmacologically similar to the amphetamines, which we will discuss in the next section, and produces similar effects, although the effects of cocaine are shorter acting and dissipate within a half hour. Users commonly report experiencing euphoria, enhanced mental and physical capacity, stimulation, and a sense of well-being accompanied by diminished fatigue.

Cocaine is most commonly "snorted" to produce a euphoric high.

Charles Gatewood/Stock, Boston, Inc.

Chronic use of cocaine can result in loss of weight, insomnia, digestive disorders, paranoia, chronic nasal problems, and hallucinations of bugs crawling under the skin, as has been reported by amphetamine users. The possibility of physical dependence is in question, but psychological dependence can occur. Although withdrawal effects are less severe than heroine or barbituates, depression may occur after taking cocaine. In contrast with the widespread "street" belief that cocaine is not a dangerous drug, accidental deaths due to cocaine, while uncommon, have been reported (Peterson, 1977).

THE "PRESCRIPTION DRUGS"

Amphetamine

> Edward K., a truck driver, has just taken a dose of a drug powerful enough to enable him to make a round trip from New York to Los Angeles without resting. Truckers have termed the dose of this drug necessary to accomplish this feat the *L.A. turnaround.*
>
> In 1969 Astronaut Gordon Cooper took a drug to increase his alertness just before he manually controlled the reentry of his Apollo space capsule.
>
> In 1964 an Olympic athlete, a gold medal hopeful competing in the 100-meter dash event, took a drug which he believed would improve his performance. Four years later the

Medical Commission of the International Olympic Organization ruled that athletes who have taken this drug must forfeit any medals they won in Olympic competition.

In 1934 a group of psychology students at the University of Minnesota took a drug in order to improve their attitude toward their work, diminish fatigue, and improve concentration while they studied for an exam. Reports suggest that this is the first use of this drug for "cramming."

As you may already have guessed, the drug taken in each of these examples was an amphetamine, one of the most widely used and misused stimulants. Stimulants are drugs that increase alertness, activity, and excitement. Amphetamines, as well as other stimulants such as coffee, cocaine, and nicotine, speed up bodily processes through their action on the central nervous system. Some of the better known drugs in the amphetamine family are amphetamine itself (e.g., benzadrine), dextroamphetamine (e.g., dexadrine), methamphetamine (e.g., methedrine), and methylphenidate (e.g., ritalin).

The therapeutic potential of the amphetamines was first recognized by Gordon Allen in 1827. His research led to the use of the drug in the benzedrine inhaler to aid in dilating the bronchial passages. Amphetamines have been used in the treatment of obesity, narcolepsy (uncontrolled fits of sleep), and hyperkinetic behavior. Since amphetamines have serious abuse potential and their contribution to the effectiveness of weight reduction programs is questionable, the FDA has recently removed amphetamines from the list of drugs for the treatment of obesity.

Despite increasingly stringent federal controls, the nonmedical use of prescription stimulants is greater than the use of prescription sedatives or tranquilizers. Furthermore, the nonmedical use of stimulants ranks second only to marijuana among young adults (Johnson, Backman, & O'Malley, 1977).

Patterns of amphetamine use. A number of patterns of amphetamine use have been identified (Amphetamine, HEW Report, 1974).

1. *Intermittent low-dose use.* The first pattern involves occasional use of small doses of oral amphetamines to postpone fatigue, elevate mood while doing an unpleasant task, help recover from a hangover, or to "experience a feeling of well-being and euphoria." The user who adopts this pattern may be any age. However, amphetamine use is not a necessary part of his life-style. The most common source of pills is friends who received a legitimate prescription.

2. *Sustained low-dose use.* In this pattern, amphetamines are obtained from a doctor for weight reduction but are used on a regular daily basis for stimulant and euphoria-producing effects. A potent psychological dependence may occur which is followed by withdrawal depression if regular use is interrupted. Dependence is reinforced by renewed use of amphetamines to alleviate withdrawal distress. Increased doses may be taken to counteract tolerance to some of the desired drug-related effects. Where intake of amphetamines gradually increases, insomnia may result and be countered by alcohol or sleeping pills. This eventuates in an "upper-downer" cycle which increases the likelihood of overdose.

3. *High-dose intravenous use.* This pattern corresponds to the behaviors

associated with the "speed-freak"—the street user who injects large doses of amphetamines intravenously in order to achieve the "flash" or "rush" of pleasure immediately following the injection.

The "speed cycle" has been described by David Smith (1969) in terms of an "action-reaction" phenomenon (see Figure 14–1).

The "action-phase" marks the onset of the drug effect. Euphoria, restlessness, talkativeness, and excitement are part of the action phase. The individual may shoot speed repeatedly to prolong the euphoria. Inability to sleep and loss of appetite also characterize the so-called speed-binge. The user may become increasingly suspicious and even develop a paranoid psychosis, similar to paranoid schizophrenia, as increasing amounts of amphetamine are accumulated within the body. Some users may begin to do peculiar things over and over, without apparent reason. And many users may become aggressive and hostile, perhaps as an expression of their paranoid feelings.

The reaction phase begins when injecting amphetamines is interrupted for reasons which include fatigue, paranoia, or lack of the drug. As drug effects diminish, the user may experience exhaustion and sleep continuously for up to two days. Following exhaustion, severe depressive symptoms may emerge which may last for as long as several weeks. The paranoid symptoms which are associated with amphetamine psychosis will also usually disappear within a few days or weeks after the drug use is stopped. But in some cases symptoms of depression, hallucinations, anxiety, and paranoia may persist for a prolonged period after use of the drug has been discontinued.

FIGURE 14–1 The Speed Cycle

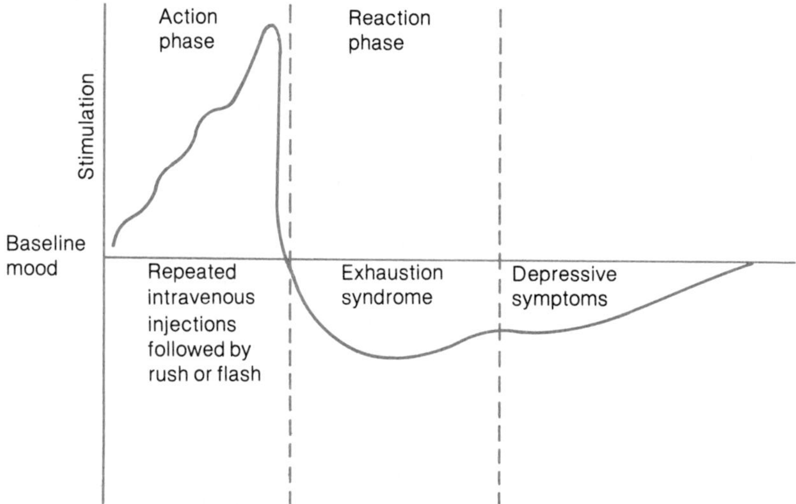

Source: Reprinted from D. E. Smith, "The Characteristics of Dependence in High Dose Amphetamine use," *International Journal of the Addiction,* 4 Marcel Dekker, Inc., N.Y. (1969), pp. 453–59, by courtesy of Marcel Dekker, Inc.

The Sedative-Hypnotics: Barbiturates

When people have problems falling asleep or when they experience the unpleasant symptoms of anxiety, they may consult a physician and obtain a sedative-hypnotic drug. The name sedative-hypnotic derives from the fact that at low doses these drugs reduce anxiety (sedative effect), while at moderate doses they induce sleep (hypnotic effect). Since the sedative-hypnotic drugs have a depressant effect on the central nervous system, they can be extremely dangerous drugs at high dosages and produce unconsciousness, coma, and death.

The sedative-hypnotics are usually grouped under three classifications: barbiturates, nonbarbiturates, and benzodiazepines. Valium, one of the benzodiazepines, is the most widely prescribed drug in the United States. It is commonly used to relieve anxiety, and its rate of abuse is increasing. Nonbarbiturates which are most commonly abused include methaqualone (Sopor, Quaalude) and meprobamate (Miltown). But of all the drugs in this class, the barbiturates are the most widely abused, and they rank third, after alcohol and tobacco, as the most frequent drugs of abuse. The most frequently abused barbiturates are secobarbitol (Seconal, or reds), pentobarbital (Nembutal), and Tuinal. Because of their abuse potential, the often fatal consequences of overdose, and the life-threatening consequences of withdrawal from barbiturates, they will serve as the focus for our discussion.

Over 2,500 barbiturates have been synthesized, but only a dozen or so are used for medical purposes. In addition to their widespread use to treat sleeplessness and anxiety, barbiturates have also been used to treat epilepsy and certain forms of cerebral palsy. They are also used as anesthetics prior to surgical operations because of their ability to produce unconsciousness.

Patterns of abuse. Physicians are the major source of barbiturates and many people who overuse barbiturates are introduced to the drug by a physician. Indeed, the ready availability of the barbiturates is one reason why they are so widely abused. In 1976, over 18 million prescriptions were written for barbiturates (Cooper, 1977).

Smith, Wesson, and Lannon (1971) have described one pattern of barbiturate abuse that is most commonly seen in persons who are introduced to barbiturates through a physician's prescription. Initially, barbiturates are taken in order to relieve anxiety or to induce sleep. However, the potential barbiturate abuser soon finds that the drug also helps him or her to cope more easily with life and to maintain an essentially tension-free state. As tolerance to the calming effects develops, such persons increase their dose—often without notifying their physician. Unaware that the patient is overusing the drug, the physician may continue to prescribe "medication." In cases where a physician refuses to prescribe barbiturates, the budding addict may consult other physicians and fail to mention his previous doctor. Eventually the abuser develops a physical dependence on barbiturates, but the problem may remain hidden from others. Barbiturate abuse may not be recognized until decreased ability to work and signs of acute intoxication like slurred speech, confusion, irritability, and a staggering walk clearly suggest a drug problem. Individuals who exhibit this pattern of abuse are likely to be 30–50 years old.

Barbiturate abuse is not limited to a

A dangerous and insidious pattern of barbiturate abuse may begin with the overuse of prescribed medication to induce sleep.

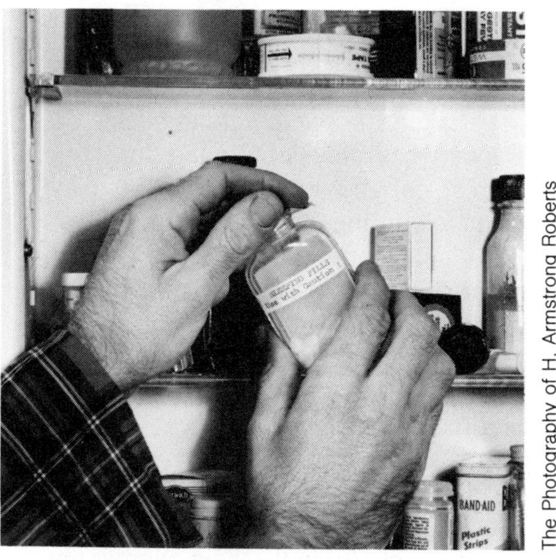

The Photography of H. Armstrong Roberts

particular age group. Survey data reveals that 17 percent of high-school seniors have tried nonprescription barbiturates (National Prescription Audit, 1976). The family medicine cabinet may be one source of barbiturates, but there also exists a black market by which access to the drugs can be obtained. In young people the pattern of abuse tends to be episodic in contrast to the pattern of chronic abuse more commonly found in adult abusers. Barbiturates produce a state of intoxication which is very similar to the effects of alcohol. Younger users may take the drug with friends in a group context to get "high," or they may use the drug on an individual basis to relieve tension or to reduce sexuality (Blum, 1969). Stimulant users occasionally take barbiturates to counteract the effects of amphetamines (Jaffe, 1970). Heroin users are known to use barbiturates when heroin is not readily available or to supplement their habit.

Long-term and adverse effects of barbiturates. Of all the psychoactive drugs we have considered, the physical dependence that develops to the barbiturates is potentially the most dangerous. Even withdrawal from heroin does not usually pose a life-threatening risk. But sudden withdrawal from barbiturates can lead to very serious physical effects which include convulsions, coma, and death. Withdrawal is usually managed by a gradual tapering off process in which the maintenance dose is reduced by about 10 percent every day or two. Most frequently this occurs in a hospital setting.

As tolerance to barbiturates develops, the danger of an overdose or suicide increases. Reported estimates of drug-related deaths attributable to barbiturates range from 17 to 39 percent (Cooper, 1977). Barbiturates can be especially lethal because unlike heroin, cocaine, and amphetamines, the lethal dose of a barbiturate does not increase with development of tolerance to the drug's effects. With barbiturates, as the dose necessary to achieve a desired effect increases, the lethal dose remains about the same. Thus, as the barbiturate abuser increases the dose in order to promote a restful sleep, to relieve anxiety, or to "get down," he approaches a dose that may have fatal consequences. Since barbiturates have a very narrow range of safe doses, they are particularly dangerous in this regard. If it takes one pill to induce sleep, it may take five pills to induce a coma, and only ten pills to cause a fatal overdose (Sikorski & Nash, 1979).

When alcohol is taken in combination with a barbiturate, it greatly increases the risk of overdose. Since both are central nervous system depressants, they multiply each others' effects. Nearly 5,000 deaths each year have been attributed to the overuse of barbiturates (AMA, 1971).

SUMMARY AND REVIEW OF EXPLANATIONS

Each of the drugs that we have described has a high potential for dependence and/ or abuse as defined by DSM III. Substance dependence is generally a more severe disorder than substance abuse. In the case of substance dependence, the user develops a tolerance to the effects of the drug. Unpleasant withdrawal symptoms are experienced when the use of the drug is discontinued.

Throughout our discussion we have touched on various explanations for drug use. Many explanations have been proposed, yet there is no one explanation for drug abuse. There are many and varied reasons for taking drugs. Let us now review some of the explanations we have considered. One of the most important factors in initial drug use is availability. If a person does not have access to a drug or contact with users, it reduces the likelihood of drug use. So, even if a person is vulnerable to substance abuse, when access is limited, a problem is unlikely to develop.

No one personality type has been consistently linked with the misuse of drugs. But drugs can be abused for a number of personal and social reasons which include the following: a search for novel experience, inability to delay gratification, peer pressure, modeling others behavior, inability to cope with one's moods and feelings in more adaptive ways, the need to compensate for a poor self-image and lack of acceptance from others, and so on. These factors may, of course, operate simultaneously to promote drug use.

Once physical dependence to a drug is created, its use may be reinforced both by the euphoria induced and the relief of withdrawal symptoms. Increased doses may be taken to counteract the effects of tolerance which develops to the drug. Psychological and social factors may play a major role in the initial stages of drug use, but after dependence has developed, powerful physiological factors may play a part in maintaining drug use. Substance abuse and dependence is a complex phenomenon. It is perhaps best viewed as having multiple determinants.

Few of the explanations we have mentioned have a sound scientific basis, but they do represent hypotheses which merit further study. In the next chapter we will see how the various perspectives on abnormal behavior have been applied to the social drugs, alcohol and tobacco.

The subjective effects of the drugs which we surveyed are determined by a complex interaction of four factors: the dosage of the drug; the setting or the psychological and social environment; the personality of the user; and the set or the user's expectations of the drug's effects and attitudes about taking the drug.

The use of all of the drugs that we have described is increasing, with the exception of LSD. Heroin use is no longer confined to large, inner-city poverty areas. Cocaine is becoming increasingly popular, and there has been a virtual explosion in the use of marijuana among young and older citizens alike. Both of these drugs are meeting wider acceptance, and marijuana is fast becoming a part of the American scene. Amphetamines rank second only to marijuana in their nonmedical use by young people. Barbiturates have not declined in popularity despite the potentially fatal consequences of their use.

Of all of these drugs, the use of heroin probably meets with the most negative societal reaction. This is probably due to the association of heroin with criminal activities in the public's eye. Recent treatment approaches to heroin abuse are promising but will probably continue to evoke controversy.

Despite the increased usage of illegal and controlled substances, there is a greater awareness of the social and personal costs of misuse. These costs can be measured not only by criminal activity, but also by the risk of overdose, health-related problems, and the danger of developing adjustment problems and psychotic-like behavior.

15

Substance Use Disorders II: The Social Drugs

INTRODUCTION

Only within the past few decades has drug abuse come to the forefront of public attention as a social problem. This is not to say that drug abuse does not have a far reaching history. It does. Drugs have always been very much with us, with all of their potential for abuse. But today, drug misuse can be considered a part of the "psychopathology of everyday life," a visible, and in some circles prominent, aspect of the American experience. Given the backdrop of recent public concern over the "drug problem," many forget that drugs like tobacco and alcohol can exact enormous costs to the individual and society. Just what are the costs of abuse of the social drugs? What are the effects of these drugs and what explanations have been offered to account for their widespread use? These are just a few of the questions and issues that we will address in this chapter.

TOBACCO

Consider the following statements which highlight some of the health hazards associated with smoking tobacco.

- A pack-a-day smoker takes more than 40,000 puffs per year and each puff delivers nicotine and other toxic chemicals into the bloodstream. Nicotine, the most active agent in tobacco, is a poison more toxic than heroine and is sometimes used as an insecticide. Nearly 500 compounds, including tars, carbon monoxide, and other gases have been isolated. The carbon monoxide content of cigarette smoke is considerably higher than Los Angeles smog on the worst day (Jarvik, 1977).
- "Last year, smoking was a major factor in 220,000 deaths from heart disease, 78,000 lung cancer deaths and 22,000 deaths from other cancers. These facts mean that people who smoke are committing slow-motion suicide." Quote by former secretary of Health, Education, and Welfare, James Califano (Lyons, 1978).
- It can now be unequivocally stated that cigarette smoking effects the developing fetus. Cigarettes increase the rate of spontaneous abortion, stillbirth, and early postpartum deaths of children (Julien, 1978).
- It has been estimated that one's life is shortened 14 minutes for every cigarette smoked. One in three smokers will die as a result of smoking (Julien, 1978).

As you read these statements you may have asked yourself questions like the ones that follow: If smoking tobacco is so dangerous—and, indeed, recent surveys suggest that 90 percent of the public believe it to be harmful to health (HEW Adult Use of Tobacco, 1976)—what factors account for the fact that 54 million Americans smoke? Why is the habit so tenacious that nearly two out of three smokers say they would like to quit, yet continue to smoke despite having tried to quit at least once? (Ray, 1978).

Before we address these questions, let us first examine some trends of smoking behavior in order to assess the impact that government initiated antismoking efforts have had on cigarette sales. Before the 1950s, when the first reported link between cigarette smoking and lung cancer was publicized, little interest was taken in the prevalence of smoking. However, with the publication of the Surgeon General's Report, in 1964, which summarized medical knowledge about the hazards to health posed by smoking, much attention was focused on smoking behavior in the general population (see Table 15–1). Indeed, growing concern about the effects of smoking spurred governmental efforts to educate the public about the consequences of smoking and led to increased restrictions placed on the user and on advertising (Ray, 1978).

TABLE 15–1 Governmental Actions on Smoking

1964	Surgeon General's report on smoking and health determines that cigarette smoking is a health hazard.
1966	Federal Cigarette Labeling and Advertising Act requires, as of January 1, cigarette packs to carry statement: CAUTION: CIGARETTE SMOKING MAY BE HAZARDOUS TO YOUR HEALTH.
1967	Federal Communications Commission rules that the "Fairness Doctrine" applies to cigarette advertising, and TV and radio must carry antismoking messages.
1970	Cigarette pack statement changed to WARNING: THE SURGEON GENERAL HAS DETERMINED THAT CIGARETTE SMOKING IS DANGEROUS TO YOUR HEALTH.
1971	Radio and TV ads banned as of January 2. Interstate Commerce Commission restricts smoking to rear five rows of interstate buses.
1972	All cigarette advertising must carry the same health warning as on packs, as well as the tar and nicotine content of a cigarette.
	The consumer Product Safety Act specifically excludes cigarettes from being considered under the act.
1973	Arizona becomes first state to prohibit smoking in all elevators, indoor theaters, libraries, art galleries, museums, concert halls, and buses; all airlines required to designate smoking and no smoking areas in planes.
1975	Minnesota passes Indoor Clean Air Act, which makes smoking illegal in all public places and public meetings except where designated.
1978	Civil Aeronautics Board bans cigar and pipe smoking on all American commercial airlines.

Source: O. Ray, *Drugs, Society, and Human Behavior,* 2d ed. (St. Louis: C. V. Mosby Company, 1978), p. 177.

Results of surveys suggest that antismoking efforts have indeed had a significant impact on smoking behavior. According to the 1975 survey by the Department of Health, Education, and Welfare (Adult Use of Tobacco, 1976), the percentage of people who classify themselves as smokers has consistently decreased over the past 15 years. A recent government study reveals that the percentage of adult smokers has fallen from 42 percent in 1964 to 33 percent in 1979 (*Columbus Dispatch,* 1979). This encouraging trend holds within every age group for men. The smoking rate for adolescent girls nearly doubled between 1968 and 1974 but is now turning downward, paralleling the pattern already established by older smokers. Another

Advertising and antismoking efforts initiated by the government have been successful in reducing the number of smokers.

indication that antismoking efforts have been successful is the switch to filter and low tar and nicotine cigarettes by more than three quarters of smokers.

Despite these encouraging trends, authorities have noted that smoking still remains the greatest public health hazard in the United States (Julien, 1978). Less than one in four smokers are successful in permanently quitting before the age of sixty (Russell, 1977). Smoking withdrawal and therapy clinics have successfully treated only about 20 percent of smokers after a one year follow-up (Hunt, Barrett, & Branch, 1971). And no one technique or therapy program has proven to be effective, although a wide range of techniques have been tried including hypnosis, nicotine chewing gum, tranquilizers, group pressure, and behavior modification.

Coan's Model of Smoking Behavior

The question of why people smoke has eluded a simple, unitary answer. Let us now consider an explanatory model proposed by Coan (1973), which emphasizes the complex, multidetermined nature of smoking behavior. The model suggests a crucial point: the variables associated with the onset of smoking may be very different from those related to the maintenance of smoking behavior. The beginning smoker may try smoking for a variety of reasons, which include curiosity, group pressure, the desire to imitate friends, or to seem mature and sophisticated. For the neophyte, smoking may have an *adjustive value,* serving particular needs such as reducing tension or anxiety, enhancing self-esteem, and providing pleasure and enjoyment. But as smoking becomes more habitual, it also tends to become automatic. And at this point, the main need that is satisfied by smoking is merely the need for another cigarette. When physical and psychological dependence develop, smoking can truly be said to be *maladjustive*—an unpleasant habit associated with an unwelcome craving for cigarettes.

A Biological Explanation: The Role of Nicotine

Some researchers believe that nicotine is the major culprit in *maintaining* smoking behavior. The primary psychological effects of nicotine consist of mild to moderate stimulation of the central nervous system (Julien, 1978). It has been hypothesized that smokers regulate their smoking in order to maintain some desirable level of nicotine, and that withdrawal symptoms appear when an optimum level of nicotine cannot be maintained (Sherman, Presson, Chassin & Olshavsky, 1979). But the evidence for this viewpoint is inconsistent and, therefore, not totally convincing. Some, but not all, studies show that smokers given low tar and nicotine cigarettes will smoke more cigarettes to equal the level of nicotine they were accustomed to. Schachter speculated that the failure to consistently find evidence for precise nicotine regulation may lie in the fact that not all smokers are addicted. Schachter (1977) found that while long-term heavy smokers showed nicotine regulation, long-term light smokers did not. Schachter concluded that long-term smokers behave as if they were addicted, while long-term light smokers are either not addicted or manage to keep their habit under tight psychological control.

Schachter and his associates have

conducted a series of studies designed to better understand the relationship between smoking and nicotine regulation. One of the hypotheses which they tested was that the acidity of the urine may mediate nicotine regulation, and that when the urine is acidified, more nicotine is flushed out of the body. Schachter and his group reasoned that if smoking serves to regulate nicotine, smokers would be expected to smoke more when the urine is acid, in order to compensate for the greater amounts of nicotine excreted. This is precisely what they found when they manipulated the acidity of the urine by the use of acidifying or alkalizing agents. There was a marked decrease in smoking when smokers were given bicarbonate to make the urine less acidic, and a dramatic increase in smoking when vitamin C was administered to acidify the urine.

Subsequent studies have demonstrated that stress and party-going, events that are commonly associated with heavy smoking, lead to increased acidification of the urine and increased smoking (Silverstein, Kozlowski, & Schachter, 1977). In the final study of the series it was found that when the urine is experimentally maintained at alkaline levels, stress had no effect on smoking. These findings not only appeared to support the general hypothesis that heavy smokers smoke for nicotine, but also that the acidity of the urine is the crucial biochemical link between stress and smoking.

But nicotine regulation does not provide a totally satisfactory explanation for the maintenance of smoking behavior. Not all smokers who cease smoking experience withdrawal symptoms. While some persons experience severe symptoms including gastric disorders, dry mouth, irritability, sleeplessness, headaches, and impaired concentration, others report no symptoms.

"My life of crime began when I gave up smoking and didn't know what to do with my hands."

Personality and Self-Concept

Sherman, et al., (1979) contend that it is important to consider other factors that may play a role in maintaining smoking. For example, McArthur, Waldron, and Dickinson (1958) found that personality variables could not account for the differences between smokers and nonsmokers, but they did have a bearing on whether a person who had already begun smoking was a heavy or a light smoker.

The nature of a person's self-concept has also been linked with habitual smoking. Sarbin and Nucci (1973) claim that people only become confirmed smokers, that is, unsuccessful quitters, when smoking becomes central to their definition of themselves. Thus, the confirmed smoker is "not merely someone who smokes cigarettes, he is a smoker" (1973, p. 183).

People may also continue smoking because they consider it to be socially desirable. A survey by the National Cancer Institute (1975) found that teenagers tended to perceive the people in cigarette advertising as attractive, young, enjoying themselves, and well-dressed. Since people may smoke in order to perceive themselves as sharing characteristics with the glamorous people portrayed in advertisements, the concern, in recent years, over cigarette advertisements is probably warranted. These findings also suggest that treatment efforts that ignore a consideration of the client's self-concept may be less than completely successful (Sherman et al., 1979).

ALCOHOL

> We arrive at the party tired and emotionally drained from the day's activities, and knock down a drink or two in order to loosen up quickly. Stress and strain begin to disappear. We feel relaxed, talkative, even euphoric.
>
> If we pay close attention to our own sensory changes we may notice a feeling of warmth and a slight numbness in the face, especially in the cheeks and lips. Then our hands, arms, and legs begin to tingle, and when they too are bordering on numbness we may, if we want, make a mental note that our blood alcohol level is approaching 0.10 percent, the legal limit of intoxication in most states (Jones & Parsons, 1975, p. 53).

The subjective effects of alcohol have long been known to man. From the time that fermented honey was made into the drink "mead" more than 8,000 years ago, alcohol has played an important role in social, religious, and medical contexts. Yet throughout history, it has been recognized that the misuse of alcohol can contribute to human misery and suffering. Almost 2,000 years ago the Roman philosopher Seneca commented that "Drunkenness is nothing but a condition of insanity purposely assumed," while others have observed that alcohol is a "curse second only to war."

Today the recreational use of alcohol is so commonplace that it is easy to forget that it is a potent and potentially dangerous psychoactive drug. Indeed, the majority of the 95 million Americans who drink are able to enjoy its effects without becoming its slave (*Time,* 1974). But for one person in ten who drinks, alcohol can not only be a serious personal problem, but it also can create problems for family, friends, employers, and with the police (NIAAA Special Report, 1975).

A special report to the U.S. Congress prepared by the National Institute of Alcohol Abuse and Alcoholism (NIAAA, 1975) provides disturbing documentation of the pervasiveness and social costs of alcohol consumption. In recent years, there has been an upsurge in drinking in society as a whole, but especially among young people and women. From 1960 to 1970, the average consumption of alcohol increased 26 percent—to the equivalent of 2.5 gallons of straight alcohol per person per year. The United States now leads all but two countries in the consumption of alcohol of the 25 countries from which reports are available. About three quarters of males and two thirds of women report using alcohol (see Figure 15–1).

But an even more disquieting trend is revealed by recent survey data: people with drinking problems are getting younger each year; and about 1.3 million youths

FIGURE 15–1 Percentage of Drinkers and Types of Drinkers, by Sex, U.S.A. 1972–1974

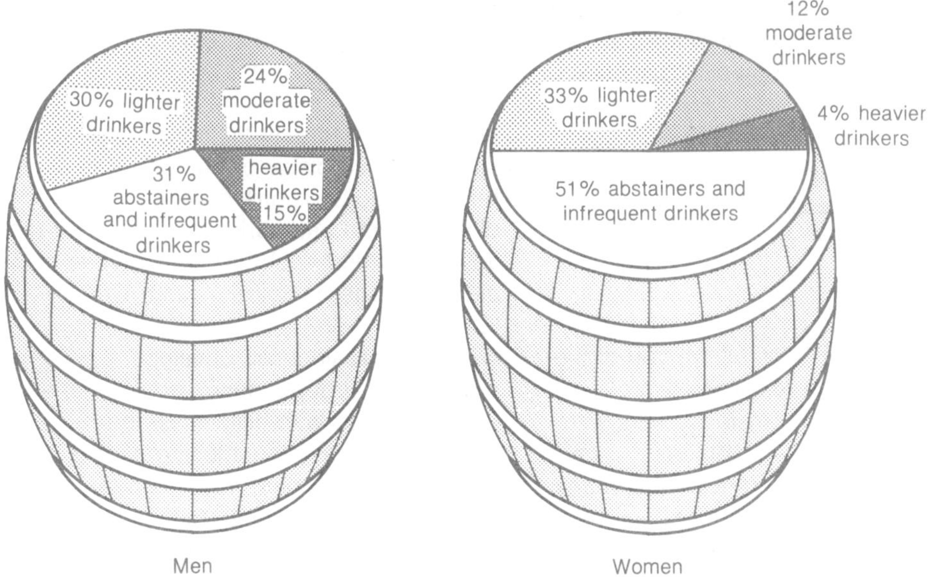

Source: U.S. Department of Health, Education, and Welfare: National Institute of Alcohol Abuse and Alcoholism (5600 Fishers Lane, Rockville, Maryland, 20852). *Second Special Report to the U.S. Congress on Alcohol and Health: New Knowledge.* DHEW Publication No. (ADM) 75–212, 1975, p. 11.

have serious drinking problems by late adolescence (*New York Times,* 1977).

Alcoholism effects a wide spectrum of the population. The NIAAA special report suggests that the stereotype of the alcoholic as a Bowery bum is inaccurate and applies to probably less than 5 percent of the alcoholics in this country. Ninety-five percent of alcoholics, who comprise 4 percent of the population, are employed or are capable of working. Persons who have high rates of alcohol problems are likely to be unmarried or divorced, live in large cities, and are both the best and least educated parts of the population (see Figure 15–2).

Although most alcoholics manage to keep their alcoholism hidden from others, the flagrant personal and dollar costs of alcoholism are more difficult to conceal.

Consider the following information gathered by NIAAA:

> Directly related to more than 86,000 deaths per year, alcohol abuse constitutes the third leading cause of death in the U.S., after heart disease and cancer. Cirrhosis, a disease which results in degeneration of the liver tissue, is the cause of most alcohol related deaths. But excessive, long-term drinking has also been linked with an increased risk of developing other medical problems which include cancer of the mouth, pharynx, and esophagus, damage to the heart muscle, brain damage and eventual dementia, ulcers, sexual impotence, malnutrition, and damage to the offspring of alcoholic mothers.

Alcohol was associated with 64 percent of all murders, 41 percent of all assaults, 34 percent of all forcible rape, and 29 percent of all other sex crimes.

In 1971, about 40 percent of the motor vehicle deaths were believed attributable to alcohol.

The economic cost associated with misuse of alcohol is estimated at $25 billion a year.

A look at Table 15–1 will inform you of the especially high costs resulting from reduced productivity of male workers with alcohol problems (NIAAA, 1975).

Despite such disturbing evidence, many people remain terribly ignorant about the effects of alcohol. Indeed, one study found that heavy drinkers were *less* likely to be knowledgeable about the effects of alcohol than light drinkers or abstainers.

The task of defining alcoholism and problem drinking is complicated by the wide range of drinking patterns and characteristics of persons who drink excessively. Nearly 20 years ago, Jellinek (1960), a pioneer in the scientific study of alcohol abuse, devised a typology of alcoholics that treats alcoholism not as a single, unified disease, but rather as a heterogeneous disorder that can be classified into categories or "alcoholisms." Jellinek named each of the five types of alcoholism he described with a Greek letter.

The alpha alcoholic develops a psychological dependence on alcohol and drinks to cope with difficulties and problems in life without losing control over alcohol intake. Alpha alcoholism may precipitate interpersonal, family, and work-related problems. In beta alcoholism, physical problems such as cirrhosis of the liver or stomach problems develop, but there are no signs of physical or psychological dependence. Gamma alcoholism is the most severe type in

FIGURE 15–2

Profile analysis of persons most likely to have no alcohol-related problems	Profile analysis of persons with high alcohol-problem rates
Lowest rates of alcohol-related problems for respondents in the 1973 national survey were found among: • Women • Persons over 50 • Widowed and married persons • Persons of Jewish religious affiliation • Residents of rural areas • Residents of the South • Persons with postgraduate education • Persons who are mostly "wine drinkers"	Highest rates of alcohol-related problems for respondents in the 1973 national survey were found among: • Men • Separated, single, and divorced persons (in that order) • Persons with no religious affiliation • Persons who are beer drinkers as compared with those who are mostly hard liquor or wine drinkers • Persons who were more likely (compared to other persons in the survey) to say: "Drunkenness is usually *not* a sign of social irresponsibility" and "Drunkenness is usually a sign of just having fun"

Source: U.S. Department of Health, Education, and Welfare: National Institute on Alcohol Abuse and Alcoholism (5600 Fishers Lane, Rockville, Maryland, 20852). *Second Special Report to the U.S. Congress on Alcohol and Health: New Knowledge.* DHEW Publication No. (ADM) 75–212. 1975, p. 19.

TABLE 15–1 Economic Costs of Alcohol Misuse and Alcoholism, U.S.A. 1971

	Billions of Dollars
Lost production	$ 9.35
Health and medical	8.29
Motor vehicle accidents	6.44
Alcohol programs and research	0.64
Criminal-justice system	0.51
Social-Welfare system	0.14
Total	$25.37

Source: R. Berry, J. Boland, J. Laxam, D. Hayler, M. Sillman, R. Fein, and P. Feldstein, "The Economic Costs of Alcohol Abuse and Alcoholism—1971." Prepared for the National Institute on Alcohol Abuse and Alcoholism under Contract No. HSM–42–73–114, Mar. 31, 1974.

This table appeared in National Institute on Alcohol Abuse and Alcoholism (NIAAA), *Alcohol and Health: 2d Special Report to the U.S. Congress, New Knowledge.* U.S. Department of Health, Education, and Welfare (DHEW Publication No. (ADM 75–212) (Washington, D.C.: U.S. Government Printing Office, 1975).

terms of health and social incapacitation. The alcoholic is unable to control his consumption once he takes a drink. But the alcoholic can still control whether or not he will take a drink, so it is possible to "go on the wagon" periodically. There is a progression from psychological to physical dependence, and withdrawal symptoms follow shortly after the alcoholic stops drinking. Gamma alcoholics are often highly motivated for treatment because with loss of control, drinking becomes more public and the ability to rationalize the use of alcohol diminishes. In delta alcoholism there is no loss of control, but psychological and physical dependence are so strong that is impossible to abstain for even relatively brief periods without suffering withdrawal. The last and perhaps most distinct type Jellinek describes is epsilon alcoholism. Here, the alcoholic engages in periodic, unpredictable binge drinking.

The richly descriptive categories proposed by Jellinek have proven useful to many workers who treat alcoholics, but they are neither precisely defined nor sufficiently independent (Wallace, 1977). The definitions of alcohol abuse and alcohol dependence presented in the new DSM III classification system include clear and specific criteria which can be used to help distinguish recreational use of alcohol from more destructive patterns of misuse. In addition, the criteria reflect the diversity of signs, symptoms, and behaviors associated with maladaptive drinking. Indeed, a look at the diagnostic criteria presented below will inform you of the kinds of indicators which may warrant a diagnosis of alcohol abuse or dependence. Alcohol abuse is diagnosed when criteria A, B, and C presented below are fulfilled. Alcohol dependence is diagnosed when criteria D is fulfilled in addition to those specified for alcohol abuse (A, B, C).

A. Continuous or episodic use of alcohol for at least one month.
B. Social complications of alcohol use: impairment in social or occupational functioning (e.g., arguments or difficulties with family or friends over excessive alcohol use, violent while intoxicated, missed work, fired), or legal difficulties (e.g., arrest for intoxicated behavior, traffic accidents while intoxicated).
C. Either *(1)* or *(2)*
   1. *Psychological dependence:* compelling desire to use alcohol; inability to cut down or stop drinking; repeated efforts to control or reduce excess drinking by "going on the wagon" (periods of temporary abstinence or restriction of drinking to certain times of the day).
   2. *Pathological pattern of use:* drinks nonbeverage alcohol; goes on binges (remains intoxicated

© William S. Nawrocki

© 1978, Rafael Macia

© Jan Halaska

© Magnum Photos Inc.

throughout the day for at least two days); occasionally drinks a fifth of spirits (or its equivalent in wine or beer); has had two or more blackouts (amnesic periods for events occurring while intoxicated).

D. Either *(1)* or *(2)*
   1. *Tolerance*
   2. *Withdrawal:* development of alcohol withdrawal (e.g., morning "shakes" and malaise relieved by drinking after cessation or reduction of drinking).

Subjective, Behavioral, and Clinical Effects of Alcohol

What are the effects of alcohol? Many of the short-term effects which you probably associate with intoxication are directly related to the concentration of alcohol in the blood. The relationship between the amount of alcohol in the blood and the intoxicating effects of alcohol are depicted in Figure 15–3.

Figure 15–3 shows that at low doses alcohol may produce talkativeness, euphoria, and diminished inhibition. Although alcohol is often misclassified as a stimulant, it is actually a depressant drug which first depresses those areas of the brain which inhibit emotion and behavior, thereby releasing them from inhibitory control. But at higher doses, the sedating effects of alcohol become more apparent as the motor centers of the brain are depressed, impairing walking and muscular coordination. Alcohol is metabolized at the rate of nearly one ounce per hour. The effects of alcohol have been found to be more pronounced when the blood alcohol is rising rather than falling (Jones & Parsons, 1975).

ALCOHOL AND EXPECTATIONS

In the last chapter we noted that the effects of drugs may be determined, in part, by the expectancies of the user. Wilson (1977) has suggested that the expectancies associated with alcohol use exert their greatest influence on complex social behaviors, such as aggression and sexuality. A number of recent studies lend support to the idea that expectancies may play an important role in influencing aggression and sexual arousal while drinking. Lang, Goeckner, Adesso, and Marlatt (1975) have studied the relationship between drinking, expectancies, and aggression. Before reviewing their study in some detail, let us consider a person who might tend to respond aggressively in a particular situation but is inhibited from engaging in aggressive behavior while sober. How might expectancies associated with the use of alcohol affect interpersonal aggression? We might expect that the person would be more likely to respond with aggression rather than with a response that would ease the interpersonal conflict if the person believes that alcohol makes him or her: (1) more likely to respond aggressively, (2) less likely to care about the opinions of others or the consequences of aggressive actions, or (3) more protected from the aggressive retaliation of another person.

Although Lang and his colleagues did not examine the relative importance of each of these beliefs in influencing interpersonal aggression, their study did show that the mere belief that one had consumed alcohol led to heightened aggressive responding. The researchers gave college students, who were heavy social drinkers, drinks which contained either alcohol (vodka and tonic) or tonic alone. The drinks were prepared in such a way that subjects could not distinguish the alcoholic drinks from the nonalcoholic drinks by the way they tasted. Within each of the groups who were given either alcoholic or a nonalcoholic drink, the experimenter told half the subjects that they had received an alcoholic beverage and the other half that they received a nonalcoholic beverage. Thus, four groups of subjects were formed: (1) told alcohol, received alcohol; (2) told alcohol, received tonic; (3) told tonic, received tonic; (4) told tonic, received alcohol. The experimenters carefully maintained the blood alcohol level of the subjects who received alcohol at the lower limit of legal intoxication for most areas of the United States.

After the subjects drank the beverages prepared for them, the researchers tested the subjects in a motor coordination task which involved working with another person. The other person was actually a confederate of the experimenters who was programmed to either parallel the performance of the subject or to surpass the subject's performance on the task and to belittle the performance and intelligence of the subject. In the second part of the study, subjects were led to believe that they were shocking the confederate as part of a learning experiment. Lang and his colleagues measured both the number of errors that the subject made on the motor coordination task and the degree of aggression displayed by the subject, as measured by the intensity and duration of shocks which the subject delivered to the confederate.

The experiment yielded two major findings. First, subjects who were given alcohol, regardless of whether they were told they were drinking alcohol or tonic, were more prone to errors at the motor coordination task. That is, the actual pharmacological properties of alcohol interfered with motor coordination even among subjects who didn't know that they were drinking alcohol. But a finding of greater interest was that even among subjects who received a nonalcoholic drink the belief that alcohol had been consumed influenced aggressive behavior. So, regardless of what the subject actually consumed, aggression was greatest when the subjects believed they had consumed alcohol. These results suggest that expectancies are more important than alcohol consumption in influencing social behaviors such as aggression than in influencing actual physical abilities such as motor coordination.

Let us now explore the relationship between expectancies associated with alcohol use and sexual expression and arousal. A widely held assumption is that alcohol serves to inhibit or decrease anxiety and guilt, thereby encouraging sexual expression (Gebhard et al., 1965). But it may be the case that people who drink alcohol experience greater relaxation simply because they expect to be more relaxed while drinking alcohol. Anthanasiou Shaver, and Tavris (1970) have argued that over time, people may have noted the associations between alcohol, relaxation, and sexual activity so that the expectation is instilled that alcohol produces sexual arousal and makes sex more enjoyable. Expectancies associated with alcohol consumption may increase the likelihood of sexual activity in another way: the knowledge that alcohol has been consumed may furnish the person with an excuse for engaging in a normally inhibited activity free from blame and reproach from others. Such alcohol related expectancies would be expected to pertain to individuals who drink moderate amounts of alcohol because it is a well-known fact that large quantities of alcohol result in a decrease in physiological sexual arousal (Bridell & Wilson, 1976; Farkas & Rosen, 1976).

Wilson and Lawson (1976) conducted research on the physiological correlates of sexual arousal using the design which we described earlier in which the experimenter manipulates alcohol content and the subject's expectancies. Their research demonstrated that male social drinkers who were led to believe that they had consumed moderate amounts of alcohol showed increased sexual arousal in response to erotic films, as compared to similar males who were led to believe that they had consumed a nonalcoholic beverage. Thus, the actual content of the drinks (alcohol versus tonic) was not a factor in determining the level of sexual arousal. But in a later study with females, Wilson and Lawson (1978) found that the alcoholic content of the drinks and not the expectancies of the subject was responsible for increased sexual arousal in female social drinkers in response to erotic films. The differences in responses between males and females suggests that researchers must exercise caution when attempting to relate their findings to people in general based on the results from research studies which are limited to the use of subjects of only one sex.

Prepared with the assistance of Larry Gorkin.

Toxic Effects

Idiosyncratic intoxication. People who regularly drink large amounts of alcohol develop a tolerance to its effects. When this occurs, it can mask an alcoholic's problems from family and friends since intoxication may not be obvious despite heavy daily consumption.

However, a small fraction of people who drink seem to have virtually no tolerance for alcohol. With small quantities of alcohol, insufficient to produce intoxification in most people, dramatic behavioral changes occur which are atypical of the person when not drinking. In what is termed *idiosyncratic intoxication,* a shy, retiring person may undergo a "personality change" in an almost Jekyll-Hyde fashion and become aggressive, boisterous, and assaultive. Curiously, the person may seem out of contact with others during the episode and have no memory for the period of intoxication.

Alcohol withdrawal syndrome. An experience which the alcoholic is unlikely to forget is the unpleasant symptoms of the alcohol withdrawal syndrome which may begin after several days of heavy drinking. Shortly after the person stops drinking or reduces his intake of alcohol, the hands, eyelids, and tongue may show a coarse tremor. One or more of the following symptoms may also be

FIGURE 15–3

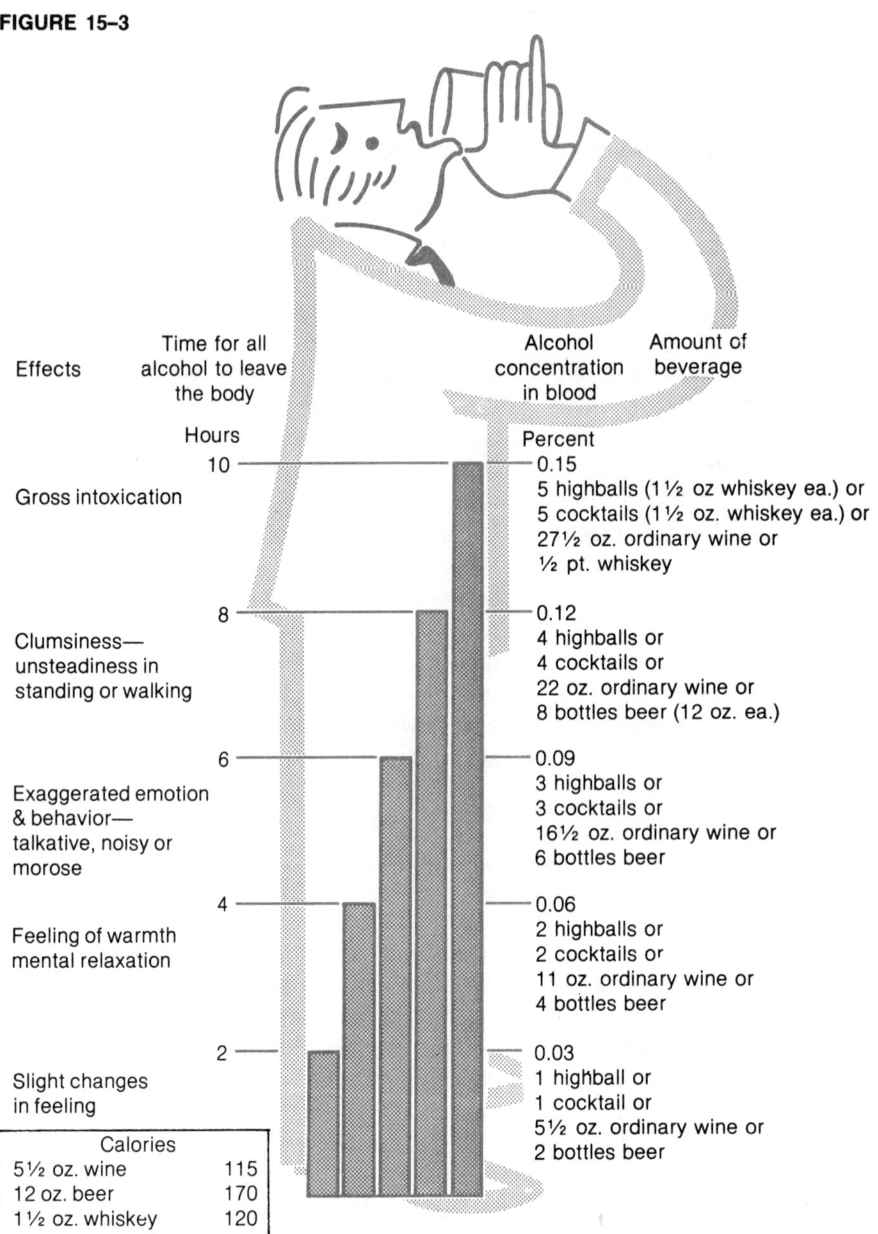

Source: Reprinted by permission from *Time,* The Weekly News Magazine; Copyright Time Inc. 1974.

prominent for the two-five days that the withdrawal persists: sleep disorders, nausea and vomiting, anxiety, depression, irritability, grand mal seizures, weakness, and elevated heart rate and blood pressure.

Alcohol withdrawal delirium (delirium tremens). Delirium tremens, a disorder which you may know as the DTs, is the most severe withdrawal phenomena. In fact, it can constitute a serious medical emergency, which prior to the advent of proper medical treatment now available, had a mortality rate as high as 15 percent (Moore, 1977). The DTs can be distinguished from the withdrawal syndrome we just discussed by the clear presence of delirium—disorientation, confusion, hallucinations, and memory problems. Agitation, sleep problems, tremor, and autonomic hyperactivity almost always accompany the delirium. The symptoms usually begin within about a week after drinking is discontinued and abate within ten days after the first signs of DTs are noticed.

Alcohol hallucinosis. The third, and final withdrawal disorder, is alcohol hallucinosis. Here, auditory hallucinations, which are sometimes accompanied by delusions, occur after a person has recovered from alcohol withdrawal. This condition is most likely to occur at least one or two weeks after a severe drinking bout. Alcohol hallucinosis may require hospitalization due to the terrifying and threatening nature of the hallucinations and an accompanying mood of fear, anger, and/or depression.

Explanations

There is no single, widely accepted explanation for alcoholism. Since alcoholics come in more "varieties" than Campbell's soup, it is not surprising that no one theory has been able to account for all types alcoholics and all aspects of alcoholism. Attempts to identify a single type of personality reliably associated with alcoholism have met with little success. As Schuckit and Hagland (1978) point out, "the general consensus of personality studies is that there is no one personality type that can be measured as being necessary and sufficient for the development of alcoholism and the range of personality types of alcoholics is not different from that found in the general population (p. 18)." Perhaps the major characteristic that alcoholics share is that they drink alcohol excessively. But the consumption of alcohol per se cannot be considered a definitive cause of alcoholism because not all persons who drink alcohol develop problems associated with its use (Moore, 1977). Explanations for alcoholism have been proposed by theorists who emphasize psychoanalytic, learning theory, sociocultural, and genetic concepts.

The psychodynamic perspective. According to psychodynamic thinking, alcoholism is related to unfulfilled needs and ways of achieving gratification which have their roots in the early years of life. One psychodynamic explanation traces the origins of alcoholism back to the oral stage of psychosexual development. During this stage, discomfort is reduced and pleasure is obtained through oral pleasures such as sucking and nursing. In times of stress, the alcoholic is believed to resort to "oral" behaviors which at one time provided security but which in adult life are no longer functional. According to this viewpoint, alcohol may serve as a pacifier for the easily frustrated, dependent, and demanding "oral character'' who has never truly matured beyond the oral stage of development. Thus, alcohol, like the oral gratifications so comforting in earlier years, may help the adult alcoholic to reduce discomfort and cope with the tension and stresses of everyday life. The fact that alcoholics tend to be heavier smokers than nonalcoholics may reflect the strong oral needs of the alcoholic (Maletzky & Klotter, 1974).

The term latent homosexual has been applied to male alcoholics by psychodynamic theorists. The origins of latent homosexuality are said to be in the phallic stage of development, during which the child experiences the Oedipal complex. According to psychodynamic thinking, Oedipal conflicts may be resolved through the process of identification with the father. If the Oedipal complex is not satisfactorily resolved, for reasons such as the father being distant or absent from the home or because he is not a very appealing model for the child, the boy may never develop a firm masculine identity. In adulthood such individuals may consume alcohol to bolster a fragile sense of masculinity.

Still other explanations for excessive alcohol use have been offered by psychodynamically oriented theorists. Alcoholics have been hypothesized to use alcohol to enhance a feeling of importance to defend against low self-esteem, to satisfy a need for punishment through self-destructive drinking patterns, to achieve a feeling of power and to better cope with anxiety and underlying depressive feelings.

While many of us may know people who misuse alcohol who fit these personality descriptions or who seem to drink to excess for some of the reasons we have noted, critics of psychoanalytic explanations argue that such theories are difficult, if not impossible, to verify. They contend that the terms and concepts are hard to define and the crucial events may have occurred long before the onset of alcoholism.

The learning perspective. Learning and reinforcement theories emphasize the rewarding aspects of alcohol consumption that are learned in the context of one's experiences with drinking. Drinking alcohol can be rewarding for a variety of reasons, which include decreasing work-related pressures, enhancing social interactions, gaining the approval of peers, and experiencing a sense of personal power (Kalin, McClelland, and Kahn 1964; Schuckit & Hagland, 1978).

But the major research focus of reinforcement theorists has been on the so-called tension-reduction model of alcoholism. This model hypothesizes that alcohol serves to reduce tension, thus reinforcing its consumption and increasing the probability of drinking (Holroyd, 1978).

Laboratory studies have assumed that if alcohol reduces tension, introducing various laboratory stressors should increase the likelihood of drinking. In two studies college students who were heavy social drinkers were found to increase their consumption of wine when they thought they would be evaluated by their peers (Higgins & Marlatt, 1975) and when their performance on a difficult anagrams test was criticized (Marlatt, Kosturn, & Lang, 1975).

But other studies provide contradictory evidence. Nathan and O'Brien (1971) compared a group of alcoholics with a matched group of nonalcoholics and found that alcohol actually produces *increases* in anxiety, tension, and depression. Higgins and Marlatt (1973) found that threat of painful electric shock had no effect on alcohol consumption. Holroyd (1978) recently reported that socially anxious college students who received negative evaluations of their social competence from peers actually drank less beer than did subjects less socially anxious and those who received positive evaluations of their social competence.

Attempting to reconcile such divergent findings, Marlatt (1976) suggests that drinking will be a response to stress only in those situations which the drinker defines as stressful and in which he believes that alcohol will be an adequate response to the stressful situation. Given these qualifications and the lack of evidence consistently supporting the model, it seems unlikely that tension-reduction is the single most important factor in the onset and maintenance of excessive drinking.

A sociocultural view. The sociocultural explanation stresses the importance of social and cultural determinants of alcohol consumption. Kinney and Leaton (1978) have identified four cultural orientations that are influential in determining societal rates of alcoholism.

Where an attitude of *total abstinence* is dominant, drinking is strictly prohibited and very low rates of alcoholism are evident, as with the Moslems or Mormons. Somewhat higher alcoholism rates are found in groups which condone *ritual use* and *convivial use.* Where ritual use is acceptable, drinking is limited to religious practice, ceremonies, and special occasions. But in other contexts, drinking is frowned upon. A pattern of convivial use describes groups in which drinking is tied to social occasions, with the emphasis on social solidarity and comraderie. Italian Americans and Jewish Americans, both from cultures in which drinking centers around the family or religious occasions,

The utilitarian use of alcohol: A Parisian family enjoys wine together at dinner.

Richard Phelps/Rapho-Photo Researchers, Inc.

drink moderately but have low rates of alcoholism (Cahalan, Cisin, & Crossley, 1969). Finally, in societies which condone *utilitarian use,* there are virtually no controls or sanctions against drinking. In France, which has the highest rate of alcoholism in the world (an estimated 10 to 12 percent of the population, including some children), drinking alcohol is seen as a healthy, useful part of daily life.

Sociocultural factors do not, however, account for individual variations within a particular culture. Alcoholics are not at all uncommon in groups with strong sanctions against drinking, and many nonalcoholics live in societies with a high prevalence of alcoholism.

The genetic explanation. Recent studies of hereditary factors and alcoholism suggest that there may indeed be support for a concept of "familial alcoholism." Nancy Cotton (1979) recently reviewed studies conducted over the last four decades and found that, on the average, almost one third of any sample of alcoholics will have had at least one parent who was an alcoholic. But as researchers in this area are quick to point out, just because alcoholism runs in families does not imply that genetic, rather than social factors, are responsible for such findings. Speaking Swahili runs in families, but not because of genetic transmission.

Evidence for the role of hereditary factors in alcoholism has come from twin studies which point to genetic control of drinking behavior. That is, identical twins tend to be more concordant for alcoholism than fraternal twins (Goodwin, 1979). Adoption studies have also provided strong support for a genetic hypothesis. Goodwin compared Danish boys and girls born of alcoholic parents who were adopted and raised by nonalcoholic parents with a similar sample of children raised by their alcoholic biological parents. Goodwin found that children of alcoholics are more likely to become alcoholics whether raised by their alcoholic parents or by nonalcoholic foster parents. Thus, alcoholism cannot simply be attributed to being reared in the same household with an alcoholic parent.

Goodwin contends that separating alcoholics into familial versus nonfamilial types may be a useful distinction. Cases of alcoholism that are likely to have a hereditary component include the following features: (1) a family history of alcoholism; (2) early onset of alcoholism, usually by age 30; (3) severe symptoms requiring treatment at an early age; and (4) absence of other conspicuous pathology.

But even if hereditary factors influence the likelihood of developing alcoholism, what is inherited? Goodwin (1979) offers a speculative answer to this question as he outlines a way in which genetic factors and learning may interact to produce alcoholism.

1. The potential alcoholic must be able to drink large quantities of alcohol without experiencing adverse physical effects in order to be an alcoholic. Thus, a *lack of intolerance* to alcohol may be inheritied.
2. Another factor that may possibly be under genetic control is the degree of euphoria from alcohol: some people experience more euphoria from alcohol than others do. Because euphoria is a positive reinforcer, Goodwin presumes that people who experience the most euphoria are the one's most likely to drink.
3. Dysphoria (unpleasant feelings) as well as euphoric effects are experienced with alcohol. Those persons who feel the most positive

effects from alcohol quite possibly also experience the most dysphoria. In order to relieve the dysphoria, and to restore a sense of euphoria, the alcoholic may increase his consumption. Both the production of euphoria and the reduction of dysphoria may be highly reinforcing to the alcoholic. This peak-valley effect may explain loss of control in drinking. The height of the peak and the depth of the valley may be genetically controlled.

4. Binge drinking may occur because alcohol use may be most reinforcing after drinking periods with the onset of withdrawal symptoms. Drinking may be resumed to relieve the dysphoria, "the morning after."
5. Finally, relapse after periods of abstinence is explained by stimulus generalization. Both the positive and the negative effects of alcohol resemble mood states and physical feelings experienced when the person is not drinking. The ups and downs induced by alcohol become associated with a wide variety of feeling states and external circumstances through the process of stimulus generalization. The circumstances and settings in which drinking is most frequent become most reliably tied to the highs and lows of drinking. These occasions and settings become conditioned stimuli for drinking behavior, along with the internal states that resemble the highs and lows of drinking. Relapse, then, represents a conditioned response to these conditioned stimuli.

As interesting and suggestive as Goodwin's theory is, it does not purport to account for all cases of alcoholism. That is, a large percentage of alcoholics—ranging from 47 to 82 percent—do not come from families in which one or both parents were alcoholics (Cotton, 1979). But none of the explanations for alcoholism which we have discussed offer an adequate accounting of the causes of alcoholism. Perhaps Cahalan is correct in saying: "There is no one overall answer . . . We are trying to exorcise a devil, but there is no one devil. There is a host of demons" (*Time,* 1974, p. 79).

Treatment

Alcoholics Anonymous.

> Alcoholics Anonymous is a fellowship of men and women who share their experience, strength and hope with each other that they may solve their common problems and help others to recover from alcoholism.
>
> The only requirement for membership is a desire to stop drinking. There are no dues or fees for A.A. membership; they are self-supporting through their own contributions.
>
> A.A. is not allied with any sect, denomination, politics, organization or institution; does not wish to engage in any controversy; neither endorses nor opposes any causes.
>
> Our primary purpose is to stay sober and help other alcoholics to achieve sobriety (Pamphlet, Alcoholics Anonymous World Services, 1978).

The beginnings of Alcoholics Anonymous can be traced to a meeting which took place over thirty years ago between two men who were struggling to control their drinking. Through their acquaintance, Bill W. a stockbroker and

Bob S. a surgeon, made an important discovery: they could help each other stay sober through mutual support. Inspired by their discovery that alcoholics could successfully help each other, they shared the story of their recoveries with other alcoholics. And within a few years, small groups of alcoholics began to meet regularly to share their drinking backgrounds, offer support, hope, and encouragement to one another, and testify that they were victims of a habit they were powerless to control.

Alcoholics Anonymous is now the largest and most successful worldwide organization for treating alcoholics, with over 22,000 chapters and an estimated 650–750,000 members (*Time,* 1974). Today, as in early days, there is an evangelic atmosphere in many A.A. meetings. A number of the Twelve Steps toward sobriety around which the program is loosely organized exhort the member to entrust his difficulties in a higher power—''God as we understand him.'' The Twelve Steps seem to have an interdenominational appeal and many believe the program facilitates gaining renewed self-respect, diminishes unproductive guilt feelings, and promotes

Alcoholics Anonymous 40th anniversary international convention in Denver, Colorado, 1975.

Courtesy of Alcoholics Anonymous

THE TWELVE STEPS OF ALCOHOLICS ANONYMOUS

1. We admitted we were powerless over alcohol—that our lives had become unmanageable.
2. Came to believe that a Power greater than ourselves could restore us to sanity.
3. Made a decision to turn our will and our lives over to the care of God as we understood him.
4. Made a searching and fearless moral inventory of ourselves.
5. Admitted to God, to ourselves and to another human being the exact nature of our wrongs.
6. Were entirely ready to have God remove all these defects of character.
7. Humbly asked Him to remove our shortcomings.
8. Made a list of all persons we had harmed, and became willing to make amends to them.
9. Made direct amends to such people wherever possible, except when to do so would injure them or others.
10. Continued to take personal inventory and when we were wrong, promptly admitted to it.
11. Sought through prayer and meditation to improve our conscious contact with God as we understood Him, praying only for knowledge of His will for us and the power to carry that out.
12. Having had a spiritual awakening as the result of these steps, we tried to carry this message to alcoholics and practice these principles in all our affairs.

behaviors which are a substitute for drinking behavior.

Many hosptials and clinics have incorporated A.A. meetings in their programs to treat alcoholics. Upon release, continued care is available through attending A.A. meetings in the community. Alcoholics Anonymous has inspired the creation of Al-anon and Alateen, groups which help the spouses and children of alcoholics cope with alcoholism.

CONTROLLED DRINKING: A VIABLE TREATMENT GOAL?

An important, yet highly controversial question is whether controlled drinking is a viable treatment goal for some alcoholics. Controlled drinking refers to the ability to use alcohol normally in some conditions without using it to excess (Ray, 1978). The traditional viewpoint, long espoused by Alcoholics Anonymous and shared by many professionals, is that lifelong abstinence is the only acceptable goal for alcoholics. The A.A. position that the problems of the alcoholic are essentially irreversible is expressed in the following quote from the book *Alcoholics Anonymous* (1939).

> But here is a man who at 55 years found he was just where he left off at 30 (the man having taken his first drink in 25 years). We have seen the truth demonstrated again and again: "once an alcoholic, always an alcoholic." Commencing to drink after a period of sobriety, we are in short time as bad as ever (p. 44).

The assumption of the irreversibility of alcoholism and the necessity of lifelong abstinence has been challenged by recent research findings. In a recent review of 74 alcohol treatment studies, Pattison, Sobell, & Sobell (1977) found that nearly one fifth of the subjects successfully engaged in controlled drinking after treatment. In contrast, only about 10 percent of the subjects were able to attain abstinence after therapy.

Such findings do not indicate that controlled drinking is possible or desirable for all alcoholics. But they suggest that for at least some problem drinkers, controlled and essentially problem-free drinking may be an attainable and even desirable treatment goal (Miller & Caddy, 1977). Miller and Caddy note that controlled drinking therapies have demonstrated considerable success (Lovibund & Caddy, 1970) and may be desirable options for certain persons for a number of reasons. Patients may be resistant to progress in treatment because they refuse to identify themselves as an alcoholic and/or protest that they can control their drinking. Miller and Caddy suggest that rather than confronting such resistant patients, it may be more helpful to "entertain the possibility of moderation." If the patient fails in achieving controlled drinking, it may be a compelling demonstration of the necessity for abstinence. In addition, controlled-drinking treatments may be useful for problem drinkers who resist seeking therapy because they do not desire total abstinence. That is, the availability of therapies with a controlled drinking goal may help problem drinkers seek help earlier than if abstinence were the only alternative. Finally, controlled drinking may be worth attempting with patients who have repeatedly failed to achieve abstinence in programs which emphasize this goal.

Miller and Caddy believe that comprehensive alcoholism treatment programs should provide services both to patients who require or request abstinence and to problem drinkers who desire greater self-control. Of course, in cases where serious physical or mental problems would be exacerbated by drinking alcohol, abstinence is the only appropriate treatment goal. Despite such interesting arguments, it is far from certain whether a goal of controlled drinking for even carefully selected patients will be accepted by the majority of professionals engaged in the treatment of alcoholics.

A biological treatment: antabuse. The use of the drug disulfiran, or antabuse, has been described as an "insurance policy against impulsive drinking for those who sincerely wish to abstain from alcohol" (Weinberg, 1977, p. 256). This description has a sound basis: when ingested with alcohol, antabuse causes a potent reaction which includes nausea, vomiting, racing heart, and flushing. Antabuse can be an effective deterrent to alcohol consumption, since even small quantities, like the amount present in cough syrup, can trigger unpleasant effects for two to three days. The effects of antabuse are the result of interference with the metabolism of alcohol and the resultant accumulation of acetaldehyde, a toxic breakdown product of alcohol.

Antabuse alone cannot cure alcoholism, since, at best, it can only postpone

THE INNER WORLD OF THE ALCOHOLIC

Alcoholics are said to be notoriously difficult to treat. In a recent survey of 384 treatment outcome studies, Emrick (1975) found that treated alcoholics were not significantly more successful in achieving abstinence than were untreated alcoholics, although treatment did significantly increase the total number of "improved" cases. If abstinence is the criterion of successful treatment, these data suggest that alcoholism is indeed difficult to treat. Why is this so?

Wallace suggests that in order to better understand the special problems of treating alcoholics we must look into the inner world of the alcoholic to see how he makes sense of his experiences and reacts to them. Wallace (1977) contends that a "fundamental delusion" lies at the heart of alcoholism: "the alcoholic believes that if he searches long and hard enough, he will find a way to control and enjoy his drinking. This belief arises directly from the alcoholic's experience of his drinking" (p. 6).

First, the alcoholic did not get drunk each and every time he drank nor were his experiences consistently negative on each drinking occasion. The "off-again, on-again" nature of the problem may be terribly confusing to an alcoholic. A second source of inner confusion is the contrast between early positive experiences with moderate drinking and the immediate experience of the unpleasant consequences of extreme intoxication. The alcoholic may continue drinking to recapture the "warm glow" of earlier drinking episodes. Third, since the category of alcoholism is so broad and includes so many different signs and symptoms, the alcoholic may not define himself as "an alcoholic." The alcoholic may say something like the following: "Well, I do drink fairly often, but since I drink only beer, I'm not an alcoholic" (p. 8). The alcoholic may also believe that in his particular case alcohol will one day be mastered because he does not experience one of the symptoms associated with alcoholism, such as blackouts. And finally the alcoholic can always point to someone who seems to be more greatly incapacitated than he.

As a means of coping with his experience of alcoholism, the alcoholic may minimize the amount of his drinking, deny that he has lost control of his drinking, rationalize his drinking bouts as resulting from his job, etc., and blame everything and everybody for his miseries except alcohol. What Wallace's observations suggest is that unless the alcoholic fully acknowledges the dimensions of the problem and affirms the need for change, therapy is unlikely to be completely successful.

drinking (Kinney & Leaton, 1978). However, when used in conjunction with therapy, it can promote a period of abstinence during which a patient can learn and implement new coping skills. Antabuse is most frequently used as an adjunct to treatment in outpatient programs that encourage or require their patients to take it regularly. But antabuse is clearly not for everybody. Its use is contraindicated with persons who suffer from certain physical disorders. And persons who are not sufficiently motivated may simply not take their "regular dose" of antabuse.

Behavioral treatments. Perhaps the best known behavioral treatment is aversive conditioning. In aversion therapy, drinking alcohol is associated with unpleasant consequences, making the experiences of drinking itself unpleasant. We will now describe a chemical aversion procedure which is used with alcoholics at Seattle's Schick's Shadel Hospital. Patients in the treatment program are first escorted to "Duffy's Tavern," a room decorated like a neighborhood bar and stocked with an ample and varied supply of liquor. Treatment takes place in a "real life" situation to promote transfer of the aversion to alcohol to the real drinking environment. The patient is then injected with the chemical, emetine, and given his favorite alcoholic beverage by the "bartender." He is instructed to savor the aroma and take a sip, but not swallow the alcohol. The timing of the procedure is arranged so that just after the patient sips the drink, the emetine produces nausea and prolonged vomiting. After three to six days of treatments, the alcoholic presumably associates nausea and alcohol.

Electrical aversion treatments follow a similar procedure. Instead of emetine the patient receives painful, yet tolerable electric shocks every time he attempts to take a drink. After the patient spits the drink out the shock is terminated.

Cautela (1966; 1970) has recently devised an aversive conditioning approach called covert sensitization which utilizes unpleasant images in place of electric shocks or chemicals. In a typical treatment session the patient is instructed to close his eyes and imagine that he is about to drink his favorite alcoholic beverage. When he reports that the image is clear and vivid, the therapist then suggests that the patient experiences sensations of nausea and vomiting. The therapist repeatedly suggests the unpleasant, graphic imagery to the patient until, presumably, a conditioned aversion is established to the sight, smell, and taste of alcohol. One advantage of covert sensitization over chemical and electrical approaches is that the patient may utilize the aversive imagery in situations where he is tempted to drink (Nathan, 1976).

Of the three treatments, therapy outcome studies favor chemical aversion as the most successful in facilitating long-term abstinence. Nausea may be the most effective aversive agent because it is more central to the drinking sequence than shock and more immediate than imagery.

A common criticism of aversion therapy is that it is a simplistic and naive approach to a complex clinical problem. It is argued that if treatment ignores the determinants of drinking behavior in the patient's living situation, therapy gains are likely to be minimal or short-lived. Thus it may be important to devote explicit attention to resolving personal, interpersonal, family, and vocational problems which contribute to excessive drinking.

At the Veterans Administration Center in Jackson, Mississippi, Miller and his colleagues (Miller, Stanford, & Hemphill, 1978) combine a number of therapeutic strategies in a "multi-modal" treatment program for alcoholics. Aversion techniques are but one part of the program and are used to "decrease the immediate reinforcing properties of alcohol." In addition, the patient is instructed in effective ways of coping with stressful situations to reduce the dependence on alcohol as a means of dealing with difficult situations. The patient, with the help of the therapist, may learn desired but previously lacking social or personal skills which are alternate behaviors to drinking. For example, it may be important for alcoholics who lack skills in asserting their feelings to learn not only how to effectively refuse drinks, but also to learn how to express assertive or angry feelings that would be unacceptable while sober. Finally, the program emphasizes family and vocational counseling to insure that the patient receives "increased satisfactions from life."

SUMMARY

In this chapter, we have noted the tremendous costs of abuse of the social drugs, alcohol and tobacco. Smoking remains the greatest public health hazard in the United States, despite the success of government efforts to reduce smoking behavior. Still, less than one in four smokers are successful in permanently quitting before the age of sixty. Treatment efforts to help smokers to quit have not proven to be effective.

No one explanation for smoking behavior is completely satisfactory. Coan (1973) has emphasized the complex, multidetermined nature of smoking behavior. The variables associated with starting to smoke may be different from those related to the maintenance of the habit. At first, smoking cigarettes may have an "adjustive value," but after it becomes habitual and automatic, physical dependence can maintain the maladaptive behavior.

Nicotine has also been seen as playing a role in maintaining smoking behavior. According to this view, smokers regulate their consumption to maintain some desirable level of nicotine. When an optimum level of nicotine cannot be maintained, withdrawal symptoms appear, establishing a "vicious circle." The evidence for this is inconsistent. Schachter and his colleagues suggest that only heavy smokers may be addicted and that the level of acidity of the urine may mediate nicotine regulation. Still other explanations that rely on personality variables have been proposed to account for smoking behavior.

Recent years have seen an upsurge in alcohol consumption and an increase in the social and personal costs related to its use. Alcoholism effects a wide spectrum of the population, yet many people remain terribly ignorant about the effects of alcohol. Jellinek has devised a typology of alcoholics that treats alcoholism as a heterogeneous disorder that can be classified. He devised five types of alcoholism and named each with a Greek letter: alpha, beta, gamma, delta, and epsilon. The new DSM III provides clearer, more specific criteria than Jellinek's classification scheme. These criteria can be used to help distinguish recreational use of alcohol from more destructive patterns of misuse.

We next considered the subjective effects of alcohol and the role which the expectancies of the user may play in complex social behaviors such as aggression and sexuality. The physical effects of alcohol are variable and depend on the pattern of alcohol use. In this context, we described idiosyncratic intoxication, the alcohol withdrawal syndrome, alcohol withdrawal delirium (DT's), and alcohol hallucinosis.

We then discussed a number of explanations of alcoholism. According to the psychodynamic perspective of alcoholism, the problem is related to unfulfilled needs and ways of achieving gratification which have their roots in the early years of life. The learning perspective emphasizes the rewarding aspects of alcohol consumption which are learned in the context of one's experiences with drinking. The sociocultural view stresses the importance of social and cultural determinants of alcohol consumption. We also discussed a genetic explanation which stresses the role of hereditary factors in alcoholism. A recently developed theory by Goodwin argues that genetic factors and learning may interact to produce alcoholism. Again, no one of these explanations provides an entirely satisfactory account of the etiology of alcoholism.

Alcoholics are very difficult to treat. Social approaches like Synanon, behavioral approaches (aversion therapy), and biological approaches (antabuse) have all been used but with limited success. There is some question and considerable debate about whether alcoholics can learn to control their drinking or whether lifelong abstinence is the only acceptable treatment goal.

PART 4

Treatment

Tony Kelly

16

The Insight Therapies

Overview

The Client
The Therapist
The Therapeutic Relationship

Insight Therapies

Dynamic Psychotherapy

Psychoanalysis
Neo-Freudian Therapy
Jung's Analytic Psychology
Sullivan's Interpersonal Psychotherapy
Summary

Humanistic-Existential Psychotherapy

Rogers' Client-Centered Therapy
Gestalt Therapy
Logotherapy

Similarities and Differences

The Challenge of Behavior Therapy

Summary

OVERVIEW

What actually is psychotherapy? Who are the people who seek psychological treatment? Who provides it? How are people helped? Does it really help? We will begin to answer these questions with a brief overview of this field. We will look at the people who undertake therapy and at the people who practice it. We will go on to show how therapy is practiced in two systems which rely on the attainment of insight as the crucial factor in psychotherapy: the psychodynamic and the humanistic. In later chapters we will consider behavior therapy, group therapy, family therapy, biological treatments, and community based treatment approaches.

Strupp (1978) defines psychotherapy as "an interpersonal process designed to bring about modifications of feelings, cognitions, attitudes, and behavior which have proven troublesome to the person seeking help from a trained professional" (p. 3). Dr. Sigmund Freud of Vienna would indeed be amazed to see some of the changes which the scope of psychotherapy has undergone in recent years. Today, there are more than 130 different systems of therapy. Psychotherapy has expanded not only the range of its theoretical and technical perspectives, but also the diversity of individuals treated. At the present time therapists are working with children, families, drug addicts, alcoholics, delinquents, the very old, psychosomatic patients, prison inmates, the terminally ill, and the physically handicapped.

Psychotic individuals, once thought to be unreachable, have been treated in both groups and individual therapy. And even people who function quite well are seeking expanded awareness, better ways of relating to others, and new, more meaningful ways of living. Such individuals are increasingly undertaking therapy or joining countless groups, "workshops," and seminars sponsored by the constantly growing number of "human potential institutes."

The number and heterogeneity of individuals practicing some form of therapy or counseling has also vastly increased. While psychiatrists, clinical psychologists, and psychiatric social workers are still the major providers of psychological services, a great number of other individuals, concerned with the mind-boggling variety of human perplexity and mental distress, have entered the field. Among other professional helpers are pastoral, marital, vocational, and rehabilitation counselors.

Volunteers with varying degrees of

training are active in crisis intervention centers where they offer supportive therapy to lonely, terrified, or suicidal people who are desperate enough in moments of crisis to reach out for help from a stranger. Recently, bachelor's level psychology students in some universities have been trained to become assistants to Ph.D. psychologists (Phares, 1979). It appears that a large part of our culture has accepted psychotherapy. Indeed, the demand for professional practitioners far outstrips the supply.

What all of these divergent "therapists" have in common is the conviction that human beings can change. And that given the right combination of client and helper and the right techniques systematically applied, individuals can be stimulated to grow and overcome their difficulties in living. But the definition of who is the "right" therapist for a particular person and which techniques are "right" for him is debatable, and is indeed frequently debated as the proponents of various systems of therapy argue in defense of their own.

The Client

Who seeks psychotherapy? As you have gathered from the material presented in earlier chapters, the experience of impaired psychological functioning is evident in almost infinite variety. Along with specific presenting problems, several common themes are often apparent: helplessness, social isolation, and a sense of failure or lack of worth (Garfield, 1978). Clients often feel that they are in the grip of forces they cannot control, prevented somehow from being the person they want to be and achieving what they want to achieve. There is a prevailing feeling of being excluded from the general stream of life, discouraged, anxious, and generally unhappy. One patient described herself as follows: Anxious about sex, feeling inadequate because her breasts are too small, feeling "left out" by her friends, worried about school performance, unable to concentrate, and hopeless about any favorable changes in her life. Another patient spoke about being "unable" to work all day without experiencing tension. He also complained about difficulties in family relationships and sexual problems.

For many people the decision to enter therapy is painful and difficult. Strupp, Fox, and Lessler (1969) in their extensive studies of patients' experiences found that over half of their subjects were aware of their problems long before they decided to act on their need for help. Many waited for over two years.

Therapy is undertaken on the basis of widely differing expectations. Some patients believe that the therapist will help them attain all they have wished for. Some dream the therapist will enlighten them and give them peace of mind, purpose, a meaningful life. Some hope to find in the therapist the loving, protective, problem-solving parent they have been seeking since childhood. Those who are more realistic anticipate that the therapist will relieve them of painful psychological states, phobias, or inhibitions. Strupp notes, "the more the client is troubled, the greater is his or her tendency to imbue the therapist with superior powers" (1978, p. 6).

Variables summarized by Phares (1979) as conducive to success in psychotherapy are the following: high ego strength, moderate degree of psychological disturbance, high motivation, relative youth, intelligence, verbal ability, and likeability.

The Therapist

A client and a therapist interact during an individual psychotherapy session.

Menninger Foundation Photo

Despite the many different theoretical orientations, despite the diversity of therapist training programs, despite the broad spectrum of individual differences among therapists, many therapists share common goals and attitudes: (1) they strive to create a warm, relaxed, confidential, and uncritical emotional climate in which trust and hope can grow; (2) they attempt to create a professional relationship and motivate the patient to work actively on the resolution of his problems; (3) they explore the origins or determinants of the client's difficulties and devise strategies for redirecting maladaptive attitudes, behavior patterns, irrational beliefs, or self-defeating ways of relating to others; (4) they cultivate an objective attitude toward the client so that their emotional reactions will not interfere with their therapeutic efforts; (5) they attempt to help the client transfer the insights and/or new behaviors acquired in therapy to their real-life situation; and (6) they attempt to provide a model of healthy attitudes and functioning.

ETHICS AND PSYCHOTHERAPY

With the practice of psychotherapy comes the professional responsibility to be sensitive to the needs and the best interests of the client. Attention to ethical concerns is of crucial importance because therapists who are insensitive, who misapply procedures, or who abuse their role and power as helpers, have the potential to harm rather than help their clients. The list below summarizes some critical ethical issues, framed in questions, which are crucial to any therapeutic endeavor.

A. Have the goals of treatment been adequately considered?
   1. To insure that the goals are explicit, are they written?
   2. Has the client's understanding of the goals been assured by having the client restate them orally or in writing?
   3. Have the therapist and client agreed on the goals of therapy?
   4. Will serving the client's interests be contrary to the interests of other persons?
   5. Will serving the client's immediate interests be contrary to the client's long-term interest?

B. Has the choice of treatment methods been adequately considered?

   1. Does the published literature show the procedure to be the best one available for that problem?
   2. If no literature exists regarding the treatment method, is the method consistent with generally accepted practice?
   3. Has the client been told of alternative procedures that might be preferred by the client on the basis of significant differences in discomfort, treatment time, cost, or degree of demonstrated effectiveness?
   4. If a treatment procedure is publicly, legally, or professionally controversial, has formal professional consultation been obtained, has the reaction of the affected segment of the public been adequately considered, and have the alternative treatment methods been more closely reexamined and reconsidered?

C. Is the client's participation voluntary?
   1. Have possible sources of coercion on the client's participation been considered?
   2. If treatment is legally mandated, has the available range of treatments and therapists been offered?
   3. Can the client withdraw from treatment without a penalty or financial loss that exceeds actual clinical costs?

D. When another person or an agency is empowered to arrange for therapy, have the interests of the subordinated client been sufficiently considered?
   1. Has the subordinated client been informed of the treatment objectives and participated in the choice of treatment procedures?
   2. Where the subordinated client's competence to decide is limited, have the client as well as the guardian participated in the treatment discussions to the extent that the client's abilities permit?
   3. If the interests of the subordinated person and the superordinate persons or agency conflict, have attempts been made to reduce the conflict by dealing with both interests?

E. Has the adequacy of treatment been evaluated?
   1. Have quantitative measures of the problem and its progress been obtained?
   2. Have the measures of the problem and its progress been made available to the client during treatment?

F. Has the confidentiality of the treatment relationship been protected?
   1. Has the client been told who has access to the records?
   2. Are records available only to authorized persons?

G. Does the therapist refer the clients to other therapists when necessary?
   1. If treatment is unsuccessful, is the client referred to other therapists?
   2. Has the client been told that if dissatisfied with the treatment, referral will be made?

H. Is the therapist qualified to provide treatment?
   1. Has the therapist had training or experience in treating problems like those of the client?

2. If deficits exist in the therapist's qualifications, has the client been informed?
3. If the therapist is not adequately qualified, is the client referred to other therapists, or has supervision by a qualified therapist been provided? Is the client informed of the supervisory relation?
4. If the treatment is administered by mediators, have the mediators been adequately supervised by a qualified therapist?

Reprinted from *Behavior Therapy* 8 (1977), V–VI.

Therapists bring into therapy their values, experiences, their own way of perceiving human beings, their particular degree of emotional maturity, sensitivity, intelligence, and mental flexibility. All of these variables may have an influence on the course of psychotherapy. Freud was well aware of this. He stated: "these diseases psychoneuroses are not cured by the drug but by the physician, that is by the personality of the physician, inasmuch as through it he exerts a mental influence" (Freud, 1904, p. 251). As Jung puts it: "It is in fact largely immaterial what sort of technique he uses, for the point is not technique . . . the personality and attitude of the doctor are of supreme importance" (1934, pp. 159–160).

With so much stress on personality, you might wonder, what attributes characterize the "ideal" therapist. According to Parloff, Waskow, and Wolfe (1978), "Prescriptions for the ideal therapist have included a litany of virtues more suited, perhaps, to the most honored biblical figures than to any of their descendants" (p. 235). But even if the ideal therapist existed, it is doubtful that he would be effective with all patients. Parloff et al. found more research support for the notion that different therapist may be effective with various types of clients. Some therapists may be more successful with children, others with psychotics and neurotics. Fromm-Reichman (1950) also cautions that while a warm, nourishing therapist might be effective with neurotic clients he or she may frighten a paranoid schizophrenic and lead him to rapid termination of therapy.

The view of therapist personality as an important therapeutic factor is discounted by some behavior therapists who believe therapy should be scientific and treatment should be largely independent of personality variables which are difficult to control. They argue that therapy should be practiced on the basis of clearly defined techniques. This position is exemplified by Krasner (1961) who describes the therapist as a "social reinforcement" machine. This human machine is programmed by his or her training to verbally condition the client's behavior in predetermined and predictable ways in accordance with the values of the therapist. He states: "The evidence is strong that the therapist . . . has the power to influence and control the behavior and values of other human beings. For the therapist not to accept this situation and to be continually unaware of the influencing effects of his behavior on his patients would be in itself unethical" (p. 69). More recently, other behavior therapists have moved away from this view. They have increasingly stressed the role of the therapeutic relationship in promoting behavior change (Wilson and Evans, 1977).

The Therapeutic Relationship

We will now consider the therapeutic relationship in which patient variables, therapist variables, and technique variables all interact to form the unique experience which each therapy situation creates. Attempts to define the therapeutic relationship vary with the theoretical orientation of the therapist.

Freud's concept of the therapist-patient relationship was clearly medical. The actual analysis was conducted by the therapist and the patient was the passive recipient of the therapist's (doctor's) effort to "cure" him.

The neo-Freudians expanded the therapeutic relationship to one of mutual responsibility for the course of treatment. For example, Whitehorn (1950) perceived psychotherapy as a cooperative enterprise, in which the patient is the most active agent, and the therapist is an "expert assistant."

The shift toward stronger emphasis upon the patient's responsibility for successful treatment and upon the therapeutic relationship as the curative instrument found its ultimate expression in Rogerian, humanistic-existential therapy. "It has become increasingly evident that the probability of therapeutic movement in a particular case depends primarily not upon the counselor's personality, nor upon his techniques, nor even upon his attitudes, but upon the way all these are *experienced by the client in the relationship*" (Rogers, 1951). (Italics mine.)

In sharp contrast to conceptions of the relationship as a valuable or major component of therapy, we have the point of view of some behavior therapists. Behavior therapists tend to agree that positive feelings between patient and therapist may motivate the patient to cooperate in their technical procedures. But many minimize the significance of the relationship per se as crucial to behavior change (Parloff, Waskow & Wolfe, 1978). This, of course, does not imply that behavior therapists lack the positive attributes of other therapists such as warmth, empathic understanding, and sensitivity. It merely reflects their difference in emphasis on the importance of the many factors involved in psychotherapy.

All of the above views of the therapeutic relationships have been formulated by therapists. We will now look at the relationship from the patient's point of view. Strupp et al. (1969) wrote: "Psychotherapy was seen by our respondents as an intensely personal experience. Most important, the therapist's warmth, his respect and interest, and his perceived competence and activity emerged as important ingredients in the amount of change reported by the patients" (p. 77). The composite view of the "good" therapist was that of a "human" expert. The patients experienced themselves to be in a "real" relationship with him. From the patient's point of view, confidence in the integrity of the therapist appeared to be the major component of an effective relationship.

INSIGHT THERAPIES

We will now attempt to answer the question: How is insight therapy actually practiced? We will introduce you to some of the more prominent approaches and attempt to briefly explain their methods.

IS PSYCHOTHERAPY EFFECTIVE?

For more than 25 years, psychologists have debated whether psychotherapy with neurotics is any more helpful than no therapy at all. The controversy about the effectiveness of psychotherapy can be traced to the publication of Hans Eysenck's review of studies of traditional therapeutic approaches to the treatment of neurosis (1952). Eysenck made the startling claim that patients who did not receive psychotherapy improved to the same extent as subjects who participated in the process. Eysenck's conclusion that traditional therapy was ineffective was based on his findings that 72 percent of patients appeared to improve without any special treatment ("spontaneous remission") after a two-year period, compared to a recovery rate of only 44 percent of patients in psychoanalysis and 66 percent of patients who participated in "eclectic" therapy. In later reviews, Eysenck argued forcefully against the notion that traditional therapy is effective and claimed that "uniformly negative" results extended to disorders other than neurotic conditions.

Eysenck's pessimism about the effectiveness of psychotherapy stimulated ardent defenses of its value. His conclusions were vigorously challenged. His reviews were criticized on both conceptual and statistical grounds. Furthermore, his opponents claim that he selected therapy studies and criteria of improvement which were biased against finding positive gains for traditional psychotherapy. It has also been argued that nontreated patients in control groups actually do receive support and advice (therapy) from friends, relatives, clergymen, and physicians. The qualities of effective psychotherapists may not be limited to licensed professionals. Individuals in the natural social environment may serve a therapeutic function for persons with neurotic disorders. Such spontaneous, unprogrammed therapy may account for some of the spontaneous remissions in nontreated individuals who seek and obtain therapeutic help from nontherapists. Thus, the recovery rates of nontreated individuals may have been inflated because neurotic persons may have received therapeutic aid in the natural environment (Bergin & Lambert, 1978).

Bergin and Lambert (1978) have argued that the rate of spontaneous remission is actually much lower than the statistic reported by Eysenck. Based on his recomputations of the data Eysenck drew from, Bergin concluded that a spontaneous remission rate of 43 percent may be more representative than the two-thirds estimate originally reported by Eysenck. Even if Eysenck's higher spontaneous remission rate were an accurate measure of improvement for nontreated neurotics, Bergin notes that the practice of psychotherapy would still be supported because patients in therapy improve in a much shorter time.

A number of more recent reviews support the conclusion that therapy is indeed effective. Mary Smith and Gene Glass (1977) at the University of Colorado in Boulder analyzed the results of 375 controlled studies that reported the therapy outcomes of nearly 25,000 men and women. Smith and Glass found that regardless of the type of therapy they examined, psychotherapy always had some beneficial effect. Based on the studies they surveyed, they determined that the typical client who received treatment was better off in some way than three quarters of those who were untreated. Patients with symptoms of fear and anxiety showed even more impressive treatment gains over untreated control patients. These patients appeared to be more improved than 83 percent of the patients who did not receive psychotherapy.

Meltzoff and Kornriech (1970) compared the recovery rates of patients in 57 studies they considered to be well-designed, with 44 studies considered less adequate. The patients in the methodologically adequate studies showed higher rates of improvement than patients in the less well-designed studies (84 percent versus 75 percent).

The results of these studies lend some degree of confidence to the assertion that psychotherapy is effective. It is unlikely, however, that even the positive findings of relatively large scale review efforts will quiet the voices of those who continue to debate the effectiveness of psychotherapy. We remain largely uncertain about which types of therapies work best with which types of patients and psychological disorders. Likewise, little is known about the specific therapeutic processes which lead to maximum change (Gottman & Markman, 1978). Answers to such questions will no doubt facilitate our understanding of the complex enterprise psychotherapy represents and improve our ability to better meet the needs of persons with problems in living.

We will begin with an overview of some of the beliefs shared by psychodynamic therapists. We will then describe Freud's psychotherapeutic techniques and the modifications in his basic therapeutic approaches which the neo-Freudians (Jung, Sullivan) developed. We will then summarize some of the humanistic-existential therapies. Expanded awareness (Freud's insight) still remains the goal of such therapies. But the orientation of the therapist and the techniques used to reach this goal depart widely from the psychodynamic approaches.

DYNAMIC PSYCHOTHERAPY

Dynamic psychotherapists share the following beliefs:

1. Much of human behavior is motivated by unconscious needs and conflicts.
2. Manifestations of abnormal behavior which appears irrational do not occur by chance; they have a cause and are meaningful.
3. The patient's present difficulties have their roots in childhood experience. Therefore, a thorough knowledge of the patient's life history is essential to treatment.
4. The patient's relationship with the therapist is an essential aspect of therapy.
5. Emotional expression and the opportunity to reexperience emotionally significant past events are important aspects of therapy.
6. When the patient achieves intellectual and emotional contact with previously

> unconscious material, the causes and the significance of his symptoms become apparent and the symptoms may disappear.

With these assumptions in mind, we will now attempt to give you a glimpse of some of the therapeutic techniques utilized by Sigmund Freud, Carl G. Jung, and Harry Stack Sullivan.

Psychoanalysis

Freud defined the goal of psychoanalytic therapy as that of making the unconscious conscious. More specifically, this means that Freudian analysts work with their patients to overcome unconscious blocks which interfere with the patient's capacity to "work well and love well."

Freud realized that his "talking cure" was not universally applicable. He clearly described the kind of patient who could benefit from it. He envisioned his ideal patient as follows: He is young, not over 50 years of age, fairly well educated, of good character, sufficiently motivated to seek therapy of his own volition, and neither psychotic, confused, or deeply depressed.

Freud limited the characteristics of the ideal psychoanalyst to two requirements: He must be a man of irreproachable character and "he must have overcome in his own mind that mixture of lewdness and prudery with which . . . many people consider sexual problems" (Freud, 1904, p. 262). This last qualification was important since Freud was convinced that sexual repression was basic to most neurotic problems.

You may wonder what occurs when the young, educated patient, of reliable character has taken his place upon the couch, and the analyst of irreproachable character has been seated behind him with "evenly hovering attention." It is at this point that psychoanalysis actually begins and continues on a five or six day a week basis for three or more years.

Let us now consider the major procedures utilized in psychoanalytic therapy.

Free association. As the patient lies on the couch in a comfortable, relaxed position, the analyst instructs him to say whatever comes to mind no matter how silly, embarrassing, or illogical. He must express every thought without selection or censorship of any kind. This is the famous "fundamental rule of psychoanalysis." The unique atmosphere of the analytic situation, with the analyst sitting out of sight and the absence of all distractions, is designed to weaken the patient's defenses and encourage the emergence of unconscious material.

The analyst gradually begins to note the connections between the client's communications and inadvertently expresses unconscious impulses and wishes. In session after session, as the patient relates whatever enters his stream of consciousness, the analyst gathers data and forms hypotheses regarding the origin and nature of the patient's difficulties. He begins to interpret such data to the patient as rapport becomes fully established and his own understandings of the client's psychodynamics is clarified. Eventually the patient begins to discover for himself the interrelationships and implications of the material which the free association process has elicited.

Dream analysis. Dream analysis is a complex, multifaceted procedure. Each dream has both manifest and latent

Freud's couch of psychoanalysis.

Historical Pictures Service, Inc., Chicago

contents. The dream, as it is recalled, represents its manifest content. The latent contents of a dream represent the emergence of repressed material in disguised form. For example, the "real" meaning of the dream may be expressed in distorted or symbolic form. Thus, the appearance of an ogre in a dream may represent a hated and feared parent. The disguise of the latent dream material is the work of *dream censorship.* The latter operates to reduce the anxiety the dreamer would experience if he or she were to encounter the repressed material directly.

In attempting to understand a dream, the analyst will view it in terms of the patient's personality. Furthermore, he will consider the relation of the dream to the patient's daytime experience and the dream's symbolic significance. Above all, the analyst will be guided by the patient's free associations to various aspects of the dream because the analyst views the dream as a logical expression of unconscious elements that strongly influence the patient's conscious life. If clearly understood, dreams contain, "the psychology of the neurosis in a nutshell" (Freud in a letter to Fleiss, 1897, appears in: Jones, 1953, p. 355).

Resistance. As treatment progresses and the patient becomes painfully aware of some previously unconscious aspects of his personality, he begins to resist further confrontation. This helps the patient to evade the anxiety which recognition of previously repressed material evokes.

The task of the therapist in overcoming resistance is perhaps the most important aspect of analysis. And it proceeds as follows: (1) The patient must be made aware of the fact that he is unconsciously resisting therapeutic efforts. (2) In each new expression of resistance, the analyst makes clear to the patient exactly *how* he is resisting the elimination of his repressions. (3) The analyst must point out to the patient just *what* it is he is avoiding (Reich, 1949).

Interpretation. Interpretation is the ultimate tool of psychoanalysis. Analytic interpretation usually takes the form of a statement formulated to help the patient understand the unconscious basis of his behavior. The analyst may also point out the disguised expression of a repressed idea, impulse, or wish. Let us consider some examples: (1) Pointing out the unconscious basis of a symptom: "Having these repeated accidents perhaps assured you of getting the attention you felt you could not get otherwise." (2) Pointing out a repressed impulse: "Could it be that your present effeminate behavior is a defense against the aggressive masculinity your mother punished when you were little?"

The analyst attempts interpretation only when he has a reasonably clear picture of the patient's personality dynamics and the historic source of his difficulties. He also must time the interpretations carefully or risk arousing anxiety and resistance if they are offered too soon. But interpretations presented when the patient is ready for them may elicit a flow of new, meaningful associations and lead to real movement in therapy.

Transference. As analysis continues, the patient begins to express toward the analyst intense, unrealistic feelings and expectations which Freud labeled *transference.* The unseen vague figure of the analyst becomes the focus of emotions once directed at the significant persons of the patient's childhood.

As the analysis progresses, the patient's view of the therapist becomes increasingly distorted by unconscious needs and wishes. The patient may project upon the analysis a gamut of unrealistic feelings. He may feel that the analyst is indifferent to him, that he is attempting to manipulate him, to hurt his feelings, and so on. Early ungratified strivings for love are also reactivated and the patient may begin to act seductive toward the analyst, bring presents, and spend hours rehearsing what he will say in the next session. This, of course, interferes with therapy.

The analyst, instead of responding warmly to the patient's advances, proceeds to interpret to him the fact that his behavior is inappropriate and he is actually resisting therapy. When this occurs, the patient may begin to experience the frustration he knew in childhood and the violent anger he once felt toward frustrating, disapproving parental figures. At this point transference often becomes negative, and the "loved" analyst may become the target for hate with all of its irrational childish intensity. Monroe (1958, p. 522) gives a dramatic example of this phenomenon:

> I admire the *sang-froid* of the analyst who looked into a gun (pointed at him) and said calmly, "This is what I meant about your murderous feelings toward your father (Laugh). Do you see it now?" According to the analyst, the patient laughed also, albeit a bit hysterically, and lay down on the couch—in such a position that the analyst could now unobtrusively wipe the sweat off his brow.

The analyst, in the example above, interpreted to the patient that his violent anger was really directed at his father and not at his doctor. The fact that this potentially dangerous situation was controlled and the patient was able to laugh about it is evidence that the interpretation was effective in reorienting the patient toward reality. Skillful use of interpretation makes the transference situation a truly therapeutic instrument.

Since the patient is emotionally re-living the painful aspects of his childhood, he is giving the analyst the opportunity to observe and interpret to him the unconscious factors which have been operating all his life to distort his perception of events and relationships. Analysis of the transference behavior permits the patient to better understand the irrational expectations and demands he brings not only to the analyst, but to people in his real-life situation.

Working through. Even when analysis seems to be successfully completed, difficulties recur. As new experiences in the patient's life threaten his new and fragile adjustment, he begins to reinstate neurotic responses which had long been interpreted as such and apparently understood and accepted as such. Resistance once more strongly operates, and "It often appears as if the patient had never heard the analyst's previous interpretation" (Menninger, 1958, p. 138). Interpretations must be repeated anew in many forms and once more related both to the patient's past and his present functioning.

Neo-Freudian Therapy

Psychoanalytically oriented therapists preserve the essence of Freud's theory, use his terminology and techniques, and strive toward the same goal: insight into the unconscious sources of the patient's difficulties. The neo-Freudians depart from Freud in their theoretical emphases (i.e., Jung), views of the therapist-patient relationship (i.e., Sullivan), and some technical modifications and innovations.

An important development has been their concern with the conscious aspects of the patient's functioning. Besides the Freudian emphasis on sexuality, the neo-Freudians recognize the impact of other powerful drives. Thus they may explore with the patient his need for love, dependence, power, status, and so on.

There is less emphasis on the past and the neo-Freudian analyst will usually delve into the patient's history only for the purpose of helping him or her understand the origin of his present irrational behavior. The technique of free association is used mainly with some specific aim. Dreams are analyzed in relation to what is presently significant in the patient's life. They are seldom used as the "royal road to the unconscious." Analysis of transference is employed largely to clarify for the patient the unrealistic aspects of his reactions to the analyst and other people in his world. The use of interpretation may vary not only with different patients but also with the same patient at various times in the course of therapy.

On the whole, the neo-Freudian therapist is much more flexible than the Freudian. The patient may be seen frequently for short intervals of time or seen less frequently over a longer period. There may also be interruptions of treatment for a specific purpose. The analyst strives to attain a therapeutic balance between the need to maintain an objective attitude and the need to provide emotional support for the patient's efforts to overcome his conflicts. He may give advice, make suggestions, or use humor to make a point. He may also call the patient's attention to what is nonverbally communicated by his body; a clenched fist, a yawn, a sigh, or averted eyes may speak more clearly than words. Occasionally, with the patient's permission, the analyst may meet with other family members on his behalf and engage in environmental manipulation to make the patient's home situation less stressful.

Carl Jung

National Library of Medicine

Jung's Analytic Psychology

Carl Jung's knowledge of mythology, alchemy, and religion imparted depth and color to his thinking and writing. His brilliance impressed Freud to the degree that he told Jung he was adopting him as "an eldest son, anointing him as successor and crown prince" (Jung, 1961, p. 316). Unfortunately the close relationship between Freud and Jung could not withstand their increasingly divergent views. Freud reacted to Jung's involvement in parapsychology and belief in precognition as "sheer nonsense"; Jung had exactly the same reaction to Freud's pervasive emphasis on sexuality. They eventually parted, bitterly disappointed in one another, their growing theoretical differences creating an everwidening gulf between them.

Unlike the Freudian analyst, the Jungian therapist is less formal, more open and accepting. He or she meets a patient in face-to-face sessions. He is willing to discuss present-day problems and freely give advice and suggestions. Jungian analysis is concerned not only with the patient's past, but also with his or her aspirations and goals for the future. Freud emphasized the infantile determinants of personality; Jung traced such determinants far back into the racial past of the individual. To Freud's concept of the personal unconscious, Jung added his conception of the *collective unconscious*. The latter is his term for the inherited memory traces which he believed are shared by the whole human race. In Jung's view the answer to the patient's problems will be found in his recognition and acceptance of the roles which both his personal and collective unconscious play in influencing present behavior and efforts toward the achievement of future goals.

Neither the personal unconscious nor the collective unconscious can be contacted directly, but Jung developed a number of methods which tap what he believed to be rich sources of potential for growth. Among the techniques Jungians use to elicit unconscious material are the following: drawing, modelling in clay, discussing day dreams and fantasies, "ideas out of the blue," and, most importantly, nocturnal dreams.

Dream analysis. Dream analysis is the principal technique of Jungian therapists. By examining Jungian dream analysis, we can better understand some of the differences between the Jungian and Freudian approaches. In Freudian dream analysis, free association created a chain of thoughts which eventually led to emotion-laden unconscious material. Jung believed his method, which he called *amplification,* to be a far broader and richer process. In Jungian dream analysis associations are not "free" but focused upon the dream material. Furthermore, such associations are given by the analyst as well as the patient. The analyst brings to dream analysis his knowledge of material found in fairy tales, myths, and legends. According to Jung, such analyses will clarify the dream content. They will direct the interpretation process toward the nucleus of the dream and the message from the unconscious the dream conveys. Jungians believe that in many cases a single dream is difficult to interpret accurately. Therefore a whole series of dreams may be considered as one unit with a single message. The example presented below shows how the analyst may use dream interpretation to help a patient achieve insight.

> An unmarried woman patient dreamed that *someone gave her a wonderful, richly ornamented, antique sword dug up out of a tumulus.*
>
> *Associations:*
>
> Her *father's* dagger, which he once flashed in the sun in front of her. It made a great impression on her. Her father was in every respect an energetic, strong-willed man, with an impetuous temperament, and adventurous in love affairs. A *Celtic* bronze sword: Patient is proud of her Celtic ancestry. The Celts are full of temperament, impetuous, passionate. The ornamentation has mysterious look about it, ancient tradition, runes, signs of ancient wisdom, ancient civilizations, heritage of mankind, brought to light again out of the grave.
>
> *Interpretation:*
>
> It is as if the patient needed such a weapon. Her father had the weapon. He was energetic, lived accordingly, and also took upon himself the difficulties inherent in his temperament. Therefore, though living a passionate exciting life, he was not neurotic. This weapon is a very ancient heritage of mankind, which lay buried in the patient and was brought to light through excavation (analysis). The weapon has to do with insight, with wisdom. It is a means of attack and defense. Her father's weapon was a passionate unbending will, with which he made his way through life. Up until now the patient has been the opposite in every respect. She is just on the point of realizing that a person can also will something and need not merely be driven, as she had always believed. The will based on a knowledge of life and on insight is an ancient heritage of the human race, which also is in her, but till now laid buried, for in this respect, too, she is her father's daughter. But she had not appreciated this till now, because her character had been that of a perpetually whining, pampered, spoilt child. She was extremely passive and completely given to sexual fantasies (Campbell, 1971, pp. 281–82).

Another helpful attribute of the dream is the *regulative activity* of the unconscious upon the conscious mind. Dreams express attitudes, impulses, thoughts, and feelings which are the opposite of conscious attitudes. Dreams influence the total psychic reality of the individual in the direction of balance and harmony.

The following example of a

"compensatory" dream is given by Jacobi (1973, pp. 77–78).

> Someone dreams that it is spring but that his favorite tree in the garden has only dry branches. This year it bears no leaves or blossoms. What the dream is trying to communicate is this: Can you see yourself in this tree? This is how you are, although you don't want to recognize it. Your nature has dried up, no tree grows within you. Such dreams are a lesson to persons whose consciousness has become autonomous and overemphasized. Of course the dream of an unusually unconscious person, living entirely by his instincts, would correspondingly emphasize his "other side." Irresponsible scoundrels often have moralizing dreams while paragons of virtue frequently have immoral dream image.

Prognostic dreams. In the Jungian view, dreams may also warn the dreamer of danger. Jung gives the following example:

> I remember the case of a man who was inextricably involved in a number of shady affairs. He developed an almost morbid passion for dangerous mountain climbing, as a sort of compensation. He was seeking to "get above himself." In a dream one night, he saw himself stepping off the summit of a high mountain into empty space. When he told me his dream, I instantly saw his danger and tried to emphasize the warning and persuade him to restrain himself. I even told him that the dream forshadowed his death in a mountain accident. It was in vain. Six months later he "stepped off into space." A mountain guide watched him and a friend letting themselves down on a rope in a difficult place. The friend had found a temporary foothold on a ledge, and the dreamer was following him down. Suddenly he let go of the rope, according to the guide, "as if he were jumping into the air." He fell upon his friend, and both went down and were killed (Jung, 1964, p. 50).

The ultimate goal of Jungian analysis is the integration of various, often opposing, aspects of the patient's personality into a harmonious "whole." Jung calls this process *individuation* and the harmonious whole, the *self.* Individuation is never complete; it is a lifelong endeavor.

Sullivan's Interpersonal Psychotherapy

Sullivan's methods are basically psychoanalytic, but they are far more flexible than Freud's, and his view of the patient is far more hopeful and optimistic. In fact, he believes that the analyst does not "cure." He merely helps the patient to become aware of the ways in which he hampers his own progress toward successful living and gratifying relationships. When this is accomplished, the patient "cures" himself (Sullivan, 1954). Thus, for Sullivan, therapy is a collaborative undertaking, and the analyst's role in it is that of a *participant observer.*

It is through his observation of the patient as the two of them interact that the analyst begins to discover and communicate to the patient the self-defeating and unrealistic aspects of his or her attitudes and behavior. Such unrealistic attitudes are termed *parataxic distortions.* Sullivan believes that the continuous analysis of such distortions strengthen the patient's capacity for reality testing and reduce the patient's dependence on the analyst.

The emphasis on interpersonal relationships is the hallmark of Sullivan's psychotherapy. And it is this emphasis that most clearly distinguishes Sullivan from his

Harry Stack Sullivan

Courtesy of the William Alanson White Psychiatric Foundation, Inc.

predecessors, Freud and Jung. For Sullivan the processes which constitute therapy take place neither in the client nor in the therapist, but in the situation which is created through the relationship.

Sullivan believed that therapy was an intensely personal and human enterprise. He brought his wry sense of humor and his profound compassion into the therapy situation where he directly faced his patient. He could, as the situation demanded, be "mildly amused," sarcastic, or profoundly supportive. He could act bored or irritated when he felt such an attitude would speed up therapy, or he could be warm and accepting when the patient revealed facts which were experienced as painful or "bad." Occasionally he used loaded questions, related anecdotes which helped him to accent a point he was making, or used deliberate silence to elicit communication from the patient.

SULLIVAN'S "MAGIC"

The following is an example of Sullivan's insight and sensitivity in his interaction with patients. Note Sullivan's spontaneity, directness, and focus on the interpersonal relationship.

Sullivan is commenting on the progress of a young schizophrenic who is delusional and uncommunicative. This boy has had a love affair which ended when the girl married someone else. Whenever the boy mentions this girl, he stresses the fact that the affair with her is of no importance to him. Sullivan states:

> There is a marvelous chance to get at a very severe disappointment of this patient if one uses as a cue these little remarks that the girl is "of the past" or she is "out of my mind," or that she was something of "no importance." If the psychiatrist swiftly comes back with something like "Nonsense, you were happy with her," he may have opened the patient's mind. It is the very speed and directness of a completely unsuspected comment like that which sometimes fixes vividly the involuntary attention of the patient. And if the psychiatrist can then move a few steps further, after he has caught the attention of the patient, he may actually reopen an issue that has in truth been treated

rather as this patient's remarks suggest—namely, the experience has been abandoned because it is a source of too great regret and grief. In a situation of this kind, once I have startled the patient into any alertness by some variant of "Nonsense, you liked her," I continue the attack by some such remark as, "And there's no reason on earth why the pleasure you had in her company should be thrown away just because the relationship didn't last forever." And if the patient is still in touch with me, I can then become a bit philosophical and say that in my experience any pleasure one has with anybody, even if it is only for a day, is something that it is good to *treasure*. There will be plenty of pain anyway. And if there was some pleasure before the pain—isn't that something to have had?

What I am really doing here is something of much theoretic complexity. Insofar as he was happy with this girl, he has proved that he can be human and enjoy life. Now that is far too important for me to leave it alone, no matter how ghastly the finish of his relationship was. It indicates that the patient has some asset which can then be extrapolated into the future—that he might again be happy with someone, even if again the relationship might end badly. This is immeasurably better than being haunted by obscure, practically transcendental horrors which probably are the most vivid experience that the patient has now (Sullivan, 1956, pp. 376–378).

How does all this help to transform the patient? Sullivan answers this question:

> The magic occurs in interpersonal relations and the real magic is done by the patient, not by the therapist. The therapist's skill and art lie in keeping things simple enough so that something can happen; in other words, he clears the field for favorable change, and then tries to avoid getting in the way of its development (Sullivan, 1954, p. 227).

Summary

We have examined three approaches to psychodynamic therapy which emphasize the influence of both conscious and unconscious factors in motivating behavior. The principal techniques which Freud used were free association, dream analysis, interpretation, analysis of resistance, analysis of transference, and working through. We have noted that Jung and Sullivan departed from Freud in both theory and practice. Jung diverged from Freud's emphasis on sexuality and stressed the role of the collective as well as the personal unconscious in influencing present behavior. For Freud's technique of free association, Jung substituted focused associations to dream material. His principal therapeutic tool, dream analysis, differed from Freud's in its emphasis on those aspects of the dream which reflected the influence of the collective unconscious. Furthermore, the associations of the therapist were also brought to bear upon the task of understanding the message brought to the patient in individual dreams as well as a whole series of dreams.

Sullivan departed from both Freud and

Jung in his use of the interaction between therapist and patient as the principal therapeutic tool. As participant observer, the therapist is engaged in a collaborative effort with the patient to discover the ways in which unrealistic attitudes block effective functioning and gratifying interpersonal relationships. Toward this goal, Sullivan utilized whatever technique he found appropriate. Some of the techniques which Sullivan used were anecdotes, humor, direct advice, instruction, and emotional support.

HUMANISTIC-EXISTENTIAL PSYCHOTHERAPY

Under the heading of humanistic-existential psychotherapy, we find a number of different approaches. We will look at three very different systems of humanistic-existential psychotherapy which have become perhaps the most prominent and widely used: Roger's client-centered therapy, Perl's Gestalt therapy, and Frankl's logotherapy. The theoretical underpinnings of these therapies are rooted in the humanistic perspective which you encountered in chapter three. There is a commitment in this orientation to the development of human potential and faith in man's basic goodness. There is a sincere desire to help people overcome the sense of alienation so prevalent in our culture; to develop sensory, intellectual, and emotional awareness; to express their creativity and to become fully alive, loving, responsible, and authentic beings.

Humanistic-existential therapists reject the interpretive techniques of psychoanalysis. Such techniques are perceived as being manipulative and ineffective. Humanistic-existentialist therapists regard people as having the freedom and capacity to choose their own goals, to make the kind of choices that are self-enhancing, and to move toward becoming the kind of person they want to become. The therapist attempts to relate to the client by assuming his frame of reference and to understand the inner world of the client through empathy and intuition. The approach to the client is *phenomenological.* This means that the therapist encounters the client as he/she is at this moment.

Humanistic-existential techniques are highly divergent. It has been said that there are as many techniques as there are humanistic-existential therapists. But techniques are considered secondary to *presence:* the being together of therapist and patient in a profound, emotionally involved, authentic relationship.

We will now turn our attention to Carl Rogers' client-centered therapy.

Rogers's Client-Centered Therapy

The therapy which Carl Rogers developed clearly exemplifies the humanistic principles we have presented. Rogers's therapy is *client-centered* because progress in therapy is directed toward the attainment of the client's own goals for himself rather than the goals the therapist may believe to be appropriate and worthy. Rogerian therapy is also *nondirective.* This means that the therapist does not define the client's problems or tell him how he might solve them. He does not make suggestions or plans for the client to follow. He lets the client conduct the therapy session, and he permits the client to use the therapeutic hour as he chooses.

Rogers firmly believed that the innate, universal human tendency is to maintain and enhance one's self. Thus, one drive,

SOME QUESTIONS FOR THE THERAPIST

Rogers was convinced that the crucial element in therapy is a unique relationship between therapist and client. Rogers's vision of an ideal therapist is vividly expressed in the form of questions the therapist might ask himself:

1. Can I be in some way which will be perceived by the other person as trustworthy, as dependable or consistent in some deep sense . . . ?
2. Can I be expressive enough as a person that what I am will be communicated unambiguously . . . ?
3. Can I let myself experience positive attitudes toward this other person—attitudes of warmth, caring, liking, interest, respect . . . ?
4. Can I be strong enough as a person to be separate from the other . . . ?
5. Am I secure enough within myself to permit him his separateness . . . ?
6. Can I let myself enter fully into the world of his feelings and personal meanings and see these as he does . . . ?
7. Can I be acceptant of each facet of this other person which he presents to me. Can I perceive him as he is? Can I communicate this attitude? Or can I only receive him conditionally, acceptant of some aspects of his feelings and silently or openly disapproving of other aspects . . . ?
8. Can I act with sufficient sensitivity in the relationship that my behavior will not be perceived as a threat . . . ?
9. Can I free him from the threat of external evaluation . . . ?
10. Can I meet this other individual as a person who is in the process of *becoming* or will I be bound by his past and by my past . . . ? (Rogers, 1961, pp. 50–55).

the drive for self-actualization, motivates behavior.

In order to be therapeutic, the therapist-client relationship must meet six conditions: (1) The client and therapist must be fully aware of one another. (2) The client must be in a state of *incongruence*. By this Rogers means that he is not freely and genuinely himself. As a result of this, the client feels vulnerable or anxious. (3) The therapist is congruent. He must be a truly authentic person who wears no mask of any kind or plays any particular role. He presents to the client exactly what he *is* in the therapeutic situation. (4) The therapist must express unconditional positive regard. The therapist listens to the client's communications with an unjudgmental attitude which permits unconditional acceptance of all feelings. An emotional climate is established where permission is given to the client to be truly himself without the threat that unless he feels, thinks, or behaves in ways which others have defined as "good," he is not a worthy person. The therapist is never morally outraged; and he can accept hostility as well as warm, positive feelings. Rogers is convinced that with unconditional positive regard the client's self-concept becomes more positive. (5) The therapist must relate to the client with

Carl Rogers

Courtesy of Carl Rogers, photo by Nozizwe S.

empathic understanding. Empathy is the capacity to feel what the client is feeling. "To sense the client's world as if it were your own, but without ever losing the 'as if' quality. This is empathy" (Rogers, 1957, p. 98). Here is an example of Rogers' (1951) empathic response to a client's expression of feelings about him:

Client: [*Begins to talk in a hard, flat voice, quite unlike her usual tone. Doesn't look at counselor. There was much repetition, but the following excerpts give the major thoughts.*] You feel I want to come, but I don't! I'm not coming any more. It doesn't do any good. I don't like you. I hate you! I wish you never were born.

Rogers: You just hate me very bitterly.*

Client: I think I'll throw you in the lake. I'll cut you up! You think people like you, but they don't . . . You think you can attract women but you can't . . . I wish you were *dead.*

Rogers: You *detest* me and you'd really like to get rid of me.*

(6) It is critically necessary for the client to feel, at least to some degree, the acceptance and understanding the therapist relates to him. Rogers wrote, "If one or more of these conditions are not present, constructive personality change will not occur" (Rogers, 1957, p. 100).

The therapy process. Rogers defines therapy as "releasing of an already existant capacity in a potentially competent individual, not the expert manipulation of a more or less passive personality" (Rogers, 1957, p. 221). Therapists make no attempt to diagnose a client's pathology or point out to him the self-defeating aspects of his personality or behavior. They are convinced that explanations or interpretations, no matter how accurate, have no enduring beneficial effects. Nor is effort expended to explore the patient's past and trace the origins of his difficulties. Rogers believes that significant emotional patterns will be revealed equally clearly in the client's present functioning (Rogers, 1942).

* Just as it is impossible to convey on paper the venom and hatred in the client's voice, so it is utterly impossible to convey the depth of empathy in the counselor's (Rogers') responses. The counselor states, "I tried to enter into and to express in my voice the full degree of the soul-consuming anger which she was pouring out. The written words look incredibly pale, but in the situation they were full of the same feelings she was so coldly and deeply expressing" (Rogers, 1951, pp. 211–212).

The principle techniques of Rogerian therapy are reflection of feelings, clarification of feelings, and expression of the therapist's feelings.

Reflection. The therapist accepts the client's feelings and communicates his understanding of them by restating them in words which attempt to mirror the very essence of what the client is trying to communicate.

> **Client:** I was small and I envied people who were large. I was—well, I took beatings by boys and I couldn't strike back . . ."
>
> **Therapist:** You've had plenty of experience in being the underdog (Rogers, 1942, p. 145–46).

Clarification of feelings. As the client progresses in his search of himself, his thinking and the expression of his feelings may become confused and incoherent. The demand on the therapist is for total attention and sensitivity so that he may understand what the client is attempting to share and help the client to express his feelings clearly.

> After a very complicated and somewhat incoherent statement by a husband, I respond, "And so, little by little, you have come to hold back things that previously you would have communicated to your wife? Is that it?"
>
> **Client:** Yes (Rogers, 1970, p. 51).

Expression of therapist's feelings. Rogers has concluded that to be really genuine, the therapist should reveal his own reaction to what the client is communicating when he feels this is appropriate.

> **Client:** I think I'm beyond help.
>
> **Therapist:** Huh? Feel as though you're beyond help. I know. You feel just completely hopeless about yourself. I can understand that. I don't feel hopeless, but I realize you do" (Meador & Rogers, 1979, p. 157).

These techniques defuse the threat inherent in the therapy situation. And, in time, the client begins to look at himself less defensively. More and more the client begins to see inconsistencies between his self-concept and his actual behavior. Feelings that were previously denied become apparent and the client begins to accept them as the therapist accepts them. Because the responsibility for making connections and drawing conclusions about himself is clearly his, the client explores himself further.

Insight achieved by the client is evident in such statements as: "I think I always saw people as being critical toward me because to make myself feel better about myself, I kept criticizing other people." Even self-destructive tendencies are now less confusing. "I kept on failing in school and losing job after job because I was sure I couldn't get anyone's approval no matter how hard I tried." (Crying softly). "I tried so hard to get my father to love me, but I couldn't ever live up to his expectations."

With increased awareness, a reorganization of the self on a new, more realistic level occurs. Behavior changes along with this reorganization. It becomes more adaptive, less anxious, and more effective. The force which motivates the client to achieve this is the "basic tendency:" self-actualization (Rogers, 1961).

Gestalt Therapy

Of Fritz Perls, founder of Gestalt therapy, it has been said, "He was the most exciting

"WHAT IS THE THERAPIST SELLING?" A PERSONAL STATEMENT BY A HUMANISTIC PSYCHOTHERAPIST

What I offer in the therapeutic encounter changes, not only from patient to patient and from hour to hour, but, with an individual patient, from moment to moment. As we proceed, the person across the desk from me may change from patient to friend, from dependent to teacher. . . .

I hold out the hope that if we can continue our dialogue, if he will permit himself to borrow some of my strength, the heaviness may lift. I argue that he *will* be able to expose to light the contents of his private Pandora's box and that he can endure the painful process of dissolution and reorganization of his personal structure—that he can find a niche to live in that has both color and tone. I promise that he and I together will do something about the message that his pain is communicating to him. I make clear that physical or psychological death is not the only solution. There are alternatives. He *can* acquire a sense of joyousness.

I believe the construct of joy is central in what I have to offer. The patient can learn that there is joy in risking, joy in the creation of meaning, joy in experiencing—even though the experiencing be painful at times. There is joy in our dialogue. To feel, to sense one's aliveness is a joyous thing. . . .

I also see pain—the ability to experience it and to incorporate it—as an essential ingredient of living. Only as you learn that to be in pain is not to die—only then can you know freedom from fear and freedom to live. Similarly, when you learn that to fail is not to die, you are free to act without constraint. This, too, I sell in my office.

Source: S. Lipkin. In *Voices: The Art and Science of Psychotherapy*, Vol. 6, American Academy of Psychotherapists (Emerson New Jersey: Emerson Quality Press, 1970), pp. 40–42.

therapist who ever lived. His was the unique ability to pierce down into a person and grasp what was most basically awry, where grief, fury, death lay deeply hidden; . . . the struggle achingly agonizing, sometimes seeming to last for centuries, sometimes finished with breathtaking rapidity. . . . The surrender to life, to wholeness, to forgiveness, release, tenderness, joy, beauty. . . . Faces now transformed, movement fluid, existence radiant and open" (Fagan, 1971, p. 16).

Some of the concepts and terminology of Gestalt therapy are borrowed directly from Gestalt psychology, a theory of perception developed in Germany by Max Wertheimer and Wolfgang Kohler. The most widely used concepts will be explained below.

Gestalt. The word *gestalt* (configuration) represents an organized whole. It is the organization of various aspects of its parts which gives it meaning. In gestalt therapy, each individual is viewed as an organized whole—a more or less complete gestalt. The striving for wholeness is here equated with the striving for self-actualization. This urge is believed to be innate and present in everyone. You probably recall that you met this concept in Jungian and Rogerian therapy. The neurotic individual represents

For many years, "Fritz" Perls was a resident at the Esalen Institute, a human growth center located in Big Sur, California. In the many workshops which he conducted, Perls worked with as many as 20 to 30 people at a time who came up one by one to relate dreams or gain insight into their problems in the "hot seat." Here an Esalen staff member tells of a dream in which he was first a Rube Goldberg cartoon figure and then a bottle of Fresca.

an incomplete gestalt because he tends to exclude from his awareness experience which triggers pain and anxiety. He also disowns aspects of his personality which he finds unacceptable.

Figure and ground. Another Gestalt psychology concept that has been applied to therapy is that of *figure and ground.* Figure is anything on which the individual's attention is focused at this moment. Ground is everything which recedes into the background when the figure holds the individual's attention. Picture a writer in the throes of creation. At this moment nothing but his book exists for him. It is the figure and everything else in his life is forgotten and becomes the ground. But right now, if someone yells: "Fire!" suddenly the fire and the need to escape from the threat becomes the figure and the book has become the ground.

Psychological health requires the ability to be flexible, to be able to shift figure and ground appropriately. For individuals Perls considered to be neurotic, this is difficult. They live with a rigid orientation to experience in which figures appear to be glued to the ground. Some examples of this are phobias, obsessions, and compulsions. The inability to form new figures is another serious block to the utilization of the individual's capacity for growth. It limits behavior which leads to new experience, the acquisition of new skills, new interests, and new relationships. The blocked individual is "stuck."

Closure. Gestalt psychologists assert that mental activity occurs in coherent wholes. When such wholeness is incomplete, there is a strong urge to complete it and create *closure.* In Gestalt therapy the urge for closure is represented by the urge to finish "unfinished business." This represents a painful or traumatic experience in the client's past which still interferes with his functioning. Unfinished business is *finished* by being brought into clear awareness, reexperienced and reformulated into a new gestalt. The new gestalt is no longer a source of pain, fear, or guilt. It is no longer a block to growth. With closure, the painful experience ceases to be a figure and fades into the ground, leaving the individual free to permit new figures to emerge. The individual is no longer "stuck."

Gestalt therapy also shows the influence of both existential and psychoanalytic concepts. As in existential analysis the approach to the client is *phenomenological.* Like Rogers, the therapist attempts to understand the client's unique world view through empathy and intuition. The concept of personal responsibility for what one does and what one becomes in the course of living is also existential. The therapist assumes that each individual is a process, always becoming and changing. The client can *choose* to remain a dependent child, spending his life in pursuit of environmental support, or he can choose to become an aware, independent, and creative self, actively working to achieve actualization.

From psychoanalysis comes the belief that expanded awareness or insight is the key to personality change, the emphasis on dream analysis, and the conviction that therapy must be an emotional experience.

Gestalt therapy is actually an expression of the humanistic-existential philosophy of life. It is transmitted to the client not by explanation but by the therapeutic process itself.

Therapeutic procedures. The "rules" of Gestalt therapy as formulated by Levitsky and Perls (1970) are the following:

1. Communicate in the present tense. Don't dwell on the past or anticipate the future. The only way to integrate the past is to bring it into the present.
2. Do not talk *at* people, talk *with* them. This may be especially relevant when Gestalt therapy is practiced in a group context.
3. Use "I" language rather than "it" language. For example: Therapist: "What is your hand doing." Client: "It is trembling." Therapist: "Say, 'I am trembling.' " By using the "I" language, the client takes responsibility for his behavior and feelings.
4. Focus on immediate experience. The therapist may repeatedly ask what the client is feeling "at this moment."
5. Do not gossip. Don't talk about someone, talk directly to him or her.
6. Don't ask questions. Instead, make a statement because the question often represents a disguised and manipulative way of stating opinions.

Levitsky and Perls also describe some of the "games" which Gestalt therapists often use to increase the client's awareness. Let us now consider several such "games".

1. *Games of dialogue.* The client is asked to have a dialog with two conflicting aspects of his personality. The *two-chair technique* is frequently used in such games. Here, the therapist asks the client to create a dialogue between two opposing forces in herself and, using two empty chairs alternately, to give both feelings full expression as if an argument were going on between them. The "good boy" versus the "spoiled brat" may be a "split" in the client's personality and serve as the focal point for a two-chair dialogue. Often, when this procedure is followed, a synthesis of the two opposing sides occurs. For example, the overcontrolled good boy, always anxious to please

others, may learn from an interchange with the spoiled brat that it is acceptable to be assertive and even demanding in certain instances. Thus, the "good-brat" may be more effective and authentic than either the good boy or the spoiled brat. A variation of this technique is for the client to occupy one chair and pretend that a significant person who is absent or dead is occupying the other one. The client addresses the absent person, expressing feelings he or she had never dared to vocalize before. The client then pretends that the imaginary person in the other chair answers, and a dialog follows. Such interaction often leads to closure because an interpersonal conflict may be resolved, or an intrapersonal situation may be clarified.

2. *"I take responsibility."* In this game the client is asked to make a statement about himself that is true and to end it with the phrase, "and I take responsibility for it." For example, "I feel depressed, and I take responsibility for it."

3. *Reversals.* A client who claims that he is shy and timid may be asked to play the role of a loud, extraverted character.

Dream analysis. Gestalt therapy utilizes dreams by having the client act out every part or selected parts of the dream. In the following example the client is a 26-year-old male attorney who describes himself as follows: "I am very good looking, successful, and smart. I don't know why I am depressed most of the time." This client related the following dream: "I see the alley which is behind the apartment where I live, but the alley is tilted up at a 45 degree angle. I am in a trash can rolling down this alley. A huge monster is chasing me. I have a feeling of fear and impending doom."

Therapist: Let yourself feel the fear and doom. How do you experience it?

Client: My chest has a tight band around it. My throat is dry and I feel constricted.

Therapist: Exaggerate these symptoms. And now let yourself become the alley. Start a sentence with "I am the alley" and tell me how you feel, and what is happening to you.

Client: I am the alley. People ride their cars over me. It is dirty.

Therapist: There is no "it." Say, "I am dirty."

Client: I am dirty. People store their garbage on me.

Therapist: How does it feel to be tilted at a 45 degree angle?

Client: I feel uncomfortable, unnatural, cramped, and not the way I should.

Therapist: Become the trash can.

Client: If I were the trash can.

Therapist: You *are* the trash can.

Client: I am dirty, rusty. I get tossed around by garbage collectors with dirty hands. Kids kick me. [*Starts crying.*]

Therapist: Stay with this feeling. Don't interrupt your experience." [*Client sobs.*]

Client: I don't think much of myself, do I?

Therapist: How do you *really* feel?

Client: I hate myself!

Therapist: Again, louder!

Client: I HATE myself! HATE! HATE! And I'm the monster, too, who is terrifying me! Destroying me! I know it now! [*Sobs.*]

The client has come in contact with feelings which he has previously been avoiding. When a breakthrough of strong negative feelings occurs the therapist responds with empathy and warmth.

Gestalt therapy is directed toward the achievement of self-knowledge and self-realization, with the therapist acting as facilitator. Perls warns that this is not an "instant cure" form of therapy. Many successive exercises involving serious emotional investment on the client's part are necessary. Equally important is creative, sensitive, and empathic behavior on the therapist's part. The message the Gestalt therapist conveys to the client is: Live in the here and now! Don't try to live up to the standards, values, and expectations of others. Listen to yourself and take responsibility for yourself. Use your eyes, ears, nose, sex organs, feelings, and thoughts to contact the world and be fully alive in it. Become what you are capable of becoming.

Logotherapy

Victor Frankl's psychotherapeutic orientation was influenced by his experiences in the dehumanizing environment of four Nazi concentration camps where he lost his parents, his brother, and his wife. Out of the suffering he experienced and witnessed, Frankl came to believe that man can preserve spiritual freedom and independence of mind even under conditions of enormous psychological and physical stress (Frankl, 1962). It is this spiritual freedom, of which no one can deprive him, that permits man to retain his dignity even in a concentration camp. It is this freedom that makes life meaningful under *any* condition and lends meaning to suffering and to man's inescapable eventual confrontation with death. When no other freedom remains, one can still choose one's own attitude toward pain or despair. Man is responsible not only for the way he behaves and the way he lives, but also for the way he suffers. Frankl defines logotherapy as the treatment of the patient's *attitude* toward his unavoidable destiny. Frankl found attitudinal treatment effective in his work with prison inmates facing the gas chamber and with terminal cancer patients (Frankl, 1969).

The literal meaning of the word *logotherapy* is meaning therapy. Even under normal conditions of life, Frankl found that often patients complain of feeling "empty" and seeing their life as meaningless. He found that such a patient can be helped to overcome the "existential vacuum" and find the meaning of his or her life in encounters with a therapist. What the therapist offers is empathy, wisdom, and a "reaching beyond himself" to the patient. Like other existentialists, Frankl stresses responsibility and the need to rise to life's challenges. He discourages patients from blaming other people or adverse circumstances for their difficulties.

Frankl has contributed two techniques to the repertoire of the therapist.

1. Paradoxical intention. Here the patient is asked to do that which he or she fears most. Consider the following example: A woman who was afraid to go shopping because she was certain she would faint, was told to enter a store and tell herself: "I am going to faint!" "I'll show everyone how well I can faint." "I'll force myself to faint all over the place!" According to Frankl, the change in attitude from one of fearful avoidance to one of direct and humorous confrontation is the curative factor.

2. De-reflection. Many people observe and analyze themselves to a degree which interferes with their capacity to live spontaneously and happily. Here is an example of how the technique of de-reflection might be used: A person who thinks her traumatic past must limit her present life *will* actually limit and restrict her life. Such patients are told to stop thinking about their past, ignore their symptoms, and attend to their everyday tasks, concerns, and relationships. In such cases, a change in attitude releases the patient's capacity for constructive living.

SIMILARITIES AND DIFFERENCES

As we have proceeded in our consideration of the psychodynamic and humanistic-existential therapies, you have no doubt noted some similarities and differences in these approaches. The approaches differ in the favored therapeutic techniques and in their concepts of psychopathology and their views of the essential nature of man.

Humanistic therapists take issue with the psychodynamic concept of psychological disturbance as some diagnosable condition to be labeled by the therapist as psychosis, neurosis, phobia, and so on. They contend that neither psychological "sickness" or health are absolute states. In all people, we can find gradations of psychological disturbances which are revealed in various ways, to varying degrees, and over varying periods of time. Humanistic-existential therapists note that the bases on which a person will be labeled "sick" or "normal" are culturally biased and relative. Often such judgments are based on the degree to which a person's behavior is perceived by others to depart from social expectations. In the humanistic perspective, therapy is not a process for healing the abnormal or sick. As Rogers notes, it is a process of "releasing an already existing capacity in a potentially competent individual" (Rogers, 1959b, p. 221).

Humanistic-existentialist therapists also oppose the pessimism of the analytic view of man. Rogers wrote: "I have little sympathy with the rather prevalent concept that man is basically irrational and that his impulses, if not controlled, will lead to destruction of others and self. Man's behavior is exquisitely rational, moving with subtle and ordered complexity toward the goals his organism is endeavoring to achieve" (Rogers, 1961a pp. 194–95).

Another criticism of psychodynamic therapy frequently voiced by those of the humanistic-existential persuasion is that its emphasis on the past provides patients with excuses for irresponsible behavior. They contend that the patient is encouraged to blame her parents or her unconscious for her difficulties: "it wasn't I who did, it was my compulsion" or "My childhood trauma is responsible" (Perls, 1971).

The neo-Freudian response to such criticism is that to ignore the patient's history and his unconscious motivation is to approach him on a very shallow basis. The crux of psychodynamic therapy is to help patients understand the unconscious meaning and the sources of their symptoms. Without such understanding, they believe, no genuine personality restructuring can occur.

Humanistic therapists have also argued that analysts see their patients as machines; as complex energy systems composed of conflicting intrapsychic forces. In the humanistic-existential view, man is not a machine to be repaired. He is, they believe, a valued and respected "being-in-the-process-of-becoming" (Allport, 1968).

What you have just read might suggest that psychodynamic therapists do not relate to their patients as positively as their humanistic-existential colleagues. This is not, however, the case. Therapists of all persuasions believe that empathy, understanding, sincerity, and unconditional positive regard are important factors in successful psychotherapy. Psychodynamic and humanistic-existential therapists also share the commitment to self-knowledge as a curative agent in psychotherapy. Although the language of the humanistic perspective stresses personal growth and self-actualization, psychodynamic therapists are equally committed to helping their patients enrich their lives in meaningful ways.

THE CHALLENGE OF BEHAVIOR THERAPY

Behavior therapists have been highly critical of both psychodynamic and humanistic psychotherapy. Indeed, early behavioral approaches were united in their opposition to the assumptions and techniques of the insight therapies we have discussed. Then, as today, behavior therapists have questioned the "economics" and effectiveness of insight therapies and the value of insight as a curative factor. Behavior therapists have argued that insight therapies are best suited to verbal, intelligent, introspective, wealthy, and relatively well-functioning individuals. The time-consuming, intellectual, and expensive insight therapies are seen as having little value to vast numbers of people, including the lower class, children, aged, and psychotics.

Behavior therapists are equally critical of insight therapists' failure to carefully evaluate the effectiveness of the therapy they practice. They note that the studies which support the effectiveness of insight therapies tend to use measures of success which lack reliability and validity. For example, the patient's self-report of progress is subjective and may be influenced by the expectancy of therapeutic gains rather than by the treatment itself. In addition, self-report data may not reflect changes in the client's actual behavior. Behavior therapists contend that well-controlled studies are lacking to support insight therapies superiority over less costly and time-consuming approaches.

Behavior therapists also fault insight therapies for focusing on the internal dynamics of the patient while virtually ignoring maladaptive behaviors. Unless the patient learns new skills or ways of responding that are more adaptive, it is unlikely that treatment gains will be maximized. The role of insight in promoting treatment gains has also been questioned by behavior therapists. They claim that patients who profit from therapy may improve because the therapist reinforces appropriate behaviors or serves as an effective model for the individual. Therapists may attribute treatment gains to insight when, in reality, other factors may be responsible for improvement.

Despite all the voices that have been raised against insight therapies, they remain viable, comprehensive, established, and widely practiced therapeutic approaches. We will now turn our attention to the behavior and biological therapies. These approaches represent a clear departure from the insight-oriented therapies.

SUMMARY

In this chapter, we presented an overview of the rapidly expanding field of psychotherapy, with special emphasis on the insight therapies. Despite their differences regarding theoretical emphases and technical procedures, therapists share many common attitudes and goals. They attempt to create a therapeutic climate in which trust and hope can grow; they explore the origins or determinants of the client's difficulties and devise strategies for cognitive, emotional, and behavioral change; they attempt to produce lasting changes which transfer to real life situations; and they serve as models of healthy attitudes and functioning in the context of a professional relationship with a client seeking help.

To understand the process of psychotherapy, it is necessary to take note of therapist, patient, and relationship variables. The therapeutic relationship is considered to be important by therapists of all persuasions, but behavior therapists see it as less crucial than psychodynamic and humanistic therapists.

The attainment of insight is a common therapeutic goal of both psychodynamic and humanistic-existential therapists. Psychodynamic therapists are united in the belief that much of human behavior is motivated by unconscious needs and conflicts. However, the Neo-Freudians (Jung and Sullivan) depart from Freud in their theoretical emphases, their views of the therapist-patient relationship, and some technical modifications and innovations. They tend to be more flexible in their use of therapeutic techniques, more concerned with conscious aspects of functioning, and more present-centered than their psychoanalytic colleagues.

We noted that the humanistic perspective on abnormal behavior provides the theoretical basis for the humanistic-existential therapies of Carl Rogers, Fritz Perls, and Victor Frankl. These therapies capture humanistic and existential psychology's emphasis on the unfolding of human potential, its view of man as a rational being, and its commitment to a phenomenological approach. Humanistic-existential therapists differ in the techniques utilized to help the client attain enhanced self-awareness. But all consider the therapist and client in an emotionally involved, authentic relationship of prime importance.

Behavior therapists have criticized and questioned insight therapy's failure to focus directly on maladaptive behavior, its lack of demonstrated effectiveness, its limited application, and insight's role as a curative factor in psychotherapy.

17

The Behavior Therapies

OVERVIEW OF BEHAVIOR THERAPY

In this chapter and the next we will examine the behavioral and biological approaches to the treatment of psychological disorders. Both of these approaches offer alternatives to insight therapies and challenge the assumption that enhanced self-knowledge is essential to successful therapy. Behavior therapists have devised many techniques for dealing with a broad range of problems in living. Biological treatments have enabled many seriously disturbed patients to leave the confines of the mental hospital and live relatively normal lives in the community.

How is behavior therapy different from traditional insight therapy? What are some general considerations which guide behavior therapists in approaching their clients? Is behavior therapy more effective than insight therapies? These are some of the questions that we will address in this chapter. We will also acquaint you with some of the most prominent and widely practiced techniques of behavior therapy. In the next chapter we will look at the biological approaches which include drug therapy, electroconvulsive therapy, and the controversial procedure of psychosurgery.

The following examples represent only a few of the many types of clients and problem behaviors treated with behavior therapy.

- David F. is a writer. Each day he spends what seems like interminable hours staring at a blank piece of paper in his typewriter. Unable to accomplish anything, he finds that his frustration mounts as he feels increasingly helpless. He wonders whether he will ever be able to finish his novel.
- Seven-year-old Frank L. wets his bed each night. When other children invite him to stay overnight, Frank refuses, goes home, and cries bitterly. More and more of Frank's friends seem to avoid him now and he asks himsef: "Do they know?"
- Barbara L. finds sweets irresistible. She alternates between periods of severe self-denial in attempts to control her weight, and eating binges in which she secretly consumes two pounds of chocolate or a whole whip cream pie. She feels frustrated and embarrassed every time that she inadvertently glances at herself in the mirror. "Do I look that bad to other people," she asks herself.
- Richard M. is a 16-year-old boy who despite his parents best efforts to "correct" his behavior continues to engage in petty thievery, come home after

his curfew, and perform below his ability level at school.

- Herman L. constantly checks the windows, doors, and stove in his house. It takes a lot of his time and energy, but he insists that "one can never be too careful."

The scope and range of application of behavior therapy techniques has expanded enormously over the past few decades. And the special needs of groups of persons like the aged and the retarded have been addressed with behavioral techniques.

The ultimate goal of all therapy is to help the client eliminate behavior patterns that are maladaptive and self-defeating. Behavior therapists take a direct path toward this goal. Unlike the psychodynamic therapists, they make no attempt to help the client understand the unconscious bases of his or her difficulties. Unlike the humanistic-existentialist therapists they do not attempt

EMERGING APPLICATIONS OF BEHAVIOR THERAPY

Kazdin (1979) has noted that behavior therapy has expanded into many applied areas that have "traditionally been outside of the treatment focus of psychiatry and clinical psychology but where behavior change represents a primary concern" (p. 647). Kazdin lists the following areas into which behavior therapy research has entered:

Education Research derived programs have been applied to students ranging from preschool to college level. The focus has been on academic skills, management problems, and curriculum design.

Child-rearing Research has addressed the full gamut of childhood problems, including thumbsucking, toilet training, complying with parental instructions, and completing homework.

Gerontology Behavioral techniques have been applied to the aged in nursing homes to increase self-care, physical activity, and social interaction.

Medicine The new area of "behavioral medicine" has shown tremendous activity where behavioral techniques are applied to medically related problems, including pain, hypertension, asthma, and seizures, to mention a few areas.

Pediatrics Health care of acute and chronic inpatient problems with children using behavioral techniques has been identified as an emergent area known as *behavioral pediatrics.*

Community work Behavior therapy techniques has been applied to a host of social and community problems, including pollution, energy and conservation, littering, and job finding.

Criminology Behavioral techniques have been applied to prisoners in institutional programs.

Business and industry Applications of incentive systems have always played an important role in business and industry, but the explicit use of behavioral programs to alter performance on the job has increased.

to show the client how "unfinished business" from the past and failure to assume responsibility for feelings block the expression of the potential for self-actualization. Instead, the behavior therapist concentrates on the specific difficulty which has led the client to undertake psychotherapy.

As we noted in Chapter 3, the theoretical basis of behavior therapy differs from other therapeutic approaches. Its roots are in learning theory which grew out of experimental investigations of learning processes in animals. However therapists of this orientation are not limited to a perception of behavior change as resulting from operant or classical reinforcing conditions. Recently there has been a trend to recognize the influence of social, cognitive, and emotional factors on behavior. Later, in our discussion, we will note how this trend is reflected in techniques based on modeling and on cognitive-behavioral approaches that directly change the client's maladaptive beliefs. Behavior therapists believe that many behaviors society labels *abnormal* result from inadequate learning of more effective responses to events and other people. Therefore they see their therapeutic effort as educative—as a training program in effective and productive behavior. What all behavior therapists share is the belief that experimental validation of the effectiveness of their technical procedures is the ultimate test of their value.

Like their psychodynamic and humanistic colleagues, the behavior therapists bring to their clients genuine interest, warmth, and understanding. A study by Sloane and his colleagues at Temple University (Sloane, Staples, Cristol, Yorkston, & Whipple, 1975) found that experienced behavior therapists were rated by their clients as equally warm, empathetic, and concrete as experienced nonbehavioral therapists. On one measure, genuineness, behavior therapists received even higher ratings than their nonbehavioral colleagues! Findings like these have helped challenge the belief that behavior therapists present themselves to their clients as cold and mechanical technicians.

Although behavior therapists do not stress the therapeutic relationship as an important aspect of therapy, they utilize their initial sessions with their clients to establish rapport and to learn the nature of the client's specific difficulties. They attempt to learn the environmental aspects of the client's experience, the nature, the degree, and the duration of the problem(s), and the client's attitudes toward them and motivation for change.

Behavior therapists do not perceive their task to be the evaluation and diagnosis of the client's degree of "mental illness." Their assessment is directed toward the recognition of the client's problem, so that specific treatment goals may be established and specific therapeutic procedures may be undertaken. Systematic evaluation of the client's progress continues throughout the course of therapy. Behavior therapists are flexible in using alternative techniques with the same client when this appears useful. The five phases of most behavior therapy efforts are nicely summarized by McNamara (1978, p. 4): (1) identification of the problem(s), (2) establishment of behavioral objectives, (3) design of a behavior change strategy, (4) program implementation, and (5) systematic evaluation of the modification effort, with feedback relating outcome data to successful intervention or the need for program modification. The client will also be encouraged to apply his or her newly acquired coping skills to everyday life situations. Behavior therapists recognize the importance of including specific procedures to help clients learn strategies and ways of behaving that will increase the likelihood of gains made in the clinic persisting in the real world.

Let us now turn our attention to some of the most prominent and widely used techniques of behavior therapy.

Joseph Wolpe

Courtesy of Joseph Wolpe

TECHNIQUES OF BEHAVIOR THERAPY

Systematic Desensitization

> We will begin treatment by helping you to become really relaxed. Then you are going to imagine scenes related to your fear, starting with ones that are only slightly frightening. Because I will be introducing the scenes in a gradual way, and because you will be relaxed when you imagine them, before long you will be able to imagine situations related to your fear of heights and actually feel comfortable at the same time. And if you can imagine flying in an airplane or looking down from a high place and still feel calm, then when you are in such a situation out there in the real world, you will find you are not afraid anymore (Adapted from Rimm & Masters, 1979).

What you have just read is a therapeutic rationale that might be presented to a client about to participate in systematic desensitization to help him overcome his fear of heights. Systematic desensitization is a widely used behavior therapy procedure that was developed by Joseph Wolpe in 1958 to help clients manage maladaptive, unrealistic anxiety. The technique has proven to be extremely effective with clients suffering from a wide range of phobic disorders. Systematic desensitization has also been successfully applied to other disorders, including insomnia (Steinmark & Borkovec, 1974), speech disorders (Walton & Mather, 1963b), and asthmatic attacks (Moore, 1965).

Wolpe's techniques are based on the reciprocal inhibition principle that the client cannot experience two conflicting responses simultaneously. Therefore he cannot feel anxiety while he is also deeply relaxed. The relaxation response inhibits the anxiety response. And this serves to desensitize the client to the anxiety provoking aspects of the stimulus.

Let us now consider how a therapist might actually proceed in treating a client with a fear of heights. With the assistance of the therapist, the client first learns deep muscular relaxation. Various approaches to inducing relaxation have been utilized, including imagining pleasant relaxing scenes, focusing on breathing and maintaining a slow breathing rate, and hypnotic suggestion. Many therapists, however, favor a technique based on progressive relaxation developed by Edmund Jacobson (1938). Jacobson's technique involves alternately tensing and relaxing various groups in a predetermined order. This procedure helps the client to tell when he is tense and when he is relaxed. Discriminating tension from relaxing presumably helps the client to attain a more profound state of relaxation. After two to six sessions, most clients are able to experience deep muscular relaxation.

Before the actual desensitization session can begin, the client constructs an anxiety hierarchy with the assistance of the therapist. The hierarchy is a series of situations or scenes that are arranged in order from the least to most anxiety evoking. Let us consider a hierarchy which was used by Rimm in the treatment of a 40-year-old man who developed a fear of heights after discharge from the Air Force during the Second World War.

1. You are beginning to climb the ladder leaning against the side of your house. You plan to work on the roof. Your hands are on the ladder and your feet are on the first rung.
2. You are halfway up the ladder, and you happen to look down. You see the lawn below you and a walkway.
3. Driving with the family, the road begins to climb.
4. Driving with the family on a California coastal highway with drop-off to the right.
5. On California seashore cliff, approximately six feet from the edge.
6. Driving with the family, approaching mountain summit.
7. In commercial airliner at the time of takeoff.
8. In airliner at an altitude of 30,000.
9. In airliner at an altitude of 30,000 with considerable turbulence.
10. On a California seaside cliff, approximately two feet (judged to be a safe distance) from the edge and looking down.
11. Climbing the water tower to assist in painting, about ten feet from the ground.
12. Same as above, but about 20 feet from the ground.
13. On the catwalk around the water tank, painting the tank (Rimm & Masters, 1979, p. 48).

After the client has learned relaxation and the anxiety hierarchy is prepared, he is ready to begin the actual desensitization session. Below is an example of a desensitization session which would take place after a client is deeply relaxed.

Therapist: Fine. Soon I shall ask you to imagine a scene. After you hear a description of the situation, please imagine it as vividly as you can, through your own eyes, as if you were actually there. Try to include all the details in the scene. While you're visualizing the situation, you may continue feeling as relaxed as you are now. If so, that's good. After 5, 10, or 15 seconds, I'll ask you to stop imagining the scene and return to your pleasant image and to just relax. But if you begin to feel even the slightest increase in anxiety or tension, please signal this to me by raising your left

> forefinger. When you do this, I'll step in and ask you to stop imagining the situation and then will help you get relaxed once more. It's important that you indicate tension to me in this way, as we want to maximize your being exposed to fearful situations without feeling anxious (Goldfield & Davison, 1976, pp. 124–125).

If the client reports anxiety at any point in the process, the procedure is interrupted. The client is asked to completely relax and return to the fantasy of the scene which preceded the one which evoked fear. When relaxation is once more completely achieved, the anxiety-provoking scene is reintroduced. In successive therapy sessions this process is continued until even the most frightening scenes in the hierarchy may be confronted without anxiety. Wolpe (1958) reported that the medium number of sessions to complete a desensitization hierarchy is eight.

There is little question that systematic desensitization is a highly effective procedure in dealing with anxiety-related disorders. In a review of the literature conducted in 1969, Paul concluded that systematic desensitization was successful in 92 percent of the cases treated. In a more recent review, Leitenberg (1976, p. 131) noted that "systematic desensitization is demonstrably more effective than both no treatment and every psychotherapy variant with which it has so far been compared."

Implosive Therapy

Implosive therapy is a behavior therapy procedure which, like systematic

DISMANTLING DESENSITIZATION

Just as behavior therapists have voiced skepticism about the value of insight in psychotherapy, they have also questioned Wolpe's reciprocal inhibition explanation of desensitization. Over the past decade, behavior therapists have searched for an answer to the question: "Why does desensitization work?" They have carefully evaluated desensitization to learn more about the mechanisms that account for the treatment's undisputed success.

One way in which a therapeutic procedure like desensitization can be evaluated is by isolating what appear to be specific components of the technique and comparing their effects with the full treatment package (Wilson & O'Leary, 1980). This enables the researcher to better understand which aspects of the treatment are essential or contribute maximally to its effectiveness. Lang (1969) has termed this method of evaluating specific techniques a *dismantling* strategy. How might this strategy be applied to desensitization? To determine whether relaxation is a necessary ingredient in desensitization, the effects of a procedure in which relaxation is omitted might be compared with a "complete" desensitization treatment. If we find that the two treatments are equally effective in reducing phobic anxiety, we might then conclude that relaxation is not an essential aspect of desensitization.

Researchers have subjected various components of desensitization to just this type of analysis. Numerous studies have cast doubt on whether any one component of desensitization (i.e., relaxation, imagery, a graduated hierarchy, low-anxiety levels) is essential (Murray & Jacobson, 1978). This has opened the door to diverse interpretations about the processes involved in the successful desensitization of phobic anxiety. Let us examine a number of accounts that have been proposed to explain the positive results produced by desensitization.

One intriguing possibility is that expectancies and cognitive factors aroused by the desensitization procedure reduce phobic anxiety. The impressive, highly credible treatment package, the optimistic treatment rationale and the scientific, yet relaxed treatment atmosphere all combine to foster positive expectancies in the client. After undergoing desensitization, the client may be convinced that he or she can overcome or better cope with troubling, yet unrealistic fears. Indeed, a number of outcome studies have shown that desensitization fares no better than a placebo control procedure specifically designed to arouse the same degree of positive expectancies as the desensitization treatment (e.g., Lick, 1975). There is little in the desensitization literature to contradict the idea that expectancies may be potent determinants of treatment gains (Kazdin & Wilcoxin, 1976).

Other cognitive views suggest that clients may come to see their attitudes toward the phobic situation as irrational or they learn to focus their attention on less threatening aspects of the object they once feared, after experiencing desensitization (Wilkins, 1971). Such adaptive changes in attitudes may promote contact with the phobic object or situation. Since phobias are actually unrealistic fears, successfully approaching the phobic object may further reinforce the belief that the fear associated with it has no objective basis.

A popular noncognitive account of desensitization's success is based on the learning theory concept of extinction. In our discussion of neurosis in chapter 6, we saw that Marks (1978) makes the strong argument that relief from phobias occurs when the person suffering from them is able to make sustained contact with those situations that evoke discomfort until the discomfort subsides. The fear response is extinguished by repeated contact with the feared stimulus in the absence of negative consequences. According to this view, we might expect that desensitization would be successful to the degree that it facilitates contact with the phobic object or situation.

In a very recent formulation of what occurs as a result of desensitization, Wilson and O'Leary (1980) combine a number of ideas. They contend that clients undergoing desensitization "(a) perceive that they are no longer upset by previously feared situations; (b) they acquire a coping skill for managing anxiety (relaxation); and (c) they rehearse in imagination the successful performance of previously feared actions" (p. 164).

The question "Why does desensitization work?" is as yet, unresolved and remains the subject of much controversy. But our brief overview reflects the active and thought-provoking efforts of contemporary behavior therapists to understand exactly why their techniques work. Much to their credit, behavior therapists subject techniques with proven value, like desensitization, to the same critical scrutiny as less well-established procedures.

desensitization, requires that the client imagine the phobic object or situation. But that is where the resemblance between these two procedures ends. Consider the following scene which might be presented to a client to visualize at the beginning of implosive treatment for a fear of heights.

> You are at the top of a tall building, looking down at the street below. Your feet are on a narrow walkway and your hands are gripping a guard rail. And you look down, you notice how small things appear and you feel a mounting sense of terror washing over you. You notice how fast your heart is beating; how your breath comes in short gasps, and yes, how you can't catch your breath. And as you think of how cold and sweaty your hands feel, you begin to feel yourself lose your grip. The slight sense of dizziness you felt as you walked up the steps to the top of the building is much greater now and everything begins to swirl around you, faster and faster, faster and faster. As you wonder whether you can hold on, your feet begin to slip, first one, then the other. Your feet slip off and your hold on the guard rail breaks. Now you're falling. You feel the wind on your face. Your thoughts quickly flash on how you will look to others lying on the concrete when they find you. Down, down you go, watching the windows go by as you fall. You know your body will hit the hard pavement in the next instant. And you imagine it all as if you're watching a slow-motion film. Your feet strike the ground first, but they can't prevent your body and head from being crushed by the hardness of the concrete. Hear your bones snap, crack, and break apart. Your guts are pouring out of the holes in your body. Look at the horrified stares of the onlookers. Shortly, they will walk away, uncaring for your lifeless body.

As you can see, the implosive therapist not only begins with a scene which is the most frightening event the client can imagine but embellishes it to prolong the anxiety at an intense level. This, of course, is a sharp contrast with the gradual approach to the fear of heights taken by a practitioner of systematic desensitization. An implosive therapist might ask the client to vividly imagine the scene or story which is suggested for as long as an hour and a half. Imagery, presumed to be related to conflicts of a psychodynamic nature, might be included in the scenes. Areas of conflict that might be touched on are: "fears, rejections, prior humiliations or deprivations, or conflicts related to the expression of fear of aggressiveness, sexual problems of various types, and guilt related behavior" (Hogan, 1968, p. 423). Between sessions, the client is instructed to imagine the scenes that were presented to him during the treatment sessions (Stampfl & Levis, 1967). Session after session, the story, or a variation of it, designed to elicit maximal anxiety, will be repeated until the client no longer reports fear in reaction to the suggested scenes.

According to the extinction theory that underlies implosive therapy, the height phobic, for example, never learns that the disasterous consequences he fears will not occur. This is because he continually avoids the phobic situation—high places. By repeatedly eliciting anxiety in the absence of any actual negative consequences, the client's fear of heights will eventually dissipate and cease to be anticipated and experienced in actual real-life situations.

Flooding

Flooding, or response prevention, as it is sometimes called, is a technique that is similar to implosive therapy but differs in one crucial respect: In flooding, the therapist does not present the anxiety producing stimuli to the client in imagery, but actually makes the client confront the fear producing stimulus in real life. Flooding has been used with success in treating numerous disorders, including obsessive-compulsive behaviors.

Myers, Robertson, and Tatlon (1975) report an interesting application of flooding procedures with a woman who felt compelled to wash her hands and change her clothes whenever she encountered anything even remotely associated with death. After it was determined that her greatest fear involved dead bodies, she and her therapist "visited" a hospital mortuary where they both handled a dead body. During the treatment, the therapist prevented the woman from engaging in compulsive rituals that previously brought her some relief from anxiety. For example, hand washing was not permitted. The woman was made to confront other sources of anxiety such as touching the picture of a man who had been shot to death in the street. The treatment, which lasted for less than two weeks, was judged to be successful over an eight month follow-up period. The compulsion to "cleanse herself" when confronted with death-related stimuli was successfully eliminated by the treatment. Another indication of the treatment's success was that the woman married a man who previously was a source of anxiety to her because his ex-wife had died before they had met.

After reviewing the research on the effectiveness of implosive therapy and flooding, Rimm and Masters (1979) concluded that there is some evidence for their usefulness, but more evidence is needed to determine just how effective they are. Rimm and Masters also urge caution against using such techniques indiscriminately. The client may prefer alternative behavior therapy techniques which are less aversive and of equal or perhaps greater effectiveness.

Modeling

From the therapist's notebook:

> Aside from the changes this client has manifested which I have previously noted, there appears to be a new tendency which is becoming increasingly evident. When looking at Ellen as she walks into my office, I am beginning to feel that I am looking at a mirror image of myself. Her new clothes are almost exact copies of mine. Her manner of speaking has changed. She is apparently imitating my way of talking and this includes my tendency to hesitate before making a statement. I have recently noticed that Ellen no longer complains endlessly in a whiney, irritating, child-like voice that used to be so characteristic of her.

In all of the therapeutic approaches you have encountered in your reading thus far, clients tend to use their therapists as models in various ways. This trend often operates to help the client learn new, more adaptive ways of behaving and interacting with others. When you read about assertion training in the next section, you will note that modeling is an important aspect of treatment.

For more than a decade now, Bandura and his colleagues have researched the applications of modeling procedures to the treatment of phobias. In one early study, Bandura, Grusec, and Menlove (1967) reduced the fear of dogs in children who observed another child gradually increase her contact with a dog by first approaching it, then touching it, petting it, and eventually playing with it.

More recently, Bandura (1971; 1977) has

By observing a model, children can learn to overcome their fears of petting and playing with a dog.

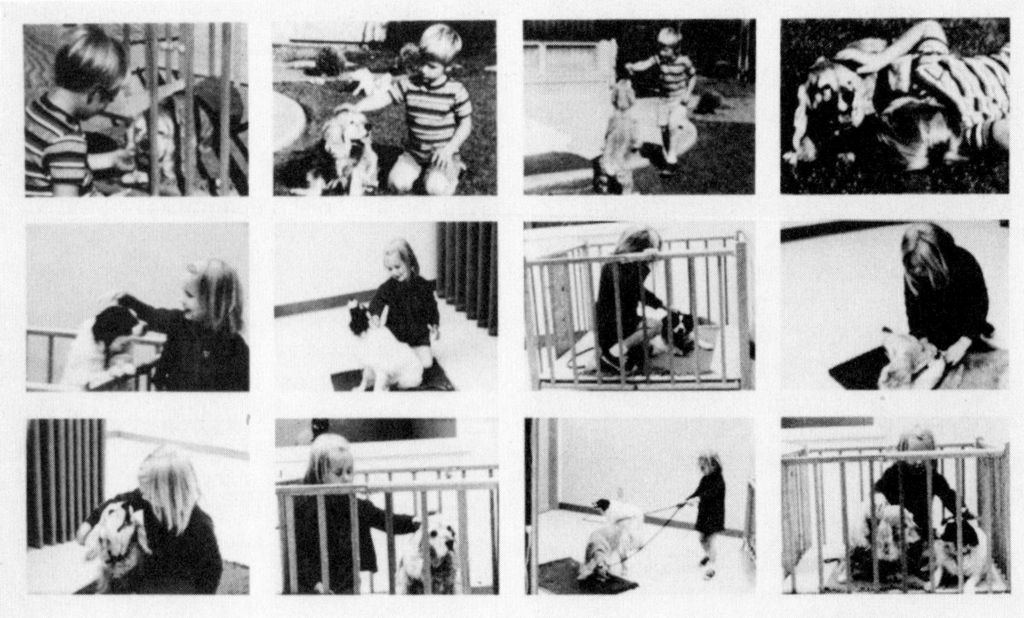

Source: Albert Bandura and Frances L. Menlove, "Factors Determining Vicarious Extinction of Avoidance Behavior through Symbolic Modeling." *Journal of Personality and Social Psychology,* 1968, *8,* 99–108. Copyright 1968 by the American Psychological Association. Reprinted by permission.

been an especially strong advocate of *participant modeling,* a technique that involves modeled demonstration along with client participation. Offering a great deal of support, praise, and reassurance, the therapist guides the patient through the same steps that he previously modeled. As the patient develops increasing confidence, the therapist's support is gradually withdrawn until the patient can cope effectively unassisted.

Bandura, Blanchard, and Ritter (1969) compared the effectiveness of participant modeling in the treatment of snake phobies with two other treatments and a no treatment control group. As Figure 17–1 shows, participant modeling was found to be superior to systematic desensitization and symbolic modeling in which subjects watched a film rather than a live model interacting with a snake. Subjects who received one of the three types of treatment showed much greater fear reduction than subjects who were untreated.

Assertion Training

Consider the following statements made by clients to therapists:

Don G: I feel like a worm. I don't stand up for myself. If I'm not for me, who will be for me, right? Just last night Maxine and I were in a restaurant and the meat we ordered was cold. I know I could have asked the waiter to take it back, but I was afraid that I'd hurt his feelings.

John G: Whenever ! ask a pretty girl out, I can't believe what happens. My face turns red, I almost lose my voice, and a couple of times I almost fainted. Maybe it's because I think she won't go out with me, but I just get tongue-tied and feel like a fool.

Judy R: I know the boss likes my work; he even told me so. But I just don't seem to be able to ask him for a raise. The funny part is, I know I deserve it.

Each of these clients might benefit from assertion training. The techniques of assertion training are used to help clients with anxieties and inhibitions related to social interactions. The goal of assertion training is to facilitate the honest and straightforward expression of thoughts and feelings in a socially appropriate manner.

FIGURE 17–1 Mean Number of Snake-approach Responses Performed by Subjects before and after Receiving Different Treatments.

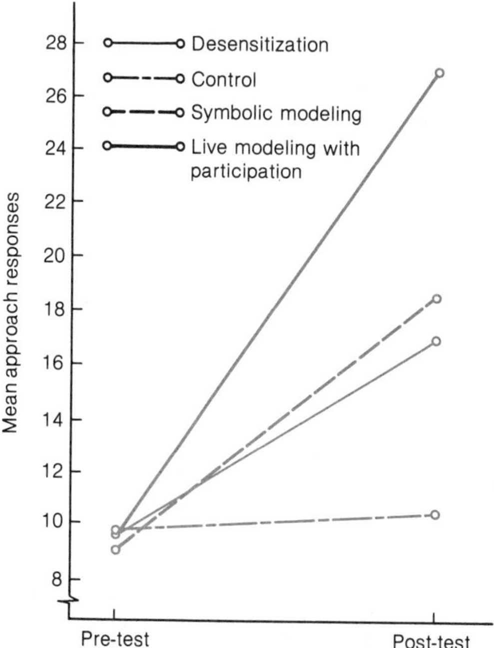

Source: A. Bandura, E. B. Blanchard, and B. Ritter, "The Relative Efficacy of Desensitization and Modeling Approaches for Inducing Behavioral, Affective, and Cognitive Changes," *Journal of Personality and Social Psychology* 13 (1969), pp. 173–99. Copyright 1969 by the American Psychological Association. Reprinted by permission.

How might a behavior therapist help his client to achieve this goal? Perhaps the most commonly used assertion training technique is behavior rehearsal or role playing (Rimm & Masters, 1979). Behavioral rehearsal involves role playing to help the client rehearse assertive responses in a particular situation (Morris, 1976). The therapist plays the role of a relevant person in the interaction such as a spouse, parent, or employer. The client then reacts to the character enacted by the therapist. The therapist provides coaching and immediate feedback about the adequacy of the client's verbal and nonverbal responses. To give the client an opportunity to model assertive behavior, the therapist and client may reverse roles, with the therapist playing the client's role.

Rimm and Masters (1979) offer the following example of behavior rehearsal with a college student who had difficulty making dates with girls.

Client: By the way [*pause*] I don't suppose you want to go out Saturday night?

Therapist: Up to actually asking for the date you were very good. However, if I were the girl, I think I might have been a bit offended when you said, "By the way." It's like your asking her out is pretty casual. Also, the way you phrased the question, you were kind of suggesting to her that she doesn't want to go out with you. Pretend for the moment I'm you. Now, how does this sound: "There is a movie at the Varsity Theater this Saturday that I want to see. If you don't have other plans, I'd very much like to take you."

Client: That sounded good. Like you were sure of yourself and liked the girl too.

Therapist: Why don't you try it.

Client: You know the movie at the Varsity? Well, I'd like to go, and I'd like to take you Saturday, if you don't have anything better to do.

Therapist: Well, that certainly was better. Your tone of voice was especially good. But the last line, "if you don't have anything better to do," sounds like you don't think you have too much to offer. Why not run through it one more time.

Client: I'd like to see the show at the Varsity, Saturday, and if you haven't made other plans, I'd like to take you.

Therapist: Much better. Excellent in fact. You were confident, forceful, and sincere.

A crucial step in behavioral rehearsal in practicing and mastering the newly acquired assertive responses in real-life situations. Since different assertive responses are required in different situations, the therapist and client usually work with one situation at a time. As in systematic desensitization, the client "moves up" a hierarchy of increasingly anxiety arousing situations. Wolpe believed that assertion training is successful because of the reciprocal inhibition principle: it is impossible for one to be assertive and passive at the same time. The client's practice of increasingly complex and difficult assertive responses inhibits anxiety and promotes self-

Noted behavior therapist Arnold Lazarus helps a couple to acquire assertive behaviors in a role-playing session.

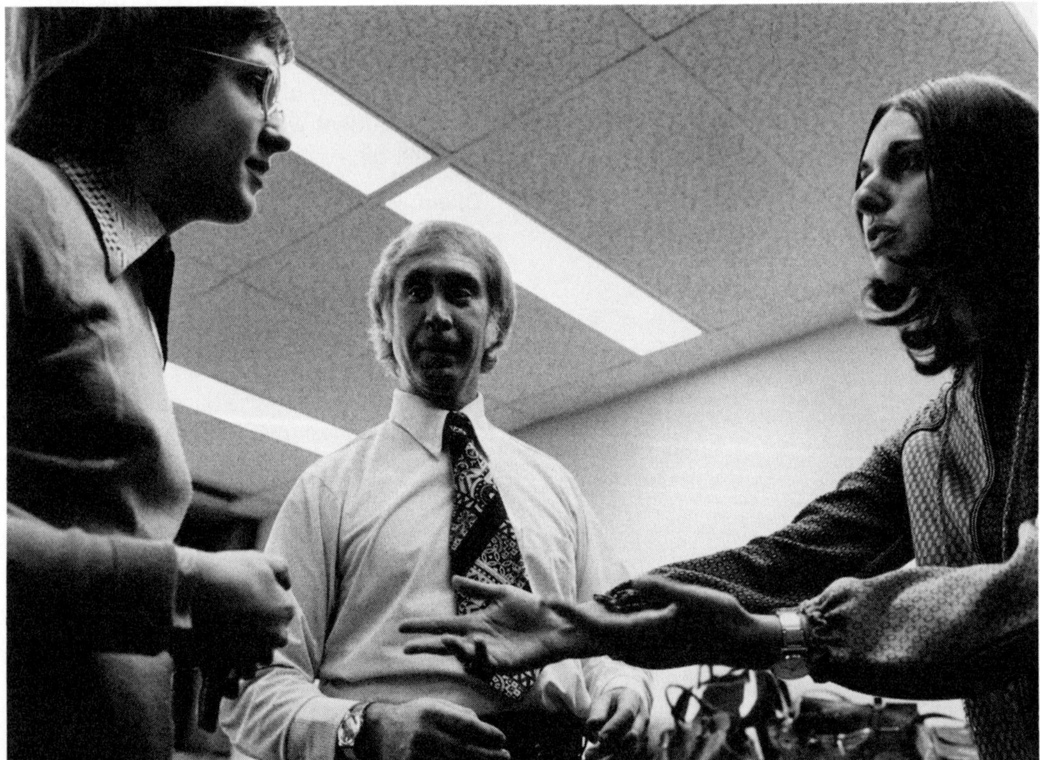

Alex Webb/Magnum Photos, Inc.

THE INTERPERSONAL CONSEQUENCES OF ASSERTION

Assertion training programs help clients to accomplish immediate goals in interpersonal situations. The guiding assumption of such programs is that behaving assertively is generally preferable to behaving in either a nonassertive or an aggressive way. But a recent study by Deborah Hull and Harold Schroeder (1979) suggests that while assertive behavior may help the client to attain immediate goals, the reactions of others to such behaviors may not be uniformly positive.

To study the interpersonal consequences of assertive behavior, the researchers looked at the responses of 42 male and 42 female college students to a partner who behaved either nonassertively, assertively, or aggressively. The subjects partner was actually a confederate whose behavior was modeled after descriptions based on clinical judgments which are commonly used in assertion training programs.

The subjects and their partners interacted in role-played situations which involved refusals and requests for behavior change.

"Has it ever occurred to you, Leland, that maybe you're too candid?"

Reprinted by permission The Wall Street Journal

In both types of situations, the desires of the confederate and the subject were in conflict. In each role-played situation, the subject read a script to initiate the interaction. The partner then responded to either a nonassertive, assertive, or aggressive way. The subject was then given a chance to respond spontaneously.

Hull and Schroeder discovered some interesting differences in the way subjects responded to their partners enacting different behaviors. Both assertive and aggressive behaviors were more effective in accomplishing immediate goals than nonassertive behaviors. But subjects rated nonassertive behavior more positively on some dimensions than both assertive and aggressive behavior. The nonassertive partners were seen as more sympathetic, friendly, and nonrevengeful than the assertive and aggressive partners. The aggressive partners were rated the most negatively, but assertive partners were seen as dominant, unsympathetic, and aggressive.

Hull and Schroeder note that the results of their study may have important implications for assertion training programs. If assertive responses are negatively evaluated, the relationship with the person asserted against may suffer. This suggests the importance of teaching clients to evaluate the likely responses of another person to assertion. Assertion training programs need to be concerned with more than training clients to accomplish their immediate goals. Indeed, assertion training programs might do well to help the client to learn to "accommodate the needs and desires of both people involved" and to recognize the importance of achieving compromises in interpersonal situations.

confidence in interpersonal situations that formerly aroused intense anxiety. Confronting situations which were previously avoided, the client learns that many of his or her fears were unrealistic.

The Token Economy: Achievement Place—A Treatment Program for Delinquent Adolescents

The *token economy* is an excellent example of how the principles of operant conditioning can be applied in treatment programs in institutional and residential settings. You probably recall that the highly effective social learning program for chronically institutionalized schizophrenics developed by Paul and Lentz (1978) involved a token economy system. As you learned in Chapter 11, one of the essential features of token reinforcement systems is that certain behaviors are consistently rewarded with tokens that can be exchanged for other, more tangible rewards, while other behaviors are ignored or not reinforced. Thus, token economy programs shape new behaviors and facilitate learning new skills by the consistent and systematic application of reinforcement principles. Rimm and Masters (1979) have specified three basic considerations involved in developing a token system: (1) identifying target behaviors; (2) defining the currency; and (3) devising an exchange system.

At this point, an example will help clarify how each of these considerations may come into play in implementing a token system. The program we have selected for our example is Achievement Place, a community-based treatment program for delinquent and predelinquent youth. Achievement Place is a home-style facility located in Lawrence, Kansas, for 12 to 16-year-old youth who are typically referred by the courts after getting in trouble with the law. Since many of the young people who participate in the program are three to four years behind academically, the focus of treatment includes improving academic performance as well as eliminating antisocial behaviors and increasing self-care and interpersonal skills. Specific target behaviors that have been identified and increased include studying school assignments, conversing, accepting criticism without aggressing, room cleaning, and saving money. Behaviors that have been decreased include the use of poor grammar, aggressive statements, tardiness in returning home to the facility, and going to bed late (Kazdin, 1978).

Modification of target behaviors is accomplished by participation in the token system and through the instructional efforts of the parent-teachers who provide the youth with specific feedback about the adequacy of his task performance, specific instructions for improvement, and verbal reinforcement and encouragement. The "currency" in the token economy is simply points which the boys receive each time they complete a task or behave appropriately. The exchange system involves trading the points earned for privileges and/or desirable objects. An examination of Table 17–1 will inform you of the relationship between various target behaviors and the points which can be earned or lost.

Each boy is responsible for recording points earned on an index card. The total number of points earned are traded each day for privileges which can be used the following day, if a minimum number of points are accumulated on that day. Boys who perform all of the target behaviors adequately which are listed on the home bulletin board and who incur few "costs," are entitled to all of the privileges. There are

TABLE 17–1 Behaviors and the Number of Points They Earn or Lose

Behaviors Earning Points	*Points*
1. Watching news on TV or reading the newspaper	300 per day
2. Cleaning and maintaining neatness in one's room	500 per day
3. Keeping one's person neat and clean	500 per day
4. Reading books	5–10 per page
5. Aiding house parents in various household tasks	20–1000 per task
6. Doing dishes	500–1000 per meal
7. Being well dressed for an evening meal	100–500 per meal
8. Performing homework	500 per day
9. Obtaining desirable grades on school report cards	500–1000 per grade
10. Turning out lights when not in use	25 per light
Behaviors Losing Points	
1. Failing grades on the report card	500–1000 per grade
2. Speaking aggressively	20–50 per response
3. Forgetting to wash hands before meals	100–300 per meal
4. Arguing	300 per response
5. Disobeying	100–1000 per response
6. Being late	10 per minute
7. Displaying poor manners	50–100 per response
8. Engaging in poor posture	50–100 per response
9. Using poor grammar	20–50 per response
10. Stealing, lying, or cheating	10,000 per response

Source: Reprinted from E. L. Phillips, "Achievement Place: Token Reinforcement Procedures on a Home-Style Setting for Pre-delinquent Boys," *Journal of Applied Behavior Analysis* 1 (1968), p. 215. Copyright 1968 by the Society for the Experimental Analysis of Behavior, Inc.

seven different kinds of privileges a youth can earn: (1) basics, including use of the telephone, tools, radio, record player, and recreation room; (2) snacks after school and before bedtime; (3) television time; (4) home time, which permits the youths to go home on weekends or to go downtown; (5) allowances of from one to five dollars a week; (6) bonds, which the youths can accumulate to buy clothes or other items they need; and (7) special privileges, which include any other privileges the youths may want. Fines have also been used to modify behavior at Achievement Place. In Figure 17–2 we can see how the number of aggressive statements, monitored every three hours, changes as a function of different conditions.

One problem Kazdin (1979) emphasizes is that, more often than not, behaviors that are learned in token economy programs are not maintained after the contingencies are withdrawn and the person confronts the "real world" where "privileges" are not exchanged for "points." How does Achievement Place deal with the potential problem of the failure to transfer what is learned in the program to everyday life situations outside of the home? As soon as the boys consistently demonstrate appropriate behavior patterns, the point system is phased out and replaced by a merit system in which all privileges are free and no points are given or taken away. Before careful plans are initiated to return the boy to his own home, he must demonstrate that he can behave appropriately without relying on the token program. Careful follow-up after the boy returns home helps

FIGURE 17–2 Number of aggressive statements by each of three youths under various conditions: baseline, correction, 20-point fines, no fines, and 50-point fines. Arrows indicate threats to fine.

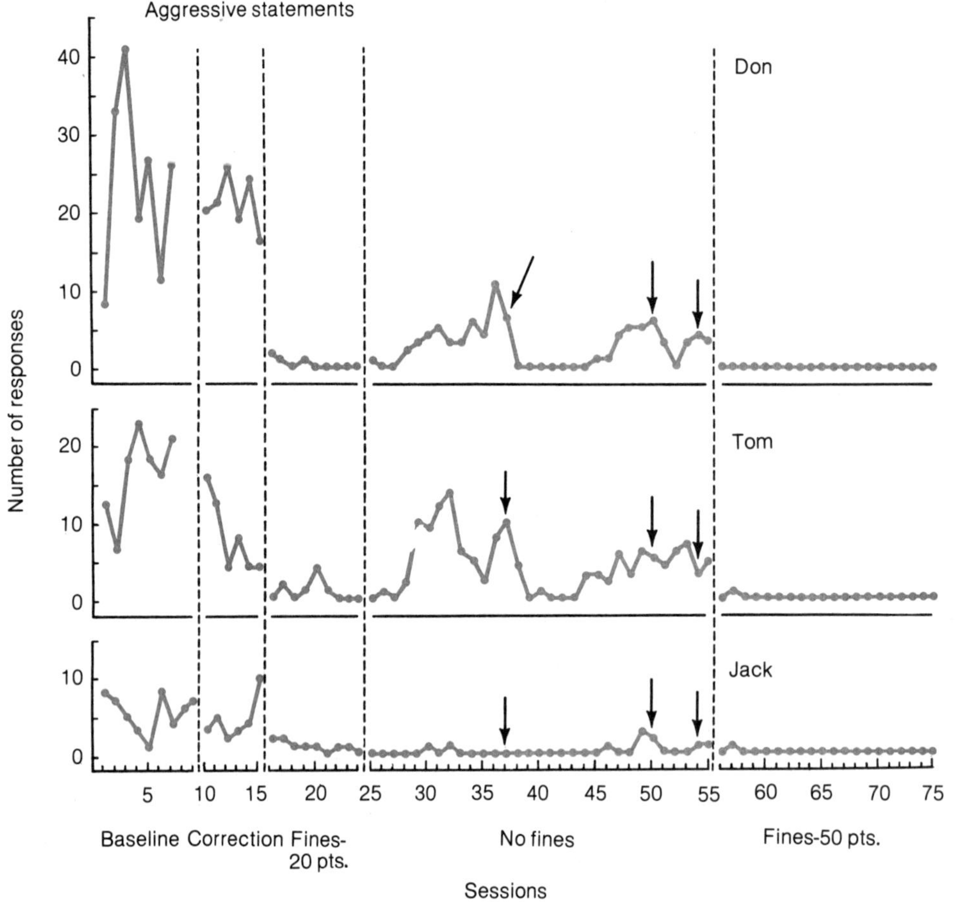

Source: E. L. Phillips, "Achievement Place: Token Reinforcement Procedures in a Long Style Rehabilitation Setting for Pre-delinquent Boys," *Journal of Applied Behavior Analysis* (1968), pp. 213–23. Copyright 1968 by the Society for the Experimental Analysis of Behavior, Inc.

to insure that continued contact with the staff is available if problems recur. Indeed, if severe problems arise, the youth may return to the program for a short period of time to resolve the difficulties with the staff's support.

Is the Achievement Place program effective in maintaining treatment gains beyond the youth's period of residence in the home? More specifically, is it effective in reducing or eliminating antisocial behaviors and contacts with the courts? The answers to both of these questions is an unqualified "Yes." Kazdin (1979) notes that "Up to two years after individuals graduated from Achievement Place, these youths showed fewer contacts with police and the courts, committed fewer acts which resulted in readjudication, and had slightly higher grades than individuals who had attended traditional institutional treatment or originally had been placed on probation" (from Fixsen, Phillips, Phillips, & Wolf, 1976).

Self-Control Procedures

Reflect for a moment on the cases of Barbara L. and David F. presented at the beginning of the chapter. You probably recall that Barbara's erratic eating patterns embarrassed and frustrated her. Her repeated attempts to decrease her food intake only reinforced her sense that she lacked control over her behavior. David's frustration increased every time he sat down at his typewriter to work on his novel. Unable to accomplish what he set out to do, his self-concept plummeted as his exasperation and feelings of helplessness increased. Despite their best intentions, both Barbara and David seem unable to control their behavior to suit their needs and wishes.

One way to increase desired behaviors (like David's time spent working productively) and to decrease undesired behaviors (like Barbara's overeating) is with operant procedures. Institutional based operant procedures such as the token economy, require considerable environmental control over the individual. Barbara and David's behavior could conceivably be modified in an institutional setting with operant procedures. But a moment's reflection suggests that this would be a drastic, restrictive, and costly course of action for their problems.

One of the more recent innovations in behavior therapy is the use of *self-control techniques* to modify behavior. Instead of relying on external controls, clients like Barbara and David can be taught to self-administer behavior change techniques in the natural environment where their problems typically occur. Like the token economy, many self-control techniques involve contingency management. Contingency management approaches modify behavior by controlling its consequences. But in the case of self-control procedures, the person arranges the reinforcement contingencies, instead of some external agent. The goal of self-control techniques is to provide the person with "active coping strategies for dealing with problem situations" (Rimm & Masters, 1979, p. 421).

In self-control programs the therapist assumes the role of a consultant. The client is instructed in self-control techniques, his progress is monitored, and the therapist offers suggestions, where appropriate. Ideally the client reaches the point where she can become her own therapist.

Watson and Tharp (1972) have outlined the basic steps that are carried out in an operant-oriented self-control program:

1. The basic idea in self-modification is to arrange situations so that desirable behavior is positively reinforced and unwanted behavior is not reinforced.
2. Reinforcement is made contingent, which means that it is gained only if some particular behavior (the target) is performed.
3. The steps in self-modification are:
   a. Specifying the target in terms of behavior in a specific situation.
   b. Making observations on how often the target behavior occurs, the antecedents that precede it, and the consequences that follow it.
   c. Forming a plan to intervene by contingently reinforcing some desirable behavior and by arranging

situations to increase the chances of performing that behavior.

d. Maintaining, adjusting, and terminating the intervention program (p. 48).

This program, like many other self-control programs, involves three stages: self-monitoring or observation, self-evaluation to determine whether there is a match between what one is doing and what one wishes to do, and the administration of self-reinforcement (Kanfer, 1975).

Let us now consider a weight reduction program developed by Richard Stuart (1967) that combines a number of self-control techniques to successfully treat obesity. Self-reward for appropriate changes in eating behavior seems to play an especially important role in weight reduction programs like Stuart's (Mahoney, Moura, & Wade, 1973). But we selected Stuart's program as an example because it relies heavily on *stimulus control* procedures. Stimulus control techniques modify behavior by rearranging environmental cues (Wilson & O'Leary, 1980). In Stuart's treatment, these techniques were initiated after subjects were first trained in self-monitoring their daily weight, the time and circumstances of eating, and their food intake. Stimulus control procedures were used to reduce the number of stimuli cueing or eliciting eating behavior. Subjects were told to eat meals only in the kitchen and to engage in

FIGURE 17–3 Weight Profile of Eight Women Undergoing Behavior Therapy for Overeating

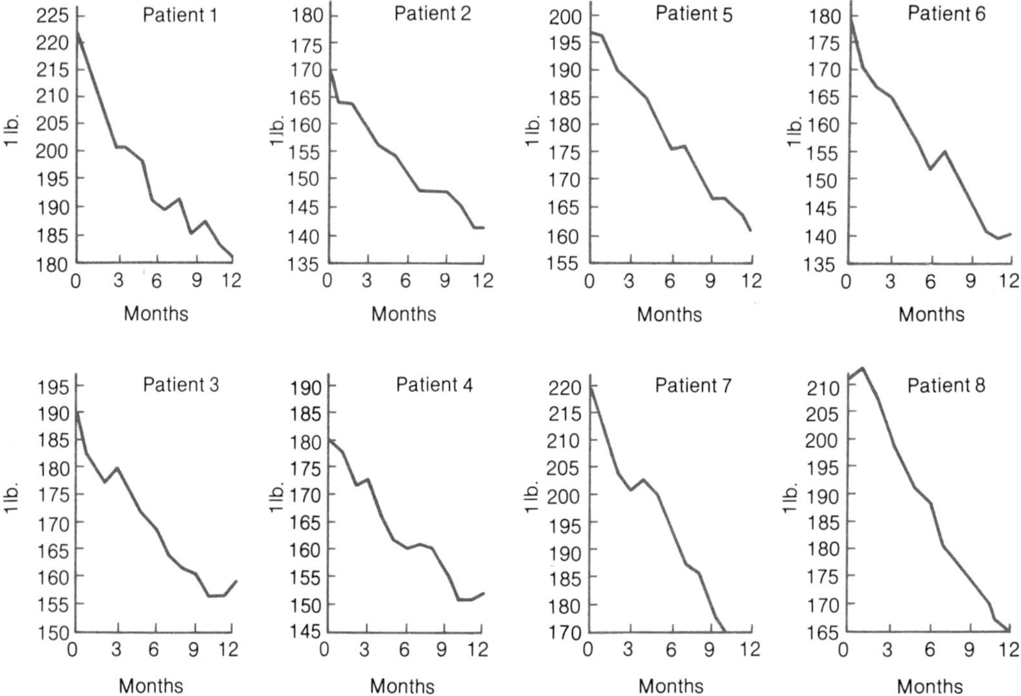

Source: Reprinted with permission from Richard B. Stuart, "Behavioral Control of Overeating," *Behavior Research and Therapy* 5 (1967), pp. 357–64. Copyright 1967, Pergamon Press, Ltd.

no other activities while eating such as watching television or reading. The goal was to make eating, a "pure" experience, restricted to only one specific setting, the kitchen. To cut down on impulsive eating, subjects were asked to eat slowly and to eat only foods which require preparation.

Stuart's treatment program was conducted over a 12-month period, with each of the self-control techniques gradually added in a stepwise fashion. An inspection of Figure 17–3 reveals that the results of Stuart's program were indeed impressive. The eight women who participated lost an average of 37.8 pounds over the course of treatment.

Self-control procedures have been successfully applied to problems like smoking (Nolan, 1968; Tooley & Pratt, 1967), poor study habits (Watson & Tharp, 1972), and insomnia (Bootzin, 1972). In chapter 9 we noted the recent surge of interest in biofeedback. Biofeedback qualifies as a self-control procedure because the client ultimately learns strategies to control a physiological response in the absence of feedback. A variety of other self-control procedures have been devised, too numerous to detail here, but they all have a common goal: fostering adaptive behavior and competencies in the absence of external control to increase the client's ability to function independently of the continued support of a therapist or a restrictive environment.

Cognitive Behavior Therapy: Rational Emotive Therapy

Cognitive behavior therapists believe that conscious thoughts play a major role in determining the way a person feels and behaves. Albert Ellis has long been one of the most forceful advocates of the cognitive behavioral approach. Since the mid-1950s, Ellis has contended that faulty or irrational patterns of thinking are at the root of much human suffering. Ellis' Rational Emotive Therapy (RET) vigorously attacks the client's irrational beliefs and stimulates an adaptive, rational approach to living. Garfield and Kurtz (1976) have observed that RET is more widely practiced than client-centered therapy. And today, RET is just one of a number of treatments that aims at so-called cognitive restructuring to help clients overcome their difficulties. Since RET is the most popular of the cognitive-behavioral treatments, we will examine its theoretical basis and its methods in some detail.

RET is based on what Ellis has termed the A-B-C theory of psychological disturbance. Psychological disturbances are not *caused* directly by events or life

Albert Ellis

Courtesy of Albert Ellis

circumstances but arise from the way the person interprets or evaluates them.

Consider the following example which illustrates Ellis' A-B-C theory. Ted and Sally are two competent and skilled workers who are fired from their jobs. Ted reacts to the loss of his job with anxiety, despair, and depression. He tells his wife that he has "given up" and that he has lost all motivation to find another job. Sally, on the other hand, reacts with disappointment but retains her sense of self-worth and actively searches for appropriate employment. Sally and Ted are responding to the identical event (called an activating event, or A), but, as you can see, the consequences of getting fired from their jobs are very different for these two individuals.

Learning something about Ted and Sally's beliefs about getting fired (B) will help you to better understand what prompted their reactions. When Ted lost his job he said something like the following to himself: "Well, that's the end of the line for me. I must be incompetent. What will people think! No one will ever hire me again. I must have this job to go on; it's a total wipeout, I'll never get it together." Now consider what Sally said to herself: "Boy, it's really too bad that I lost my job, what a drag. But life will go on. It's going to be tough, but I know I can handle this. It may be some rough going, but I'll find another job, I'm sure I will."

In considering this example, we can see that the differences in the way Tom and Sally feel and behave are mediated by the views and beliefs they hold about losing their jobs. In RET language, A (activating event) does not directly cause C (emotional and behavioral consequences); B (one's beliefs about A) does (Ellis, 1977).

To correct problems related to irrational beliefs, the client must actively confront and ultimately modify his or her thinking patterns. The first task confronting the therapist is to identify the activating events and irrational beliefs which interfere with the client's coming to terms with "objective reality." Rational beliefs are

TWELVE "IRRATIONAL" IDEAS

Ellis has identified 12 irrational ideas which he believes are quite common in our culture. You might find it interesting to see which of these beliefs you have entertained at one time or another in your life. Since such ideas are so much a part of many people's thinking, it would not be at all unusual to agree with a number of the beliefs listed below.

1. The idea that you must, yes, must have sincere love and approval almost all the time from all the people you find significant.
2. The idea that you must prove yourself thoroughly competent, adequate, and achieving; or that you must at least have real competence or talent at something important.
3. The idea that people who harm you or commit misdeeds rate as generally bad, wicked, or villainous individuals, and that you should

severely blame, damn, and punish them for their sins.

4. The idea that life proves awful, terrible, horrible, or catastrophic when things do not go the way you would like them to go.
5. The idea that emotional misery comes from external pressures and that you have little ability to control your feelings or rid yourself of depression and hostility.
6. The idea that if something seems dangerous or fearsome, you must become terribly occupied with and upset about it.
7. The idea that you will find it easier to avoid facing many of life's difficulties and self-responsibilities than to undertake some rewarding forms of self-discipline.
8. The idea that your past remains all-important and that, because something once strongly influenced your life, it has to keep determining your feelings and behavior today.
9. The idea that people and things should turn out better than they do; and that you have to view it as awful and horrible if you do not quickly find good solutions to life's hassles.
10. The idea that you can achieve happiness by inertia and inaction or by passively and uncommittedly "enjoying yourself."
11. The idea that you must have a high degree of order or certainty to feel comfortable; or that you need some supernatural power on which to rely.
12. The idea that you give yourself a global rating as a human and that your general worth and self-acceptance depend upon the goodness of your performance and the degree that people approve of you (Ellis, 1977, p. 10).

those which enable the person to "live amicably in a social group, relate intimately to a few members of this group, engage in productive work, and enjoy selectively chosen recreational pursuits" (Ellis, 1976, p. 21).

To modify the client's irrational beliefs, the therapist assumes the role of an active, directive teacher. The client may be persuaded, encouraged, and cajoled into rethinking the assumptions, conclusions, and personal philosophy which underlies the psychological disturbance. The therapist may assign "homework" to insure that the client engages in behaviors that are consistent with an increasingly "rational" philosophy of life. For example, shy clients may be given an "assignment" to talk to an attractive man or woman who might previously have been avoided, or a person who is anxious when speaking in groups may be encouraged to inject comments in various group situations.

Ellis, along with therapists of other persuasions, is careful to point out that successful treatment involves not only change in the way in which people "think" about their problems, but also the way they behave. Using the example of a client with an airplane phobia, Ellis (1976) notes that we can consider the client "cured" when he or she no longer avoids plane trips, is no longer anxious when thinking about traveling in planes, and when it is possible to apply what is learned in RET sessions to cope with similar phobias "inflicted on oneself" in the future.

Another cognitive behavioral approach is stress inoculation training, which we described in Chapter 10. As you recall, this procedure was developed by Meichenbaum (1975) to increase an individual's ability to deal with the pathological effects of stress. In Meichenbaum's approach, there is an emphasis on examining individual differences in coping with stressful events, instead of focusing attention on specific irrational beliefs, as Ellis does. Although cognitive behavioral therapists may differ in the specific procedures they employ, they tend to agree that changing maladaptive thought patterns is a central therapeutic goal (Mahoney & Arnkoff, 1978). Cognitive behavioral methods have been used with considerable success in treating numerous problems and disorders, including test anxiety (Holroyd, 1976), institutionalized schizophrenics (Meichenbaum & Cameron, 1976), lack of dating skills (Glass, Gottman, & Shmurak, 1976) and chronic anger (Novoco, 1976). In one of the few studies comparing behavior therapy with drug treatment, cognitive behavior therapy was found to be superior to an antidepressant drug, imiprimine, in the treatment of outpatient depressives (Rush, Beck, Kovacs, & Hollon, 1977).

Although cognitive therapists resemble insight therapists in their attention to mental events, they feel that it is unnecessary to postulate hidden motivations or unconscious processes to modify behavior. Other therapeutic techniques like desensitization and modeling have cognitive or symbolic aspects, but it is cognitive behavior therapy's direct focus on conscious thinking patterns that most distinguishes it from other techniques.

SOME COMMON PATHWAYS TO CHANGE IN PSYCHOTHERAPIES

Are there certain features, goals, and processes that are common to both traditional and behavior therapy? Murray and Jacobson (1978) contend that there are. What, then, are some of the common factors which they believe unite these and other approaches to helping?

The first basic process common to different therapies is the expectation of help instilled in the client. The promise of help offered to the demoralized client who seeks therapy serves to boost morale. Murray and Jacobson note that this amounts to a "psychological placebo effect" which may give the client a realistic expectancy that change can occur. This, in itself, may be beneficial, as we noted earlier in our discussion of desensitation.

Recently, Bandura (1977) has argued that clients who acquire expectancies that they can successfully perform new behaviors may be more likely to engage in the behaviors (both within and outside therapy) than clients who do not develop such expectations of "self-efficacy." Bandura believes that any successful therapy program serves to enhance the client's self-efficacy. Efficacy expectations may be induced by the specific procedures used by the therapist, so in this sense, therapeutic interventions can function as more than mere placebos. For example, Bandura believes that the most convincing source of information about one's ability to successfully perform a task derives from actual performance accomplishments. Techniques like participant modeling, then, would be expected to be highly effective because they enhance the client's self-efficacy expectations. And as we have noted, participant modeling is more effective than modeling and systematic desensitization in reducing certain fears. Since any credible treatment may arouse self-efficacy expectations, it is essential to compare the success of any treatment with an equally credible placebo control treatment.

Correcting maladaptive beliefs about the world is a second pathway to change. The psychodynamic therapist's permissive attitude may encourage the client to rethink views about sexual behavior, for example. The rational-emotive therapists' focus on "irrational" thinking may not only lead to changes in beliefs, but also to behavioral change. Behavioral techniques like systematic desensitization and flooding may change the client's beliefs about the phobic object or situation. And modeling and operant procedures may inform the client about real-world reinforcement contingencies.

In addition to coming to view the world differently, clients also come to alter their beliefs about themselves as a result of therapy. Therapists of all persuasions strive to convey an unconditional acceptance of the person. Humanistic-existential therapists are the most explicit about the importance of the relationship as a vehicle for enhanced self-esteem. But Murray and Jacobson note that behavior therapists also communicate a basic acceptance by their efforts to positively change socially undesirable behavior. Cognitive therapists deal in a direct fashion with beliefs about the self.

Virtually all therapies help the client to develop competencies in social living. In behavioral and insight therapies, the therapist models socially appropriate behavior. Gestalt and client-centered therapists reflect feelings and thoughts and provide feedback about social relationships. Assertion training deals in a most direct way with developing social competencies.

Murray and Jacobson are careful to point out that each of the changes they have described interact with one another. They conclude by stating that, "Therapy operates on a complex cognitive, emotional, and social system of human behavior" (p. 683).

Our discussion suggests that although the techniques of behavioral and insight therapies are very different, the similarities between these two approaches may outweigh the differences (Farkas, 1980). Behavior therapists' values and ideals concerning the need to evaluate the effectiveness of techniques and the factors responsible for therapeutic change may be the one factor that eventually distinguishes their approach from others (Farkas, 1980; McNamara, 1980).

INSIGHT VERSUS BEHAVIOR THERAPY: THE ISSUE OF OUTCOME

Behavior therapists have devised numerous techniques specifically designed to treat a multitude of problems in living. Our brief review of some of the more prominent techniques reveals that behavioral approaches are quite effective in treating phobias and obsessive compulsive disorders. Kazdin and Wilson (1978) claim that behavior therapy may be more effective than insight therapy in helping clients with these problems. In this and other chapters, we have seen that behavior therapy has been successfully applied to sexual problems, assertion difficulties, juvenile delinquents, substance abuse disorders, and a host of other difficulties. Behavior therapy has made inroads in helping groups of persons such as the mentally retarded and autistic children who usually are neglected by other forms of therapy.

Despite the proven effectiveness of some behavioral techniques, the superiority of these methods over traditional psychotherapy has yet to be demonstrated. Studies that have used experienced therapists who practiced behavioral, psychodynamic, and client-centered approaches have found that all were more successful in helping clients than no treatment at all (DiLoretto, 1971; Sloane, et al., 1975). Smith and Glass's (1977) large-scale review of hundreds of therapy outcome studies mentioned in the previous chapter found no firm evidence for the superiority of behavior therapy over traditional therapy. Kazdin (1979) has noted that much more research is needed to show that gains derived from behavior therapy persist over long-time intervals. Whether behavior therapy fosters long-term gains to a greater degree than insight therapy has yet to be determined.

According to Kazdin and Wilson (1978), statements about the relative effectiveness of behavioral and traditional approaches are premature because the two approaches have not been compared on a number of important criteria. They argue that the criteria used in most therapy outcome studies to gauge the success of treatment are too narrowly defined. That is, the value of a particular technique can be judged on criteria other than the average number of clients who "improve" at the end of treatment, as is most often the case. For example, Kazdin and Wilson suggest that the importance of the changes, the breadth of the changes, and the durability of the changes attributed to therapy are relevant criteria which are often ignored. Other important criteria which could be considered are the cost effectiveness of the technique, the ease of administration, the appeal of the procedure to the client, and the time required to treat the client with a particular treatment mode. Behavioral and insight-oriented techniques may fare differently across various measures of treatment outcome.

The use of multiple criteria would help us to better understand the complex ways in which different treatments affect clients. Using a broader range of outcome measures, we may learn more about the impact of different therapeutic techniques and which ones are most suited to the individual client's problem. In some cases, behavioral techniques may be better suited to the specific problems, needs, and desires of a client, whereas in other cases, insight therapy may be the treatment of choice. Perhaps the question therapy outcome researchers should address is not simply: "Is behavior therapy more effective than insight therapy." Instead, it might be more productive to ask: "What is the potential value of a treatment in relation to specific therapeutic and social goals." Given the state of the art of psychotherapy outcome research, we are a long way from answering this complex question.

SUMMARY

Behavior therapy has contributed numerous techniques that have been applied to many different problems and populations. The roots of behavior therapy are in the learning perspective, but we noted that behavior therapists are not limited to a narrow view of behavior change as resulting only from operant or classical conditioning. As the learning perspective has expanded to encompass social learning and cognitive views, behavior therapy has developed techniques that reflect recent developments in the learning field. Behavior therapists proceed by conducting a careful behavioral assessment of the client's specific difficulties, establishing specific treatment objectives, designing a behavior change program which can be effectively implemented, and systematically evaluating and monitoring their efforts to determine whether modifications are necessary to maximize treatment gains.

We discussed in some detail a number of the most prominent and widely used behavior therapy techniques. Systematic desensitization was developed by Wolpe to help clients cope with maladaptive, unrealistic anxiety. It is based on the reciprocal-inhibition principle that clients cannot experience anxiety while they are deeply relaxed. In recent years this explanation has been challenged by alternate accounts of its effectiveness, which rely on cognitive factors and extinction models among others. Why desensitization works is still an unresolved question, but its effectiveness is virtually undisputed.

Implosive therapy and flooding confront the client with the most feared stimuli to elicit maximal anxiety so that it can eventually be extinguished with repeated and prolonged exposure. Flooding has been shown to be effective with obsessive-compulsive disorders. However, both flooding and implosive therapy may be less desirable than other techniques, which clients might find less aversive.

In many treatments clients model their therapists. Bandura and his colleagues have developed specific modeling procedures that have proven quite effective in treating phobias. Participant modeling, which involves modeled demonstration along with client participation, may be especially effective.

Assertion training procedures seem to be helpful with anxieties and inhibitions related to social interactions. Behavioral rehearsal or role playing is perhaps the most central technique in assertion training.

Operant procedures like the token economy have been used extensively in institutional settings with diverse populations. Achievement Place, a community-based treatment program for delinquent and predelinquent youth, has reduced or eliminated antisocial behaviors in this population. Many self-control procedures also utilize contingency management, but the person self-administers these techniques in the absence of external controls to effect desired behavior changes.

Cognitive-behavioral approaches are among the most popular recent innovations in behavior therapy. We described Albert Ellis' approach in some detail, but numerous other cognitive behavioral treatments have been developed in recent years. While specific techniques may differ, cognitive-behavior therapists are united in their belief that maladaptive thinking patterns are important targets of treatment efforts.

We noted that although the techniques of behavior and insight therapies are very different, the similarities between these two approaches may outweigh the differences. Behavior therapy has proven effectiveness with certain disorders, but it is probably premature to conclude that behavior therapy is generally superior to more traditional approaches.

18

The Biological Treatments

Both insight and behavioral therapies have enhanced the quality of life and diminished the distress of clients suffering from psychological disorders. But some of the most cost-effective and efficient treatments for very serious mental disorders directly alter the physiology of the person to effect cognitive, emotional, and behavioral change. While the psychotherapies have proven helpful with neurotic conditions, psychophysiological disorders, and sexual and substance abuse disorders, the biological treatments appear to be far more powerful therapeutic agents in the treatment of the psychoses and severe affective disorders. We will begin our discussion of the biological treatments with a description of antipsychotic drugs that have revolutionalized the treatment of schizophrenia.

ANTIPSYCHOTIC DRUGS

The 1950s were years of tremendous excitement for physicians practicing psychiatry with seriously disturbed mental patients. Before that decade, many of the more than 560,000 patients confined in hospitals had little hope of leaving that setting and returning to the community. Medical treatments for schizophrenia and severe depression consisted of little more than palliative measures to sedate and calm agitated, disorganized, and assaultive patients. Smoking and drinking alcohol were sometimes employed to calm the more aggressive and assaultive patients. Mania was treated with hot packs, restraints, needle showers, and hydrotherapy. Amphetamines were the only pharmaceuticals used in the treatment of depression. Agitated schizophrenic patients often required the not so gentle restraint of the straight jacket. Liberal doses of barbiturates merely served to temporarily suppress the behavior of patients who were incapable of responding to the reasoned logic of the hospital staff. And more often than not, when the restraints were removed or the effect of the drug wore off, another cycle of disruptive behavior and unsuccessful, frustrating attempts to treat it would begin. Psychoanalysis and other forms of psychotherapy proved to be equally ineffective with the majority of seriously disturbed patients (Hackett, 1979).

But with the demonstration of the effectiveness of chlorpromazine in the treatment of schizophrenia by Delay, Deniker, and Harl, in 1952, came new hope for treating seriously disturbed mental patients. Chlorpromazine

(Thorazine) calmed agitated schizophrenics and eased symptoms such as delusions, hallucinations, disordered thinking, and social withdrawal. Sensing the promise of antipsychotic medications, pharmaceutical companies were quick to synthesize other drugs in the phenothiazine family, such as trifluoperazine (Stelazine), thoridazine (Mellaril), fluopenazine (Prolixin), and prochlorperazine (Compazine). Potent medications which altered mood and combated anxiety were synthesized only a few years after the value of chlorpromazine in treating schizophrenia was recognized. These developments ushered in the "pharmacological revolution" in the treatment of serious mental disorders. For the first time physicians could choose from a variety of medications to treat a variety of mental disorders. Chemical treatments came to enjoy widespread appeal and application. And the search for different and more potent medications continues. For example, a recently developed drug, haloperidol (Haldol) is quite effective in treating acute psychotic episodes.

Today, the antipsychotics, or major tranquilizers as they are sometimes called, are the primary form of treatment for persons diagnosed as psychotic. MacDonald and Tobias (1976) have estimated that 87 percent of all psychiatric inpatients are maintained on psychotropic drugs. One measure of the impact of antipsychotic medications is the fact that at the beginning of the 1980s, there are nearly 300,000 fewer

Powerful antipsychotic drugs have revolutionized the treatment of schizophrenia.

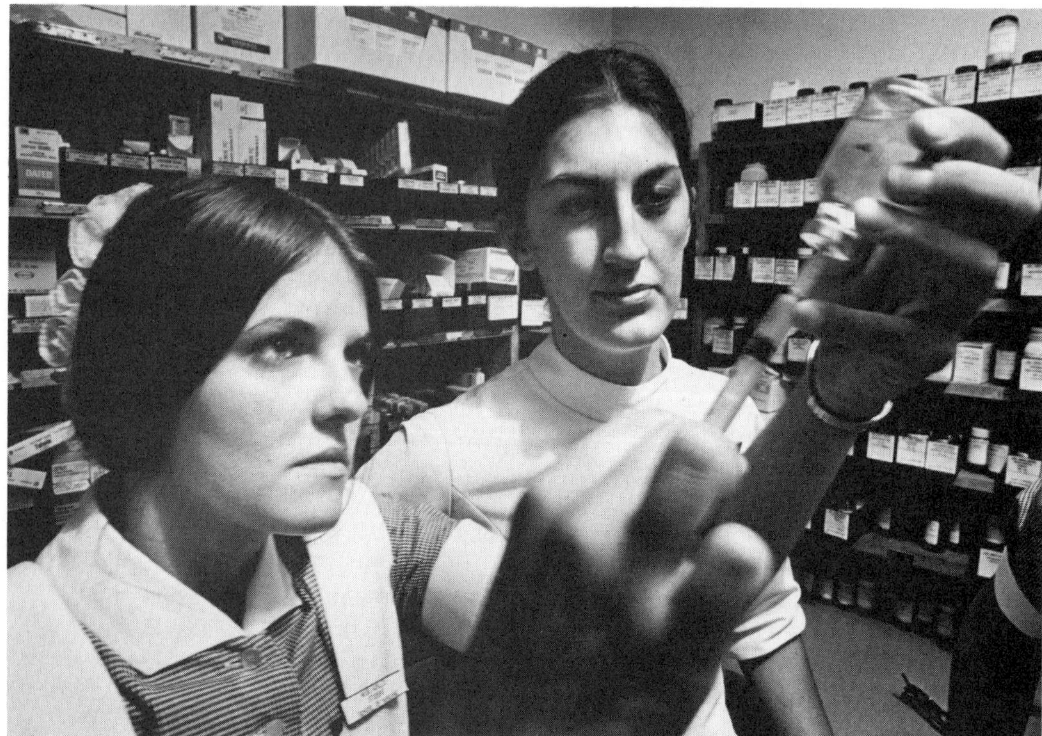

Ellis Herwig/Stock, Boston, Inc.

mental patients residing in mental institutions than in the early 1950s (see Figure 18–1).

Despite the dramatic changes in the treatment of seriously disturbed patients over the past 30 years, antipsychotic medications have not provided the long sought after "cure" for schizophrenia. Although many patients are able to leave the hospital, they are not entirely symptom-free when they return to the community. Symptoms tend to persist, but in milder form, leaving the patient with some difficulties in speech and cognition and with social liabilities (Klerman & Izen, 1978). In order to help prevent a relapse, about 80 percent of psychiatric outpatients receive some form of maintenance drug therapy (Gunderson & Mosher, 1975). But some patients seem to deteriorate even with continued drug therapy and must

FIGURE 18–1 Number of Psychiatric Patients in VA Hospitals (Based on Data from the Veterans Administration).

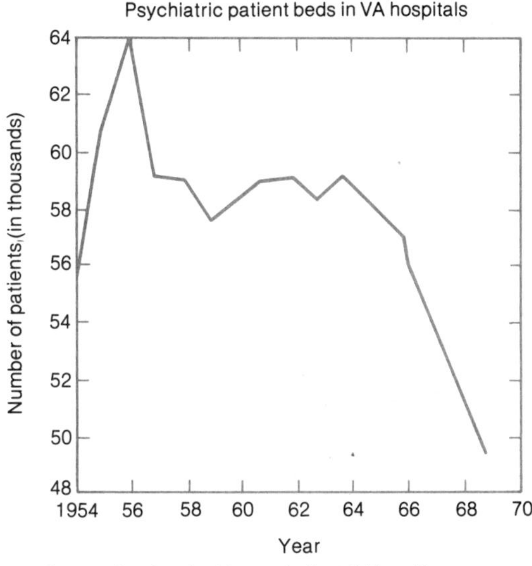

Source: Reprinted with permission of Macmillan Publishing Co., Inc., from W. L. Witters, and P. Jones-Witters, *Drugs and Sex,* (New York: Macmillan, 1975), p. 209. Copyright © 1975 by Weldon L. Witters.

return to the hospital. Hogarty (1977) has cited a relapse rate of 37 percent for patients receiving maintenance doses of antipsychotic medication. About one fifth of patients diagnosed as schizophrenic do not seem to be helped at all by drug treatment. In addition, serious side effects and complications of antipsychotic drug treatment can be harfmul to certain patients. But even with the limitations we have mentioned, the efficiency of antipsychotic medication relative to alternative approaches has great appeal. Before we turn our attention to how a physician might go about prescribing medication to a schizoprehnic patient, let us consider the important issue of the side effects of antipsychotic drugs.

Side Effects and Complications of Antipsychotic Drugs

A number of side effects, which are usually temporary and reversible, occur within the first month or so of treatment with drugs, if not sooner. These include feelings of muscle weakness and fatigue, slow initiation of movements, soft monotonous speech, muscle contractions and abnormal posturing, and difficulties in sleeping and extreme restlessness. Even if untreated these symptoms will usually disappear, and, if they do not, drug treatments are available to counter these unpleasant side effects. The broad spectrum of antipsychotic side effects can be seen in Table 18–1.

A far more serious side effect of major tranquilizers is *tardive dyskinesia,* a neurological disorder. The symptoms include grotesque involuntary movements of the facial muscles and mouth, and twitching of the neck, arms, and legs. Most often the disorder begins after

TO TREAT OR NOT TO TREAT, THAT IS A QUESTION

Is it advisable to treat schizophrenics without antipsychotic medication? Should chronic schizophrenics be gradually withdrawn from their medication? These are some of the questions that Marian MacDonald and her colleagues (MacDonald, Lidsky, & Kern, 1979) have addressed in a recent paper that critically examines the value of antipsychotic medication with schizophrenics.

MacDonald's group came to the following conclusions based on their interpretation of the literature on the effects of antipsychotic medication with schizophrenics: (1) the severity of side effects resulting from antipsychotic medications does not justify prolonged maintenance for a significant proportion of schizophrenic patients; (2) a significant proportion of schizophrenics might not be worse off if their medications were withdrawn, especially if active treatment efforts accompany gradual withdrawal; and (3) the physiological and psychological effects of antipsychotic medication may reduce the effectiveness of learning based therapeutic programs.

Based on these conclusions, MacDonald and her colleagues have argued that patients should receive antipsychotic medication only when they are a clear and present danger to themselves and/or others. For first admission psychotic patients, they advocate crisis intervention in a setting that emphasizes community return, in place of drug treatment. They contend that schizophrenic patients who are receiving maintenance doses of antipsychotics should be exposed to therapeutic learning experiences as they are gradually withdrawn from their medication. For more chronic schizophrenics, they recommend learning-based, drug-free programs to prepare them for independent community life. As you can see, these authors express a clear preference for learning-based programs over chemotherapy for schizophrenic patients.

MacDonald and her colleague's recommendations are indeed thought-provoking. But is their position realistic or overoptimistic? Only carefully conducted studies, which compare how medicated versus drug free patients who participate in therapeutic programs fare in the community, will help to answer this question.

several years of high dosage treatment, but it has occasionally been observed after only a few months of therapy at low dosages (Simpson & Kline, 1976). Studies examining the incidence of tardive dyskinesia have reported widely differing rates, ranging from 0.5 percent to 56 percent of those on antipsychotic medication (Jus et. al., 1976; Crane, 1973). In spite of different estimates, it is clear that significant proportions of schizophrenics, especially older and more long-term patients, develop tardive dyskinesia. Because the symptoms of tardive dyskinesia are often noticed when dosages are reduced or the drug is withdrawn, many experts argue that it is essential to take patients off antipsychotic

TABLE 18–1 The Spectrum of Antipsychotic Side Effects

Behavioral
Fatigue
Lethargy
Weakness
Psychomotor retardation
Insomnia
Nightmares
Confusion
Delirium
Neuromuscular
Tardive dyskinesia
Reduced seizure threshold
Akinesia
Akathisia
Parkinsonain Reactions
Reduced arm accessory movements
Mask-like facies
Resting tremor
Shuffling gait
Rigidity
Excessive salivation
Other Bodily Reactions
Blurred vision
Other visual problems
Changes in cardiac rhythms
Dizziness postural hypotension
Itching
Eczema
Pallor
Flushing
Photosensitivity
Urticaria
Dryness of mouth
Decreased sweating
Urinary retention
Difficulty in voiding urine
Difficulty with erection
Delayed ejaculation
Constipation
Liver problems
Blood changes
Weight gain
Irregular menstruation
Breast enlargement
Decreased sex drive

Source: Adapted from J. G. Bernstein, "Prescribing Antipsychotics," *Drug Therapy*. 9 (1979) p.79.

medication periodically to check for early signs of tardive dyskinesia (Crane, 1972; Gardos & Cole, 1976; Prien & Caffey, 1975). Early detection is very important because the symptoms may otherwise become long term or irreversible (Quitkin, Rifkin, & Gochfeld, 1977). Our discussion of the complications of antipsychotic drug treatment suggests that those patients treated by short-term drug treatment are likely to experience fewer risks than those on long-term maintenance therapy. This points to the need for careful monitoring of the patient's condition and an accurate assessment by the physician of the risk factors involved in treating the patient. Let us now examine some of the considerations a physician might have in prescribing antipsychotic medication.

Prescribing Antipsychotic Medication: Treatment Considerations

Denber (1979) has described a number of "general rules" for prescribing medication for patients with mental disorders such as schizophrenia. Denber emphasizes the importance of a treatment plan in the pharmacological treatment of schizophrenia. It is essential that the treatment plan be tailored to the patient.

The first step in developing a treatment strategy is to conduct a thorough evaluation of the patient and to establish an accurate diagnosis. The physician collects information about the patient's past history, prior drug usage, and response to chemotherapy. The probable course of the psychological problem and the response to drug therapy are also assessed. The evaluation guides the physician in the development of the treatment plan. The plan includes the appropriate medication and dosage level, alternate drug treatments if the initial medication proves ineffective, a determination of the drug's possible side effects, and plans for integrating psychotherapy, family therapy, and other therapeutic interventions into the treatment plan. If the patient is hospitalized, the staff are informed of the details of the plan; in all cases, the patient and the family are informed about what to anticipate and how to recognize side effects of treatment.

Antipsychotic drug therapy can be thought of as consisting of three phases (Bernstein, 1979). In the initial phase of treatment, the dosage is increased over the first week to bring psychotic symptoms, such as hallucinations, delusions, and disordered thinking, under control. This phase of treatment is called *pharmacolysis* of psychosis, because its goal is to relieve psychotic symptoms pharmacologically. As we noted in Chapter 11, one possible mechanism by which the major tranquilizers reduce psychotic symptoms is by blocking dopamine activity within the central nervous system. Thus, it has been hypothesized that when drug levels reach a high enough concentration, psychotic symptoms will diminish.

During the next phase of treatment, termed *stabilization,* the physician gradually reduces the dosage of the medication after the acute symptoms of psychosis begin to disappear. The goal of this phase is to begin to gain enduring control of the psychotic symptoms.

The third and final phase is termed *maintenance.* The goal of this phase of treatment is to maintain the patient free of psychotic symptoms with the minimal dosage of antipsychotic medication. Ideally the patient can be "weaned" from the

PATIENTS' RIGHTS AND INFORMED CONSENT*

Protecting the rights of patients in the mental health setting is an important but difficult task. Critics of our mental health system, such as psychiatrist Thomas Szasz (1970), have claimed that the system robs people of their freedom of choice by subjecting them, without their consent, to the effects of mind-controlling drugs and other treatments. They argue that patients should have the freedom to decide whether or not they should receive treatment.

Because the disorders patients suffer from can be considered mind-controlling in their own right, the issue of when a patient's rights are being protected becomes very complicated. Take, for example, the case of a schizophrenic patient whom we shall call "Brad." Brad was hospitalized following a suicide attempt. When interviewed he reported that he tried to kill himself in an attempt to silence voices inside of himself which were constantly tormenting him. Brad was afraid to accept treatment because of what the voices would do to him and consequently refused all attempts to help him. Brad's psychiatrist implemented antipsychotic drug treatment over his objections. As a result of this treatment, the voices disappeared and with them, Brad's desire to commit suicide.

Was the psychiatrist correct in treating Brad without his consent? In this case

* Prepared with the assistance of Errol Liebowitz.

apparently yes. The problem is, we are making this decision knowing the results of treatment. The psychiatrist treating Brad believed treatment would help, but he could not be sure. Brad could have gotten worse, he could have developed severe reactions to the drugs or any of a number of other possibilities. Would we still judge the psychiatrist's decision as being correct under different circumstances?

A number of legal and ethical guidelines have been established to help decide when a psychiatrist can administer treatment over a patient's objections. The most frequently used criterion is that of dangerousness to one's self or others. This was the criteria that was used in Brad's case. Another criterion used is that of rationality. That is, for a patient's refusal to be considered valid, the patient's reason for refusal must be logical and based on an understanding of the likely results of accepting or not accepting treatment. However, the rationality criterion is not always accepted by the law. For example, in one recent case (Rogers vs. Okin, 1979) patients sued their psychiatrists for the right to refuse medication. The judge ruled that patients could refuse drugs as long as they were not a threat to themselves or others. Even patients who were "irrational" or who would remain ill without drugs could refuse medication.

Guidelines have also been established for psychiatrists to follow in informing patients about treatment. Before they ask a patient to accept treatment, they are required to give patients information about the risks and benefits of the proposed treatment, what the alternatives are, and what is likely to happen if the patient decides to refuse all treatment. When a patient is not capable of understanding the information, for whatever reason, the psychiatrist is supposed to inform a relative or other guardian who then decides about treatment for the patient.

How do psychiatrists feel about these guidelines? There is considerable controversy within the psychiatric community concerning what treatments patients' rights guidelines should cover and with what patients. A study by Liebowitz and McNamara (1980) examined circumstances under which psychiatrists favored providing information and accepting refusal of medication by schizophrenic patients. They found several factors related to psychiatrists' beliefs. One factor was the impact psychiatrists believed information would have on patients. When they believed that patients would understand the information and that it would help treatment, they reported being more willing to inform patients than when they thought information would create fear and anxiety in the patient. Another factor was their beliefs about the risks and benefits of antipsychotic drugs. Psychiatrists were most partial to treatment refusal when they believed there was risk associated with the use of medication. When they believed drug treatment was safe and routine, they appeared to be less likely to allow treatment refusal. A third factor was whether they believed other treatments also worked. When this was the case, they were also more likely to accept treatment refusal.

In general, it appears that psychiatrists believe their primary responsibility is to heal the patient. They are in favor of permitting treatment refusal if it does not result in significant conflict with this responsibility. The question is, do psychiatrists, as a group, underestimate the importance of the individual to choose his or her own fate. There are many who believe so.

drug by gradually decreasing the dosage until there is no longer a need for continued medication. But many patients, as we have indicated, may need long-term, perhaps indefinite, chemotherapy. It is very important to establish an effective, yet minimal dosage level, since the risk of harmful side effects is greater with high dosage, long-term treatment.

ANTIDEPRESSANT DRUGS

Since the antidepressant drugs were introduced in the early 1950s, they have enjoyed widespread acceptance and use. Today, more than 30 million prescriptions are written for antidepressant drugs each year in the United States (Gelenberg, 1979). In Chapter 9 you were introduced to the two main classes of antidepressant drugs: the tricyclic compounds and the monoamine oxidase inhibitors (MAOI) (see Table 18–2). As you recall, the tricyclics are more widely used than the MAOIs because they tend to produce fewer side effects. Thus the tricyclics are generally regarded as the "first line" drugs for treating depression.

Since the antidepressant drugs were developed, knowledge has been gained regarding which symptoms are most likely to respond positively to medication. Table 18–3 presents the factors associated with

TABLE 18–2

Generic Name	*Brand Name*
Tricyclic agents:	
Amitriptyline	Amitid, Amitril, Elavil, Endep, SK-Amitriptyline
Desipramine	Norpramin, Pertofrane
Doxepin	Adapin, Sinequan
Imipramine	Antipress, Imavate, Janimine, Presamine, SK-Pramine, Tofranil
Nortriptyline	Aventyl, Pamelor
Protriptyline	Vivactil
MAO inhibitors:	
Isocarboxazid	Marplan
Phenelzine	Nardil
Tranylcypromine	Parnate
*Combination agents**	
Amitriptyline and chlordiazepoxide	Limbitrol
Amitriptyline and perphenazine	Etrafon, Triavil

* These agents include tranquilizers in addition to the antidepressant.

Source: A. J. Gelenberg, "Treating Depression," *Drug Therapy*, 9, (11) (1979), p. 113.

TABLE 18–3 Factors Correlating with Likelihood of Response to Tricyclic Antidepressants

Positive Correlation

Consistent sadness and depression
Feelings of hopelessness, helplessness, worthlessness
Feelings of guilt
Sleep disturbance, particularly with early morning awakening
Depression worse in the mornings
Loss of appetite
Weight loss
Diminished libido
Change from normal personality
Depressions present over a period of weeks

Negative Correlation

Histrionics
Feelings of anger and resentment
Self-pity
Longstanding character pattern of unhappiness
Emotional lability
Manipulativeness

No Correlation

Presence or absence of precipitating event

Source: A. J. Gelenberg, "Prescribing Antidepressants," *Drug Therapy* (1979), 9 (11) p. 96.

the likelihood of response to tricyclic antidepressants. This pattern of symptoms has been identified with the so-called endogenous type of depression. The MAOIs are used most often in patients who do not respond favorably to treatment with tricyclics. There are indications that the MAO inhibitors may be the treatment of choice with a subtype of depressive patients with "atypical depression." In contrast with the patient who responds favorably to tricyclic medication, the patient with atypical depression is likely to have difficulty falling asleep, overeat as a way of coping with depression, and feel more depressed in the evening rather than in the morning.

Neither the tricyclics nor the MAOIs are indicated in treating mild episodes of sad or depressed feelings and brief depressions related to situational stresses. Although a trial of antidepressant medication may be considered in these cases, brief supportive psychotherapy or a change in the patient's living situation may be more helpful (Gelenberg, 1979).

THE ANTIDEPRESSANTS: WORDS FROM A PHYSICIAN

In order to gain a better sense of what it might be like to be treated with an antidepressant drug, consider the following statements about tricyclic drug therapy which a physician might relate to a patient experiencing depression:

> The drug which you are being treated with is a tricyclic antidepressant drug. It is called a tricyclic because of the three-ring chemical structure of the compound. The drug will not relieve your depression overnight. It's going to take time—anywhere from two to four weeks. In the beginning the drug may help you sleep, but you may feel the side effects before you start feeling better. Even then, the first signs of improvement are likely to be short-lived or limited to one or two symptoms. Because the results of antidepressant therapy are not going to be apparent immediately, it is all too easy to become discouraged. However, only by persisting with the treatment regimen which is prescribed for you, will it ultimately be successful. Never increase or decrease the dosage or stop taking the drug on your own. If you have any problems or feel uncomfortable, be sure to let me know about it. Once this initial stage is over, overall progress will probably become much more obvious.
>
> During the first week of therapy, I will be gradually increasing the dose to build up your tolerance to the drug's side effects. Side effects are common adverse reactions to the presence of a foreign chemical substance in your body. Although mildly uncomfortable, these reactions will let you know that the drug is in your system and working.
>
> What sort of effects can you expect? Most people being treated with the drug I have prescribed experience one or more of the following: drowsiness, dryness of the mouth, constipation, morning "hangover," dizziness, blurred vision, difficulty in urinating. As a rule, these symptoms will diminish or disappear as you continue to take the drug at the

prescribed dosage. If you find these effects particularly unpleasant or disabling, don't hesitate to call me.

As I mentioned earlier, the first signs of improvement should begin to appear two to four weeks after you start therapy, although a close friend or family member may notice the improvement a few days or a week before you do. Initially, you may notice that you sleep better, are able to concentrate more, have more energy, or your appetite has increased and you are beginning to gain weight. With time, the sadness, helplessness, and emptiness you have been feeling will also diminish. To be sure, this will not happen all at once, and good periods may sometimes be followed by a return of depressive symptoms. But once you have begun to improve, the odds are that you will continue to get better (Adapted from Gelenberg, 1979).

The fact that the tricyclics may not begin to reach their peak effectiveness for upwards of two weeks can be a drawback in the treatment of patients who are seriously depressed and where there is a risk of suicide. With such patients electroconvulsive therapy might be utilized because it can produce quicker results and diminish the likelihood of a suicide. But with most patients suffering from depression, a trial of antidepressant medication is prescribed before electroconvulsive therapy is considered.

Antidepressant drugs have been found to be effective in treating depression. The majority of studies have shown a superiority for tricyclic drugs over placebos in treating depression. The MAOIs have not been shown to be consistently superior to placebos, but, overall, the antidepressant drugs appear to benefit about 70 percent of those patients treated (Morris & Beck, 1974).

LITHIUM

In a fascinating study, Dawson, Moore, and McGanitz (1970) found an intriguing relationship between concentrations of lithium in drinking water and the number of mental hospital admissions in Texas. They discovered an inverse relationship between amounts of lithium in residential drinking water and the incidence of admissions and readmissions to state mental hospitals.

In chapter 8 we noted that lithium, an element present in trace amounts in water throughout the world, has important and widespread applications. Patients with mood disorders can be treated with lithium while their behavior and metabolism are carefully monitored. Manic episodes and bipolar affective disorders are especially susceptible to treatment with lithium. Table 18–4 suggests that it may be useful in the treatment of other disorders.

A manic episode, you recall, can produce severe problems in social and occupational functioning. Acutely manic patients may require hospitalization before their mood can be stablized with lithium and maintenance treatment in the community is feasible. But after about two weeks of lithium treatment, 70 to 80 percent of even acutely agitated patients seem to improve (Baldessarini, 1977). Normal functioning can be restored in many patients who, before taking lithium, were severely disturbed and distressed.

Lithium can also have a ''protective''

TABLE 18–4 Psychiatric Indications for and Uses of Lithium A reviewer's assessment of the extent to which the evidence supports the effect claimed: ++ effect established, + effect likely, ? effect dubious but possible, —— lack of effect established.

Suggested Indication	*Reviewer's Assessment*
Mania and hypomania	++
Depression	+
Schizophrenia	——
Recurrent affective disorder, bipolar	++
Recurrent affective disorder, monopolar	++
Recurrent affective disorder, schizo-affective	++
Pathological emotional instability in children and adolescents	+
Pathological periodic aggressiveness	+
Periodic alcoholism with depression	+
Opiate addiction	?
Obsessive-compulsive neurosis	——
Acute anxiety	——
Premenstrual dysphoria	——

Source: Excerpt, from A. Villeneuve, ed., *Lithium in Psychiatry, A Synopsis* (Quebec: Les Presses De L'Université Laval, 1976), p. 50.

TABLE 18–5 Rate of Recurrence of Mania or Depression in Bipolar Manic-Depressives with Lithium or Placebo

	Percent of Relapses[a]	
Treatment	*Manic (120)*	*Depressive (63)*
Lithium	29.2	36.5
Placebo	70.8	63.5
"Protection Ratio" (Placebo:Lithium)	2.4	1.7

[a] Data are mean percent of patients relapsing in the manic or depressive phases of bipolar affective illnesses during treatment with lithium or placebo. The results are derived from the only two controlled studies that provided sufficient data to evaluate the differential effects of the treatment on the two phases of the illness. Lithium appears to produce a protective effect against both types of relapse, but the results are too few to permit statistical analysis. It is interesting to note that about two-thirds of all 183 relapses were manic in type regardless of the treatment.

Source: R. J. Baldessarini, *Chemotherapy in Psychiatry*, (Cambridge: Harvard University Press, 1977), p. 63.

effect. The results presented in Table 18–5 show that lithium can prevent relapses of both manic and depressive episodes in bipolar disorders. Mood swings tend to occur less often and, if they do occur, are less debilitating (Van Praag, 1978).

Despite the remarkable personality and mood changes that often accompany treatment with lithium, some physicians are reluctant to prescribe it. Managing patients on a lithium regimen can prove difficult. The levels of lithium in the blood must be monitored and carefully regulated. Recall that in Fieve's "metabolic ward," which you read about in Chapter 8, bodily functions were closely monitored so that dosages could be adjusted on an individual basis. Lithium is a drug with a very narrow "safe" range. If the dose is not properly adjusted, it can act as a toxic agent, impairing various bodily processes. Overdosage can produce quite serious complications, and very depressed, suicidal patients can take a lethal dose of lithium.

Over the years, however, the popularity of lithium has increased, and more and more physicians feel comfortable prescribing it to patients whom they believe will benefit from its use. Still, some have argued that as many as 20 times the number of patients currently taking lithium could benefit from it (Baldessarini, 1977). Yet few psychiatrists would take serious issue with the observation that lithium treatment is one of the "great success stories of modern psychiatry" (Newsweek, 1979, p. 100).

ANTIANXIETY DRUGS

There is perhaps no greater testimony to the wide-ranging impact of the "drug revolution" than the prescription of antianxiety medications to millions of Americans each year. Primary care physicians routinely prescribe medication when anxiety, irritability, and agitation become severe enough to interfere with their patients' daily functioning.

The most frequently prescribed antianxiety agents are the *benzodiazepines,* or anxiolytics, as they are sometimes called. This family of drugs includes the most commonly prescribed drug Valium along with a number of other frequently prescribed drugs such as Librium and Serax. The meprobamate drug group (Miltown, Equanil) and the barbiturates (phenobarbital) are less routinely used, and their effectiveness in treating anxiety is less well established than the benzodiazepines.

Whatever drug the physician prescribes, it is likely that it will be suggested only after other approaches like support, reassurance, and advice fail to help the patient. The use of anxiolytics is most common among women, the elderly, and patients suffering from chronic medical problems (Uhlenhuth, Balter, and Lipman, 1978). Unlike antipsychotic medication, anxiolytics medication is most likely to be prescribed on a time-limited basis. Treatment with these drugs is usually limited to periods of stress which produce noticeable discomfort in the patient.

Because of the potential of abuse and dependence, the prescribing physician should carefully monitor and adjust the dosage in response to changing levels of stress and tension. Where it is clear that the drugs have little impact on the individual's level of anxiety, their use should be reevaluated. Psychotherapy or alteration of the patient's life-style and environment may be indicated rather than continued drug treatment.

PSYCHOLOGICAL COMPLICATIONS OF DRUG TREATMENT

Before the Food and Drug Administration (FDA) will grant approval for the marketing of a new drug, it first must undergo extensive clinical tests to insure its clinical value and safety. Even after a drug has met the rigorous licensing standards of the FDA, it still may produce side effects in certain patients. We have noted many of the physical side effects that are produced by drugs used to treat a variety of psychological disorders. But many of these drugs also induce psychological side effects that may change or compound the patient's symptoms. Such side effects are easily neglected or overlooked in a psychiatric population. A worsening of the patient's condition may be attributed to the "natural course" of the disorder, instead of drug-related complications.

Flaherty (1979) has summarized the psychological side effects of the antipsychotics, the antianxiety agents, and the antidepressant drugs. Let us now consider some of the major complications that can be induced by drugs in each of these classes.

Antipsychotic drugs The major groups of antipsychotics are all capable of worsening the symptoms of psychosis by producing visual hallucinations, disorientation, and autonomic symptoms. In some cases antipsychotic medications can induce a fairly serious depression with insomnia, suicidal thoughts, and slowed motor activity. Reducing the dosage or substituting another drug may be helpful when such side effects are detected.

Antianxiety agents Antianxiety drugs can heighten anxiety in patients with agitated depressions and increase the severity of depressed symptoms in patients who are depressed as well as anxious. Antianxiety drugs like the barbiturates have a fairly high abuse potential. If their use is abruptly discontinued for some reason in an addicted patient, a dangerous withdrawal syndrome may develop which requires prompt medical attention and treatment.

Antidepressant drugs Tricyclic antidepressants can, in some patients, increase irritability. An acute manic episode may be triggered in patients with a history of mania. Schizophrenic symptoms may increase in severity if they are present during the course of administration of antidepressants (Flaherty, 1979).

These examples suggest that drug treatment for psychological disorders is not as straightforward as many people think. The very drugs that are used to treat a particular disorder may actually make the condition worse or create other problems for the patient. Over the entire course of treatment, careful monitoring of the psychological as well as the physical condition of the patient appears to be an absolute necessity.

John Thoeming/Dorsey Press

Indeed, in many instances, psychotherapy may be a more appropriate treatment than drug treatment for anxiety. The real source of the person's anxiety may be masked by the calming effects of the medication. Patients whose treatment is limited to drug therapy may never get in touch with the causes of their anxiety. Thus they may be deprived of an opportunity to learn how to better manage internal conflicts or stressful situations. On the other hand, when anxiety seriously disrupts the patient's ability to function, anxiolytic medication may be a valuable adjunct to psychotherapy and an effective treatment in its own right.

SOME CONCLUDING COMMENTS ON CHEMOTHERAPY

As chemotherapy has gained increasing acceptance, thought-provoking questions about the proper use, effectiveness, and limitations of drug treatments have been raised. One frequently voiced criticism of chemotherapy is the overuse of medication. Even advocates of drug treatment acknowledge that medications sometimes are prescribed with "excessive zeal" (Baldessarini, 1977). Consider Baldessarini's (1977) comments on this point:

> In busy clinics or office practice, it is particularly tempting to allow the "ritualization" of chemotherapy to displace sensitive and honest attention to painful and difficult psychological and social issues, needs, and wishes of the patient (p. 153).

Such "ritualization" of practice arises, in part, from the fact that drugs are easy to administer, nondemanding of the physician's time, and generally effective. Unfortunately, routine reissuing of prescriptions may substitute for regular evaluation of the patient's condition and thoughtful consideration of alternate treatments.

The physician's enthusiastic promotion of chemotherapy may foster an unhealthy dependence on medication. Patients may attribute positive changes to the medications they are taking. They may come to invest drugs with almost magical powers, overvaluing their effects. The patient's belief in a drug's curative powers may reinforce the physician's tendency to prescribe drugs on a routine basis.

The overvaluation of medication may effect the patient in other ways. Treatment gains may be more long-lasting when people believe that their own efforts, rather than a chemical agent, are responsible for positive changes (MacDonald, Lidsky, & Kern, 1979). This suggests that by encouraging patients to attribute gains to themselves, physicians may promote more enduring positive changes.

Critics of chemotherapy have pointed out that drug treatments offer little value in helping the patient to learn social skills, to modify self-defeating behaviors, or to cope more adaptively with conflict-producing situations. Unless patients learn effective coping skills, or are able to change their environment in beneficial ways, they may be no better off after drug treatment than they were before it was started. Psychotherapy, vocational counseling, and learning-based social skills programs all may promote adjustment in the community when combined with drug treatments.

But just as drugs have their limitations, psychotherapeutic approaches are not without their own shortcomings. Indeed, in the areas where chemotherapy appears to be most effective, psychotherapy seems to have the least proven value. Michel Hersen (1979), a well-known behavior therapist, notes that many psychologists and behavior therapists have strong, preconceived biases against the use of drugs with very disturbed patients. Hence they are inclined to minimize the very real contributions of drugs to the treatment of certain disorders. For example, the treatment of choice in bipolar affective disorders appears to be lithium carbonate. Severe depressions may be more effectively treated with tricyclic antidepressants than with behavioral or other psychotherapeutic approaches. And schizophrenic symptoms seem most amenable to treatment with the antipsychotic agents.

Hersen also points out that drugs may be used to bring symptoms under control so that psychotherapeutic procedures may be more readily applied. Schizophrenic patients, for example, may be distracted by hallucinations and delusions that minimize their potential to learn new behaviors. Hersen has found that unless the dosage of antipsychotic medication is finely adjusted, schizophrenics do not seem to derive benefit from a social skills training program.

The value of drugs can also be seen in their ability to enhance certain therapeutic techniques like systematic desensitization (Liberman & Davis, 1975) and flooding (Marks, Viswanathan, Lipsedge, & Gardiner, 1972). There is still much to be learned about how various drugs and therapeutic approaches can be combined to maximize treatment effects. And we can expect new and exciting innovations in this area. It is likely that chemotherapy will continue to have both ardent defenders and detractors, but drug therapy's contribution to the treatment of serious psychological disorders seems difficult to dispute.

ELECTROCONVULSIVE THERAPY

> Strapped to a stretcher, you are wheeled into the ECT room. The electroshock machine is in clear view. It is a solemn occasion; there is little talk. The nurse, the attendant, and the anesthetist go about their preparation methodically. Your psychiatrist enters. He seems quite matter-of-fact, businesslike—perhaps a bit rushed. "Everything is going to be just fine. I have given hundreds of these treatments. No one has ever died." You flinch inside. Why did he say that? But there is no time to dwell on it. They are ready. The electrodes are in place. The long clear plastic tube running from the bottle above ends with a needle in your vein. An injection is given. Suddenly—terrifyingly—you can no longer breathe; and then . . . You awaken in your hospital bed. There is a soreness in your legs and a bruise on your arm you can't explain. You are confused to find it so difficult to recover memories. Finally your stop struggling in the realization that you have no memory for what has transpired. You were scheduled to have ECT, but something must have happened. Perhaps it was postponed. But the nurse keeps coming over to you and asking, "How are you feeling?" You think to yourself: "It must have been given"; but you can't remember. Confused and uncomfortable, you begin the dread return to the ECT room. You have forgotten, but something about it remains. You are frightened (Taylor, 1975).

It has been estimated that electroconvulsive therapy is administered about 10,000 times a day in the United States (Pitts, 1972). We have already encountered this treatment in our discussion of depression in Chapter 9. We noted that no one knows exactly why ECT has its therapeutic effects, but some evidence does exist to suggest that endogenous depressions are relatively more benefited by ECT treatments. We also noted that memory loss, a side effect of electroconvulsive therapy, can have a negative effect on the recovery of certain patients.

But a recent review of 60 studies

Electroconvulsive therapy should be cautiously prescribed, but its results can be impressive with severely depressed patients.

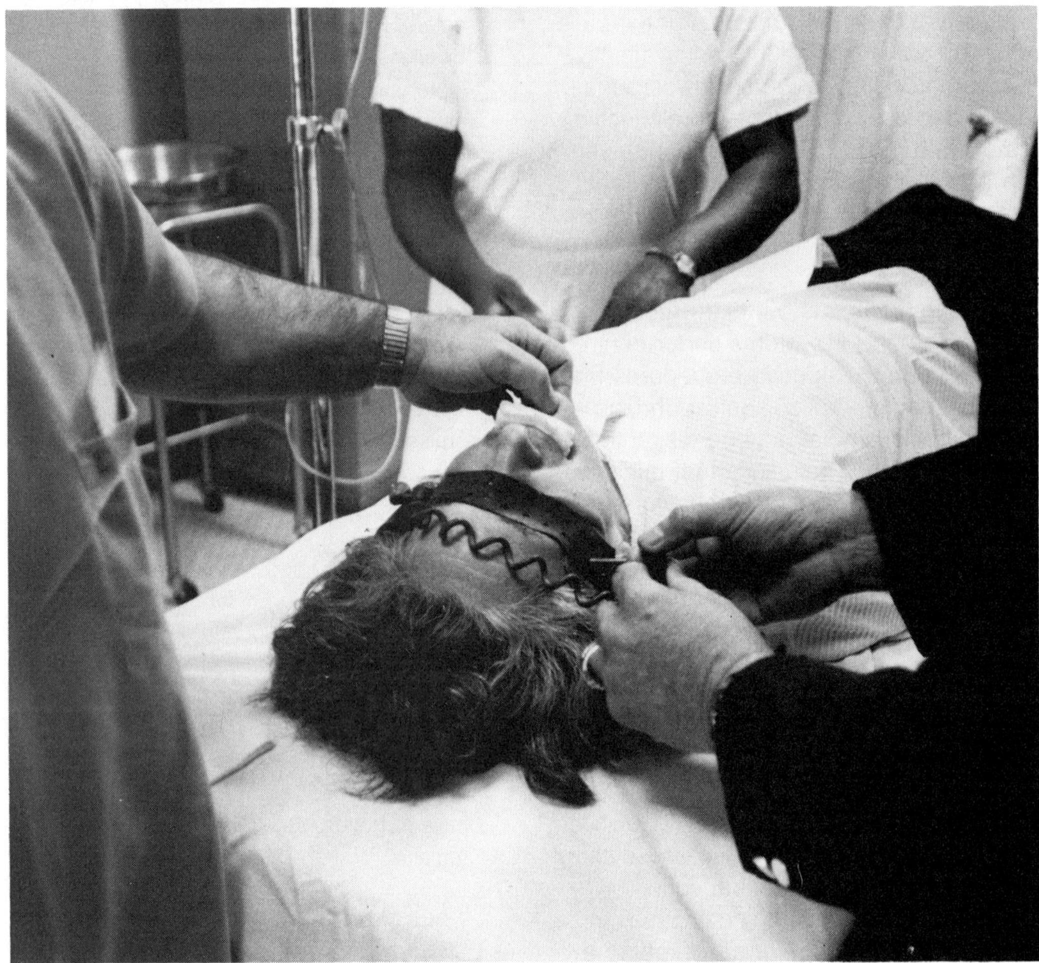

Paul Fusco/Magnum Photos, Inc.

comparing ECT with control procedures or alternative treatments suggests that ECT may be more effective for certain patients than was previously believed. For example, Scovern and Kilmann (1980) note that ECT appears to be markedly superior to drug treatments with patients who suffer from endogenous depressions and additionally are severely disturbed or deluded. Involutional and manic-depressive patients also appear to respond quite favorably to ECT treatments. The fast action of ECT can make it a lifesaving treatment for depressed patients at serious risk for suicide. ECT may be the treatment of choice in such cases because, as you recall, antidepressant medication may not be maximally effective for upwards of two weeks after treatment is initiated.

ECT is not so effective with other disorders. The treatment appears to be of little value in relieving the symptoms of the less severe, or "neurotic," depressions. While ECT may help certain schizophrenics, in that it may aid their depressive symptoms which may complicate the symptom picture, it does not appear to alter the primary symptoms of thought disorder. Scovern and Kilmann's review also suggests that the value of ECT in the treatment of depression may be limited to altering the patient's subjective experience of depression. Although patients tend to report feeling better after ECT treatments, parallel changes in intellectual, perceptual, and motoric retardation are typically not observed. Further research is needed to determine which symptoms are most affected by electroconvulsive therapy.

In prescribing electroconvulsive therapy for any patient, the task challenging the physician is to determine whether the potential therapeutic gains outweigh the potential costs associated with the treatment. As we mentioned earlier, ECT can adversely affect memory. In his review of the literature, Fink (1977) was unable to disconfirm the belief that ECT can cause permanent brain damage. Thus, given what is known about ECT, the physician is probably wise to prescribe ECT "only with utmost care" (Scovern & Kilmann, 1980, p. 299).

PSYCHOSURGERY

There is little doubt that psychosurgery is the most dramatic biological treatment for psychological disorders. As you might imagine, the "therapeutic" destruction of brain tissue to control behavior and emotion has been the focus of much controversy. Critics of psychosurgery have raised questions about the effectiveness of the treatment, the use of psychosurgery for social control, and the fundamental values which underlie behavioral control. Psychosurgical procedures are usually regarded as a treatment of the "last resort" for disorders seemingly untreatable by other methods. Schizophrenia, depression, and severe obsessive-compulsive neuroses are some of the disorders that have been treated with psychosurgery.

The results of psychosurgery are not always predictable. Consider the following two cases of patients who received psychosurgical operations:

> L.W. is an obese, 32-year-old unmarried and unemployed woman, inarticulate to the point of near muteness, with a history of over ten years of intermittent hospitalizations for what has been described as both "chronic schizophrenia" and "depression." When she was in her early 20s, L.W. began to have episodes of destructive rage and irrational speech and became unable to care for herself. She had three psychosurgical operations without apparent success. Her parents indicate some moderate improvement after the first operation, but it was short-lived. There was no improvement after either of the subsequent operations. The patient is profoundly hypokinetic, cannot give any history, cannot be tested except with operant methods. She has had an undetermined number of shock treatments and is on many different drugs.
>
> T.M. is a married woman of 37, also overweight (220 lbs.), with a similar diagnostic history of schizophrenia and depressive hallucinations. Her first psychotic episode occurred when she was in her early 20s.
>
> T.M. was married shortly afterwards, at age 22. Soon after that, during her first and

> only pregnancy, she grew increasingly suspicious and agitated. She was given three to four ECTs and hospitalized for two years. She had her first psychosurgery (a cingulotomy) at age 30—because of suicidal tendencies—and reportedly felt tremendous relief. She was still suspicious, but no longer felt "as if encased in a plastic cube." There were no side effects, she insists, except perhaps for weight gain (80 pounds in the first six months post op).
>
> T.M. says she functioned fairly well for five years as a school teacher, but then got worse again and began drinking heavily in the latter part of 1974. She and her husband made a trip West to seek the help of a neurosurgeon in California from whom she received a psychosurgical operation. This was in January, 1975. Immediately afterwards, the patient reported that she was no longer suspicious, but still felt fearful . . . She went back to her psychiatrist in the East, who suggested one more operation. She received this third psychosurgical operation the following August, after which, except for one six-week regression, she reports being entirely well.
>
> Previously, this patient had received 27 ECTs and 60 insulin coma treatments. Asked for her views of psychosurgery and whether she would recommend it to others, she says emphatically, "I would tell them to snap it up as quick as they could. It's a godsend, it is, I cannot say enough about them (the operations). I don't know why they work or how they work, but they are a true godsend. They gave me back my life" (Adapted from the APA Monitor, 1976).

In examining these two cases, it is apparent that the treatment outcomes are very different. Negative views of psychosurgery arise, in part, from a lack of data about which patients respond most favorably to treatment. Concerns about harmful side effects have also contributed to skepticism about the safe and effective use of psychosurgical procedures. It is often unclear when the benefits of psychosurgery outweigh the risks of impairing memory, blunting the personality, diminishing emotion and creativity, and the ordinary dangers of brain surgery (Neville, 1976).

But as is often the case with new treatments, when psychosurgery was first introduced, it was hailed as a promising innovation. Indeed, Egas Moniz, the Portuguese neurologist who developed psychosurgery techniques in the early 1930s, won a Nobel Prize for his surgical operations and studies of the brain. Freeman and Watts introduced psychosurgery in this country and published highly favorable reports about their successful treatment of thousands of patients.

The early psychosurgical operations were termed lobotomies. The technique consisted of severing the fibers between the frontal lobes and the lower portions of the brain. Valenstein (1973) notes that the pressing need to treat psychiatrically disturbed veterans during and after World War II played a significant role in the widespread adoption of psychosurgical procedures. Psychosurgery remained a popular technique until the mid-1950s, after which time, "the tide receded in the face of a strong reaction against psychosurgery precipitated by reports of 'dehumanized zombies,' the overuse of the surgical approach, and the availability of psychoactive drugs as an alternative to surgery" (p. 269).

In the 1960s a new form of psychosurgery came into prominence. The procedure involves creating small lesions in the amygdala or in the other parts of the limbic system of the brain, which is

Psychosurgery is a dramatic and highly controversial procedure.

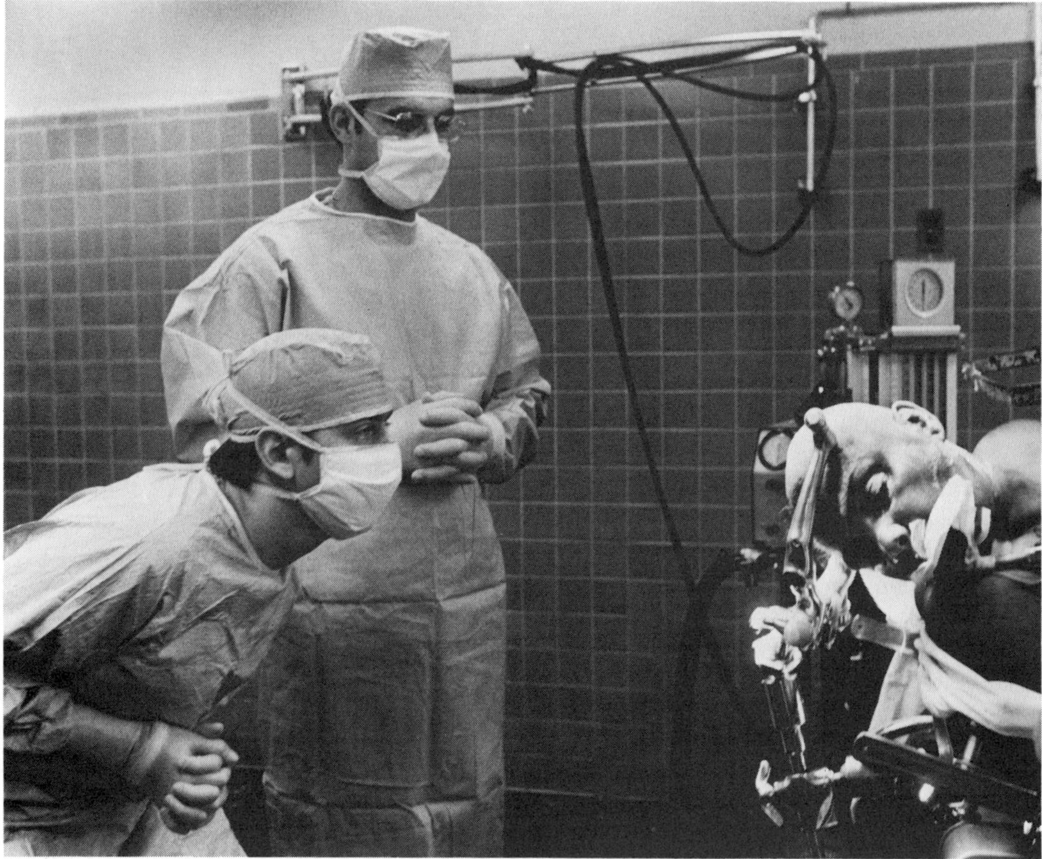

© Mitchell Payne/Jeroboam, Inc.

thought to control emotions. Primitive surgical procedures have been replaced by ultrasound, electricity, freezing of tissues, and implants of radioactive materials. New stereotactic or automated surgical devices have added precision to delicate brain surgery.

Despite certain advances in psychosurgery, it still remains an experimental technique with potential for misuse. Critics of psychosurgery note that the motives for conducting such operations may not always be benign. Indeed, in the past, it has been used with violent sexual criminals, with homosexual child abusers, and in prisons to control violent inmates whose behavior was judged irrational. Punitive and therapeutic motives may, in some instances, be difficult to separate. This raises the possibility that social goals (the control of behavior) may be confused with therapeutic goals which best serve the interests of the patient.

Questions also have been raised about when to perform psychosurgery. As we have indicated, psychosurgery is performed as a treatment of "last resort." But it is not always clear when alternative, less drastic, treatment procedures have been exhausted. Recognizing the need to protect the interests of the patient, the federal government has recommended establishing institutional review boards in hospitals where psychosurgery is performed. Valenstein (1973) has argued that in submitting recommendations to such review boards, "the burden of proof that alternative treatments have been adequately explored should always be on those recommending psychosurgery" (p. 339). Institutional review boards would help insure that there was a clear rationale for the operation, that the patient received an appropriate preoperative and postoperative evaluation, that the patient was informed about the surgery and consented to the operation, and that the operating physician is competent to conduct the surgical procedures.

It is important to keep in mind the fact that psychosurgery is still an experimental procedure. It is not a treatment for any specific psychological disorder (Kalinowsky, 1978). Careful evaluations of psychosurgery will hopefully guide future decisions about where its use may help alleviate psychic pain, and where its use represents an unacceptable risk to the patient.

SUMMARY

Over the past three decades, biological treatments have made great contributions to the treatment of severely disturbed patients. Since the introduction of antipsychotic drugs, many patients have been able to leave the hospital and live relatively normal lives in the community. The antipsychotics are the primary form of treatment for persons diagnosed as psychotic. Although many patients who take antipsychotic drugs improve enough to leave the hospital, their symptoms tend to persist, but in milder form. Antipsychotic drugs also have rather serious side effects that need to be taken into consideration when prescribing these potent medications. The most serious side effect is *tardive dyskinesia,* a neurological disorder. Estimates of patients with tardive dyskinesia vary, but it is clear that significant proportions of schizophrenics, especially older and more long-term patients develop it. Patients treated by short-term drug treatment are less likely to experience side effects than those on long-term maintenance therapy.

Denber (1979) has described three phases of treatment with antipsychotic medication. In the first phase, *pharmacolysis,* the goal is to relieve psychotic symptoms within about the first week by gradually increasing the dosage. During *stabilization,* dosage is regulated to gain enduring control of the psychotic symptoms. In the third phase, *maintenance,* a minimal dosage of the drug is administered to maintain the patient free of psychotic symptoms.

The tricyclic antidepressant drugs are more widely used than the MAOI's because they tend to produce fewer side effects. The use of MAOIs is the treatment of choice of "atypical depression," but otherwise, tricyclics are the "first line" drugs. Antidepressant medication is usually prescribed for serious depressions, but not for mild or brief depressive episodes. Alternative biological treatments like ECT may be indicated in severe depressions where there is a serious risk of suicide, because drugs may not reach peak effectiveness for up to three weeks.

Antianxiety drugs are frequently prescribed, but their use is best limited to conditions where other supportive measures fail to help the patient. Dependence on antianxiety agents may be a greater risk than the potential benefit of such drugs.

Electroconvulsive therapy is a widely

practiced, yet still controversial treatment. It is especially effective with endogenous depressions, where evidence suggests that it may be superior to drug treatment. Given potential side effects and risks associated with ECT administration, its use is warranted only after carefully weighing the risks and benefits.

Psychosurgical procedures are the most dramatic and controversial of the biological treatments. Generally it is regarded as a treatment of "last resort," with its use indicated only for disorders seemingly untreatable by other methods. Its effects are quite unpredictable, but new surgical procedures have increased its credibility to some degree. But despite certain advances in technical procedures, it still remains an experimental technique with potential for misuse. Careful evaluations of psychosurgery may guide future decisions regarding where its use might be maximally beneficial.

19

Group, Family, and Community Based Treatment

OVERVIEW OF GROUP THERAPY

About nine people file into a room slowly, tentatively. Each has seen only one other person in the room: the therapist, a week earlier in a diagnostic interview. Some appear reluctant, some enthusiastic, but all have come to this first meeting with at least the willingness to go along with the therapist's belief that the group could be useful to them. They sit in a circle, quiet and expectant. Their posture reveals a bit of anxiety. What will go on here? What can go on here? What will the therapist do? Several in the group have had previous psychotherapy. One woman begins the interaction by describing her current predicament and the disappointments she experienced in previous treatments. Others chime in. Sympathetic offerings of similar tales of woe are heard from various people in the room. From time to time the therapist comments, pointing out the expectations of the various group members. People are beginning to get to know one another. Each of the people is attending for a different reason, but they all share some similar concerns. Will the group members accept me? Are there other people in this room with similar problems and concerns? Will I be really understood? Can I take risks with these people? After the first session all of the group members have had an opportunity to express why they came and what their expectations are for future meetings. This is but one of many different types of groups. But for this group, for these people, group therapy begins (Adapted from Lieberman, 1975).

What does group treatment have to offer? How are groups conducted? Is group therapy effective? These are some of the important questions and issues which we will address in our overview of group treatment methods. As you are no doubt aware, group treatment methods utilize the skills of a helping person with two or more persons at a time. In this section we will consider a number of group treatment approaches. We will also take a close look at family therapy—a form of group therapy conducted with members of the same family. But first let us take note of the dramatic increase in the popularity of group approaches to treatment.

The popularity of group approaches has paralleled the increased demand for psychological services in the general population—a trend which became especially apparent in the years following World War II. Today there seems to be a group experience tailored to suit the interests and meet the needs of virtually anyone who seeks psychotherapy, personal growth, or simply support and companionship from others. Most of you have probably participated in or know of someone who has been involved in one of the myriad forms of group experience available today. If you have not had direct or indirect contact with a group like Alcoholics Anonymous, a "consciousness raising" group, a religious inspirational group, an encounter group, or a weight control group, you may be in the minority of your peers. As this brief listing suggests, the diversity of group approaches is impressive. Approaches range from self-help groups like Alcoholics Anonymous to groups which adapt psychoanalytic principles and techniques to the group setting. In recent years the encounter group has become very popular. There seems to be a move towards using group methods to promote personal growth in individuals with no serious psychological disturbances. Lieberman has noted that by 1975 more than 5 million Americans had participated in encounter groups aimed at personal growth and change.

The popularity of groups can also be seen in their extension to numerous settings. Groups conducted in homes, hospitals, businesses, weekend retreats, community agencies, and professional offices reach people of all races, ages, economic levels, and so on.

But apart from their popularity and the real human needs which group methods address, their place in the spectrum of therapeutic methods is assured for another reason: group methods are efficient, time-saving, and less costly than individual treatment methods. Levine (1979) has commented that "group therapy can help with most anything that individual therapy can, providing an appropriate group is available and the individual will accept the group as the mode of treatment" (p. 11). The virtues of group therapy have been recognized by therapists of every major theoretical orientation, although different therapists may work very differently within a group framework.

Some therapists, for example, adopt psychoanalytic principles by encouraging free associations of group members and interpreting transference reactions between the therapist and individual patients. Other therapists administer behavior therapy procedures such as systematic desensitization and assertiveness training. Such therapists are likely to play a very active, directive role in groups which they conduct. Still other therapists focus on communication and styles of relating between group members, emphasizing interpersonal relationships as a key vehicle for change and growth. But despite differences in therapist style and approach to group treatment, there are some common elements in diverse groups which contribute to their effectiveness.

Curative Factors in Group Therapy

Yalom (1975) has contributed to our understanding of the usefulness of group methods by specifying "curative factors" that are believed to be common to diverse group approaches. A consideration of the following list of curative factors in group therapy will help us to answer one of the questions which we posed earlier: What do group treatments have to offer?

1. Imparting information. In every therapy group there is ample access

to information provided by the therapist and other group members. Group members, then, have an opportunity to receive suggestions, advice, or direct guidance from the group. Didactic instructions may be formally incorporated into the group, or may arise from the dynamics of group life as the members interact and share experiences that are relevant to commonly held problems or concerns.

2. Instilling hope. Hope is an essential ingredient of any successful therapeutic approach. If there is no hope of a favorable treatment outcome, it is unlikely that maximum benefit will be derived from therapy. Observing other group members who have coped successfully with similar problems or dilemmas may be a potent source of inspiration. Contact with persons who have improved is especially important in groups, like Alcoholics Anonymous, that rely heavily on personal testimonials and the exemplary activity of members.
3. Universality. As group members share intimate feelings and disclosures, it may be comforting to learn that others share similar fears and concerns, have endured equally difficult situations, and have surmounted hurdles in life that some of the group members are only beginning to confront. The very knowledge that one is not alone in one's suffering and in one's struggles to cope effectively with life's challenges may be a source of relief as well as an impetus for change and growth.
4. Altruism. Clients often enter group treatment demoralized, unsure of themselves, and lacking in self-esteem. But over the course of the group experience, members can learn

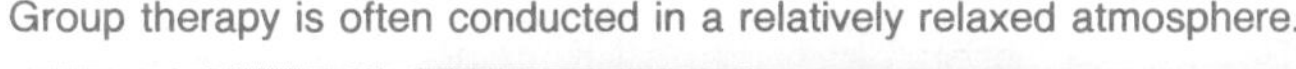

Group therapy is often conducted in a relatively relaxed atmosphere.

Josiah Hornblower/Globe Photos, Inc.

a valuable lesson: that they can be of help and value to others. The contribution to the personal growth of other group members can lead to a greater sense of self-worth and a heightened awareness of personal resources.

5. Interpersonal learning. The complex interplay of relationships and personalities which fashion the shape of the group affords an excellent context for learning about interpersonal relationships, social skills, sensitivity to others, and conflict resolution.
6. Imitative behavior. Group members may acquire new behaviors by modeling desired and effective behaviors. Group members can learn from one another as well as from the individual designated as the therapist.
7. Corrective recapitulation of the primary family. The group experience may offer the client a unique opportunity to explore and resolve conflicts and problems related to family members which continue to be expressed in relationships outside the family context. Insight into the way one reenacts past family dramas and scripts for behaving that stem from the primary family may be an important first step in breaking free from the hold of the past. Behaviors which may have been rewarded and even functional in the family of origin may come to be viewed as maladaptive and inappropriate in the context of the treatment group.
8. Catharsis. The open expression of feelings toward others is an essential part of the group process. Learning how to express feelings in an open, honest, and straightforward way may lead to closer bonds between group members and a greater sense of mutual trust and understanding.
9. Group cohesiveness. Group cohesiveness is one of the primary curative factors. It is the sense of "groupness" that binds individuals together, serving much the same function as the relationship in individual therapy. In a tightly knit group where members feel close to one another and a sense of trust exists, members may more freely take risks, accept feedback from one another, and experience a sense of self-esteem that derives from acceptance by the group. There is likely to be the free flow of feeling and interpersonal exchange which is so essential to the emergence of the other curative factors we have mentioned.

A moment's reflection on the curative factors Yalom describes suggests that groups provide a rich context for change and growth. You probably noted that the group experience may help foster a sense of personal validation and self-worth. It may provide the impetus for interpersonal learning and the opportunity to profit from the experiences of others, and it may offer the group member an opportunity to help others in their quest for change and growth.

Let us now turn to another question: How is group therapy conducted? Actually no *one* answer applies to all types of groups. But we hope that an inspection of several very different types of groups will give you a sense of the interplay of curative factors in group treatments and the range of techniques employed by group therapists.

The roots of group therapy as practiced today are often traced back to the efforts of Joseph Pratt, a Boston internist, who worked with groups of tubercular patients in the early 1900s. Meeting with his patients in a class format, Pratt described his work in this way: "The class meeting is a pleasant social hour for members . . . made up as a membership of widely different races and sexes, they have a common bond in a common disease. A fine spirit of camaraderie has developed. They never discuss their symptoms and are almost invariably in good spirits. . . .". (1907) The inspiration of hope, the identification with other patients experiencing a similar plight, and the camaraderie, mutual support and group cohesiveness all seem to be important "therapeutic ingredients" in Pratt's early groups. Groups like Alcoholics Anonymous, Weight Watchers, and Synanon have an inspirational quality reminiscent of Pratt's "classes."

Like Pratt's groups, self-help groups like Alcoholics Anonymous tend to be composed of people who share a similar problem. However, self-help groups are not led by professionals and draw their "therapists," or leaders, from their own ranks.

Psychodrama

Jacob Moreno, a psychiatrist who first used the term *group therapy,* developed a group treatment known as psychodrama in the early 1920s in Vienna. Psychodrama uses techniques of dramatic play and unrehearsed acting to stimulate the spontaneous expression of feeling. The dramatic techniques utilized tend to obscure the distinction between fantasy and reality and seem to provide a sense of security because new behaviors and attitudes can be explored in the "safety" of a play-acting situation. J. M. Sacks (in Rabin & Rosenbaum, 1976) provides us with a concise description of a psychodrama session:

> The psychodrama group meets in a small threater-like room. The therapist, called the director, begins with a "warm up" or a structuring of the session to prepare the members for action. In the second phase of the session, the dramatic production, a protagonist is selected who enacts relevant scenes from his past, present, or future. He may take his own role or roles of other people. "Auxiliary egos" play the complementary roles and may either be group members or trained professionals. They may play roles opposite the protagonist or accompany him as his extension or "double." In the "mirror" technique the protagonist watches the auxiliaries play out scenes from his life. The director frequently calls for a "role reversal" in which the protagonist and antagonist change their positions to experience the scene from the other's point of view. During the third and final phase a general discussion is held in the "light of the drama" (p. 60).

Through role reversal and role playing techniques, the group member, or protagonist, as he or she is called, may gain greater self-awareness, explore previously hidden conflicts, and engage in new and experimental behaviors under the guidance of the "director." The audience, in turn, may furnish valuable feedback and make observations regarding the "performance" which may add to the impact of the "production." Psychodrama continues to be practiced by therapists in the United States and abroad, but the techniques of role playing and role reversal have been more widely adopted by behavior therapists in assertiveness

WORKING WITH THE ALTER EGO: A PSYCHODRAMA TECHNIQUE

Mintz (1970) offers the following example of an "alter ego" technique as might be used in a psychodrama group:

"Susan, a young woman married to Don, a medical student, wishes him to accept her father's help during their financially difficult years. They discuss the problem, reverse roles, then interact with another participant who impersonates the father and expresses feelings of hatred and rejection. After the situation has been played out on a realistic level, several group members volunteer to function as what Moreno has termed 'alter egos,' speaking for the secret thoughts and feelings of one of the participants as they guess them to be. The role playing proceeds:

Susan: Why shouldn't I have a comfortable way to live? Daddy wants to help us and he certainly can afford it.

Susan's alter ego (standing behind her): You're just angry because daddy's rich and can afford to give me the things you can't. Why I believe you're jealous.

Don: You're my wife and I want to support you. It wouldn't hurt for you to live economically for a few years.

Don's alter ego (standing behind him): I feel castrated by you and your father.

Father: It hurts my feelings you won't let me help you.

Father's alter ego: I want to prove I'm a better man than that young fellow who's my son-in-law!

The alter ego technique, as used in this episode, brought it to the open what Don and Susan believed to be one another's underlying attitudes and Don's suspicions about the concealed attitude of his father-in-law. It is impossible to see the consequences of an alter ego psychodrama. In this case, once Don's anxiety and suspicions had been ventilated, he decided that they were not justified, and a compromise was reached which satisfied both wife and husband" (p. 63–64).

training and by Gestalt therapists and leaders of encounter groups who stress emotional expressiveness as a pathway to personal growth. Psychodrama rarely makes use of the group as a whole. Instead, it focuses attention on the drama centering around an individual, thereby deemphasizing interpersonal interactions within the group.

T–Groups

A more contemporary development in group methods is the T–group ("T" stands for training). T–groups were stimulated by the efforts of Kurt Lewin, a scientist who believed that human behavior could be changed by working with individuals in groups to improve problem-solving skills and the quality of interpersonal relationships. At the request of the Connecticut Interracial Commission, Lewin and his colleagues, Leland Bradford, Kenneth Benne, and Ronald Lippit, conducted a workshop to reduce racial tensions. The workshop stressed group training in human relations and was viewed by the participants as an extremely positive experience. Impressed by the success of group methods in reducing intergroup tensions, Lewin's colleagues established the National Training Laboratories (NTL) after his death in 1946. NTL became a center for human relations training. The T–group developed as an outgrowth of research in group dynamics at NTL and soon became an accepted instrument for teaching interpersonal interaction skills. Within several years, hundreds of people received human relations training through workshops conducted by NTL staff and T–groups began to be conducted in industry and in the community. Executives received training in social skills, businesspeople were trained in leadership and decision making skills, and workers in industry and in the community were urged to discuss problems encountered in their work, explore possible alternatives, and ponder the consequences of the alternatives presented.

Buchanan (1964) describes the T–group as follows:

> Training approaches meriting the name laboratory (or T–group) utilize: (1) face-to-face, largely unstructured group as a primary vehicle for learning, (2) planned activities involving interaction between individuals and/or between groups, (3) systematic and frequent feedback and analysis of information regarding what happened in the here and now and what effect it had, (4) dilemmas or problems for which "odd ways" of behaving for most of the participants do not provide effective courses of action (and thus for which innovative or "search" behavior is required), and (5) generalization, or reformulation of concepts and values based upon the analysis of direct experience (p. 216).

The group usually consists of 8 to 16 members and a leader or trainer. The participants meet for varying time periods in the "laboratory," at each others' homes, or at a resort; the important aspect of the environment is that it is away from their workaday world and everyday stresses. The interaction process in each group is varied with its purpose; the emotional depths probed range in a continuum which extends from the problem-solving executive group in the shallow end to the intensive, highly charged groups usually referred to as encounter groups, which we will discuss next.

Encounter Groups

The encounter group emerged from attempts to expand the range of the T–groups functions and goals to include increasing the individual's capacity for enriched experience and personal improvement. Stoller has noted that the goals of encounter groups are "growth and change, new behavioral directions, the realization of potential, heightened self-awareness, and a richer perception of one's circumstances as well as the circumstances of others" (p. 3). Thus in encounter groups, the emphasis is shifted away from learning about social behavior in groups to learning about oneself (Korchin, 1976). Encounter groups are seen by their proponents as having universal applicability. Unlike traditional group psychotherapy which implies psychological disturbance and patient status, encounter groups are considered by many to be relevant to "normal" personalities who want to "grow, change, and develop" (Lieberman, 1975, p. 440).

Encounter groups tend to stress emotional aspects of individual functioning and utilize techniques to amplify feelings. A gamut of techniques including body

"In the city this would be called a group therapy session and it would be costing us fifteen bucks apiece."

Reprinted by permission The Wall Street Journal

awareness, fantasy, dream analysis, and psychodrama may be used. Nonetheless, the relationships that develop in the group and cognitive learning are also essential to self-exploration and change.

Carl Rogers (1970) acknowledges the great diversity in encounter groups yet speculates that certain "practical hypotheses" tend to be shared by groups with widely divergent activities and emphases. Here is Rogers' attempt to formulate one such set of "practical hypotheses" that account for basic aspects of group experience:

1. "A facilitator can develop, in a group which meets intensively, a psychological climate of safety in which freedom of expression and reduction of defensiveness gradually occur.
2. In such a psychological climate many of the immediate feeling reactions of each member toward others, and of each member toward himself, tend to be expressed.
3. A climate of mutual trust develops out of this mutual freedom to express real feelings, positive and negative. Each member moves toward greater acceptance of his total being—emotional, intellectual, and physical—as it *is,* including its potential.
4. With individuals less inhibited by defensive rigidity, the possibility of change in personal attitudes and behavior, in professional methods, in administrative procedures and relationships, becomes less threatening.
5. With the reduction of defensive rigidity, individuals can hear each other, can learn from each other, to a greater extent.
6. There is a development of feedback from one person to another, such that each individual learns how he appears to others and what impact he has in interpersonal relationships.
7. With this greater freedom and improved communication, new ideas, new concepts, new directions emerge. Innovation can become a desirable rather than a threatening possibility.
8. These learnings in the group experience tend to carry over, temporarily or more permanently, into the relationships with spouse, children, students, subordinates, peers, and even superiors following the group experience."

Rogers' description conveys the optimism of the human potential movement

SOME ENCOUNTER GROUP EXERCISES

Many encounter groups use structured group exercises, especially in the early stages of the group. Structured exercises may be used to ease the "entry" of individuals into the group, to facilitate communication, to increase feedback among group members, and to amplify and intensify feelings. It is important to emphasize that structured group exercises are not really an end in themselves. This point is nicely illustrated by what Jerrold Shapiro has coined the "Golden Rule of Structured Experiences": "It is far less important to complete the exercise than to deal with whatever behaviors and feelings are generated by the exercise or the suggestion of the exercise" (1978, p. 193). Thus structured exercises are perhaps best thought of as catalysts which help to initiate the processes considered to be of great importance in encounter groups. Here are a number of structured group exercises which Shapiro suggests are appropriate for encounter-type groups.

1. Introductory exercises
   a. Leader: Let's start by giving our names and saying briefly why we're here. Please share, if you'd like, what you hope to get out of this group and what you fear from this group.
   b. Leader: Please choose a name you'd like to be called during this group. It can be a real name or something you've always wanted to be called. Don't tell why you've chosen this name or whether it's your real name or not. Write the name on a 4 by 6 card and put the card in front of you.
   c. Each person gives a first name and a personality descriptive adjective or adverb beginning with the same letter, such as "Sexy Sadie," or "Angry Arnie." Each person will then say the names and adjectives of each preceding individual, in reverse order. For example, "I'm 'Good Guy,' and this is 'Sexy Sadie,' and this is 'Horrible Harmon,' and so on. Introductions end when the first person gives the names of all others.
   d. Leader: Since it's easier to begin talking to one person than a group of people, please choose one partner. Somebody here you don't know or someone you would like to get to know better. (When everyone has paired off, the leader continues.) Okay, now decide who will talk first and who will talk second. The person who will talk second is to interview, try to get to know the person in a personal way, not just status or occupation but values, attitudes, feelings, likes, dislikes, and so on. When this is done you'll be asked to introduce your partner to the group.
2. A trust exercise: The blind walk
   Leader: This exercise is called a blind walk. Each person should choose a partner. After you have a partner chosen you will be blindfolded. Place the blindfold across the eyes of one person. From now on there should be no verbal communication until the exercise is completed. Your task is to lead the blindfolded person around,

giving him as full a sensory experience as you can, safely. Each person will lead for 20 minutes. Everyone should be back in this room in 40 minutes and we'll discuss this experience.

3. Exchanging feedback: The truth pillow
Leader: As a way of increasing our communication I'd like to recommend this exercise (picking up a pillow). This pillow will have special qualities for awhile. If someone throws this pillow to you, you're required to give them positive and negative feedback. Say something you like and something you don't like about them in this group. For example, if I were to throw this to Tom, he would give me feedback. Then Tom could throw it to whomever he wanted to receive feedback from. Okay, let's begin (throwing it to a member).
Adapted from Shapiro (1978, p. 196–205).

regarding the ability of the group member to exchange authentic responses for more rigid, stereotyped behavior, given the appropriate facilitative conditions. In addition, we can clearly see the dynamic interplay of the curative factors which Yalom believes are operative in all groups. Perhaps you noted that the high level of cohesiveness which can be achieved in encounter groups seems to promote a sense of universality and hope and stimulates interpersonal learning, catharsis, and exchange of information.

Marathon Groups

The marathon group is a kind of extended one-session, encounter-type group developed by H. Stoller and George Boch. Stoller experimented with marathon groups for the first time in 1963 with a group of seriously disturbed, psychotic patients. Since then, the technique has been used with individuals of varying degrees of adjustment, including "normals." The group is planned to continue for 24 to 30 hours, or longer. It assumes that participants are capable of tolerating undiluted intense experience and do not require carefully measured exposure to psychotherapy. Virtually no limits are placed upon the intensity of emotional experience in such groups.

In a marathon group, the 10 to 15 participants are requested to react to each other immediately and spontaneously at all times. Feedback from others informs the person of the nature of the impact he or she has on the group. Labels such as doctor or lawyer are avoided, so that individuals may not fall back on a particular role for security, and are forced to build their security from their participation in the group. The group is instructed to remain together for the duration of the session, and psychological jargon is not permitted. The goal of interactions is not to be understood but to be reacted to.

Schwartz & Schwartz (1969) believe that the marathon group offers a uniquely effective emotional experience for the following reasons: (1) There is intensity of participation as each individual reveals his own life drama and, in the presence of the group, gives up long-held defenses. Tolerance for anxiety increases with the mounting cumulative emotionality expressed in the group and eventually permits the expression of intense feelings such as love, grief, and despair; (2) Deprived of their usual environment where roles and life-styles are fixed, the participants are less apt to rely upon stereotyped reactions and habitual defenses. Thus their behavior becomes more flexible and open to change; (3) Fatigue, constantly growing toward the end of the marathon period, becomes a disinhibitory factor, breaking down resistance and leading to authentic, spontaneous responses; and (4) Toward the end of the marathon, with the knowledge that this experience will soon be terminated, there is an urgency to "get from the marathon what he came for" and a "release of emotion seldom seen in any other setting."

FAMILY THERAPY

Consider for a moment, Bloch and LaPerriere's (1973) definition of family therapy as

> Face to face psychotherapy of a natural system, natural in contrast to a group formed specifically for the purposes of therapy. The therapist or a team of therapists, directly engages the family, or some substantial elements of the family, of the index patient. . . . What unites all family therapists is the view that change, which is significant to the psychotherapeutic endeavor, takes place in the family system. With this unifying thread, they may vary considerably as to the size of the elements of the family they engage, the techniques they employ, and the theory to which they adhere (p. 1).

As you may have noted, unlike practitioners of group psychotherapy, family therapists strive to change problem behavior in the system in which it "naturally" occurs—the family system. Since family therapists see most problems as having their roots in a dysfunctional family system, it is not surprising that they believe that treatment must focus on the family context out of which the problems arise. Thus in family therapy, the patient—the focus of treatment—is the family unit itself. In order to create change in the family system and thereby in the individual, family therapists often focus on communication and patterns of interaction between family members. Our discussion of family therapy techniques will center on a very popular treatment approach termed *conjoint family therapy,* developed by Virginia Satir (1964). Satir's therapeutic approach emphasizes modifying communication and interaction patterns within the family to bring about change. We have chosen to present Satir's approach because we believe that it has been more influential than any other in the burgeoning field of family therapy.

Satir's Conjoint Family Therapy

Before therapy is actually initiated, the conjoint family therapist needs to know something about the family members experience of the problem and who feels hurt or threatened on account of the problem. The therapist will learn something about the family's expectations about therapy and will share with the family his guiding belief: the problems or symptoms of any family members involve and concern the whole family (Sorrells & Ford, 1969).

Therapy usually begins with an evaluation of the communication patterns and interactions between family members. The therapist might be interested in such things as how messages are given, received, and verified; how direct, specific, and clear the family communications are; and finally, how feedback is given and received by different family members. The therapist might also learn something about the self-concepts of the family members by observing the way in which the family makes decisions, resolves or fails to resolve differences, and by the way members of the family express their uniqueness. One way in which the therapist develops hypotheses regarding communications processes and the family rules which govern interactions is through the use of a structured interview.

Although one family member may be singled out as the "identified patient" with *the* problem, the real source of difficulties lies in the dysfunctional ways in which family members communicate and relate to one another. The goals of family therapy, then, relate to removing the barriers to effective, meaningful

EVALUATION IN FAMILY THERAPY: THE STRUCTURED INTERVIEW

The structured interview consists of a set of tasks which provide an opportunity for the therapist to learn more about how the family displays many of its rules and communication patterns. Sorrells and Ford (1969) provide the following example of a structured interview, as utilized by Virginia Satir.

1. "What is the main problem in your family at this point in time?" This question is asked to each family member individually and is then posed as a matter for family discussion.
2. "Plan something that you could do together." This task is given to the whole family and to various segments of the family, such as parents alone, children alone, males, etc.
3. The marital couple is asked, "How did you two, out of all the people in the world, get together?"
4. The parents are given the proverb, "A rolling stone gathers no moss." They are asked to discuss the proverb, come to some conclusion about its meaning, then to teach the proverb to the children.
5. Main fault, main asset. Each person in the family is asked to write on a card the main fault, as he sees it, of the person on his left. The members are arranged in the order of husband, wife, and then children in descending chronological order. The therapist then reads the cards, changing the wording to preserve anonymity. Each person is asked to vote for whom he thinks each item applies to most in the family. Each member is then asked to specify what he thinks is his own main fault.
6. Each person is asked, "Who's in charge of this family?"
7. Similarities and differences.
   a. Each parent is asked which child he thinks is most like himself and which child is most like the spouse.
   b. Each child is asked which parent he perceives himself as being most like. After making this choice, the

child is then asked how he is like the other parent and how he is different from the parent he chose.

c. Both spouses are asked how they are alike and how they are different (from each other).

8. A relatively unstructured overview of the meeting completes the format. Most therapists are interested in finding out how the interview was experienced by all the family members. In addition, the therapist may wish to draw attention to parts of the interview which seemed significant for future work and to insure that each member leaves the interview with a feeling of "completed transactions" (i.e., that the therapist heard and understood what was said).

communication between family members. Sorrells and Ford (1969) have specified the following goals of family therapy which are closely aligned with Satir's therapeutic approach:

1. That the family be able to communicate with clarity, specificity, directness, and congruence;
2. that the family adopt and manifest the value of completed transactions so that each member is always sure that he is both heard, seen, and understood;
3. that each member be able to give feedback to other family members and accept feedback about himself without distortion, denial, or disqualification;
4. that the family value the unique contribution of each individual member;
5. that the family strive to make decisions that provide for the needs and wants of each individual affected;
6. and that the family use the ways in which individuals differ as a means for growth rather than as a barrier to understanding.

There goals are accomplished by first creating a "safe" therapeutic atmosphere in which each person is willing to take risks and share intimate feelings. The therapist models and encourages appropriate communication in his own interactions with family members. In each session, an effort is made to help each family member to feel included and valued. The therapist stresses the value of feedback and teaches clients that feedback can be given or received as a "gift" rather than as an assault. Clients are discouraged from assigning blame to others, and family members are asked to avoid use of words like always or never. Each family member may be asked to make a commitment to believing in the possibility of change on the part of the whole family or any individual member (Sorrells & Ford, 1969).

When family members are secure about not being judged negatively by others in the group, the therapist attempts to foster insight into the patterns of words and actions that tend to inhibit communication and problem resolution. Once the patterns are made clear, the therapist and family members must arrive at some agreements about how family members would prefer to be dealt with, how problem solving might take place with minimum conflict, and how family members will continue to practice any new behaviors or alternatives that

Family therapy can be an opportunity for new openness among family members.

have been defined in the family itself. (McPeak, 1979).

Structured Family Therapy

Before we leave the topic of family therapy, let us briefly consider another treatment approach: structured family therapy (Minuchin, 1974). In their efforts to help a troubled family, structured family therapists alter the way in which relationships and interactions between family members are structured and organized. In contrast with the less active, communications-oriented conjoint family therapist, the structured family therapist actively immerses himself in the everyday activities of the family to make planned changes in the way family members interact with each other. Rossman, Minuchin, and Liebman (1975) provide an example:

> Eating lunch with the family provides exceptional opportunities to observe family members' transactions around eating and to make on-the-spot interventions to change the patterning of these interactions. This session also serves broader diagnostic purposes, since structural and dysfunctional characteristics of the family are more readily apparent in this context (p. 846).

The structured family therapy approach is further illustrated by Aponte and Hoffman's (1973) successful treatment of a 14-year-old girl who refused to eat. The therapists first carefully observed the relationships and communications patterns of the family. They noted that the girl, Laura, was able to successfully compete for her father's attention by refusing to eat. By not eating, Laura was able to exercise considerable power in the family. The goal of the therapists was to help Laura and the rest of the family members to express their needs and wants in a straightforward manner. And eventually Laura was able to express in words the message that her refusal to eat conveyed indirectly. When Laura was better able to verbalize her wants and needs directly, she no longer resorted to refusing to eat to attain the affection she so desired.

EVALUATION OF GROUP AND FAMILY THERAPY

After surveying a number of divergent group approaches, including family therapy, we now come to the final question which we posed at the beginning of the section: Does group therapy work? Recent reviews of the group and family therapy literature suggest that a preliminary answer to the question is a qualified "Yes." Reviewing the group therapy literature, Bednar and Kaul (1978) conclude that group therapy seems to help people to attain more positive and perhaps more healthy evaluations of themselves and others than no treatment and placebo treatments. Further, in some circumstances, group therapies have been found to be more effective than other psychological treatments with which they have been compared. In their comprehensive review of the family therapy literature, Gurman and Kniskern (1978) are equally, if not more, optimistic: "family therapy appears to be at least as effective and possibly more effective than individual therapy for a wide variety of problems, both with apparent "individual" difficulties and more obvious family conflicts" (p. 883).

But given the limitations of some of the studies which were reviewed, it is premature to conclude that group and family therapy are generally superior to individual therapy. In addition, much more research is needed to determine the extent to which self-reported positive changes in self-concept and personality are reflected in actual behavioral changes outside the group and family situation that persist over time. More research is also needed to evaluate the relationship between the various curative factors we have discussed and the outcome of various group treatments.

Bednar and Kaul (1978) caution against accepting the conclusion that group therapy "works" without also heeding the following qualification: not all groups have uniformly positive and beneficial results. This observation appears to be warranted. Data provided by Lieberman, Yalom, and Miles (1973) regarding the experiences of over 200 Stanford University students who participated in ten different types of group therapy (psychodrama, Gestalt therapy, NTL-T–group, psychoanalytically oriented groups, etc.) suggests that very disparate reactions may be elicited by group therapy. At least in terms of the subjects self-report of attitudes, self-concepts, and social values, a high degree of gains were experienced by a third of the group participants.

But just as groups apparently stimulated positive changes in some individuals, in others, negative, and even harmful effects were experienced as a result of their group participation. Eight percent of the participants were considered to be "psychiatric casualties." Their very negative reactions ranged from psychotic episodes to experiences of great discomfort and distress. Clearly negative, but less serious problems and experiences, were reported by another 11 percent of the sample studied. Thus participants in group therapy do not uniformly experience positive benefits from their group experience.

Lieberman and his colleagues completed a more fine grained analysis of the experiences of group members and discovered that the style of the group leader and the group atmosphere he created were related to the experience of the group members. Casualties tended to occur in groups where leaders displayed an attacking, confronting, "energizing" style in which strong pressures were exerted on members to express emotions and to make intimate, highly personal self-disclosures. The leaders who were most successful rewarded caring in the group and provided students with a cognitive framework for change, often translating feelings and experiences into ideas for the members of the group. Thus Lieberman and his colleagues found that it was not the type of group so much as the leadership style that accounted for differences in outcome.

Research like Lieberman's emphasizes the need for an even greater understanding of the processes that lead to constructive change in group therapy. We are only beginning to learn about what types of people are likely to make gains in divergent groups and much more research is needed to answer this important question. Prescreening of participants for serious disturbances seems to be indicated before vulnerable personalities are exposed to excessively stressful interpersonal situations. But with adequately screened clientele and with trained and competent leaders, groups may be a remarkably effective means of maximizing services to a wide variety of people in need of help.

NEW WAYS OF HELPING: MENTAL HEALTH AND THE COMMUNITY

If you were to imagine the treatment of an emotionally disturbed person, you would, most likely think of a person talking with a mental health professional. We all have a culturally determined image of how abnormal behavior should be treated. Perhaps, if you know a bit more than the average person, you are likely also to think that treatment may include the administration of tranquilizers or that it might also occur in group psychotherapy or in some other setting. It has certainly not always been this way.

Think back, for a moment, to our discussion of the history of abnormal behavior in Chapter 2. There we related how people displaying odd or disturbed behavior were once treated as witches or common criminals and often, unceremoniously, thrown into dungeons. Many people mark the beginning of the "first revolution in mental health" from the time in 1792 when Pinel broke the chains on the inmates in the Paris hospital called the Bicetre as a symbolic act of humanitarian reform.

Certainly the development of the psychological point of view by Sigmund Freud, at the turn of this century and throughout the beginning of the 20th century, marks a "second revolution" in the field of mental health. Freud's brilliant insights into the nature of psychological dynamics and his development of a treatment technology, psychoanalysis, truly revolutionized our thinking about the nature and treatment of abnormal behavior.

In fact, we are still living, to some degree at least, with the remnants of that second revolution in the field of mental health. Most people still think that individual problems in living and various forms of abnormal behavior are best dealt with over long periods of time in intensive individual psychological treatment. The analysts couch has replaced the mental hospital in the public mind as the most appropriate way of dealing with abnormal behavior. Freud's views have dominated during most of the 20th century. Still, treatment for human distress on the analysts couch has been only available for those with the economic means to buy it. There has been no real way for the poor or for minority groups to receive the benefits of the second mental health revolution.

But in 1946 the National Institute of Mental Health was formed and the Public Mental Health Act was instituted. This signified the beginning of an effort in the United States to serve every citizen. Also, by the middle of the 1950s, the major tranquilizers had come into use and mental hospitals had begun to change as a result. It was then possible to reduce the size of the staff and to bring psychotic symptoms under control more quickly. Soon patients began to be released more quickly from the hospital and a "revolving door" phenomenon began to develop. People leaving the mental hospital, with their symptoms under temporary control, soon found themselves back in a community that was not necessarily ready to receive them. So new crises would ensue and many of these people found themselves reentering the mental hospital. By 1961 a Joint Commission on Mental Health and Mental Illness was instituted to investigate these problems and to think systematically about how we could produce a third revolution in mental health in this country.

A ground breaking book by Gurin, Veroff, and Feld entitled *Americans View Their Mental Health* (1960) documented, for the first time, the degree to which most of us in this country saw persons suffering from mental illness as stigmatized people. The knowledge that someone was suffering from psychological problems was often hidden, an embarrassment to the sufferer. Gurin, Veroff, and Feld's results showed us that there existed natural helpers in the community, people who were able, through their individual skills and dedication, to help others even though they did not possess conventional psychiatric degrees. These helpers were the clergy, bartenders, and even hairdressers. They were people who, through their day-to-day sympathetic contacts with others, often provided help for those who were not financially privileged enough or inclined to hire a therapist.

The results of the studies of the Joint Commission on Mental Illness and Mental Health included recommendations for (1) increased emergency care for people suffering from psychological crises, (2) improved care for chronic mental patients, (3) expanded care in the community for people who had been discharged from mental hospitals, and (4) mental health education for the public so that people who were suffering from psychological difficulties would be better understood. Then, in 1963, President John F. Kennedy instituted the Community Mental Health Center Act, a "bold new approach" to the development of community mental centers throughout the country.

These developments have been called the "third revolution in mental health." But as we pointed out earlier, history can be written in such a way as to lead us to believe that every new development is a victory in the march of progress. This march of progress view of history can lead to self-deception. A more judicious and thoughtful view of the recent history of mental health care is one that recognizes the "third revolution" as a real change in our orientation to treatment, but whether it reflects "progress" only time and careful research will tell.

Characteristics of Community Mental Health Today

In the remainder of this chapter we will discuss some of the innovative treatment practices associated with community mental health today. For the moment, however, we will discuss some of the major dimensions of the third revolution in mental health. Bloom (1977) suggests a number of characteristics of the community health movement today. Let us consider some of them briefly.

First, community mental today emphasizes practice in the community. The underlying premise is that the community itself should be responsible for the mental health of its own citizens. One consequence of this goal has been a movement toward deinstitutionalization. As we will see, attempts are being made to provide a new life in the community for patients who have spent many years in public mental hospitals. These programs raise a variety of complex and difficult questions. How would you yourself feel living next to a person who had just been discharged from a mental hospital? Would you be willing to volunteer to help provide community based programs for such people?

A second emphasis of the community mental health movement is a focus on *total populations* rather than individuals. Thus the "client," as Denner and Price (1973) note, is no longer the individual, or even a family unit, but entire communities and populations of people. This is an entirely new way for individually oriented psychologists to think about their work and it will be many years before this becomes a natural part of our thinking.

Another important characteristic of community mental health today is an emphasis on prevention rather than treatment. The goal is to reduce the incidence of disturbed behavior rather than merely to treat new cases. Some innovative programs are already underway to help populations who are at risk for the development of a variety of psychological disorders. Widows suffering from depression are being helped by other widows. Programs to teach children interpersonal problem-solving skills are being developed in school systems. We will return to discuss prevention later in this chapter.

Yet another important characteristic of the community mental health movement is an emphasis on *indirect rather than direct services.* Many mental health professionals have knowledge that they can provide to other community helpers, including teachers, clergymen, public health nurses, and others. These people see far more of the public than do most psychologists or psychiatrists. They can then use the mental health knowledge and skills provided by the mental health professional to enhance their own effectiveness. Thus by "helping the helpers" the mental health professional can produce a "multiplier effect" and expand his or her own impact. For example, police who often find themselves in the middle of psychological emergencies when they intervene in a family crisis can be trained to intervene more effectively in family disputes. It has already been shown that such training programs delivered by mental health professionals to police can reduce the risk of injury to the police and improve the quality of service to disturbed families (Bard 1970).

Community mental health also seeks to develop innovative clinical strategies. Rather than thinking about long-term psychotherapy as the single method of choice, crisis intervention services can be developed, and hotlines, call-in services, and suicide prevention lines are being offered to whole new populations within a community.

Finding new sources of person power to deliver mental health services is another goal. As Albee (1968) has noted, there will never be enough professionals trained to meet the mental health needs of people in

This suicide prevention center is providing a training seminar to teach volunteers to evaluate the nature of callers problems, assess the seriousness of a suicide threat, and to develop a plan of action while still on the phone with the caller. Such efforts are part of the community mental health movements' attempt to find new sources of nonprofessional help in the community.

Courtesy of San Francisco Suicide Prevention, Inc.

the community. As our population continues to increase, the number of mental problems will certainly increase as well. We must begin to think about new populations of people who are able to deliver mental health services. They may be housewives, who, in many cases, can work effectively in the delivery of certain kinds of treatment. They may be volunteers who work in community mental health centers. They may be college students who serve as peer counselors to other students, in their own university, who are finding it difficult to adjust to the demands of university life.

Finally, community mental health research is oriented to identifying sources of stress within the community. Unemployment, for example, can be a source of stress with major mental health implications. The community mental health movement is oriented to identifying these sources of stress and developing methods of helping people cope with them.

This is a new way to think about mental health in the community. As an approach to the provision of mental health services, it deserves our serious and thoughtful examination. We will consider some examples in more detail in the remainder of this chapter. And we will also consider evidence for the effectiveness of these new approaches. Innovations should always be looked at with a critical eye. The innovations of yesterday, such as the mental hospital, quickly become the institution that we wish to reform tomorrow.

From Mental Hospital to Community

You will recall that in the middle of the 19th century asylums began to be built all over the United States. As Rothman (1971) observed, these new asylums were viewed as sanctuaries from the chaos and uncertainty of a social environment that was assumed to be the major cause of psychological difficulties.

The first asylums were relatively orderly and supportive institutions in which care for the severely disturbed could be obtained. But by the end of the nineteenth century, mental hospitals began to take on a new function. People who were socially or intellectually disabled for a wide variety of different reasons began to be placed in mental hospitals. The hospitals became crowded and the quality of care deteriorated. Thus, by the beginning of the 20th century, the well-ordered asylum of the Jacksonian era had become an institution in which conditions of crowding, poor treatment, and even maltreatment predominated. Most large public mental hospitals had few rehabilitative programs and little resembled the early asylums of the Jacksonian era.

In fact, during this period, as Price and Denner (1973) have noted, people were often removed from their community for various forms of odd behavior and committed to mental institutions where they received little help. If, indeed, they were released, they often found themselves rejected and stigmatized in the community. Mental hospitals began to receive substantial criticism at this time and studies by the Joint Commission on Mental Illness and Mental Health (1961) reinforced the public concern about the quality of care in mental institutions.

A recent study by Price and Moos (1975) gives us some idea about the quality of the social climate in various psychiatric hospital wards. The climate of the wards was measured using the Ward Atmosphere Scale, WAS, which measures the residents own perceptions of ward atmosphere on ten dimensions.

Price and Moos (1975) analyzed results

of the WAS from 144 different hospital wards in sixteen states. By clustering WAS results in terms of profile similarity, Price and Moos were able to discover six distinctive types of ward social environemnts. The types are shown as WAS profiles in Figure 19–1 below.

For our present purposes the importance of these results is that a large proportion of the hospital wards were oriented primarily to social control of patients. We called these "control oriented" wards. On the other hand, fewer by far of the treatment environments we studied were oriented toward therapeutic relationships or even the practical concerns of teaching patients life skills for survival in the community. Although our sample was not a strict probability sample and therefore may not be precisely representative of all psychiatric wards, its large size and geographic dispersion suggests that it is broadly representative of the nature and quality of mental hospital wards in the early 1970s.

Experiments in community living. Concern with the quality of treatment in hospitals and a strong national policy shift toward "deinstitutionalization" has, in recent years, led to increased efforts to return residents of mental hospitals to the community.

Earlier, in discussing the treatment of schizophrenia, we described an important demonstration project conducted by Paul and his colleagues (Paul et al., 1978). Paul's behaviorally oriented program was explicitly designed to help chronic schizophrenic patients learn living skills that would allow them to function relatively independently in the community.

Another important innovation which

FIGURE 19–1

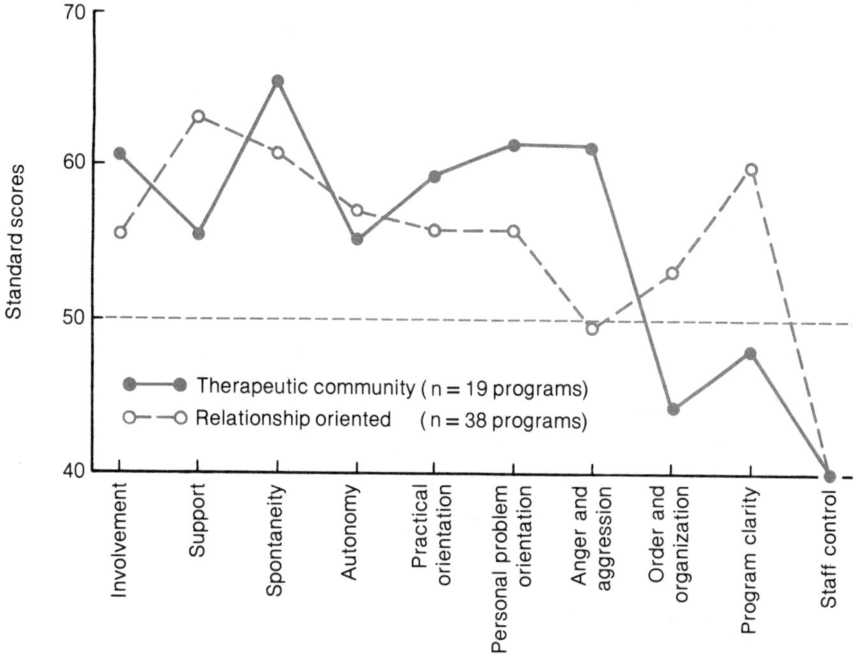

A. Mean ward atmosphere scale profiles for therapeutic community and relationship - oriented treatment program clusters.

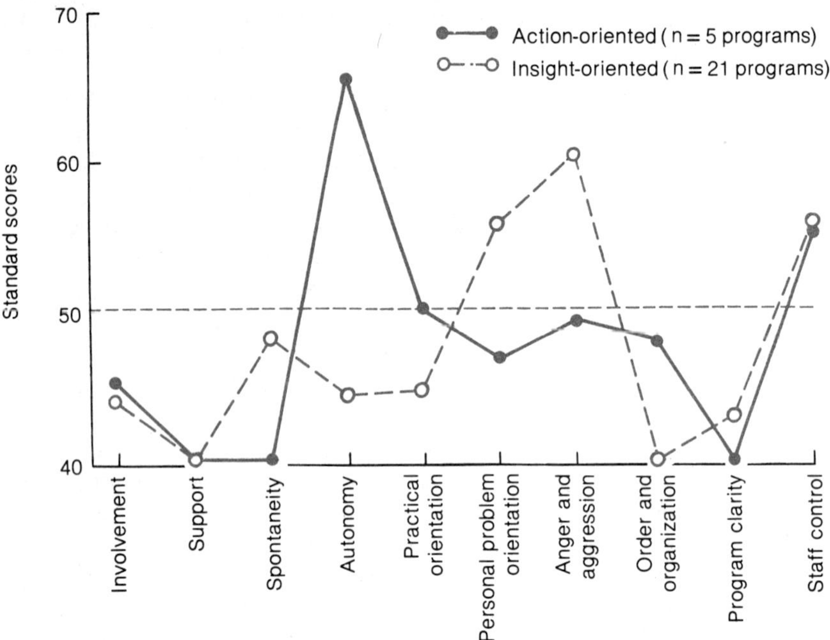

B. Mean ward atmosphere scale profiles for action-oriented and insight-oriented treatment program clusters.

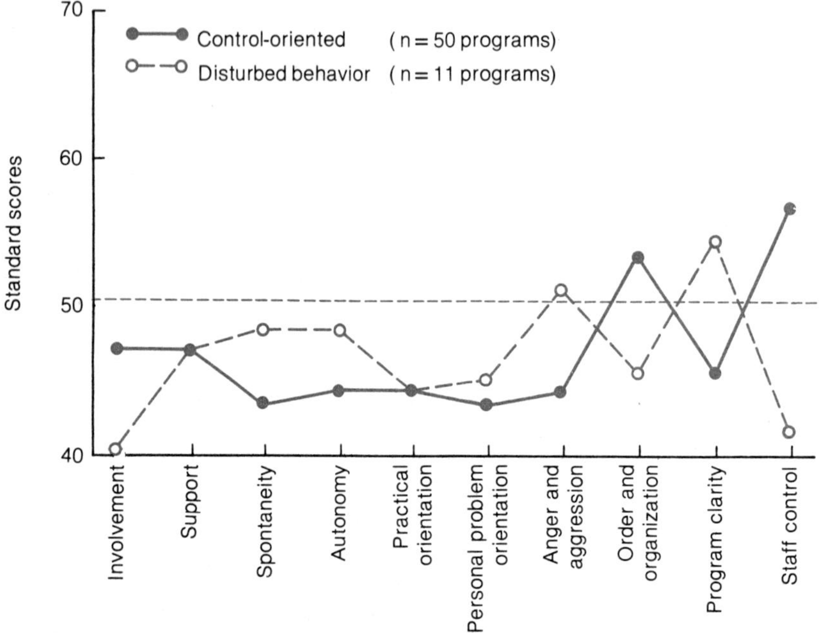

C. Mean ward atmosphere scale profiles for control-oriented and disturbed behavior treatment program clusters.

Source: Figures from Price and Moos, "Toward a Taxonomy of Inpatient Treatment Environments," *Journal of Abnormal Psychology,* 1975, *84,* pp. 181–88. Copyright 1975 by the American Psychological Association. Reprinted by permission.

demonstrated that mental patients can be taught to live effectively in the community is that of Fairweather and his colleagues (Fairweather 1964; Fairweather, Sanders, Maynard, & Cressler, 1969). These researchers conducted a series of carefully designed field experiments in which they hoped to demonstrate that small groups of severely disturbed mental patients could live in the community in small communal living situations. Fairweather later called these houses "lodges." Hospitalized patients were first taught skills in group decision making and problem solving. When Fairweather compared the group that received this training with groups that were treated in more conventional ways, it was shown that they could be discharged more readily from the hospital with their newly found social skills. Fairweather then moved his experimental group to a lodge within the community and they began to cope with their new community role. They received training in jobs as gardeners and janitors and became relatively self-sufficient.

One of the outstanding qualities of Fairweather's innovation is that it is far more than a demonstration project. Throughout the development of Fairweather's program, he carefully compared the lodge innovation with appropriate control groups so that the relative effectiveness of the lodge could actually be compared with more conventional approaches to treatment. Fairweather did not feel that placement in the community was necessarily a "good in itself." Results had to be demonstrated.

In this initial set of studies, Fairweather was able to demonstrate the lodge group's ability to avoid rehospitalization was substantially greater than that of a control group. The control group used outpatients clinics and other typically available community resources. In Figure 19–2 below you can see that the lodge group's time spent in the community rather than back in the hospital over a 40-month period was between 80 percent and 100 percent, whereas the control groups median time in the community was only 20 percent. Similarly, Figure 19–3 below shows that lodge group members were employed for much larger proportions of the time than were the control group.

Since these early demonstrations by Fairweather and his colleagues, Fairweather has attempted to disseminate his lodge model throughout the country as a supplement to public mental hospital treatment. Although a relatively small proportion of public mental hospitals have been receptive to the development of Fairweather's lodges, those that have shown relatively good success in maintaining patients in the community.

Another similar demonstration project is called Training in Community Living (Marx, Test, & Stein, 1973; Fields, 1978), a program developed by the Mendota Mental Health Institute in Madison, Wisconsin. The orientation of the staff in the Training in Community Living Program is to help patients "make it" in the community. Staff go grocery shopping with patients, teach them how to cook or do laundry, find them a place to live, and talk to clerks, landlords, employers, and police to prepare the way for a community living situation for people who have been hospitalized sometimes for as much as 20 or 30 years. The program includes the opportunity for patients to return to the hospital if it is needed.

In the past, research has shown that community treatment for patients has produced an extremely high drop-out rate (Fields, 1978). This so called "revolving door" phenomenon was a major concern in the late sixties and early seventies when

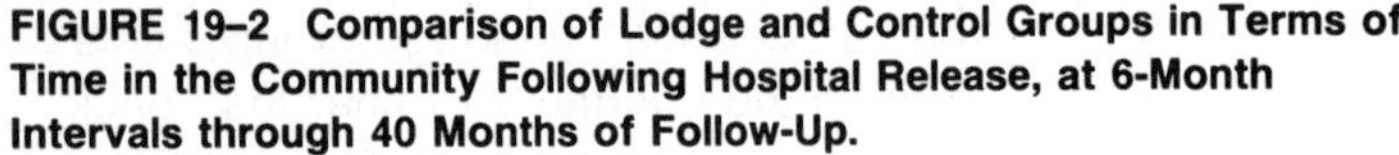

FIGURE 19–2 Comparison of Lodge and Control Groups in Terms of Time in the Community Following Hospital Release, at 6-Month Intervals through 40 Months of Follow-Up.

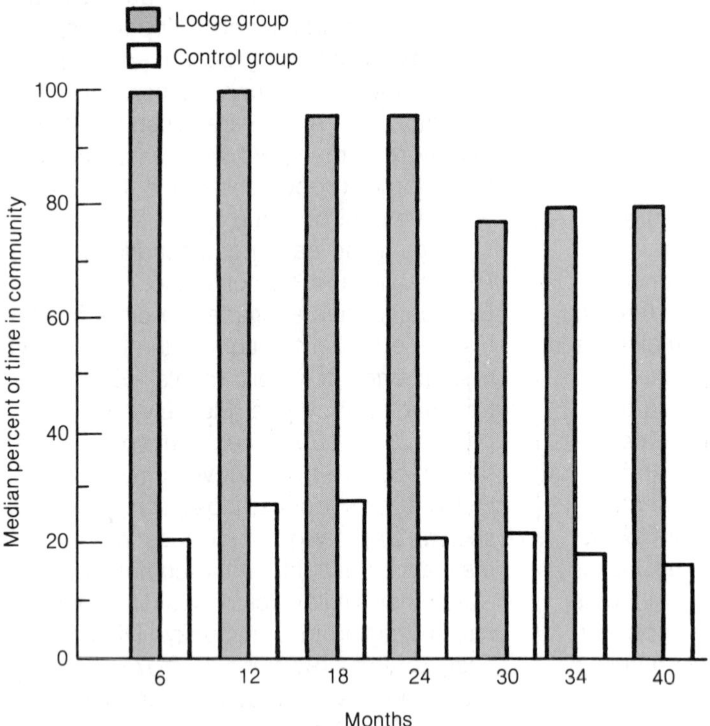

Source: From *Community Life for the Mentally Ill: An Alternative to Institutional Care,* by G. W. Fairweather, D. H. Sanders, H. Maynard, and D. L. Cressler. Copyright 1969 by Aldine Publishing Company. Reprinted by permission.

more and more patients were moved into the community. However, an active support system for patients in the community of the sort developed by the Training in Community Living Program can make a substantial difference.

Research on this program began with a random sample of patients from Mendota State Hospital who, although they were seen as needing hospital care, were placed directly in the community. Staff worked with these patients developing their coping skills and supporting them. At the end of the five months they were much more successful in the community than a comparable control group that did not receive the skill training and support. However, once the support program was withdrawn, many of these patients returned to the hospital. Continuing support in the community is necessary for many of these patients. The results of a second larger study in which community support was sustained for 14 months and in which patients were carefully linked with community agencies, produced several important findings. At the end of a year the TCL group spent very little time in institutions as compared with control groups, and they were significantly better

FIGURE 19–3 Comparison of Lodge and Control Groups on Employment, Following Hospital Release, at 6-Month Intervals through 40 Months of Follow-Up.

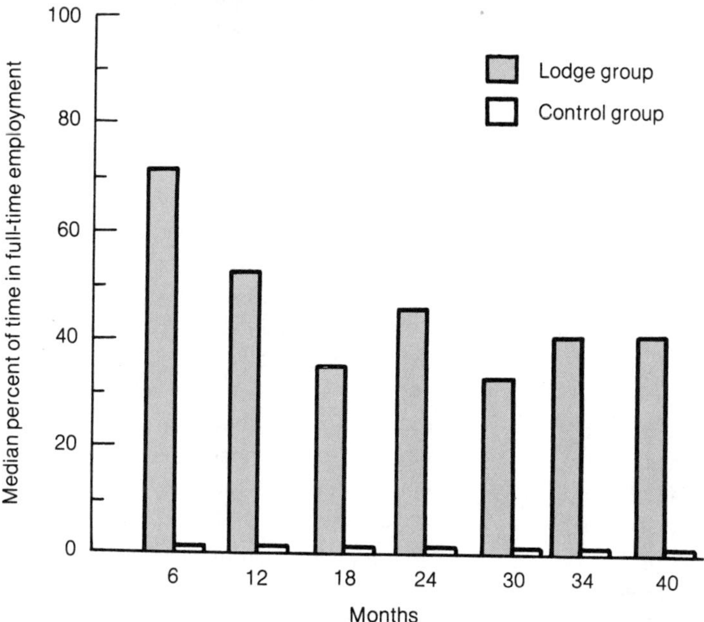

Source: From *Community Life for the Mentally Ill: An Alternative to Institutional Care,* by G. W. Fairweather, D. H. Sanders, H. Maynard, and D. L. Cressler. Copyright 1969 by Aldine Publishing Company. Reprinted by permission.

TRAINING IN COMMUNITY LIVING

Time: 2:30–3:30 p.m. Changing shifts.

Place: Training in Community Living headquarters.

Scene: A psychiatrist, psychologist, two nurses, an occupational therapist, five aides, and three trainees sit around a large rectangular table and sift through a stack of files, their case load of about 50 clients. (Case loads vary from about 40 to 60 patients at any one time, two thirds of them diagnosed schizophrenics and one third, personality disorders.) They discuss each patient and their last conversation with him or her. Most program planning and change take place at cross-shift meetings. Staff see some of their clients regularly; others, who have been in the program for a long time, require only minimum supervision. It is staff responsibility, however, to know if any patients are having problems getting along in the community, at work, at home, in recreational activities or in therapy. They find out at staff meetings.

Sharing the Information

Johnathan is doing fine. He's attending classes. Seems stabilized on his medicine. He's active in a men's group. Even likes cooking classes. Plans to go to the football game on Saturday.

Brenda was hostile when she came in for her meds today. Might be an issue in her therapy this afternoon.

Jerry was late coming home yesterday. I left a note saying I was there and that I'll call him this morning. When I called to check in, he said he was sorry he missed me. He stopped off for a cup of coffee at Rennebaum's, where he transferred buses.

I'm really worried about Bert. He's hearing voices again. He said, 'I don't want to take meds today because my voices are talking too loud.' He started a new task at the sheltered workshop yesterday and I think he found it too stressful. We sat there stapling papers together, but he didn't want to staple. I thought he was ready to move on to something more, but he got scared. Even though we moved back to paper stacking I think he felt too much pressure from the other task. Also, he's been having lots of friends over and playing his music very loud. It's possible he got hold of some drugs. I'm going back to his rooming house this evening to see how he's doing. I left him with some friends. He was talking a lot about the war inside himself. 'I can't fail God's test,' he kept saying. I might have to take him into the hospital today, if the voices overwhelm him.

I went shopping with Derek this morning and he picked out some good apples and some eggs and onions. He said he wanted to make an omelette with me tomorrow when I go there for breakfast. He seems to be caring more about himself. The last time we had breakfast he didn't want to make anything. He poured some cereal in a bowl but then he recognized he was out of milk. Today he made a big deal out of buying milk.

Alice is working well at her volunteer work at the Heart Association.

Jimmy is bugging his family again. He wants to move back with them, but they're holding firm. He was sitting in their driveway when they came home last night. I had a long talk with his mother this morning and she thinks we're doing right to remain firm about him living in a rooming house. She needs lots of support, though, because she frequently feels guilty about not taking care of him.

Naturally. She said he was always her favorite child and she worries about who will take care of him after she dies.

She really wants to take him with her.

There is a groan at the familiarity of this story and some jokes about the "soap opera of schizophrenics." The entire staff knows about Jimmy and his mother.

A staff member mediates a problem with a patient, her landlord, and a policeman.

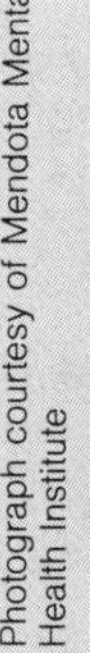

As the session moves on, it is difficult for a visitor to identify the different roles of the team members. Who is the doctor, nurse, social worker, or aide? Everyone seems to contribute to the discussions of the perils and small triumphs in the lives of Amy, Buddy, Dolores, Meredith, Lee, Al, Lucy (Fields, 1978, p. 4–5).

adjusted to their homes in the community. In terms of employment and social relationships, they also experienced greater satisfaction with their lives than did the control group. In addition, when one compares the TCL project with that of the hospitalized group, there is little difference in cost of care.

As Fields (1978) notes, the Training in Community Living project is really a "floating hospital ward." In the project, staff are highly motivated to work hard to retain patients in the community. But, as with all demonstration projects designed to show that such services actually can be provided, we must ask whether enough commitment and skill and resources can be brought to bear to repeat the Training in Community Living Program on a large scale, throughout the country.

Crisis Intervention

Caplan (1970) has suggested that we all experience at least two kinds of crises in

TWO IMAGES OF DEINSTITUTIONALIZATION: "DUMPING" OR COMMUNITY SUPPORT?

Studies like those of Fairweather (1964) and Paul et al. (1978) and the TCL project clearly indicate that with enough resources and effort even chronically institutionalized mental patients can be supported in the community. From examining these studies alone we might be inclined to conclude that our efforts at deinstitutionalization have been a success. But how widespread are the sorts of projects that we just described?

Another, much less optimistic perspective has been offered by Koenig (1978). He notes that nearly 40,000 poor chronic mental patients have been "dumped" in New York City alone. Patients who have been dependent on life in a

Social workers do their best to help deinstitutionalized patients with their problems in living, but sometimes there's not enough help to go around.

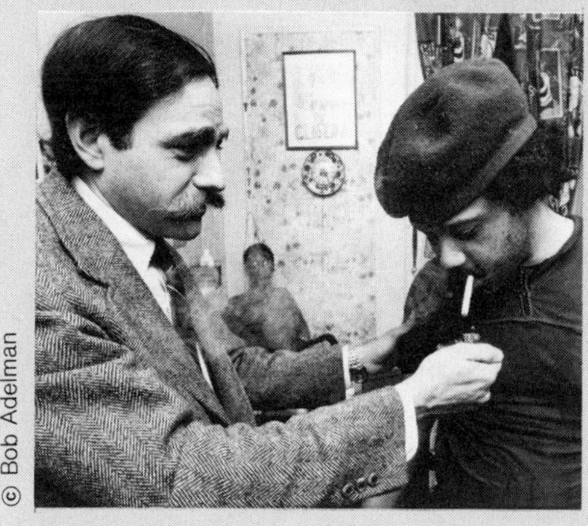

© Bob Adelman

mental hospital for as much as 20 years have been placed in "single room occupancy hotels" where they receive little or no care, live on public assistance funds, and only occasionally receive the support of one overworked social worker.

Which image is true? It is fair to say that so far, projects like the Training In Community Living project are the exception rather than the rule. The fact is that most patients discharged from mental hospitals will not find themselves with a rich array of community supports.

In fact, Scull (1977) argues that the "decarceration" of dependent individuals from institutional settings does not have the quality of benevolent reform that some would claim. Instead, Scull argues that decarceration is actually supported because it is more inexpensive to return mental patients to the community than it is to provide them with institutional care.

Whether Scull is correct or not, there is little question that our efforts to develop an effective community support program for hospitalized patients to replace the mental hospital is only beginning. The National Institute of Mental Health's development of a community support program (Turner and TenHoor, 1978) suggests that a national program is now getting underway. Such a program will have to contend with the extensive needs of chronically hospitalized patients as well as with communities who may resist the placement of ex-mental patients in their neighborhoods. There is little question that we are in the midst of a major experiment in social change in the field of community mental health. And the outcome is still uncertain.

This 35-year-old mental outpatient, like many others, drifts from S.R.O. to S.R.O. After a few months at the Continental, he recently moved to a hotel in Harlem.

From *New York Times Magazine*, May 21, 1978, p. 16.

our normal life development. The first of these are *developmental crises* that occur at predictable times in our life cycle. Examples of such developmental crises might include the birth of a child, entry into school, leaving school to take one's first job, and so on. The second type of crisis can be thought of as an *accidental crisis.* These are unpredictable and can occur in a variety of different forms. The death of a loved one, the onset of a severe physical illness, the loss of a job are all examples of accidental crises.

Earlier we noted that many times in the face of a psychological emergency or crisis, people have had nowhere to turn. Only a few years ago psychological help in the face of a personal crisis was often unavailable to the average person. Long waiting lists for conventional psychotherapy were commonplace. Admission to a psychiatric hospital did not necessarily mean that constructive help with a personal crisis would be available. Today, suicide prevention services, hotlines, and crisis intervention services are much more readily available than they were even ten years ago.

But what are the elements of a successful crisis intervention? Rappaport (1977) and McGee (1974) suggest that successful crisis intervention services typically use nonprofessional personnel and professional mental health workers as consultants. They are imbedded in a network of agencies, and they are committed to evaluating their own effectiveness.

Let us consider an example. McGee's own work, as exemplified by the Suicide and Crisis Intervention Service in Gainesville, Florida, began with the assumption that immediate face-to-face contact between trained volunteers and people who were in crisis was a crucial ingredient in the service itself. They were oriented to "respond to every request to participate in the solution of any human problem whenever and wherever it occurs" (McGee, 1974, p. 181).

McGee's crisis intervention team often acted as *advocates* on the behalf of people in crisis. They played a variety of different helping roles that were considerably more diverse than conventional therapist. They might, as Rappaport (1977) suggests, go to court to tell a judge that they are trying to help the person in crisis find a job or they might attempt to reestablish contact between a young person and his or her parents. They might intervene in family disputes, or, in some cases, help with direct human needs such as the provision of clothing and shelter.

This crisis intervention worker is talking with a young woman who has found herself confused and upset in a strange town. The police had called in the crisis intervention team.

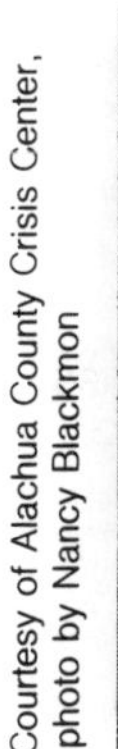
Courtesy of Alachua County Crisis Center, photo by Nancy Blackmon

When the crisis intervention team opened a case, their first goal was to establish communication with the person in crisis and to develop an action plan. During early intervention the team tries to establish a close working relationship with the person in crisis, determine if they are suicidal, and assess their resources in the community. Once the crisis intervention team has moved into action, it attempts to establish realistic mutual goals between the person and the worker with whom the person will continue to communicate.

A key aspect of this sort of crisis intervention work is that the crisis intervention worker attempts to find whatever other sort of resources exist for the person in the community and to mobilize those resources to help the person. Thus, rather than a lonely and private relationship, as in psychotherapy, crisis intervention invovles a broad range of collaborative efforts designed to help the client overcome their crisis situation.

Typical problems found in crisis intervention centers, hotlines, and suicide

MENTAL HEALTH EDUCATION

Our account so far has suggested that an increasingly broad array of activities is being undertaken in the name of mental health. We have examined community support systems for chronic mental patients, emergency services and hotlines for people in psychological crisis, and programs to improve the skills of other professional groups who work with the public such as the police.

Broad-based educational efforts can also serve community mental health needs. In a recent review, Bloom (1980) describes important new efforts in the field of mental health education. Community education regarding mental health issues can be directed at correcting stereotypes regarding the nature of psychological disorders, informing the public about the availability of new or specialized services, or helping people understand their own personal problems or relationships better.

Mental health education can be an important positive force in the field of community mental health.

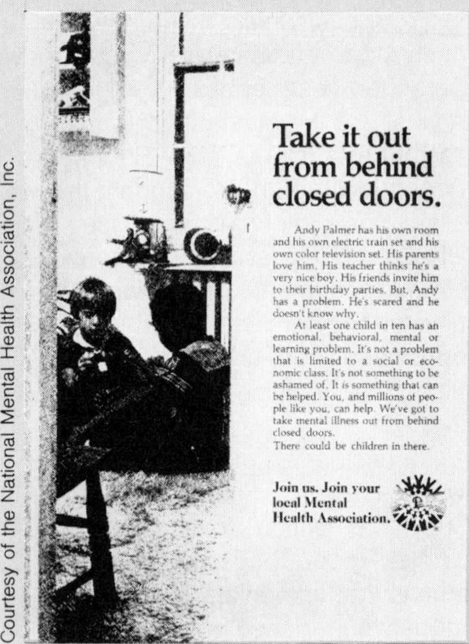

Courtesy of the National Mental Health Association, Inc.

An informative example of a mental education efforts is the Alternatives Project (Sundel & Schanie, 1978). The Alternatives Project used radio and TV messages in an educational attempt to improve public attitudes toward mental health issues, to increase the public's awareness of what mental health resources existed in the community, and to increase the use of these resources.

The study was conducted in Louisville, Kentucky, during a 60-week period in 1973–1974. The educational campaign itself consisted of 21 brief radio and television messages describing a local crisis and information center and included the telephone number of the center.

In order to evaluate the impact of the project, Sundel and his colleagues examined the pattern of telephone calls to the crisis information center and also conducted a telephone survey of Louisville households before the mass media program began and then again each 20 weeks during the program. The investigators found that the TV messages did indeed increase the number of adults calling the crisis information center and increased the public's knowledge of community mental health resources available to them.

Initially better educated people in the community seemed to have a great deal more information about mental health resources than less well-educated people, but as the campaign continued, the gains in knowledge were greatest for the less educated people. Thus it appears that mental health education efforts can aid people in the community to gain access to mental health resources and to understand their own problems in living.

prevention centers include marital and family problems, alcoholism and drug abuse, juvenile problems, vocational and school adjustment problems, homosexual problems, loneliness, alienation, and others.

The important point here is that significant psychological help can be provided for a wide variety of emergency or crisis situations. In most cases, that help can be provided by trained volunteers. In fact, McGee notes that almost 80 percent of the personnel surveyed in over 200 crisis intervention centers across the country were nonprofessional volunteers. Thus, on a number of dimensions, crisis intervention is sharply contrasted with our conventional image of long-term psychotherapy.

The Promise of Prevention

Unquestionably our greatest victories over disease and suffering have been those involving prevention rather than treatment. In fact, many of these victories occurred long before we had sophisticated laboratories and biochemical knowledge of disease (Caplan, 1964). Consider the following examples:

> The British Admiralty was impressed by reports that sailors on ships that were well stocked with citrus fruits and vegetables did not suffer from scurvy. They ordered that fruits and vegetables be included in the diets of sailors and scurvy virtually disappeared.
>
> A London physician in the 19th century named Snow suspected that the water supply might have something to do with the epidemic of cholera raging in the city at the time. He noted the addresses of the people developing cholera all drew water from the Broad Street pump. Furthermore, he noticed that people who drew their water from other sources did not contract the disease. His prevention strategy was as simple as it was effective. He simple removed the handle from the pump! The cholera epidemic was brought under control and new cases of the disease were prevented from occurring.

One of the most difficult challenges in the field of mental health is in finding methods for preventing the development of abnormal behavior. It remains to be seen whether we will be able to find the handle to our own Broad Street pump. In this section we will examine some of the key concepts emerging in the field of prevention of abnormal behavior as well as some examples of prevention programs. Finally, we will consider research strategies that hold promise in discovering new ways of preventing abnormal behavior.

Key concepts in prevention. Many of the fundamental concepts in the field of prevention have been derived from the fields of public health and community mental health. They are based on the premise that our efforts need to focus not on individuals who have already developed a disorder, but groups or populations of people who are *at risk* for disorder. Goldenberg (1977) notes that:

> Prevention programs are based upon: (1) a commitment to a public health model with its focus on whole community *populations* rather than individuals; (2) a concern with *reducing the incidence* (number of new cases) and prevalence (total number of existing cases) of psychological disorders in the community; and (3) an effort to locate particularly *vulnerable individuals* who, because of genetic background, unique personal experiences or exposure to excessive environmental stresses, are thought to have especially high potential for developing abnormal behavior (p. 36, emphasis added).

This seems reasonable enough, but how might we actually create programs that accomplish these goals? The strategies of individual treatment are familiar enough, but the strategies of prevention may be less so.

Bloom (1968) distinguishes between three different types of preventive efforts. The first involves community wide efforts where all residents in a community are exposed to the program. In the field of public health it is easy to identify such *community wide* preventive efforts. Heller and Monahan (1977) point out that water purification to eliminate typhoid fever or the supervision of food and water processing are public health measures which provide community wide prevention programs. Psychologically oriented community wide prevention programs might involve newspaper or television public information programs to educate people in more effective parenting skills or to eliminate corporal punishment in the schools.

A second type of prevention program is called a *milestone program.* As Heller and Monahan (1977) note that in the milestone approach citizens are exposed to the program at specified intervals in their lives and "residents of a specified area march, as it were, past the program, prior to reaching it they are not protected" (Bloom, 1971, p. 118). An example of a milestone prevention program in public health might be smallpox vaccination required upon admission to school. Psychological milestones, suggested Heller and Monahan (1977), might include critical developmental periods in a person's life, such as the birth of a sibling, school entry, the first year of a marriage, or the birth of one's first child. The stresses of these critical periods of social development could be reduced by helping people to gain skills that would help them cope with the life transition (as in the case of marriage or parenthood) or by changing the social environment associated with the transition, as in the case of school entry.

The third type of prevention strategy is called the *high risk* program. It focuses on populations of people who are, for genetic or environmental reasons, vulnerable to specific disorders. An example offered by Heller and Monahan is that of a program in a school system that provides special support to children who are beginning to show signs of emotional disorders. Other high risk populations might be the children of mental patients, children who experience the death of a parent at an early age, or the survivors of natural disasters such as earthquakes, floods, or plane crashes.

In Table 19–1, Bowers (1963) provides us with a variety of examples of "normal emotional hazard" that are encountered throughout life that might suggest appropriate high risk or milestone oriented preventive interventions.

TABLE 19–1 Suggestions for Possible Primary Prevention Programs Applicable to Various Institutions and Agencies

Institutions and Agencies	*Normal Emotional Hazard*	*Possibilities for Preventive Action*
1. Family	Loss of father through death, divorce, or desertion	Reinforcement of childcare services for working mothers
	Loss of mother	Reinforcement of fosterhome services
	Adolescence	Increase in staff and professionalization of high school counselors, deans, and vice-principals
	Birth of sibling	Pediatric or well-baby clinic counseling
	Death	Management of grief—religious or community agency worker
2. Public health	Phenylketonuria (a form of mental retardation)	Detection and diet
	Childhood illnesses	Vaccination, immunization
	Stress caused by children—economic, housing, etc.	Reinforcement of well-baby clinic through mental health consultation to staff
	Pregnancy	Adequate prenatal care for mothers of lower socioeconomic status
3. School	Birth of sibling	Recognition of event by school and appropriate intervention
	School entrance of child	Screening vulnerable children
	Intellectual retardation	Special classes and assistance
	Teacher concern and anxiety about a child's behavior	Consultation by mental health specialists
	School failure	Early identification and prevention through appropriate school program
4. Religion	Marriage	Counseling by clergy
5. Job or profession	Promotion or demotion	Opportunity to define role through services of a mental health counselor
6. Recreation	Appropriate and rewarding use of leisure time	Active community and city recreational programs
7. Housing	Lack of space, need for privacy	Working with architects and housing developers

Source: Reprinted with permission from E. M. Bower, "Primary Prevention of Mental and Emotional Disorders: A Conceptual Framework and Action Possibilities," *American Journal of Orthopsychiatry* 33(5) (October 1963), pp. 832–48.

The idea that mental health professionals could actually develop programs that would prevent rather than merely treat psychological disorder is an extremely appealing one. Indeed, the President's Commission on Mental Health (1978) argues that such programs can be developed, but that they must be based on a strong research base. Prevention remains a goal and few convincing demonstrations are yet available. Nevertheless, the demonstrations that we do have are instructive. Let us consider several different examples of attempts to prevent rather than merely treat psychological disorders.

Anticipatory coping with a stressful event. Unavoidable surgical procedures, especially for young children, can produce a genuinely stressful emotional hazard, and programs focused on helping the child anticipate and cope with the stress may prevent later severe emotional reactions.

A study by Cassel (1965) focused on children between the ages of 3 and 11 who were about to undergo a serious diagnostic experience called cardiac catheterization. The experience of being in a strange operating room and having this procedure carried out can be stressful indeed. Cassel rehearsed the operating room procedure with the child by acting it out in a puppet play. The puppet was actually dressed in a hospital gown, had electrodes attached to it, and went through the steps involved in administering anesthetic. After the child watched this procedure, the roles were reversed and the child played the part of the doctor with the therapist acting the role of the frightened child and asking reassurance from the child who was now playing the doctor.

Compared with a control group that did not receive this experience, the children who received anticipitory guidance showed much less emotional upset during the procedure itself and were more willing to return to the hospital for further treatment. But, interestingly, as Heller and Monahan (1977) note, the intervention effect was no different when the children in the two groups were compared at home or later in the hospital. Thus, many intervention effects may be highly specific in their impact. Careful research on the actual impact of such efforts is needed if we are to succeed in achieving prevention goals.

Skill training to reduce vulnerability. An example of a different sort of prevention program is offered by the work of Spivak and Shure (1974). The rationale for their research was that it should be possible to provide children with interpersonal and cognitive problem-solving skills early in their school development. These skills included the ability to sense problems, to identify feelings, and to look for alternative solutions. Spivak and Shure reasoned that training of this kind should help children to cope with interpersonal problems effectively in the future and therefore reduce a child's vulnerability to later psychological distress. The investigators provided children four years of age with 46 such lessons over a ten-week period. The children did appear to acquire the key skills and their behavioral adjustment was also shown to improve. A year later, when these children were followed in new class settings, program improvements were maintained over time (Spivak & Shure, 1975).

Early identification of children with emotional problems. Still another strategy for prevention is to identify children with early signs of emotional disorder and to intervene to reduce the possibility of the disorder becoming more severe. Technically this type of effort is "secondary prevention" (Caplan, 1964) since its goal is to reduce the *duration* of psychological problems rather than to reduce the incidence of new cases.

As part of the Primary Mental Health Project, Cowen and his colleagues have conducted a series of studies (Cowen et al. 1963; 1966; 1974) that identify children who show signs of disorder as judged by their peers and their mothers and other observers. The children's case folders were "red tagged" and singled out for special help and companionship by teachers aides and other paraprofessional helpers.

Cowen et al. (1972) have reported what they believe is a reduction in the rate of worsening among red tagged children, although as Heller and Monahan (1977) point out, several interpretations of these findings are possible. Nevertheless, the Primary Mental Health Project (PMHP) represents an important effort in using community volunteers to prevent the worsening of incipient psychological disorder (Cowen et al., 1980). This and

ETHICAL PROBLEMS IN IDENTIFYING HIGH RISK CASES

Heller and Monahan (1977) have argued that prevention efforts often require that we identify cases that are "at risk" for the development of some psychological disorder. But we know that our ability to predict who will and who won't develop a disorder is far from perfect. Are there psychological costs in being identified as being "at risk?" In the example of Cowen's Primary Mental Health Program, children's case folders were "red tagged" as being vulnerable to future problems and singled out for special attention. Is it possible that being singled out this way might actually lead teachers or others to see the child as a problem and reject the child still further?

In order to avoid this problem Heller and Monahan suggest a series of steps to be followed to avoid these problems. They state:

> We would suggest that prevention programs based on the early identification of problem cases should pass through four stages of evaluation.
>
> Stage one: The precise "end-state" that one wishes to prevent must be defined. What cannot be defined cannot be predicted.
>
> Stage two: The reliability of case identification and the validity of the predictive scheme being used must be assessed. Can different people agree that this is a potential problem case? If they can agree, does their common prediction have any basis in fact (i.e., without intervention, will the "early-identified" case turn into a "full-fledged" case later)?
>
> Stage three: Is an effective intervention program available for those people correctly predicted to be problem cases? Do those people who receive the prevention program in fact have lower rates of the problem during their lives than people who do not participate in the program?
>
> Stage four: What effect does the prevention program (or merely the screening process) have on those people incorrectly identified as future problem cases?
>
> Only when the issues raised in these four stages are answered can one begin the complex ethical weighing that leads to a decision as to whether to undertake a secondary prevention program (p. 140).

future efforts of the PMHP are likely to tell us a great deal about our potential for preventing emotional distress in the developing lives of children.

The Challenge of Research for Prevention

Despite the ethical problems reviewed in the featured article and our relative lack of knowledge, the goal of primary prevention is a worthy one. The question, however, of turning the goal into operational programs, with demonstrated effectiveness is far from solved. In reviewing the strategies for doing research on prevention, the President's Commission on Mental Health suggests that five questions should be answered by research to help us in our pursuit of valid and effective prevention programs. They are: (1) What groups of people are at high risk for the disorder? (2) What is the relative importance of specific risk factors? (3) Can we effectively reduce or eliminate the most important risk factors? (4) Does eliminating these risk factors effectively lower the rate of disorder? and (5) If the disorder can be prevented, are the costs of the intervention justified by the degree of prevention obtained (p. 1818)?

But where are we to begin? Heller, Price, & Shur (1980) suggest three "boot-strapping" strategies for evaluating the effects of primary prevention programs. The first of these strategies is to identify clearly an end state for which prevention efforts are justified. In the field of public health these are fairly easy to identify: brain damage as a result of being poisoned by lead-based paints, infection associated with syphilis, or the consequences of certain genetic diseases. Other end states may be defined by a changed social status rather than by a disease. Examples of these would be school failure or delinquency. In the end state approach, an operational definition of the end state itself must be developed. Following this, a method for identifying cases at risk must be provided, and an intervention strategy then mounted to prevent the end state followed by rigorous evaluation of the effect of the intervention.

A second strategy is to attempt to identify a group which appears to be at risk for one or several negative outcomes. Such high risk groups might include single parents, widows, children entering the hospital for a surgical procedure, or children experiencing divorce in their family. Beginning with such a potential high risk group, the second step is to discover what the risk factors actually are. A program must then be mounted to reduce these risks and finally an evaluation of the program must be developed.

A third strategy involves beginning with a program that demonstrates the potential for building competence or effectiveness. Many such educational programs already exist. The question, then, becomes what effects the program actually has. Even if positive effects occur, we should still ask if any negative outcomes are actually prevented. These are research strategies that will require large amounts of time and human effort to implement, and yet they are critical in deciding about the relative effectiveness of any prevention strategy.

SUMMARY

We have seen that the group therapies offer psychological help in a wide variety of settings for a number of different types of psychological and interpersonal problems. Despite their diversity, the group therapies offer a set of common characteristics that include practical information, hope, a context for learning from others, and a sense of belonging. The special advantages of group therapy go beyond the fact that a number of people can be simultaneously helped by a single professional. The social learning and modeling processes that are critical ingredients of the group process offer an added dimension to the therapeutic process.

Family therapy provides still another context for helping. It occurs in a natural system, the family, which may contain some of the roots of disturbance as well as an arena for the development of new adaptive behavior. Family therapies usually focus upon communication and interaction patterns within the family and, in some cases, be structured to alter the way in which relationships and interactions among family members are organized.

An examination of research on the effectiveness of group therapy suggest that group-oriented approaches to treatment can indeed produce beneficial effects, although it is currently unclear whether they are actually superior to individual approaches. But like all interventions into the life of a person, group approaches can produce casualties as well. The style of the group leader as well as characteristics of people who fail to benefit or experience harmful effects are likely to be important factors in the degree of benefit derived by group-oriented treatment.

Over the past three decades, our perspective on the ways in which people may receive psychological help has been considerably broadened. The community mental health movement has opened up new possibilities for helping in a variety of community contexts that go beyond the traditional view of individual psychotherapy. Rather than replacing individual treatment, however, the community mental health approach has emphasized (1) an orientation to larger populations and groups rather than individuals, (2) short-term emergency oriented crisis treatment, and (3) pioneering experiments in community living for many hospital patients who previously had been thought to be treatable only in institutional settings.

The research on the effectiveness of these new approaches is only now beginning to yield a substantial body of scientific literature. In addition, efforts to deinstitutionalize mental patients have not always produced humane community treatment and require careful preparations for community support and community living. Nevertheless, the community mental health approach to coping with psychological problems offers new strategies for treatment that promise to reach a wider range of people suffering from psychological distress.

The community mental health approach also suggests that prevention programs may provide still other avenues for reducing the incidence of psychological distress. These innovative programs are directed at people who are judged to be vulnerable to psychological distress. We have seen that such programs are being developed and evaluated for children, people experiencing major life transitions, and other vulnerable groups. Solid experimental research on preventive approaches is badly needed and represents one of the major challenges facing researchers concerned with alleviating human misery and reducing psychological distress in our communities.

Glossary

Abnormal behavior: Behavior that is disturbing to others, subjectively distressing, or psychologically handicapping to the person displaying it.
Abreaction: Expression of pent-up emotions.
Acquired reinforcers: Stimuli which through a learning process come to reinforce certain behaviors.
Acrophobia: Fear of high places.
Acute: A disorder of sudden onset and relatively short duration.
Acutely suicidal: Sudden onset of self-destructive thoughts and behaviors.
Adoption studies: An experimental procedure in which genetic factors are separated from environmental factors by observing children adopted away from their natural parents.
Adoptive studies: Genetic studies in which environmental and genetic effects are separated by examining persons with the genetic factor but in a new adoptive home environment.
Affective disorders: Mood disturbances in which feelings of sadness or elation become intense and unrealistic.
Agoraphobia: Fear of open places.
Alcohol hallucinosis: Severe and distressing hallucinations, usually auditory, occurring about two weeks after abrupt cessation of alcohol use.
Alcohol withdrawal: Pattern of physiological responses to abrupt cessation of alcohol use, usually following a period of chronic use. Symptoms can be severe and life threatening.
Alcoholism: Excessive use of alcohol, usually associated with psychological and physical dependency, which impairs ability to function in several areas of life.
Alcoholics Anonymous: A self-help organization to rehabilitate alcoholics.
Ambivalence: Existence of simultaneous contradictory emotional attitudes toward the same person or object; for example, love and hate.
Amnesia: The partial or total loss of memory for past experiences. May be associated with either organic brain disorders or dissociative reaction.
Amotivational syndrome: Apathy and lack of life goal purported to be related to use of marijuana.
Amphetamine: Drug that produces a physiologically and psychologically stimulating effect.
Amphetamine psychosis: A usually temporary, psychotic-like reaction to high levels of amphetamine in the blood stream. Paranoid ideation is prominent.
Amplification: In Jungian analysis, a technique of dream interpretation in which the analyst and the patient provide associations which are focused on the dream material, as opposed to the "free" association technique used by Freud.
Anaclitic depression: Profound depression in an infant when separated from its primary caretaker for a prolonged period.
Anesthesia: Loss of sense of touch or numbness in part of the body surface.
Anginal syndrome: Chest pain sometimes associated with cardiac insufficiency.
Anticipatory coping: Helping people to prepare for predictable life change or crisis through provision of information and social support.
Antidepressant drugs: Drugs which elevate mood and relieve depression.
Antisocial personality: Classification applied to people who display repeated conflicts with society, do not experience guilt, and are incapable of loyalty to others (synonymous with "sociopath" and "psychopath").
Anxiety: State of increased arousal and generalized feelings of fear and apprehension usually without a specific object of fear.
Anxiety disorders: Disorders listed in DSM III, in which anxiety plays an important role. Examples include phobic disorders, anxiety states, and obsessive compulsive disorders.
Antabuse: A drug which, when present in the blood

stream, causes severe body distress when the individual ingests alcohol.

Arousal: Either behavioral or physiological state of activation.

Asexual homosexuals: According to Bell and Weinberg's typology, homosexuals who are secretive and withdrawn, who are not highly sexually active, and who may not be exclusively homosexual or well adjusted.

Assertive training: A therapeutic technique, usually involving behavior rehearsal, in which persons learn to assert themselves appropriately.

Associative disturbance: Disturbance in the association of ideas which is often reflected in unusual speech patterns or patterns of logic. Characteristic of schizophrenic disorders.

Asthma: A respiratory disorder.

Attachment behavior: Behavior reflecting strong emotional bond between infant and his/her caretaker.

Autism: See Infantile autism.

Auxillary egos: Members of a psychodrama group or trained professionals who enact the role of the protagonist or interact in an opposite role.

Barbiturates: Sedatives used to induce sleep or relaxation.

"Barnum effect": The impression of accuracy produced by a test or other assessment method because the traits used to describe the person are characteristic of most people in the population and are therefore trivially accurate.

Base rate: The prevailing proportion of an event or object in the total population.

Behavior therapy: A method of psychotherapy that uses learning principles such as reinforcement, extinction, and modeling to change behavior.

Biochemical research: The search for the cause of a disorder in the biochemistry of the brain.

Biofeedback: A technique by which individuals can monitor their own physiological processes such as pulse, blood pressure, and brain waves with mechanical aid.

Biological preparedness: The idea that certain objects may for biological reasons be prepotent targets for phobias.

Bipolar episode: An affective disorder involving both depressive and manic episodes.

Blood alcohol levels: A measure of the amount of alcohol in the blood stream.

Bodily humors: The theory formulated by Hippocrates that inbalances in four body fluids (blood, black bile, yellow bile, and phlegm) cause depression and other mood changes.

Booster treatments: Additional treatment sessions administered during a follow-up period to bolster treatment gains.

Career: The sequence of movements from one position to another in a social or occupational system.

Case history: The collection of historical or biographical information on a single person for the purpose of discovering or illustrating psychological principles.

Catatonic schizophrenia: Form of schizophrenia characterized by a disturbance in motor behavior, often with alternating periods of immobility and extreme agitation.

Catecholamines: The neurotransmitters, together as a class.

Catharsis: Similar to abreaction; refers to expression of pent-up emotion.

Carthartic method: Discharge of emotional tension associated with repressed material by talking it out.

Childhood schizophrenia: Childhood disorder which occurs after a period of normal development. The child shows disturbances in social adjustment and in reality contact.

Chronic: Disorder of lengthy duration, often irreversible.

Classical conditioning: A form of learning in which a neutral stimulus (conditioned stimulus) is associated with an unconditioned stimulus to bring about a conditioned response.

Client-centered therapy: A therapy approach developed chiefly by Carl Rogers that is directed toward the attainment of the client's own goals in an accepting, empathic, and warm therapeutic atmosphere.

Clinical observation: Noting and recording abnormal behavior as it occurs.

Clinical experiment: Experiments conducted to illuminate the nature of acquisition, maintenance, and change of abnormal behavior.

Close coupled homosexuals: According to Bell and Weinberg's typology, homosexuals who live in quasi-marriages and tend to be well adjusted.

CNS (central nervous system) depressants: Drugs which have a sedative or hypnotic (sleep inducing) effect on an organism. Overdose leads to anesthesia, coma, and, finally, death.

Cocaine: A stimulant made from the coca plant that produces feelings of euphoria.

"Cold turkey" withdrawal: Usually refers to quitting heroin use abruptly, without support of other medication.

Collective unconscious: A term coined by Carl Jung to refer to the inherited memory traces, which are part of the unconscious and which are shared by the whole human race.

Compulsion: Irrational and repetitive impulse to perform some act or behavior.

Compulsive personality: A personality disorder characterized by preoccupation with matters of rules, order, organization, efficiency, detail, indecision, and restricted ability to express warm and tender emotions.

Concordance: In genetic research, the occurrence of the same disorder or behavior in two subjects.

Conditioned response: A simple response to a neutral stimulus that is the result of repeatedly pairing the neutral stimulus with another nonneutral stimulus that would have naturally elicited the response.

Conditioned stimulus: The neutral stimulus which elicits a particular response as a result of repeated pairings with a nonneutral or unconditioned stimulus that naturally elicits that response.

Conditions of worth: A person's view of his or her own experiences as being more or less worthy of respect. In the humanistic perspective, a predisposing factor in the development of abnormal behavior.

Conflict: Simultaneous arousal of opposing impulses, desires, or motives.

Conjoint family therapy: Therapeutic intervention with the entire family to alter family dynamics viewed as a total system.

Control group: Those subjects in an experiment who are not exposed to whatever experimental conditions are being studied and who serve as a comparison to assess the effects of the experimental manipulations.

Controlled drinking: An approach to alcoholism treatment which sanctions ingestion of small amounts of alcohol recreationally. This is in contrast to the more traditional abstinance approach.

Controlled drug: Substance defined as illegal to possess without medical prescription.

Controlled experiment: An experiment in which one variable is manipulated while all others are held constant.

Conversion reaction: A reaction involving bodily symptoms, usually of the skeletal musculature and sensory functions with no detectable tissue damage.

Correlation of causal factors: The degree to which factors occur together.

Correlational approach: Research in which the relationships between two or more variables are examined but no manipulations of the variables are used.

Co-twin: Term used in genetic research to refer to the twin of the index case.

Countertransference: Arousal of feelings of transference on the part of the analyst during the course of psychoanalytic therapy in response to behavior or characteristics of the client.

Coverage: Degree to which a classification or diagnosis is capable of identifying a significant segment of the population in question.

Covert sensitization: A behavioral technique in which the client imagines repulsive, aversive associations to eliminate a target behavior.

Crisis intervention: Methods for rendering immediate therapeutic assistance to people in acute distress.

Cross-fostering: An experimental procedure in which observations are made on normal children who are raised by disordered adopting parents.

Defense mechanism: In psychoanalysis, behavior which protects the person from anxiety provoked by sexual and aggressive impulses.

Deinstitutionalization: The policy of removing patients from hospitals and transferring their care to the community. In part, this treatment policy stems from a recognition of the debilitating effects of long-term hospitalization and the negative effects of the patient role.

Delirium: State of mental confusion characterized by confusion, disorientation, restlessness, excitement, and at times hallucinations.

Delirium tremens: Delirium associated with prolonged alcoholism and characterized by anxiety, hallucinations, and tremors.

Delusion: A usually persistent belief that is contrary to the consensus of other people.

Dementia: Severe mental disorder involving impairment of mental ability including memory and reasoning ability.

Dementia praecox: A term used by Emil Kraepelin to refer to a form of psychotic behavior now called schizophrenia.

Depression: A disorder characterized by apathy, dejection, sadness, and self-blame.

De-reflection: A therapeutic technique devised by Victor Frankl in which the person's capacity to live spontaneously is enhanced by instructions to ignore symptoms, focus on the present, and attend to everyday concerns and relationships.

Detoxification: Treatment for alcoholism consisting of removing alcohol from the patient's system.

Diathesis-stress: An hypothesis that asserts that individuals predisposed toward a particular psychological disorder will be affected by stress and will then manifest abnormal behavior.

Direct therapy: Behaviorally oriented sex therapy programs based on the idea that sexual dysfunctions can be treated directly without focusing on in-depth personality changes.

Displacement: Defense mechanism in which an emotional attitude or symbolic meaning is transferred from one object or concept to another.

Displacement: A defense mechanism that redirects emotion to less-dangerous objects.

Disregulation: Hypothesis that psychophysiological disorders are the result of disruption in the brain's regulatory feedback system with various other organ systems.

Dissociative disorders: Psychological disorders resulting from the apparent splitting off of some psychological function from the rest of conscious thought.

Dizygotic twins (DZ twins, fraternal twins): Twins that develop from two eggs fertilized by two different sperm and who have only approximately 50 percent of their genes in common, as do other sibling pairs.

Dopamine hypothesis: A theory that schizophrenia is caused by an increased level of the brain neurotransmitter, dopamine.

Double bind: An interpersonal relationship in which the person is confronted by mutually inconsistent messages to which he must respond.

Draw-a-person test: Projective test requiring that a picture of a person be drawn; inferences regarding the characteristics of the subject are then drawn.

Dream analysis: The interpretation of the patient's dreams in psychotherapy.

Dream censorship: In psychoanalytic theory, the process or manner in which the latent dream material is disguised to reduce the anxiety of the dream and permit undisturbed sleep.

Drift hypothesis: Hypothesis that psychologically disabled people, especially schizophrenics, "drift" to lower social status rather than that lower social status plays a direct causal role in the development of the disorder.

Drive: Internal conditions directing organism toward a specific goal, usually involving biological rather than psychological motives.

Drug addiction: Reliance on a drug developed through continual use; characterized by increased tolerance and withdrawal symptoms and physiological dependence.

Drug combination (interaction): The way in which two or more drugs affect the individual when the drugs are taken concurrently.

Drug detoxification: Usually refers to the process of medical and psychological support necessary after initial cessation of drug use.

Drug-induced euphoria: Intense feeling of pleasure and power produced following ingestion of drug.

DSM III: "Diagnostic and Statistical Manual of Mental Disorders," published by the American Psychiatric Association. The official list of diagnostic terms and definitions.

Dynamic viewpoint: The view of abnormal behavior in which intrapsychic conflicts are thought to be the cause.

Dysfunctional homosexuals: According to Bell and Weinberg's typology, homosexuals who are poorly adjusted sexually, socially, and psychologically.

Eccentric personality disorders: One of the clusters of personality disorders listed in DSM III which includes paranoid, introverted, and schizotypal personality disorders.

Ecology: The study of the relation or interaction between organisms and their physical or behavioral environment.

Ego: That part of the psychological structure that is usually described as the "self." It is the aspect of the personality that mediates between the needs of the id and reality.

Ego ideal: The person or "self" the individual thinks he could and should be.

Ego-dystonic homosexuality: A recent addition to the list of psychosexual disorders (indexed in DSM III) which involves homosexual thoughts and/or feelings which are personally distressing and unwanted.

Electroshock (EST) or electroconvulsive therapy (ECT): Use of the electric shock to the brain as treatment, usually for depression.

Empathy: The ability to appreciate and share the emotional or mental state of mind of another person.

Encounter group: Group including features of the T-group and the sensitivity group; emphasizes personal growth.

Endogenous: Resulting from or referring to internal causes.

Endogenous depression: Depression attributable to internal rather than external causes. No reasonable precipitating external cause can be found.

"Entrance" life events: Life events that involve moving into the social field (e.g. engagement, marriage, birth). Depressives and normals have the same number of entrance life events.

Epidemiological: The study of the distribution of illnesses in populations or geographic areas.

Epinephrine: Hormone secreted by the adrenal glands that acts as a stimulant. It is released when the body experiences stress.

Erratic personality disorders: One of the clusters of personality disorders listed in DSM III which includes histrionic, narcissistic, antisocial, and borderline personality disorders.

Ethnocentrism: Belief that one's own country, culture, and race are superior to other countries, cultures, and races.

Etiology: Cause or determinant.

Evoking stimuli (ES): In Mark's (1977) terminology, the stimuli that trigger a phobic response.

Exhibitionism: Displaying one's genitals to an involuntary observer for the purpose of sexual arousal.

Existential therapy: Therapy based on existential concepts, emphasizing the development of a sense of self-direction and meaning in one's existence.

"Exit" life events: Life events that involve some removal from the social field (e.g. death, divorce, or family member leaving home).

Exogenous: Resulting from or referring to external causes.

Exogenous depression: Depression attributable to external causes (death in family, separation from loved one).

Exorcism: Techniques practiced in medieval times for casting "evil spirits" out of the possessed or afflicted.

Experimental analogue: Experimental study of a phenomenon different from but analogous to the actual interests of the investigator.

Experimental group: In research, the group on which the manipulation of interest is performed.

Experimental neurosis: Maladaptive behavior produced in animals in the laboratory by inescapable conflicts and other types of stress.

Extinction: Gradual disappearance of conditioned response when it is no longer reinforced.

Family hypothesis: The idea that schizophrenia is caused by dysfunctional family functioning.

Family sacrifice: The idea that schizophrenia in a child is caused by rejection by his/her family.

Fearful personality disorder: One of the clusters of personality disorders listed in DSM III which includes avoidant, compulsive, and passive-aggressive personality disorders.

Fetishism: Use of an object or nongenital body part for sexual arousal and satisfaction.

Fixation: In psychoanalysis, developmental arrest at a childhood level of psychosexual development.

Flashback: Usually disturbing, brief, vivid, and intense reliving of a drug experience days, weeks, or months after the actual drug ingestion.

Flight of ideas: Characteristic of manic disorders. Rapid and irrational series of thoughts and/or images.

Flooding: Therapeutic technique in which the person is made to confront the stimuli that arouse anxiety until the anxiety extinguishes.

Follow-up study: Research procedure in which individuals are studied over a period of time or are recontacted at a later time after initial study.

Free-association: Psychoanalytic technique in which the analysand is instructed to say whatever comes to mind, without selection or censorship of any kind; the goal is to examine and clarify the implication of the material elicited.

Fugue: A type of dissociative reaction in which the person moves to a new locale, begins a new life, and is amnesic of his previous life.

Functional analysis: An analysis of the frequency of particular behaviors, the situations in which they occur, and their consequences. Used by behaviorally oriented clinicians and researchers.

Functional dyspareunia: Painful intercourse not caused exclusively by organic factors.

Functional homosexuals: According to Bell and Weinberg's typology, highly sexually active "swinging" homosexuals who tend to have a good psychological adjustment.

Functional psychosis: Severe disturbance in thought, behavior, and emotional behavior without known damage to the brain or other organ systems.

Gender identity disorders: Psychological disorders in which discomfort and inappropriateness about the person's anatomic sex is expressed and in which the behavior is generally congruent with the "opposite" sex.

General adaptation syndrome: A pattern of reaction to excessive stress; consists of the alarm reaction, the stage of resistance, and the stage of exhaustion.

General sexual dysfunction: The absence or weakness of the physiological changes in women that normally accompany the excitement phase of sexual response.

Generalized other: A concept developed by Mead (1934) which is used to summarize the way each person develops an idea of how other people will react to his or her behavior.

Genetic factors: Inherited genetic material which causes disorder.

Genetic heterogeneity: The theory that specific genes in specific combinations cause disorder.

Genetic marker: A known genetic characteristic which allows prediction of risk for a disorder.

Genetics: Scientific study of heredity.

Gestalt therapy: An approach to psychotherapy emphasizing the integration of thought, feeling, and action.

Glove anesthesia: A form of dissociative reaction in which the person reports a numbness in his or her hand from the tips of the fingers to a clear cut-off point at the wrist which does not conform to the neurological pattern to be expected if nerve damage were the cause.

Grandiose ideas: Exaggerated expression of self-importance and/or power.

Group therapy: Treating psychological disorders by having several persons seen simultaneously by a single therapist. Group interaction is an important therapeutic agent.

Hallucination: Perception in any sensory modality (but particularly auditory, visual, and tactile) without adequate external stimuli.

Hallucinogenic: Capable of producing hallucinations.

Hebephrenic schizophrenia: Schizophrenic pattern characterized by severe personality disintegration, confusion, and giggling.

Hidden observer: A part of consciousness, described by Hilgard, which continues to monitor external circumstances even though a person remains deeply hypnotized.

High-risk method: Research following persons believed to be at risk for developing a disorder over time, usually in comparison to a low-risk group for the purpose of identifying characteristics of the high-risk group that may play a causal role in the disorder.

High-risk strategy: A means of studying a disorder in which children judged at risk for the disorder are observed prospectively. Events which precede the disorder can hopefully be examined.

Hives: Skin condition characterized by itching patches. Often considered a stress-related disorder.

Homeostasis: The process whereby equilibrium or balance is maintained in a dynamic system such as the organism.

Homosexuality: Sexual attraction toward one's own sex.

Hot line: Telephone service where people in trouble can call and receive immediate attention and advice from trained volunteers.

Humanistic perspective: A view of abnormal behavior that emphasizes personal growth and emphasis on the whole person. Includes self-theories, some elements of existentialism, and some elements of phenomenology.

Hypnosis: Trancelike state resembling sleep, characterized by increased suggestibility.

Hypertension: A chronic elevation of blood pressure due to constriction of the arteries. Often a stress-related physical disorder.

Hypochondriasis: A psychological disorder in which an individual converts anxiety into a preoccupation with bodily functioning.

Hypothesis: Proposition tested in an experiment. May be denied or supported by empirical results but never proved conclusively.

Hysteria: A physical disability (paralysis or sensory loss) for which no organic causes can be found.

Id: The reservoir of instinctual drives in the psychological structure of the individual. It is the most primitive and most inaccessible structure of the personality.

Idiosyncratic intoxification: A radical and abrupt personality shift in an individual following substantial ingestion of alcohol.

Illness perspective: A view of abnormal behavior in which the language and concepts of physical medicine are used as a model to describe deviant behavior.

Implosive therapy: Form of flooding therapy.

Implosion therapy: A technique for reducing fears; the client is induced to imagine himself/herself in the most frightening situations and to visualize bizarre images.

Impotence: Absence or weakness of the physiological changes that produce an erection.

Incest: Sexual relations between close relatives.

Incidence: The rate at which new cases occur in a given place at a given time.

Incongruence: A discrepancy or conflict that the organism experiences. The discrepancy is between the self as the individual perceives it and the actual experience of the organism. For example, one may perceive oneself as having one set of characteristics, but an accurate symbolization of one's experience would indicate a different set of characteristics. A state of incongruence in the organism may be characterized as internal confusion or tension.

Index case (proband case): In genetic research, the individual in the family who has the diagnosed case of the disorder.

Infantile autism: A disorder in children in which the primary symptom, from infancy onward, seems to be the inability to relate to others. Also, speech disturbances and stereotyped behaviors are apparent.

Informed consent: Procedure for obtaining permission of research subjects to participate in an experiment after assuring that the subject is aware of the demands and risks of participating.

Inhibited orgasm: According to DSM III, the sexual disorders defined by persistent and repeated delay or absence of orgasm in males and females who are responsive to sexual stimuli and capable of experiencing a normal sexual excitement phase.

Inhibited sexual excitement: According to DSM III, a sexual disorder characterized by failure to attain or maintain sexual excitement until the sexual act is completed; commonly termed *impotence* in the male, and *frigidity* in the female.

Instrumental conditioning: Process of development of behavior in which the organism must emit the response before reinforcement can occur. Therefore, the response is instrumental in receiving reinforcement.

Interpretation: Statement made by an analyst to help the patient understand the unconscious basis of his behavior which repression and resistance have kept him from perceiving.

Interrater reliability: The extent to which independent observers can agree on ratings or other scores for a set of observations.

Interview: A psychological method of assessment involving a face-to-face conversation between subject and interviewer.

La belle indifference: Lack of concern and indifference about a physical symptom, often displayed by persons suffering from conversion disorders.

Latent content: In psychoanalytic theory, the unconscious or "real" meaning of a dream which is expressed in disguised, distorted, or symbolic form.

Learned helplessness: A concept referring to passive acceptance of discomfort and lack of responsiveness after responses do not provide a means of escape or alter the situation.

Learning perspective: A view of abnormal behavior that describes both a formulation of abnormal behavior as well as a relatively well-defined program of treatment based upon the principles of learning theory.

Lesbianism: Female homosexuality.

Lethal dose: A dose or amount of a drug that will result in death when ingested.

Lethality: The likelihood of fatal outcome for particular methods of suicide.

Life events: Common problems which temporarily engender stress and sadness in most individuals but which do not usually result in serious psychological disturbance.

Lithium carbonate: A drug shown to be useful in treating affective disorders.

Logotherapy: Viktor Frankl's existential therapy which involves helping the patient to assume responsibility for his or her life and his or her attitudes for it and to find personal meaning and value in everyday life.

Longitudinal study: A type of study which involves observations of a sample population at regular time intervals over an extended period of time.

Low rate of response: In the learning theory of depression the depressed person is not receiving reinforcement for the behaviors he emits. This results in an impoverishment of responses to the environment.

Lysergic acid diethylamide-25 (LSD): A potent hallucinogen.

Machiavellianism: As defined by Christie and Geis (1970), a personality trait characterized by manipulating others, lack of concern with conventional morality, lack of gross pathology, and low ideological commitment.

Magnetic fluids: Invisible energy which Anton Mesmer hypothesized was the reason some of his patients were cured.

Maintaining factors: Factors which reinforce abnormal behavior and thus maintain it over time.

Malleus Maleficarum: *The Witch Hammer,* a book written by two monks during the Middle Ages. Although the book purported to identify witches, it resulted in the persecution of poor people who happened to behave in a peculiar manner.

Mania: A form of psychosis involving extreme euphoria, hyperactivity, grandiose thinking, and sleep disturbances.

Manic episode: A period during which the person experiences euphoria, along with associated characteristics of mania. This period usually lasts more than one week.

Manifest content: In psychoanalytic theory, the content of the dream as recalled by the patient.

Marathon group: A form of group therapy run for long periods of time, the assumption being that defenses can be worn down by the fatigue produced through intensive and continuous group interaction.

March of progress school of history: A view of history which stresses breakthroughs and famous persons in each century.

Marijuana: Drug derived from the plant cannabis sativa, often used in cigarettes.

Marital schism: Marriage relationship characterized by conflict and discord which threatens continuation of marital relationship.

Marital skew: Marriage maintained at expense of distorted relationship in favor of one of the partners.

Masochism: Sexual deviation in which an individual obtains sexual gratification from having pain inflicted upon him/her.

Medical view: View that mental illness is attributable to organic or mental disease of some sort.

Mesmerism: Theory of hypnosis invoking "animal magnetism" advanced by Anton Mesmer.

Methadone: A synthetic addictive narcotic for treating heroin addicts; acts as a substitute for heroin.

Method lethality: The probability of death connected with a specific means of self-destruction.

Migraine headache: A form of headache associated with contractions of the cranial arteries and dilation of blood vessels in the brain.

Milieu therapy: Therapy in which disturbed patients live together in an atmosphere designed to maximize their sense of independence, their activity level, and their sense of dignity and participation.

Model: An analogy that helps a scientist order his findings and see important relationships among them.

Model psychoses: Psychoticlike states produced: by hallucinogenic drugs such as LSD and thought to be analogous to naturally occurring psychoses.

Model psychosis: Psychotic symptoms induced by drugs which are thought to provide a model for the study of the disorder itself.

Modeling: Behavior learned through imitation.

Monoamine oxidase inhibitors: Antidepressant drugs which prevent the enzyme monoamine oxidase from deactivating neurotransmitters of the brain and central nervous system.

Monogenic theory: Hypothesis that a disorder is transmitted by a single gene at one location on a chromosome.

Monozygotic twins (MZ twins): Twins who develop from a single fertilized egg and have exactly the same genotype.

Moral anxiety: In Freudian theory, the result of conflict between the id impulses and the superego. A person feeling moral anxiety will often feel intense shame or guilt.

Moral treatment: The treatment of the American asylum movement in the 19th century. It was assumed that the peace and serenity of the country and removal from the rapid pace of the city was essential to cure. The heart of moral treatment was disciplined routine.

Motor symptoms: In neurotic disorders, apparent loss of motor function with no apparent tissue damage (e.g., paralysis).

Multiaxial classification: Classification of disorders on multiple dimensions or aspects of behavior. The method employed by DSM III.

Multiple personality: Dissociative reaction characterized by the development of two or more relatively independent personalities in the same individual.

Narcotic drugs: Drugs such as morphine which may lead to physiological dependence and increased tolerance.

Narcotic antagonists: A group of drugs which block and reverse the effects of opiates.

Need: Biological or psychological condition whose gratification is necessary for the maintenance of homeostasis or for self-actualization.

Neuroleptic drugs: Tranquilizing drugs used in the treatment of schizophrenia.

Neurology: Field concerned with study of brain and nervous system.

Neuroses: Term previously used to denote conditions in which maladaptive behaviors serve as a protection against sources of unconscious anxiety.

Neurotransmitter: A chemical that transmits electrical signals between brain cells.

Nicotine: A mild stimulant found in tobacco.

Nondirective therapy: An approach to the client (usually associated with Rogerian therapy), in which the therapist does not define the client's problems or tell him or her how they might be solved.

Norepinephrine (noradrenalin): A hormone or biogenic amine that plays a role in transmitting neural impulses in many parts of the body, including the brain.

Norepinephrine depletion: A theory of depression held by Weiss, which states that depression is a result of lowered levels of the neurotransmitter norepinephrine.

Obsession: Recurrent idea or thought which intrudes and seems uncontrollable to the person experiencing it.

Obsessive-compulsive disorder: Preoccupation with unwelcome thoughts (obsession) and/or stereotyped, involuntary repetition of an unnecessary action (compulsion).

Oedipus complex: In psychoanalytic theory, belief that boys desire sexual relations with their mothers.

Open coupled homosexuals: According to Bell and Weinberg's typology, independent, nonattached homosexual couples.

Operant conditioning: Form of learning in which the correct response is rewarded and then becomes more likely to occur.

Operational definition: Defining a concept on the basis of the set of operations that are used to measure and observe it.

Opiates: Drugs derived from opium including heroin, morphine, and codeine.

Opium: Chemical substance derived from the opium poppy; one of the narcotic drugs.

Oral character: A personality type purportedly fixated at an early stage of psychosexual development (oral). Such persons are purported to be prone to develop alcoholism.

Organic brain syndrome: Psychological, behavioral, and physical disturbances caused by some known physical disease or injury.

Organic psychosis: A disorder in which intellectual or emotional functioning are impaired due to dysfunction.

Paradigm: A basic conceptual framework specifying concepts considered legitimate and procedures to be used in the collection and interpretation of data.

Paradigm clash: The conflict or clash between the prevailing view of normal science and a new, emerging conceptual scheme. Often the new paradigm produces a shift in the problems available for scientific investigation and transforms the ways in which the scientist sees the world.

Paradoxical intention: One of Viktor Frankl's techniques in which the patient is asked what he or she fears most and exaggerate a symptom to further a greater sense of mastery or control over the symptom.

Paranoid personality disorder: A personality disorder defined by suspiciousness and mistrust.

Paranoid schizophrenia: A type of schizophrenia characterized by delusions, hallucinations, and some personality disorganization.

Paraphilias: Psychosexual disorders included in DSM III which involve variations from the norms of conventional choice of sexual objects and choice of sexual activity in which the person is hindered in his or her capacity to engage in close, affectionate sexual relations.

Parataxic distortion: Unrealistic attitude or misperceptions of reality, with roots in childhood and carried over into adult relationships. The term was coined by H. S. Sullivan.

Partial penetrance: Theory that a known genotype does not always manifest itself phenotypically.

Participant observer: The collaborative role which the therapist assumes in treatment in Sullivan's interpersonal psychotherapy.

Pedophilia: Preference for obtaining sexual gratification through contact with children.

Penetrance: Percent of cases who manifest the trait in question.

Performance anxiety: Anxiety and concern about

performance which contributes to sexual dysfunctions.

Personality disorder: An inflexible pattern of behavior that may cause impairment in social or occupational functioning, presumably developed at an early age and of long duration.

Perspective: A theoretical point of view organized around a central conception which provides a framework for understanding phenomena.

Phenomenological: Referring to the immediate experience of the individual.

Phenothiazines: A class of drug found effective in the treatment of schizophrenia.

Phenotype: The observable characteristics that result from the combination of a person's genotype with environmental influences.

Phobia: Irrational fear, often associated with avoidance of specific objects and situations, such as crowds or heights.

Placebo effect: Any behavioral or psychological effect caused by creating a belief or expectancy that a change will occur.

Pleasure principle: In psychoanalytic theory, the desire or instinctual need to be immediately gratified regardless of reality constraints.

Polygenic theory: Hypothesis that a disorder is transmitted by two or more genes on a chromosome.

Polygene threshold model: Theory that genes causing a disorder exert a cumulative effect. However, only when a threshold number of genes is reached will the disorder occur.

Possession (spirit): Belief that people who behaved in a particular manner were inhabited by evil spirits.

Posthypnotic suggestion: Suggestion given during the hypnotic trance to be carried out by the person after he is brought out of the trance.

Precipitating environmental events: External stresses or events which are thought to act as a catalyst in causing disorders.

Preconscious: In Freudian theory the second level of consciousness which consists of contents the person can recall without great difficulty.

Predictive validity: Degree to which a test or measure is capable of predicting some future state or status of an individual.

Predisposing factor: Factor which lowers the individual's stress tolerance and paves the way for the appearance of a disorder.

Premack Principle: The Premack Principle states that the occurrence of a high-frequency behavior can be used to reinforce a low-frequency behavior.

Premature ejaculation: According to DSM III, the absence of voluntary control of ejaculation and orgasm during sexual activity, so that ejaculation occurs before it is desired.

Premorbid: Usually refers to adjustment of persons before they develop behavior problems.

Prevalence: In epidemiological studies of a disorder, the proportion of a population that has the disorder at a given time.

Primary prevention: Establishing environmental conditions designed to prevent occurrence of mental disorders.

Primary process: Usually refers to modes of thinking that are primitive, illogical, and perceptually vivid. Primary process may also refer to drive energy that is mobile and can be displaced onto other objects.

Primary sexual disorders: The term for sexual disorders in which a sexual history suggests that the person never functioned normally with respect to the disorder being evaluated.

Process-reactive dimension: Classification of schizophrenics according to whether the onset of the disorder is gradual (process) or sudden and precipitated by some traumatic event (reactive).

Prognosis: In diagnosis, a prediction of the future course and outcome of the patient's problem.

Prognostic dreams: According to Carl Jung, dreams which foretell a future event or warn the dreamer.

Projection: A defense mechanism in which the person disowns some impulse and attributes it to another person or object.

Projective test: Psychological tests using unstructured stimuli like ink blots or figures.

Prospective research: A method of research in which data is gathered before the phenomenon understudy has occurred.

Protagonist: A member of a psychodrama group who enacts relevant scenes from his/her past, present, or future, playing the role of himself or herself or other people.

Psychedelic drugs: Mind expanding or altering drugs, such as LSD, which may result in hallucinations.

Psychiatrist: A physician who specializes in the treatment of psychological disorders.

Psychoactive drug: Substance that affects the person's behavior or subjective experience.

Psychoanalysis: Theoretical model of psychological functioning and therapy technique developed by Sigmund Freud.

Psychoanalyst: Person who has received specialized training at a psychoanalytic institute.

Psychodrama: A group treatment developed by Jacob Moreno which uses techniques of dramatic play and unrehearsed acting to stimulate the spontaneous expression of feeling.

Psychological approach: An approach to abnormal behavior which de-emphasizes physicalistic explanations. Events in the person's life and intrapsychic interpretations of these events are viewed as important.

Psychological test: An assessment technique in

which the subject is presented with a series of stimuli to which he or she is asked to respond.

Psychosexual dysfunctions: Psychological disorders that are characterized by a failure to enjoy and/or achieve accepted sexual behaviors.

Psychosurgery: Brain surgery used to treat psychological disorders.

Psychotherapy: As defined by Strupp (1970), an interpersonal process designed to bring about changes of feelings, cognitions, attitudes, and behavior which have proven troublesome to the person seeking help from a trained professional.

Psychomimetic: Resembling psychosis.

Rape: To force sexual relations upon another person.

Rapid cycling of mood: Short-lived alternations between euphoria and depression.

Rapport: Relationship characterized by an attitude of cooperation, confidence, and harmony.

Rational-emotive therapy: Therapeutic approach developed by Albert Ellis that emphasizes cognitive-change techniques and change in irrational beliefs.

Reaction formation: According to dynamic theory, a state in which a person represses feelings that arouse anxiety and then professes the exact opposite of these feelings.

Reality anxiety: A state in which a person is threatened by something actual in the outside world.

Reality principle: Awareness of the demands of the environment and adjustment of behavior to meet these demands.

Recessive gene: Gene which has effect when it is paired with an identical gene.

Recreational use: Occassional use of alcohol or other drugs without pathology or serious disruption of life experiences.

Reform movement: Humanitarian spirit arising from American and French revolutions which resulted in kinder treatment and improved living conditions for mental patients.

Regulative activity: In Jungian thinking, the unconscious, through activities like dreams, works toward achieving psychic harmony and balance.

Reinforcement: The process by which response strength (i.e., the probability of a response) is changed as a result of either classical conditioning or operant conditioning.

Reliability: The extent to which a test or observation method is consistent in measuring whatever it does measure.

Repression: Defense mechanism in which impulses threatening to the ego are pushed out of awareness and into the unconscious.

Resistance: In psychoanalytic thinking, the tendency to resist treatment to avoid the anxiety which recognition of previously repressed material evokes.

Role theory (antisocial personality): An account offered by Gough which argues that the antisocial personality is undersocialized, lacking in empathy, and unable to evaluate behavior from the point of view of another.

Rorschach: A projective personality and diagnostic test making use of inkblots.

Sadism: Sexual deviation in which sexual gratification is obtained by inflicting pain upon others.

Satir's structured interview: An interview format developed by Virginia Satir which is used in family therapy and consists of a set of tasks which enables the therapist to learn about the family's rules and communication problems.

Schemas: In depression theory, schemas are habitual ways of thinking that actually reinforce the negative experiences the depressive typically reports.

Schizomimetic conditions: Conditions which produce behavior that is similar to schizophrenia.

Schizophrenia: A group of psychoses marked by severe disorganization of thought, distortion of perception, and of affect, by bizarre behavior, and frequently by social withdrawal.

Schizophrenogenic mother: A mother who is capable of causing schizophrenia in an offspring.

Secondary pain: Indirect benefit from symptoms.

Secondary prevention: Efforts to reduce the severity or rate of an existing disorder.

Secondary process: In Freudian thinking, usually refers to thinking that is logical or rational. It is also used to refer to drive or drive energy that is bound to specific objects or ideas.

Secondary sexual disorders: The term for sexual disorders in which a sexual history suggests that the person has functioned normally in the past with respect to the disorder being evaluated.

Self: In Jungian terminology, the "ultimate individuation"—the psychological organization that embodies all of the different and sometimes opposing elements of the psyche.

Self-actualization: Important theme of the humanistic movement. A process described by Maslow and others in which one develops the ability to perceive reality efficiently, be detached and objective, be interested in one's fellow human beings, and discriminate between means and ends. Self-actualized people are creative, have a sense of humor, and are able to resist the forces of the culture in which they live.

Self-esteem: A sense of personal worth.

Semantic differential: A rating scale with contrasting adjectives at each end of the scale.

Sensate focus: A series of gradual steps of specific sexual behaviors that are used in direct sex therapy programs to increase sexual pleasure and reduce performance demands and anxiety.

Sensory symptoms: In neurotic disorders, apparent loss of sensory function with no apparent tissue damage (i.e., apparent blindness, deafness, numbness).

Separation anxiety: Anxiety which may be intensely experienced, related to separation from a parent, caretaker, or significant other.

Sex role stereotype: Fixed conception of the behavior patterns and role characteristics of men or women.

Sexual inadequacy: Impaired ability to experience or give sexual gratification.

Sexual response cycle: The phases of physiological responses manifested by males and females to sexual stimulation as orgasm is approached and attained.

Sick role: Role provided by society for individual suffering from physical or mental disorder.

Single-subject experiments: Experiments conducted with a single individual, often using instrumental conditional methods.

Situational reaction: Maladaptive response to newly experienced life situations which are especially difficult or trying.

Social drift hypothesis: A theory used to explain the relationship between socioeconomic class and schizophrenia; schizophrenics naturally drift into the low socioeconomic class due to their reduced abilities to function effectively.

Social norms: Group or societal standards concerning behaviors viewed as appropriate or inappropriate.

Social perspective: A view of abnormal behavior that emphasizes the role of society in judging whether mental illness exists. This perspective looks to context and social reactions rather than symptoms in isolation.

Social role: Pattern of behavior expected of individual occupying given position in group.

Social stress hypothesis: A theory used to explain the relationship between socioeconomic class and schizophrenia. Lower social class and poverty create stress which creates schizophrenia.

Social support system: The available resources a person may turn to during times of stress. These resources may include family, friends, clubs, or community agencies.

Socialization: The process by which individuals adapt to and learn to cope with the demands of society over the course of the life span.

Sodomy: Sexual intercourse via the anus.

Somatic: Referring to the body.

Somatic weakness hypothesis: Beliefs that a particular organ is vulnerable to psychological stress, thus producing particular psychophysiological disorder.

Somatization disorder: "Neurotic" disorder in which physical complaints are prominent.

Somatoform: A "neurotic" disorder characterized by physical symptoms.

Somnambulism: Sleepwalking.

Specific emotion hypothesis: The hypothesis that specific attitudes or feeling states are associated with particular psychophysiological disorder.

Specific etiology: That causal condition which is necessary but not sufficient for an illness to occur; it does not by itself produce the illness.

Speed-freak: A person who abuses or is dependent on amphetamines or other stimulants.

Spontaneous remission (recovery): Recovery of a person with a psychological disorder in the absence of therapy or with minimal treatment.

Stimulants: Drugs that increase alertness and reduce fatigue.

Stimulus generalization: Tendency to respond to similar stimuli other than the original stimuli to which one learned to respond.

Stress: Any adjustive demand that requires coping behavior on part of individual or group.

Stressful "triggering" effects (depression): Events associated with employment, health-related events, and marital events which are related to depression.

Structured family therapy: A method of family therapy devised by Salvador Minuchin in which the therapist alters the way relationships and interactions between family members are structured and organized.

Stupor: State unresponsiveness, with partial or complete unconsciousness.

Substance abuse: Nonpathological use of a substance; episodes of intoxication without definite patterns of pathological use.

Substance dependence: Use of substance in a pattern that impairs social or occupational functioning. Usually tolerance or withdrawal effects are evident.

Suicidal ideation: Persistent thoughts or desires to kill oneself.

Suicidal risk: The probability that a person will commit suicide based on observed predictors.

Suicide: Intentionally taking one's own life.

Superego: That structure of the personality that is concerned with ethical and moral feelings and attitudes. The superego is usually identified with the "conscience."

Symptom: A sign or manifestation of a physical or psychological disorder.

Synapse: The gap between two neurons where the nerve impulse passes.

Syndrome: Patterns or constellations of symptoms that are typical of a disorder.

Systematic desensitization: A behavioral technique for eliminating anxiety responses to particular situations or stimuli.

T-group: Training group in which participants learn about the dynamics of effective group functioning and apply the principles to their own interactional problems.

Tardive dyskinesia: A neuromuscular disorder caused by the antipsychotic drugs, the phenothiazines.

Test-retest reliability: The degree to which test or measure is consistent in its measurement over repeated occasions.

THC (Tetrahydrocannabinol): The chemical which many chemists feel is the active ingredient in marijuana.

Thought disorder: Synonym for schizophrenia.

Token economy: A behavioral treatment of hospitalized patients in which desired behaviors are rewarded by tokens; the tokens can then be exchanged for a range of rewards from which the patients choose.

Tolerance (to drugs): A condition in which the continued use of some drugs results in the need for larger and larger doses to produce the same effect.

Tranquilizers: Drugs used for reduction of anxiety and tension or to reduce psychotic symptoms.

Transference: The analysand's feelings, attitudes, and expectations which are projected onto the analyst and which were once directed at significant persons in the patient's past.

Transmission of schizophrenia: The passing of schizophrenia from parent to child.

Transsexualism: Gender identification with the opposite sex or belief that one is of opposite sex.

Transvestism: The practice of dressing in the clothing of the opposite sex usually for the purpose of sexual stimulation.

Trephining: A practice of the stone age, in which a hole was cut in the skull of a person who was behaving strangely to allow the escape of evil spirits.

Tricyclic drug: One of a group of antidepressant drugs.

Twin studies: An experimental procedure in which twins, judged at risk for a disorder, are observed as sharing or not sharing the disorder.

Ulcer: An open sore or lesion in the wall of the stomach or in a portion of the small intestine produced by abnormally high levels of gastric activity.

Unconditional positive regard: Positive regard experienced toward an individual irrespective of that individual's values or behavior. As Rogers (1959) puts it: "If self-experiences of another are perceived by me in such a way that no self-experience can be discriminated as more or less worthy of positive regard than any other, then I am experiencing unconditional positive regard for this individual" (p. 208).

Unconditioned response: A natural, unlearned response to a stimulus.

Unconditioned stimulus: A stimulus which elicits a natural or unconditioned response.

Unconscious: The portion of the psychological structure of the individual where repressed or forgotten memories or desires reside. These memories or desires are not directly available to consciousness but can be made available through psychoanalysis or hypnosis.

Undue risk: Exposure of experimental subjects to unethical dangers or risks.

Upper-downer cycle: A pattern of drug use in which the person uses depressants to get to sleep, then uses stimulants to overcome depressant hangover; more depressants are then needed for sleep.

Validity: The degree to which a test is consistent with other sources of information about the same attributes or characteristics.

Variable: A measure of a characteristic that may take on one of a set of different qualities.

Vicarious conditioning: Learning by observing the reactions of others to stimuli or events.

Victorian morality: Pervasive social norms of the 19th century in Western Europe which stressed work, diligence, and achievement and discouraged outward expression of sexuality.

Voyeurism: Achievement of sexual pleasure through "peeping"; usually watching other persons disrobe and/or engage in sexual activities.

Vulnerability model: The idea that susceptability to schizophrenia is determined by genetic and acquired factors but triggered by life events.

Well-ordered asylum: Because early 19th-century American society viewed mental illness as stemming from social pressures and environmental tensions, institutions in America emphasized orderly, regular, and disciplined routine.

Withdrawal syndrome: Result of physical dependency on drugs in which an intense physical reaction occurs when the drug is discontinued.

Working through: In psychoanalytic therapy, the term refers to the need to confront resistance until satisfactory adjustment is achieved.

X-Factor: An unknown chemical that is thought to cause schizophrenia.

Zone of Transition: The slum area of a city heavily populated by schizophrenics.

References

Abelson, H. I., Fishburne, P. M., & Cisin, I. H. National survey on drug abuse, 1977: A nationwide study—youth, young adults, and older adults. Princeton, N.J.: Response Analysis Corporation, 1977.

Aguilera, D., & Messick, J. M. *Crisis Intervention,* 3d ed. St. Louis: The C. V. Mosby Co., 1978.

Akiskal, H. S., & McKinney, W. T. Overview of recent research in depression. *Archives of General Psychiatry,* 1975, *32* 285–305.

Albee, G. W. Conceptual models and manpower requirements in psychology. *American Psychologist,* 1968, *23,* 317–320.

Alexander, F. *Psychosomatic medicine: Its principles and applications.* New York: Norton, 1950.

Allen, K. E., Hart, B., Buell, J. S., Harris, F. R., & Wolf, M. M. Effects of social reinforcement on isolate behavior of a nursery school child. *Child Development,* 1964, *35,* 511–518.

American Medical Association. Failure to diagnose barbiturate intoxication. *The Citation,* 1971, *24,* 22–23.

American Psychiatric Association. *Diagnostic and statistical manual of mental disorders* (DSM III) (3rd ed.). Washington, D.C.: American Psychiatric Association, 1980.

American Psychiatric Association, Task Force on Nomenclature and Statistics. *Diagnostic and statistical manual of mental disorders* (3rd ed.). Washington, D.C.: American Psychiatric Association, 1980.

Andrasik, F., & Holroyd, K. A test of the specific effects in the treatment of tension headache. Paper presented at the *Association for the Advancement of Behavior Therapy Convention,* Chicago, November, 1978.

Annon, J. S. *The behavioral treatment of sexual problems.* Honolulu: Kapiolani Health Services, 1974.

Anonymous. *Alcoholics Anonymous.* New York: Works Publishing, Inc., 1939.

Athanasiou, R., Shaver, P., & Tavris, C. Sex. *Psychology Today,* 1970, *4,* 37–52.

APA Monitor. Here to stay? Marijuana. *APA Monitor,* January 1976, *5, 10.*

Aponte, H., & Hoffman, L. The open door: A structural approach to a family with an anorectic child. *Family Process,* 1973, *12,* 1–44.

Arieti, S. Manic-depressive psychosis. In S. Arieti (Ed.), *American handbook of psychiatry.* New York: Basic Books, 1959.

Aronow, E., & Reznikoff, M. *Rorschach content interpretation.* New York: Grune & Stratton, 1976.

Bakal, D. Headache: A biopsychological perspective. *Psychological Bulletin,* 1975, *82,* 369–382.

Baldessarini, R. J. *Chemotherapy in psychiatry.* Cambridge, Mass: Harvard University Press, 1977.

Ball, J. C., Smith, J. P., & Graff, H. (Eds.). International survey. *Addictive Diseases,* 1977, *3,* 1–138.

Bandura, A. A social learning interpretation of psychological dysfunctions. In Perry Landon and David Rosenhan (Eds.), *Foundations of Abnormal Psychology.* New York: Holt, Rinehart & Winston, 1968.

Bandura, A. Psychotherapy based on modeling principles. In A. E. Bergin & S. L. Garfield (Eds.), *Handbook of psychotherapy and behavior change.* New York: Wiley, 1971.

Bandura, A. Self-efficacy: Toward a unifying theory of behavioral change. *Psychological Review,* 1977, *84,* 191–215.

Bandura, A. Social learning analysis of aggression. In E. Ribes-Inesta (Ed.), *Analysis of delinquency and aggression.* Hillsdale, N.J.: Erlbaum, 1976.

Bandura, A., Blanchard, E. B., & Ritter, B. The relative efficacy of desensitization and modeling approaches for inducing behavioral, affective, and cognitive changes. *Journal of Personality and Social Psychology,* 1969, *13,* 173–199.

Copyright 1969 by the American Psychological Association.

Bandura, A., Grusec, J. E., & Menlove, F. L. Vicarious extinction of avoidance behavior. *Journal of Personality and Social Psychology,* 1967, *5,* 16–23.

Bandura, A., & Rosenthal, T. L. Vicarious classical conditioning as a function of arousal level. *Journal of Personality and Social Psychology,* 1966, *3,* 54–62.

Barber, B. The ethics of human experimentation with human subjects. *Scientific American,* 1976, *234,* 25–31.

Barber, T. X. *LSD, marijuana, yoga, and hypnosis.* Chicago: Aldine, 1970.

Bard, M. *Training police as specialists in family crisis intervention.* Washington, D.C.: U.S. Government Printing Office, 1970.

Bard, M., & Berkowitz, B. Training police as specialists in family crisis intervention: A community psychology action program. *Community Mental Health Journal,* 1967, *3,* 315–317.

Bateson, G., Jackson, D. D., Haley, J., & Weakland, J. Toward a theory of schizophrenia. *Behavioral Science,* 1956, *1,* 251–264.

Baumgold, J. Agoraphobia: Life ruled by panic. *New York Times Magazine,* December 4, 1977, 46. © 1977 by The New York Times Company. Material reprinted by permission.

Beck, A. T. Cognition, affect, and psychopathology. *Archives of General Psychiatry,* 1971, *24,* 495–500.

Beck, A. T. Cognitive therapy: Nature and relation to behavior therapy. *Behavior Therapy,* 1970, *1,* 184–200.

Beck, A. T. *Depression: Clinical, experimental, and theoretical aspects.* New York: Hoeber (Harper & Row), 1967.

Beck, A. T., Beck, R., & Kovacs, M. Classification of suicidal behaviors: I. Quantifying intent and medical lethality. *American Journal of Psychiatry,* 1975, *132,* 285–287.

Beck, A. T., Kovacs, M., & Weissman, A. Assessment of suicidal intention: The scale for suicide ideation. *Journal of Clinical and Consultant Psychology,* 1979, *47,* 243–252.

Beck, A. T., Resnik, H. L. P., & Lettieri, D. J. (Eds.). *The prediction of suicide.* Bowie, Md.: Charles Press, 1974.

Beck, S. J., Beck, A. L., Levitt, E. E., & Molish, H. B. *Rorschach's test I. Basic processes* (3rd ed.). New York: Grune & Stratton, 1961.

Becker, H. S. Becoming a marijuana user. *American Journal of Sociology,* 1953, *59,* 235–242.

Bednar, R. L., & Kaul, T. J. Experiential group research: Current perspectives. In S. L. Garfield & A. E. Bergin (Eds.), *Handbook of psychotherapy and behavior change* (2nd ed.). New York: Wiley, 1978.

Bell, A. *Homosexuality.* Lecture delivered at the Institute for Sex Research Summer Program, Bloomington, Indiana, July 13, 1973.

Bell, A. P., & Weinberg, M. S. *Homosexualities: A study of diversity among men and women.* New York: Simon and Schuster, 1978. Copyright © 1978 by Alan P. Bell and Martin S. Weinberg. Material reprinted by permission of Simon & Schuster, a Division of Gulf & Western Corporation.

Belliveau, F., & Richter, L. *Understanding human sexual inadequacy.* New York: Bantam, 1970. Copyright © 1970 by Fred Belliveau and Lin Richter.

Benjamin, H. *The transsexual phenomenon.* New York: Julien Press, 1966.

Bentler, P. A typology of transsexualism: Gender identity theory and data. *Archives of Sexual Behavior,* 1976, *5,* 567–584.

Bergin, A. E., & Lambert, M. J. The evaluation of therapeutic outcomes. In S. L. Garfield & A. E. Bergin (Eds.), *Handbook of psychotherapy and behavior change* (2nd ed.). New York: Wiley, 1978.

Bernard, J. Kurt Lewin Memorial address. *American Psychological Association,* 1976.

Bernstein, J. G. Prescribing antipsychotics. *Drug Therapy for the Family Physician,* 1979, *9,* 71–88.

Bieber, I., Dain, H. J., Dince, O. R., Drelich, M. G., Grand, H. G., Grundlack, R. H., Kremer, M. W., Rifkin, A. H., Wilbur, C. B., & Bieber, T. B. *Homosexuality: A psychoanalytic study.* New York: Basic Books, 1962.

Blashfield, R. K., & Draguns, J. G. Evaluative criteria for psychiatric classification. *Journal of Abnormal Psychology,* 1976, *85,* 140–150.

Bleuler, E. *Dementia praecox, or the group of schizophrenias.* J. Zinkin (Trans.). New York: International Universities Press, 1950. (Originally published in 1911.)

Block, D., & LaPerriere, K. Techniques of family therapy: A conceptual frame. In D. Block (Ed.), *Techniques of family psychotherapy: A primer.* New York: Grune & Stratton, 1973.

Bloom, B. *Community Mental Health,* Monterey, Calif.: Brooks-Cole, 1977.

Bloom, B. L. *Social and community interventions. Annual Review of Psychology,* 1980, *31,* 111–142.

Bloom, B. L. Strategies for the prevention of mental disorders. In Division 27, American Psychological Association, Task Force on Community Mental Health, *Issues in community psychology and preventive mental health.* New York: Behavioral Publications, 1971.

Blum, R. *Utopiates.* New York: Atherton, 1964.

Blum, R. H., & Associates. *Students and drugs* (Vol. 2). San Francisco: Jossey Bass, 1969.

Boekelheide, P. D. Incest and the family physician. *Journal of Family Practice,* 1978, *6,* 87–90.

Bootzin, R. A stimulus control treatment for insomnia. Proceedings of the American Psychological Association, 1972, *1,* 395–396.

Bower, E. M. Primary prevention of mental and emotional disorders: A conceptual framework and active possibilities. *American Journal of Orthopsychiatry,* 1963, *33,* 832–848. Copyright 1963 by the American Orthopsychiatric Association, Inc.

Bowers, K. S. *Hypnosis for the seriously curious.* Monterey, Calif.: Brooks-Cole, 1976.

Bowlby, J. *Attachment and loss: Separation, anxiety and anger* (Vol. 2). New York: Basic Books, 1973.

Brady, J. V. Ulcers in "executive" monkeys. *Scientific American,* October 1958, 95–100.

Brenner, M. H. *Mental illness and the economy.* Cambridge, Mass.: Harvard University Press, 1973.

Bridell, D. W., & Wilson, G. T. The effects of alcohol and expectancy set on male sexual arousal. *Journal of Abnormal Psychology,* 1976, *85,* 225–234.

Brody, J. E. Study finds some homosexuals are happier than heterosexuals. *The New York Times,* Sunday, July 9, 1978.

Broverman, I. K., Broverman, D. M., & Clarkson, F. E. Sex-Pole stereotypes and clinical judgments of mental health. *Journal of Consulting and Clinical Psychology,* 1970, *34,* 1–7.

Brown, G. W., Birley, J. L. T., & Wing, J. K. Influence of family on the course of schizophrenic disorders: A replication. *British Journal of Psychiatry,* 1972, *121,* 241–258.

Buchanan, P. C. Innovative organizations: A study in organizational development. In *Applying behavioral science research in industry.* New York: Industrial Relations Counselor, 1964.

Buchwald, A. M., & Young, R. D. Some comments on the foundations of behavior therapy. In C. M. Franks (Ed.), *Behavior therapy: appraisal and status.* New York: McGraw-Hill, 1969.

Buck, J. A., & Graham, J. R. The 4–3 MMPI profile type: A failure to replicate. *Journal of Consulting and Clinical Psychology,* 1978, *46,* 344.

Bucklew, J. *Paradigms for psychopathology: A contribution to case history analysis.* Chicago: J. B. Lippincott, 1960.

Burns, R. S., & Lerner, S. E. Perspectives: Acute phencyclidine intoxication. *Clinical Toxicology,* 1976, *4,* 14–18.

Buss, A. H. *Psychopathology.* New York: Wiley, 1966.

Cadoret, R. J. Psychopathology in adopted away offspring of biologic parents with antisocial behavior. *Archives of General Psychiatry,* 1978, *35,* 176–184.

Cahalan, D., Cisin, I. H., & Crossley, H. M. *American drinking practices: A national study of drinking behaviors and attitudes.* New Brunswick, N.J.: Rutgers Center of Alcohol Studies, 1969.

Cameron, N. *Personality development and psychopathology: A dynamic approach.* Boston: Houghton Mifflin, 1963. Copyright © 1963 by Houghton Mifflin Company. Material reprinted by permission of the publishers.

Campbell, J. (Ed.). *The portable Jung.* New York: Viking Press, 1971.

Cannon, W. B. The role of emotion in disease. *Annals of Internal Medicine,* 1936, *9,* 1453–1456.

Cannon, W. B. *The wisdom of the body.* New York: W. W. Norton, 1939.

Caplan, G. *Principles of preventive psychiatry.* New York: Basic Books, 1964.

Caplan, G. *The theory and practice of mental health consultation.* New York: Basic Books, 1970.

Caplan, R. B. *Psychiatry and the community in nineteenth century America.* New York: Basic Books, 1969.

Caprio, F. S. "Fetishism." In A. Ellis & A. Abarbanel (Eds.), *Encyclopedia of sexual behavior.* New York: Jason Aronson, 1973.

Carr, A. T. Compulsive neurosis: A review of the literature. *Psychological Bulletin,* 1974, *81,* 311–318.

Casey, R. L., Masuda, M., and Holmes, T. H. Quantitative study of recall of life events. *Journal of Psychosomatic Research,* 1967, *11,* 239–247.

Cass, L. K., & Thomas C. B. *Childhood pathology and later adjustment: The question of prediction.* New York: Wiley, 1979. Copyright 1979 John Wiley & Sons, Inc.

Cassell, S. Effect of brief puppet therapy upon the emotional responses of children undergoing cardiac catheterization. *Journal of Counsulting Psychology,* 1965, *29,* 1–8.

Cautela, J. R. The treatment of alcoholism by covert sensitization. *Psychotherapy: Theory, Research, and Practice,* 1970, *7,* 86–90.

Cautela, J. R. Treatment of compulsive behavior by covert sensitization. *Psychological Record,* 1966, *16,* 33–41.

Chapman, J. The early symptoms of schizophrenia. *British Journal of Psychiatry,* 1966, *112,* 225–251.

Choron, J. *Suicide.* New York: Charles Scribner and Sons, 1972.

Christie, R., & Geis, F. *Studies in Machiavellianism.* New York: Academic Press, 1970.

Clayton, P., Halikas, J., & Maurice, W. The

depression of widowhood. *British Journal of Psychiatry,* 1972, *120,* 71–77.

Cleckley, H. *The mask of sanity* (5th ed.). St. Louis: C. V. Mosby, 1976.

Cleckley, H. Psychopathic personality. In O. L. Sills (Ed.), *International encyclopedia of the social sciences* (Vol. 13). New York: Macmillan Co., 1968.

Coan, R. W. Personality variables associated with cigarette smoking. *Journal of Personality and Social Psychology,* 1973, *26,* 86–104.

Coggins, W. J. Costa Rica Cannabis Project: An interim report on the medical aspects. In M. C. Braude & S. Szarn (Eds.), *Pharmocology of marijuana.* New York: Raven Press, 1976.

Cohen, S. Angel dust. *Journal of the American Medical Association,* 1977, *238,* 515–516.

Cohen, W., & Paul, G. L. Current trends and recommended changes in extended-care placement of mental patients: The Illinois system as a case in point. *Schizophrenia Bulletin,* 1976.

Cole, J. O. Schizophrenia: The therapies, a broad perspective. In J. D. Cole & L. E. Hollister (Eds.), *Schizophrenia.* MEDCOM, Inc., 1970.

Columbus Dispatch. Teen smoking rate dips, government study shows. *Columbus Dispatch,* April 26, 1979, A–5.

Cooper, J. R. (Ed.). *Sedative-hypnotic drugs: Risks and benefits.* U.S. Department of Health, Education, and Welfare, DHEW Publication No. (ADM) 78–592. Washington, D.C.: U.S. Government Printing Office, 1977.

Cory, D. W., & LeRoy, J. P. *The homosexual and his society: A view from within.* New York: Citadel, 1964.

Cotton, N. S. The familial incidence of alcoholism: A review. *Journal of Studies on Alcohol,* 1979, *40,* 89–116.

Cowen, E. L., Gesten, R. L., & Weissberg, R. P. An integrated network of preventively oriented school-based mental health approaches. In R. H. Price and P. E. Politser (Eds.), *Evaluation and action in the social environment.* New York: Academic Press, 1980.

Cowen, E. L., Izzo, L. D., Miles, H., Telschow, E. F., Trost, M. A., & Zax, M. A preventive mental health program in the school setting: Description and evaluation. *Journal of Psychology,* 1963, *56,* 307–356.

Cowen, E. L., Trost, M. A., Lorion, R. P., Dorr, D., Izzo, L. D., & Isaacson, R. V. *New ways in school mental health: Early detection and prevention of school maladaption.* New York: Human Sciences, 1975.

Cowen, E. L., Zax, M., Izzo, L. D., & Trost, M. A. Prevention of emotional disorders in the school setting: A further investigation. *Journal of Consulting Psychology,* 1966, *30,* 381–387.

Cox, A., et al. A comparative study of infantile autism and specific developmental receptive language disorder: II. Parental characteristics. *British Journal of Psychiatry,* 1975, *126,* 146.

Coyne, J. C. Depression and the response of others. *Journal of Abnormal Psychology,* 1976, *85,* 186–193.

Coyne, J. C. Toward an interactional description of depression. *Psychiatry,* 1976, 1976, *39,* 14–27.

Crane, G. E. Persistence of neurological symptoms due to neuroleptic drugs. *American Journal of Psychiatry,* 1971, *127,* 1407–1410.

Crane, G. E. Persistent dyskinesia. *British Journal of Psychiatry,* 1973, *122,* 395–405.

Dabrowski, K. In J. Aronson (Ed.), *Positive distintegration.* Boston: Little, Brown, 1964.

Da Fonseca, A. F. *Analise heredo-clinica des perturbacoes affectivas* (Doctoral dissertation, Universidade do Porto, Portugal, 1959.

Davis, J. M. Overview: Maintenance therapy in psychiatry: II. Affective disorders. *American Journal of Psychiatry,* 1976, *133,* 1–13.

Davis, W. E. Race and the differential power of the MMPI. *Journal of Personality Assessment,* 1975, *39,* 138–40.

Dawson, E. B., Moore, T. D., & McGanity, W. J. The mathematical relationship of drinking water, lithium, and rainfall to mental hospital admissions. *Diseases of the Nervous System,* 1970, *31,* 811–820.

Delay, J., Deniker, P., & Harl, J. Utilization therapeutique psychiatrique d'une phenothiazine d'action centrale elective (4560 RP). *Annals of Medical Psychology,* 1952, *110,* 112–117.

DeLong, J. V. The methadone habit. *New York Times Magazine,* March 16, 1975, 16, 78, 80, 86, 90, 91, 93.

DeMyer, M. K., et al. Parental practices and innate activity in normal, autistic, and brain-damaged infants. *The Journal of Autism and Childhood Schizophrenia,* 1972, *2,* 49.

Denber, H. C. B. *Textbook of clinical psychopharmacology.* New York: Stratton Intercontinental Medical Book Corporation, 1979.

Denner, B., & Price, R. H. (Eds.). *Community mental health: Social action and community reaction.* New York: Holt, Rinehart & Winston, 1973.

Densen-Gerber, J., & Benward, J. *Incest is a causative factor in antisocial behavior: An exploratory study. Contemporary Drug Problems,* 1975, *4,* 323–340.

DePiano, F. A., & Salzberg, H. C. Clinical applications of hypnosis to three psychosomatic disorders. *Psychological Bulletin,* 1979, *86,* 1223–1235.

DeLoreto, A. O. *Comparative psychotherapy: An experimental analysis.* Chicago: Aldine-Atherton, 1971.

Dollard, J., & Miller, N. E. *Personality and psychotherapy.* New York: McGraw-Hill, 1950.

Dooley, D., & Catalano, R. Economic change as a cause of behavior disorder. *Psychological Bulletin,* 1980, *87,* 450–468.

Drugs and psychiatry: A new era. Newsweek, November 12, 1979, 98–106.

Dunham, H. W. *Community and schizophrenia: An epidemiological analysis.* Detroit: Wayne State University Press, 1965.

DuPont, R. L. *Current national heroin use trends.* Paper presented at the Scientific Program of the Annual Meeting, American Psychiatric Association, Miami, Florida, May 10–14, 1976.

Dupont, R. I., Goldstein, A., & O'Donnell, J. Treatment modalities for narcotics addicts. In R. Dupont, A. Goldstein, & J. O'Donnell (Eds.), *Handbook on drug abuse.* Washington, D.C.: National Institute on Drug Abuse, U.S. Government Printing Office, 1979.

Durkheim, E. *Suicide* (J. A. Spaulding & G. Simpson, trans.). London: Routledge & Kegan Paul, 1952.

Eastman, C. Behavioral formulations of depression. *Psychological Review,* 1976, *83,* 277–291.

Edinburg, G., Zinberg, N., & Kelson, W. *Clinical interviewing and counseling: Principles and techniques.* New York: Appleton, 1975.

Eisenberg, L. The autistic child in adolescence. *American Journal of Psychiatry,* 1956, *112,* 607.

Eisenberg, L. School phobia: A study in the communication of anxieties. *American Journal of Psychiatry,* 1958, *114,* 712–718.

Ellis, A. The basic clinical theory of rational-emotive therapy. In A. Ellis & R. Grieger (Eds.), *Handbook of rational-emotive therapy.* New York: Springer Publishing Co., 1977. Copyright © 1977 by Springer Publishing Company, Inc. Material used by permission.

Ellis, A. Rational emotive therapy. In V. Binder, A. Binder, & B. Rimland (Eds.), *Modern therapies.* Englewood Cliffs, N.J.: Prentice-Hall, 1976.

Emrick, C. D. A review of psychologically oriented treatment of alcoholism: II. The relative effectiveness of different treatment approaches and the effectiveness of treatment vs. no treatment. *Journal of Studies on Alcohol,* 1975, *36,* 88–108.

Engel, B. P. Clinical applications of operant conditioning techniques in the control of cardiac arrhythmias. *Seminars in Psychiatry,* 1973, *5,* 433–438.

Ethical issues for human services. *Behavior Therapy,* 1977, *8,* V–VI.

Etzioni, A. Methadone: Best hope for now. *Smithsonian Magazine,* April 1973, *48,* 67–74.

Eysenck, H. J. The effects of psychotherapy: An evaluation. *Journal of Consulting Psychology,* 1952, *16,* 319–324.

Fagen, J. The importance of Fritz Perls having been. *Voices,* Spring 1971, *7,* 16–20.

Fairweather, G. W. (Ed.) *Social psychology in treating mental illness: An experimental approach.* New York: Wiley, 1964.

Fairweather, G. W., Sanders, D. H., Cressler, D. L., & Maynard, H. *Community life for the mentally ill: An alternative to institutional care.* Chicago: Aldine, 1969.

Faris, R. E. L., & Dunham, H. W. Mental disorders in urban areas: An ecological study of schizophrenia and other psychoses. Chicago: University of Chicago Press, 1939.

Farkas, G. M., & Rosen, R. C. The effect of alcohol on elicited male sexual response. *Journal of Studies on Alcohol,* 1976, *37,* 265–272.

Farkas, G. M. An ontological analysis of behavior therapy. *American Psychologist,* 1980, *35,* 364–374.

Federal Commission OK's psychosurgery. *APA Monitor,* November 1976, 4–5.

Ferster, C. B. A functional analysis of depression. *American Psychologist,* 1973, *28,* 857–870.

Fields, S. Folk healing for the wounded spirit. *Innovations.* 1976, *3,* 3–18.

Fields, S. Support and succor for the "walking wounded." *Innovations* Spring 1978, *5*(1), 2–15.

Fieve, R. R. *Moodswing: The third revolution in psychiatry.* New York: Bantam, 1975. Copyright © 1975 by Ronald R. Fieve. Material reprinted by permission of William Morrow & Company.

Fink, M. Myths of "Shock Therapy." *American Journal of Psychiatry,* 1977, *134,* 991–996.

Fixsen, D. L., Phillips, E. L., Phillips, E. A., & Wolf, M. M. The teaching-family model of group home treatment. Paper presented at the meeting of the American Psychological Association, Honolulu, Hawaii, September 1972.

Flaherty, J. A. Psychiatric complications of medical drugs. *The Journal of Family Practice,* 1979, *9,* 243–254.

Folstein, S., & Rutter, M. Genetic influences and infantile autism. *Nature,* 1977, *265,* 726.

Foltz, E. L., & Millett, F. E. Experimental psychosomatic disease states in monkeys: I. Peptic ulcer-executive monkeys. *Journal of Surgical Research,* 1964, *4,* 445–453.

Footlick, J. K., & Lowell, J. The ten phases of Billy. *Newsweek,* December 18, 1978, 106.

Ford, C. S., & Beach, F. A. *Patterns of sexual behavior.* New York: Harper and Bros., 1952.

Foucault, M. *Madness and civilization* (R. Howard, Trans.). New York: Random House, 1965.

Frank, J. D. Persuasion and Healing, 2d ed. Baltimore: Johns Hopkins University Press, 1973.

Frankl, V. E. *The doctor and the soul: From psychotherapy to logotherapy.* New York: Knopf, 1965.

Frankl, V. E. *Man's search for meaning: An introduction to logotherapy.* New York: Washington Square Press, 1971.

Frankl, V. E. *The will to meaning.* New York: New American Library, 1970.
Freud in a letter to Fleiss, 1897. In E. Jones, *The life and works of Sigmund Freud* (Vol. 1). New York: Basic Books, 1953.
Freud, S. Letter to an American mother. *American Journal of Psychiatry,* 1951, *102,* 786.
Freud, S. *New Introductory lectures on psychoanalysis.* New York: Norton, 1933.
Freud, S. On psychotherapy. In E. Jones (Ed.), *Sigmund Freud Collected papers.* (Vol. 1). New York: Basic Books, Hogarth Press, Ltd., 1959. (Originally published, 1904.)
Friar, L. R., & Beatty, J. Migraine: Management by trained control of vasoconstriction. *Journal of Consulting and Clinical Psychology,* 1976, *44,* 46–53.
Fromm-Reichman, F. *Principles of intensive psychotherapy.* Chicago: University of Chicago Press, 1950.
Gagnon, J. H. *Human sexualities.* Glenview, Ill.: Scott Foresman, 1977.
Gallup, G. *Three part series on the homosexual in U.S. society.* Unpublished paper, Princeton, New Jersey, July, 1977.
Gardos, G., & Cole, J. O. Maintenance antipsychotic therapy: Is the cure worse than the disease? *American Journal of Psychiatry,* 1976, *133,* 323–336.
Garfield, S. L. Research on client variables. In S. Garfield & A. Bergin (Eds.), *Handbook of psychotherapy and behavior change.* New York: Wiley, 1978.
Garfield, S. L., & Kurtz, R. Clinical psychologists in the 1970s. *American Psychologist,* 1976, *31,* 1–9.
Gebhard, P. H. Fetishism and sadomasochism. *Science and Psychoanalysis,* 1969, *15,* 71–80.
Gebhard, P. H., Gagnon, J. H., Pomeroy, W. B., & Christenson, C. V. *Sex Offenders.* New York: Harper & Row, 1965.
Gelenberg, A. J. Prescribing antidepressants. *Drug Therapy,* 1979, *9,* 95–112.
Glass, C. R., Gottman, J. M., & Shmurak, S. H. Response acquisition and cognitive self-statement modification approaches to dating skills training. *Journal of Counseling Psychology,* 1976, *23,* 520–526.
Goffman, E. *Asylums: Essays on the social situation of mental patients and other inmates.* Garden City, N.J.: Anchor, 1961.
Gold, R. Stop it, you're making me sick. Paper (expanded version) presented at the American Psychiatric Association, Honolulu, Hawaii, May 9, 1973.
Goldberg, S., & Lewis, M. Play behavior in the year-old infant: Early sex differences. *Child development,* 1969, *40,* 21–31.
Goldenberg H. *Abnormal psychology: A social/community approach.* Monterey, Calif.: Brooks-Cole, 1977.
Goldfried, M. R., & Daviso G. C. *Clinical behavior therapy.* New York: Holt, Rinehart & Winston, 1976.
Goldfried, M. R., & Sprafkin, J. N. *Behavioral personality assessment.* Morristown, N.J.: General Learning Press, 1974. © 1974 General Learning Corporation. Material reprinted by permission of Silver Burdett Company.
Goldfried, M. R., Stricker, G., & Weiner, I. B. *Rorschach handbook of clinical and research applications.* Englewood Cliffs, N.J.: Prentice-Hall, 1971.
Goodwin, D. W. Alcoholism and heredity. *Archives of General Psychiatry,* 1979, *36,* 57–64. Copyright 1979, American Medical Association.
Gordon, J. S. Who is mad? Who is sane? R. D. Laing: In search of a new psychiatry. *The Atlantic,* January 1971, 50–66.
Gottesman, I. I., & Shields, J. A polygenic theory of schizophrenia. *Proceedings of the National Academy of Sciences,* 1967, *58,* 199–205.
Gottman, J., & Markman, H. Experimental designs in psychotherapy research. In S. L. Garfield & A. E. Bergin (Eds.), *Handbook of psychotherapy and behavior change* (2nd ed.). New York: Wiley, 1978.
Gough, H. G. A sociological theory of psychopathy. *American Journal of Sociology,* 1948, *53,* 359–366.
Gould, L. C. Berberian, R. M., Kasl, S. V., Thompson, W. D., & Kleber, H. D. Sequential patterns of multiple-drug use among high school students. *Archives of General Psychiatry,* 1977, *34,* 216–222.
Gove, W. R. (Ed.) *The labeling of deviance: Evaluating a perspective.* Beverly Hills, Calif.: Sage, 1975.
Grace, W. J., & Graham, D. T. Relationship of specific attitudes and emotions to certain bodily diseases. *Psychosomatic Medicine,* 1952, *14,* 243–251.
Graham, D. T., Kabler, J. D., & Graham, F. K. Physiological response to the suggestion of attitudes specific for hives and hypertension. *Psychosomatic Medicine,* 1962, *24,* 159–169.
Graham, D. T., Stern, J. A., & Winokur, G. Experimental investigation of the specificity of attitude hypothesis in psychosomatic diseases. *Psychosomatic Medicine,* 1958, *20,* 446–447.
Grant, V. W. A case study of fetishism. *Journal of Abnormal and Social Psychology,* 1953, *48,* 142–149. Copyright 1953 by the American Psychological Association. Excerpt in text reprinted by permission.
Green, R. *Sexual identity conflict in children and adults.* Baltimore: Penguin Books, 1974.
Grimshaw, L. Obsessional disorder and neurological illness. *Journal of Neurology,*

Neurosurgery and Psychiatry, 1964, *27,* 229–231.

Gunderson, J. G., & Mosher, L. R. The cost of schizophrenia. *Archives of General Psychiatry,* 1975, *132,* 901–906.

Gurin, G., Veroff, J., & Feld, S. *Americans view their mental health.* New York: Basic Books, 1960.

Gurman, A. S., & Kniskern, D. P. Research on marital and family therapy: Progress, perspective, and prospect. In S. L. Garfield & A. E. Bergin (Eds.), *Handbook of psychotherapy and behavior change* (2nd ed.). New York: Wiley, 1978.

Gutheil, T. G., & Avery, G. Multiple overt incest as family defense against loss. *Family Process,* 1977, *16,* 105–116.

Gynther, M. D. White norms and black MMPI's: A prescription for discrimination? *Psychological Bulletin,* 1972, *78,* 386–402.

Hackett, T. P. Editorial: The rational use of psychotropic drugs. *Drug Therapy for the Family Physician,* 1979, *9,* 39–40.

Hæberle, E. J. *The sex atlas.* New York: Seabury Press, 1978. Material used by permission of The Continuum Publishing Corporation, New York.

Hare, E. H. Mental illness and social conditions in Bristol. *Journal of Mental Science,* 1956, *102,* 349–357.

Harlow, H. F., & Harlow, M. K. Effects of various mother-infant relationships on rhesus monkey behaviors. In B. M. Foss (Ed.), *Determinants of infant behavior IV.* London: Methuen, 1969.

Hathaway, S. R., & McKinley, J. C. *Minnesota multiphasic personality inventory: Manual.* New York: Psychological Corporation, 1943.

Haughton, E., & Ayllon, T. Production and elimination of symptomatic behavior. In L. Ullmann & L. Krasner (Eds.), *Case studies in behavior modification.* New York: Holt, Rinehart & Winston, 1965, pp. 94–98.

Hauser, S. L., DeLong, G. K., & Rosman, N. P. Pneumographic findings in the infantile autism syndrome. *Brain,* 1975, *98,* 667.

Heilbrun, A. B., Jr. Psychopathy and violent crime. *Journal of Consulting and Clinical Psychology,* 1979, *47,* 517–524.

Heller, K., & Monahan, J. *Psychology and community change.* Homewood, Ill.: Dorsey Press, 1977.

Heller, K., Price, R. H., & Sher, K. J. Research and evaulation in primary prevention. In R. H. Price, R. F. Ketterer, B. C. Bader, & J. Monahan (eds.), *Prevention in mental health.* Beverly Hills, London: Sage Publications, 1980.

Hersen, M. Limitations and problems in the clinical application of behavioral techniques in psychiatric settings. *Behavior Therapy,* 1979, *10,* 65–80.

Hersov, L. A. Persistent non-attendance at school. *Journal of Child Psychology and Psychiatry,* 1960, *1,* 130–136.

H.E.W. Report

Higgins, R. L., & Marlatt, G. A. Effects of anxiety arousal on the consumption of alcohol by alcoholics and social drinkers. *Journal of Consulting and Clinical Psychology,* 1973, *41,* 426–433.

Higgins, R. L., & Marlatt, G. A. Fear of interpersonal evaluation as a determinant of alcohol consumption in male social drinkers. *Journal of Abnormal Psychology,* 1975, *84,* 644–651.

Hilgard, E. R. *Introduction to Psychology,* 3d ed. New York: Harcourt, Brace & World, 1962.

Hilgard, E. R. *Divided consciousness: Multiple controls in human thought and action.* New York: Wiley, 1977.

Hogan, D. R. The effectiveness of sex therapy: A review of the literature. In J. Lopiccolo and L. Lopiccolo (Eds.), *Handbook of sex therapy.* New York: Plenum, 1978.

Hogan, R. A. The implosive technique. *Behavior Research and Therapy,* 1968, *6,* 423–432.

Hogarty, G. E. Treatment and the course of schizophrenia. *Schizophrenia Bulletin,* 1977, *3,* 587–599.

Hogarty, G. E., Goldberg, S. C., Schooler, N. R., & Ulrich, R. F., & the collaborative study group: Drug and sociotherapy in the aftercare of schizophrenic patients: II. Two year relapse rates. *Archives of General Psychiatry,* 1974, *31,* 603–608 (a).

Hogarty, G. E., Goldberg, S. C., Schooler, N. R., Ulrich, R. F., & the Collaborative Study Group. Drug and sociotherapy in the aftercare of schizophrenic patients: III. Adjustment of nonrelapsed patients. *Archives of General Psychiatry,* 1974, *31,* 609–618 (b).

Hollingshead, A. B., & Redlich, F. C. *Social class and mental illness.* New York: Wiley, 1958.

Holmes, T. H., & Masuda, M. Psychosomatic syndromes. *Psychology Today,* April 1972, 71–106.

Holmes, T. H., & Rahe, R. H. The social adjustment rating scale. *Journal of Psychosomatic Research,* 1967, *11,* 213–218.

Holroyd, K. A. Cognition and desensitization in the group treatment of test anxiety. *Journal of Consulting and Clinical Psychology,* 1976, *44,* 991–1001.

Holroyd, K. A. Effects of social anxiety and social evaluation on beer consumption and social interaction. *Journal of Studies on Alcohol,* 1978, *39,* 737–744.

Holroyd, K. A. Stress, coping and the treatment of stress related illness. In J. R. McNamara (Ed.), *Behavioral approaches in medicine: Application and analysis.* New York: Plenum, 1979.

Holroyd, K., Andrasik, F., & Westbrook, K.

Cognitive control of tension headache. *Cognitive therapy and research,* 1977, *1,* 121–133.

Hook, S. Science and mythology in psychoanalysis. In S. Hook (Ed.), *Psychoanalysis, scientific method, and philosophy.* New York: New York University Press, 1959.

Holzman, P. S. *Psychoanalysis and psychopathology.* New York: McGraw-Hill, 1970.

Hull, D. B., & Schroeder, H. E. Some interpersonal effects of assertion, nonassertion, and aggression. *Behavior Therapy,* 1979, *10,* 14–19.

Humphreys, L. *Tearoom trade: Impersonal sex in public places.* Chicago: Aldine-Atherton, 1970.

Hunt, W. A., Barnett, J., & Branch, L. G. Relapse rates in addiction programs. *Journal of Clinical Psychology,* 1971, *27,* 455–456.

Jacobi, J. *The psychology of C. G. Jung.* New Haven, Conn.: Yale University Press, 1973.

Jacob, M. S., Marshman, J. A., & Carlen, P. L. *Clinical toxicology of phencyclidine.* Toronto, Ontario: Addiction Research Foundation, 1976.

Jacob, T. Family interaction in distrubed and normal families: A methodological and substantive review. *Psychological Bulletin,* 1975, *82,* 33–65.

Jacobson, E. *Progressive relaxation.* Chicago: University of Chicago Press, 1938.

Jaffe, J. H. Drug addiction and drug abuse. In L. S. Goodman & A. Gilman (Eds.), *The pharmacological basis of therapeutics* (4th ed.). New York: Macmillan, 1970.

Janeway, E. Witches and witch hunts. *Atlantic Monthly,* 1975, 80–84. Copyright © 1975, by The Atlantic Monthly Company, Boston. Material reprinted with permission.

Jarvik, M. E. Biological factors underlying the smoking habit. In *Research on smoking behavior* (NIDA Research monograph series: 17) U.S. Department of Health, Education, and Welfare. Washington, D.C.: U.S. Government Printing Office, 1977.

Jarvik, M. The role of nicotine in the smoking habit. In W. Hunt (Ed.), *Learning mechanisms in smoking.* Chicago: Aldine, 1970.

Jeans, R. F. I. An independently validated case of multiple personality. *Journal of Abnormal Psychology,* 1976, *85,* 249–255.

Jellinek, E. M. *The disease concept of alcoholism.* New Haven, Conn.: College and University Press and Hillhouse Press, New Brunswick, N.J., 1960.

Jersild, A. T., & Holmes, F. B. Children's fears. *Child Development Monographs,* 1935, No. 20.

Jessor, R. Marijuana: A review of recent psychosocial research. In R. I. Dupont, A. Goldstein, & J. O'Donnell (Eds.), *Handbook on drug abuse.* Washington, D.C.: National Institute on Drug Abuse, U.S. Government Printing Office, 1979.

Johnson, L. D., Bachman, J. G., & O'Malley, P. M. Highlights from: *Drug use among American high school students 1975–1977.* Washington, D.C.: National Institute on Drug Abuse, 1977.

Joint commission on mental health and illness. *Action for mental health.* New York: Wiley, 1961.

Jones, B. M., & Parsons, O. Alcohol and consciousness: Getting high, coming down. *Psychology Today,* 1975, *8,* 53–60.

Jones, M. Community care for chronic mental patients: The need for a reassessment. *The Journal of Hospital and Community Psychiatry,* 1975, *26,* 94–98.

Julien, R. M. *A primer of drug action* (2nd ed.). San Francisco, Calif.: Freeman and Company, 1978.

Jung, C. G. Approaching the unconscious. In C. G. Jung et al. (Eds.), *Man and his symbols.* London: Aldus Books, 1964. Copyright 1964, Aldus Books Limited.

Jung, C. G. *Memories, dreams, and reflections.* New York: Random House, 1909/1961.

Jung, C. G. The state of psychotherapy today. *Collected works, Vol. 10: Civilization in transition.* Princeton, N.J.: Princeton University Press, 1964. Copyright © 1960, 1969 by Princeton University Press. Excerpts reprinted by permission.

Jung, C. G. The transcendent function. In J. Campbell (Ed.), *The portable Jung.* New York: Penguin, 1971.

Jus, A., Pineau, R., Lachance, R., Pelchat, G., Jus, K., Pires, P., & Villeneuve, R. Epidemiology of tardive dyskinesia, Part I. *Diseases of the Nervous System,* 1976, *37,* 310–314.

Kahn, J. H., & Narsten, J. P. School refusal: A comprehensive view of school phobia and other failures of school attendance. *American Journal of Orthopsychiatry,* 1962, *32,* 707–718.

Kalin, R., McClelland, D. C., & Kahn, M. The effects of male social drinking on fantasy. *Journal of Personality and Social Psychology,* 1964, *4,* 441–452.

Kalinowsky, L. Psychosurgery. In A. Freedman, H. Kaplan, & B. Saddock (Eds.), *Comprehensive textbook of psychiatry* (Vol. 2). Baltimore: Williams & Wilkins, 1975.

Kallmann, F. J. A comparative twin study on the genetic aspects of male homosexuality. *Journal of Nervous and Mental Diseases,* 1952, *115,* 283–298.

Kanfer, F. H. Self-management methods. In F. H. Kanfer, & A. P. Goldstein (Ed.), *Helping people change.* New York: Pergamon Press, Inc., 1975.

Kanner, L. Autistic disturbances of affective contact. *Nervous Child,* 1942, *2,* 217.

Kantor, R. E., Wallner, J. M., & Winder, C. L. Process and reactive schizophrenia. *Journal of Consulting and Clinical Psychology,* 1953, *17,* 157–162.

Kaplan, N. M. *Your blood pressure—the most deadly high: A physician's guide to controlling your hypertension.* New York: MEDCOM, 1974.

Kaplan, H. S. Hypoactive sexual desire. *Journal of Sex and Marital Therapy,* 1977, Spring, 1–11. Copyright 1977, Human Sciences Press.

Kaplan, H. S. *The new sex therapy: Active treatment of sexual dysfunctions.* New York: Quadrangle, 1974.

Katchadourian, H. A., & Lunde, D. T. *Fundamentals of human sexuality.* New York: Holt, Rinehart & Winston, 1972.

Kaufman, I., Peck, A. L., & Taguiri, C. K. The family constellation and overt incestuous relations between father and daughter. *American Journal of Orthopsychiatry,* 1954, *24,* 266–277.

Kazdin, A. E. The application of operant techniques in treatment, rehabilitation, and education. In S. L. Garfield & A. E. Bergin (Eds.), *Handbook of psychotherapy and behavior change* (2nd ed.). New York: Wiley, 1978.

Kazdin, A. E. Fictions, factions, and functions of behavior therapy. *Behavior Therapy,* 1979, *10,* 629–654.

Kazdin, A. E., & Wilcoxin, L. A. Systematic desensitization and nonspecific treatment effects: A methodological evaluation. *Psychological Bulletin,* 1976, *83,* 729–758.

Kazdin, A. E., & Wilson, T. W. Criteria for evaluating psychotherapy. *Archives of General Psychiatry,* 1978, 35, 407–416.

Keith, S. J., Gunderson, J. G., Reifman, A., Buchsbaum, S., & Mosher, L. R. Special report: Schizophrenia, 1976. *Schizophrenia Bulletin,* 1976, *2,* 510–565.

Kendell, R. E. The classification of depressive illness: The uses and limitation of multivariate analysis. *Psychiatria, Neurologia and Neurochirurgia,* 1969, *72,* 207–216.

Kennedy, W. A. School phobia: Rapid treatment of 50 cases. *Journal of Abnormal Psychology,* 1965, *70,* 285–289.

Kessler, S. The etiological question in mental illness. *Science,* September 26, 1969, 1341–1342.

Kety, S. S. Current biochemical approaches to schizophrenia. *New England Journal of Medicine,* 1967, *276,* 325–331.

Kety, S. S., Rosenthal, D., Wender, P. H., & Schulsinger, F. The types and prevalence of mental illness in the biological and adoptive families of adopted schizophrenics. In D. Rosenthal, & S. S. Kety, (Eds.), *The transmission of schizophrenia.* Oxford: Pergamon Press Ltd., 1968, 345–362.

Kidd, K. K., & Cavalli-Sforza, L. L. An analysis of the genetics of schizophrenia. *Social Biology,* 1973, *20,* 254–265.

Kinney, J., & Leaton, G. *Loosening the grip: A handbook of alcohol information.* St. Louis: Mosley, 1970.

Kinsey, A. C., Pomeroy, W. B., Martin, C. E., & Gebhard, P. H. *Sexual behavior in the human female.* Philadelphia: Saunders, 1953.

Kinsey, A. C., Pomeroy, W. B., & Martin, C. E. *Sexual behavior in the human male.* Philadelphia: Saunders, 1948.

Kisker, G. W. *The disorganized personality.* McGraw-Hill, 1964. Copyright © 1964 by McGraw-Hill. Excerpt in text used with the permission of McGraw-Hill Book Company.

Klerman, G. L., & Izen, J. E. Psychopharmacology. In W. T. Reich (Ed.), *Encyclopedia of bioethics* (Vol. 3). New York: Free Press, 1978.

Knight, R. A., Roff, J. D., Barnett, J., & Moss, J. L. Concurrent and predictive validity of thought disorder affectivity: A 22-year follow-up of acute schizophrenics. *Journal of Abnormal Psychology,* 1979, *88,* 1–13.

Koenig, P. The problem that can't be tranquilized. *New York Times Magazine,* May 21, 1978, 14–16.

Kohn, M. L. *Class and conformity: A study in values.* Homewood, Ill.: Dorsey Press, 1969.

Kolb, L. S. Therapy of homosexuality. In J. Mosserman (Ed.), *Current psychiatric therapies* (Vol. 3). New York: Grune & Stratton, 1963.

Kolvin, et al., Studies in the childhood psychoses: I–VI. *British Journal of Psychiatry,* 1971, *118,* 381.

Korchin, S. K. *Modern clinical psychology.* New York: Basic Books, 1976.

Krasner, L. The therapist as a social reinforcement machine. In H. H. Strupp & L. Luborsky (Eds.), *Research in psychotherapy* (Vol. 2). Washington, D.C.: American Psychological Association, 1962.

Kroger, W. S. *Clinical and experimental hypnosis* (2nd ed.). Philadelphia: J. B. Lippincott, 1977.

Kuhn, T. S. *The structure of scientific revolutions.* Chicago: University of Chicago Press, 1962.

Lachman, S. J. *Psychosomatic disorders: A behavioristic interpretation.* New York: Wiley, 1972.

Laing, R. D. *The divided self.* London: Tavistock, 1959.

Laing, R. D. *The politics of experience.* New York: Ballantine, 1967.

Laing, R. D., & Esterson, A. *Sanity, madness, and the family.* New York: Basic Books, 1971.

Lang, A. R., Goeckner, D. J., Adesso, V. J., & Marlatt, G. A. Effects of alcohol on aggression in male social drinkers. *Journal of Abnormal Psychology,* 1975, *84,* 508–518. Copyright 1975 by the American Psychological Association. Text quote reprinted by permission.

Lang, P. E. The mechanics of desensitization and the laboratory study of fear. In C. M. Franks (Ed.), *Behavior therapy: Appraisal and status.* New York: McGraw-Hill, 1969.

Langer, E. J., Abelson, R. P. A patient by any other name . . . : Clinician group difference in labeling bias. *Journal of Consulting and Clinical Psychology,* 1974, *42,* 4–9.

Larsen, S. R. *Strategies for reducing phobic behavior* (Doctoral dissertation, Stanford University, 1965.

Laughlin, H. P. *The neuroses in clinical practice.* Philadelphia: W. B. Saunders Co., 1965.

Lazarus, A. A. *Multimodal behavior therapy.* New York: Springer, 1976.

Leff, J. P. Schizophrenia and sensitivity to the family environment. *Schizophrenia Bulletin,* 1976, 566–574.

Leighton, D. C., Harding, J. S., Macklin, D. B., Hughes, C. C., & Leighton, A. H. Psychiatric findings of the Sterling County study. *American Journal of Psychiatry,* 1963, *119,* 1021–1026.

Leitenberg, H. *Handbook of behavior modification and behavior therapy.* Englewood Cliffs, N.J.: Prentice-Hall, 1976.

Levine, B. *Group psychotherapy: Practice and development.* Englewood Cliffs, N.J.: Prentice-Hall, 1979.

Levitsky, F., & Perls, F. S. The rules and games of Gestalt Therapy. In J. Fagan & I. L. Sheperd (Eds.), *Gestalt therapy now: Therapy, techniques, application.* Palo Alto, Calif.: Science and Behavior Books, 1970.

Levitt, E. E. Sadomasochism. *Sexual Behavior,* 1971, *1,* 68–80.

Levitt, E. E., & Lubin, B. *Depression: Concepts, controversies and some new facts.* New York: Springer, 1975.

Lewinsohn, P. M. A behavioral approach to depression. In R. J. Friedman & M. M. Katz (Eds.), *The psychology of depression: Contemporary theory and research.* Washington, D.C.: V. H. Winston, 1974(a).

Lewinsohn, P. M. Clinical and theoretical aspects of depression. In K. S. Calhoun, H. E. Adams, & K. M. Mitchell (Eds.), *Innovative treatment methods in psychopathology.* New York: Wiley, 1974(b).

Lewis, M., & Ban, P. Stability of attachment behavior: A transformational analysis. Paper presented at The Society for Research in Child Development, April 1971, Minneapolis.

Lewis, M. L., & Sorrel, P. M. Some psychological aspects of seduction, incest, and rape in childhood. *Journal of the American Academy of Child Psychiatry,* 1969, *8,* 606.

Liberman, R. P., & Davis, J. Drugs and behavior analysis. In M. Hersen, R. M. Eisler, & P. M. Miller (Eds.), *Progress in behavior modification* (Vol. 1). New York: Academic Press, 1975.

Liberman, R. P., & Raskin, D. E. Depression: A behavioral formulation. *Archives of General Psychiatry,* 1971, *24,* 515–523. Copyright 1971, American Medical Association.

Lick, J. Expectancy, false galvanic skin response feedback, and systematic desensitization in the modification of phobic behavior. *Journal of Consulting and Clinical Psychology,* 1975, *43,* 557–567.

Lidz, T., Fleck, S., & Cornelison, A. *Schizophrenia and the family.* New York: International Universities Press, 1965.

Liebowitz, E., & McNamara, J. R. Neuroleptics and the need for informed consent with schizophrenic patients. Preliminary report to the Ohio Department of Mental Health, Office of Program Evaluation and Research, 1980.

Lieberman, M. A., Yalom, I. D., & Miles, M. B. *Encounter groups: First facts.* New York: Basic Books, 1973.

Lieberman, M. A. Group methods. In F. H. Kanfer & A. P. Goldstein (Eds.), *Helping people change.* New York: Pergamon Press, 1975.

Linton, H. B., & Langs, R. J. Subjective reactions to lysergic acid diethylamide (LSD–25) measured by a questionnaire. *Archives of General Psychiatry,* 1964, *10,* 469–485.

Lopiccolo, J., & Lopiccolo, L. (Eds.), *Handbook of sex therapy.* New York: Plenum, 1978.

Loraine, J. A., Ismael, A. A., Adamopoulous, P. A., & Dove, G. A. Endocrine functions in male and female homosexuals. *British Medical Journal,* 1970, *4,* 406.

Lotter, V. Epidemiology of autistic conditions in young children. *Social Psychiatry,* 1966, *1,* 124 and 163.

Lovass, I. O. *The autistic child.* New York: Irvington Publishers, 1977.

Lovibond, S. H., & Caddy, G. R. Discriminated aversive control in the moderation of alcoholics' drinking behavior. *Behavior Therapy,* 1970, *1,* 437–444.

Luisada, P. V. *The PCP psychosis: A hidden epidemic.* Paper presented at the VI World Congress of Psychiatry, Honolulu, Hawaii, August 1977.

Lukianowicz, N. "Incest." *British Journal of Psychiatry,* 1972, *120,* 301–313.

Lykken, D. T. A study of anxiety in the sociopathic personality. (Doctoral dissertation, University of Minnesota, 1955.) University Microfilms No. 55–944.

Lykken, D. T. A study of anxiety in the sociopathic personality. *Journal of Abnormal and Social Psychology,* 1957, *55,* 6–10.

Lynn, S. J., & Freedman, R. R. Transfer and evaluation of biofeedback treatment. In A. P. Goldstein and F. Kanfer (Eds.), *Maximizing treatment gains: Transfer enhancement in psychotherapy.* New York: Academic Press, 1979.

Lyons, R. D. Califano in drive to end smoking; calls habit "slow motion suicide." *New York Times,* January 12, 1978, A14.

McArthur, C., Waldron, E., & Dickinson, J. The psychology of smoking. *Journal of Abnormal and Social Psychology,* 1958, *56,* 267–275.

McClelland, D. C. Testing for competence rather than "intelligence." *American Psychologist,* 1973, *28,* 1–14.

MacDonald, M. L., Lidsky, T. I., & Kern, J. M. Drug instigated effects. In A. P. Goldstein & F. Kanfer (Eds.), *Maximizing treatment gains: Transfer enchancement in psychotherapy.* New York: Academic Press, 1979.

MacDonald, M. L., & Tobias, L. L. Withdrawal causes relapse? Our response. *Psychological Bulletin,* 1976, *83,* 448–451.

McGee, R. K. *Crisis intervention in the community.* Baltimore: University Park Press, 1974.

McGlothlin, Witt., Anglin, M. D., & Wilson, B. D. Narcotic addiction and crime. *Criminology,* 1978.

McPeak, W. R. Family therapies. In A. P. Goldstein & F. H. Kanfer (Eds.), Maximizing treatment gains: *Transfer enhancement in psychotherapy.* New York: Academic, 1979.

McNamara, J. R. Behavior therapy in the seventies: Some changes and current issues. *Psychotherapy: Theory, Research, and Practice,* 1980, *17,* 2–9.

McNamara, J. R. Socioethical considerations in behavior therapy research and practice. *Behavior Modification,* 1978, 2, 3–24.

McNaught, B. A response to Anita Bryant . . . Why bother with gay rights? *Humanist,* 1977, *37,* 34–36.

McWhorter, W. L. *The naked man in open raincoat: A sociological perspective of exhibitionism.* Unpublished manuscript, Virginia Polytechnic Institute and State University, Blacksburg, Virginia, 1976.

Maher, B. The chattered language of schizophrenia. *Psychology Today,* 1968, *2*(6), 30–64.

Maher, B. A. *Principles of psychopathology.* New York: McGraw-Hill, 1966.

Maher, B. A., McKean, K., & McLaughlin, B. Studies in psychotic language. In P. Stone (Ed.), *The general inquirer: A computer approach to content analysis.* Cambridge, Mass.: Massachusetts Institute of Technology, 1966.

Mahoney, M. J., & Arnkoff, D. Cognitive and self-control therapies. In S. L. Garfield & A. E. Bergin (Eds.), *Handbook of psychotherapy and behavior change* (2nd ed.). New York: Wiley, 1978.

Mahoney, M. J., Moura, N. G., & Wade, T. C. Relative efficiency of self-reward, self-punishment, and self-monitoring techniques for weight loss. *Journal of Consulting and Clinical Psychology,* 1973, *40,* 404–407.

Maletzky, B. M., & Klotter, J. Smoking and alcoholism. *American Journal of Psychiatry,* 1974, *131,* 445–447.

Margolese, M. Androsterone/etiochalanolone ratios in male homosexuals. *British Medical Journal,* 1973, *3,* 207–210.

Marks, I. Behavioral psychotherapy of adult neurosis. In S. L. Garfield and A. E. Bergin (Eds.), *Handbook of psychotherapy and behavior change: An empirical analysis* (2nd. ed.). New York: Wiley, 1978.

Marks, I. M. *Fears and phobias.* New York: Academic Press, 1969.

Marks, I. M. Phobias and obsessions. In J. Maser & M. Seligman (Eds.), *Experimental psychopathology.* New York: Wiley, 1977.

Marks, I. M., Viswanathan, R., Lipsedge, M. S., & Gardiner, R. Enhanced relief of phobias by flooding during waning diazepam effect. *British Journal of Psychiatry,* 1972, *121,* 493–505.

Marlatt, G. A. Alcohol, stress, and cognitive control. In C. D. Spielberger & G. Sarason (Eds.), *Stress and anxiety* (Vol. 3). Washington, D.C.: Hemisphere Publishing Co., 1976.

Marlatt, G. A., Kosturn, C. F., & Lang, A. R. Provocation to anger and opportunity for retaliation as determinants of alcohol consumption in social drinkers. *Journal of Abnormal Psychology,* 1975, *84,* 652–659.

Marmor, J. Homosexuality in males. *Psychiatric Annals,* 1971, *4,* 45–59.

Marx, A. J., Test, M. A., & Stein, L. I. Extrahospital management of severe mental illness. *Archives of General Psychiatry,* 1973, *29,* 505–511.

Maslow, A. H. *Motivation and personality.* New York: Harper & Row, 1954.

Maslow, A. Synanon eupsychia. *Journal of Humanistic Psychology,* Spring 1967, 28–35.

Masters, W. H., & Johnson, V. E. *Homosexuality in perspective.* Boston: Little, Brown, 1979.

Masters, W. H., & Johnson, V. E. *Human sexual inadequacy.* Boston: Little, Brown, 1970.

Masters, W. H., & Johnson, V. E. *Human sexual response.* Boston: Little, Brown, 1966.

Mathis, J. L. The exhibitionist. *Medical Aspects of Human Sexuality,* 1969, June, 89–101.

May, P. R. A. *Treatment of schizophrenia: A comparative study of five treatment methods.* New York: Science House, 1968.

Mayer-Gross, W., Slater, E., & Roth, M. *Clinical psychiatry,* 3d ed. Baltimore: Williams & Wilkens, 1969. Revised and reprinted 1977, Bailliere, Tindall London.

Mead, G. H. *Mind, self, and society* (C. W. Morris, Ed.). Chicago: University of Chicago Press, 1934.

Meador, B. D., & Rogers, C. R. Person centered therapy. In J. R. Corsini (Ed.), *Current psychotherapies.* Itasca, Ill.: Peacock, 1979.

Mednick, S. A. A longitudinal study of children with high risk for schizophrenia. *Mental Hygiene,* 1966, *50,* 522–535. Material reprinted by permission of The National Mental Health Association.

Meehl, P. E. Schizotypy, schizophrenia. *American Psychologist.* 1962, *17,* 827–838.

Meichenbaum, D. *Cognitive-behavior modification.* New York: Plenum, 1977.

Meichenbaum, D. H., & Cameron, R. Training schizophrenics to talk to themselves: A means of developing attentional controls. *Behavior Therapy,* 1973, *4,* 515–534.

Meltzoff, J., & Kornreich, M. *Research in psychotherapy.* New York: Atherton, 1970.

Mendels, J. *Concepts of depression.* New York: Wiley, 1970.

Menninger, K. *Theory of psychoanalytic technique.* New York: Basic Books, 1958.

Mercer, J. R., & Lewis, J. *System of multi-cultural pluralistic assessment.* New York: Psychological Corporation, 1977.

Meyer, J. K., & Reter, D. J. Sex reassignment. *Archives of General Psychiatry,* 1979, *36,* 1010–1015.

Meyer, V., Robertson, J., & Tallon, A. Home treatment of an obsessive-compulsive disorder by response prevention. *Journal of Behavior Therapy and Experimental Psychiatry,* 1975, *6,* 37–38.

Miller, I. W., & Norman, W. H. Learned helplessness in humans: A review and attribution theory model. *Psychology Bulletin,* 1979, *86,* 93–118.

Miller, N. E. Biofeedback and visceral learning. In *Annual Review of Psychology* (Vol. 29). Palo Alto, Calif.: Annual Reviews, Inc., 1978.

Miller, P. M., Stanford, A. G., & Hemphill, D. P. A comprehensive social learning approach to alcoholism treatment. *Social Casework,* 1978, *59,* 240–251.

Miller, W. R., & Caddy, G. R. Abstinence and controlled drinking in the treatment of problem drinkers. *Journal of Studies on Alcohol,* 1977, *38,* 986–1003.

Mintz, E. *Marathon groups: Reality and symbol.* New York: Appleton-Century-Crofts, 1971.

Minuchin, S. *Families and family therapy.* Cambridge, Mass.: Harvard University Press, 1974.

Mischel, W. Continuity and change in personality. *American Psychologist,* 1969, *24,* 1012–1018.

Mohr, J. W., & Turner, R. E. Sexual deviations part IV—pedophilia. *Applied Therapeutics,* 1967, *9,* 362–365.

Monroe, R. *Schools of psychoanalytic thought.* New York: Dryden, 1955.

Moore, N. Behavior therapy in bronchial asthma. *Journal of Psychosomatic Research,* 1965, *9,* 257–276.

Moore, R. Dependence on alcohol. In S. N. Pradhan & S. N. Dutta (Eds.), *Drug abuse: Clinical and basic aspects.* St. Louis: Mosby, 1977.

Morris, J. *Conundrum.* New York: Harcourt Brace Jovanovich, 1974.

Morris, J. B., & Beck, A. T. The efficacy of antipsychotic drugs. *Archives of General Psychiatry,* 1974, *30,* 667–671.

Murray, E. J., & Jacobson, L. I. Cognititon and learning in traditional and behavioral therapy. In S. L. Garfield & A. E. Bergin (Eds.), *Handbook of psychotherapy and behavior change* (2nd ed.). New York: Wiley, 1978.

Murray, J. J., & Trotter, A. B. Treatment in drug abuse: Counseling approaches and special programs. In R. E. Hardy & J. G. Cull (Eds.), *Drug dependence and rehabilitation approaches.* Springfield, Ill.: Charles C Thomas, 1973.

Nash, M. R., Johnson, L. S., & Tipton, R. D. Hypnotic age regression and the occurrence of transitional object relationships. *Journal of Abnormal Psychology,* 1979, *88,* 547–554.

Nathan, P. E. Alcoholism. In H. Leitenberg (Ed.), *Handbook of behavior modification.* New York: Appleton-Century-Crofts, 1976.

Nathan, P. E., & O'Brien, J. S. An experimental analysis of the behavior of alcoholics and nonalcoholics during prolonged experimental drinking. *Behavior Therapy,* 1971, *2,* 455–476.

National Cancer Institute. *Cigarette smoking among teenagers and young women.* U.S. Department of Health, Education, and Welfare, Public Health Service, DHEW, 1975.

National Clearinghouse for drug abuse information. *Narcotic antagonists* (Report Series 26). Washington, D.C.: U.S. Government Printing Office, 1975.

National Institute on Alcohol Abuse and Alcoholism (NIAAA). *Alcohol and health: 2nd special report to the U.S. Congress, new knowledge.* U.S. department of Health, Education and Welfare, DHEW Publication No. (ADM) 75–212. Washington, D.C.: U.S. Government Printing Office, 1975.

National Institute on Drug Abuse. *Marijuana Research Findings.* Washington, D.C.: U.S. Department of Health, Education, and Welfare, Research Monograph, 1976, No. 14.

National Prescription Audit, 1976. Ambler, Penn.: IMS America Ltd., 1976.

Neisworth, J. T., & Moore, F. Operant treatment of asthmatic responding with the patient as therapist. *Behavior Therapy,* 1972, *3,* 95–99.

Neuringer, C. Rorschach ink blot test assessment of suicidal risk. In C. Neuringer (Ed.), *Psychological assessment of suicidal risk.* Springfield, Ill.: Charles Thomas, 1974.

Neville, R. Psychosurgery. In W. Reich (Ed.), *Encyclopedia of bioethics, Vol. 3.* New York: The Free Press, 1978.

New York Times. Study finds drinking—often to excess—now starts at earlier age. *New York Times,* March 27, 1977, 38.

Nolan, J. D. Self-control procedure in the modification of smoking behavior. *Journal of Consulting and Clinical Psychology,* 1968, *32,* 92–93.

Novoco, R. W. Treatment of chronic anger through cognitive and relaxation controls. *Journal of Consulting and Clinical Psychology,* 1976, *44,* 681.

Nuckolls, C. B., Cassell, J., & Kaplan, B. H. Psycho-social assets, life crises and the prognosis of pregnancy. *American Journal of Epidemiology,* 1972, *95,* 431–441.

Nurco, D. N. A choice of treatments. In C. C. Brown & C. Savage (Eds.), *The drug abuse controversy.* Baltimore: National Educational Consultant, 1971.

Nurco, D. N. Etiological aspect of drug abuse. In R. I. Dupont, A. Goldstein, & J. O.'Donnell (Eds.), *Handbook on drug abuse.* Washington, D.C.: National Institute on Drug Abuse, U.S. Government Printing Office, 1979.

Ohman, A., Eriksson, A., Fredriksson, N., Hugdahl, K., & Oloffson, C. Habituation of the electrodermal at orienting reaction to potentially phobic and supposedly neutral stimuli in normal human subjects. *Biological Psychology,* 1974, *2,* 85–92.

Oi, M., Oshida, K., & Sugimura, A. The location of gastric ulcer. *Gastroenterology,* 1959, *36,* 45–56.

Osgood, C. E., Luria, Z., & Smith, S. W., II. A blind analysis of another case of multiple personality using the semantic personality technique. *Journal of Abnormal Psychology,* 1976, *85,* 256–270.

Pahnke, W. N., Kurland, A. A., Unger, S., Savage, C., & Grof, S. The experimental use of psychedelic (LSD) psychotherapy. In J. R. Gamage & E. L. Zerkin (Eds.), *Hallucinogenic drug research: Impact on science & society.* Beloit, Wis.: Stash Press, 1970.

Pamphlet. Alcoholics Anonymous. Alcoholics Anonymous World Services, 1978.

Parloff, M. B., Waskow, E., & Wolper, B. E. Research on therapist variables in relation to process and outcome. In S. Garfield & A. Bergin (Eds.), *Handbook of psychotherapy and behavior change.* New York: Wiley, 1978.

Patsiokas, A. J., Clum, G. A., & Luscomb, R. L. Cognitive characteristics of suicide attempts. *Journal of Consulting and Clinical Psychology,* 1979, *47,* 478–484.

Pattison, E. M., Sobell, M. B., & Sobell, L. C. *Emerging concepts of alcohol dependence.* New York: Springer, 1977.

Paul, G. L., & Lentz, R. J. *Psychosocial treatment of chronic mental patients; Milieu vs. social learning programs,* Cambridge, Mass.: Harvard University Press, 1978.

Paykel, E., Myers, J., Dienalt, M., et al. Life events and depression. *Archives of General Psychiatry,* 1970, *21,* 753–760.

Paykel, E. S., & Weisman, M. M. Social adjustment and depression. *Archives of General Psychiatry,* 1973, *28,* 659–663.

Pelletier, K. R. *Mind as healer, mind as slayer.* New York: Dell, 1977.

Perls, F. S. *The gestalt approach and eye witness to therapy.* New York: Bantam Books, 1976.

Perls, F. S. *Gestalt therapy verbatim.* New York: Bantam Books, 1971.

Perry, J. W. Reconstitutive process in the psychopathology of the self. *Annals of the New York Academy of Sciences,* 1962, *96,* 853–876.

Peterson, R. C. Cocaine: An overview. In R. C. Peterson & R. C. Stillman (Eds.), *Cocaine 1977.* Washington, D.C.: U.S. Government Printing Office, 1977.

Phares, E. J. *Clinical psychology.* Homewood, Ill.: Dorsey Press, 1979.

Phillips, E. L. Achievement place: Token reinforcement procedures in a home-style rehabilitation setting for "predelinquent" boys. *Journal of Applied Behavior Analysis,* 1968, *1,* 213–223.

Philips, L. Case history data and prognosis in schizophrenia. *Journal of Nervous and Mental Disease,* 1953, *117,* 515–525.

Pierce, A. The economic cycle and the social suicide rate. *American Sociological Review,* 1967, *32,* 457–462.

Pitts, F. N. Medical aspects of ECT. *Seminars in Psychiatry,* 1972, *4,* 27–32.

Pollit, J. Natural history of obsessional states. *British Medical Journal,* 1957, *1,* 195–198.

Pope, H. G., & Lipinski, J. F. Diagnosis in schizophrenia and manic-depressive illness. *Archives of General Psychiatry,* 1978, *35,* 811–828.

Pratt, J. H. The class method of treating consumption in the homes of the poor. *Journal of the American Medical Association,* 1907, *49,* 755–759.

President's Commission on Mental Health, Report to the President, Vol I. Washington, D.C.: U.S. Government Printing Office, 1978.

Price, R. H. *Abnormal behavior: Perspectives in conflict* (2nd ed.). New York: Holt, Rinehart & Winston, 1978.

Price, R. H. Analysis of task requirements in schizophrenic concept identification performance. *Journal of Abnormal Psychology,* 1968, *73,* 285–293.

Price, R. H. Etiology, the social environment, and the prevention of psychological dysfunction. In

P. Insel & R. H. Moos (Eds.), *Health and the social environment.* Lexington, Mass.: D. C. Heath & Co., 1974.

Price, R. H. Signal detection methods in personality and perception. *Psychological Bulletin,* 1966, *66,* 55–62.

Price, R. H., & Bouffard, D. L. Behavioral appropriateness and situational constraint as dimensions of social behavior. *Journal of Personality and Social Psychology,* 1974, *30,* 579–586.

Price, R. H., & Denner, B. (Eds.). *The making of a mental patient.* New York: Holt, Rinehart & Winston, 1973.

Price, R. H., & Eriksen, D. W. Size constancy in schizophrenia: A reanalysis. *Journal of Abnormal Psychology,* 1966, *71,* 155–160.

Price, R. H., & Moos, R. H. Toward a taxonomy of inpatient treatment environments. *Journal of Abnormal Psychology,* 1975, *84,* 181–188.

Prien, R., & Caffey, E. Guidelines for antipsychotic drug use. *Resident and Staff Physician,* 1975, *9,* 165–172.

Prince, C. A survey of 504 cases of transvestism. *Psychological Reports,* 1972, *31,* 903–917.

Prince, M. *The dissociation of a personality.* New York and London: Longmans Green, 1906.

Pronko, N. H. *Abnormal psychology.* Baltimore: Williams & Wilkens, 1963.

Purcell, K., Brady, K., Chai, H., Muser, J., Molk, L., Gordon, N., & Means, J. The effect on asthma in children of experimental separation from the family. *Psychosomatic Medicine,* 1969, *31,* 144–164.

Quitkin, F., Rifkin, A., & Gochfeld, L. Tardive dyskinesia: Are first signs reversible? *American Journal of Psychiatry,* 1977, *134,* 84–86.

Rabin, H. M., & nbaum, M. *How to begin a psychotherapy group: Six approaches.* New York: Gordon and Breash Science Publishers, 1976.

Rabkin, J. G., & Struening, E. L. Life events, stress, and illness, *Science,* 1976, *194,* 1013–1020.

Rachman, S. J., & Hodgson, R. J. *Obsessions and compulsions.* Englewood Cliffs, N.J.: Prentice-Hall, © 1980. Material reprinted by permission.

Rappaport, J. *Community psychology: Values research and action.* New York: Holt, Rinehart & Winston, 1977.

Rapaport, D., & Gill, M. M. The points of view and assumptions of metapsychology. In Merton M. Gill (Ed.), *Collected papers of David Rapaport.* New York: Basic Books, 1967.

Raskin, M., Johnson, G., & Rodestvedt, J. W. Chronic anxiety treated by feedback induced muscle relaxation. *Archives of General Psychiatry,* 1973, *23,* 263–267.

Ray, O. S. *Drugs, society, and human behavior.* (2nd ed.) St. Louis: Mosby, 1978.

Redlich, F. C., & Freedman, D. X. *The theory and practice of psychiatry.* New York: Basic Books, 1966.

Rees, L. The importance of psychological, allergic, and infective factors in childhood asthma. *Journal of Psychosomatic Research,* 1964, *7,* 253–262.

Reich, W. *Character analysis.* New York: Orgone Institute Press, 1949.

Reiss, A. J. The social integration of queers and peers. *Social Problems,* 1961 (Fall), *9,* 102–120.

Reyher, J. Hypnosis in research on psychopathology. In J. E. Gordon (Ed.), *Handbook of clinical and experimental hypnosis.* New York: Macmillan, 1967.

Richter, C. P. On the phenomenon of sudden death in animals and man. *Psychosomatic Medicine,* 1957, *19,* 191–198.

Richter, C. P. The phenomenon of unexplained sudden death in animals and man. In W. H. Gant (Ed.), *Physiological basis of psychiatry.* Springfield, Ill: Charles Thomas, 1958, 148–171.

Rickers-Ovsiankina, M. A. (Ed.). *Rorschach psychology.* New York: Wiley, 1960.

Riegel, K. F. Influence of economic and political ideologies on the development of developmental psychology. *Psychological Bulletin,* 1972, *78,* 129–141.

Rimm, D. C., & Masters, J. C. *Behavior therapy: Techniques and empirical findings* (2nd ed.). New York: Academic Press, 1979.

Roback, H. B., Strassberg, D. S., McKee, E., & Cunningham, J. Self-concept and psychological adjustment differences between self-identified male transsexuals and male homosexuals. *Journal of Homosexuality,* 1977, *3,* 15–19.

Robins, L. N. Addict Careers. In R. I. Dupont, A. Goldstein, & J. O'Donnell (Eds.), *Handbook on drug abuse.* Washington, D.C.: National Institute on Drug Abuse, U.S. Government Printing Office, 1979.

Robins, N. L. *Deviant children grown up.* Baltimore: Williams & Wilkins, 1966.

Rogers, C. R. *Client-centered therapy.* Boston: Houghton Mifflin, 1951., Copyright © 1951, renewed 1978, Houghton Mifflin Company. Material reprinted by permission of the publishers.

Rogers, C. R. *Counseling and psychotherapy.* New York: Houghton Mifflin, 1942.

Rogers, C. R. The necessary and sufficient conditions of therapeutic personality change. *Journal of Consulting Psychology,* 1957, *21,* 95–103.

Rogers, C. R. *On becoming a person.* Boston: Houghton Mifflin, 1961. Copyright © 1961 by Houghton Mifflin Company. Material reprinted by permission of the publishers.

Rogers, C. *On encounter groups.* New York: Harper

& Row, 1970. Copyright © 1970 by Carl R. Rogers. Excerpt in text reprinted by permission of Harper & Row, Publishers, Inc.

Rogers, C. R. A theory of therapy, personality, and interpersonal relationships as developed in client-centered framework. In S. Koch (Ed.), *Psychology: A study of a science (Vol. III) Formulation of the person in the social context.* New York: McGraw-Hill, 1959.

Rogers vs. Okin. Civil Action 75–1610–T. (OC Mass.) October 29, 1979.

Roney, J. G., & Nall, M. L. *Medication practices in a community: An exploratory study, research report.* Menlo Park, Calif.: Stanford Research Institute, 1966.

Rosen, G. *Madness in society.* New York: Harper & Row, 1968.

Rosenberg, P. The effects of mood altering drugs: Pleasures and pitfalls. In R. E. Hardy & J. G. Cull (Eds.), *Drug dependence and rehabilitation approaches.* Springfield, Ill.: Charles C Thomas, 1973. Material reprinted courtesy of Charles C Thomas, Publisher.

Rosenhan, D. L. On being sane in insane places. *Science,* 1973, *179,* 250–258. Copyright 1973 by the American Society for the Advancement of Science.

Rosenthal, D. *Genetic theory and abnormal behavior.* New York: McGraw-Hill, 1970. Copyright © 1970 McGraw-Hill. Excerpt in text used with permission of McGraw-Hill Book Company.

Rosenthal, D. Evidence for a spectrum of schizophrenic disorders. Presented at the Annual Meeting of the American Psychological Association. Montreal, Canada, August 1973.

Rosenthal, D. *Genetic theory and abnormal behavior.* New York: McGraw-Hill, 1970.

Rossman, B., Minuchin, S., & Liebman, R. Family lunch session: An introduction to family therapy in anorexia nervosa. *American Journal of Orthopsychiatry,* 1975, *45,* 846–853.

Rothman, D. *The discovery of the asylum.* New York: Little, Brown, 1971.

Rush, A. J., Beck, A. T., Kovacs, M., & Hollon, S. Comparative efficacy of cognitive therapy and pharmacotherapy in the treatment of depressed outpatients. *Cognitive Therapy and Research,* 1977, *1,* 17–37.

Russell, M. A. H. Smoking problems: An overview. In *Research on smoking behavior,* NIDA Research Monograph Series: 17, U.S. Department of Health, Education, and Welfare. Washington, D.C.: U.S. Government Printing Office, 1977.

Rutter, M., Greenfeld, D., & Lockyer, L. A five to fifteen year follow-up study of infantile psychosis: II. Social and behavioural outcome. *British Journal of Psychiatry,* 1967, *113,* 1183.

Rutter, M., & Lockyer, L. A five to fifteen year follow-up study of infantile psychosis: I. Description of sample. *British Journal of Psychiatry,* 1967, *113,* 1169.

Saddock, V. A., & Saddock, B. J. Dual sex therapy. In B. J. Saddock, H. I. Kaplan & A. M. Freedman (Eds.), *The sexual experience.* Baltimore: Williams & Wilkins, 1976.

Saghir, M. T. & Robins, E. *Male and female homosexuality.* Baltimore: Williams & Wilkins, 1973.

Salzinger, K. Behavioral Analysis. In M. R. Rosenzweig & L. W. Porter (Eds.), *Annual Review of Psychology,* 1975, *26,* 623–629.

Sandler, J., & Hazari, A. The "obsessional": On the psychological classification of obsessional character traits and symptoms. *British Journal of Medical Psychology,* 1960, *33,* 113–122.

Sarbin, R. R., & Nucci, L. P. Self-reconstitution processes: A proposal for reorganizing the conduct of confirmed smokers. *Journal of Abnormal Psychology,* 1973, *81,* 182–195.

Sarbin, T. R. Schizophrenia is a myth born of metaphor, meaningless. *Psychology Today,* June 1972, 18–27.

Satir, V. *Conjoint family therapy: A guide to therapy and technique.* Palo Alto, Calif.: Science and Behavior Books, 1964.

Schact, T., & Nathan, P. E. But is it good for psychologists? Appraisal and status of DSM III. *American Psychologist,* 1977, *32,* 1017–1025.

Schachter, S. *Emotion, obesity and crime.* New York: Academic Press, 1971.

Schachter, S. Nicotine regulation in heavy and light smokers. *Journal of Experimental Psychology* (General), 1977, *106,* 5–12.

Schachter, S., Silverstein, B., Kozlowski, L. T., Herman, C. P., & Liebling, B. Effects of stress of cigarette smoking and urinary ph. *Journal of Experimental Psychology* (General), 1977, *106,* 24–30.

Schechter, M., & Roberge, L. Sexual exploitation. In R. E. Helfer & H. Kempe (Eds.), *Child abuse and neglect, the family and community.* Houston: Houston Law Review, 1976.

Scheff, T. J. (Ed.). *Labeling madness.* Englewood Cliffs, N.J.: Prentice-Hall, 1975.

Scheff, T. J. *Being mentally ill: A sociological theory.* Chicago: Aldine, 1966.

Schildkraut, J. J., & Ketty, S. S. Biogenic amines and emotion. *Science,* 1967, *156,* 21–30.

Schneidman, E. S., Farberow, N. L., & Litman, R. E. (Eds.) *The psychology of suicide.* New York: Jason Aronson, 1970.

Schneidman, E. S., & Farberow, N. L. A psychological approach to the study of suicide notes. In E. S. Schneidman, N. L. Farberow, & R. E. Litman (Eds.), *The psychology of suicide.* New York: Jason Aronson, 1970.

Schov, M. Current status of lithium therapy in affective disorders and other diseases. In A.

Villeneuve (Ed.), *Lithium in psychiatry, a synopsis*. Quebec: Les Presses De L'Universite Laval, 1976.

Schuckit, M. A., & Haglund, R. M. J. An overview of the etiological theories of alcoholism. In N. J. Estes & M. E. Heinman (Eds.), *Alcoholism: Development, consequences, and interventions.* St. Jouis: Mosby, 1977.

Schwartz, G. E. Biofeedback as therapy: Some theoretical and practical issues. *American Psychologist,* 1973, *28,* 666–673.

Schwartz, G. E. Psychosomatic disorders and biofeedback: A psychobiological model of disregulation. In J. D. Maser and M. E. P. Seligman (Eds.), *Psychopathology: Experimental models.* San Francisco: Freeman, 1977.

Schwartz, G. E. Voluntary control of human cardiovascular integration and differentiation through feedback and reward. *Science,* 1972, *175,* 90–93.

Schwartz, J. J., & Schwartz, R. Growth encounters. *Voices,* Fall–Winter 1969, *5,* 7–16.

Scovern, A. W., & Kilmann, P. R. Status of electroconvulsive therapy: Review of the outcome literature. *Psychological Bulletin,* 1980, *87,* 260–303.

Scull, A. T. Community treatment and the deviant: A radical view. *Decarceration.* Englewood Cliffs, N. J.: Prentice-Hall, 1977.

Seligman, M. E. P. *Helplessness: On depression, development and death.* San Francisco: Freeman, 1975.

Selling, L. S. *Men against madness.* New York: Greenberg, 1940.

Selye, H. *The stress of life.* New York: McGraw-Hill, 1956.

Selye, H. On the real benefits of eustress. *Psychology Today,* March 1978, pp. 60–63; 69–70.

Shapiro, A. P., Schwartz, G., Ferguson, D., Kedmand, D., and Weiss, S. M. Behavioral approaches to the treatment of hypertension: Clinical status. *Annals of Internal Medicine,* 1977, *86,* 626–636.

Shapiro, D. *Neurotic styles.* New York: Basic Books, 1965.

Shapiro, J. L. *Methods of group psychotherapy and encounter: A tradition of innovation.* Itasca, Ill.: F. E. Peacock Publishers, 1978.

Sherman, S. J. Presson, C., Chassin, L., & Olshavsky, R. *Social psychological factors in adolescent smoking.* Grant application, submitted to the U.S. Department of Health, Education, and Welfare, 1979.

Sikorski, K., & Nash, M. *Substance abuse: Training tapes and manual.* Columbia, Mo.: Everyday People, Inc., 1979.

Silverman, L. H. Psychoanalytic theory: The reports of my death are greatly exaggerated. *American Psychologist,* September 1976, *31*(9), 621. Copyright 1976 by the American Psychological Association. Text quote reprinted by permission.

Silverstein, B., Kozlowski, L. T., & Schachter, S. Social life, cigarette smoking, and urinary ph. *Journal of Experimental Psychology* (General), 1977, *106,* 20–23.

Simpson, G. M., & Kline, N. S. Tardive dyskinesia: Manifestations, etiology, and treatment. In M. D. Yahr (Ed.) *The basal ganglia.* New York: Raven Press, 1976.

Sinclair-Gieben, A. H. C., & Chambers, C. Evaluation of treatment of warts by hypnosis. *Lancet,* 1959, *2,* 480–482.

Skinner, B. F. *Science and Human Behavior.* New York: Macmillan, 1953.

Skinner, B. F. *Beyond freedom and dignity.* New York: Knopf, 1971. Copyright ©1971 by B. F. Skinner. Material reprinted by permission of Alfred A. Knopf, Inc.

Slager-Jorné, P. Counseling sexually abused children. *Personnel and Guidance Journal,* 1978, *12,* 103–105.

Slater, E. Clinical aspects of genetic mental disorders. In J. N. Cummings & M. Kremer (Eds.), *Biochemical aspects of neurological disorders* (2nd Series). Oxford: Blackwell Scientific Publications, Ltd., 1965.

Slater, E. *Psychotic and neurotic illnesses in twins.* London: Her Majesty's Stationary Office, 1953.

Slater, E., & Glithero, E. A follow-up of patients diagnosed as suffering from hysteria. *Journal of Psychosomatic Research,* 1965, *9,* 9–13.

Sloane, R. B., Staples, F. R., Cristol, A. H., Yorkston, N., & Whipple, K. *Psychotherapy versus behavior therapy.* Cambridge, Mass.: Harvard University Press, 1975.

Smith, E. The characteristics of dependence in high dose amphetamine abuse. *International Journal of the Addiction,* 1969, *4,* 453–459.

Smith, M. L., & Glass, G. V. Meta-analysis of psychotherapy outcome studies. *American Psychologist,* 1977, *32,* 752–760.

Smith, R. J. *The psychopath in society.* New York: Academic Press, 1978.

Smith, D. E., Wesson, D. R., & Lannon, R. A. New development in barbiturate abuse. *Clinical Toxicology,* 1970, *3,* 57–65.

Snyder, S. H. *Madness and the brain.* New York: McGraw-Hill, 1975.

Sorrells, J. M., & Ford, F. Toward an integrated theory of families and family therapy. *Psychotherapy: Theory, research, and practice,* 1969, *9,* 150–161.

Spengler, A. *Sadomasochists and their subculture: Results of an empirical study.* Paper presented at the Annual Meeting, International Academy of Sex Research, Hamburg, Germany, August 24, 1976.

Spitzer, R. L., & Endicott, J. Diagno: A computer program for psychiatric diagnosis utilizing the differential diagnosis procedure. *Archives of General Psychiatry,* 1968, *28,* 746–756.

Spitzer, R. L., Endicott, J., & Robins, E. Clinical criteria for psychiatric diagnosis and DSM III. *American Journal of Psychiatry,* 1975, *132,* 1187–1192.

Spitzer, R. L., Endicott, J., & Robins, E. *Research diagnostic criteria,* New York: Biometrics Research, 1975.

Spivack, G., & Shure, M. B. *Social adjustment of young children: A cognitive approach to solving real life problems.* San Francisco, Calif.: Jossey-Bass, 1974.

Srole, L., Langner, T. S., Michael, S. H., Opler, M. K., & Rennie, T. A. C. *Mental health in the metropolis: The midtown Manhattan study.* New York: McGraw-Hill, 1962.

Stampfl, T. G., & Levis, D. J. Essentials of implosive therapy: A learning theory-based psychodynamic behavioral therapy. *Journal of Abnormal Psychology,* 1967, *72,* 496–503.

Stefansson, J. G., et al. Hysterical neurosis, conversion type. *Acta Psychiatrica Scandinavia,* 1976, *53,* 119–138.

Steinmark, W. W., & Borkovec, T. D. Active and placebo treatment effects on moderate insomnia under counterdemand and positive demand instructions. *Journal of Abnormal Psychology,* 1974, *83,* 157–163.

Sterling-Smith, R. S. *A special study of drivers most responsible in fatal accidents.* Summary for Management Report, Contract No. DOTHS 310–3–595, April 1976.

Stewart, M. A., & Gath, A. *Psychological disorders of children: A handbook for primary care physicians.* Baltimore: Williams & Wilkins, 1978.

Stoller, F. H. A stage for trust. In A. Burton (Ed.), *Encounter.* San Francisco, Calif.: Jossey-Bass, 1970.

Stoller, R. J. The term "transvestism." *Archives of General Psychiatry,* 1971, *24,* 230–237. Copyright 1971, American Medical Association.

Strassberg, D., Roback, H., Cunningham, J., & McKee, E. TSCS-indicated psychopathology in self-identified female transsexuals, homosexuals, and heterosexuals. *Archives of Sexual Behavior,* in press.

Strupp, H. H. Psychotherapy research and practice. In S. Garfield & A. Bergin (Eds.), *Handbook of psychotherapy and behavior change.* New York: Wiley, 1978.

Strupp, H. H., Fox, R. E., & Lessler, K. *Patients view their therapy.* Baltimore: Johns Hopkins Press, 1969.

Stuart, R. B. Behavioral control of overeating. *Behavior Research and Therapy,* 1967, *5,* 357–365.

Sullivan, H. S. *Clinical studies in psychiatry* (Part II). In H. S. Perry, & M. C. Gaywell (Eds.), *The collected works of Harry Stack Sullivan.* New York: Norton, 1956. Copyright by the William Alanson White Psychiatric Foundation.

Sullivan, H. S. *The psychiatric interview.* New York: Norton, 1954. Copyright, The William Alonson White Psychiatric Foundation.

Sundberg, N. D., Snowden, L. R., & Reynolds, W. M. Toward assessment of personal competence and incompetence in life situations. *Annual Review of Psychology,* 1978, *29,* 179–221.

Sundel, M., & Schanie, C. F. Community mental health and mass media preventive education: The alternatives project. *Social Services Review,* 1978, *52,* 297–306.

Swift, C. *Sexual assault of children and adolescents.* Paper presented to the Domestic and International Scientific Planning, Analysis, and Cooperation Subcommittee of the Committee of Science and Technology of the U.S. House of Representatives, New York, January 11, 1978.

Szasz, T. *The manufacture of madness.* New York: Harper & Row, 1970.

Szasz, T. S. *The myth of mental illness.* New York: Dell, 1967.

Szasz, T. S. *Schizophrenia: The sacred symbol of psychiatry.* New York: Basic Books, 1976.

Taylor, R. Electroconvulsive treatment (ECT): The control of therapeutic power. *Exchange,* May/June 1975, 32–37.

Thigpen, Z. H., & Cleckley, H. *The three faces of Eve.* Kingsport, Tenn.: Kingsport Press, 1954.

Time Magazine. Alcoholism: New victims, new treatment. *Time Magazine,* April 22, 1974, 75–81.

Time Magazine. PCP: "A terror of a drug." *Time Magazine,* December 19, 1977, 53.

Torrey, E. F. *The death of psychiatry.* New York: Penguin Books, 1975.

Torrey, E. F., Hersh, S. P., & McCabe, K. D. Early childhood psychosis and bleeding during pregnancy: A prospective study of gravid women and their offspring. *Journal of Autism and Childhood Schizophrenia,* 1975, *5,* 287.

Tooley, J. T., & Pratt, S. An experimental procedure for the extinction of smoking behavior. *Psychological Record,* 1967, *17,* 209–218.

Tsuang, M. Schizophrenia around the world. *Comparative Psychiatry,* 1976, *17,* 477–481.

Turner, J., & Ten Hoor, W. The NIMH community support program pilot approach to a needed social reform. *Schizophrenia Bulletin,* 1978, *4,* 319–344.

Uhlenhuth, E. H., Balter, M. B., & Lipman, R. S. Minor tranquilizers: Clinical correlates of use in an urban population. *Archives of General Psychiatry,* 1978, *35,* 650–655.

Ullmann, L. P., & Krasner, L. *A psychological approach to abnormal behavior.* Englewood Cliffs, N.J.: Prentice-Hall, 1969.

Ullmann, L. P., & Krasner, L. *A psychological approach to abnormal behavior* (2nd ed.). Englewood Cliffs, N.J.: Prentice-Hall, 1975.

Unger, S. M. Mescaline, L. S. D., psilocybin, and personality change. *Psychiatry,* 1963, *26,* 111-125.

U.S. Department of Health, Education, and Welfare. *Adult use of tobacco—1975.* Public Health Service, Center for Disease Control, National Clearinghouse for Smoking and Health, 1976.

U.S. Department of Health, Education, and Welfare. Amphetamine. DHEW Publication No. (ADM) 75–52, Maryland, 1975.

U.S. News and World Report, 85(1), July 10, 1978.

Valenstein, E. S. *Brain control.* New York: Wiley, 1973.

Valentine, C. W. The innate bases of fear. *Journal of Genetic Psychology,* 1930, *37,* 394–419.

Van Praag, H. M. *Psychotropic drugs: A guide for practitioners.* New York: Brunner/Mozel, 1978.

Vaughn, C. E., & Leff, J. P. The influence of family and social factors on the course of psychiatric illness: A comparison of schizophrenic and depressive-neurotic patients. *British Journal of Psychiatry,* 1976, *129,* 127–137.

Vonnegut, M. *The Eden Express.* New York: Praeger, 1975. Copyright © 1975 by Praeger Publishers, Inc. Excerpt in text reprinted by permission of Holt, Rinehart and Winston, Publishers.

Wallace, A. F. C. Mental illness, biology and culture. In Frances, L. K. Hsu (Ed.), *Psychological anthropology.* Cambridge, Mass.: Schenkman Publishing Co., 1972.

Wallace, J. Alcoholism from the inside out: A phenomenological analysis. In N. J. Estes & M. E. Heinman (Eds.), *Alcoholism: Development, consequences and interventions.* St. Louis: Mosby, 1977.

Walters, D. *Physical and sexual abuse of children: Causes and treatment.* Bloomington: Indiana University Press, 1975.

Walton, D., & Mather, M. D. The relevance of generalization techniques to the treatment of stammering and phobic symptoms. *Behavior Research and Therapy,* 1963, *1,* 121–125.

Waring, M., & Ricks, D. Family patterns of children who become adult schizophrenics. *Journal of Nervous and Mental Disease,* 1965, *140,* 351-364.

Waters, W. E. Migraine: Intelligence, social class and familial prevalence. *British Medical Journal,* 1971, *2,* 77–78.

Watson, D. L., & Tharp, R. G. Self-directed behavior: Self-modification for personal adjustment. Monterey, Calif.: Brooks/Cole, 1972. Copyright © 1972 by Wadsworth, Inc. Material reprinted by permission of the publisher.

Watson, J. B., & Rayner, R. Conditioned emotional reactions. *Journal of Experimental Psychology,* 1920, *3,* 1–14.

Weinberg, J. R. Counseling the person with alcohol problems. In N. J. Estes & M. E. Heinman (Eds.), *Alcoholism: Development, consequences and interventions.* St. Louis: Mosby, 1977.

Weinberg, S. K. *Incest behavior.* New York: Citadel, 1955.

Weiner, H., Thaler, M., Reiser, M. F., & Mirsky, J. A. Etiology of duodenal ulcer. *Psychosomatic Medicine,* 1957, *19,* 1–10.

Weiss, J. M. Effects of coping behavior in different warning signal conditions on stress pathology in rats. *Journal of Comparative and Physiological Psychology,* 1971, *77,* 1–13(a).

Weiss, J. M. Effects of coping behavior with and without a feedback signal on stress pathology in rats. *Journal of Comparative and Physiological Psychology,* 1971, *77,* 22–30(b).

Weiss, J. M. Effects of punishing the coping response (conflict) on stress pathology in rats. *Journal of Comparative and Physiological Psychology,* 1971, *77,* 14–21(c).

Weiss, J. M., Glazer, H. I., & Pohorecky, L. A. Coping behavior and neurochemical changes: An alternative explanation for the original "learned helplessness" experiments. In G. Serban and A. Kling (Eds.), *Relevance of the animal model to the human.* New York: Plenum, 1976, 141–173.

Weiss, J. M., Stone, E. A., & Harrell, N. Coping behavior and brain norepinephrine level in rats. *Journal of Comparative and Physiological Psychology,* 1970, *72*(1), 153–160.

Weissman, M. M., & Paykel, S. *The depressed women: A study of social relationships.* Chicago: University of Chicago Press, 1974.

Wender, P. H., Rosenthal, D., Kety, S. S., Schulsinger, F., & Welner, J. Crossfostering: A research strategy for clarifying the role of genetic and experiential factors in the etiology of schizophrenia. *Archives of General Psychiatry,* 1974, *30,* 121–128.

Wender, P. H., Rosenthal, D., Kety, S. S., Schulsinger, F. & Welner, J. Social class and psychopathology in adoptees: A natural experimental method for separating the roles of genetic and experiential factors. *Archives of General Psychiatry,* 1973, *28,* 318–325.

Whitehorn, J. C. *Psychodynamic considerations in the treatment of psychotic patients.* London, Ont.: The University of Western Ontario Press, 1951.

Wilkins, W. Desensitization: Social and cognitive factors underlying the effectiveness of Wolpe's procedure. *Psychological Bulletin,* 1971, *76,* 311-317.

Will, O. A. Analytic etiology: A primer. In J. O. Cole & L. E. Hollister (Eds.), *Schizophrenia.* New York: MEDCOM, 1970.

Wilson, G. T. Alcohol and human sexual behavior. *Behaviour Research and Therapy,* 1977, *15,* 239–252.

Wilson, G. T., & Evans, I. M. The therapist-client relationship in behavior therapy. In A. S. Gurman & A. M. Razin (Eds.), *Effective psychotherapy: A handbook of research.* New York: Pergamon, 1978.

Wilson, G. T., & Lawson, D. M. Expectancies, alcohol and sexual arousal in male social drinkers. *Journal of Abnormal Psychology,* 1976, *85,* 587–594.

Wilson, G. T., & Lawson, D. M. Expectancies, alcohol, and sexual arousal in women. *Journal of Abnormal Psychology,* 1978, *87,* 358–367.

Wilson, G. T., & O'Leary, K. D. *Principles of behavior therapy.* Englewood Cliffs, N.J.: Prentice-Hall, 1980.

Winokur, G. Genetic aspects of depression. In J. P. Scott and E. C. Senay (Eds.), *Separation and depression: Clinical and research aspects.* Washington, D.C.: American Association for the Advancement of Science, 1973.

Winokur, G., & Clayton, P. Family history studies: I. Two types of affective disorders separated according to genetic and clinical factors. In *Recent Advances in Biological Psychiatry, 9.* New York: Plenum, 1967.

Witters, W. L., & Jones-Witters, P. *Drugs & sex.* New York: Macmillan, 1975.

Wohlberg, G. W., & Kornetsky, C. Sustained attention in remitted schizophrenics. *Archives of General Psychiatry, 28,* 533–537, 1973.

Wolff, S., & Chess, S. An analysis of the language of fourteen schizophrenic children. *Journal of Child Psychology and Psychiatry,* 1973, *6,* 29.

Wolpe, J. *Psychotherapy by reciprocal inhibition.* Stanford: Stanford University Press, 1958.

Wolpe, J., & Rachman, S. Psychoanalytic "evidence": A critique based on Freud's case of Little Hans. *Journal of Nervous and Mental Diseases,* 1960, *130,* 135–148.

Woolsey, R. M. Hysteria: 1875 to 1975. *Diseases of the Nervous System,* 1976, *37,* 379–386.

Wynne, L. C. Communication disorders and the quest for relatedness in families of schizophrenics. *American Journal of Psychoanalysis.* 1970, *30,* 100–114.

Yalom, D. Aggression and forbiddenness in voyeurism. *Archives of General Psychiatry,* 1960, *3,* 305–319.

Yalom, I. *The theory and practice of group psychotherapy.* New York: Basic Books, 1975.

Yates, A. J. *Behavior therapy.* New York: Wiley, 1970.

Zax, M., & Cowen, L. *Abnormal Psychology: Changing conceptions* (2nd ed.). New York: Holt, Rinehart & Winston, 1972.

Zetner, J. L. The recreational use of LSD–25 and drug prohibition. *Journal of Psychedelic Drugs,* 1976, *8,* 299–305.

Zigler, E., & Phillips, L. Psychiatric diagnosis and symptomatology. *Journal of Abnormal and Social Psychology,* 1961, *63,* 69–75.

Zubin, J., Eron, L. D., & Schumer, F. *An experimental approach to projective techniques.* New York: Wiley, 1965.

Zubin, J., Salzinger, K., Fleiss, J. L., Gurland, B., Spitzer, R. L., Endicott, J., & Sutton, S. Biometric approach to psychopathology: Abnormal and clinical psychology—statistical, epidemiological, and diagnostic approaches. In M. R. Rosenzweig and L. W. Porter (Eds.), *Annual Review of Psychology.* Palo Alto, Calif.: Annual Reviews, 1975, 647.

Zubin, J., & Spring, B. Vulnerability: A new view of schizophrenia. *Journal of Abnormal Psychology,* 1977, 103–126.

Name Index

Subject Index

D

N

O

P–Q

T

This book has been set CAP in 10 and 9 point Spectra Light, leaded 2 and 3 points. Part numbers are set in 16 and 64 point Spectra; part titles are set in 28 point Spectra. Chapter numbers are set in 48 point Spectra; chapter titles are set in 24 point Spectra. The size of the type page is 33½ by 47½ picas.